Cooking Light®
complete meals in minutes

Cooking Light®

complete
meals in
minutes

over 700 great recipes

Oxmoor House®

ISBN-13: 978-0-8487-3647-7
ISBN-10: 0-8487-3647-8
Library of Congress Control Number: 2009937183

Printed in the United States of America
Second Printing 2012

Be sure to check with your health-care provider before making any changes in your diet.

Oxmoor House

VP, Publishing Director: Jim Childs
Editorial Director: Susan Payne Dobbs
Brand Manager: Terri Laschober Robertson
Managing Editor: Laurie S. Herr

Cooking Light® Complete Meals in Minutes

Senior Editor: Heather Averett
Project Editor: Diane Rose
Senior Designer: Melissa Jones Clark
Director, Test Kitchens: Elizabeth Tyler Austin
Assistant Director, Test Kitchens: Julie Christopher
Test Kitchens Professionals: Allison E. Cox,
  Julie Gunter, Kathleen Royal Phillips,
  Catherine Crowell Steele, Ashley T. Strickland
Photography Director: Jim Bathie
Senior Photo Stylist: Kay E. Clarke
Associate Photo Stylist: Katherine Eckert Coyne
Production Managers: Theresa Beste-Farley,
  Tamara N. Wilder

Contributors

Compositor: Carol Damsky
Copy Editor: Norma Butterworth-McKittrick
Proofreaders: Jacqueline B. Giovanelli,
  Carmine B. Loper
Indexer: Mary Ann Laurens
Nutritional Analyses: Lauren Page, R.D.
Interns: Sarah Bélanger, Chris Cosgrove,
  Georgia Dodge, Perri K. Hubbard, Allison Sperando,
  Lindsey Vaughan
Food Stylists: Alyson Haynes, Iris O'Brien,
  Laura Zapalowski
Photographer: Lee Harrelson
Photo Stylists: Cathy Still Johnson, Rose Nguyen

Cooking Light®

Editor: Scott Mowbray
Creative Director: Carla Frank
Deputy Editor: Phillip Rhodes
Food Editor: Ann Taylor Pittman
Special Publications Editor: Mary Simpson
  Creel, M.S., R.D.
Nutrition Editor: Kathy Kitchens Downie, R.D.
Associate Food Editors: Timothy Q. Cebula,
  Julianna Grimes
Associate Editors: Cindy Hatcher, Brandy Rushing
Test Kitchen Director: Vanessa T. Pruett
Assistant Test Kitchen Director: Tiffany Vickers Davis
Senior Food Stylist: Kellie Gerber Kelley
Recipe Testers and Developers: SaBrina Bone, Deb Wise
Art Director: Fernande Bondarenko
Deputy Art Director: J. Shay McNamee
Junior Deputy Art Director: Alexander Spacher
Photo Director: Kristen Schaefer
Senior Photographer: Randy Mayor
Senior Photo Stylist: Cindy Barr
Photo Stylist: Leigh Ann Ross
Copy Chief: Maria Parker Hopkins
Assistant Copy Chief: Susan Roberts
Research Editor: Michelle Gibson Daniels
Editorial Production Director: Liz Rhoades
Production Editor: Hazel R. Eddins
Art/Production Assistant: Josh Rutledge
Administrative Coordinator: Carol D. Johnson
CookingLight.com Editor: Allison Long Lowery

To order additional publications,
call 1-800-765-6400 or 1-800-491-0551.

For more books to enrich your life,
visit **oxmoorhouse.com**

To search, savor, and share thousands of recipes,
visit **myrecipes.com**

Cover:
Chicken Breasts with Tomatoes and Olives (page 281), Pesto Shrimp Pasta (page 128), Filet Mignon with Sherry-Mushroom Sauce (page 214)

table of contents

About This Book

Cooking Light **Complete Meals in Minutes** is a must-have collection of over 700 fast and delicious recipes that go from kitchen to table in 30 minutes or less. Enjoy appetizers and beverages, pasta and pizza, meats and poultry, soups and sandwiches, sides and desserts, and much more. Over 500 beautiful color photos showcase rich, delicious food at its finest, helping speed your selection for dinner tonight.

Check out these fantastic features that will guide you in selecting and preparing **Complete Meals in Minutes:**

- **Colorful icons** highlight recipe prep times for at-a-glance searching.

- **Make It a Meal** tips suggest ways to round out your meals by offering options for everything from sides to breads and beverages to desserts.

- **Make It Faster** ideas offer information on how to make our recipes even quicker—giving you tips you can use to simplify your own recipes that may use the same (or similar) ingredients.

- **Ingredient Spotlights** showcase purchasing tips, storing guidelines, and nutritional information for recipe ingredients.

- **Cooking Class** how-to boxes and photos show you the fundamentals of healthy, quick cooking, guiding you in preparation of specific ingredients or recipes.

- **Shortcut Spotlight** boxes tout our editors' picks for favorite convenience gadgets that save time but won't break your budget.

APPETIZERS & BEVERAGES

Creamy Asian Dip

15 MINUTES

Lemon-Parsley Hummus

Tahini, a thick paste made from ground sesame seeds, is similar in texture to natural peanut butter. Serve the hummus with baked pita chips and raw veggies.

1   (16-ounce) can chickpeas
    (garbanzo beans), rinsed and drained
⅓   cup fresh lemon juice
¼   cup fresh parsley sprigs
2   tablespoons water
2   tablespoons tahini
1   tablespoon olive oil
1   garlic clove
½   teaspoon ground cumin

1. Place all ingredients in a food processor; process until smooth, occasionally scraping down sides of bowl. **Yield:** 14 servings (serving size: 2 tablespoons).

CALORIES 39; FAT 2.4g (sat 0.3g, mono 1.3g, poly 0.8g); PROTEIN 1.4g; CARB 3.6g; FIBER 0.8g; CHOL 0mg; IRON 0.4mg; SODIUM 33mg; CALC 12mg

15 MINUTES

Creamy Asian Dip

You can make this party-pleasing dip a day ahead and store it in the refrigerator.

1   cup light mayonnaise
½   cup reduced-fat sour cream
¼   cup chopped fresh basil
¼   cup low-sodium soy sauce
2   tablespoons rice vinegar
4   teaspoons sesame seeds, toasted
2   teaspoons sugar
2   teaspoons minced fresh ginger
4   teaspoons sesame oil
1   teaspoon dry mustard
¼   teaspoon ground red pepper
¼   teaspoon salt
¼   teaspoon freshly ground black pepper

1. Combine all ingredients in a small bowl; stir well. Cover and chill. **Yield:** 16 servings (serving size: 2 tablespoons).

CALORIES 80; FAT 7.5g (sat 1.8g, mono 3.5g, poly 2g); PROTEIN 0.6g; CARB 2.5g; FIBER 0.2g; CHOL 8mg; IRON 0.3mg; SODIUM 294mg; CALC 18mg

Lemon-Parsley Hummus

20 MINUTES

Roasted Red Pepper Dip

1	ounce sun-dried tomatoes packed without oil (about 8 tomatoes)
3/4	cup boiling water
1	(12-ounce) jar roasted red bell peppers, drained and chopped
1/2	cup (4 ounces) 1/3-less-fat cream cheese, softened
1/2	cup reduced-fat sour cream
2	tablespoons chopped fresh parsley
1	tablespoon lemon juice
2	teaspoons bottled minced garlic
1/4	teaspoon salt
1/4	teaspoon black pepper

1. Combine tomatoes and boiling water in a small bowl; let stand 5 minutes. Drain.
2. Place tomatoes, chopped red bell peppers, and remaining ingredients in a food processor. Process 15 seconds; scrape sides of bowl. Process an additional 20 seconds or until smooth. Transfer to a bowl; cover and chill. **Yield:** 20 servings (serving size: 2 tablespoons).

CALORIES 30; FAT 1.8g (sat 1.2g, mono 0.3g, poly 0.1g); PROTEIN 1g; CARB 2.6g; FIBER 0.2g; CHOL 6mg; IRON 0.2mg; SODIUM 138mg; CALC 6mg

Bacon–Blue Cheese Dip

Use a good-quality blue cheese, such as Maytag blue cheese, for a dip that is full of the cheese's distinct flavor.

½ cup light sour cream
⅓ cup ⅓-less-fat cream cheese, softened
1 garlic clove, finely minced
⅛ teaspoon hot sauce (such as Tabasco)
¾ cup (3 ounces) crumbled blue cheese
2 slices fully-cooked bacon (such as Oscar Mayer), crumbled

1. Combine first 4 ingredients in a small bowl; stir until smooth. Fold in blue cheese. **2.** Spoon dip into a serving bowl; sprinkle with crumbled bacon. Serve with fresh vegetables.**Yield:** 10 servings (serving size: 2 tablespoons).

CALORIES 70; FAT 5g (sat 3.8g, mono 0.9g, poly 0.1g); PROTEIN 3.5g; CARB 2.2g; FIBER 0g; CHOL 19mg; IRON 0.1mg; SODIUM 184mg; CALC 76mg

Green Pea and Feta Dip

Green peas add fiber, color, and a subtle sweetness to this hummuslike dip. Serve with pita wedges or fresh-cut veggies, or use it as a spread for sandwiches.

1¾ cups frozen petite green peas, thawed
¾ cup (3 ounces) crumbled reduced-fat feta cheese
2 tablespoons chopped fresh mint
1 small garlic clove
1 tablespoon water
1 tablespoon extra-virgin olive oil
2 teaspoons fresh lemon juice
½ teaspoon freshly ground black pepper

1. Place all ingredients in a blender or food processor; process until combined but not smooth. **Yield:** 12 servings (serving size: 2 tablespoons).

CALORIES 42; FAT 2.2g (sat 0.8g, mono 0.9g, poly 0.2g); PROTEIN 2.6g; CARB 3.3g; FIBER 1g; CHOL 2mg; IRON 0.4mg; SODIUM 122mg; CALC 23mg

Edamame Hummus

Instead of chickpeas, this hummus features edamame, making the color of the dip similar to guacamole. Serve this hummus with pita wedges or fresh vegetables.

1½ cups frozen shelled edamame (green soybeans)
3 garlic cloves
1 tablespoon olive oil
½ teaspoon ground cumin
¼ teaspoon kosher salt
¼ teaspoon freshly ground black pepper
¼ cup chopped fresh cilantro
¼ cup fresh lemon juice
3 tablespoons tahini (sesame-seed paste)
2 tablespoons water

1. Cook edamame in boiling water 5 to 7 minutes or until tender. Drain. **2.** Place garlic and next 4 ingredients in a food processor, and pulse 3 times or until chopped. Add edamame, cilantro, and remaining ingredients; process until smooth. **Yield:** 12 servings (serving size: 2 tablespoons).

CALORIES 60; FAT 4.2g (sat 0.4g, mono 1.8g, poly 1.8g); PROTEIN 2.8g; CARB 3.9g; FIBER 1.4g; CHOL 0mg; IRON 0.6mg; SODIUM 48mg; CALC 20mg

Edamame are immature soybeans that are picked green and served fresh. You'll find them in season from late July to September. However, frozen edamame are available year-round, both in the pod and shelled.

INGREDIENT SPOTLIGHT

Southwestern Salsa Dip

process until smooth. Stir in reserved black beans and ¹/₄ cup salsa. Serve immediately, or cover and chill for up to 1 week. Garnish with cilantro sprig, if desired. **Yield:** 7 servings (serving size: ¹/₄ cup).

CALORIES 53; FAT 1.5g (sat 0.2g, mono 1g, poly 0.2g); PROTEIN 2.3g; CARB 8.2g; FIBER 2.7g; CHOL 0mg; IRON 0.9mg; SODIUM 147mg; CALC 31mg

MINUTES

Layered Bean Dip

We used refrigerated fresh salsa—found in the deli department or produce section of the supermarket—because it has less than half the sodium of most bottled salsas.

1 (16-ounce) can fat-free spicy refried beans
¹/₄ cup fat-free sour cream
1 (8-ounce) container refrigerated guacamole
1 cup refrigerated fresh salsa
1 cup (4 ounces) preshredded reduced-fat 4-cheese Mexican blend cheese
¹/₂ cup diced tomato
2 tablespoons chopped green onions

1. Combine beans and sour cream in a small bowl, stirring well. Spread mixture into bottom of a shallow 1-quart serving dish. Spread guacamole over bean mixture. Top with salsa; sprinkle with cheese, tomato, and green onions. Cover and chill. **Yield:** 16 servings (serving size: ¹/₄ cup).

CALORIES 74; FAT 3.2g (sat 1.9g, mono 1g, poly 0.1g); PROTEIN 4.2g; CARB 7.1g; FIBER 3g; CHOL 3mg; IRON 1.1mg; SODIUM 305mg; CALC 59mg

MINUTES

Southwestern Salsa Dip

Serve this south-of-the-border inspired salsa dip with Fiesta Tortilla Chips (recipe on page 21).

1 (15-ounce) can black beans, rinsed and drained
³/₄ cup fresh salsa, divided
¹/₂ cup fresh cilantro leaves
2 teaspoons extra-virgin olive oil
2 drops of hot sauce
Cilantro sprig (optional)

1. Set aside ¹/₄ cup black beans; place remaining beans, ¹/₂ cup salsa, cilantro, oil, and hot sauce in a food processor;

COOKING CLASS: *how to dice tomatoes*

To dice a tomato means to cut it into small cubes that are about ¹/₄ inch in size. Use a chef's knife to cut the tomatoes into slices of desired thickness, and then cut the slices into strips of the same thickness. Stack the strips with the ends flush, and cut them crosswise into small cubes.

Chunky Tomato-Asparagus Dip

Scoop up this chunky dip with a twist—blue corn tortilla chips. The fun, festive color contrast of the dip and chips will make this appetizer anything but ordinary.

1	pound asparagus spears, trimmed and cut into 1-inch pieces
½	cup finely chopped onion
1	medium tomato, chopped
1	garlic clove, minced
2	tablespoons minced fresh cilantro
2	tablespoons fresh lime juice
¼	teaspoon salt
¼	teaspoon freshly ground black pepper

Dash of ground red pepper

1. Cook asparagus in boiling water to cover in a large saucepan 5 minutes or until crisp-tender. Rinse under cold water; drain well.

2. Place asparagus in a food processor; process 1 minute or until smooth, scraping sides of bowl occasionally. Spoon asparagus into a bowl, and stir in onion and remaining ingredients. Serve immediately, or cover and chill until ready to serve. **Yield:** 11 servings (serving size: ¼ cup).

CALORIES 14; FAT 0.1g (sat 0g, mono 0g, poly 0.1g); PROTEIN 0.9g; CARB 2.7g; FIBER 0.9g; CHOL 0mg; IRON 0.7mg; SODIUM 55mg; CALC 11mg

Hot Fiesta Dip

Hot Fiesta Dip

Serve this dip with baked tortilla chips.

1   (10-ounce) package frozen whole-kernel corn
1½ cups refrigerated fresh salsa
¾   cup (3 ounces) preshredded reduced-fat 4-cheese Mexican blend cheese
2   tablespoons chopped green onions

1. Microwave frozen corn according to package directions. Drain.
2. Combine corn and salsa in a microwave-safe 9-inch pie plate. Cover with plastic wrap; vent. Microwave at HIGH 2 minutes or until bubbly.
3. Sprinkle cheese over corn mixture; cover and let stand 5 minutes or until cheese melts. Top with chopped onions. **Yield:** 10 servings (serving size: ¼ cup).

CALORIES 63; FAT 1.9g (sat 1.4g, mono 0.1g, poly 0.1g); PROTEIN 3g; CARB 7.9g; FIBER 0.6g; CHOL 5mg; IRON 0.2mg; SODIUM 158mg; CALC 99mg

Hot Crabmeat Dip

1   (8-ounce) package ⅓-less-fat cream cheese
2   tablespoons light mayonnaise
1   tablespoon fresh lemon juice
¼   teaspoon garlic powder
¼   teaspoon freshly ground black pepper
⅛   teaspoon salt
8   ounces lump crabmeat, shell pieces removed
2   tablespoons chopped fresh chives
2   teaspoons chopped fresh parsley

1. Combine first 6 ingredients in a medium saucepan; cook over medium heat, stirring constantly, until cheese melts.
2. Stir in crabmeat, chives, and parsley; cook over medium heat, stirring constantly, until thoroughly heated. **Yield:** 16 servings (serving size: 2 tablespoons).

CALORIES 54; FAT 3.8g (sat 3.2g, mono 0.3g, poly 0.1g); PROTEIN 4.2g; CARB 0.8g; FIBER 0g; CHOL 22mg; IRON 0mg; SODIUM 138mg; CALC 24mg

Artichoke Pesto

Artichoke Pesto

2   (14-ounce) cans quartered artichoke hearts, rinsed and drained
½   cup (2 ounces) grated fresh Parmigiano-Reggiano cheese
¼   cup finely chopped fresh parsley
2   teaspoons grated fresh lemon rind
1   tablespoon fresh lemon juice
1   tablespoon olive oil
¼   teaspoon salt

1. Place artichokes in a food processor; pulse 5 times or until finely chopped. Add cheese and remaining ingredients; pulse to combine. Serve immediately, or cover and chill until ready to serve. **Yield:** 9 servings (serving size: ¼ cup).

CALORIES 59; FAT 3.3g (sat 1.9g, mono 1.1g, poly 0.2g); PROTEIN 3.4g; CARB 4.5g; FIBER 0.8g; CHOL 6mg; IRON 0.8mg; SODIUM 253mg; CALC 70mg

When it comes to finely grating foods, nothing works better than a Microplane® grater. It's perfect for grating lemon rind, such as in this pesto.

SHORTCUT SPOTLIGHT

2O
MINUTES

Mediterranean Goat Cheese Spread

Gently fold the olives and tomatoes into the cheese mixture; overmixing may turn the spread an unappetizing purplish pink. Serve on melba toast rounds.

4   sun-dried tomatoes, packed without oil
¼   cup water
¼   cup (2 ounces) goat cheese
3   tablespoons fat-free sour cream
⅛   teaspoon salt
6   pitted kalamata olives, finely chopped

1. Combine sun-dried tomatoes and water in a microwave-safe bowl, and microwave at HIGH 1 minute or until water boils. Remove from microwave; cover with plastic wrap and let stand 10 minutes to soften.
2. While tomatoes stand, place cheese in a microwave-safe bowl; microwave at HIGH 15 seconds or until soft. Add sour cream and salt; stir until well blended. Fold in olives.
3. Drain tomatoes; finely chop, and fold into goat cheese mixture. Serve immediately, or cover and chill until ready to serve. **Yield:** 8 servings (serving size: 1 tablespoon).

CALORIES 36; FAT 2.5g (sat 1.2g, mono 1g, poly 0.2g); PROTEIN 1.8g; CARB 1.6g; FIBER 0.3g; CHOL 4mg; IRON 0.3mg; SODIUM 113mg; CALC 23mg

Rosemary-Garlic
White Bean Spread

15 MINUTES

Rosemary-Garlic White Bean Spread

Use this flavorful high-fiber spread as an accompaniment to toasted baguette slices or as a dip for pita bread, carrot sticks, or cucumber slices. It also makes a terrific spread for pita sandwiches. If you don't have a food processor, simply mash the bean mixture with a fork; the spread, will have a slightly chunkier consistency.

2   tablespoons olive oil
4   garlic cloves, coarsely chopped
1   (15-ounce) can Great Northern beans, rinsed and drained
2   tablespoons fresh lemon juice
1   teaspoon finely chopped fresh rosemary
¼   teaspoon salt
Rosemary sprig (optional)

1. Heat oil in a small skillet over medium heat. Add garlic; sauté 1 minute. Place garlic mixture, beans, and next 3 ingredients in a food processor; process until smooth. Serve immediately, or cover and chill until ready to serve. Garnish with rosemary sprig, if desired. **Yield:** 8 servings (serving size: 2 tablespoons).

CALORIES 70; FAT 3.5g (sat 0.5g, mono 2.5g, poly 0.4g); PROTEIN 2.5g; CARB 7.6g; FIBER 1.6g; CHOL 0mg; IRON 0.4mg; SODIUM 74mg; CALC 13mg

MINUTES

Smoked Trout Spread

Look for smoked trout in the section of the grocery store where you find fresh fish.

1   (8-ounce) package smoked trout (such as Ducktrap)
1   (8-ounce) block fat-free cream cheese, softened
2   tablespoons finely chopped red onion
1   tablespoon fresh lemon juice
2   teaspoons extra-virgin olive oil
1   teaspoon prepared horseradish
1   teaspoon Dijon mustard
⅛   teaspoon salt
2   drops of hot sauce (such as Tabasco)

1. Flake trout with a fork; discard any skin and bones.
2. Place fish and cream cheese in a food processor; process until smooth. Spoon into a bowl. Add onion and remaining ingredients, stirring until blended. Cover and chill. **Yield:** 16 servings (serving size: 2 tablespoons).

CALORIES 46; FAT 1.8g (sat 0.5g, mono 0.7g, poly 0.3g); PROTEIN 6g; CARB 1.1g; FIBER 0g; CHOL 12mg; IRON 0.1mg; SODIUM 105mg; CALC 27mg

In Latin, rosemary means "dew of the sea"—appropriate since it is indigenous to the Mediterranean. Rosemary is one of the most aromatic and pungent of all herbs. Its needlelike leaves have a pronounced lemon-pine flavor that pairs well with olive oil, garlic, lemon juice, and white beans.

INGREDIENT SPOTLIGHT

MINUTES

Ginger Fruit Salsa

Keep the prep time short by buying precut fresh fruit from your supermarket's produce section. Pair with gingersnaps or Cinnamon Crisps with Honey (recipe on page 22).

1½ cups coarsely chopped cantaloupe
1 cup chopped pineapple
½ cup dried cranberries (such as Craisins)
¼ cup chopped fresh mint
2 tablespoons fresh lemon juice
1 teaspoon grated peeled fresh ginger
1 jalapeño pepper, seeded and finely chopped

1. Combine all ingredients in a medium bowl, tossing gently. Let stand 5 minutes before serving. **Yield:** 12 servings (serving size: ¼ cup).

CALORIES 29; FAT 0.1g (sat 0g, mono 0g, poly 0g); PROTEIN 0.3g; CARB 7.7g; FIBER 0.6g; CHOL 0mg; IRON 0.1mg; SODIUM 4mg; CALC 6mg

MINUTES

Salsa Verde

Salsa verde is a traditional Mexican salsa made from tomatillos; the tomatillos and green chiles give it a bright green hue. Here, salsa verde is a dip for tortilla chips, but you can also serve it with tacos or grilled meats and fish.

8 tomatillos (about 12 ounces)
¼ cup chopped green onions
¼ cup chopped fresh cilantro
½ teaspoon salt
1 jalapeño pepper, seeded and quartered
1 (4.5-ounce) can chopped green chiles, undrained

1. Discard husks and stems from tomatillos. Place tomatillos and remaining ingredients in a food processor; pulse until coarsely chopped. **Yield:** 8 servings (serving size: ¼ cup).

CALORIES 16; FAT 0.4g (sat 0.1g, mono 0.1g, poly 0.2g); PROTEIN 0.5g; CARB 3.2g; FIBER 1g; CHOL 0mg; IRON 0.3mg; SODIUM 334mg; CALC 4mg

MINUTES

Fresh Peach Salsa

Serve this fruity salsa with baked scoop-shaped tortilla chips for a fresh-tasting appetizer or snack. If you have leftovers, serve it alongside grilled chicken or fish.

1 large tomato, chopped
2 medium peaches, peeled and chopped
⅓ cup chopped sweet onion (such as Walla Walla or Vidalia)
2 tablespoons chopped fresh cilantro
1 garlic clove, sliced
2 teaspoons apple cider vinegar
½ teaspoon fresh lime juice
⅛ teaspoon freshly ground black pepper
1 (4.5-ounce) can chopped green chiles, drained

1. Place first 5 ingredients in a food processor; pulse 5 times. Add vinegar and remaining ingredients to food processor; pulse 2 times or until blended. Serve immediately, or cover and chill. **Yield:** 10 servings (serving size: ¼ cup).

CALORIES 21; FAT 0.2g (sat 0g, mono 0g, poly 0.1g); PROTEIN 0.7g; CARB 5.1g; FIBER 1g; CHOL 0mg; IRON 0.3mg; SODIUM 41mg; CALC 10mg

Without a doubt, this salsa is best prepared when peaches are at their peak—from May to late September. When fresh peaches aren't in season, use 1 cup chopped refrigerated peaches instead.

INGREDIENT SPOTLIGHT

Fresh Peach Salsa

MINUTES

Texas Caviar

2 tablespoons chopped fresh cilantro
3 tablespoons red wine vinegar
2 tablespoons canola oil
2 tablespoons hot sauce
1 garlic clove, minced
½ teaspoon salt
2 (15.8-ounce) cans black-eyed peas, rinsed
   and drained
1⅓ cups diced red onion
1 cup diced seeded tomato
1 cup diced green bell pepper

1. Combine first 6 ingredients in a large bowl; stir well with a whisk. Add peas and remaining ingredients; toss gently to coat. **Yield:** 20 servings (serving size: ¼ cup).

CALORIES 43; FAT 1.6g (sat 0.2g, mono 0.8g, poly 0.5g); PROTEIN 1.7g; CARB 5.8g; FIBER 1.4g; CHOL 0mg; IRON 0.4mg; SODIUM 150mg; CALC 11mg

MINUTES

Fresh Green Veggie Salsa

½ cup finely chopped tomatillos (about
   2 medium)
½ medium cucumber, peeled, seeded, and
   chopped (about ½ cup)
⅓ cup chopped fresh cilantro
½ medium celery stalk, finely chopped (about
   ¼ cup)
3 tablespoons fresh lime juice (about 2 limes)
1 green onion, thinly sliced (about 2
   tablespoons)
1 tablespoon extra-virgin olive oil
¼ teaspoon salt
1 ripe avocado, chopped

1. Combine all ingredients in a medium bowl. Serve immediately, or cover and chill. **Yield:** 8 servings (serving size: ¼ cup).

CALORIES 53; FAT 4.7g (sat 0.6g, mono 3.4g, poly 0.7g); PROTEIN 0.9g; CARB 3.2g; FIBER 2g; CHOL 0mg; IRON 0.2mg; SODIUM 79mg; CALC 8mg

MINUTES

Fiesta Tortilla Chips

Bake up a batch of these flavorful chips to accompany Southwestern Salsa Dip (recipe on page 12).

4 (7-inch) flour tortillas (such as Azteca)
Cooking spray
1½ teaspoons salt-free Mexican seasoning
⅛ teaspoon salt

1. Preheat oven to 425°.
2. Stack tortillas on a work surface. Cut stack into 6 wedges. Arrange wedges in a single layer on a parchment paper–lined baking sheet. Coat wedges with cooking spray. Sprinkle with Mexican seasoning and salt. Coat again lightly with cooking spray.
3. Bake at 425° for 3 minutes or just until chips become golden. Turn chips, and bake 2 minutes. Remove from oven, and let stand on baking sheet until crisp. **Yield:** 4 servings (serving size: 6 chips).

CALORIES 77; FAT 1.7g (sat 0.3g, mono 0.8g, poly 0.3g); PROTEIN 2g; CARB 13.5g; FIBER 1g; CHOL 0mg; IRON 0.8mg; SODIUM 233mg; CALC 0mg

Fresh Green Veggie Salsa

Tomato-Basil Bruschetta

Tomato-Basil Bruschetta

Bruschetta is an appetizer of toasted bread that is usually topped with some type of cheese, vegetable, or herb. Here, fresh basil leaves add beauty and an extra punch of flavor.

18   (¼-inch-thick) slices diagonally cut
        whole-grain French baguette
Cooking spray
⅓   cup light mayonnaise
⅓   cup tub-style light cream cheese
1   tablespoon chopped fresh basil
18   (¼-inch-thick) slices diagonally cut plum
        tomato (about 5 large plum tomatoes)
¼   teaspoon freshly ground black pepper
18   fresh basil leaves

1. Preheat oven to 400°.
2. Place baguette slices on a baking sheet; coat slices with cooking spray. Bake at 400° for 5 minutes or until bread is toasted; set aside.
3. Combine mayonnaise, cream cheese, and chopped basil in a small bowl; stir well.
4. Spread 1 teaspoon cheese mixture on each bread slice; top with tomato slices, and sprinkle with pepper. Top each tomato slice with a basil leaf. **Yield:** 18 servings (serving size: 1 bruschetta).

CALORIES 52; FAT 2.4g (sat 0.8g, mono 0.9g, poly 0.5g); PROTEIN 1.3g; CARB 6g; FIBER 1g; CHOL 4mg; IRON 0.5mg; SODIUM 121mg; CALC 20mg

Cinnamon Crisps with Honey

These sweet crisps are reminiscent of sopaipillas—a crispy Mexican pastry—but they are much easier to prepare and much healthier, too. They're perfectly suited for eating by themselves, but equally as good for scooping up Ginger Fruit Salsa (recipe on page 18).

4   (8-inch) fat-free flour tortillas
Butter-flavored cooking spray
2   tablespoons sugar
1   teaspoon ground cinnamon
2   tablespoons honey

1. Preheat oven to 350°.
2. Stack tortillas; cut stack into 4 wedges. Separate wedges, and place in a single layer on a large baking sheet lined with parchment paper; coat wedges with cooking spray.
3. Combine sugar and cinnamon. Sprinkle wedges with sugar mixture. Bake at 350° for 15 minutes or until golden and crisp. Serve with honey. **Yield:** 4 servings (serving size: 4 crisps and ½ tablespoon honey).

CALORIES 172; FAT 0.5g (sat 0.3g, mono 0g, poly 0g); PROTEIN 3.1g; CARB 39.4g; FIBER 1.3g; CHOL 0mg; IRON 1.3mg; SODIUM 341mg; CALC 8mg

Cutting bread for crostini is easy if you use a serrated knife. With its scalloped toothlike edge, this knife is ideal for cutting through foods that have a hard exterior and a softer interior, such as a loaf of crusty bread.

SHORTCUT SPOTLIGHT

20 MINUTES

Tomato–Blue Cheese Crostini

You can toast slices of bread for crostini ahead and store them in an airtight container at room temperature. Crostini are especially good in the summer and early fall when tomatoes are at their ripest.

24 (¼-inch-thick) slices diagonally cut French baguette

Cooking spray

⅓ cup tub-style light cream cheese

¼ cup (1 ounce) crumbled blue cheese

½ teaspoon minced garlic

⅛ teaspoon coarsely ground black pepper

1 cup finely chopped tomato

2 tablespoons chopped fresh basil

⅛ teaspoon salt

1. Preheat oven to 400°.

2. Place baguette slices on a baking sheet; coat slices with cooking spray. Bake at 400° for 5 minutes or until bread is toasted; set aside.

3. While bread bakes, combine cream cheese and blue cheese in a small microwave-safe bowl. Microwave at HIGH 15 seconds or until softened. Add garlic and pepper; stir until combined.

4. Combine tomato, basil, and salt in a small bowl. Spread about 1 teaspoon cheese mixture on each bread slice, and top each with 2 teaspoons tomato mixture. **Yield:** 24 servings (serving size: 1 crostino).

CALORIES 42; FAT 1.2g (sat 0.7g, mono 0.2g, poly 0.1g); PROTEIN 1.6g; CARB 5.9g; FIBER 0.4g; CHOL 3mg; IRON 0.3mg; SODIUM 108mg; CALC 20mg

Mini Pizza Margheritas

MINUTES

Pesto Bread Rounds

The nutty flavor of the Asiago cheese balances the sharp, salty taste of the Parmesan cheese in this rustic hors d'oeuvre. Accompany these cheesy toasts with a glass of wine, a cup of soup, or a salad.

20   (½-inch-thick) slices French bread baguette
½   cup light mayonnaise
¼   cup (1 ounce) shredded fresh Parmesan cheese
2   tablespoons grated fresh Asiago cheese
1   tablespoon commercial pesto
⅛   teaspoon black pepper

1. Preheat broiler.
2. Place bread slices on a baking sheet; broil 2 minutes or until toasted. Turn bread slices over.
3. Combine mayonnaise and next 4 ingredients in a medium bowl. Spread about 2 teaspoons mayonnaise mixture on untoasted side of each bread slice. Broil 2 minutes or until cheese is bubbly and edges of bread are browned. **Yield:** 20 servings (serving size: 1 slice).

CALORIES 63; FAT 3.1g (sat 1g, mono 1.3g, poly 0.6g); PROTEIN 2g; CARB 6.7g; FIBER 0.3g; CHOL 4mg; IRON 0.4mg; SODIUM 145mg; CALC 28mg

 MINUTES

Devilish Eggs

You can prepare these eggs up to a day in advance. Just cover and store them in the refrigerator until you're ready to serve them.

6   hard-cooked large eggs
½   cup prepared hummus
2   tablespoons fat-free sour cream
1½   teaspoons prepared mustard
¼   teaspoon black pepper
1   tablespoon sweet or dill pickle relish

1. Cut eggs in half lengthwise; remove yolks. Place 3 yolks in a small bowl; reserve

remaining yolks for another use. Add hummus and next 3 ingredients to yolks; mash with a fork until smooth. Stir in pickle relish. Spoon egg mixture into egg white halves. **Yield:** 12 servings (serving size: 1 stuffed egg half).

CALORIES 59; FAT 3.6g (sat 1g, mono 1.6g, poly 0.7g); PROTEIN 4.1g; CARB 2.5g; FIBER 0.6g; CHOL 106mg; IRON 0.4mg; SODIUM 85mg; CALC 16mg

 MINUTES

Pickled Shrimp

For an appetizer, spoon the shrimp into a serving bowl, and let guests spear the shrimp with wooden picks. As a first course, spoon the shrimp and onion mixture onto individual lettuce-lined salad plates.

1   large lemon
1½   cups water
½   cup light olive oil vinaigrette
1   teaspoon pickling spice
1   pound cooked, peeled medium shrimp
1   medium red onion, thinly sliced

1. Thinly slice half of lemon; set aside. Squeeze remaining half of lemon over a small bowl to measure 2 tablespoons juice; add water, vinaigrette, and pickling spice.
2. Layer shrimp, onion, and lemon slices in a shallow dish or wide-mouthed jar. Pour lemon juice mixture over layers. Cover and refrigerate at least 24 hours. **Yield:** 8 servings (serving size: about 7 shrimp and ¼ cup onion).

CALORIES 103; FAT 4g (sat 0.3g, mono 2.3g, poly 1.2g); PROTEIN 14.3g; CARB 2.8g; FIBER 0.2g; CHOL 115mg; IRON 1.2mg; SODIUM 283mg; CALC 44mg

Make this recipe ahead because it needs to sit 24 hours for the flavors to meld. You can save prep time by buying cooked and peeled shrimp.

MAKE IT FASTER

Jalapeño Boats

Perfect for your next game-day gathering, these "boats" can be made ahead and chilled until you're ready to serve them. The cream cheese calms the heat of the peppers, leaving just enough kick to excite the palate. If jalapeño peppers have too much heat for your taste, try using poblano chiles or quartered green bell peppers.

½ cup frozen whole-kernel corn, thawed
½ cup (4 ounces) ⅓-less-fat cream cheese, softened
1 tablespoon chopped green onions
2 teaspoons chopped fresh cilantro
½ teaspoon chili powder
¼ teaspoon salt
6 large jalapeño peppers, halved lengthwise and seeded

1. Combine first 6 ingredients in a small bowl. Spoon about 1 tablespoon cream cheese mixture evenly into each jalapeño half. **Yield:** 12 servings (serving size: 1 stuffed jalapeño half).

CALORIES 34; FAT 2.3g (sat 2g, mono 0g, poly 0.1g); PROTEIN 1.3g; CARB 2.4g; FIBER 0.4g; CHOL 7mg; IRON 0.2mg; SODIUM 90mg; CALC 9mg

Chicken Lettuce Wraps

Serve these wraps with an Asian dipping sauce or peanut sauce, if desired.

2	garlic cloves, finely minced
¼	cup fresh lime juice
3	tablespoons low-sodium soy sauce
2	teaspoons sugar
1	teaspoon sesame oil
¼	teaspoon crushed red pepper
2	cups shredded cooked chicken breast
¼	cup chopped fresh cilantro
2	tablespoons chopped fresh mint
12	small, tender Bibb or iceberg lettuce leaves, rinsed, drained, and dried

1. Combine first 6 ingredients in a large bowl, stirring well with a whisk. Add chicken, cilantro, and mint; toss to combine. Let stand 5 minutes.

2. Spoon about 2½ tablespoons chicken mixture in center of each lettuce leaf. **Yield:** 12 servings (serving size: 1 chicken-filled lettuce wrap).

CALORIES 50; FAT 1.3g (sat 0.3g, mono 0.4g, poly 0.4g); PROTEIN 7.6g; CARB 1.9g; FIBER 0.2g; CHOL 20mg; IRON 0.5mg; SODIUM 151mg; CALC 10mg

MAKE IT EASIER Use rotisserie chicken from your grocery store's deli department to save time.

MINUTES

Shrimp Salad–Stuffed Endive

Belgian endive is a small, cigar-shaped head of compact, pointed leaves that's grown in complete darkness. It has a slightly bitter flavor and crunchy leaves that are perfect for stuffing, scooping, or dipping.

½   pound cooked peeled shrimp, coarsely chopped (about 1½ cups)
¼   cup chopped celery
¼   cup chopped red bell pepper
¼   cup chopped red onion
¼   cup light mayonnaise
3   tablespoons chopped green onions
1   teaspoon fresh lemon juice
¼   teaspoon salt
⅛   teaspoon freshly ground black pepper
2   heads Belgian endive (about 10 ounces), separated into leaves
2   teaspoons chopped fresh dill

1. Combine first 9 ingredients in a bowl, stirring to combine.
2. Spoon 1 rounded tablespoonful of shrimp salad onto end of each endive leaf; sprinkle evenly with dill. **Yield:** 18 servings (serving size: 1 stuffed endive leaf).

CALORIES 27; FAT 1.3g (sat 0.3g, mono 0.6g, poly 0.3g); PROTEIN 2.8g; CARB 1g; FIBER 0.3g; CHOL 26mg; IRON 0.4mg; SODIUM 89mg; CALC 8mg

 MINUTES

Shrimp and Mango Lettuce Wraps with Lime-Peanut Sauce

The fruity shrimp mixture blends nicely with the salty peanut sauce in these crunchy lettuce wraps.

⅓   cup flaked sweetened coconut
1   pound chopped cooked shrimp
2   cups diced peeled mango
3   tablespoons fresh lime juice, divided
1   tablespoon chopped fresh mint
8   Bibb lettuce leaves
½   cup bottled peanut sauce (such as Bangkok Padang)
2   tablespoons wasabi- and soy sauce–flavored almonds, chopped (such as Blue Diamond)

1. Heat a small nonstick skillet over medium-high heat. Add coconut; cook 3 minutes or until golden brown and fragrant, stirring constantly.
2. Combine coconut, shrimp, mango, 2 tablespoons lime juice, and mint in a medium bowl. Spoon shrimp mixture evenly onto lettuce leaves.
3. Stir remaining 1 tablespoon lime juice into peanut sauce. Drizzle sauce evenly over lettuce wraps, and sprinkle with almonds. **Yield:** 8 servings (serving size: 1 wrap).

CALORIES 84; FAT 3g (sat 0.8g, mono 1.2g, poly 0.8g); PROTEIN 7.1g; CARB 7.1g; FIBER 0.8g; CHOL 55mg; IRON 1.1mg; SODIUM 201mg; CALC 22mg

15 MINUTES

Greek Tuna Bites

A packet of lemon-pepper tuna is the key ingredient in these Mediterranean-inspired hors d'oeuvres. If you plan to prepare this recipe ahead, chill the tuna mixture by itself, and fill the shells right before serving.

1 (5-ounce) package lemon-pepper tuna
⅓ cup light mayonnaise
¼ cup chopped sun-dried tomato, packed without oil (about 5 sun-dried tomatoes)
2 tablespoons chopped fresh dill
2 tablespoons crumbled reduced-fat feta cheese
½ teaspoon Greek seasoning
1 (2.1-ounce) package mini phyllo shells (such as Athens)
Sliced ripe olives (optional)
Dill sprigs (optional)

1. Drain tuna; pat dry with paper towels.
2. Combine tuna and next 5 ingredients in a medium bowl; cover and chill, if desired.
3. Fill each phyllo shell with 1 tablespoon tuna mixture. Top each with an olive slice and a dill sprig, if desired. **Yield:** 15 servings (serving size: 1 tuna bite).

CALORIES 53; FAT 3g (sat 0.4g, mono 1.7g, poly 0.6g); PROTEIN 2.6g; CARB 3.8g; FIBER 0.2g; CHOL 6mg; IRON 0.4mg; SODIUM 115mg; CALC 3mg

20 MINUTES

Chutney-Glazed Chicken Skewers

To get those tasty grill marks on the chicken, make sure your grill is hot. For a great main dish, thread 2 chicken strips onto each of 8 (12-inch) metal skewers.

2 teaspoons canola oil
1½ teaspoons chili powder
¼ teaspoon salt
¼ teaspoon ground cumin
4 (6-ounce) skinless, boneless chicken breast halves
1 (9-ounce) bottle mango chutney, divided
Cooking spray

1. Prepare grill.
2. Combine first 4 ingredients in a medium bowl.
3. Place chicken breast halves between 2 sheets of heavy-duty plastic wrap; pound to ½-inch thickness using a meat mallet or small heavy skillet. Cut each breast lengthwise into 4 strips. Add chicken to oil mixture; toss well. Thread 1 chicken strip onto each of 16 (6-inch) metal skewers. Brush chicken with 3 tablespoons chutney.
4. Place chicken on grill rack coated with cooking spray. Grill 2 minutes on each side or until done. Serve with remaining chutney. **Yield:** 16 servings (serving size: 1 skewer and 1½ teaspoons chutney).

CALORIES 83; FAT 1.6g (sat 0.3g, mono 0.7g, poly 0.4g); PROTEIN 8.6g; CARB 7.2g; FIBER 0g; CHOL 25mg; IRON 0.3mg; SODIUM 168mg; CALC 5mg

Wooden skewers require a good soaking in water for at least 30 minutes before using them to prevent burning. If you grill often and want to skip that step, invest in a set of metal skewers, which are reusable and don't require soaking.

SHORTCUT SPOTLIGHT

Chicken Tenders with Pita Coating

You can use whatever flavor of pita chips you prefer. In addition to the Parmesan, garlic, and herb-flavored variety, we also like pesto and sun-dried tomato–flavored chips.

½   cup egg substitute
½   teaspoon freshly ground black pepper
1½ cups Parmesan, garlic, and herb–flavored
      pita chips (such as Stacy's), finely crushed
1   tablespoon salt-free Italian seasoning (such
      as Mrs. Dash)
8   (2-ounce) chicken breast tenders
Cooking spray
½   cup tomato-basil pasta sauce (such as
      Classico), warmed

1. Preheat oven to 400°.
2. Heat a large baking sheet in oven 5 minutes.
3. While baking sheet heats, combine egg substitute and pepper in a shallow dish. Combine chips and Italian seasoning in another shallow dish. Dip chicken in egg mixture; dredge in chip mixture. Coat preheated baking sheet with cooking spray, and place chicken on pan.
4. Bake at 400° for 15 minutes or until done. Serve with pasta sauce. **Yield:** 8 servings (serving size: 1 chicken breast tender and 1 tablespoon pasta sauce).

CALORIES 97; FAT 2.6g (sat 1.1g, mono 0.7g, poly 0.5g); PROTEIN 14.3g; CARB 3.7g; FIBER 0.5g; CHOL 33mg; IRON 0.8mg; SODIUM 120mg; CALC 13mg

30 MINUTES

Peach and Brie Quesadillas with Lime-Honey Dipping Sauce

This intriguing appetizer is savory-sweet. Ripe—but firm—peaches work best; if they're too soft, they'll make the tortillas soggy. Placing the fillings on one side of the tortilla and folding the other half over (like a taco) makes the quesadillas easier to handle.

Sauce:
2   tablespoons honey
2   teaspoons fresh lime juice
½   teaspoon grated lime rind
Quesadillas:
1   cup thinly sliced peeled firm ripe peaches
     (about 2 large peaches)
1   tablespoon chopped fresh chives
1   teaspoon brown sugar
3   ounces Brie cheese, thinly sliced
4   (8-inch) fat-free flour tortillas
Cooking spray
Chive strips (optional)

1. To prepare sauce, combine first 3 ingredients, stirring with a whisk; set aside.
2. To prepare quesadillas, combine peaches, 1 tablespoon chives, and sugar, tossing gently to coat. Heat a large nonstick skillet over medium-high heat. Arrange one-fourth of cheese and one-fourth of peach mixture over half of each tortilla; fold tortillas in half. Coat pan with cooking spray. Place 2 quesadillas in pan; cook 2 minutes on each side or until tortillas are lightly browned and crisp. Remove from pan; keep warm. Repeat procedure with remaining quesadillas. Cut each quesadilla into 3 wedges; serve with sauce. Garnish with chive strips, if desired. **Yield:** 6 servings (serving size: 2 quesadilla wedges and about 1 teaspoon sauce).

CALORIES 157; FAT 4g (sat 2.5g, mono 1.2g, poly 0.1g); PROTEIN 5.3g; CARB 25.5g; FIBER 0.7g; CHOL 14mg; IRON 0.9mg; SODIUM 316mg; CALC 30mg

COOKING CLASS: *how to revive tortillas*

If tortillas are not stored properly, they tend to dry out and become difficult to separate. You can revive dry tortillas by wrapping them in damp paper towels and microwaving them at HIGH for 10 seconds. This will keep them from cracking when you fold them in half.

 MINUTES

Smoked Salmon and Dill Quesadillas

Havarti is a mild semisoft Danish cheese. Look for light Havarti cheese in the deli department of your grocery store. You may substitute light provolone or part-skim mozzarella for the Havarti, if desired.

4   (8-inch) flour tortillas
Olive oil–flavored cooking spray
1   (4-ounce) package cold-smoked salmon
1   cup (4 ounces) shredded light Havarti cheese
4   teaspoons chopped fresh dill

1. Heat a large nonstick skillet over medium heat. Coat 1 side of each tortilla with cooking spray. Place 1 tortilla, coated side down, in pan; top with 1 ounce smoked salmon, 1/4 cup cheese, and 1 teaspoon dill. Fold tortilla in half. Repeat procedure with 1 more tortilla for other side of pan.
2. Cook 2 to 3 minutes on 1 side; turn tortillas over, and cook 1 more minute or until golden and cheese is melted. Repeat procedure with remaining ingredients.
3. Cut each quesadilla into 4 wedges. Serve immediately. **Yield:** 8 servings (serving size: 2 wedges).

CALORIES 135; FAT 4.7g (sat 2.1g, mono 1.9g, poly 0.5g); PROTEIN 8.7g; CARB 12.6g; FIBER 0.8g; CHOL 11mg; IRON 0.9mg; SODIUM 368mg; CALC 135mg

 MINUTES

Chicken Quesadillas

Here's a traditional Mexican classic with a healthful update of fat-free refried beans, 40% less-sodium taco seasoning, and whole wheat tortillas.

1   cup fat-free refried beans
1   tablespoon 40%-less-sodium taco seasoning
2   cups chopped cooked chicken breast
1/2   cup bottled chunky salsa
6   (7-inch) whole wheat tortillas
Cooking spray
1   cup (4-ounces) shredded reduced-fat cheddar cheese with jalapeño peppers

1. Preheat broiler.
2. Combine beans and seasoning in a small bowl; set aside. Combine chicken and salsa in another small bowl.
3. Place tortillas on a baking sheet coated with cooking spray. Spread about 3 tablespoons bean mixture on each tortilla. Spoon chicken mixture evenly over beans; sprinkle each tortilla with about 3 tablespoons cheese. Fold tortillas in half.
4. Lightly coat tops with cooking spray. Broil 3 minutes or until cheese melts and tortillas begin to brown. Cut each tortilla into 4 wedges. **Yield:** 12 servings (serving size: 2 wedges).

CALORIES 130; FAT 5g (sat 2.7g, mono 0.8g, poly 1.2g); PROTEIN 13.3g; CARB 9g; FIBER 2.8g; CHOL 20mg; IRON 1.2mg; SODIUM 330mg; CALC 116mg

15 MINUTES

Cappuccino

While it may sound like a fancy coffee-house drink, cappuccino can easily be prepared on your stovetop at home by using instant espresso granules. Look for them at large supermarkets or specialty coffee shops.

2 teaspoons instant espresso granules
³/₄ cup boiling water
³/₄ cup 1% low-fat milk
Ground cinnamon or nutmeg (optional)

1. Combine espresso granules and boiling water.
2. Place milk in a small saucepan; cook over medium heat 2 minutes or until a thermometer registers between 140° and 160°, stirring constantly with a whisk. Remove from heat; stir vigorously with a whisk 30 seconds or until foamy.
3. Divide milk (with froth) and espresso equally between 2 mugs. Sprinkle with cinnamon, if desired. **Yield:** 2 servings (serving size: ³/₄ cup).

CALORIES 47; FAT 1.1g (sat 0.7g, mono 0.3g, poly 0g); PROTEIN 3.1g; CARB 5.9g; FIBER 0g; CHOL 5mg; IRON 0.1mg; SODIUM 53mg; CALC 111mg

Cappuccino

For the freshest coffee with the best flavor, buy whole beans. Keep the whole beans in the bag and store in an airtight container. The coffee will stay fresh up to six weeks once opened.

INGREDIENT SPOTLIGHT

15 MINUTES

Coffee Royale

For a nonalcoholic version, omit the amaretto and increase the coffee to 3¼ cups.

1¼ cups 1% low-fat milk
1 tablespoon sugar
¼ teaspoon ground cinnamon
2³/₄ cups hot strong brewed coffee
½ cup amaretto (almond-flavored liqueur)

1. Combine first 3 ingredients in a medium saucepan. Place over medium heat; cook 2 minutes or until sugar dissolves, stirring constantly.
2. Remove from heat, and stir in coffee and amaretto. Serve warm. **Yield:** 6 servings (serving size: ³/₄ cup).

CALORIES 98; FAT 0.6g (sat 0.3g, mono 0.2g, poly 0.1g); PROTEIN 1.9g; CARB 13.1g; FIBER 0.1g; CHOL 3mg; IRON 0.1mg; SODIUM 26mg; CALC 64mg

Mexican Marshmallow Mocha

We added marshmallow creme to make this mocha drink especially rich.

2 cups 1% low-fat milk
¼ cup unsweetened cocoa
3 tablespoons sugar
2½ teaspoons instant coffee granules
¼ teaspoon ground cinnamon
½ cup marshmallow creme
½ teaspoon vanilla extract

1. Heat milk in a medium saucepan over medium heat; bring to a simmer (do not boil).

2. Combine cocoa and next 3 ingredients in a small bowl, and stir well. Add cocoa mixture to milk mixture in pan, stirring with a whisk until smooth. Stir in marshmallow creme. Cook mixture over medium heat 3 minutes or until thoroughly heated, stirring constantly with a whisk. Reduce heat to low, and simmer 1 minute, stirring vigorously with a whisk to froth mixture. Remove from heat; stir in vanilla. Pour into mugs. **Yield:** 3 servings (serving size: about ³⁄₄ cup).

CALORIES 189; FAT 2.6g (sat 1.6g, mono 0.8g, poly 0.1g); PROTEIN 7.1g; CARB 37.8g; FIBER 2.5g; CHOL 8mg; IRON 1.1mg; SODIUM 86mg; CALC 207mg

Peppermint White Hot Chocolate

MINUTES

Peppermint White Hot Chocolate

End a festive holiday meal by serving this lusciously rich, minty dessert beverage.

2   cups 1% low-fat milk
5   hard peppermint candies, divided
¼   cup white chocolate chips
¼   teaspoon pure peppermint extract
1½ teaspoons light-colored corn syrup
3   tablespoons frozen fat-free whipped topping, thawed

1. Cook milk in a heavy saucepan over medium heat until warm (do not boil). Crush 3 peppermint candies; add to warm milk, stirring until candies dissolve. Add white chocolate, stirring with a whisk until chocolate melts. Cook until tiny bubbles form around edge of pan (do not boil), stirring constantly with a whisk. Remove from heat; stir in extract.
2. Finely crush 1 peppermint. Coat rims of 3 mugs with corn syrup. Place finely crushed peppermint in a saucer, and dip rim of each mug in peppermint to coat.
3. Coarsely crush remaining peppermint. Pour ⅔ cup hot chocolate into each mug, and top each serving with 1 tablespoon whipped topping. Sprinkle coarsely crushed peppermint evenly over topping. **Yield:** 3 servings.

CALORIES 178; FAT 6.3g (sat 3.8g, mono 2.1g, poly 0.2g); PROTEIN 6.2g; CARB 23.1g; FIBER 0g; CHOL 7mg; IRON 0.1mg; SODIUM 107mg; CALC 200mg

MINUTES

Hot Cranberry-Apple Cider

4   cups apple cider
3   cups reduced-calorie cranberry-apple juice drink
2   (3-inch) cinnamon sticks
1   teaspoon whole cloves
1   small lemon, thinly sliced

1. Combine all ingredients in a large Dutch oven. Cover and bring to a boil. Reduce heat, and simmer, uncovered, 15 minutes. Remove from heat, and discard cinnamon sticks, cloves, and lemon slices.
2. Pour beverage into individual cups. Serve cider immediately. **Yield:** 8 servings (serving size: ¾ cup).

CALORIES 89; FAT 0g; PROTEIN 0.6g; CARB 22.4g; FIBER 0.2g; CHOL 0mg; IRON 0mg; SODIUM 2mg; CALC 4mg

MINUTES

Spicy Hot Ginger Tea

Ginger beer is a nonalcoholic carbonated beverage that tastes very similar to ginger ale but with a more pronounced ginger flavor. Enjoy this ginger-spiked tea both hot and over ice.

1   (12-ounce) bottle Jamaican-style ginger beer (such as Reed's)
1   cup water
2   tablespoons turbinado sugar
½   (3-inch) cinnamon stick
4   black tea bags

1. Bring first 4 ingredients to a boil in a medium saucepan, stirring until sugar dissolves. Remove pan from heat; add tea bags, and steep 5 minutes. Remove cinnamon stick and tea bags with a slotted spoon (do not squeeze tea bags). Serve hot or chilled. **Yield:** 2 servings (serving size: about 1 cup).

CALORIES 99; FAT 0g; PROTEIN 0g; CARB 26.9g; FIBER 0g; CHOL 0mg; IRON 0mg; SODIUM 2mg; CALC 0mg

Turbinado sugar is a dry, pourable sugar that has been only partially refined and steam cleaned. Blond in color and consisting of large, coarse crystals, it has a subtler molasses flavor than brown sugar.

INGREDIENT SPOTLIGHT

Iced Spiced Latte

Lemon and Mint Iced Tea

This twist on sweet Southern iced tea is refreshingly tart. Serve well chilled.

4	cups water
3	family-sized tea bags
1	fresh mint sprig (about ¼ cup leaves)
¾	cup sugar
¼	cup fresh lemon juice
4	cups cold water
8	lemon slices (optional)
8	fresh mint sprigs (optional)

1. Bring 4 cups water to a boil in a medium saucepan. Add tea bags and mint to pan; steep 10 minutes. Remove and discard tea bags and mint.
2. Combine sugar and juice in a glass measuring cup. Add ½ cup hot tea mixture; stir until sugar dissolves. Pour sugar mixture into a 2-quart pitcher. Pour remaining hot tea mixture into pitcher. Add 4 cups cold water; stir. Serve over ice. Garnish with lemon slices and mint sprigs, if desired.
Yield: 8 servings (serving size: 1 cup).

CALORIES 75; FAT 0g; PROTEIN 0g; CARB 19.4g; FIBER 0g; CHOL 0mg; IRON 0mg; SODIUM 5mg; CALC 5mg

Iced Spiced Latte

Make the brewed coffee ahead, and chill it to prevent the ice from melting too quickly.

½	cup ground dark roast coffee
4	teaspoons pumpkin pie spice
4	cups water
4	cups crushed ice
1	cup fat-free half-and-half
1	cup refrigerated fat-free dairy whipped topping (such as Reddi-wip)

Ground cinnamon (optional)

1. Combine ground coffee and pumpkin pie spice, stirring well. Brew ground coffee mixture with 4 cups water in a coffeemaker according to manufacturer's directions.
2. For each serving, spoon 1 cup crushed ice into a tall glass. Pour 1 cup brewed coffee and ¼ cup half-and-half over ice in each glass; top with whipped topping, and sprinkle with ground cinnamon, if desired. Serve immediately. **Yield:** 4 servings (serving size: 1¼ cups).

CALORIES 55; FAT 0.2g (sat 0.1g, mono 0g, poly 0g); PROTEIN 0.1g; CARB 9.3g; FIBER 0.3g; CHOL 0mg; IRON 0.3mg; SODIUM 61mg; CALC 77mg

INGREDIENT SPOTLIGHT

We use tea bags for some of our recipes and loose tea for others. Tea bags are convenient and easy to use. We test with supermarket brands so there's no need to visit a specialty shop.

Lemon and Mint Iced Tea

Fresh Ginger Beer

Fresh Ginger Beer

If you like ginger ale, you'll love this tangy beverage. Add your favorite rum to create a memorable cocktail. If you can't find superfine sugar, place granulated sugar in a blender, and process it until fine. You can find bottled ground fresh ginger in the produce section of your supermarket.

2   cups cold water
1   cup fresh lime juice
4   teaspoons bottled ground fresh ginger
    (such as Spice World)
¾   cup superfine sugar
3   cups sparkling water
Lime slices (optional)

1. Place water, juice, and ginger in a blender; process until blended.
2. Line a strainer with cheesecloth. Strain mixture over a pitcher; discard solids. Add sugar to pitcher; stir until dissolved.
3. Add sparkling water just before serving. Serve over ice. Garnish with lime slices, if desired. **Yield:** 8 servings (serving size: 1 cup).

CALORIES 81; FAT 0g; PROTEIN 0.1g; CARB 21.5g; FIBER 0.1g; CHOL 0mg; IRON 0mg; SODIUM 3mg; CALC 21mg

Raspberry Lemonade

If you've been raspberry picking, here's a perfect recipe to use your bounty. You may want to consider doubling the recipe as we found it's so good you'll be craving more than four cups!

3   cups cold water, divided
1   cup fresh raspberries
1   (6-ounce) can thawed lemonade
    concentrate, undiluted
Mint sprigs (optional)

1. Place ¾ cup water and raspberries in a blender; process until smooth. Strain mixture through a sieve into a medium bowl; discard seeds. Combine raspberry liquid, 2 ¼ cups water, and lemonade concentrate in a pitcher; chill. Serve garnished with mint, if desired. **Yield:** 4 servings (serving size: 1 cup).

CALORIES 92; FAT 0.3g (sat 0g, mono 0g, poly 0.1g); PROTEIN 0.4g; CARB 23.6g; FIBER 2.5g; CHOL 0mg; IRON 0.5mg; SODIUM 2mg; CALC 10mg

MAKE IT FASTER

Lemonade concentrate is a frozen juice product that should be used by the "best if used by" date on the bottom of the lid. Save prep time by thawing the concentrate ahead of time in the refrigerator. Once thawed, the lemonade will stay fresh for five days if it remains refrigerated.

15 MINUTES

White Cranberry–Peach Spritzers

Be sure to use fresh peaches when they're in season. Once fresh are no longer available, frozen peaches make a good substitute.

2   cups white cranberry–peach juice (such as Ocean Spray)
²/₃   cup peach nectar
²/₃   cup sparkling water
½   cup fresh or frozen sliced peaches
4   lime wedges

1. Combine first 3 ingredients in a pitcher; stir gently. Pour about ³/₄ cup juice mixture into each of 4 tall glasses. Divide peach slices evenly among glasses, and squeeze a lime wedge into each glass. Fill glasses with ice. Serve immediately. **Yield:** 4 servings (serving size: ³/₄ cup juice mixture, about 2 peach slices, and 1 lime wedge).

CALORIES 91; FAT 0g; PROTEIN 0.3g; CARB 23.5g; FIBER 0.4g; CHOL 0mg; IRON 0.1mg; SODIUM 21mg; CALC 3mg

Pomegranates are noted for their astounding antioxidant benefits—which help prevent cancer and heart disease. They're also a good source of potassium, which helps lower blood pressure. Pomegranate juice is great in marinades, desserts, and beverages, and it is featured in this fabulous fizzer.

INGREDIENT SPOTLIGHT

15 MINUTES

Pomegranate Fizzers

Add the diet ginger ale to the beverage just before serving to make sure you get the most fizz. This recipe is easily doubled or tripled if you plan to serve a crowd.

1   (16-ounce) bottle pomegranate juice (such as POM Wonderful)
1   cup mixed berry juice (such as Dole's Berry Blend)
2   tablespoons lime juice
1   cup diet ginger ale
Lime wedges (optional)

1. Combine first 3 ingredients in a pitcher; cover and chill, if desired.
2. Stir in ginger ale just before serving. Serve over ice. Garnish with lime wedges, if desired. **Yield:** 4 servings (serving size: 1 cup).

CALORIES 99; FAT 0g; PROTEIN 0.5g; CARB 24.9g; FIBER 0g; CHOL 0mg; IRON 0.2mg; SODIUM 35mg; CALC 21mg

White Cranberry–Peach Spritzers

Pomegranate Fizzers

Cherry-Lemonade Slush

15 MINUTES

Cherry-Lemonade Slush

This icy refresher is a quick thirst quencher on hot summer days.

1½ cups frozen pitted dark sweet cherries
1   cup water
2   tablespoons maraschino cherry juice
1½ teaspoons sugar-free pink lemonade drink
       mix (such as Crystal Light)
1   cup crushed ice
Mint sprigs (optional)

1. Place first 5 ingredients in a blender; process until smooth. Pour into glasses and garnish with mint, if desired. **Yield:** 2 servings (serving size: 1¼ cups).

CALORIES 97; FAT 0g (sat 0g, mono 0g, poly 0g); PROTEIN 1.4g; CARB 24.1g; FIBER 0.5g; CHOL 0mg; IRON 0.3mg; SODIUM 23mg; CALC 19mg

A blender is a must-have when making quick frozen beverages, sensational smoothies, and slushy drinks.
If you make frozen beverages often, choose a blender with an ice-crushing mode.

SHORTCUT SPOTLIGHT

15 MINUTES

Cranberry-Orange Spritzers

Serve this tangy beverage to brunch guests or to your family for an afternoon treat.

4½ cups reduced-calorie cranberry juice
       cocktail, chilled
3   tablespoons orange juice
3½ cups diet lemon-lime carbonated beverage
       (such as Sprite Zero), chilled

1. Combine juices in a large pitcher. Cover and chill. Stir in lemon-lime beverage just before serving. Serve over crushed ice. **Yield:** 8 servings (serving size: 1 cup).

CALORIES 29; FAT 0g; PROTEIN 0.1g; CARB 6.7g; FIBER 0g; CHOL 0mg; IRON 0.1mg; SODIUM 4mg; CALC 13mg

20 MINUTES

Pineapple-Ginger Punch

This refreshing beverage features sweet pineapple juice with a kick of mint and peppery ginger.

4   (6-ounce) cans pineapple juice
2   large fresh mint sprigs
2   (12-ounce) cans diet ginger ale

1. Combine juice and mint sprigs in a medium saucepan. Bring to a boil; remove from heat, and cool to room temperature. Discard mint sprigs.
2. Transfer pineapple juice to a pitcher; gently stir in ginger ale. Serve immediately over ice. **Yield:** 6 servings (serving size: about 1 cup).

CALORIES 66; FAT 0.1g (sat 0g, mono 0g, poly 0.1g); PROTEIN 0.5g; CARB 16.1g; FIBER 0.3g; CHOL 0mg; IRON 0.4mg; SODIUM 17mg; CALC 16mg

15 MINUTES

Blueberry-Lime Slush

Not only is this beverage a thirst quencher, but it also packs a nutritional punch. Look for light limeade with the other refrigerated juices.

2   cups frozen blueberries
2   cups crushed ice
1½   cups light limeade (such as Minute Maid)
1   (12-ounce) can diet citrus soda (such as
       original Fresca), chilled
Lime slices (optional)

1. Place first 3 ingredients in a blender; process until smooth. Pour into a pitcher, and stir in soda. Pour into glasses, and garnish with lime slices, if desired. **Yield:** 5 servings (serving size: 1 cup).

CALORIES 37; FAT 0.4g (sat 0g, mono 0.1g, poly 0.2g); PROTEIN 0.3g; CARB 8.8g; FIBER 1.7g; CHOL 0mg; IRON 0.1mg; SODIUM 5mg; CALC 5mg

Blueberry-Lime Slush

Of all the popular summer fruits, blueberries have an advantage, nutritionally speaking. They've earned the distinction of one of the most potent sources of antioxidants, which help counteract heart disease, cancers, and other types of illnesses. Blueberries are also full of fiber and high in vitamin C.

INGREDIENT SPOTLIGHT

15 MINUTES

Cranberry Smoothie

This cool, fruity drink doubles as a delicious breakfast beverage or a refreshing snack.

½   cup light cranberry juice
1   cup sliced strawberries
1   frozen banana

1. Place all ingredients in a blender. Process until smooth. **Yield:** 1 serving (serving size: 1¾ cups).

CALORIES 178; FAT 0.9g (sat 0.2g, mono 0.1g, poly 0.3g); PROTEIN 2.4g; CARB 44.7g; FIBER 6.4g; CHOL 0mg; IRON 1mg; SODIUM 12mg; CALC 33mg

MINUTES

Raspberry-Banana Smoothies

The beautiful color of this quick smoothie makes a cheery treat.

1   small banana
1   cup frozen unsweetened raspberries
1   (6-ounce) carton vanilla fat-free yogurt
1   tablespoon fat-free milk

1. Place all ingredients in a blender, and process until smooth. Serve immediately. **Yield:** 2 servings (serving size: about $^3/_4$ cup).

CALORIES 173; FAT 1g (sat 0.2g, mono 0.1g, poly 0.5g); PROTEIN 6.8g; CARB 37.3g; FIBER 9.4g; CHOL 2mg; IRON 1mg; SODIUM 63mg; CALC 174mg

MINUTES

Banana-Berry Smoothies

This fruity treat, chock-full of potassium and antioxidants, is sure to jump-start your morning.

1   cup fresh blueberries
1   small banana, frozen
1   (6-ounce) carton vanilla fat-free yogurt

1. Place all ingredients in a blender; process until smooth, scraping sides of bowl once. Serve immediately. **Yield:** 2 servings (serving size: about $^3/_4$ cup).

CALORIES 158; FAT 0.5g (sat 0.2g, mono 0.1g, poly 0.1g); PROTEIN 5.4g; CARB 36g; FIBER 3g; CHOL 1mg; IRON 0.4mg; SODIUM 59mg; CALC 158mg

Raspberry-Banana Smoothies

Mango Lassi

COOKING CLASS: *how to cut a mango*

To cut a mango, use a sharp knife to trim about half an inch from the top and bottom to create a sturdy surface for cutting. Hold the mango in one hand, and use a vegetable peeler to slice the skin from the flesh. Cut the flesh from around the pit with two curved cuts down the plumpest sides, and then trim the remaining sides. Cut the fruit's flesh as desired—diced or sliced.

15 MINUTES

Mango Lassi

Lassi is a time-honored Indian yogurt drink that is often served to cool the heat of the spicy curries characteristic of Indian cuisine. Plain or flavored, its consistency is similar to that of a thick milk shake. We prefer the more intense flavor of the mango nectar, but you can substitute 1⅓ cups of pureed fresh mango (about 2 ripe mangoes).

2   cups ice
2   cups vanilla fat-free yogurt
1⅓ cups mango nectar
2   tablespoons honey
2   tablespoons fresh lemon juice
Mint sprigs (optional)

1. Place first 5 ingredients in a blender; process until smooth. Garnish with mint, if desired. **Yield:** 5 servings (serving size: 1 cup).

CALORIES 106; FAT 0.1g (sat 0g, mono 0g, poly 0g); PROTEIN 4.2g; CARB 25.2g; FIBER 0.5g; CHOL 2mg; IRON 0.1mg; SODIUM 56mg; CALC 124mg

15 MINUTES

Easy Sangria Slush

This sangria is great for entertaining because you can make it ahead and then transfer it to a pitcher for serving. This recipe is easily doubled or tripled if you're preparing it for a party.

3   cups zinfandel or other fruity dry red wine
½   cup orange juice
½   cup pineapple juice
⅓   cup thawed lemonade concentrate
1   cup sparkling water or club soda

1. Combine first 3 ingredients in a 4-cup glass measure. Pour liquid evenly into ice cube trays. Freeze 8 hours or until firm.
2. Place frozen juice cubes in a food processor; process 30 seconds or until coarsely chopped. Add lemonade concentrate and sparkling water; process 1 minute or until smooth. Pour into a pitcher to serve. **Yield:** 5 servings (serving size: 1 cup).

CALORIES 185; FAT 0.1g (sat 0g, mono 0g, poly 0.1g); PROTEIN 0.4g; CARB 19g; FIBER 0.1g; CHOL 0mg; IRON 0.3mg; SODIUM 11mg; CALC 10mg

MINUTES

Classic Mojito

*This Cuban drink is fast becoming an
American favorite. The mint and sugar are
ideal complements.*

2   tablespoons sugar
15   fresh mint leaves
¼   cup white rum
1½   tablespoons fresh lime juice
¼   cup club soda, chilled
½   cup ice

1. Place sugar and mint in a 2-cup glass measure; crush with a wooden spoon. Add rum
and juice; stir until sugar dissolves. Just
before serving, stir in club soda. Place ice in
an 8-ounce glass; pour mint mixture over
ice. **Yield:** 1 serving (serving size: about
1 cup).

CALORIES 234; FAT 0g; PROTEIN 0.1g; CARB 27.2g; FIBER 0.2g; CHOL 0mg;
IRON 0.1mg; SODIUM 14mg; CALC 7mg

If you have access
to Key limes, use
those for the most
authentic flavor.
One medium lime
will give you 1½
tablespoons of fresh
juice, which is what we call
for in this recipe. To get
the most juice out of a lime,
bring it to room temperature
before squeezing it.

INGREDIENT SPOTLIGHT

MINUTES

Strawberry Mojitos

*Blend up a batch of these rejuvenating
cocktails the next time you entertain
outdoors.*

1   (16-ounce) package frozen unsweetened
       whole strawberries
1   (10-ounce) can frozen mojito mix (such as
       Bacardi)
1   (25-ounce) bottle lime-flavored sparkling
       water
1   cup white rum
Fresh strawberries (optional)
Mint sprigs (optional)

1. Place half of strawberries and mojito mix
in a blender; process until slushy. Pour into
a large pitcher. Repeat with remaining
strawberries and mojito mix. Stir in sparkling water and rum. Garnish with fresh
strawberries and mint sprigs, if desired.
Yield: 12 servings (serving size: 1 cup).

CALORIES 119; FAT 0g; PROTEIN 0.2g; CARB 20.5g; FIBER 0.8g; CHOL 0mg;
IRON 0.3mg; SODIUM 3mg; CALC 7mg

MINUTES

Madras Spritzers

*You can make this drink ahead, but wait to
add the sparkling water until just before
serving to prevent it from going flat. For a
kid-friendly drink, substitute orange juice
for the liqueur.*

3   cups light cranberry juice cocktail, chilled
⅓   cup Grand Marnier (orange-flavored liqueur)
3   cups orange sparkling water (such as Poland
       Spring), chilled

1. Combine juice and liqueur in a pitcher;
stir. Add sparkling water just before serving. **Yield:** 6 servings (serving size: about
1 cup).

CALORIES 67; FAT 0g; PROTEIN 0g; CARB 9.3g; FIBER 0g; CHOL 0mg; IRON 0mg;
SODIUM 38mg; CALC 0mg

Strawberry Mojitos

Bloody Mary

For a twist on this drink, you can use rum or tequila instead of vodka. Tomato juice is a concentrated source of lycopene; a ½ cup serving supplies one-third of your daily lycopene dose.

4   cups tomato juice
1   cup vodka
2   tablespoons fresh lemon juice
1   to 1½ tablespoons prepared
    horseradish
2   teaspoons hot sauce
2   teaspoons Worcestershire sauce
¼   teaspoon freshly ground black pepper
½   teaspoon brown sugar
¼   teaspoon ground celery seeds
Fresh lemon slices and celery sticks

1. Combine first 9 ingredients in a pitcher, stirring to combine. Serve over ice. Garnish with lemon wedges and celery sticks. **Yield:** 10 servings (serving size: ½ cup).

CALORIES 76; FAT 0.1g (sat 0g, mono 0g, poly 0g); PROTEIN 0.8g; CARB 5g;
FIBER 0.5g; CHOL 0mg; IRON 0.5mg; SODIUM 284mg; CALC 13mg

FISH & SHELLFISH

Curried Amberjack

Since it's full of flavor and has a firm flesh, amberjack is ideal for grilling, broiling, and, in this recipe, pan-frying. Amberjack is available in fillets or steaks year-round, especially in the South, since it comes primarily from the Gulf of Mexico.

1½ tablespoons all-purpose flour
1½ teaspoons curry powder
½ teaspoon salt
¼ teaspoon black pepper
4 (6-ounce) amberjack fillets (about 1 inch thick)
2 teaspoons canola oil
⅓ cup hot mango chutney
2 tablespoons raisins
2 tablespoons flaked coconut
1 tablespoon water
Sliced green onions (optional)

1. Combine first 4 ingredients in a shallow bowl. Dredge each fillet in flour mixture.
2. Heat oil in a nonstick skillet over medium-high heat. Add fish; cook 4 to 5 minutes on each side or until fish flakes easily when tested with a fork.
3. Combine chutney and next 3 ingredients. Spoon chutney mixture over fish, and sprinkle evenly with green onions, if desired. Serve immediately. **Yield:** 4 servings (serving size: 1 fillet and 2 tablespoons chutney mixture).

CALORIES 300; FAT 6.2g (sat 1.7g, mono 2.7g, poly 1.5g); PROTEIN 36.8g; CARB 22.7g; FIBER 1.3g; CHOL 75mg; IRON 0.8mg; SODIUM 695mg; CALC 14mg

Sautéed Bass with Shiitake
Mushroom Sauce

Sautéed Bass with Shiitake Mushroom Sauce

2 teaspoons canola oil
⅛ teaspoon salt
⅛ teaspoon black pepper
4 (6-ounce) skinned bass fillets
2 cups sliced shiitake mushroom caps
1 teaspoon dark sesame oil
2 teaspoons bottled ground fresh ginger (such as Spice World)
1 teaspoon bottled minced garlic
1 cup chopped green onions
¼ cup water
¼ cup low-sodium soy sauce
1 tablespoon lemon juice

1. Heat canola oil in a large nonstick skillet over medium-high heat. Sprinkle salt and pepper over fish. Add fish to pan; cook 2½ minutes on each side or until fish flakes easily when tested with a fork or until desired degree of doneness. Remove fish from pan; cover and keep warm.
2. Add mushrooms and sesame oil to pan; sauté 2 minutes. Add ginger and garlic to pan; sauté 1 minute. Add green onions and remaining ingredients to pan; sauté 2 minutes. Serve sauce with fish. **Yield:** 4 servings (serving size: 1 fillet and ¼ cup sauce).

CALORIES 247; FAT 7.6g (sat 1.2g, mono 3.2g, poly 2.4g); PROTEIN 33.2g; CARB 6.9g; FIBER 1.7g; CHOL 140mg; IRON 2.9mg; SODIUM 629mg; CALC 49mg

15 MINUTES

Catfish Fajitas

make it a meal *Serve these fajitas with baked chips and tropical fruit salad from the deli for a speedy supper.*

1	pound catfish fillets, cut into 8 strips
2	teaspoons fajita seasoning
2	teaspoons olive oil
1	cup sliced red bell pepper
1	cup sliced green bell pepper
1	cup sliced onion
1	tablespoon chopped pickled jalapeño peppers
1	teaspoon bottled minced garlic
½	cup chopped plum tomato (about 2)
1	tablespoon low-sodium soy sauce
4	(8-inch) fat-free flour tortillas
½	cup bottled pico de gallo

1. Sprinkle both sides of fish evenly with fajita seasoning. Heat oil in a large nonstick skillet over medium-high heat. Add fish to pan; cook 2 minutes on each side or until fish flakes easily when tested with a fork. Remove fish from pan. Add bell peppers and next 3 ingredients to pan; cook 3 minutes, stirring occasionally. Add tomato; cook 2 minutes. Stir in soy sauce; cook 1 minute. Add fish; cook 1 minute or until thoroughly heated. Remove from heat.
2. Warm tortillas according to package directions. Spoon about 1 cup fish mixture down center of each tortilla; top each serving with 2 tablespoons pico de gallo. Serve immediately. **Yield:** 4 servings (serving size: 1 fajita).

CALORIES 334; FAT 11.3g (sat 2.4g, mono 5.8g, poly 2.2g); PROTEIN 22.7g; CARB 35.3g; FIBER 3.7g; CHOL 53mg; IRON 2.2mg; SODIUM 908mg; CALC 29mg

COOKING CLASS: *how to separate eggs*

Crack an egg, and let the white run through your fingers into a bowl instead of pouring the yolk from one half of the shell to the other (which increases the likelihood of the shell breaking the yolk and the chance of transferring bacteria). Wash your hands before and after.

Crispy Baked Catfish

When breading fish, use one hand for the wet ingredients, such as the egg whites, and the other hand for the dry ingredients. You'll use fewer breadcrumbs, and the process will take less time.

4	(6-ounce) catfish fillets
1	teaspoon seafood seasoning blend (such as Chef Paul Prudhomme's Seafood Magic)
¼	teaspoon salt
3	large egg whites
1	cup dry breadcrumbs

Cooking spray
Lemon wedges (optional)

1. Preheat oven to 450°.
2. Rinse fillets; pat dry with paper towels to remove excess moisture. Sprinkle both sides of fillets with seasoning blend and salt. Lightly beat egg whites in a shallow dish. Place breadcrumbs in a shallow dish. Dip each fillet in egg white; dredge lightly in breadcrumbs. Repeat procedure with remaining egg white and breadcrumbs so that each fillet is dipped twice.
3. Coat a foil-lined baking sheet with cooking spray. Place fish on pan, and bake at 450° for 12 minutes or until fish flakes easily when tested with a fork. Serve immediately with lemon wedges, if desired. **Yield:** 4 servings (serving size: 1 fillet).

CALORIES 285; FAT 6.3g (sat 2.1g, mono 2.1g, poly 1.9g); PROTEIN 34.6g; CARB 20.2g; FIBER 1.2g; CHOL 80mg; IRON 0.5mg; SODIUM 629mg; CALC 25mg

Cod with Tangy Tartar Sauce

1.1	ounces all-purpose flour (about ¼ cup)
1	teaspoon kosher salt
½	teaspoon freshly ground black pepper
¼	teaspoon paprika
4	(6-ounce) cod fillets

Cooking spray
Tangy Tartar Sauce

1. Combine first 4 ingredients in a shallow dish. Pat fish dry. Dredge both sides of fish in flour mixture, shaking off excess flour.
2. Heat a large nonstick skillet over medium-high heat. Coat pan with cooking spray. Place fish in pan, reduce heat to medium, and cook 5 minutes. Turn fish, and cook 4 minutes or until fish flakes easily when tested with a fork. Serve with Tangy Tartar Sauce. **Yield:** 4 servings (serving size: 1 fillet and 3 tablespoons sauce).

CALORIES 240; FAT 6.5g (sat 1.4g, mono 3.5g, poly 1.5g); PROTEIN 32g; CARB 11.8g; FIBER 0.4g; CHOL 81mg; IRON 0.9mg; SODIUM 853mg; CALC 69mg

tangy tartar sauce

⅓	cup fat-free sour cream
¼	cup light mayonnaise
2	tablespoons drained dill pickle relish
1	teaspoon chopped fresh parsley
1	teaspoon drained capers, chopped
½	teaspoon finely grated fresh lemon rind
1	teaspoon fresh lemon juice
¼	teaspoon garlic powder

Dash of ground red pepper

1. Combine all ingredients. **Yield:** ³/₄ cup.

Per Tablespoon: CALORIES 71; FAT 5.2g (sat 0.9g, mono 3.2g, poly 1g); PROTEIN 1.2g; CARB 4.8g; FIBER 0.1g; CHOL 3mg; IRON 0mg; SODIUM 291mg; CALC 32mg

Mediterranean Cod

make it a meal *Serve this fish main dish with Spinach and Onion Couscous (recipe on page 439). To make prep work even faster, save time by using tender and mild baby spinach in the couscous. There's no need to trim the stems from the leaves.*

2	tablespoons chopped fresh parsley
4	oil-packed sun-dried tomato halves, drained and finely chopped
6	pitted kalamata olives
4	teaspoons oil from oil-packed sun-dried tomatoes, divided
4	(6-ounce) cod fillets (about 1¼ inches thick)
¼	teaspoon salt
¼	teaspoon freshly ground black pepper

1. Combine first 3 ingredients and 1 teaspoon sun-dried tomato oil in a small bowl; set aside. Sprinkle fish with salt and pepper.
2. Heat remaining 1 tablespoon sun-dried tomato oil in a large nonstick skillet over medium-high heat. Add fish to pan; cook 2 to 3 minutes on each side or until fish flakes easily when tested with a fork. Transfer fish to a serving platter; top with tomato mixture. Serve immediately. **Yield:** 4 servings (serving size: 1 fillet and about 1½ tablespoons tomato mixture).

CALORIES 203; FAT 7.6g (sat 1.2g, mono 4.9g, poly 1.3g); PROTEIN 30.6g; CARB 1.4g; FIBER 0.3g; CHOL 73mg; IRON 0.9mg; SODIUM 338mg; CALC 34mg

Flounder with Cilantro-Curry Topping and Toasted Coconut

make it a meal *Serve this fish with brown basmati rice and sautéed sliced carrots. You can substitute tilapia or snapper for flounder, if you like.*

½ teaspoon salt, divided
4 (6-ounce) flounder fillets
Cooking spray
2 tablespoons flaked sweetened coconut
1 cup fresh cilantro sprigs
2 tablespoons fresh lemon juice
2 tablespoons extra-virgin olive oil
1 teaspoon curry powder
3 garlic cloves, peeled
1 jalapeño pepper, halved and seeded
Lemon wedges (optional)

1. Preheat broiler.
2. Sprinkle ¼ teaspoon salt over fish. Heat a large nonstick skillet over medium-high heat; coat pan with cooking spray. Add fish to pan; cook 4 minutes on each side or until fish flakes easily when tested with a fork or until desired degree of doneness.
3. Place coconut on a baking sheet, and broil 2 minutes or until toasted, stirring occasionally.
4. Place remaining ¼ teaspoon salt, cilantro, and next 5 ingredients in a food processor; process until finely chopped. Spoon 2 tablespoons cilantro mixture over each fillet; sprinkle each serving with 1½ teaspoons coconut. Garnish with lemon wedges, if desired. **Yield:** 4 servings.

CALORIES 234; FAT 9.5g (sat 2g, mono 5.4g, poly 1.3g); PROTEIN 32.5g; CARB 3.3g; FIBER 0.7g; CHOL 82mg; IRON 1mg; SODIUM 442mg; CALC 41mg

Apricot-Glazed Flounder

Quickly thaw the frozen fish in the microwave at 30% power for 5 to 6 minutes. Be careful not to overheat the fish because it will begin to cook.

Cooking spray
4 (3-ounce) frozen flounder fillets, thawed
¼ teaspoon salt
¼ teaspoon freshly ground black pepper
¼ cup reduced-sugar apricot preserves
3 tablespoons water
1 teaspoon low-sodium soy sauce
¼ teaspoon grated peeled fresh ginger

1. Heat a large nonstick skillet over medium-high heat; generously coat pan with cooking spray. Sprinkle fish with salt and pepper. Add 2 fillets to pan; cook 2 minutes on each side or until fish flakes easily when tested with a fork. Remove fish from pan; keep warm. Repeat with remaining fillets.
2. Reduce heat to medium. Add apricot preserves and remaining ingredients to pan. Cook 30 seconds or until hot. Pour glaze over fish, and serve immediately. **Yield:** 2 servings (serving size: 2 fillets and about ¼ cup glaze).

CALORIES 208; FAT 2g (sat 0.5g, mono 0.5g, poly 0.7g); PROTEIN 32.3g; CARB 12.4g; FIBER 0.1g; CHOL 82mg; IRON 0.6mg; SODIUM 529mg; CALC 32mg

Although sole are actually members of the flounder family, the word "sole" and "flounder" are often used interchangeably. You're likely to see flounder at the market and sole at a restaurant.

INGREDIENT SPOTLIGHT

20 MINUTES

Flounder Piccata with Spinach

You can substitute any flaky white fish,
such as tilapia or sole, in this elegant dish.

1   (3½-ounce) bag boil-in-bag long-grain rice
½   teaspoon salt, divided
¼   teaspoon black pepper, divided
4   (6-ounce) flounder fillets
2   tablespoons all-purpose flour
2   teaspoons olive oil
⅓   cup dry white wine
2   tablespoons fresh lemon juice
1   tablespoon drained capers, chopped
2   tablespoons butter
4   cups fresh baby spinach

1. Cook rice according to package directions, omitting salt and fat. Place rice in a medium bowl; stir in ¼ teaspoon salt and ⅛ teaspoon pepper.

2. Sprinkle fish with remaining ¼ teaspoon salt and remaining ⅛ teaspoon pepper. Dredge fish in flour.

3. Heat oil in a large nonstick skillet over medium-high heat. Add fish to pan; cook 1½ minutes on each side or until fish flakes easily when tested with a fork or until desired degree of doneness.

4. Add wine, juice, and capers to pan; cook 1 minute. Add butter to pan, stirring until butter melts. Remove fish and sauce from pan; keep warm. Wipe pan clean with a paper towel. Add spinach to pan; sauté 1 minute or until wilted. Place ½ cup rice onto each of 4 plates. Top each serving with about ⅓ cup spinach, 1 fillet, and 1 table-spoon sauce. **Yield:** 4 servings.

CALORIES 332; FAT 10.2g (sat 4.4g, mono 3.5g, poly 1.2g); PROTEIN 31.3g;
CARB 27.4g; FIBER 1.9g; CHOL 95mg; IRON 3mg; SODIUM 713mg; CALC 51mg

Seared Grouper with
Tomato-Tarragon Salsa

Grilled Grouper with Tomato Salsa

*If you can't find grouper, use another firm
white fish, such as red snapper or halibut.*

1   cup chopped tomato
3   tablespoons finely chopped red onion
2   tablespoons chopped fresh cilantro or parsley
1   tablespoon lime juice
4   (6-ounce) grouper fillets
2   teaspoons olive oil
1/2 teaspoon salt
1/4 teaspoon freshly ground black pepper
Olive oil–flavored cooking spray

1. Prepare grill.
2. Combine first 4 ingredients, tossing
gently; set aside.
3. Brush fish with olive oil; sprinkle with
salt and pepper. Place fish on grill rack
coated with cooking spray. Cover and grill 4
to 5 minutes on each side or until fish flakes
easily when tested with a fork.
4. Place fish on serving plates. Top each
serving with tomato salsa. **Yield:** 4 servings
(serving size: 1 fillet and 1/4 cup salsa).

CALORIES 189; FAT 4.1g (sat 0.8g, mono 2.5g, poly 0.8g); PROTEIN 33.5g;
CARB 2.9g; FIBER 0.7g; CHOL 63mg; IRON 1.7mg; SODIUM 388mg; CALC 54mg

Seared Grouper with Tomato-Tarragon Salsa

1   cup chopped cherry tomatoes
2   tablespoons finely chopped green onions
2   tablespoons chopped fresh parsley
2   tablespoons capers
1   tablespoon olive oil
1   tablespoon balsamic vinegar
1/4 teaspoon dried tarragon
1/4 teaspoon salt
4   (6-ounce) grouper fillets
2   teaspoons blackened seasoning
Cooking spray

1. Combine first 8 ingredients in a small
bowl. Stir to blend, and set aside.
2. Sprinkle both sides of fillets with blackened seasoning.
3. Heat a large nonstick skillet over
medium-high heat. Coat pan with cooking
spray; add fillets, and cook 3 to 4 minutes
on each side or until fish flakes easily when
tested with a fork.
4. Remove from heat; place 1 fillet on each
of 4 dinner plates. Spoon salsa evenly over
fillets. **Yield:** 4 servings (serving size: 1 fillet and 1/4 cup salsa).

CALORIES 202; FAT 5.3g (sat 1g, mono 3g, poly 1.1g); PROTEIN 33.6g; CARB 3.4g;
FIBER 1g; CHOL 63mg; IRON 1.9mg; SODIUM 602mg; CALC 61mg

Capers add a distinct, tart
flavor to many recipes.
You can find capers in
the condiment section
of your supermarket.
Choose capers jarred in
liquid rather than dry-packed
in coarse salt. Once opened, a jar
of capers will stay fresh for several
months in the refrigerator.

INGREDIENT SPOTLIGHT

Halibut with Coconut–Red Curry Sauce

20 MINUTES

Braised Halibut with Bacon and Mushrooms

Smoky bacon complements slightly sweet halibut. If you can't find fresh halibut, substitute snapper.

1   (3½-ounce) bag boil-in-bag long-grain rice
4   slices applewood-smoked bacon
⅓   cup prechopped onion
1   tablespoon chopped fresh thyme
8   ounces presliced mushrooms
2   teaspoons olive oil
4   (6-ounce) halibut fillets
½   teaspoon salt
¼   teaspoon black pepper
1   cup dry white wine
2   tablespoons chopped fresh parsley

1. Cook rice according to package directions, omitting salt and fat. Drain and keep warm.
2. Cook bacon in a large nonstick skillet over medium heat until crisp. Remove bacon from pan; crumble. Add onion, thyme, and mushrooms to drippings in pan; sauté 3 minutes. Remove mushroom mixture from pan.
3. Heat oil in pan over medium heat. Sprinkle fish with salt and pepper. Add fish to pan, and cook 2 minutes on each side or until browned. Return mushroom mixture to pan. Stir in wine, and cook 3 minutes or until fish flakes easily when tested with a fork or until desired degree of doneness. Sprinkle with crumbled bacon and parsley. Serve over rice. **Yield:** 4 servings (serving size: 1 halibut fillet, 6 tablespoons mushroom mixture, and ½ cup rice).

CALORIES 388; FAT 11.1g (sat 2.7g, mono 5.2g, poly 2.1g); PROTEIN 43.1g; CARB 27.3g; FIBER 1.3g; CHOL 64mg; IRON 3.2mg; SODIUM 617mg; CALC 103mg

30 MINUTES

Halibut with Coconut–Red Curry Sauce

2   teaspoons canola oil, divided
4   (6-ounce) halibut fillets
1   cup chopped onion
½   cup chopped green onions
1   tablespoon grated peeled fresh ginger
1   cup light coconut milk
1   tablespoon sugar
1   tablespoon fish sauce
¾   teaspoon red curry paste
½   teaspoon ground coriander
1   tablespoon chopped fresh basil
2   teaspoons fresh lime juice

1. Heat 1 teaspoon oil in a large nonstick skillet over medium-high heat. Add fish to pan; cook 5 minutes on each side or until fish flakes easily when tested with a fork or until desired degree of doneness. Remove fish from pan; keep warm.
2. Add remaining 1 teaspoon oil to pan. Add onion, green onions, and ginger; sauté 2 minutes. Stir in coconut milk and next 4 ingredients. Bring to a boil; cook 1 minute. Remove from heat. Stir in basil and juice.
Yield: 4 servings (serving size: 1 fillet and about ⅓ cup sauce).

CALORIES 278; FAT 9.3g (sat 3.6g, mono 2.7g, poly 2g); PROTEIN 37.1g; CARB 10.9g; FIBER 1.1g; CHOL 54mg; IRON 2mg; SODIUM 475mg; CALC 102mg

2O
M I N U T E S

Spanish-Style Halibut

1	slice applewood-smoked bacon
1/2	teaspoon salt
1/2	teaspoon smoked paprika
1/4	teaspoon black pepper
4	(6-ounce) skinless halibut fillets
2	teaspoons bottled minced garlic
1	(6-ounce) package fresh baby spinach

1. Cook bacon in a large nonstick skillet over medium heat until crisp. Remove bacon from pan, and crumble. Set aside.
2. Combine 1/2 teaspoon salt, smoked paprika, and 1/4 teaspoon black pepper in a small bowl. Sprinkle spice mixture evenly over fish. Add fish to drippings in pan, and cook 3 minutes on each side or until fish flakes easily when tested with a fork or until desired degree of doneness. Remove fish from pan, and keep warm.

3. Add 2 teaspoons garlic to pan, and cook 1 minute, stirring frequently. Stir in bacon. Add spinach to pan, and cook 1 minute or until spinach begins to wilt. Serve with fish. **Yield:** 4 servings (serving size: 1 fillet and 1/2 cup spinach mixture).

CALORIES 214; FAT 5.1g (sat 1g, mono 2.7g, poly 1.3g); PROTEIN 37.4g; CARB 2.4g; FIBER 1.2g; CHOL 57mg; IRON 2.9mg; SODIUM 475mg; CALC 124mg

Smoked paprika contrasts nicely with the sweet halibut. Dried over smoldering oak logs, smoked paprika has a strong, smoky flavor. And the aroma is deep, intense, sweet, and spicy. The color is a striking deep red that spreads throughout any dish to which it is added.

INGREDIENT SPOTLIGHT

Pesto Halibut Kebabs

20 MINUTES

Pesto Halibut Kebabs

make it a meal *Serve this dish with Israeli couscous tossed with toasted sliced almonds, dried cranberries, and chopped fresh parsley.*

1½ pounds halibut, cut into 1-inch chunks
1 large red bell pepper, cut into 1-inch chunks
3 tablespoons prepared basil pesto
2 tablespoons white wine vinegar
½ teaspoon salt
Cooking spray
4 lemon wedges

1. Preheat broiler.
2. Place fish and bell pepper in a shallow dish. Drizzle pesto and vinegar over fish mixture; toss to coat. Let fish mixture stand 5 minutes.
3. Thread fish and pepper alternately onto each of 4 (12-inch) skewers; sprinkle evenly with salt. Place skewers on a jelly-roll pan coated with cooking spray. Broil 8 minutes or until desired degree of doneness, turning once. Serve with lemon wedges. **Yield:** 4 servings (serving size: 1 skewer and 1 lemon wedge).

CALORIES 239; FAT 7.9g (sat 1.2g, mono 2.3g, poly 2.9g); PROTEIN 36.3g; CARB 4g; FIBER 1.2g; CHOL 55mg; IRON 1.8mg; SODIUM 514mg; CALC 104mg

Popular because of its mild flavor, halibut is a flaky white fish. Halibut is plentiful and available fresh from March to November; it's sold frozen the rest of the year.

INGREDIENT SPOTLIGHT

30 MINUTES

Macadamia-Crusted Mahimahi

4 (6-ounce) mahimahi or other firm white fish fillets
¼ teaspoon freshly ground black pepper
Cooking spray
1 tablespoon butter, melted
¼ cup finely chopped macadamia nuts
½ cup panko (Japanese breadcrumbs)
2 tablespoons light coconut milk

1. Preheat oven to 450°.
2. Sprinkle fish evenly with pepper. Place fish on a baking sheet coated with cooking spray. Bake at 450° for 5 minutes.
3. Combine butter and remaining ingredients in a bowl; stir well. Press mixture on top of fish; bake an additional 10 minutes or until crust is browned and fish flakes easily when tested with a fork. **Yield:** 4 servings (serving size: 1 fillet).

CALORIES 254; FAT 9.7g (sat 3.5g, mono 5.5g, poly 0.7g); PROTEIN 33.2g; CARB 6.7g; FIBER 0.9g; CHOL 132mg; IRON 2.1mg; SODIUM 194mg; CALC 31mg

15 MINUTES

Parmesan-Dill Orange Roughy

4 (6-ounce) orange roughy fillets
Cooking spray
3 tablespoons freshly shredded Parmesan cheese
1 teaspoon dried dill
¼ teaspoon salt
¼ teaspoon black pepper

1. Preheat oven to 450°.
2. Place fish on a jelly-roll pan coated with cooking spray. Sprinkle fish evenly with Parmesan cheese, dill, salt, and pepper. Bake at 450° for 9 to 11 minutes or until fish flakes easily when tested with a fork. **Yield:** 4 servings (serving size: 1 fillet).

CALORIES 151; FAT 2.7g (sat 1g, mono 1g, poly 0.4g); PROTEIN 29.4g; CARB 0.4g; FIBER 0.1g; CHOL 105mg; IRON 1.9mg; SODIUM 332mg; CALC 67mg

30 MINUTES

Fish and Vegetable Dinner

Baking the fish and vegetables in a foil packet traps steam inside to keep the fish moist and the vegetables tender.

Cooking spray
4   (6-ounce) orange roughy fillets
¼   teaspoon freshly ground black pepper
½   cup light buttermilk ranch dressing
2   cups broccoli florets
1   cup chopped red bell pepper (about 1 medium)
1   cup chopped onion (about 1 small)

1. Preheat oven to 450°.
2. Cut 4 (12 x 12–inch) squares of foil, and lightly coat with cooking spray. Place 1 fillet on each sheet.
3. Sprinkle each fillet evenly with pepper; brush with 2 tablespoons dressing. Top each with ½ cup broccoli, ¼ cup bell pepper, and ¼ cup onion.
4. Fold foil in half over each fillet to form a packet, and crimp edges tightly to seal. Place foil packets on a baking sheet.
5. Bake at 450° for 20 minutes or until fish flakes easily when tested with a fork. Remove fish and vegetables from foil; transfer to plates. Serve immediately. **Yield:** 4 servings (serving size: 1 packet).

CALORIES 245; FAT 8.5g (sat 6.9g, mono 0.9g, poly 0.4g); PROTEIN 29.8g; CARB 10.9g; FIBER 2.5g; CHOL 112mg; IRON 2.3mg; SODIUM 435mg; CALC 45mg

The recipe at right calls for **MAKE IT FASTER** ½ cup matchstick-cut carrots. Purchase prepackaged matchstick-cut carrots from your grocer to avoid having to slice your own.

Orange Roughy with Leeks

30 MINUTES

Orange Roughy with Leeks

Orange roughy is a fish from New Zealand, but is becoming quite common in the United States. It's a firm white fish with a mild flavor that's low in fat.

½   cup matchstick-cut carrots
½   cup thinly sliced leek
4   (6-ounce) orange roughy fillets
1   teaspoon dried tarragon
½   teaspoon salt
¼   teaspoon freshly ground black pepper
Olive oil–flavored cooking spray

1. Preheat oven to 475°. Place a baking sheet in oven while preheating.
2. Cut 4 (12-inch) squares of foil. Spoon carrot and leek evenly into center of each foil square; top each with a fish fillet. Sprinkle fish with tarragon, salt, and pepper. Coat each fillet with cooking spray. Fold foil over fillets to make packets, and seal edges tightly.
3. Place packets on hot baking sheet. Bake at 475° for 14 minutes. Transfer fish and vegetables to serving plates, and serve immediately. **Yield:** 4 servings (serving size: 1 fillet and about ¼ cup vegetables).

CALORIES 148; FAT 1.5g (sat 0g, mono 0.8g, poly 0.4g); PROTEIN 28.3g; CARB 3.2g; FIBER 0.7g; CHOL 102mg; IRON 2.1mg; SODIUM 430mg; CALC 29mg

Broiled Salmon with Marmalade-Dijon Glaze

make it a meal *Although quick enough for a hectic weeknight, this dish will impress guests, too. Serve with salad and roasted potatoes.*

½ cup orange marmalade
1 tablespoon Dijon mustard
½ teaspoon garlic powder
½ teaspoon salt
¼ teaspoon black pepper
⅛ teaspoon ground ginger
4 (6-ounce) salmon fillets
Cooking spray

1. Preheat broiler.
2. Combine first 6 ingredients in a small bowl, stirring well. Place fish on a jelly-roll pan coated with cooking spray. Brush half of marmalade mixture over fish; broil 6 minutes. Brush fish with remaining marmalade mixture; broil 2 minutes or until fish flakes easily when tested with a fork or until desired degree of doneness. **Yield:** 4 servings (serving size: 1 fillet).

CALORIES 377; FAT 13.4g (sat 3.1g, mono 5.8g, poly 3.3g); PROTEIN 36.6g; CARB 27.3g; FIBER 0.4g; CHOL 87mg; IRON 0.8mg; SODIUM 488mg; CALC 42mg

Broiled Salmon with Peppercorn-Lime Rub

make it a meal *Try a fresh, quick, and satisfying quinoa-vegetable salad with your broiled fish to round out the meal.*

4   (6-ounce) salmon fillets (about ¾ inch thick)
Cooking spray
2   teaspoons grated lime rind
½   teaspoon kosher salt
½   teaspoon cracked black pepper
1   garlic clove, minced
Lime wedges (optional)

1. Preheat broiler.
2. Place fish, skin sides down, on a broiler pan coated with cooking spray. Combine remaining ingredients except lime wedges; sprinkle over fish. Broil 7 minutes or until fish flakes easily when tested with a fork or until desired degree of doneness. Serve with lime wedges, if desired. **Yield:** 4 servings (serving size: 1 fillet).

CALORIES 318; FAT 18.5g (sat 3.7g, mono 6.6g, poly 6.7g); PROTEIN 34.1g; CARB 2.2g; FIBER 0.6g; CHOL 100mg; IRON 0.8mg; SODIUM 336mg; CALC 28mg

20 MINUTES

Salmon with Spicy Cucumber Salad and Peanuts

The spicy-sweet vinegar dressing in the salad complements the salmon seasoned with just salt and pepper.

4	cups sliced seeded peeled cucumber (about 2 large)
1/4	cup seasoned rice vinegar
2	tablespoons chopped fresh parsley
2	teaspoons sugar
1/2	teaspoon crushed red pepper
1/2	teaspoon salt, divided
	Cooking spray
1/4	teaspoon black pepper
4	(6-ounce) salmon fillets
4	teaspoons chopped unsalted, dry-roasted peanuts

1. Combine first 5 ingredients in a medium bowl; stir in 1/4 teaspoon salt.
2. Heat a large nonstick skillet over medium-high heat. Coat pan with cooking spray. Sprinkle remaining 1/4 teaspoon salt and black pepper over fish. Add fish to pan; cook 4 minutes on each side or until fish flakes easily when tested with a fork or until desired degree of doneness. Place 1 fillet in each of 4 shallow bowls, and top each serving with 1/2 cup cucumber salad and 1 teaspoon peanuts. **Yield:** 4 servings.

CALORIES 262; FAT 11g (sat 1.7g, mono 3.8g, poly 4.2g); PROTEIN 30.5g; CARB 8.9g; FIBER 1.3g; CHOL 81mg; IRON 1.7mg; SODIUM 666mg; CALC 41mg

15 MINUTES

Orange-Glazed Salmon Fillets with Rosemary

Fresh rosemary and a little maple syrup infuse aromatic and faintly sweet flavor into this speedy seafood dish.

4	(6-ounce) salmon fillets (1 inch thick)
1/2	teaspoon kosher salt
1/4	teaspoon freshly ground black pepper
	Cooking spray
2	tablespoons minced shallots
1/4	cup dry white wine
1/2	teaspoon chopped fresh rosemary
3/4	cup fresh orange juice (about 2 oranges)
1	tablespoon maple syrup

1. Sprinkle fillets evenly with salt and pepper. Heat a large nonstick skillet over medium-high heat; coat pan with cooking spray. Add fillets; cook 2 minutes on each side or until fish flakes easily when tested with a fork or until desired degree of doneness. Remove from pan.
2. Recoat pan with cooking spray. Add shallots; sauté 30 seconds. Stir in wine and rosemary; cook 30 seconds or until liquid almost evaporates. Add juice and syrup; bring to a boil, and cook 1 minute. Return fillets to pan; cook 1 minute on each side or until thoroughly heated. **Yield:** 4 servings (serving size: 1 fillet and 1 1/2 tablespoons sauce).

CALORIES 226; FAT 5.6g (sat 1.4g, mono 2g, poly 1.7g); PROTEIN 30.4g; CARB 9.5g; FIBER 0.2g; CHOL 70mg; IRON 1.1mg; SODIUM 311mg; CALC 70mg

COOKING CLASS: *how to seed a cucumber*

To easily seed a cucumber, peel it, cut it in half lengthwise, and scrape the seeds out with a spoon.

COOKING CLASS: *how to seed a pepper*

To seed a pepper, slice off the stem end, and cut the pepper in half lengthwise. Remove the seeds by running your finger along the inside of the vein, scraping off the seeds.

20 MINUTES

Pan-Seared Salmon with Pineapple-Jalapeño Relish

make it a meal *Tangy, spicy, and fruity, this inviting recipe belies its simple preparation. Seed the jalapeño pepper if you prefer a milder dish, and serve the relish over coconut rice accompanied by a crunchy salad.*

2   cups chopped pineapple
¼   cup finely chopped red onion
¼   cup finely chopped red bell pepper
1   tablespoon fresh lemon juice
2   teaspoons sugar
1   finely chopped seeded jalapeño pepper
½   teaspoon salt, divided
Cooking spray
1   teaspoon chili powder
¼   teaspoon black pepper
4   (6-ounce) salmon fillets

1. Combine first 6 ingredients in a medium bowl; stir in ¼ teaspoon salt.
2. Heat a large nonstick skillet over medium-high heat. Coat pan with cooking spray. Combine remaining ¼ teaspoon salt, chili powder, and black pepper, stirring well; sprinkle evenly over fish. Add fish to pan, skin side up; cook 4 minutes on each side or until fish flakes easily when tested with a fork or until desired degree of doneness. Serve with pineapple mixture. **Yield:** 4 servings (serving size: 1 fillet and about ½ cup pineapple mixture).

CALORIES 308; FAT 15.6g (sat 3.2g, mono 5.7g, poly 5.7g); PROTEIN 28.8g; CARB 11.7g; FIBER 1.3g; CHOL 80mg; IRON 0.7mg; SODIUM 394mg; CALC 31mg

15 MINUTES

Salmon with Sweet Chile Sauce

make it a meal *Serve the salmon with soba noodles tossed with low-sodium soy sauce and dark sesame oil. Add steamed broccoli florets on the side.*

4   (6-ounce) salmon fillets, skinned
1   teaspoon ground coriander
½   teaspoon salt
Cooking spray
2   tablespoons honey
1   tablespoon fresh lime juice
2   teaspoons low-sodium soy sauce
½   to 1 teaspoon Sriracha (hot chile sauce, such as Huy Fong)
4   teaspoons thinly sliced green onions

1. Sprinkle fish evenly with coriander and salt. Heat a large nonstick skillet over medium-high heat; coat pan with cooking spray. Add fish to pan; cook 4 minutes on each side or until fish flakes easily when tested with a fork or until desired degree of doneness.
2. Combine honey, juice, soy sauce, and Sriracha; drizzle over fish. Sprinkle with green onions. **Yield:** 4 servings (serving size: 1 fillet, 1 tablespoon sauce, and 1 teaspoon green onions).

CALORIES 262; FAT 10.5g (sat 2.5g, mono 4.6g, poly 2.5g); PROTEIN 31.2g; CARB 9.5g; FIBER 0.1g; CHOL 80mg; IRON 0.6mg; SODIUM 460mg; CALC 18mg

MINUTES

Grilled Pesto Salmon

make it a meal *Unexpected guests?*
No problem. Present an elegant meal of
salmon, orzo, and steamed green beans in
15 minutes. While the salmon grills,
prepare the orzo and beans.

4   (6-ounce) salmon fillets
¼   teaspoon salt
¼   teaspoon freshly ground black pepper
3   tablespoons commercial pesto
3   tablespoons dry white wine
Cooking spray

1. Heat a large grill pan over medium heat.
2. Sprinkle fish evenly with salt and pepper, and set aside.
3. Combine pesto and wine in a bowl, and stir well.
4. Coat pan with cooking spray. Add fish to pan, and cook 6 minutes on each side or until fish flakes easily when tested with a fork. Serve fish with pesto sauce. **Yield:** 4 servings (serving size: 1 fillet and 1½ tablespoons pesto sauce).

CALORIES 279; FAT 11.6g (sat 3.2g,,mono 3.1g, poly 5.2g); PROTEIN 38.3g;
CARB 2.5g; FIBER 0.3g; CHOL 91mg; IRON 1.9mg; SODIUM 438mg; CALC 54mg

Red Snapper with
Ginger-Lime Butter

 MINUTES

Red Snapper with Ginger-Lime Butter

make it a meal *Serve with long-grain rice tossed with green onions.*

1½ tablespoons butter, softened
1 tablespoon chopped fresh cilantro
1 teaspoon minced seeded jalapeño pepper
½ teaspoon grated lime rind
¼ teaspoon bottled fresh ground ginger
¾ teaspoon salt, divided
4 (6-ounce) red snapper or other firm white fish fillets
¼ teaspoon black pepper
Cooking spray
Lime wedges (optional)

1. Combine first 5 ingredients in a bowl. Stir in ¼ teaspoon salt. Cover and chill.
2. Heat a large nonstick skillet over medium-high heat. Sprinkle both sides of fish with remaining ½ teaspoon salt and black pepper. Coat pan with cooking spray. Add fish to pan; cook 3 minutes on each side or until fish flakes easily when tested with a fork or until desired degree of doneness. Place 1 fillet on each of 4 plates, and top each serving with 1½ teaspoons butter mixture. Serve with lime wedges, if desired. **Yield:** 4 servings.

CALORIES 202; FAT 6.5g (sat 3.2g, mono 1.5g, poly 0.9g); PROTEIN 33.6g; CARB 0.2g; FIBER 0.1g; CHOL 71mg; IRON 0.3mg; SODIUM 546mg; CALC 53mg

MINUTES

Snapper with Basil-Mint Sauce

make it a meal *Serve with jasmine rice and sautéed green beans.*

4 (6-ounce) snapper fillets
Cooking spray
¼ teaspoon salt
⅛ teaspoon freshly ground black pepper
1 cup fresh basil leaves
¼ cup fresh mint leaves
2 tablespoons chopped seeded jalapeño pepper
2 tablespoons olive oil
2 tablespoons water
2 teaspoons fresh lime juice
⅛ teaspoon salt
1 garlic clove, chopped

1. Preheat broiler.
2. Arrange fish in a single layer on a broiler pan lightly coated with cooking spray. Sprinkle fish with ¼ teaspoon salt and pepper. Broil 6 minutes or until fish flakes easily when tested with a fork or until desired degree of doneness.
3. Place basil and remaining ingredients in a food processor; process 1 minute or until smooth. Serve with fish. **Yield:** 4 servings (serving size: 1 fillet and about 1 tablespoon sauce).

CALORIES 237; FAT 9.1g (sat 1.4g, mono 5.4g, poly 1.6g); PROTEIN 35.3g; CARB 1.4g; FIBER 0.7g; CHOL 63mg; IRON 0.8mg; SODIUM 328mg; CALC 77mg

The most prized member of the large snapper family is American red snapper, which has a pronounced sweet flavor similar to shrimp. Many varieties are available year-round, and though they may not be as sweet as American red snapper, they're excellent substitutions.

INGREDIENT SPOTLIGHT

Sautéed Snapper with Plum Tomatoes and Spinach

make it a meal *If you can't find snapper, purchase another mild, firm white fish, such as cod or halibut. Serve alongside your favorite pasta tossed with pesto.*

1 tablespoon olive oil, divided
4 (6-ounce) snapper fillets
¼ teaspoon salt
¼ teaspoon black pepper
1½ cups diced plum tomato (about 6 tomatoes)
2 teaspoons bottled minced garlic
¼ cup dry white wine
3 cups baby spinach leaves

1. Heat 1½ teaspoons oil in a large nonstick skillet over medium-high heat. Sprinkle fish evenly with salt and pepper. Add fish to pan; cook 2 minutes on each side. Remove fish from pan.

2. Heat remaining 1½ teaspoons olive oil in pan over medium-high heat. Add tomato and garlic; sauté 1 minute. Stir in wine; simmer 2 minutes. Add spinach to pan; cook 1 minute or just until spinach wilts. Return fish to pan. Spoon tomato mixture over fish; cook 1 minute or until fish flakes easily when tested with a fork or until desired degree of doneness. **Yield:** 4 servings (serving size: 1 fillet and about ½ cup spinach mixture).

CALORIES 225; FAT 5.9g (sat 1g, mono 2.9g, poly 1.3g); PROTEIN 36.5g; CARB 5.2g; FIBER 1.7g; CHOL 63mg; IRON 1.3mg; SODIUM 280mg; CALC 90mg

MINUTES

Seared Snapper Provençale

2 cups grape tomatoes, halved
½ cup chopped bottled roasted red bell peppers
¼ cup kalamata olives, pitted and coarsely
   chopped
3 tablespoons chopped fresh basil
2 tablespoons chopped shallots
1 tablespoon balsamic vinegar
2 teaspoons extra-virgin olive oil
¼ teaspoon salt, divided
Cooking spray
4 (6-ounce) red snapper fillets
¼ teaspoon black pepper

1. Combine first 7 ingredients in a bowl; sprinkle with ⅛ teaspoon salt. Toss well.
2. Heat a large nonstick skillet over medium-high heat. Coat pan with cooking spray. Sprinkle fish with remaining ⅛ teaspoon salt and pepper. Add fish to pan; cook 4 minutes on each side or until fish flakes easily when tested with a fork or until desired degree of doneness. Serve with tomato mixture. **Yield:** 4 servings (serving size: 1 fillet and about ¾ cup tomato mixture).

CALORIES 260; FAT 8.6g (sat 1.3g, mono 5g, poly 1.6g); PROTEIN 36.4g; CARB 7.4g; FIBER 1.4g; CHOL 63mg; IRON 1mg; SODIUM 743mg; CALC 77mg

Snapper with Grilled Mango Salsa

degree of doneness. Serve with mango mixture. Garnish with mint sprigs, if desired. **Yield:** 4 servings (serving size: 1 fillet and ¹/₃ cup salsa).

CALORIES 246; FAT 6.1g (sat 1g, mono 3g, poly 1.2g); PROTEIN 35.8g; CARB 11.2g; FIBER 1.6g; CHOL 63mg; IRON 0.6mg; SODIUM 402mg; CALC 67mg

20 MINUTES

Pan-Grilled Snapper with Orzo Pasta Salad

Orzo is a small rice-shaped pasta. It cooks quickly and soaks up flavor from the vinaigrette. Double the vinaigrette and spoon some over the top of the fish, if you'd like.

1½ cups uncooked orzo (rice-shaped pasta)
Cooking spray
4   (6-ounce) red snapper fillets
½   teaspoon salt, divided
¼   teaspoon black pepper, divided
1½ tablespoons minced shallots
1   tablespoon chopped fresh parsley
1   tablespoon fresh lemon juice
2   teaspoons orange juice
1   teaspoon Dijon mustard
2½ tablespoons extra-virgin olive oil

1. Cook pasta according to package directions, omitting salt and fat. Drain and keep warm.
2. Heat a grill pan over medium-high heat. Coat pan with cooking spray. Sprinkle fish evenly with ¹/₄ teaspoon salt and ¹/₈ teaspoon pepper. Add fish to pan; cook 3 minutes on each side or until fish flakes easily when tested with a fork or until desired degree of doneness.
3. Combine remaining ¹/₄ teaspoon salt, remaining ¹/₈ teaspoon pepper, shallots, parsley, lemon juice, orange juice, and mustard in a small bowl, stirring well. Slowly add olive oil, stirring constantly with a whisk. Drizzle shallot mixture over pasta; toss well to coat. **Yield:** 4 servings (serving size: 1 fillet and ³/₄ cup pasta mixture).

CALORIES 398; FAT 11.2g (sat 1.8g, mono 6.9g, poly 1.6g); PROTEIN 32.7g; CARB 39.3g; FIBER 1.9g; CHOL 47mg; IRON 0.4mg; SODIUM 409mg; CALC 46mg

20 MINUTES

Snapper with Grilled Mango Salsa

make it a meal *Grilling the mango brings out its sweetness, which perfectly balances the flavor of the fish. Serve it with orange-scented couscous.*

6   (½-inch-thick) mango wedges (1 mango)
3   (¼-inch-thick) slices red onion
2   teaspoons olive oil, divided
Cooking spray
¼   cup diced peeled avocado
1   tablespoon chopped fresh mint
2   teaspoons fresh lemon juice
½   teaspoon salt, divided
¼   teaspoon freshly ground black pepper, divided
4   (6-ounce) yellowtail snapper or other firm white fish fillets
Mint sprigs (optional)

1. Prepare grill to medium-high heat.
2. Brush mango and onion with 1 teaspoon oil. Place mango and onion on grill rack coated with cooking spray; cover and grill 3 minutes on each side or until tender. Chop onion and mango. Combine onion, mango, avocado, mint, juice, ¹/₄ teaspoon salt, and ¹/₈ teaspoon pepper in a medium bowl.
3. Brush fish with remaining 1 teaspoon oil; sprinkle with ¹/₄ teaspoon salt and ¹/₈ teaspoon pepper. Place fish on grill rack; grill 4 minutes on each side or until fish flakes easily when tested with a fork or until desired

Swordfish Siciliana

make it a meal *This fish is tasty and impressive enough to serve company. You can substitute tuna for swordfish. Serve with orzo tossed with chopped fresh basil and toasted pine nuts.*

Cooking spray
4   (6-ounce) swordfish steaks
½   teaspoon salt
½   teaspoon freshly ground black pepper
1   tablespoon sliced almonds
2   teaspoons bottled minced garlic
2   tablespoons raisins
2   tablespoons fresh orange juice
1½   tablespoons chopped pitted kalamata olives
1½   tablespoons chopped bottled roasted red bell peppers

1. Heat a large nonstick skillet over medium-high heat; coat pan with cooking spray. Sprinkle fish evenly with salt and black pepper. Add fish to pan; sauté 5 minutes on each side or until fish flakes easily when tested with a fork or until desired degree of doneness. Remove fish from pan; cover and keep warm.
2. Recoat pan with cooking spray; add nuts and garlic to pan. Sauté 30 seconds. Add 2 tablespoons raisins, orange juice, kalamata olives, and bell pepper to pan; cook 1 minute or until liquid evaporates. Serve with fish. **Yield:** 4 servings (serving size: 1 fish steak and 2 tablespoons olive mixture).

CALORIES 246; FAT 8.3g (sat 2g, mono 3.6g, poly 1.9g); PROTEIN 34.6g; CARB 6.5g; FIBER 0.7g; CHOL 66mg; IRON 1.8mg; SODIUM 503mg; CALC 23mg

Moroccan Swordfish with Caper-Yogurt Sauce

make it a meal *Couscous or rice would make a nice pairing with this main dish, which is seasoned with spices frequently used in North African cuisine.*

Sauce:
½   cup plain low-fat yogurt
1   tablespoon chopped fresh mint
1½   teaspoons capers, drained
¼   teaspoon bottled minced garlic
Dash of salt
Dash of freshly ground black pepper
Fish:
1   teaspoon paprika
½   teaspoon ground coriander
¼   teaspoon salt
¼   teaspoon ground ginger
¼   teaspoon ground cumin
¼   teaspoon ground cinnamon
⅛   teaspoon ground red pepper
4   (6-ounce) swordfish steaks (about ¾ inch thick)
Cooking spray
Mint chiffonade (optional)

1. To prepare sauce, combine first 6 ingredients in a small bowl.
2. To prepare fish, heat a nonstick grill pan over medium-high heat. Combine paprika and next 6 ingredients; sprinkle over both sides of fish. Lightly coat both sides of fish with cooking spray; add fish to pan. Cook 4 minutes on each side or until fish flakes easily when tested with a fork or until desired degree of doneness. Serve with sauce. Garnish with mint, if desired. **Yield:** 4 servings (serving size: 1 steak and 2 tablespoons sauce).

CALORIES 222; FAT 7.2g (sat 2.1g, mono 2.7g, poly 1.6g); PROTEIN 34.3g; CARB 3.1g; FIBER 0.6g; CHOL 66mg; IRON 1.8mg; SODIUM 383mg; CALC 73mg

Fish Tacos with Cabbage Slaw

The sturdy texture of corn tortillas works best for these tacos, but you can use flour tortillas. Since the recipe makes more slaw than necessary for the tacos, serve the extra on the side.

4   cups very thinly presliced green cabbage
1   cup chopped plum tomatoes
⅓   cup thinly sliced green onions
¼   cup chopped fresh cilantro
2   tablespoons fresh lime juice
5   teaspoons extra-virgin olive oil, divided
½   teaspoon salt, divided
1   pound tilapia fillets
1   teaspoon chili powder
8   (6-inch) corn tortillas

1. Combine first 4 ingredients in a large bowl. Add juice, 1 tablespoon oil, and ¼ teaspoon salt; toss well to combine.
2. Heat remaining 2 teaspoons oil in a large nonstick skillet over medium-high heat. Sprinkle fish evenly with chili powder and remaining ¼ teaspoon salt. Add fish to pan; cook 3 minutes on each side or until fish flakes easily when tested with a fork or until desired degree of doneness. Remove from heat, and cut fish into bite-sized pieces.
3. Warm tortillas according to package directions. Spoon about ¼ cup cabbage mixture down the center of each tortilla. Divide fish evenly among tortillas; fold in half. Serve tacos with remaining cabbage mixture. **Yield:** 4 servings (serving size: 2 tacos and about 1 cup cabbage mixture).

CALORIES 305; FAT 9.8g (sat 2g, mono 4.9g, poly 1.2g); PROTEIN 26.5g; CARB 30.1g; FIBER 4.4g; CHOL 75mg; IRON 1.4mg; SODIUM 445mg; CALC 162mg

Quick Fish Fillets

Skillet Fillets with Cilantro Butter

make it a meal *Any mild white fish such as cod, flounder, or orange roughy would also be delicious in place of tilapia. Serve these brightly flavored fillets with sautéed spinach or a green salad.*

¼   teaspoon salt
¼   teaspoon ground cumin
⅛   teaspoon ground red pepper
4   (6-ounce) tilapia fillets
Cooking spray
1   lemon, quartered
2   tablespoons butter, softened
2   tablespoons finely chopped fresh cilantro
½   teaspoon grated lemon rind
¼   teaspoon paprika
⅛   teaspoon salt

1. Combine first 3 ingredients, and sprinkle over both sides of fish. Heat a large nonstick skillet over medium-high heat. Coat pan with cooking spray. Coat both sides of fish with cooking spray; place in pan. Cook 3 minutes on each side or until fish flakes easily when tested with a fork or until desired degree of doneness. Place fish on a serving platter; squeeze lemon quarters over fish.
2. Place butter and remaining ingredients in a small bowl; stir until well blended. Serve with fish. **Yield:** 4 servings (serving size: 1 fillet and about 2 teaspoons cilantro butter).

CALORIES 194; FAT 6.9g (sat 3.1g, mono 2.5g, poly 0.6g); PROTEIN 30.5g; CARB 1.2g; FIBER 0.2g; CHOL 88mg; IRON 0.7mg; SODIUM 354mg; CALC 32mg

Quick Fish Fillets

¼   cup dry breadcrumbs
½   teaspoon paprika
¼   cup plain yogurt
1   teaspoon prepared mustard
2   (6-ounce) tilapia or orange roughy fillets (¾ inch thick)
Cooking spray
Lemon wedges (optional)
1   teaspoon chopped fresh parsley (optional)

1. Preheat oven to 450°.
2. Combine breadcrumbs and paprika in a shallow dish. Combine yogurt and mustard in another shallow dish. Dip fish in yogurt mixture, and dredge in breadcrumb mixture. Place fish on a baking sheet coated with cooking spray.
3. Bake at 450° for 10 minutes or until fish flakes easily when tested with a fork. Serve immediately with lemon wedges and sprinkle with parsley, if desired. **Yield:** 2 servings (serving size: 1 fillet).

CALORIES 205; FAT 3g (sat 1g, mono 1.4g, poly 0.4g); PROTEIN 31.1g; CARB 11.7g; FIBER 0.9g; CHOL 104mg; IRON 1.8mg; SODIUM 271mg; CALC 99mg

Cilantro leaves are often mistaken for flat-leaf parsley, so read the tag to verify that you're buying the correct herb.

INGREDIENT SPOTLIGHT

15 MINUTES

Tilapia with Celery Leaf Relish

Buy celery with the leaves attached instead of trimmed celery hearts. The pale green leaves, with their delicate flavor, make a wonderful addition to relishes and salsas.

Cooking spray
4   (6-ounce) tilapia or orange roughy fillets
¼   teaspoon salt
¼   teaspoon freshly ground black pepper
1   pint grape tomatoes, halved
½   cup loosely packed celery leaves, coarsely chopped
½   cup pimiento-stuffed olives, halved
¼   cup coarsely chopped walnuts, toasted
2   tablespoons olive oil
1¾   teaspoons grated lemon rind
2   tablespoons fresh lemon juice
Additional freshly ground black pepper (optional)

1. Preheat oven to 425°.
2. Heat a large ovenproof skillet over medium-high heat. Coat skillet with cooking spray.
3. Sprinkle fish with salt and ¼ teaspoon pepper. Add fish to hot pan, and cook 2 minutes; turn fish over in pan. Transfer pan to oven. Bake at 425° for 6 to 8 minutes or until fish flakes easily when tested with a fork.
4. While fish bakes, combine tomatoes and next 6 ingredients. Serve with fish. Sprinkle with freshly ground pepper, if desired.
Yield: 4 servings (serving size: 1 fillet and about ½ cup relish).

CALORIES 320; FAT 17g (sat 3.1g, mono 8.4g, poly 5.2g); PROTEIN 35.9g;
CARB 5.3g; FIBER 1.8g; CHOL 85mg; IRON 1.2mg; SODIUM 666mg; CALC 43mg

15 MINUTES

Sautéed Tilapia with Honey-Scallion Dressing

Dressing:

2½ tablespoons fresh lemon juice
2 tablespoons chopped green onions
1 tablespoon honey
1 tablespoon low-sodium soy sauce
1 teaspoon bottled ground fresh ginger (such as Spice World)
¼ teaspoon dark sesame oil

Fish:

1 tablespoon canola oil
4 (6-ounce) tilapia fillets
½ teaspoon salt
⅛ teaspoon black pepper
4 cups gourmet salad greens

1. To prepare dressing, combine first 6 ingredients in a bowl, stirring well with a whisk.
2. To prepare fish, heat canola oil in a large nonstick skillet over medium-high heat. Sprinkle fish evenly with salt and pepper. Add fish to pan; cook 3 minutes on each side or until fish flakes easily when tested with a fork or until desired degree of doneness. Arrange 1 cup greens on each of 4 plates. Top each serving with 1 fish fillet; drizzle with 2 tablespoons dressing. **Yield:** 4 servings.

CALORIES 230; FAT 7.7g (sat 1.8g, mono 3.9g, poly 1.4g); PROTEIN 34.2g; CARB 7.5g; FIBER 1.4g; CHOL 113mg; IRON 1.4mg; SODIUM 485mg; CALC 35mg

make it a meal *Serve this sautéed fish with fast-cooking rice noodles to round out your meal.*

15 MINUTES

Tilapia Piccata

A traditional piccata dish is meat (usually veal) that's dredged in flour, quickly sautéed, and then served with a pan sauce made with lemon juice and herbs. Here, we've used tilapia. You can substitute most any flaky white fish, or use veal or chicken cutlets.

8   ounces uncooked orzo (about 1½ cups)
¾   cup grape tomatoes, halved
½   teaspoon salt, divided
3   tablespoons chopped fresh parsley
¼   teaspoon black pepper, divided
3   tablespoons all-purpose flour
4   (6-ounce) tilapia fillets
3   tablespoons butter, divided
¼   cup white wine
3   tablespoons fresh lemon juice
1   tablespoon drained capers

1. Cook pasta according to package directions, omitting salt and fat. Drain; stir in tomatoes, ¼ teaspoon salt, parsley, and ⅛ teaspoon pepper. Set aside and keep warm.
2. Combine remaining ¼ teaspoon salt, remaining ⅛ teaspoon pepper, and flour in a large shallow dish. Dredge fish in flour mixture. Melt 1 tablespoon butter in a large nonstick skillet over medium-high heat. Add fish to pan; cook 1½ minutes on each side or until fish flakes easily when tested with a fork or until desired degree of doneness. Remove fish from pan, and keep warm.
3. Add wine, juice, and capers to pan; cook 30 seconds. Remove from heat. Add remaining 2 tablespoons butter to pan; stir until butter melts. Serve fish with sauce and pasta. **Yield:** 4 servings (serving size: 1 fillet, ¾ cup pasta mixture, and about 1 tablespoon sauce).

CALORIES 461; FAT 12.5g (sat 6.4g, mono 3.1g, poly 1.1g); PROTEIN 41.7g; CARB 45.3g; FIBER 2.6g; CHOL 108mg; IRON 1.6mg; SODIUM 512mg; CALC 30mg

15 MINUTES

Spicy Tilapia with Pineapple-Pepper Relish

make it a meal *Serve with coconut rice (substitute light coconut milk for some of the water to cook it). Round out your menu with a romaine lettuce salad tossed with lime dressing.*

2   teaspoons canola oil
1   teaspoon Cajun seasoning
¼   teaspoon kosher salt
¼   teaspoon ground red pepper
4   (6-ounce) tilapia fillets
1½   cups chopped fresh pineapple chunks
⅓   cup chopped onion
⅓   cup chopped plum tomato
2   tablespoons rice vinegar
1   tablespoon chopped fresh cilantro
1   small jalapeño pepper, seeded and chopped
4   lime wedges

1. Heat oil in a large nonstick skillet over medium-high heat. Combine Cajun seasoning, salt, and pepper in a small bowl. Sprinkle fish evenly with spice mixture. Add fish to pan, and cook 2 minutes on each side or until fish flakes easily when tested with a fork or until desired degree of doneness.
2. Combine pineapple and next 5 ingredients in a large bowl, stirring gently. Serve pineapple mixture with fish. Garnish with lime wedges. **Yield:** 4 servings (serving size: 1 fillet, about ½ cup relish, and 1 lime wedge).

CALORIES 228; FAT 5.5g (sat 1.2g, mono 2.2g, poly 1.4g); PROTEIN 34.9g; CARB 11.2g; FIBER 1.5g; CHOL 85mg; IRON 1.2mg; SODIUM 328mg; CALC 29mg

Fresh pineapple chunks, now widely available in the produce section of supermarkets, speed the prep for this relish.

MAKE IT FASTER

Spicy Lemon Trout

15 MINUTES

Pecan Trout

⅓ cup chopped pecans
10 saltine crackers
1 garlic clove, chopped
¼ teaspoon salt
3 tablespoons fat-free milk
2 (6-ounce) trout fillets
Cooking spray
2 teaspoons canola oil, divided
Lemon wedges

1. Place first 4 ingredients in a food processor, and process until finely ground. Place cracker mixture in a shallow dish.
2. Place milk in a separate shallow dish. Dip fish in milk; then dredge in cracker mixture. Coat fish with cooking spray.
3. Heat 1 teaspoon oil in a large nonstick skillet over medium-high heat. Add 1 fillet; cook 2 to 3 minutes on each side or until fish flakes easily when tested with a fork. Remove fillet from pan; keep warm. Repeat procedure with remaining 1 teaspoon oil and fillet. Serve with lemon wedges. **Yield:** 2 servings (serving size: 1 fillet).

CALORIES 320; FAT 19.5g (sat 2.5g, mono 10.3g, poly 6.4g); PROTEIN 24.2g; CARB 12.6g; FIBER 1.6g; CHOL 100mg; IRON 1.2mg; SODIUM 394mg; CALC 116mg

15 MINUTES

Spicy Lemon Trout

make it a meal *Serve with a spinach-mushroom salad and French bread. Chardonnay's oak tones help it remain bright and fruity when paired with this dish. Its fresh mineral qualities complement the delicate flavors of the fish.*

2 teaspoons fresh lemon juice
2 teaspoons olive oil
4 (6-ounce) dressed trout fillets
1 teaspoon dried thyme
½ teaspoon salt
½ teaspoon Spanish smoked paprika
¼ teaspoon ground red pepper
12 thin lemon slices (about 2 lemons)
Cooking spray

1. Preheat broiler.
2. Combine juice and oil, and brush inside of fish. Combine thyme, salt, paprika, and pepper; sprinkle evenly inside cavity of each fish. Place 3 lemon slices into cavity of each fish. Place fish on broiler pan coated with cooking spray; broil 4 minutes on each side or until fish flakes easily when tested with a fork or until desired degree of doneness. **Yield:** 4 servings (serving size: 1 fillet).

CALORIES 374; FAT 15.7g (sat 4g, mono 5.6g, poly 4.5g); PROTEIN 52.7g; CARB 6.4g; FIBER 2.8g; CHOL 156mg; IRON 1.8mg; SODIUM 424mg; CALC 235mg

Trout's flavor ranges from subtle and mild to sweet. Most of the trout sold at markets is rainbow trout, although you'll also see other varieties such as brook trout. At its best, trout is subtle; prepare it simply to avoid masking its flavor.

INGREDIENT SPOTLIGHT

15 MINUTES

Tuna with Jalapeño Sour Cream

make it a meal *Look for packages of fillets in the frozen seafood section of your supermarket. If you use frozen fish, thaw according to the package directions before starting the recipe. Frozen packages of fish fillets can range in size within each bag. You can count two 3-ounce fillets as a 6-ounce portion. To make this a meal serve with sugar snap peas and brown rice.*

½   cup reduced-fat sour cream
1   jalapeño pepper, seeded and finely chopped
1   tablespoon fresh lime juice (½ lime)
¼   cup chopped fresh cilantro
¼   teaspoon salt
1   tablespoon chili powder
¼   teaspoon salt
4   (6-ounce) tuna steaks (about 1 inch thick)
Cooking spray

1. Combine first 5 ingredients; set aside.
2. Combine chili powder and ¼ teaspoon salt; rub over fish. Coat fish with cooking spray.

3. Heat a large nonstick grill pan over medium-high heat; add fish. Cook 3 minutes on each side or until desired degree of doneness. Serve with sour cream mixture. **Yield:** 4 servings (serving size: 1 steak and 2 tablespoons sour cream mixture).

CALORIES 220; FAT 5.4g (sat 2.8g, mono 1.6g, poly 0.7g); PROTEIN 38.4g; CARB 2.2g; FIBER 0.5g; CHOL 92mg; IRON 2.2mg; SODIUM 421mg; CALC 86mg

15 MINUTES

Thai-Style Roasted Trout

make it a meal *Fresh lime juice complements the sweet taste of trout. Steamed asparagus and jasmine rice make good sides.*

2   tablespoons fresh lime juice
1   tablespoon fish sauce
2   teaspoons dark sesame oil
½   teaspoon crushed red pepper
4   (6-ounce) trout fillets
Cooking spray
¼   cup coarsely chopped fresh cilantro
Lime slices (optional)
Cilantro sprigs (optional)

1. Preheat oven to 450°.
2. Combine first 4 ingredients in a small bowl; stir well.
3. Arrange trout on a jelly-roll pan coated with cooking spray. Brush half of juice mixture inside of fish. Bake at 450° for 5 minutes. Brush remaining juice mixture over fish. Bake an additional 5 minutes or until fish flakes easily when tested with a fork or until desired degree of doneness. Sprinkle with chopped cilantro; garnish with lime slices and cilantro sprigs, if desired. **Yield:** 4 servings (serving size: 1 fish and 1 tablespoon cilantro).

CALORIES 280; FAT 12.2g (sat 3.1g, mono 3.9g, poly 4.1g); PROTEIN 39.3g; CARB 1g; FIBER 0.1g; CHOL 117mg; IRON 0.7mg; SODIUM 443mg; CALC 150mg

Tuna with Jalapeño Sour Cream

Coriander-Crusted Tuna with Black Bean Salsa

make it a meal *This Southwestern tuna has a spicy crust made with coriander, cumin, and black pepper. Serve it with warm flour tortillas, and garnish with sliced avocado.*

1	tablespoon ground coriander
1	teaspoon ground cumin
³⁄₄	teaspoon kosher salt, divided
¹⁄₄	teaspoon black pepper
4	(6-ounce) tuna steaks (about 1 inch thick)
1	tablespoon olive oil
1	cup diced plum tomato (about 3 tomatoes)
¹⁄₂	cup chopped yellow bell pepper
¹⁄₄	cup sliced green onions
3	tablespoons chopped fresh cilantro
2	tablespoons fresh lime juice
1	(15-ounce) can no-salt-added black beans, rinsed and drained

Cilantro sprigs (optional)

1. Combine coriander, cumin, ¹⁄₂ teaspoon salt, and black pepper in a small bowl.

Rub spice mixture evenly over both sides of fish.

2. Heat oil in a large nonstick skillet over medium-high heat. Add fish to pan; cook 2 minutes on each side or until desired degree of doneness. Remove from heat.

3. Combine tomato and next 5 ingredients in a medium bowl. Stir in remaining ¹⁄₄ teaspoon salt, and toss well. Serve salsa with fish. Garnish with cilantro sprigs, if desired. **Yield:** 4 servings (serving size: 1 tuna steak and about ³⁄₄ cup salsa).

CALORIES 356; FAT 12.3g (sat 2.6g, mono 5.2g, poly 2.9g); PROTEIN 43.9g; CARB 15.4g; FIBER 4.9g; CHOL 65mg; IRON 3.1mg; SODIUM 501mg; CALC 64mg

Fresh Tuna Tacos

This is a great dish for a casual supper; let everyone assemble their own tacos.

¾ teaspoon chili powder
½ teaspoon ground cumin
½ teaspoon sugar
¼ teaspoon salt
⅛ teaspoon chipotle chile powder or chile powder
1 pound Yellowfin tuna fillet (about ¾ inch thick)
Cooking spray
8 (6-inch) corn tortillas
1 cup sliced peeled avocado (about 1 medium)
½ cup vertically sliced onion
¼ cup fresh cilantro leaves
24 pickled jalapeño slices
8 teaspoons reduced-fat sour cream
4 lime wedges

1. Combine first 5 ingredients in a small bowl; sprinkle the spice mixture evenly over both sides of tuna.
2. Heat a grill pan over high heat; coat pan with cooking spray. Add tuna; cook 2 minutes on each side or until medium-rare or until desired degree of doneness. Cut tuna into ¼-inch-thick slices.
3. Warm tortillas according to package directions. Divide tuna evenly among tortillas; top each with 2 tablespoons avocado, 1 tablespoon onion, 1½ teaspoons cilantro, and 3 jalapeño slices. Top each with 1 teaspoon sour cream. Serve tacos with lime wedges. **Yield:** 4 servings (serving size: 2 filled tacos and 1 lime wedge).

CALORIES 331; FAT 9g (sat 2g, mono 4.1g, poly 1.7g); PROTEIN 31.5g; CARB 32.3g; FIBER 5.3g; CHOL 55mg; IRON 2.3mg; SODIUM 408mg; CALC 138mg

Tuna Steaks with Wasabi-Ginger Glaze

make it a meal *Add jasmine rice and steamed fresh asparagus to complete the meal. Chinese-style hot mustard has a sharp, spicy bite and can be used in place of wasabi paste. The glaze would also pair well with salmon, chicken thighs, or pork.*

2 tablespoons low-sodium soy sauce, divided
4 (6-ounce) tuna steaks (1 inch thick)
2 tablespoons ginger marmalade (such as Dundee)
2 teaspoons wasabi paste
Cooking spray
2 tablespoons chopped fresh cilantro

1. Spoon 1 tablespoon soy sauce over fish; let stand 5 minutes.
2. Combine remaining 1 tablespoon soy sauce, ginger marmalade, and 2 teaspoons wasabi paste in a small bowl, stirring with a whisk.
3. Heat a grill pan over medium-high heat; coat pan with cooking spray. Add fish to pan; cook 2 minutes on each side. Spoon marmalade mixture over tuna; cook 1 minute or until medium-rare or until desired degree of doneness. Remove tuna from pan; sprinkle with cilantro. **Yield:** 4 servings (serving size: 1 steak and 1½ teaspoons cilantro).

CALORIES 281; FAT 2.3g (sat 0.5g, mono 0.3g, poly 0.6g); PROTEIN 51.4g; CARB 7.7g; FIBER 0.1g; CHOL 98mg; IRON 1.8mg; SODIUM 397mg; CALC 37mg

A grill pan is a good alternative to a gas or charcoal grill. Meat and fish turn out juicy, with no need for added fat, and you save time by not having to heat up a traditional grill.

SHORTCUT SPOTLIGHT

15 MINUTES

Sesame Tuna with Spicy Slaw

make it a meal *There isn't a good substitute for the one-of-a-kind flavor of fish sauce, though many cooks will use soy sauce in a pinch. Pair this dish with rice noodles.*

1   tablespoon dark sesame oil
4   (6-ounce) tuna steaks
2   tablespoons low-sodium soy sauce
2   teaspoons coarsely ground black pepper
1   teaspoon sesame seeds
2   tablespoons water
2   teaspoons sugar
1   teaspoon Sriracha (hot chile sauce, such as Huy Fong)
¾   teaspoon fish sauce
½   teaspoon rice vinegar
½   teaspoon bottled ground fresh ginger (such as Spice World)
4   cups packaged angel hair slaw
2   tablespoons thinly sliced green onions

1. Heat oil in a large nonstick skillet over medium-high heat. Brush fish with soy sauce. Combine 2 teaspoons pepper and sesame seeds; sprinkle evenly over fish. Add fish to pan, and cook 2 minutes on each side or until fish flakes easily when tested with a fork or until desired degree of doneness.
2. Combine 2 tablespoons water and next 5 ingredients in a small bowl. Combine slaw and onions in a large bowl. Drizzle vinegar mixture over slaw mixture; toss to coat. Serve with fish. **Yield:** 4 servings (serving size: 1 tuna steak and about ¾ cup slaw).

CALORIES 247; FAT 5.5g (sat 1g, mono 1.8g, poly 2.1g); PROTEIN 40.1g; CARB 7.9g; FIBER 2.1g; CHOL 74mg; IRON 2mg; SODIUM 427mg; CALC 75mg

Sriracha chile sauce can be found in the ethnic foods aisle in large supermarkets or in Asian groceries. If you can't find Sriracha, substitute half the amount of Tabasco or other hot sauce.

INGREDIENT SPOTLIGHT

15 MINUTES

Sautéed Clams Parmesan

make it a meal *Serve this speedy entrée over angel hair pasta to soak up the flavorful broth.*

4   pounds littleneck clams
¼   cup fresh lemon juice
½   teaspoon black pepper
½   cup (2 ounces) preshredded fresh Parmesan cheese
2   tablespoons dry breadcrumbs
2   tablespoons chopped fresh basil
2   tablespoons chopped fresh oregano
2   tablespoons chopped fresh parsley
2   teaspoons olive oil

1. Combine clams, lemon juice, and pepper in a large nonstick skillet. Cover and cook over medium heat 8 minutes or until shells open. Discard any unopened shells.
2. While clams cook, combine cheese and next 4 ingredients in a small bowl; set aside.
3. Transfer clam mixture to a large bowl. Sprinkle with cheese mixture, and drizzle with oil. **Yield:** 3 servings (serving size: 20 clams, ½ cup broth, and about ½ teaspoon oil).

CALORIES 414; FAT 9.4g (sat 3.8g, mono 4g, poly 0.8g); PROTEIN 19.5g; CARB 8.8g; FIBER 0.5g; CHOL 44mg; IRON 13.3mg; SODIUM 406mg; CALC 308mg

Sautéed Clams Parmesan

Steamed Clams and Tomatoes with Angel Hair Pasta

make it a meal *Store-bought clam juice adds great flavor to a quick pasta dish. Serve with crusty bread and a simple green salad to round out dinner.*

1	(9-ounce) package fresh angel hair pasta
1	tablespoon olive oil
1	cup chopped tomato
1	tablespoon bottled minced garlic
¼	teaspoon crushed red pepper
⅓	cup dry white wine
1	(8-ounce) bottle clam juice
2	dozen littleneck clams, scrubbed
1	tablespoon butter
4	teaspoons chopped fresh flat-leaf parsley

1. Cook pasta according to package directions, omitting salt and fat. Drain and keep warm.

2. Heat oil in a large nonstick skillet over medium-high heat. Add tomato, garlic, and pepper to pan; sauté 1 minute. Stir in wine and juice; bring to a boil. Add clams. Cover and cook 7 minutes or until shells open. Discard any unopened shells. Remove clams from pan with a slotted spoon; add butter to pan, stirring until butter melts. Place 1 cup pasta in each of 4 shallow bowls; top each serving with about 6 clams, ½ cup broth, and 1 teaspoon parsley. **Yield:** 4 servings.

CALORIES 302; FAT 9.4g (sat 3.2g, mono 3.3g, poly 0.8g); PROTEIN 15.6g; CARB 39g; FIBER 2.2g; CHOL 63mg; IRON 9.5mg; SODIUM 194mg; CALC 54mg

COOKING CLASS: *how to clean clams*

Cleaning clams is an important process that you need to be familiar with. If you don't properly clean clams before cooking them, you can end up eating salty, sandy clams. Cleaning them is quick and easy: Scrub clams under cold running water with a stiff brush to remove sand and dirt.

15 MINUTES

Steamed Clams with Pico de Gallo

The pico de gallo in this recipe makes a great salsa to serve with baked tortilla chips as well as a condiment for grilled chicken, pork, and fish.

1   cup water
4   dozen fresh littleneck clams
1   (8-ounce) container prechopped tomato, green bell pepper, and onion mix
1   tablespoon chopped fresh cilantro
2   teaspoons fresh lime juice
¼   teaspoon salt

1. Bring 1 cup water to a boil in a large skillet. Scrub clams; discard any clams that are open. Add clams to pan; cover and cook 5 minutes or until clams open. Discard any unopened clams.
2. While clams cook, combine vegetable mix and next 3 ingredients in a small bowl; set aside.
3. Carefully remove clams from pan to individual serving bowls. Spoon tomato mixture over clams. Serve immediately. **Yield:** 4 servings (serving size: 1 dozen clams and about ¼ cup pico de gallo).

CALORIES 184; FAT 2.3g (sat 0.5g, mono 0.9g, poly 0.7g); PROTEIN 29.7g; CARB 9.5g; FIBER 0.9g; CHOL 76mg; IRON 32mg; SODIUM 278mg; CALC 114mg

15 MINUTES

Crab Quesadillas

These quesadillas finish in the oven under the broiler. If you prefer, brown them in a nonstick skillet coated with cooking spray. Serve sour cream and salsa on the side.

¼   cup chopped green onions
1   tablespoon minced fresh cilantro
2   tablespoons fat-free sour cream
¾   teaspoon bottled minced garlic
1   jalapeño pepper, seeded and finely chopped
½   pound lump crabmeat, shell pieces removed
½   cup (2 ounces) shredded Monterey Jack cheese
4   (8-inch) fat-free flour tortillas

1. Preheat broiler.
2. Combine first 6 ingredients, stirring well. Sprinkle 2 tablespoons cheese over each tortilla. Divide crab mixture evenly among tortillas. Fold in half, pressing gently to seal.
3. Place filled tortillas on a baking sheet. Broil 1 minute or until tortilla is lightly browned. **Yield:** 4 servings (serving size: 1 quesadilla).

CALORIES 275; FAT 8.6g (sat 3.7g, mono 3.2g, poly 0.9g); PROTEIN 18.5g; CARB 30g; FIBER 2g; CHOL 58mg; IRON 2.2mg; SODIUM 484mg; CALC 187mg

15 MINUTES

Crab Cakes with Rémoulade

make it a meal *Serve with a green salad.*

Crab Cakes:

2 teaspoons olive oil
1 cup dry breadcrumbs
½ cup thinly sliced green onions
½ pound lump crabmeat, shell pieces removed
1 (4-ounce) jar diced pimiento, drained
1 tablespoon Dijon mustard
1 tablespoon fresh lemon juice
¼ teaspoon salt
1 large egg

Rémoulade:

⅓ cup low-fat mayonnaise
2 teaspoons 2% reduced-fat milk
1 teaspoon capers, chopped
⅛ teaspoon ground red pepper
1 small garlic clove, minced

1. To prepare crab cakes, heat oil in a large nonstick skillet over medium-high heat. Combine breadcrumbs, onions, crabmeat, and pimiento in a medium bowl. Combine mustard, juice, salt, and egg, stirring with a whisk. Add egg mixture to crab mixture, tossing gently to combine. Divide crab mixture into 4 equal portions, shaping each into a 1-inch-thick patty.
2. Add crab cakes to skillet; cook 2 minutes. Turn cakes; reduce heat to medium. Cook 3 minutes or until golden brown.
3. To prepare rémoulade, combine mayonnaise and remaining ingredients, stirring

Crab Cakes with Rémoulade

with a whisk. Serve with crab cakes. **Yield:** 4 servings (serving size: 1 crab cake and 2 tablespoons rémoulade).

CALORIES 246; FAT 7.4g (sat 1.4g, mono 2.2g, poly 2.9g); PROTEIN 16.1g; CARB 28.5g; FIBER 1.6g; CHOL 97mg; IRON 3.1mg; SODIUM 870mg; CALC 136mg

30 MINUTES

Boiled Lobster

3 gallons water
¾ cup salt
4 (1½-pound) live Maine lobsters

1. Bring water and salt to a boil in a 5-gallon stockpot; add lobsters. Cover; cook 12 minutes or until shells are bright orange-red and tails are curled. **Yield:** 4 servings (serving size: 1 lobster).

CALORIES 111; FAT 0.7g (sat 0.1g, mono 0.2g, poly 0.1g); PROTEIN 23.2g; CARB 1.5g; FIBER 0g; CHOL 82mg; IRON 0.5mg; SODIUM 2189mg; CALC 70mg

COOKING CLASS: *how to eat a lobster*

To get meat from a cooked lobster, separate the tail from the rest of the body by bending the lobster backward. Snap off the flippers, and push the meat out of the shell using a fork at the flipper end of the tail. Twist off the claws, and gently move the pincher from side to side until you feel it snap. Gently pull it away. Gently crack the claws open with a nutcracker to release the meat. Pluck off the legs. Crack the body of the lobster open to remove the meat.

30 MINUTES

Coconut and Basil Steamed Mussels

2 teaspoons canola oil
¼ cup minced shallots
2 teaspoons bottled minced garlic
1 cup light coconut milk
⅔ cup water
⅓ cup fat-free, less-sodium chicken broth
¼ cup torn fresh basil
1 tablespoon fresh lime juice
1 teaspoon dark brown sugar
1 teaspoon fish sauce
½ to 1 teaspoon Sriracha (hot chile sauce, such as Huy Fong)
24 mussels (about 1 pound), scrubbed and debearded
Thinly sliced fresh basil (optional)

1. Heat a Dutch oven over medium heat. Add oil to pan, swirling to coat. Add shallots and garlic to pan; cook 2 minutes or until tender, stirring frequently. Stir in coconut milk and next 7 ingredients; bring to a boil. Add mussels to pan; cover and cook 5 minutes or until shells open. Discard any unopened shells.

2. Remove mussels from pan with a slotted spoon, reserving broth mixture. Divide mussels between 2 serving bowls; keep warm. Bring broth mixture to a boil; cook 5 minutes. Pour 1 cup sauce over each bowl. Sprinkle with sliced basil, if desired. **Yield:** 2 servings.

CALORIES 308; FAT 15.1g (sat 6.8g, mono 5g, poly 3.2g); PROTEIN 25.5g; CARB 19.4g; FIBER 0.5g; CHOL 54mg; IRON 8.8mg; SODIUM 996mg; CALC 75mg

Steamed Mussels in Saffron Broth

make it a meal *Saffron adds its characteristic bittersweet earthiness to the broth, though the dish is good without it, too. Serve with toasted slices of French bread.*

1 teaspoon olive oil
1 cup chopped onion
1 teaspoon bottled minced garlic
¼ teaspoon saffron threads, crushed
3 tablespoons tomato paste
1½ tablespoons whipping cream
1 (8-ounce) bottle clam juice
4 pounds mussels, scrubbed and debearded

1. Heat oil in a large saucepan over medium-high heat. Add onion to pan; sauté 1 minute. Add garlic, and sauté 30 seconds. Add saffron; sauté 15 seconds. Stir in tomato paste, whipping cream, and clam juice; bring to a boil. Cook 1 minute, stirring occasionally. Add mussels to pan. Cover and cook 5 minutes or until mussels open; discard any unopened shells. **Yield:** 4 servings (serving size: 1 pound mussels).

CALORIES 318; FAT 10g (sat 2.7g, mono 3g, poly 2g); PROTEIN 37.2g; CARB 17.9g; FIBER 1g; CHOL 93mg; IRON 12.4mg; SODIUM 991mg; CALC 99mg

20 MINUTES

Mussels and Clams with Curry-Coconut Sauce over Noodles

If you don't have a serrano chile, substitute ¼ teaspoon crushed red pepper.

1   (7-ounce) package rice noodles
1   tablespoon olive oil
1   teaspoon bottled minced garlic
1   serrano chile, seeded and thinly sliced
1   cup fat-free, less-sodium chicken broth
1   tablespoon green curry paste
1   teaspoon bottled ground fresh ginger (such as Spice World)
1   (14-ounce) can light coconut milk
1½   pounds mussels, scrubbed and debearded
1½   pounds littleneck clams, scrubbed
2   cups grape or cherry tomatoes
1   cup chopped fresh cilantro, divided
¼   cup fresh lime juice
4   lime wedges

1. Cook noodles according to package directions, omitting salt and fat. Drain; set aside.
2. While noodles cook, heat olive oil in a large Dutch oven over medium heat. Add garlic and serrano chile, and sauté 1 minute. Stir in chicken broth, curry paste, ginger, and coconut milk; bring to a boil.
3. Add mussels and clams. Cover, reduce heat, and simmer 5 minutes or until shells open; discard any unopened shells. Remove from heat. Stir in tomatoes, ½ cup cilantro, and juice; toss well. Place 1 cup noodles in each of 4 shallow bowls; top each serving with 4 mussels and 4 clams. Drizzle sauce evenly over shellfish; sprinkle each serving with 2 tablespoons cilantro. Serve with lime wedges. **Yield:** 4 servings.

CALORIES 405; FAT 11.3g (sat 5.3g, mono 3.3g, poly 1g); PROTEIN 19.6g; CARB 56.7g; FIBER 2.1g; CHOL 49mg; IRON 6.3mg; SODIUM 548mg; CALC 69mg

20 MINUTES

Thai Green Curry Mussels

1   (3½-ounce) bag boil-in-bag long-grain white rice
1   cup water
1   teaspoon grated lime rind
2   tablespoons fresh lime juice
1   teaspoon sugar
1½   teaspoons green curry paste
1   teaspoon fish sauce
1   (13.5-ounce) can light coconut milk
1   (8-ounce) bottle clam juice
80   mussels (about 2 pounds), scrubbed and debearded
⅓   cup chopped fresh cilantro
Lime wedges (optional)

1. Cook rice according to the package directions, omitting salt and fat.
2. Combine 1 cup water and next 7 ingredients in a large Dutch oven over medium-high heat. Add mussels to pan; bring to a boil. Cover; steam 5 minutes or until mussels open. Discard any unopened shells. Stir in cilantro. Place about ½ cup rice in each of 4 bowls; ladle about 20 mussels and 1 cup coconut mixture over rice. Garnish with lime wedges, if desired. **Yield:** 4 servings.

CALORIES 349; FAT 9.6g (sat 5.2g, mono 1.2g, poly 1.4g); PROTEIN 30.5g; CARB 34.8g; FIBER 0.1g; CHOL 65mg; IRON 10.3mg; SODIUM 954mg; CALC 70mg

INGREDIENT SPOTLIGHT

Always buy fresh mussels, and use them within a day. Choose tightly closed shells or those that are slightly open and snap shut when tapped. Avoid broken and chipped shells. Once home, remove the mussels from the packaging and store them wrapped in a moist towel in the fridge to keep them fresh.

MINUTES

Seared Scallops with Lemon Orzo

make it a meal *Sear the scallops while the orzo cooks. Serve this easy but impressive meal with a green salad, garlic bread, and a crisp white wine.*

Cooking spray
½ cup prechopped onion
1 cup uncooked orzo (rice-shaped pasta)
1 cup fat-free, less-sodium chicken broth
½ cup dry white wine
¼ teaspoon dried thyme
2 tablespoons chopped fresh chives
2 tablespoons fresh lemon juice
2 teaspoons olive oil
1½ pounds sea scallops
¼ teaspoon salt
¼ teaspoon black pepper

1. Heat a medium saucepan over medium-high heat; coat pan with cooking spray. Add onion to pan; sauté 3 minutes. Stir in pasta, broth, wine, and thyme; bring to a boil. Cover, reduce heat, and simmer 15 minutes or until liquid is absorbed and pasta is al dente. Stir in chopped chives and lemon juice. Keep warm.
2. Heat oil in a large cast-iron skillet over medium-high heat. Sprinkle scallops evenly with salt and pepper. Add scallops to pan, and cook 3 minutes on each side or until desired degree of doneness. Serve with pasta mixture. **Yield:** 4 servings (serving size: 4½ ounces scallops and about ¾ cup pasta mixture).

CALORIES 480; FAT 5.1g (sat 1.7g, mono 1.9g, poly 0.7g); PROTEIN 60.9g; CARB 45.5g; FIBER 2.2g; CHOL 122mg; IRON 1.1mg; SODIUM 875mg; CALC 95mg

 MINUTES

Seared Scallops with Fresh Linguine and Romano Cheese

1 (9-ounce) package refrigerated linguine
¼ cup plus 2 tablespoons (about 1½ ounces) finely grated fresh Romano cheese, divided
2 tablespoons olive oil, divided
2 tablespoons chopped fresh basil
½ teaspoon black pepper
⅛ teaspoon salt
1½ pounds sea scallops
4 lemon wedges

1. Cook pasta according to package directions, omitting salt and fat. Drain pasta in a colander over a bowl, reserving 2 tablespoons pasta water. Combine pasta, reserved 2 tablespoons pasta water, ¼ cup cheese, 1 tablespoon oil, chopped basil, and pepper in a large bowl; toss well.
2. Heat remaining 1 tablespoon oil in a large cast-iron skillet over high heat. Sprinkle salt evenly over scallops; add scallops to pan. Cook 1 minute on each side or until golden.
3. Place 1 cup pasta mixture on each of 4 plates; top each serving with about 3 scallops and 1½ teaspoons remaining cheese. Serve with lemon wedges. **Yield:** 4 servings.

CALORIES 495; FAT 12.5g (sat 3g, mono 5.8g, poly 1.5g); PROTEIN 51.7g; CARB 42.4g; FIBER 1.9g; CHOL 110mg; IRON 5.6mg; SODIUM 872mg; CALC 177mg

The ability of cast-iron cookware to withstand and maintain very high cooking temperatures makes it ideal for quickly cooking scallops.

SHORTCUT SPOTLIGHT

Scallops in Champagne Sauce

Champagne or sparkling wine lends this simple French-inspired sauce delicate flavor. Tarragon, with its anise-like overtones, is a classic herb seasoning in this dish.

1½ tablespoons olive oil
1½ pounds sea scallops
1   cup sliced shiitake mushroom caps
    (about 4 ounces)
1½ tablespoons chopped shallots
½   cup Champagne or sparkling wine
1   tablespoon Dijon mustard
¼   teaspoon salt
¼   teaspoon dried tarragon
¼   cup reduced-fat sour cream

1. Heat oil in a large nonstick skillet over medium-high heat. Pat scallops dry with a paper towel. Add scallops to pan; cook 3 minutes on each side or until done. Remove from pan; keep warm.

2. Add mushrooms and shallots to pan; sauté 3 minutes or until liquid evaporates and mushrooms darken. Stir in Champagne, mustard, salt, and tarragon, scraping pan to loosen browned bits. Remove from heat; stir in sour cream. Serve with scallops. **Yield:** 4 servings (serving size: about 4 ounces scallops and 3 tablespoons sauce).

CALORIES 238; FAT 8.6g (sat 2g, mono 3.9g, poly 1.1g); PROTEIN 30.3g; CARB 8.1g; FIBER 0.4g; CHOL 64mg; IRON 1.3mg; SODIUM 534mg; CALC 76mg

2O
MINUTES

Soy Citrus Scallops with Soba Noodles

make it a meal *Entertain dinner guests with a flavorful scallop supper served on a bed of tender noodles. Steamed peas vinaigrette round out the plate.*

3	tablespoons low-sodium soy sauce
1	tablespoon fresh orange juice
1	tablespoon rice vinegar
1	tablespoon honey
½	teaspoon bottled ground fresh ginger
¼	teaspoon chili garlic sauce (such as Lee Kum Kee)
1	tablespoon dark sesame oil, divided
1	pound large sea scallops
4	cups hot cooked soba (about 6 ounces uncooked buckwheat noodles)
⅛	teaspoon salt
¼	cup thinly sliced green onions

1. Combine first 6 ingredients and 1 teaspoon oil in a shallow baking dish; add scallops to dish in a single layer. Marinate 4 minutes on each side.

2. Heat remaining 2 teaspoons oil in a large skillet over medium-high heat. Remove scallops from dish, reserving marinade. Add scallops to pan; sauté 1 minute on each side or until almost done. Remove scallops from pan; keep warm. Place remaining marinade in pan; bring to a boil. Return scallops to pan; cook 1 minute. Toss noodles with salt and green onions. Place 1 cup noodle mixture on each of 4 plates. Top each serving with about 3 scallops, and drizzle with 1 tablespoon sauce. **Yield:** 4 servings.

CALORIES 315; FAT 4.5g (sat 0.6g, mono 1.5g, poly 1.5g); PROTEIN 28g; CARB 42.7g; FIBER 1.9g; CHOL 37mg; IRON 1.3mg; SODIUM 653mg; CALC 41mg

COOKING CLASS: *how to sear scallops*

For the best sear, pat scallops dry with paper towels before seasoning them, and cook them in a very hot pan.

MINUTES

Seared Scallops with Warm Tuscan Beans

make it a meal *Pair this one-dish meal with a side of garlic bread. It's perfect for sopping up every last drop of the delicious sauce.*

2   tablespoons olive oil, divided
1½   pounds sea scallops
¼   teaspoon salt
1   cup prechopped onion
⅛   teaspoon crushed red pepper
2   garlic cloves, minced
¼   cup dry white wine
1   cup fat-free, less-sodium chicken broth
1   (19-ounce) can cannellini beans or other white beans, rinsed and drained
1   (6-ounce) package fresh baby spinach
2   tablespoons chopped fresh basil

1. Heat 1 tablespoon oil in a large nonstick skillet over medium-high heat. Sprinkle scallops evenly with salt. Add scallops to pan, and cook 2 minutes on each side or until done. Remove scallops from pan, and keep warm.
2. Add remaining 1 tablespoon oil and onion to pan; sauté 2 minutes. Add pepper and garlic; cook 20 seconds, stirring constantly. Stir in wine; cook 1 minute or until most of liquid evaporates. Stir in broth and beans; cook 2 minutes. Add spinach; cook 1 minute or until spinach wilts. Remove from heat; stir in basil. **Yield:** 4 servings (serving size: about 4 ounces scallops and ¾ cup bean mixture).

CALORIES 314; FAT 8.7g (sat 1.2g, mono 5.1g, poly 1.8g); PROTEIN 33.7g;
CARB 24.8g; FIBER 6.1g; CHOL 56mg; IRON 3.2mg; SODIUM 781mg; CALC 112mg

MINUTES

Caramelized Scallops

make it a meal *Save this recipe for your next date night at home. Scallops cook quickly and are packed with delicious flavor. Serve with wide rice noodles and sugar snap peas.*

3½   teaspoons sugar, divided
5   teaspoons water, divided
1   tablespoon fish sauce
1   teaspoon minced fresh ginger
2   teaspoons fresh lime juice
½   teaspoon minced fresh garlic
⅛   teaspoon crushed red pepper
Cooking spray
⅛   teaspoon freshly ground black pepper
6   large sea scallops (about 12 ounces)
1   teaspoon chopped fresh mint
2   lime wedges

1. Combine ½ teaspoon sugar, 1 tablespoon water, fish sauce, and next 4 ingredients in a small bowl.
2. Combine remaining 1 tablespoon sugar and remaining 2 teaspoons water in a small heavy saucepan over medium-high heat; cook until sugar dissolves. Continue cooking 2 minutes or until golden (do not stir). Remove from heat; carefully add fish sauce mixture, stirring constantly. Keep warm.
3. Heat a medium skillet over medium-high heat. Coat pan with cooking spray. Sprinkle black pepper over scallops; add scallops to pan. Cook 1½ minutes on each side or until desired degree of doneness. Add sauce; toss well. Sprinkle with mint. Serve with lime. **Yield:** 2 servings (serving size: 3 scallops).

CALORIES 185; FAT 1.3g (sat 0.1g, mono 0.1g, poly 0.5g); PROTEIN 29.2g;
CARB 13.2g; FIBER 0.4g; CHOL 56mg; IRON 0.6mg; SODIUM 844mg; CALC 44mg

20 MINUTES

Shrimp Skewers with Mango Dipping Sauce

1½   cups cherry tomatoes (about 12 ounces)
1   pound peeled, deveined large shrimp
1   medium red onion, cut into 1½-inch pieces (about 1 cup)
1   medium green pepper, cut into 1½-inch pieces (about 1 cup)
Cooking spray
¼   cup fresh lime juice, divided
¼   teaspoon black pepper
⅛   teaspoon salt
½   cup mango chutney
¼   cup chopped green onions
2   tablespoons low-sodium soy sauce
½   teaspoon bottled minced garlic

1. Preheat broiler.
2. Thread tomatoes, shrimp, onion, and pepper alternately onto each of 8 skewers. Place skewers on a wire rack coated with cooking spray; place rack on a roasting pan. Drizzle with 2 tablespoons juice; sprinkle with black pepper and salt. Broil 4 minutes or until shrimp are done, turning once.
3. Combine remaining 2 tablespoons juice, chutney, and remaining ingredients in a small bowl, stirring well. Serve sauce with skewers. **Yield:** 4 servings (serving size: 2 skewers and about ¼ cup sauce).

CALORIES 217; FAT 2.4g (sat 0.5g, mono 0.4g, poly 1g); PROTEIN 25.4g; CARB 24.8g; FIBER 3g; CHOL 172mg; IRON 3.8mg; SODIUM 522mg; CALC 98mg

make it a meal *Set the finished skewers atop hot cooked rice tossed with chopped fresh cilantro.*

Shrimp Chalupa with Mango Salsa

This is our version of a Mexican dish in which tortilla dough is shaped like a boat and fried until crisp; in fact, chalupa means "boat" in Spanish. Regular chili powder is a blend that tastes mostly of cumin. Chipotle chile powder is pure ground dried chiles, and it packs a hot punch. For more heat use all chipotle powder, or tame the spice by substituting all chili powder.

1   cup chopped peeled mango
3   tablespoons prechopped red onion
2   tablespoons chopped fresh cilantro
1   tablespoon fresh lime juice
³⁄₄ teaspoon salt, divided
¹⁄₂ teaspoon chili powder
¹⁄₄ teaspoon chipotle chile powder
32   large peeled, deveined shrimp (about
     1¹⁄₄ pounds)
1¹⁄₂ tablespoons olive oil, divided
8   (6-inch) corn tortillas

1. Combine first 4 ingredients in a bowl, and stir in ¹⁄₄ teaspoon salt. Set aside.
2. Combine remaining ¹⁄₂ teaspoon salt, chili powder, chipotle powder, and shrimp in a large bowl. Heat 1¹⁄₂ teaspoons oil in a large nonstick skillet over medium-high heat. Add shrimp to pan; cook 2 minutes on each side or until shrimp are done. Remove shrimp from pan; keep warm.
3. Wipe pan clean with a paper towel. Return pan to heat; add 1 teaspoon oil to pan. Place 3 tortillas in pan; cook 30 seconds on each side or until tortillas puff slightly. Repeat procedure with remaining oil and tortillas.
4. Place 2 tortillas on each of 4 plates, and arrange 4 shrimp on each tortilla. Top shrimp with about 2 tablespoons mango mixture, and serve immediately. **Yield:** 4 servings (serving size: 2 chalupas).

CALORIES 215; FAT 7.2g (sat 0.9g, mono 3.9g, poly 1.4g); PROTEIN 13.7g;
CARB 26.6g; FIBER 2.9g; CHOL 85mg; IRON 1.5mg; SODIUM 542mg; CALC 56mg

Chipotle Shrimp Tacos

make it a meal *Try serving these Southwestern-style shrimp tacos with fresh orange sections and beer.*

2   teaspoons chili powder
1   teaspoon sugar
¹⁄₂ teaspoon salt
¹⁄₂ teaspoon ground cumin
¹⁄₄ teaspoon ground chipotle chile powder
32   peeled and deveined large shrimp (about
     1¹⁄₂ pounds)
1   teaspoon olive oil
8   (6-inch) white corn tortillas
2   cups shredded iceberg lettuce
1   ripe avocado, peeled and cut into 16 slices
³⁄₄ cup salsa verde

1. Combine first 5 ingredients in a large bowl; add shrimp, tossing to coat.
2. Heat oil in a large nonstick skillet over medium-high heat. Add shrimp mixture to pan; cook 1¹⁄₂ minutes on each side or until done. Remove from heat.
3. Heat tortillas in microwave according to package directions. Place 2 tortillas on each of 4 plates; arrange 4 shrimp on each tortilla. Top each tortilla with ¹⁄₄ cup lettuce, 2 avocado slices, and 1¹⁄₂ tablespoons salsa. **Yield:** 4 servings (serving size: 2 filled tacos).

CALORIES 366; FAT 11.8g (sat 1.6g, mono 5.5g, poly 2.6g); PROTEIN 37.7g;
CARB 28.2g; FIBER 5.4g; CHOL 259mg; IRON 4.6mg; SODIUM 747mg; CALC 121mg

30
MINUTES

Shrimp Fried Rice

3   (3½-ounce) bags boil-in-bag long-grain rice
1   (10-ounce) package frozen green peas
Cooking spray
2   large eggs, lightly beaten
1   tablespoon canola oil
1   cup chopped green onions
1   tablespoon bottled ground fresh ginger (such as Spice World)
12 ounces medium shrimp, peeled and deveined
2   tablespoons rice vinegar
2   tablespoons low-sodium soy sauce
1   teaspoon dark sesame oil
¼   teaspoon salt
Dash of crushed red pepper

1. Cook rice according to package directions, omitting salt and fat. Drain. Remove rice from bags; return to pan. Add peas to pan, stirring well. Cover and keep warm.
2. Heat a nonstick skillet over medium-high heat; coat pan with cooking spray. Add eggs to pan; cook 1 minute or until set. Remove eggs from pan; coarsely chop. Return pan to heat; add canola oil to pan. Add onions and ginger to pan; sauté 1 minute. Add shrimp to pan, and sauté 2 minutes or until shrimp are done.

3. Add shrimp mixture and eggs to rice mixture; stir well. Combine vinegar and remaining ingredients, stirring well. Drizzle vinegar mixture over rice mixture; stir well. **Yield:** 6 servings (serving size: about 1½ cups).

CALORIES 392; FAT 6.7g (sat 1.1g, mono 2.8g, poly 1.9g); PROTEIN 19.3g; CARB 61.9g; FIBER 3.2g; CHOL 155mg; IRON 4.9mg; SODIUM 478mg; CALC 67mg

20
MINUTES

Lowcountry Shrimp Pilaf

make it a meal *Serve this quick dish with a green salad and crusty bread for a delicious meal inspired by the cuisine of South Carolina.*

1½ tablespoons canola oil
1½ cups prechopped green bell pepper
1   cup prechopped onion
1   tablespoon bottled minced garlic
2   teaspoons Old Bay seasoning
1   pound peeled and deveined large shrimp
½   cup dry white wine
1   (8-ounce) bottle clam juice
1½ cups instant white rice
2   tablespoons chopped fresh thyme, divided
1   (14.5-ounce) can diced tomatoes with jalapeños, undrained

1. Heat oil in large nonstick skillet over medium-high heat. Add bell pepper and onion to pan; sauté 2 minutes. Add garlic and Old Bay seasoning to pan; sauté 1 minute. Add shrimp, wine, and clam juice; bring to a boil. Stir in rice; cover and remove from heat. Let stand 5 minutes or until liquid is absorbed.
2. Place pan over medium-high heat. Stir in 1 tablespoon thyme and tomatoes; cook 2 minutes or until thoroughly heated, stirring occasionally. Sprinkle with remaining 1 tablespoon thyme. **Yield:** 4 servings (serving size: 1½ cups).

CALORIES 365; FAT 8g (sat 0.8g, mono 3.5g, poly 2.4g); PROTEIN 27.8g; CARB 44.7g; FIBER 3.9g; CHOL 174mg; IRON 6mg; SODIUM 756mg; CALC 117mg

Made from fermented soybeans and wheat, the flavor of soy sauce varies by manufacturer and aging process. We use light or low-sodium versions to keep the sodium levels in our recipes lower. Light or low-sodium soy sauces have 500-600 milligrams of sodium per tablespoon.

INGREDIENT SPOTLIGHT

 MINUTES

Smoky Shrimp and Parmesan-Polenta Cakes

1	tablespoon olive oil
1	pound peeled and deveined medium shrimp
¼	cup dry white wine
1	tablespoon chopped fresh chives
1	tablespoon fresh lemon juice
¼	teaspoon Spanish smoked paprika
1	(17-ounce) tube polenta, cut into 8 (½-inch) slices

Cooking spray

8	teaspoons marinara sauce
8	teaspoons grated fresh Parmesan cheese
1	tablespoon chopped fresh flat-leaf parsley

1. Preheat broiler.
2. Heat olive oil in a large skillet over medium-high heat. Add shrimp to pan, and sauté 3 minutes or until done, stirring frequently. Remove from heat, and stir in wine, chives, juice, and paprika, tossing to coat. Keep warm.
3. Place polenta slices on a baking sheet coated with cooking spray. Top each slice with 1 teaspoon sauce and 1 teaspoon cheese; broil 3 minutes or until cheese melts. Place 2 polenta slices on each of 4 plates; top each serving evenly with shrimp mixture. Sprinkle with parsley.
Yield: 4 servings.

CALORIES 231; FAT 5.4g (sat 1.3g, mono 2.9g, poly 0.8g); PROTEIN 21.7g;
CARB 18.8g; FIBER 2.4g; CHOL 171mg; IRON 3.7mg; SODIUM 386mg; CALC 75mg

make it a meal *Use smoked paprika, which is available in supermarkets, to spice up sour cream, eggs, or rice. Its pungency offsets the shrimp's sweetness. Serve with bagged prewashed salad greens splashed with vinaigrette.*

30 MINUTES

Shrimp and Sausage Paella

Here's a recipe that's great for weeknights, leftovers, and group gatherings.

2   links Spanish chorizo sausage (about 6 1/2 ounces) or turkey kielbasa, cut into 1/2-inch-thick slices
1   cup chopped onion
1   cup chopped green bell pepper (about 1 medium)
2   teaspoons bottled minced garlic
1/4   teaspoon black pepper
1/4   teaspoon crushed saffron threads
1 1/2 cups instant rice
3/4   cup water
1/2   teaspoon dried marjoram
1   (14 1/2-ounce) can no-salt-added diced tomatoes (undrained)
1   (8-ounce) bottle clam juice
8   ounces medium shrimp, peeled and deveined

1. Heat a large nonstick skillet over medium-high heat. Add sausage to pan; sauté 1 minute. Add onion and bell pepper to pan; sauté 4 minutes. Stir in garlic, black pepper, and saffron; sauté 1 minute. Stir in rice, 3/4 cup water, marjoram, tomatoes, and clam juice; bring to a boil. Cover, reduce heat, and simmer 4 minutes or until rice is almost tender. Stir in shrimp. Cover and simmer 3 minutes or until shrimp are done. **Yield:** 4 servings (serving size: about 1 1/2 cups).

CALORIES 390; FAT 13.2g (sat 4.6g, mono 5.8g, poly 1.5g); PROTEIN 23.3g; CARB 41.8g; FIBER 2.7g; CHOL 114mg; IRON 5.1mg; SODIUM 626mg; CALC 66mg

20 MINUTES

Chile-Garlic Shrimp

make it a meal *Inspired by the bright flavors of Spain, this dish calls for whole lemon slices to be sautéed with the shrimp, resulting in a bold citrus punch. Serve with a small bowl of green olives and a crisp salad for a quick weeknight dinner.*

1   (3 1/2-ounce) bag boil-in-bag brown rice
1/2   teaspoon salt
1/8   teaspoon black pepper
1 1/2 pounds peeled and deveined large shrimp (about 32)
1 1/2 tablespoons olive oil
1/4   teaspoon crushed red pepper
3   large garlic cloves, sliced
1   bay leaf
1/2   cup dry white wine
4   (1/4-inch-thick) lemon slices
2   tablespoons chopped fresh parsley
1   tablespoon butter
Lemon wedges (optional)

1. Cook rice according to package directions, omitting salt and fat.
2. Sprinkle salt and black pepper evenly over shrimp. Heat oil in a large skillet over medium heat. Add shrimp, red pepper, garlic, and bay leaf to pan; cook 3 minutes, stirring frequently. Add wine and lemon to pan. Increase heat to medium-high, and bring to a simmer; cook until liquid is reduced to 1/2 cup (about 3 minutes). Remove from heat. Discard bay leaf and lemon. Add parsley and butter, stirring until butter melts. Serve shrimp and sauce over rice. Serve with lemon wedges, if desired. **Yield:** 4 servings (serving size: about 8 shrimp, 1/2 cup rice, and 2 tablespoons sauce).

CALORIES 344; FAT 11.4g (sat 3.1g, mono 4.9g, poly 1.8g); PROTEIN 36.9g; CARB 21.9g; FIBER 1.5g; CHOL 266mg; IRON 4.8mg; SODIUM 581mg; CALC 99mg

INGREDIENT SPOTLIGHT

Saffron has always been the world's most expensive spice, but you need only a few dried stigmas to color a dish golden yellow and impart a warm, aromatic quality.

COOKING CLASS: *how to drain tofu*

Tofu is packed in water to keep it fresh. But you need to press some of the moisture out with paper towels in order to create a crisp, browned exterior when sautéing or stir-frying it.

15 MINUTES

Sweet and Sour Shrimp

This Chinese favorite can be on your table in a flash using traditional sweet-and-sour ingredients. Add crunch, not fat, by coating shrimp and tofu with cornstarch, and then pan-fry them.

1   (3½-ounce) bag boil-in-bag rice
8   ounces firm light tofu
2   tablespoons cornstarch, divided
8   ounces peeled large shrimp
¼   cup fat-free, less-sodium chicken broth
¼   cup low-sodium soy sauce
2   tablespoons sugar
3   tablespoons rice vinegar
1   tablespoon chile paste with garlic
2   teaspoons dark sesame oil
2   teaspoons canola oil
1   cup prechopped onion
½   cup prechopped green bell pepper
1   tablespoon ground fresh ginger
1   (8-ounce) can pineapple chunks in juice, drained

1. Cook rice according to package directions, omitting salt and fat; set aside.
2. Place tofu between paper towels until barely moist; cut into ½-inch cubes. Combine tofu, 1 tablespoon cornstarch, and shrimp. Combine remaining cornstarch, broth, and next 4 ingredients; set aside.
3. Heat sesame oil in a large nonstick skillet over medium-high heat. Add shrimp mixture to pan; sauté 3 minutes. Place shrimp mixture in a bowl. Heat canola oil in pan over medium-high heat. Add onion, bell pepper, ginger, and pineapple to pan; sauté 2 minutes. Add shrimp mixture; cook 1 minute. Add broth mixture to pan, and cook 1 minute. Serve over rice. **Yield:** 4 servings (serving size: 1 cup shrimp and ½ cup rice).

CALORIES 318; FAT 6.8g (sat 1g, mono 2.7g, poly 1.3g); PROTEIN 19.8g; CARB 45.4g; FIBER 2.7g; CHOL 86mg; IRON 2.7mg; SODIUM 681mg; CALC 89mg

MINUTES

Szechuan Shrimp with Spinach

make it a meal *Serve this tasty dish with hot cooked rice to soak up the garlicky sauce.*

2   tablespoons bottled minced garlic
2   tablespoons dry sherry
1½   tablespoons bottled ground fresh ginger (such as Spice World)
1½   tablespoons low-sodium soy sauce
1   tablespoon chili garlic sauce (such as Lee Kum Kee)
1   teaspoon sugar
24   large shrimp, peeled and deveined (about 1 pound)
½   cup fat-free, less-sodium chicken broth
2   teaspoons cornstarch
1   tablespoon canola oil
2   (6-ounce) packages fresh baby spinach

1. Combine first 6 ingredients in a bowl, stirring well. Add shrimp to bowl; toss to coat. Let stand 5 minutes. Remove shrimp with a slotted spoon, and reserve marinade. Combine broth and cornstarch in a small bowl, stirring with a whisk.
2. Heat oil in a large nonstick skillet over medium-high heat. Add shrimp to pan; sauté 3 minutes or until done. Remove shrimp from pan. Add reserved marinade to pan; cook 1 minute or until slightly thick. Add broth mixture to pan; bring to a boil. Add spinach to pan; cook 1 minute or until spinach wilts. Serve with shrimp. **Yield:** 4 servings (serving size: about 6 shrimp and ½ cup spinach).

CALORIES 216; FAT 5.5g (sat 0.6g, mono 2.4g, poly 1.8g); PROTEIN 26g; CARB 15.2g; FIBER 4.4g; CHOL 172mg; IRON 5.9mg; SODIUM 712mg; CALC 131mg

MINUTES

Shrimp and Broccoli Stir-Fry

¼   cup fat-free, less-sodium chicken broth
2   tablespoons rice vinegar
2   tablespoons low-sodium soy sauce
2   teaspoons cornstarch
½   teaspoon dark sesame oil
¼   teaspoon crushed red pepper
1   tablespoon canola oil, divided
1   tablespoon minced peeled fresh ginger
1   tablespoon bottled minced garlic
1   pound peeled and deveined large shrimp
¼   teaspoon salt
4   cups small broccoli florets
1   cup vertically sliced onion

1. Combine first 6 ingredients in a small bowl, stirring with a whisk.
2. Heat 2 teaspoons canola oil in a large nonstick skillet over medium-high heat. Add ginger and garlic to pan; stir-fry 30 seconds. Sprinkle shrimp with salt. Add shrimp to pan, and stir-fry 3 minutes or until done. Remove shrimp mixture from pan.
3. Add remaining 1 teaspoon canola oil to pan. Add broccoli and onion to pan; stir-fry 4 minutes or until broccoli is crisp-tender. Add shrimp mixture and broth mixture to pan; cook 1 minute or until thickened, stirring constantly. **Yield:** 4 servings (serving size: 1 cup).

CALORIES 220; FAT 6.7g (sat 0.8g, mono 2.4g, poly 1.9g); PROTEIN 26.2g; CARB 11.8g; FIBER 2.8g; CHOL 172mg; IRON 3.6mg; SODIUM 577mg; CALC 105mg

Pick up prepackaged bags of broccoli florets from the produce section of your local market and save time by not having to cut up a broccoli crown.

MAKE IT FASTER

Lemon Pepper Shrimp Scampi

Simple ingredients, fantastic flavor. Here's a quick weeknight meal that will have the whole family smiling. It will be your new go-to shrimp recipe.

1	cup uncooked orzo
2	tablespoons chopped fresh parsley
1/2	teaspoon salt, divided
7	teaspoons unsalted butter, divided
11/2	pounds peeled and deveined jumbo shrimp
2	teaspoons bottled minced garlic
2	tablespoons fresh lemon juice
1/4	teaspoon black pepper

1. Cook orzo according to package directions, omitting salt and fat. Drain. Place orzo in a medium bowl. Stir in parsley and 1/4 teaspoon salt; cover and keep warm.

2. While orzo cooks, melt 1 tablespoon butter in a large nonstick skillet over medium-high heat. Sprinkle shrimp with remaining 1/4 teaspoon salt. Add half of shrimp to pan; sauté 2 minutes or until almost done. Transfer shrimp to a plate. Melt 1 teaspoon butter in pan. Add remaining shrimp to pan; sauté 2 minutes or until almost done. Transfer to plate.

3. Melt remaining 1 tablespoon butter in pan. Add garlic to pan; cook 30 seconds, stirring constantly. Stir in shrimp, juice, and pepper; cook 1 minute or until shrimp are done. **Yield:** 4 servings (serving size: 1/2 cup orzo mixture and about 7 shrimp).

CALORIES 403; FAT 10.4g (sat 4.8g, mono 2.2g, poly 1.4g); PROTEIN 40.1g; CARB 34.7g; FIBER 1.7g; CHOL 276mg; IRON 4.3mg; SODIUM 549mg; CALC 97mg

Greek-Style Scampi

make it a meal *This quick, filling weeknight meal relies on easy-to-find ingredients. Add a spinach-mushroom salad to round out the menu.*

6	ounces uncooked angel hair pasta
1	teaspoon olive oil
½	cup chopped green bell pepper
2	teaspoons bottled minced garlic
1	(14.5-ounce) can diced tomatoes with basil, garlic, and oregano, undrained
⅛	teaspoon black pepper
1	pound peeled and deveined medium shrimp
⅛	teaspoon ground red pepper
6	tablespoons (about 1½ ounces) crumbled feta cheese

1. Cook pasta according to package directions, omitting salt and fat. Drain and keep warm.

2. Heat oil in a large nonstick skillet over medium-high heat. Add green bell pepper to pan; sauté 1 minute. Add garlic and tomatoes, and cook 1 minute. Add black pepper and shrimp; cover and cook 3 minutes or until shrimp are done. Stir in red pepper; remove from heat. Place 1 cup pasta on each of 4 plates. Top each serving with 1 cup shrimp mixture and 1½ tablespoons cheese. **Yield: 4 servings.**

CALORIES 379; FAT 8.5g (sat 3g, mono 2.8g, poly 1.7g); PROTEIN 31.7g; CARB 43.3g; FIBER 2.6g; CHOL 185mg; IRON 4.1mg; SODIUM 139mg; CALC 656mg

Feta is a Greek cheese that is tangy and salty as a result of the brine in which it's cured. It's traditionally made from sheep's milk but can also be made from goat's or cow's milk.

INGREDIENT SPOTLIGHT

Gnocchi with Shrimp, Asparagus, and Pesto

Gnocchi, small Italian dumplings made with potatoes, are a hearty alternative to pasta in this satisfyingly quick and easy recipe.

2	quarts plus 1 tablespoon water, divided
1	(16-ounce) package vacuum-packed gnocchi (such as Vigo)
4	cups (1-inch) slices asparagus (about 1 pound)
1	pound peeled and deveined large shrimp, coarsely chopped
1	cup fresh basil leaves
2	tablespoons pine nuts, toasted
2	tablespoons preshredded Parmesan cheese
2	teaspoons fresh lemon juice
2	teaspoons bottled minced garlic
4	teaspoons extra-virgin olive oil
¼	teaspoon salt

1. Bring 2 quarts water to a boil in a Dutch oven. Add gnocchi to pan; cook 4 minutes or until done (gnocchi will rise to surface). Remove gnocchi with a slotted spoon; place in a large bowl. Add asparagus and shrimp to pan; cook 5 minutes or until shrimp are done. Drain. Add shrimp mixture to gnocchi.

2. Place remaining 1 tablespoon water, basil, and next 4 ingredients in a food processor; process until smooth, scraping sides. Drizzle oil through food chute with food processor on; process until well blended. Add salt and basil mixture to shrimp mixture; toss to coat. Serve immediately. **Yield: 4 servings (serving size: 2 cups).**

CALORIES 355; FAT 9.3g (sat 1.6g, mono 4.5g, poly 2.5g); PROTEIN 26.5g; CARB 42.7g; FIBER 3g; CHOL 170mg; IRON 5.7mg; SODIUM 894mg; CALC 108mg

Spicy Mustard Shrimp

make it a meal *Serve with sautéed sliced zucchini and orzo tossed with chopped fresh flat-leaf parsley.*

2	teaspoons canola oil
1	pound peeled and deveined large shrimp
1	tablespoon whole-grain Dijon mustard
1½	teaspoons chipotle hot pepper sauce (such as Tabasco)
⅔	cup (3-inch) diagonally cut green onions
1	cup diced peeled mango (about 1 medium)
¼	cup chopped fresh cilantro
4	lime wedges

1. Heat oil in a large nonstick skillet over medium-high heat. Add shrimp to pan; sauté 1 minute. Add mustard and pepper sauce to pan; sauté 2 minutes, stirring frequently. Stir in onions; cook 1 minute. Remove from heat; stir in diced mango. Sprinkle with cilantro. Serve with lime wedges. **Yield:** 4 servings (serving size: about 1 cup shrimp mixture, 1 tablespoon cilantro, and 1 lime wedge).

CALORIES 181; FAT 4.5g (sat 0.6g, mono 1.7g, poly 1.5g); PROTEIN 23.5g; CARB 10.3g; FIBER 1.9g; CHOL 172mg; IRON 3.1mg; SODIUM 247mg; CALC 82mg

MINUTES

Three Chile–Dusted Shrimp with Quick Corn Relish

make it a meal *Here's a good quick and easy meal that's great paired with rice and a salad. There's just enough spice to make this dish intriguing without overpowering your taste buds.*

3½ teaspoons sugar, divided
2 teaspoons chili powder
1 teaspoon ancho chile powder
¼ teaspoon chipotle chile powder
½ teaspoon salt, divided
1½ pounds peeled and deveined large shrimp
5 teaspoons olive oil, divided
½ cup chopped onion
½ cup chopped red bell pepper
2 teaspoons bottled minced garlic
2 teaspoons bottled minced ginger
1 (10-ounce) package frozen whole-kernel corn
1½ tablespoons cider vinegar
½ cup chopped green onions

1. Combine 2 teaspoons sugar, chili powder, chile powders, and ¼ teaspoon salt in a shallow dish. Add shrimp to spice mixture; toss well to coat.
2. Heat 1 tablespoon oil in a large nonstick skillet over medium-high heat. Add ½ cup onion, bell pepper, garlic, and ginger to pan; sauté 3 minutes. Add remaining 1½ teaspoons sugar and corn to pan; cook 3 minutes, stirring occasionally. Stir in vinegar; cook 30 seconds. Transfer corn mixture to a bowl; stir in remaining ¼ teaspoon salt and ½ cup green onions.
3. Wipe pan with a paper towel. Heat remaining 2 teaspoons oil in pan over medium-high heat. Add shrimp to pan; sauté 3 minutes or until done, turning once. Serve with corn mixture. **Yield:** 4 servings (serving size: 4½ ounces shrimp and about ¾ cup corn mixture).

CALORIES 342; FAT 9.6g (sat 1.5g, mono 4.8g, poly 2.2g); PROTEIN 37.9g; CARB 28g; FIBER 3.7g; CHOL 259mg; IRON 5.3mg; SODIUM 569mg; CALC 114mg

MINUTES

Roasted Rosemary Shrimp with Arugula and White Bean Salad

make it a meal *Baked shrimp, marinated in fresh rosemary, lemon juice, and garlic, top a crisp salad of arugula drizzled with a homemade lemon-and-garlic vinaigrette. Serve with garlic ciabatta.*

Shrimp:
2 tablespoons olive oil
1 tablespoon fresh lemon juice
2 teaspoons minced fresh rosemary
½ teaspoon kosher salt
¼ teaspoon black pepper
3 garlic cloves, crushed
1½ pounds jumbo shrimp, peeled and deveined
Salad:
2 tablespoons fresh lemon juice
1 tablespoon extra-virgin olive oil
½ teaspoon minced fresh garlic
¼ teaspoon kosher salt
⅛ teaspoon black pepper
5 cups arugula leaves
½ cup vertically sliced red onion
1 (15-ounce) can cannellini beans, rinsed and drained

1. Preheat oven to 400°.
2. To prepare shrimp, combine first 6 ingredients in a medium bowl; stir with a whisk. Add shrimp to bowl; toss well. Cover and refrigerate 10 minutes.
3. Arrange shrimp on a jelly-roll pan. Bake at 400° for 10 minutes or until shrimp are done.
4. To prepare salad, combine 2 tablespoons juice and next 4 ingredients in a large bowl; stir with a whisk. Add arugula, onion, and beans to bowl; toss well. Place salad and shrimp on each of 4 plates. **Yield:** 4 servings (serving size: 1½ cups salad and about 6 shrimp).

CALORIES 334; FAT 13.6g (sat 2g, mono 7.8g, poly 2.5g); PROTEIN 37.7g; CARB 13.6g; FIBER 3g; CHOL 259mg; IRON 5.4mg; SODIUM 690mg; CALC 156mg

PIZZA & PASTA

Fresh Tomato, Basil, and Cheese Pizza

3. Bake at 450° for 8 to 10 minutes or until crust is golden. Remove pizza to a cutting board, and top with fresh basil leaves. Cut into 12 rectangular pieces. **Yield:** 6 servings (serving size: 2 pieces).

CALORIES 276; FAT 8.5g (sat 4.2g, mono 2.7g, poly 1.3g); PROTEIN 12.2g; CARB 38g; FIBER 2.8g; CHOL 7mg; IRON 2.3mg; SODIUM 629mg; CALC 232mg

15 MINUTES

Barbecue Shrimp Pizza

We've replaced traditional pizza sauce with a store-bought barbecue sauce for this quick-to-prepare pizza. Bake the crust directly on the rack to give it a crisp texture and golden color.

¼ cup barbecue sauce
1 (10-ounce) Italian cheese-flavored thin pizza crust (such as Boboli)
½ pound cooked peeled shrimp, coarsely chopped
⅓ cup presliced red onion
¾ cup (3 ounces) shredded part-skim mozzarella cheese
2 tablespoons chopped fresh cilantro

1. Preheat oven to 450°.
2. Spread barbecue sauce over pizza crust. Arrange shrimp and onion over sauce; sprinkle evenly with cheese. Place pizza crust directly on oven rack. Bake at 450° for 12 minutes or until lightly browned and bubbly. Sprinkle fresh cilantro over pizza. Cut into 8 slices. **Yield:** 8 servings (serving size: 1 slice).

CALORIES 184; FAT 4.6g (sat 2.4g, mono 1.2g, poly 0.8g); PROTEIN 12.5g; CARB 22.2g; FIBER 0.7g; CHOL 61mg; IRON 2mg; SODIUM 385mg; CALC 140mg

15 MINUTES

Fresh Tomato, Basil, and Cheese Pizza

This pizza features the very best that summer has to offer—vine-ripened tomatoes, garden-fresh basil, and savory garlic. The 14-ounce pizza crust is the same diameter as a 10-ounce crust, but it's thicker.

1 (14-ounce) Italian cheese-flavored pizza crust (such as Boboli)
2 teaspoons olive oil
½ cup grated fresh Parmesan cheese, divided
3 tomatoes (about 1½ pounds), cut into ¼-inch slices
6 garlic cloves, thinly sliced
¼ teaspoon salt
⅛ teaspoon black pepper
¼ cup fresh basil leaves

1. Preheat oven to 450°.
2. Place pizza crust on a baking sheet. Brush crust with olive oil. Sprinkle with ¼ cup Parmesan cheese, leaving a ½-inch border around edge of crust. Arrange tomato slices over cheese, overlapping edges; top with garlic slices, remaining ¼ cup cheese, salt, and pepper.

Pesto and Goat Cheese Pizza

Prep time is super-quick, and the final result is much healthier than delivery.

1   (10-ounce) Italian cheese-flavored thin pizza crust (such as Boboli)
3   tablespoons commercial pesto
3   plum tomatoes, thinly sliced
¾   cup (3 ounces) crumbled goat cheese or crumbled feta cheese
¼   teaspoon crushed red pepper

1. Preheat oven to 450°.
2. Place pizza crust on a baking sheet. Spread pesto over crust, leaving a ½-inch border. Top with tomatoes and cheese; sprinkle with crushed red pepper.
3. Bake at 450° for 13 minutes or until crust is golden. Cut into 8 wedges. **Yield:** 4 servings (serving size: 2 wedges).

CALORIES 335; FAT 14.3g (sat 5.9g, mono 3.4g, poly 4.7g); PROTEIN 13.9g; CARB 37.7g; FIBER 2.2g; CHOL 14mg; IRON 3.2mg; SODIUM 580mg; CALC 217mg

Goat cheese—or *chèvre*, French for "goat"—is a fresh, unripened goat's milk cheese that has a fruity flavor early on but develops a sharper and slightly tart quality as it ages. Crumble it over salads, or use it as a topping for pizzas, quesadillas, or open-faced sandwiches.

INGREDIENT SPOTLIGHT

Speedy Greek Pizza

Here's a quick and easy pie that features flavorful sun-dried tomatoes, spinach, goat cheese, and basil.

¼   cup oil-packed sun-dried tomato halves
1   (10-ounce) Italian cheese-flavored thin pizza crust (such as Boboli)
1   cup fresh baby spinach
1   (4-ounce) package crumbled goat cheese
¼   cup thinly sliced fresh basil

1. Preheat oven to 450°.
2. Drain tomatoes, reserving 1 tablespoon oil. Cut tomatoes into strips. Place crust on a baking sheet; brush with reserved oil. Top with tomatoes, spinach, and cheese. Bake at 450° for 8 to 10 minutes. Top with basil. Cut into 8 slices. **Yield:** 4 servings (serving size: 2 slices).

CALORIES 304; FAT 11.3g (sat 6.3g, mono 3g, poly 1.8g); PROTEIN 13.3g; CARB 37g; FIBER 2g; CHOL 13mg; IRON 3.2mg; SODIUM 536mg; CALC 152mg

Goat Cheese and Asparagus Pizza

For a crispier pizza, lightly coat the crust with cooking spray before adding the toppings.

⅓   cup commercial pesto
1   (14-ounce) Italian cheese-flavored pizza crust (such as Boboli)
2   plum tomatoes, thinly sliced
8   asparagus spears, cut into 1-inch pieces
¾   cup (3 ounces) crumbled goat cheese

1. Preheat oven to 450°.
2. Spread pesto over pizza crust, and top with tomatoes, asparagus, and cheese.
3. Place pizza directly onto center rack in oven; bake at 450° for 10 to 12 minutes or until asparagus is crisp-tender and cheese melts. **Yield:** 6 servings (serving size: 1 slice).

CALORIES 301; FAT 14g (sat 6.9g, mono 1.1g, poly 5.3g); PROTEIN 12.2g; CARB 31.2g; FIBER 1.7g; CHOL 16mg; IRON 2.8mg; SODIUM 543mg; CALC 257mg

Goat Cheese and Asparagus Pizza

Rustic Tomato-Olive Pizza

MINUTES

Rustic Tomato-Olive Pizza

Use parchment paper to keep your baking sheet clean.

2   teaspoons yellow cornmeal
1   (14-ounce) Italian cheese-flavored pizza crust (such as Boboli)
Cooking spray
1   (28-ounce) can fire-roasted diced tomatoes, drained
1   cup (4 ounces) shredded mozzarella and Asiago with roasted garlic cheese blend (such as Sargento)
¼   cup sliced pitted kalamata olives
Chopped fresh oregano

1. Preheat oven to 450°.
2. Cover a large baking sheet with parchment paper; sprinkle with cornmeal. Place crust on top of cornmeal; lightly coat crust with cooking spray. Arrange tomatoes, cheese, and olives on crust.
3. Bake at 450° for 10 minutes or until lightly browned. Sprinkle with oregano. **Yield:** 8 servings (serving size: 1 slice).

CALORIES 223; FAT 6.8g (sat 3.2g, mono 1.4g, poly 2.1g); PROTEIN 9.5g; CARB 30.1g; FIBER 1.6g; CHOL 8mg; IRON 1.9mg; SODIUM 513mg; CALC 179mg

MINUTES

Rosemary, Goat Cheese, and Mushroom Pizzas

Olive oil–flavored cooking spray
1   (8-ounce) package presliced mushrooms
¼   teaspoon salt
¼   teaspoon freshly ground black pepper
¼   cup (2 ounces) crumbled goat cheese
2   tablespoons reduced-fat cream cheese
1   tablespoon chopped fresh rosemary
3   (2-ounce) whole wheat mini bagel squares, split and toasted

1. Heat a large nonstick skillet over medium-high heat; coat pan with cooking spray. Add mushrooms, salt, and pepper. Sauté 8 minutes or until tender.

2. While mushrooms cook, combine goat cheese, cream cheese, and rosemary in a small bowl.
3. Spread goat cheese mixture over cut side of each bagel square. Top evenly with mushrooms. Serve immediately. **Yield:** 3 servings (serving size: 2 pizzas).

CALORIES 251; FAT 6.9g (sat 4g, mono 1.4g, poly 1.3g); PROTEIN 12.1g; CARB 37.8g; FIBER 7.5g; CHOL 20mg; IRON 2.5mg; SODIUM 603mg; CALC 52mg

MINUTES

Roasted Bell Pepper and Mushroom Pizza

1   (10-ounce) Italian cheese-flavored thin pizza crust (such as Boboli)
1   cup tomato-basil pasta sauce
1   (8-ounce) package presliced mushrooms
½   cup bottled roasted red bell peppers, thinly sliced
¾   cup (3 ounces) preshredded reduced-fat 4-cheese Mexican blend cheese

1. Preheat oven to 450°.
2. Place pizza crust on a baking sheet. Spread sauce over crust, leaving a ½-inch border; top with mushrooms and roasted red bell peppers. Sprinkle with cheese. Bake at 450° for 10 minutes. Cut into 8 slices. **Yield:** 4 servings (serving size: 2 slices).

CALORIES 312; FAT 8.4g (sat 4.7g, mono 0.7g, poly 2.9g); PROTEIN 15.6g; CARB 43.7g; FIBER 3.8g; CHOL 15mg; IRON 3.1mg; SODIUM 798mg; CALC 309mg

INGREDIENT SPOTLIGHT

Keep packaged Italian cheese-flavored pizza crusts on hand for fun, last-minute suppers. We recommend lightly coating the crust with cooking spray before baking it to give the crust a golden color and a crisp texture. Olive oil–flavored cooking spray adds extra flavor.

The Works Pizza

3. Remove pizza crust from oven; place on an ungreased baking sheet. Lightly coat crust with cooking spray. Spoon sauce over crust, leaving a 1-inch border around outside edge. Top with burger crumble mixture; sprinkle with cheese.

4. Bake at 425° for 12 minutes or until cheese melts. Cut into 6 slices. **Yield:** 6 servings (serving size: 1 slice).

CALORIES 260; FAT 9.3g (sat 5.2g, mono 3.5g, poly 0.4g); PROTEIN 18.7g; CARB 30.2g; FIBER 5.3g; CHOL 15mg; IRON 2.1g; SODIUM 582mg; CALC 312mg

20 MINUTES

The Works Pizza

make it a meal *Serve this irresistible pizza with a side salad.*

1   (10-ounce) 100% whole wheat Italian cheese-flavored thin pizza crust (such as Boboli)
1   teaspoon olive oil
Olive oil–flavored cooking spray
2   garlic cloves, pressed
1   cup frozen meatless burger crumbles (such as Morningstar Farms)
1   cup prechopped onion
1   cup presliced mushrooms
⅓   cup prechopped green bell pepper
⅛   teaspoon salt
⅓   cup tomato-basil pasta sauce (such as Classico)
1½ cups (6 ounces) shredded part-skim mozzarella cheese

1. Place pizza crust directly on middle rack in oven while preheating to 425°.

2. While pizza crust bakes, heat oil in a large nonstick skillet coated with cooking spray over medium-high heat. Add garlic and burger crumbles; sauté 2 minutes, stirring frequently, or until burger crumbles thaw. Add onion, mushrooms, and bell pepper; sauté 3 minutes. Remove from heat; sprinkle with salt.

15 MINUTES

Kalamata-Artichoke Pita Pizzas

1   (14-ounce) can quartered artichoke hearts, drained and coarsely chopped
12 pitted kalamata olives, coarsely chopped
¼   cup chopped red onion
½   teaspoon dried basil
6   (6-inch) whole wheat pitas
¾   cup commercial hummus
2   plum tomatoes, sliced
⅓   cup (1.3 ounces) crumbled reduced-fat feta cheese with basil and sun-dried tomatoes

1. Preheat broiler.

2. Combine first 4 ingredients in a bowl.

3. Place pitas on a baking sheet, concave side up. Spread 2 tablespoons hummus on each pita; top each with ⅓ cup artichoke mixture. Divide tomato evenly among pizzas, and sprinkle evenly with cheese.

4. Broil 7 minutes or until cheese melts and edges are brown. **Yield:** 6 servings (serving size: 1 pizza).

CALORIES 273; FAT 7.2g (sat 1.4g, mono 3.4g, poly 2.4g); PROTEIN 11.1g; CARB 44.3g; FIBER 7g; CHOL 3mg; IRON 3.1mg; SODIUM 714mg; CALC 67mg

Cut down on your prep time by purchasing prechopped red onion from the produce section of your supermarket.

MAKE IT FASTER

15 MINUTES

Mini White Pizzas with Vegetables

For a Greek-inspired variation, substitute hummus for the spreadable cheese.

4   (6-inch) whole wheat pitas
Olive oil–flavored cooking spray
1   medium zucchini, thinly sliced
¼   cup thinly sliced red onion, separated into rings
¼   teaspoon freshly ground black pepper
⅛   teaspoon salt
½   cup light garlic-and-herbs spreadable cheese (such as Alouette Light)
6   tablespoons shredded Asiago cheese

1. Preheat broiler.
2. Place pitas on a baking sheet; broil 3 minutes.
3. Heat a nonstick skillet over medium-high heat; coat pan with cooking spray. Add zucchini, onion, black pepper, and salt; sauté 3 minutes or until vegetables are crisp-tender.
4. Remove pitas from oven, and spread 2 tablespoons garlic-and-herbs spreadable cheese over each pita. Top evenly with vegetables and Asiago cheese. Broil 3 minutes or until edges are lightly browned and cheese melts. **Yield:** 4 servings (serving size: 1 pizza).

CALORIES 222; FAT 8.7g (sat 6.3g, mono 1.4g, poly 0.9g); PROTEIN 11.9g; CARB 39.2g; FIBER 5.5g; CHOL 24mg; IRON 2.2mg; SODIUM 564mg; CALC 137mg

30 MINUTES

Sausage, Pepper, and Mushroom Pizza

1	(4-ounce) sweet Italian sausage link
1	cup thinly sliced onion
½	cup thinly sliced red bell pepper
1	(8-ounce) package presliced exotic mushroom blend (such as shiitake, cremini, and oyster)
2	garlic cloves, minced
1	(14-ounce) Italian cheese-flavored pizza crust (such as Boboli)
½	cup fat-free pasta sauce
¾	cup (3 ounces) shredded part-skim mozzarella cheese
2	tablespoons thinly sliced fresh basil

1. Preheat oven to 450°.
2. Remove casing from sausage. Cook sausage in a large nonstick skillet over medium-high heat until browned, stirring to crumble. Add onion, pepper, and mushrooms to pan; sauté 8 minutes or until tender. Stir in garlic; sauté 1 minute. Place crust on a large baking sheet. Spread pasta sauce evenly over crust, leaving a ¼-inch border. Top evenly with mushroom mixture. Sprinkle evenly with cheese. Bake at 450° for 8 minutes. Remove from oven; sprinkle evenly with basil. Cut pizza into 8 wedges. **Yield:** 4 servings (serving size: 2 wedges).

CALORIES 400; FAT 10.9g (sat 4.6g, mono 4.7g, poly 0.9g); PROTEIN 23.8g; CARB 52g; FIBER 3g; CHOL 20mg; IRON 3.5mg; SODIUM 943mg; CALC 451mg

A garlic press is a quick time-saver. It crushes garlic right into your pan or bowl. You don't even have to peel the clove.

SHORTCUT SPOTLIGHT

Tomato-Mozzarella Pizza

30
MINUTES

Tomato-Mozzarella Pizza

make it a meal *Round out the meal with a tossed green salad. Pancetta is Italian cured bacon; you can substitute regular bacon, if you wish.*

1   (11-ounce) can refrigerated French bread dough
2   tablespoons yellow cornmeal
Cooking spray
1½ pounds plum tomatoes, thinly sliced
1   garlic clove, minced
1   cup (4 ounces) shredded part-skim mozzarella cheese, divided
¼   teaspoon black pepper
2   ounces pancetta
¼   cup thinly sliced fresh basil

1. Preheat oven to 450°.
2. Place dough on a baking sheet sprinkled with cornmeal; press dough into a 12-inch circle. Crimp edges of dough with fingers to form a rim. Lightly spray surface of dough with cooking spray. Bake at 450° for 8 minutes. Remove from oven.
3. Arrange tomato slices on paper towels. Cover with additional paper towels; let stand 5 minutes. Sprinkle garlic evenly over surface of dough; sprinkle ½ cup cheese evenly over dough. Arrange tomato slices on top of cheese, and sprinkle with pepper. Top with remaining ½ cup cheese. Bake at 450° for 5 minutes.
4. Chop pancetta. Cook pancetta in a non-stick skillet over medium heat until crisp; drain. Sprinkle pancetta over pizza; bake an additional 1 minute or until crust is golden. Sprinkle basil over pizza; let stand 2 minutes. Cut into 6 wedges. **Yield:** 6 servings (serving size: 1 wedge).

CALORIES 243; FAT 8.6g (sat 4.2g, mono 1.1g, poly 0.2g); PROTEIN 11.5g; CARB 31.7g; FIBER 2.4g; CHOL 16.9mg; IRON 1.9mg; SODIUM 560mg; CALC 153mg

20
MINUTES

Mexican Pizza

1   (13.8-ounce) can refrigerated pizza crust dough
Butter-flavored cooking spray
1   cup mild black bean dip (such as Guiltless Gourmet)
1   cup (4 ounces) preshredded reduced-fat 4-cheese Mexican blend cheese
4   cups preshredded iceberg lettuce
½   cup refrigerated fresh salsa
Reduced-fat sour cream (optional)

1. Preheat oven to 450°.
2. Unroll pizza dough onto a large baking sheet coated with cooking spray. Press dough into a 15 x 12–inch rectangle. Bake at 450° for 10 minutes. Remove pizza crust from oven.
3. Spread bean dip over crust, leaving a ½-inch border; sprinkle with cheese. Carefully slide crust directly onto bottom oven rack. Bake at 450° for 3 to 5 minutes or until cheese melts and bottom of crust is brown and crisp. Remove from oven; cut into 8 rectangles. Top each rectangle with ½ cup lettuce, 1 tablespoon salsa, and sour cream, if desired. Serve immediately. **Yield:** 8 servings (serving size: 1 rectangle).

CALORIES 197; FAT 3.9g (sat 2.8g, mono 0g, poly 1g); PROTEIN 10.2g; CARB 29.5g; FIBER 1.6g; CHOL 9mg; IRON 1.9mg; SODIUM 619mg; CALC 123mg

Artichoke and Arugula
Pizza with Prosciutto

20 MINUTES

Artichoke and Arugula Pizza with Prosciutto

Move the oven rack to the lowest level for a crisp crust on the pizza.

Cooking spray
1 tablespoon cornmeal
1 (13.8-ounce) can refrigerated pizza crust dough
2 tablespoons commercial pesto
¾ cup (3 ounces) shredded part-skim mozzarella cheese
1 (9-ounce) package frozen artichoke hearts, thawed and drained
1 ounce thinly sliced prosciutto
2 tablespoons shredded Parmesan cheese
1½ cups arugula leaves
1½ tablespoons fresh lemon juice

1. Position oven rack to lowest setting. Preheat oven to 500°.
2. Coat a baking sheet with cooking spray, and sprinkle with cornmeal. Unroll dough onto prepared baking sheet, and pat into a 14 x 10–inch rectangle. Spread pesto evenly over dough, leaving a ½-inch border. Sprinkle mozzarella cheese over pesto. Place baking sheet on bottom oven rack; bake at 500° for 5 minutes. Remove pizza from oven.
3. Coarsely chop artichokes. Arrange artichokes on pizza; top with sliced prosciutto. Sprinkle with Parmesan. Return pizza to bottom oven rack; bake an additional 6 minutes or until crust is browned.
4. Place arugula in a bowl. Drizzle juice over arugula; toss gently. Top pizza with arugula mixture. Cut pizza into 4 (7 x 5–inch) rectangles; cut each rectangle diagonally into 2 wedges. **Yield:** 4 servings (serving size: 2 wedges).

CALORIES 419; FAT 13g (sat 4.4g, mono 6.4g, poly 0.6g); PROTEIN 20.1g; CARB 55.3g; FIBER 5.7g; CHOL 20mg; IRON 3.6mg; SODIUM 1001mg; CALC 265mg

15 MINUTES

Ham and Tomato Pizza

Ham is salty. Be sure to choose wisely, and pick a ham that is low in sodium to keep your nutritional values in check.

1 (10-ounce) Italian cheese-flavored thin pizza crust (such as Boboli)
Cooking spray
6 tablespoons part-skim ricotta cheese
1 (14.5-ounce) can diced tomatoes with basil, garlic, and oregano, drained
1 cup (4 ounces) shredded mozzarella and Asiago with roasted garlic cheese blend (such as Sargento)
¾ cup diced or chopped ham
Chopped fresh basil (optional)

1. Preheat oven to 450°.
2. Place crust on an ungreased baking sheet, and lightly coat crust with cooking spray. Spread ricotta over crust. Arrange tomatoes over ricotta, and sprinkle with cheese blend and ham.
3. Bake at 450° for 10 minutes or until lightly browned. Sprinkle with fresh basil, if desired. **Yield:** 8 servings (serving size: 1 slice).

CALORIES 185; FAT 6g (sat 3.7g, mono 1.2g, poly 1g); PROTEIN 10.8g; CARB 21.9g; FIBER 0.9g; CHOL 18mg; IRON 1.7mg; SODIUM 572mg; CALC 190mg

MINUTES

Maui French Bread Pizza

Some people like the simplicity of plain old French bread pizza, but we've perked it up for a Hawaiian-inspired variation with ham and pineapple.

1	(16-ounce) loaf French bread, cut in half horizontally

Cooking spray

1½	cups marinara sauce, divided
¾	cup pineapple tidbits, drained
6	tablespoons deli ham, diced
1½	teaspoons bottled minced garlic
6	tablespoons sliced green onions
¾	cup (3 ounces) shredded part-skim mozzarella cheese, divided

1. Preheat oven to 450°.
2. Cut each bread half crosswise into 3 pieces. Coat cut sides of bread with cooking spray; place bread, cut sides up, on a baking sheet. Bake at 450° for 3 to 5 minutes or until lightly browned.
3. Spread ¼ cup marinara sauce on each piece of bread. Top each piece with 2 tablespoons pineapple, 1 tablespoon ham, ¼ teaspoon garlic, and 1 tablespoon green onions. Sprinkle each with 2 tablespoons cheese. Bake at 450° for 5 minutes or until cheese melts. **Yield:** 6 servings (serving size: 1 piece).

CALORIES 291; FAT 4.6g (sat 2.3g, mono 1.2g, poly 0.8g); PROTEIN 13.9g; CARB 49.4g; FIBER 2.2g; CHOL 11mg; IRON 3.5mg; SODIUM 745mg; CALC 166mg

Everyone needs a pizza cutter for cutting pizza. But it also works great for cutting toast, focaccia, and even pancakes or waffles.

SHORTCUT SPOTLIGHT

Pizza with Chicken and Artichokes

1   (10-ounce) Italian cheese-flavored thin pizza crust (such as Boboli)
1   (6-ounce) package diced, cooked chicken breast (such as Tyson)
1¼ cups roasted garlic pasta sauce (such as Barilla)
1   (14-ounce) can quartered artichoke hearts, drained
1   cup prechopped green, yellow, and red bell pepper mix
2   tablespoons sliced ripe olives
¾   cup (3 ounces) shredded part-skim mozzarella cheese

1. Preheat oven to 450°.
2. Place crust directly on oven rack (you do not have to wait for oven temperature to reach 450°); bake 9 minutes or until golden. Remove crust from oven, and place on baking sheet.
3. Preheat broiler.
4. While broiler preheats, place chicken on a microwave-safe plate; microwave at HIGH 30 seconds. Spread pasta sauce over pizza crust. Arrange chicken, artichoke hearts, bell pepper mix, and olives over sauce; sprinkle with cheese. Broil pizza 2 to 3 minutes or until cheese melts; serve immediately. **Yield:** 8 servings (serving size: 1 wedge).

CALORIES 221; FAT 6.3g (sat 4.2g, mono 0.8g, poly 1.1g); PROTEIN 14.5g; CARB 26g; FIBER 2g; CHOL 20mg; IRON 2mg; SODIUM 503mg; CALC 137mg

20 MINUTES

Grilled Chicken, Artichoke, and Feta Pizza

1 (13.8-ounce) can refrigerated pizza crust dough
Olive oil–flavored cooking spray
½ cup prepared pizza sauce (such as Boboli)
1 (14-ounce) can artichoke hearts, drained and chopped
2 cups chopped cooked chicken breast
1 cup (4 ounces) crumbled feta cheese
½ teaspoon freshly ground black pepper

1. Prepare grill.
2. Unroll dough; place on an 18 x 12–inch sheet of heavy-duty aluminum foil coated with cooking spray. Starting at center, press out dough to form a 13 x 9–inch rectangle; coat dough with cooking spray.
3. Invert dough onto grill rack; peel off foil. Cover and grill 3 minutes or until bottom of dough is browned. Turn dough over; cover and grill 2 minutes or until bottom is set. Carefully remove crust from grill to an aluminum foil-lined baking sheet. Spread sauce over crust; top with artichokes and chicken. Sprinkle with cheese and pepper. Remove pizza from foil-lined pan, and return to grill rack.
4. Cover and grill 5 minutes or until crust is done and cheese is melted. Cut into 6 squares. Serve immediately. **Yield:** 6 servings (serving size: 1 square).

CALORIES 304; FAT 7.8g (sat 4.3g, mono 1.9g, poly 1.6g); PROTEIN 23.9g; CARB 34.5g; FIBER 0.1g; CHOL 56mg; IRON 3.1mg; SODIUM 777mg; CALC 119mg

Refrigerated pizza crust dough stars in this pizza. It cuts down on prep time compared to making your own crust, and it bakes up a nice golden brown.

INGREDIENT SPOTLIGHT

Southwestern Chicken Pizza

20 MINUTES

Southwestern Chicken Pizza

1 (10-ounce) Italian cheese-flavored thin pizza crust (such as Boboli)
Cooking spray
1 cup refried beans
1 (4.5-ounce) can chopped green chiles, drained
1½ cups shredded cooked chicken breast
1 cup (4 ounces) preshredded reduced-fat Mexican cheese blend
½ cup refrigerated fresh salsa
2 tablespoons chopped green onions
1 tablespoon chopped fresh cilantro

1. Preheat oven to 475°.
2. Place pizza crust on an ungreased baking sheet; lightly coat crust with cooking spray. Bake at 475° for 5 minutes.
3. Meanwhile, combine beans and chiles in a microwave-safe bowl. Microwave at HIGH 1½ minutes or until thoroughly heated.
4. Spread bean mixture evenly over baked crust. Arrange chicken over beans. Sprinkle evenly with cheese.
5. Bake at 475° for 9 minutes or until cheese melts and crust is golden. Spoon salsa onto pizza. Top with green onions and cilantro. Cut into 8 slices. **Yield:** 8 servings (serving size: 1 slice).

CALORIES 230; FAT 6.6g (sat 3.8g, mono 1.6g, poly 1g); PROTEIN 18g; CARB 24.2g; FIBER 3.1g; CHOL 32mg; IRON 2.8mg; SODIUM 488mg; CALC 200mg

Individual Thai Chicken Pizzas

This exotically seasoned pizza is piled high with chicken, veggies, and cheese. Look for peanut sauce and Thai chili garlic paste in the ethnic food aisle of your supermarket. Thai chili garlic paste is rather fiery, so adjust the amount to suit your personal taste.

¼	cup hoisin sauce
3	tablespoons peanut sauce (such as House of Tsang)
1	teaspoon Thai chili garlic paste (such as Dynasty)
4	(6-inch) pitas
1	cup diced cooked chicken
1	cup matchstick-cut carrots
1	cup fresh bean sprouts
¼	cup sliced green onions
¾	cup (3 ounces) shredded part-skim mozzarella cheese
2	tablespoons chopped fresh cilantro

1. Preheat oven to 450°.

2. Combine first 3 ingredients; stir well with a whisk. Spread 2 tablespoons sauce mixture on each pita. Place pitas on a large baking sheet. Top each pita with ¼ cup chicken, ¼ cup carrots, ¼ cup bean sprouts, and 1 tablespoon green onions. Sprinkle shredded cheese evenly over each pita. Bake at 450° for 8 minutes or until golden brown around edges and cheese melts. Sprinkle evenly with cilantro. **Yield:** 4 servings (serving size: 1 pizza).

CALORIES 367; FAT 8g (sat 3.6g, mono 2.9g, poly 1.3g); PROTEIN 25.8g; CARB 47.9g; FIBER 2.5g; CHOL 42mg; IRON 3.7mg; SODIUM 780mg; CALC 218mg

Pizza Provençal

Chicken-Alfredo Pizza

Commercial light Alfredo sauce melds beautifully with cooked chicken, spinach, and garlic, resulting in an easy, yet gourmet, pizza.

1	cup diced cooked chicken breast
1	(10-ounce) package frozen chopped spinach, thawed, drained, and squeezed dry
1	large garlic clove, minced
½	teaspoon crushed red pepper
½	cup refrigerated light Alfredo sauce (such as Buitoni)
1	(10-ounce) Italian cheese-flavored thin pizza crust (such as Boboli)
1	cup (4 ounces) shredded part-skim mozzarella cheese

1. Preheat oven to 450°.
2. Combine first 4 ingredients in a bowl; stir well. Spread Alfredo sauce evenly over crust; top with chicken mixture. Sprinkle with cheese.
3. Place pizza directly on middle oven rack. Bake at 450° for 11 minutes or until crust is crisp and golden. Cut into 6 wedges. **Yield:** 6 servings (serving size: 1 wedge).

CALORIES 275; FAT 9.4g (sat 6.5g, mono 1.6g, poly 1.2g); PROTEIN 19.9g; CARB 27.6g; FIBER 2.3g; CHOL 35mg; IRON 2.8mg; SODIUM 538mg; CALC 289mg

Pizza Provençal

¼	cup niçoise olives, pitted
3	tablespoons fresh basil leaves
3	tablespoons drained oil-packed sun-dried tomatoes
1	teaspoon grated lemon rind
2	tablespoons fresh lemon juice
1½	teaspoons minced fresh garlic
1	teaspoon water
1	(16-ounce) loaf Italian bread, split in half horizontally
2	cups thinly sliced roasted skinless, boneless chicken breast (about 6 ounces)
¾	cup (3 ounces) crumbled goat cheese
2	tablespoons chopped fresh basil

1. Preheat oven to 450°.
2. Place first 7 ingredients in a food processor; process until smooth. Place bottom half of bread, cut side up, on a baking sheet (reserve top half for another use). Spread olive mixture over bread. Arrange chicken over bread; sprinkle with cheese. Bake at 450° for 10 minutes or until heated. Sprinkle with basil. Cut into 4 pieces. **Yield:** 4 servings (serving size: 1 piece).

CALORIES 330; FAT 10.7g (sat 4.4g, mono 3.8g, poly 1.6g); PROTEIN 23.2g; CARB 34.4g; FIBER 2.3g; CHOL 46mg; IRON 3mg; SODIUM 595mg; CALC 98mg

An easy-to-use pitter is the perfect tool to handily remove olive and cherry pits.

SHORTCUT SPOTLIGHT

Chicken and Spinach Pizza

If you don't have leftover cooked chicken on hand, pick up a rotisserie chicken from your supermarket's deli for this pizza. Keep in mind that one rotisserie chicken will yield approximately 3 cups of chopped chicken.

1 (10-ounce) Italian cheese-flavored thin pizza crust (such as Boboli)
1 (10-ounce) package frozen chopped spinach, thawed, drained, and squeezed dry
1 cup spicy spaghetti sauce (such as Newman's Own Fra Diavolo)
1½ cups chopped cooked chicken breast
1½ cups (6 ounces) shredded part-skim mozzarella cheese
Chopped fresh basil (optional)

1. Preheat oven to 450°.
2. Place crust on an ungreased baking sheet.
3. Combine spinach and spaghetti sauce in a bowl; spoon evenly over crust. Top with chicken, and sprinkle with cheese.
4. Bake at 450° for 12 minutes or until crust is browned and cheese melts. Top with basil, if desired; cut into 8 wedges. **Yield:** 8 servings (serving size: 1 wedge).

CALORIES 236; FAT 8g (sat 4.9g, mono 1.8g, poly 1.1g); PROTEIN 18.9g; CARB 21.7g; FIBER 1.8g; CHOL 36mg; IRON 2.5mg; SODIUM 507mg; CALC 267mg

Peppery Monterey Jack Pasta Salad

Acini di pepe [ah-CHEE-nee dee-PAY-pay] are tiny pasta rounds that resemble peppercorns. Use ditalini (very short tube-shaped macaroni) or any other small pasta shape if you can't find acini di pepe in your supermarket. Serve with breadsticks.

6 ounces uncooked acini di pepe pasta (about 1 cup)
2¼ cups diced plum tomato (about 14 ounces)
⅓ cup capers, rinsed and drained
¼ cup finely chopped red onion
¼ cup sliced pickled banana peppers
¼ cup chopped fresh parsley
2 tablespoons cider vinegar
1 tablespoon extra-virgin olive oil
½ teaspoon dried oregano
⅛ teaspoon salt
2 ounces Monterey Jack cheese, cut into ¼-inch cubes
1 (16-ounce) can navy beans, rinsed and drained
1 ounce salami, chopped
1 garlic clove, minced

1. Cook pasta according to package directions, omitting salt and fat. Drain.
2. Combine tomato and remaining ingredients in a large bowl. Add pasta to tomato mixture, tossing well to combine. **Yield:** 4 servings (serving size: about 1½ cups).

CALORIES 371; FAT 11.6g (sat 4.7g, mono 5.3g, poly 1.4g); PROTEIN 16.6g; CARB 51.7g; FIBER 6.3g; CHOL 21mg; IRON 3.5mg; SODIUM 919mg; CALC 164mg

Peppery Monterey Jack Pasta Salad

COOKING CLASS: *how to mince garlic*

To mince garlic, loosen the papery skin. Place the flat side of a chef's knife on an unpeeled garlic clove. To crush, press down with the heel of your hand. Peel off the skin. Remove the tough end with a knife. Make lengthwise cuts through the clove, and then cut the strips crosswise for minced pieces.

MINUTES

Pesto Shrimp Pasta

(pictured on cover)

This delectable pasta dish features swirls of tender angel hair, plump shrimp, and grape tomatoes tossed with pesto. Garnish with sprigs of basil just before serving for extra color and a burst of freshness.

4   ounces uncooked angel hair pasta
6   cups water
1¼   pounds peeled and deveined large shrimp
¼   cup commercial pesto, divided
1   cup halved grape tomatoes
¼   cup (1 ounce) shaved fresh Parmesan cheese
Basil sprigs (optional)

1. Cook pasta according to package directions, omitting salt and fat; drain.
2. While pasta cooks, bring 6 cups water to a boil in a large saucepan. Add shrimp, and cook 2 to 3 minutes or until done. Drain shrimp; toss with 2 tablespoons pesto and tomatoes. Stir in pasta and 2 tablespoons pesto. Top with cheese. Garnish with basil, if desired. **Yield:** 4 servings (serving size: 1 cup shrimp pasta and 1 tablespoon cheese).

CALORIES 320; FAT 11g (sat 2.7g, mono 6.3g, poly 1.7g); PROTEIN 31.4g; CARB 23.6g; FIBER 1.9g; CHOL 220mg; IRON 4.7mg; SODIUM 505mg; CALC 189mg

MINUTES

Artichoke Pasta

Add grilled shrimp or chopped cooked chicken to this pasta for a heartier main dish.

1   (9-ounce) package fresh angel hair pasta
2   teaspoons olive oil
1   tablespoon minced garlic
2   (6-ounce) jars marinated quartered artichoke hearts, undrained
1   cup (4 ounces) preshredded reduced-fat Italian blend cheese
½   cup chopped fresh basil
Freshly ground black pepper

1. Cook pasta according to package directions, omitting salt and fat. Drain and return to pan.
2. While pasta cooks, heat oil in a small nonstick skillet over medium-high heat. Add garlic; sauté 1 minute. Add artichoke hearts, and cook 1 minute or until thoroughly heated. Pour artichoke mixture over pasta; add cheese and basil, and toss well. Sprinkle with freshly ground pepper. Serve immediately. **Yield:** 5 servings (serving size: 1 cup).

CALORIES 335; FAT 10.7g (sat 5.6g, mono 2.7g, poly 2.1g); PROTEIN 15.8g; CARB 46g; FIBER 4.3g; CHOL 12mg; IRON 1.3mg; SODIUM 444mg; CALC 183mg

Shrimp Marinara with Angel Hair Pasta

Angel Hair Pasta with Prosciutto and Mushroom Cream Sauce

1   (9-ounce) package refrigerated angel hair
    pasta
Olive oil–flavored cooking spray
1   (8-ounce) package mushrooms, quartered
¼   cup julienne-cut ready-to-eat sun-dried
    tomatoes (such as California Sun Dry)
1½ tablespoons minced garlic (about 5 cloves)
2   ounces very thinly sliced prosciutto (about
    4 slices), sliced crosswise into ½-inch strips
½   cup dry white wine or fat-free, less-sodium
    chicken broth
½   cup fat-free, less-sodium chicken broth
1   cup frozen baby green peas, thawed
½   teaspoon freshly ground black pepper
1   (10-ounce) container refrigerated
    light Alfredo sauce (such as Buitoni)
¼   cup preshredded fresh Parmesan cheese

1. Cook pasta according to package directions, omitting salt and fat. Drain and
keep warm.
2. While pasta cooks, heat a large nonstick
skillet over medium-high heat; coat pan
with cooking spray. Add mushrooms, and
sauté 5 minutes or until tender. Add sun-
dried tomatoes, garlic, and prosciutto;
sauté 2 minutes. Add wine and broth, and
bring to a boil. Boil 3 minutes or until liquid
is reduced to ½ cup. Stir in peas, pepper,
Alfredo sauce, and pasta, and toss gently
to coat.
3. Spoon pasta into individual bowls, and
sprinkle with cheese. Serve immediately.
Yield: 6 servings (serving size: 1 cup pasta
and 2 teaspoons cheese).

CALORIES 269; FAT 7.8g (sat 6.5g, mono 0.4g, poly 0.8g); PROTEIN 15.4g;
CARB 34.1g; FIBER 2.5g; CHOL 49mg; IRON 1.7mg; SODIUM 621mg; CALC 150mg

Shrimp Marinara with Angel Hair Pasta

*This hearty pasta gets a dash of heat from
crushed red pepper. A splash of lime juice
helps balance the flavors.*

1   (9-ounce) package refrigerated angel hair
    pasta
1   teaspoon olive oil
Olive oil–flavored cooking spray
2   garlic cloves, minced
1½ pounds peeled and deveined large shrimp
1   (15.5-ounce) jar marinara sauce
1   tablespoon fresh lime juice
1   teaspoon crushed red pepper
Chopped fresh basil or parsley (optional)

1. Cook pasta according to package directions, omitting salt and fat. Drain.
2. While pasta cooks, heat oil in a large nonstick skillet coated with cooking spray over
medium heat. Add garlic; cook 1 minute,
stirring constantly. Add shrimp; cook 5
minutes or until shrimp are done, stirring
often. Add marinara sauce, lime juice, and
red pepper; cook until thoroughly heated.
Serve over pasta. Sprinkle with chopped
fresh basil or parsley, if desired. **Yield:**
5 servings (servings size: ¾ cup shrimp
mixture and ¾ cup pasta).

CALORIES 352; FAT 6.5g (sat 2.4g, mono 2.5g, poly 1.5g); PROTEIN 35.6g;
CARB 38g; FIBER 1.4g; CHOL 236mg; IRON 5.1mg; SODIUM 573mg; CALC 87mg

Bow Ties with Tomatoes, Feta, and Balsamic Dressing

6   ounces uncooked farfalle (bow tie pasta)
2   cups grape tomatoes, halved
1   cup seedless green grapes, halved
⅓   cup thinly sliced fresh basil leaves
2   tablespoons white balsamic vinegar
2   tablespoons chopped shallots
2   teaspoons capers
1   teaspoon Dijon mustard
½   teaspoon bottled minced garlic
½   teaspoon salt
¼   teaspoon freshly ground black pepper
4   teaspoons extra-virgin olive oil
1   (4-ounce) package crumbled reduced-fat
    feta cheese

1. Cook pasta according to package directions, omitting salt and fat. Drain. Combine cooked pasta, tomatoes, grapes, and basil in a large bowl.

2. While pasta cooks, combine vinegar and next 6 ingredients in a small bowl, stirring with a whisk. Gradually add oil to vinegar mixture, stirring constantly with a whisk. Drizzle vinaigrette over pasta mixture; toss well to coat. Add cheese; toss to combine.

Yield: 4 servings (serving size: 2 cups).

CALORIES 320; FAT 9.9g (sat 3.8g, mono 3.6g, poly 0.7g); PROTEIN 14g;
CARB 45.6g; FIBER 3.4g; CHOL 10mg; IRON 2mg; SODIUM 822mg; CALC 130mg

Bow Tie Pasta and Kalamata Olive Toss

2½ cups uncooked bow tie pasta
1½ cups halved grape tomatoes
1 cup (4 ounces) diced part-skim mozzarella cheese
16 kalamata olives, pitted and coarsely chopped
½ cup thinly sliced fresh basil
2 tablespoons red wine vinegar
2 tablespoons extra-virgin olive oil
2 garlic cloves, minced
½ teaspoon salt
¼ teaspoon crushed red pepper

1. Cook pasta according to package directions, omitting salt and fat.
2. In a large bowl, toss pasta with remaining ingredients. **Yield:** 6 servings (serving size: 1¼ cups).

CALORIES 343; FAT 11.2g (sat 3.7g, mono 6.5g, poly 0.8g); PROTEIN 13.2g; CARB 47.5g; FIBER 2.6g; CHOL 12mg; IRON 2.2mg; SODIUM 450mg; CALC 184mg

Bow tie pasta is also known as farfalle pasta. Three cups (or 8 ounces) will yield about 4 cups of cooked pasta. Bow tie pasta on average takes about 11 minutes to cook.

INGREDIENT SPOTLIGHT

Hamburger Stroganoff

make it a meal *Add a tossed green salad for a satisfying fall meal.*

8 ounces uncooked medium egg noodles
1 teaspoon olive oil
1 pound ground beef, extra lean
1 cup prechopped onion
1 teaspoon bottled minced garlic
1 (8-ounce) package presliced cremini mushrooms
2 tablespoons all-purpose flour
1 cup fat-free, less-sodium beef broth
1¼ teaspoons kosher salt
⅛ teaspoon black pepper
¾ cup reduced-fat sour cream
1 tablespoon dry sherry
3 tablespoons chopped fresh parsley

1. Cook pasta according to package directions, omitting salt and fat. Drain and rinse under cold water; drain.
2. Heat oil in a large nonstick skillet over medium-high heat. Add beef to pan; cook 4 minutes or until browned, stirring to crumble. Add onion, garlic, and mushrooms to pan; cook 4 minutes or until most of liquid evaporates, stirring frequently. Sprinkle with flour; cook 1 minute, stirring constantly. Stir in broth; bring to a boil. Reduce heat, and simmer 1 minute or until slightly thick. Stir in salt and pepper.
3. Remove from heat. Stir in sour cream and sherry. Serve over pasta. Sprinkle with parsley. **Yield:** 6 servings (serving size: about ½ cup stroganoff, ⅔ cup pasta, and 1½ teaspoons parsley).

CALORIES 322; FAT 9.8g (sat 4.4g, mono 3.5g, poly 1.1g); PROTEIN 23.9g; CARB 35.1g; FIBER 2.1g; CHOL 82mg; IRON 3.2mg; SODIUM 541mg; CALC 70mg

Fettuccine with Bacon, Peas, and Parmesan

Fettuccine with Bacon, Peas, and Parmesan

make it a meal *Garlic bread and a romaine salad with grape tomatoes will complete the menu.*

1   (9-ounce) package fresh fettuccine pasta
2   slices smoked center-cut bacon
½   cup chopped onion
2   teaspoons bottled minced garlic
1   tablespoon chopped fresh thyme
½   cup frozen green peas
½   cup chopped green onions
⅓   cup half-and-half
2   teaspoons butter
½   teaspoon salt
⅛   teaspoon black pepper
¼   cup shredded Parmesan cheese

1. Cook pasta according to package directions, omitting salt and fat. Drain pasta, reserving ¾ cup cooking liquid.
2. Cook bacon in a large nonstick skillet over medium heat until crisp. Remove bacon from pan, reserving drippings in pan; crumble. Add ½ cup chopped onion, bottled minced garlic, and chopped fresh thyme to drippings in pan; sauté 2 minutes. Stir in green peas; sauté 1 minute. Add green onions to pan, and sauté 1½ minutes. Add pasta, reserved cooking liquid, and half-and-half to pan; cook 1 minute or until

thoroughly heated, tossing to combine. Remove from heat. Add butter, salt, and pepper to pan; toss until butter melts. Sprinkle with crumbled bacon and Parmesan cheese. **Yield:** 4 servings (serving size: 1¼ cups).

CALORIES 313; FAT 9.9g (sat 4.5g, mono 3.8g, poly 0.4g); PROTEIN 14.2g; CARB 43.1g; FIBER 3.7g; CHOL 22mg; IRON 0.7mg; SODIUM 747mg; CALC 145mg

20 MINUTES

Spicy Shrimp-and-Artichoke Pasta

8   ounces uncooked fettuccine
2   teaspoons olive oil
1   pound peeled and deveined large shrimp
1   (9-ounce) package frozen artichoke hearts, thawed and squeezed dry
2   garlic cloves, minced
⅓   cup dry white wine
1   (7-ounce) jar sliced pimiento, drained
1   teaspoon dried oregano
½   teaspoon crushed red pepper
½   teaspoon salt
½   teaspoon freshly ground black pepper
2   cups arugula leaves
½   cup (2 ounces) crumbled feta cheese

1. Cook fettuccine according to package directions, omitting salt and fat. Drain well, reserving ¼ cup pasta water. Keep pasta and reserved water warm.
2. While pasta cooks, heat oil in a large nonstick skillet over medium-high heat. Add shrimp, artichokes, and garlic; sauté 5 minutes or until shrimp are done. Stir in wine, scraping pan to loosen browned bits. Add pimiento and next 4 ingredients; cook over medium-low heat 2 minutes or until thoroughly heated.
3. Place arugula in a large bowl; add drained pasta, reserved pasta water, and shrimp mixture. Toss well. Sprinkle with feta cheese. Serve immediately. **Yield:** 5 servings (serving size: 1⅓ cups).

CALORIES 354; FAT 7.2g (sat 3.5g, mono 2.4g, poly 1.2g); PROTEIN 28.1g; CARB 43.6g; FIBER 5.3g; CHOL 151mg; IRON 4.9mg; SODIUM 631mg; CALC 163mg

Chicken, Artichoke, and Mushroom Fettuccine

Jam-packed with veggies and roasted chicken, this pasta is easy enough for weeknight fare but special enough for entertaining, too.

1   (9-ounce) package fresh fettuccine
Cooking spray
1   (8-ounce) package presliced mushrooms
1   small red bell pepper, seeded and sliced
2   tablespoons light stick butter
1   tablespoon all-purpose flour
1   cup fat-free milk
⅛   teaspoon salt
¼   teaspoon freshly ground black pepper
2   cups shredded skinless rotisserie chicken breast
1   (14-ounce) can artichoke hearts, drained and cut in half
2   tablespoons fresh lemon juice
¼   cup chopped green onions (optional)
Shredded fresh Parmesan cheese (optional)

1. Cook pasta according to package directions, omitting salt and fat. Drain and keep warm.

2. While pasta cooks, heat a large nonstick skillet over medium heat; coat pan with cooking spray. Add mushrooms and red bell pepper, and sauté 5 minutes or until mushrooms are tender and liquid evaporates, stirring frequently. Remove from pan, and keep warm.

3. Add butter to pan, and cook over medium heat 1 minute or until butter melts. Add flour, and stir with a whisk; cook 1 minute or until bubbly. Add milk, salt, and black pepper; cook 3 minutes or until thick, stirring constantly.

4. Add reserved mushroom mixture, chicken, and artichokes to pan, stirring gently. Cook 3 minutes or until thoroughly heated. Add lemon juice and, if desired, green onions. Toss chicken mixture with pasta. Sprinkle with Parmesan cheese, if desired. **Yield:** 5 servings (serving size: 1½ cups).

CALORIES 328; FAT 6.1g (sat 3g, mono 1.7g, poly 1.3g); PROTEIN 27.6g; CARB 37.6g; FIBER 3.1g; CHOL 53mg; IRON 1.6mg; SODIUM 372mg; CALC 63mg

Quick Bouillabaisse Pasta

COOKING CLASS: *how to cook pasta*

Perfectly cooked pasta has a firm, tender consistency, called *al dente,* which means "to the tooth." When testing for doneness, remove a piece of pasta from the water and bite into it. It should offer resistance but no brittleness. Here are examples of undercooked pasta (left), al dente pasta (middle), and overcooked pasta (right).

 MINUTES

Quick Bouillabaisse Pasta

make it a meal *Toss together a salad, and serve with slices of crusty bread.*

1   (9-ounce) package refrigerated fettuccine
1   tablespoon olive oil
1   teaspoon bottled minced garlic
2   teaspoons all-purpose flour
½   teaspoon herbes de Provence
¼   teaspoon ground turmeric
1   (14.5-ounce) can diced tomatoes, undrained
1   (8-ounce) bottle clam juice
12 medium mussels, cleaned and debearded
8   ounces medium shrimp, peeled and deveined
1   (8-ounce) halibut fillet, cut into 1-inch pieces
Chopped fresh basil (optional)

1. Cook refrigerated fettuccine according to package directions, omitting salt and fat. Drain and keep warm.
2. Heat oil in large nonstick skillet over medium-high heat. Add garlic to pan; cook 1 minute. Add flour to pan; cook 30 seconds, stirring constantly with a whisk. Stir in herbes de Provence, turmeric, tomatoes, and clam juice; bring to a boil. Stir in mussels, shrimp, and fish. Cover, reduce heat, and simmer 5 minutes or until mussels open. Discard any unopened shells.
3. Place 1 cup pasta in each of 4 bowls; top each serving with about ⅓ cup fish mixture and 3 mussels. Garnish with basil, if desired. **Yield:** 4 servings.

CALORIES 407; FAT 8.3g (sat 1.2g, mono 3.5g, poly 2g); PROTEIN 37.5g;
CARB 41.5g; FIBER 3.6g; CHOL 119mg; IRON 4.4mg; SODIUM 632mg; CALC 96mg

 MINUTES

Fettuccine Alfredo with Vegetables

Creamy pasta and vegetables are always a great combination.

1   (9-ounce) package refrigerated fettuccine
1   (16-ounce) package frozen steam-in-bag broccoli stir-fry vegetables (such as Birds Eye)
1   (10-ounce) container refrigerated light Alfredo sauce (such as Buitoni)
¼   cup grated fresh Parmesan cheese
¼   teaspoon freshly ground black pepper

1. Cook fettuccine according to package directions, omitting salt and fat; drain well.
2. While fettuccine cooks, microwave vegetables according to package directions.
3. Place Alfredo sauce in a large microwave-safe serving bowl; microwave at HIGH 1 minute or until thoroughly heated.
4. Add pasta, vegetables, cheese, and pepper to Alfredo sauce, and toss well. Serve immediately. **Yield:** 4 servings (serving size: 1¼ cups).

CALORIES 343; FAT 9.7g (sat 6.9g, mono 1.1g, poly 1.6g); PROTEIN 16.5g; CARB 46.4g;
FIBER 3.9g; CHOL 63mg; IRON 1.8mg; SODIUM 591mg; CALC 246mg

Fettuccine translates to "small ribbons." Eight ounces of uncooked fettuccine will yield 4 cups of cooked—in about 10 minutes.

INGREDIENT SPOTLIGHT

COOKING CLASS: *how to trim sugar snap peas*

Trimming sugar snap peas is time-consuming, so look for 6-ounce packages of fresh, trimmed sugar snap peas in the produce section of your supermarket. If you can't find trimmed peas, gather the peas with like ends facing the same direction, and slice off all of the tips at once with a chef's knife.

MINUTES

Fettuccine Alfredo with Salmon and Sugar Snap Peas

Think spring. This fresh fettuccine capitalizes on some quintessential springtime favorites: salmon, sugar snaps, dill, and a creamy white sauce.

1   (9-ounce) package refrigerated fettuccine
1   (6-ounce) package fresh sugar snap peas
1   (10-ounce) container refrigerated
     light Alfredo sauce
½   cup thinly sliced smoked salmon
1   teaspoon chopped fresh dill
½   teaspoon freshly ground black pepper

1. Cook fettuccine according to package directions, omitting salt and fat; add sugar snap peas during last 1 minute of cooking time. Drain well.
2. Place Alfredo sauce in a large microwave-safe serving bowl; microwave at HIGH 1 minute or until thoroughly heated. Add pasta mixture, salmon, dill, and pepper to Alfredo sauce; toss. **Yield:** 4 servings (serving size: about 1 cup).

CALORIES 323; FAT 8.5g (sat 6.2g, mono 0.5g, poly 1.7g); PROTEIN 16.5g; CARB 43.6g; FIBER 2.6g; CHOL 68mg; IRON 2.1mg; SODIUM 583mg; CALC 141mg

MINUTES

Spinach and Mushroom Fettuccine Alfredo

For even more flavor, add chopped onion and bell pepper to the garlic and mushroom mixture.

1   (9-ounce) package refrigerated fettuccine
Cooking spray
½   teaspoon bottled minced garlic
1   (8-ounce) package presliced mushrooms
1   (10-ounce) container refrigerated
     light Alfredo sauce
1   (7-ounce) package fresh baby spinach
¼   teaspoon freshly ground black pepper

1. Cook fettuccine according to package directions, omitting salt and fat. Drain well. Transfer to a large bowl.
2. While pasta cooks, heat a large nonstick skillet over medium-high heat; coat pan with cooking spray. Add garlic and mushrooms; sauté 5 minutes or until mushrooms are tender. Add Alfredo sauce, stirring well. Add spinach; cover and cook 3 minutes or just until spinach wilts. Remove from heat, and stir.
3. Add Alfredo mixture to pasta; toss well. Sprinkle with black pepper. Serve immediately. **Yield:** 4 servings (serving size: about 1 cup).

CALORIES 312; FAT 7.9g (sat 6g, mono 0.2g, poly 1.5g); PROTEIN 14.6g; CARB 46.2g; FIBER 4.5g; CHOL 64mg; IRON 3.3mg; SODIUM 483mg; CALC 179mg

Pasta with Ham and Peas

Fresh pasta cooks more quickly than dried pasta, so we've used it here to keep the cook time to a minimum.

2	(9-ounce) packages refrigerated fettuccine
2	cups fat-free half-and-half, divided
2	tablespoons all-purpose flour
1	teaspoon butter
1½	cups chopped cooked ham
1	cup frozen petite green peas, thawed
½	teaspoon salt
¼	teaspoon black pepper
1	cup freshly grated Romano cheese

1. Cook pasta according to package directions, omitting salt and fat; drain.
2. While pasta cooks, combine ¼ cup half-and-half and flour; stir until smooth. Add mixture to remaining half-and-half. Set aside.
3. Melt butter in a large nonstick skillet. Add ham, and cook 2 minutes. Add half-and-half mixture to pan. Cook, stirring constantly, 5 minutes or until thickened. Stir in peas, salt, and pepper.
4. Combine pasta and ham mixture; toss well, and stir in cheese. Serve immediately. **Yield:** 6 servings (serving size: 1⅓ cups).

CALORIES 422; FAT 9g (sat 7.1g, mono 1.6g, poly 0.1g); PROTEIN 21.9g; CARB 59.5g; FIBER 3.2g; CHOL 76mg; IRON 2.4mg; SODIUM 827mg; CALC 257mg

Beefy Skillet Pasta

Beefy Skillet Pasta

make it a meal *Here's a quick and easy stovetop supper that you can have on the table in a flash. Add a mixed greens salad to round out the meal.*

6	ounces uncooked fusilli (short twisted spaghetti)
1	pound ground sirloin
2	cups tomato-basil pasta sauce (such as Bertolli)
¼	teaspoon freshly ground black pepper
½	cup (2 ounces) shredded part-skim mozzarella or reduced-fat cheddar cheese

1. Cook fusilli according to package directions, omitting salt and fat. Drain.
2. While pasta cooks, cook beef in a large nonstick skillet over medium-high heat until browned, stirring to crumble. Drain and return beef to pan.
3. Add pasta sauce and pepper; cook 2 minutes. Add pasta; cook 2 minutes. Sprinkle with cheese; cook 1 minute or until cheese melts. **Yield:** 5 servings (serving size: 1 cup).

CALORIES 305; FAT 9.8g (sat 5.5g, mono 3.1g, poly 1.1g); PROTEIN 27g; CARB 28.2g; FIBER 2.9g; CHOL 56mg; IRON 2.1mg; SODIUM 943mg; CALC 175mg

To save prep time, buy prechopped ham and pregrated Romano cheese. If you can't find Romano, use Parmesan.

MAKE IT FASTER

Sesame Noodles with Chicken

Creamy Cajun Shrimp Linguine

make it a meal *Shrimp and pasta combine with a creamy sauce for a quick and delicious dish. Round out the meal with a Caesar salad.*

1	cup water
1	(14-ounce) can fat-free, less-sodium chicken broth
6	ounces uncooked linguine
1	pound medium shrimp, peeled and deveined
1½	tablespoons butter
1	(8-ounce) package presliced mushrooms
1	large red bell pepper, cut into (¼-inch-thick) slices
2	teaspoons all-purpose flour
1	teaspoon Cajun seasoning
¼	teaspoon salt
⅔	cup half-and-half
¼	cup chopped fresh flat-leaf parsley

1. Combine 1 cup water and broth in a Dutch oven; bring to a boil. Break pasta in half; add to pan. Bring mixture to a boil. Cover, reduce heat, and simmer 8 minutes. Add shrimp to pan. Cover and simmer 3 minutes or until shrimp are done; drain.
2. Melt butter in a large skillet over medium-high heat. Add mushrooms and pepper to pan; sauté 4 minutes or until moisture evaporates. Add flour, seasoning, and salt to pan; sauté 30 seconds. Stir in half-and-half; cook 1 minute or until thick, stirring constantly. Remove from heat. Add pasta mixture and parsley to pan; toss. **Yield:** 4 servings (serving size: 1½ cups).

CALORIES 365; FAT 10.9g (sat 5.9g, mono 2.7g, poly 0.8g); PROTEIN 27.4g; CARB 38.1g; FIBER 2.2g; CHOL 194mg; IRON 4.1mg; SODIUM 685mg; CALC 101mg

Sesame Noodles with Chicken

8	ounces uncooked linguine
1	cup matchstick-cut carrots
⅔	cup organic vegetable broth (such as Swanson Certified Organic)
½	cup reduced-fat peanut butter
2	tablespoons rice vinegar
2	tablespoons low-sodium soy sauce
1	tablespoon bottled ground fresh ginger (such as Spice World)
2	teaspoons Sriracha (hot chile sauce, such as Huy Fong)
2	cups chopped cooked chicken breast
1	cup thinly sliced green onions
2	tablespoons sesame seeds, toasted

1. Cook pasta according to package directions, omitting salt and fat. Add carrots to pasta during the last 3 minutes of cooking. Drain well.
2. Place broth and next 5 ingredients in a food processor; process until smooth. Combine pasta mixture, chicken, and onions in a large bowl. Drizzle broth mixture over pasta mixture; toss well. Sprinkle with sesame seeds. **Yield:** 5 servings (serving size: 1 cup).

CALORIES 456; FAT 13.9g (sat 3g, mono 6.1g, poly 4.1g); PROTEIN 31.1g; CARB 52.8g; FIBER 5.2g; CHOL 48mg; IRON 3.2mg; SODIUM 645mg; CALC 47mg

COOKING CLASS: *how to toast almonds*

While this recipe calls for sliced almonds (not slivered), the technique for toasting is the same. Spread the almonds on a baking sheet, and bake at 350° for 6 to 8 minutes. Be sure to watch them carefully—they go from toasted to burned quickly.

20 MINUTES

Pasta with Zucchini and Toasted Almonds

make it a meal *Pair flavorful pasta with olive tapenade breadsticks for a superfast and delicious meal in minutes.*

2 cups cherry tomatoes, halved
2 tablespoons minced shallots
1 teaspoon minced fresh thyme
2 teaspoons fresh lemon juice
3/4 teaspoon kosher salt
1/2 teaspoon freshly ground black pepper
1/4 teaspoon sugar
5 teaspoons extra-virgin olive oil, divided
1 (9-ounce) package refrigerated linguine
1 1/2 teaspoons bottled minced garlic
3 cups chopped zucchini (about 1 pound)
3/4 cup fat-free, less-sodium chicken broth
3 tablespoons chopped fresh mint, divided
1/3 cup (1 1/2 ounces) grated fresh pecorino Romano cheese
3 tablespoons sliced almonds, toasted

1. Combine first 7 ingredients in a medium bowl. Add 2 teaspoons oil, tossing to coat.
2. Cook pasta according to package directions, omitting salt and fat. Drain well.
3. Heat a large nonstick skillet over medium-high heat. Add remaining 1 tablespoon oil to pan, swirling to coat. Add garlic to pan; sauté 30 seconds. Add zucchini; sauté 3 minutes or until crisp-tender. Add broth; bring to a simmer. Stir in pasta and 1 1/2 tablespoons mint; toss well. Remove from heat; stir in tomato mixture. Place 1 1/2 cups pasta mixture in each of 4 bowls; top evenly with remaining 1 1/2 tablespoons mint. Sprinkle each serving with 4 teaspoons cheese and 2 teaspoons almonds. **Yield:** 4 servings.

CALORIES 344; FAT 12.7g (sat 3.1g, mono 6.6g, poly 2g); PROTEIN 14g; CARB 45.5g; FIBER 5.3g; CHOL 58mg; IRON 3.4mg; SODIUM 601mg; CALC 163mg

Linguine with Asparagus, Parmesan, and Bacon

Start with hot tap water, and cover the pot with the lid—the water for cooking the pasta will come to a boil faster. Look for prechopped onion in the produce section.

3   cups (1-inch) sliced asparagus (about 1 pound)
1   (9-ounce) package refrigerated linguine
4   bacon slices (uncooked)
1   cup chopped onion
2   teaspoons bottled minced garlic
1   teaspoon dried oregano
2   cups grape or cherry tomatoes
¾   cup fat-free, less-sodium chicken broth
1   tablespoon butter
¼   teaspoon salt
¼   teaspoon freshly ground black pepper
2   tablespoons fresh lemon juice
½   cup (2 ounces) preshredded Parmesan cheese
Shaved Parmesan cheese (optional)

1. Cook asparagus and pasta according to pasta package directions, omitting salt and fat. Drain; set aside.

2. Cook bacon in a large nonstick skillet over medium-high heat until crisp; cool slightly. Remove bacon from pan, reserving 2 teaspoons drippings in pan. Crumble bacon. Add onion, garlic, and oregano to drippings in pan; sauté 4 minutes or until onion is lightly browned. Add tomatoes; cook 2 minutes. Add broth; bring to a boil. Stir in butter, salt, and pepper; remove from heat. Place asparagus mixture in a large bowl; add tomato mixture and juice, tossing well. Top with bacon and shredded cheese. Garnish with shaved Parmesan, if desired. **Yield:** 4 servings (serving size: 2 cups pasta mixture and 2 tablespoons cheese).

CALORIES 360; FAT 11.9g (sat 5.3g, mono 3.9g, poly 0.8g); PROTEIN 16.9g; CARB 46.1g; FIBER 5.6g; CHOL 23mg; IRON 1.3mg; SODIUM 683mg; CALC 171mg

Linguine with Spicy
and Clam Sauce

20 MINUTES

Linguine with Garlicky Clams and Peas

make it a meal *Crusty bread and a tossed green salad will round out the meal.*

1   (9-ounce) package fresh linguine
2   tablespoons olive oil
1½   teaspoons bottled minced garlic
3   (6½-ounce) cans chopped clams, undrained
1   cup organic vegetable broth (such as Swanson Certified Organic)
¼   cup dry white wine
¼   teaspoon crushed red pepper
1   cup frozen green peas
½   cup (2 ounces) preshredded Parmesan cheese
2   tablespoons chopped fresh basil

1. Cook pasta according to package directions, omitting salt and fat. Drain and keep warm.
2. Heat oil in a large nonstick skillet over medium-high heat. Add garlic to pan; sauté 1 minute. Drain clams, reserving clams and ½ cup juice. Add reserved clam juice, broth, wine, and pepper to pan; bring to a boil. Reduce heat, and simmer 5 minutes, stirring occasionally. Add clams and peas to pan; cook 2 minutes or until thoroughly heated. Add pasta to pan; toss well. Sprinkle with cheese and basil. **Yield:** 4 servings (serving size: 1½ cups pasta mixture, 2 tablespoons cheese, and 1½ teaspoons basil).

CALORIES 368; FAT 11.9g (sat 3g, mono 6.9g, poly 0.9g); PROTEIN 19.8g; CARB 46.5g; FIBER 4.3g; CHOL 24mg; IRON 1.9mg; SODIUM 961mg; CALC 166mg

20 MINUTES

Linguine with Spicy Red Clam Sauce

1   (9-ounce) package fresh linguine
1   tablespoon olive oil
½   cup chopped onion
1   tablespoon bottled minced garlic
½   teaspoon crushed red pepper
2   tablespoons tomato paste
1   (14.5-ounce) can no-salt-added diced tomatoes, undrained
2   (6.5-ounce) cans minced clams, undrained
2   tablespoons chopped fresh parsley
1   tablespoon chopped fresh basil
1   tablespoon chopped fresh oregano

1. Cook pasta according to package directions, omitting salt and fat. Drain.
2. Heat olive oil in a large nonstick skillet over medium-high heat. Add onion, garlic, and crushed red pepper to pan; sauté 3 minutes or until onion is lightly browned. Stir in tomato paste and tomatoes; cook 4 minutes or until thick, stirring constantly. Stir in clams; cook 2 minutes or until thoroughly heated. Remove from heat; stir in parsley, basil, and oregano. Serve with pasta. **Yield:** 4 servings (serving size: 1 cup pasta and about 1 cup sauce).

CALORIES 292; FAT 5.4g (sat 0.5g, mono 2.5g, poly 0.8g); PROTEIN 15.5g; CARB 45.1g; FIBER 3.6g; CHOL 17mg; IRON 3.9mg; SODIUM 806mg; CALC 47mg

Canned clams are ideal for recipes that call for clams. You can buy them whole or chopped. Be aware that, as with most canned products, canned clams are high in sodium.

INGREDIENT SPOTLIGHT

MINUTES

Shrimp and Scallop Arrabbiata

Arrabbiata, *which is Italian for "angry,"* *often refers to the classic combination of* *tomatoes, pancetta, and hot pepper.* *Substitute bacon for the pancetta, if you* *prefer.*

1	(9-ounce) package fresh linguine
2	tablespoons olive oil, divided
8	ounces peeled and deveined large shrimp
8	ounces bay scallops
¼	teaspoon salt
1	cup prechopped onion
2	teaspoons bottled minced garlic
¼	teaspoon fennel seeds, crushed
¼	teaspoon crushed red pepper
1	ounce pancetta, chopped
4	(14.5-ounce) cans organic stewed tomatoes, undrained (such as Muir Glen)
3	tablespoons chopped fresh basil

1. Cook pasta according to package directions, omitting salt and fat. Drain. Set aside and keep warm.
2. Heat 1 tablespoon oil in a large nonstick skillet over medium-high heat. Add shrimp and scallops to pan; sprinkle with salt. Sauté 3 minutes or until almost done. Remove shrimp mixture from pan.
3. Heat remaining 1 tablespoon oil in pan over medium-high heat. Add onion, garlic, fennel seeds, pepper, and pancetta to pan; sauté 1 minute. Stir in tomatoes; bring to a boil. Cook 2 minutes, stirring occasionally. Return shrimp mixture to pan; cook 1 minute or until thoroughly heated. Remove from heat. Serve shrimp mixture over pasta. Sprinkle with basil. **Yield:** 4 servings (serving size: 1 cup pasta, 2 cups shrimp mixture, and 2 teaspoons basil).

CALORIES 480; FAT 11.9g (sat 2.2g, mono 5.1g, poly 1.3g); PROTEIN 33.2g; CARB 55.4g; FIBER 5.7g; CHOL 110mg; IRON 4.2mg; SODIUM 718mg; CALC 59mg

COOKING CLASS: *how to debeard a mussel*

Debearding mussels mean removing the byssal threads (or beard), which connect the mussel to rocks or pilings in the sea. Grab the fibers with your fingers, and pull them out, tugging toward the hinged point of the shell.

 MINUTES

Linguine with Pancetta and Parmesan

1   (9-ounce) package fresh linguine
Cooking spray
1   cup prechopped onion
²∕₃ cup chopped pancetta or ham (about 2 ounces)
½   teaspoon bottled minced garlic
1   (25.5-ounce) bottle fat-free Italian herb pasta sauce (such as Muir Glen Organic)
¼   cup chopped ripe olives
1   tablespoon capers
¼   cup (1 ounce) preshredded fresh Parmesan cheese

1. Cook pasta according to package directions, omitting salt and fat.
2. While pasta cooks, heat a large nonstick skillet over medium-high heat; coat pan with cooking spray. Add onion, pancetta, and garlic; sauté 5 minutes. Add pasta sauce; cook 5 minutes. Stir in olives and capers. Add pasta; toss well, and sprinkle with cheese. **Yield:** 4 servings (serving size: 1½ cups pasta mixture and 1 tablespoon cheese).

CALORIES 352; FAT 6.9g (sat 4.6g, mono 1.4g, poly 0.8g); PROTEIN 18.6g; CARB 57.3g; FIBER 2.3g; CHOL 46mg; IRON 3.9mg; SODIUM 1,000mg; CALC 169mg

 MINUTES

Linguine and Mussels Marinara

make it a meal *Here's a restaurant-style recipe that's simple to prepare. Add fresh Italian bread on the side to sop up the sauce.*

1   pound mussels (about 21 mussels)
1   (9-ounce) package fresh linguine
2   cups tomato-basil pasta sauce
⅛   teaspoon crushed red pepper
¼   cup chopped fresh basil

1. Rinse mussels in cold water; scrub shells thoroughly with a brush. Remove beards on mussels, and discard any opened or cracked shells.
2. Cook pasta according to package directions, omitting salt and fat.
3. While pasta cooks, combine mussels, sauce, and pepper in a large deep skillet. Cover and bring to a simmer over medium heat; cook 7 minutes or until mussels open. Discard any unopened shells.
4. Serve mussels and sauce over pasta; sprinkle with basil. **Yield:** 3 servings (serving size: about 7 mussels, ²∕₃ cup sauce, and 1 cup pasta).

CALORIES 447; FAT 7.3g (sat 4.3g, mono 1.5g, poly 1.3g); PROTEIN 31g; CARB 66.6g; FIBER 4.9g; CHOL 88mg; IRON 8.9mg; SODIUM 972mg; CALC 171mg

20 MINUTES

Linguine with Creamy Chicken and Walnuts

1   (9-ounce) package refrigerated linguine
1   tablespoon water
2   teaspoons all-purpose flour
2   teaspoons olive oil
1   (8-ounce) package presliced mushrooms
2   garlic cloves, minced
1   cup fat-free milk
1   cup fat-free, less-sodium chicken broth
3/4 cup (6 ounces) block-style 1/3-less-fat cream cheese, cubed and softened
1/2 teaspoon freshly ground black pepper
1/4 teaspoon salt
3   cups chopped cooked chicken (about 1 pound)
1/4 teaspoon ground nutmeg
2   teaspoons butter
3   tablespoons coarsely chopped walnuts, toasted

1. Cook pasta according to package directions, omitting salt and fat. Drain and keep warm.
2. While pasta cooks, place 1 tablespoon water and flour in a small bowl; stir with a whisk until smooth, and set aside.
3. Heat oil in a large nonstick skillet over medium-high heat; add mushrooms and garlic. Sauté 4 minutes or until mushrooms are tender; add milk and next 4 ingredients. Bring mixture to a boil; cook, stirring constantly, 2 minutes or until cream cheese melts and sauce is smooth. Stir in flour mixture; cook 1 minute, stirring constantly. Stir in chicken and nutmeg; reduce heat, and simmer, uncovered, 4 minutes or until thoroughly heated, stirring frequently. Add butter, stirring until butter melts. Add pasta; toss gently to coat. Sprinkle each serving with walnuts. **Yield:** 7 servings (serving size: about 1 1/3 cups pasta and 1 1/2 teaspoons walnuts).

CALORIES 331; FAT 12.9g (sat 6.2g, mono 3.9g, poly 2.6g); PROTEIN 29.2g; CARB 24.5g; FIBER 1.5g; CHOL 90mg; IRON 1.7mg; SODIUM 332mg; CALC 80mg

15 MINUTES

Shrimp and Orzo with Cherry Tomatoes and Romano Cheese

1   cup uncooked orzo (rice-shaped pasta)
2   tablespoons olive oil, divided
3/4 teaspoon salt, divided
1/4 teaspoon black pepper, divided
1   pound medium shrimp, peeled and deveined
1   cup chopped Vidalia or other sweet onion
1   tablespoon bottled minced garlic
1/4 teaspoon crushed red pepper
2   cups cherry tomatoes, halved
1/3 cup (about 1 1/2 ounces) grated fresh pecorino Romano cheese
1/3 cup chopped fresh basil

1. Cook pasta according to package directions, omitting salt and fat.
2. While pasta cooks, heat 1 tablespoon oil in a large skillet over medium-high heat. Sprinkle 1/2 teaspoon salt and 1/8 teaspoon black pepper evenly over shrimp. Add shrimp to pan; cook 1 1/2 minutes on each side or until done. Remove from pan.
3. Add remaining 1 tablespoon olive oil to pan. Add onion, garlic, and red pepper; cook 2 minutes, stirring frequently. Add tomatoes, and cook 3 minutes or until tomatoes begin to soften, stirring occasionally. Stir in pasta and shrimp; cook 1 minute or until thoroughly heated. Remove from heat, and stir in 1/4 teaspoon salt, 1/8 teaspoon black pepper, cheese, and basil. **Yield:** 4 servings (serving size: 1 1/4 cups).

CALORIES 414; FAT 11.9g (sat 2.9g, mono 6g, poly 1.6g); PROTEIN 33.1g; CARB 43.6g; FIBER 3.1g; CHOL 181mg; IRON 4.9mg; SODIUM 721mg; CALC 178mg

Orzo is a versatile pasta used in sides, soups, and salads. The rice-shaped pasta is available in short, plump "grains" and long, thin "grains."

INGREDIENT SPOTLIGHT

20 MINUTES

Cheesy Macaroni

Both kids and adults will love this hearty one-dish meal. It's so quick and easy, you'll turn to this recipe over and over again.

8   ounces uncooked small elbow macaroni

1   pound ground sirloin

1¼ cups prechopped onion

2   garlic cloves, minced

1   (26-ounce) jar tomato-basil pasta sauce (such as Classico)

1   cup (4 ounces) reduced-fat shredded sharp cheddar cheese, divided

1. Cook pasta according to package directions, omitting salt and fat. Drain and keep warm.

2. While pasta cooks, heat a large nonstick skillet over medium-high heat until hot. Add beef, onion, and garlic; sauté 6 minutes or until beef is browned, stirring to crumble. Drain, if necessary, and return beef mixture to pan.

3. Add pasta sauce to beef mixture; cook 2 minutes or until hot. Stir in pasta and ½ cup cheese; cook 1 minute or until cheese melts. Remove from heat; sprinkle with remaining ½ cup cheese. **Yield:** 8 servings (serving size: 1 cup).

CALORIES 258; FAT 6.9g (sat 3.5g, mono 2.6g, poly 0.8g); PROTEIN 20.4g; CARB 30.9g; FIBER 2.8g; CHOL 38mg; IRON 2.5mg; SODIUM 324mg; CALC 201mg

Bacon and Sun-Dried Tomato Alfredo Pasta

With a combination of pasta, sun-dried tomatoes, bacon, and a creamy alfredo sauce, this is comfort food at its finest.

8 ounces uncooked multigrain penne (such as Barilla Plus)
1 (10-ounce) package refrigerated light Alfredo sauce (such as Buitoni)
½ cup sun-dried tomatoes, packed without oil and cut into julienne strips
10 slices precooked bacon
¼ cup chopped fresh basil
¼ teaspoon freshly ground black pepper

1. Cook pasta according to package directions, omitting salt and fat; drain and keep warm.

2. While pasta cooks, combine Alfredo sauce and sun-dried tomatoes in a saucepan. Cook over low heat, stirring occasionally, 6 to 8 minutes or until thoroughly heated and tomatoes are juicy and plump. While sauce cooks, microwave bacon according to package directions. Crumble bacon, and set aside.

3. Combine cooked pasta and Alfredo sauce mixture in a large serving bowl. Top with crumbled bacon, basil, and black pepper. **Yield:** 5 servings (serving size: 1 cup).

CALORIES 315; FAT 9.5g (sat 6.5g, mono 0.2g, poly 2.7g); PROTEIN 15.6g; CARB 40.5g; FIBER 4.9g; CHOL 29mg; IRON 11.7mg; SODIUM 535mg; CALC 98mg

15 MINUTES

Penne with Asparagus, Spinach, and Bacon

make it a meal *This pasta toss comes together in a snap on busy weeknights. Complement it with a glass of white wine, such as sauvignon blanc, and garlic-Parmesan breadsticks.*

8   ounces uncooked penne pasta
2   bacon slices
½   cup chopped sweet onion
2½ cups (1-inch) slices asparagus (about 1 pound)
1½ cups fat-free, less-sodium chicken broth
4   cups bagged baby spinach leaves
½   cup (2 ounces) preshredded Parmesan cheese, divided
¼   teaspoon black pepper

1. Cook pasta according to package directions, omitting salt and fat. Drain and keep warm.
2. Cook bacon in a large nonstick skillet over medium heat until crisp. Remove bacon from pan; crumble. Add onion to drippings in pan; sauté 1 minute. Add asparagus and broth to pan; bring to a boil. Reduce heat, and simmer 5 minutes or until asparagus is crisp-tender. Add pasta, spinach, ¼ cup cheese, and pepper to pan; toss well. Sprinkle with remaining ¼ cup cheese and bacon. **Yield:** 4 servings (serving size: about 1½ cups pasta mixture and 1 tablespoon cheese).

CALORIES 363; FAT 10.2g (sat 4.2g, mono 3.6g, poly 0.8g); PROTEIN 17.8g; CARB 49.1g; FIBER 4.6g; CHOL 18mg; IRON 4.3mg; SODIUM 501mg; CALC 239mg

To quickly prepare this meal, use precooked bacon. Typically precooked bacon will be higher priced than traditional, but we think the time saved is worth the splurge.

MAKE IT FASTER

20 MINUTES

Penne with Bacon, Cheese, and Tomato

Use the same pan to cook the bacon and the white sauce; the reserved bacon drippings in the pan boost the flavor of the sauce.

2   cups uncooked penne
2   tablespoons all-purpose flour
1   cup fat-free milk
4   center-cut bacon slices
2   garlic cloves, minced
1   cup (4 ounces) shredded Gruyère cheese
½   teaspoon salt
¼   teaspoon freshly ground black pepper
¼   cup chopped fresh basil
½   (6-ounce) package fresh baby spinach (about 3 cups packed)
1   pint grape tomatoes
3   tablespoons preshredded fresh Parmesan cheese

1. Cook pasta according to package directions, omitting salt and fat. Drain and keep warm.
2. While pasta cooks, place flour in a small bowl, and gradually add milk, stirring with a whisk until well blended.
3. Cook bacon in a medium saucepan over medium heat until crisp. Remove bacon from pan, reserving 1 teaspoon drippings in pan; crumble bacon, and set aside. Add garlic to pan; sauté 30 seconds. Add milk mixture, and cook over medium heat, stirring occasionally, 4 minutes or until thick. Remove pan from heat; add Gruyère, salt, and pepper, stirring until cheese melts.
4. Combine pasta, cheese sauce, bacon, basil, spinach, and tomatoes in a large serving bowl. Sprinkle with Parmesan cheese. Serve immediately. **Yield:** 7 servings (serving size: 1 cup).

CALORIES 257; FAT 8.3g (sat 4.5g, mono 2.9g, poly 0.6g); PROTEIN 13.8g; CARB 32.9g; FIBER 2.8g; CHOL 24mg; IRON 2.3mg; SODIUM 393mg; CALC 264mg

20 MINUTES

Roasted Chicken and Vegetable Pasta Primavera

Roasting the vegetables deepens their flavors. A small amount of cream per serving is the ticket to an incredibly rich and tasty—yet healthful—pasta dish.

1½ pounds thin asparagus spears
1 cup matchstick-cut carrots
½ medium-size sweet onion, halved and thinly sliced (about 1 cup)
1 teaspoon bottled minced garlic
1 teaspoon olive oil
½ teaspoon salt
¼ teaspoon freshly ground black pepper
1 pint grape tomatoes
8 ounces uncooked penne
2 cups sliced rotisserie chicken breast
¾ cup whipping cream
⅔ cup (2.7 ounces) shaved fresh Parmesan cheese

1. Preheat oven to 450°.
2. Snap off tough ends of asparagus, and cut asparagus into 2-inch pieces. Combine asparagus and next 3 ingredients in a large roasting pan. Drizzle with olive oil, and sprinkle with salt and pepper; toss gently to coat. Bake at 450° for 10 minutes or until vegetables begin to brown; stir vegetables. Add tomatoes, and cook 5 minutes.
3. While vegetables roast, cook pasta according to package directions, omitting salt and fat. Drain well, reserving ⅓ cup pasta water. Keep pasta and reserved water warm.
4. Combine chicken, vegetables, pasta, reserved ⅓ cup pasta water, and whipping cream; toss gently to coat. Sprinkle with cheese. Serve immediately. **Yield:** 8 servings (serving size: 1¼ cups).

CALORIES 325; FAT 14.2g (sat 8.9g, mono 3.8g, poly 1.4g); PROTEIN 20.9g; CARB 29.5g; FIBER 3.3g; CHOL 67mg; IRON 2.6mg; SODIUM 346mg; CALC 181mg

Penne with Sausage and Roasted Pepper Sauce

20 MINUTES

Penne with Sausage and Roasted Pepper Sauce

Water will come to a boil faster over high heat with the lid on the pot. However, once pasta is added to the water, don't replace the lid. Bring the water back to a boil, and cook, uncovered, until the pasta is done, stirring occasionally.

2 cups uncooked penne or other tube-shaped pasta
6 ounces 50%-less-fat pork sausage
1¼ cups bottled spaghetti sauce with mushrooms and ripe olives
½ cup diced bottled roasted red bell peppers
¾ teaspoon sugar

1. Cook pasta according to package directions, omitting salt and fat. Drain well.
2. While pasta cooks, cook sausage in a large nonstick skillet over medium heat 6 minutes or until brown, stirring to crumble. Drain; return to pan.
3. Add spaghetti sauce and bell peppers to pan; bring to a boil. Reduce heat. Simmer, uncovered, 5 minutes or until slightly thick. Remove from heat; stir in sugar. Serve over pasta. **Yield:** 4 servings (serving size: 1 cup pasta and ½ cup sauce).

CALORIES 355; FAT 9.4g (sat 2.7g, mono 2.7g, poly 3.9g); PROTEIN 15.5g; CARB 53.8g; FIBER 2.1g; CHOL 30mg; IRON 2.2mg; SODIUM 720mg; CALC 25mg

Penne with Sausage, Peppers, and Tomatoes

6   ounces uncooked penne
Cooking spray
8   ounces sweet Italian turkey sausage, cut into
     ½-inch slices (about 2 sausages)
3   garlic cloves, minced
1   (14½-ounce) can no-salt-added whole
     tomatoes, undrained and chopped
1   (7-ounce) bottle roasted red bell peppers,
     drained and diced
½   teaspoon freshly ground black pepper
¼   cup grated Parmesan cheese

1. Cook pasta according to package directions, omitting salt and fat. Drain and keep warm.
2. While pasta cooks, heat a large nonstick skillet over medium heat; coat pan with cooking spray. Add sausage, and cook, stirring frequently, 8 to 10 minutes or until browned; drain well. Set sausage aside. Wipe drippings from pan with a paper towel.
3. Coat pan with cooking spray; add garlic, and sauté 1 minute. Add sausage and tomatoes. Bring to a boil; reduce heat, and simmer until most of liquid evaporates. Stir in roasted bell peppers and ground black pepper. Remove from heat.
4. Place pasta in a large bowl; add sausage mixture, and toss. Sprinkle servings with cheese. **Yield:** 4 servings (serving size: 1½ cups pasta and 1 tablespoon cheese).

CALORIES 306; FAT 8.2g (sat 2.8g, mono 2.9g, poly 2.3g); PROTEIN 19.3g; CARB 37.2g; FIBER 1.9g; CHOL 52mg; IRON 2.6mg; SODIUM 623mg; CALC 137mg

Pesto Chicken with Penne

Commercial pesto boosts the flavor of this simple chicken and pasta dish.

2¼ cups (8 ounces) uncooked penne pasta
1   pound skinless, boneless chicken breasts,
     cut into 1-inch pieces
½   teaspoon salt
¼   teaspoon freshly ground black pepper
Cooking spray
⅓   cup commercial pesto

1. Cook pasta according to package directions, omitting salt and fat.
2. While pasta cooks, sprinkle chicken with salt and pepper. Heat a large nonstick skillet over medium-high heat; coat pan with cooking spray. Add chicken to pan; cook, stirring frequently, 5 to 7 minutes or until chicken is done.
3. Drain pasta. Add pesto and chicken to warm pasta; toss lightly. **Yield:** 5 servings (serving size: about 1 cup).

CALORIES 347; FAT 10.4g (sat 3.1g, mono 3.1g, poly 4g); PROTEIN 25.7g; CARB 34.3g; FIBER 1.4g; CHOL 58mg; IRON 1.7mg; SODIUM 420mg; CALC 50mg

Chopping the canned tomatoes with kitchen shears while they are still in the can is a quick way to speed up your prep time.

MAKE IT FASTER

Zesty Cheese Ravioli

make it a meal *For a complete meal, add crusty bread and a favorite dessert.*

½ cup water
1 (14.5-ounce) can no-salt-added diced tomatoes, undrained
1 garlic clove, minced
1 (9-ounce) package fresh cheese ravioli (such as Contadina)
2 cups finely chopped spinach (5 ounces)
⅛ teaspoon sugar
⅛ teaspoon coarsely ground black pepper
1 tablespoon grated Parmesan cheese

1. Combine first 3 ingredients in a large saucepan; bring to a boil. Add ravioli; cover and cook 5 minutes. Uncover and cook an additional 5 minutes or until done.
2. Stir in spinach, sugar, and pepper; cover and cook 2 minutes. Remove from heat, and let stand 5 minutes. Sprinkle with Parmesan cheese. **Yield:** 2 servings (serving size: 2 cups).

CALORIES 505; FAT 14.5g (sat 8g, mono 4.1g, poly 0.4g); PROTEIN 25.8g; CARB 69.7g; FIBER 7.4g; CHOL 107mg; IRON 5.6mg; SODIUM 640mg; CALC 476mg

Spicy Asian Noodles with Chicken

MINUTES

Spicy Asian Noodles with Chicken

1   tablespoon dark sesame oil, divided
1   tablespoon grated peeled fresh ginger
2   garlic cloves, minced
2   cups chopped roasted skinless, boneless
     chicken breasts
½   cup chopped green onions
¼   cup chopped fresh cilantro
3   tablespoons low-sodium soy sauce
2   tablespoons rice vinegar
2   tablespoons hoisin sauce
2   teaspoons sambal oelek (ground fresh chile
     paste)
1   (6.75-ounce) package thin rice sticks
     (rice-flour noodles)
2   tablespoons chopped dry-roasted peanuts

1. Heat 2 teaspoons oil in a small skillet over
medium-high heat. Add ginger and garlic to
pan; cook 45 seconds, stirring constantly.
Place in a large bowl. Stir in remaining 1 teaspoon oil, chicken, and next 6 ingredients.
2. Cook noodles according to package directions. Drain and rinse under cold water;
drain. Cut noodles into smaller pieces. Add
noodles to bowl; toss well to coat. Sprinkle
with peanuts. **Yield:** 4 servings (serving
size: 1¾ cups).

CALORIES 381; FAT 8.1g (sat 1.5g, mono 3.2g, poly 2.7g); PROTEIN 27.5g;
CARB 47.1g; FIBER 2.3g; CHOL 60mg; IRON 3.1mg; SODIUM 614mg; CALC 55mg

MINUTES

Chili and Basil Chicken Noodle Stir-Fry

1   (6-ounce) package Japanese noodles (such
     as Chuka Soba), uncooked and crumbled
3   tablespoons low-sodium soy sauce
2   tablespoons fresh lime juice
1   tablespoon chili garlic sauce
2   teaspoons fish sauce
1   pound skinless, boneless chicken breasts,
     thinly sliced
¼   cup fat-free, less-sodium chicken broth
1   teaspoon cornstarch
1   tablespoon canola oil
3   green onions, diagonally cut
⅓   cup fresh small basil leaves

1. Cook noodles according to package directions, omitting salt and fat. Drain and
keep warm.
2. While pasta cooks, combine soy sauce and
next 3 ingredients. Combine chicken and 2
tablespoons soy sauce mixture. Add chicken
broth and cornstarch to remaining soy sauce
mixture; set aside.
3. Heat oil in a large nonstick skillet over
medium-high heat. Add chicken; cook 5
minutes or until done, stirring occasionally.
Add noodles and soy sauce mixture; cook
1 minute or until sauce thickens. Top with
green onions and basil. Serve immediately. **Yield:** 4 servings (serving size: about
1 cup).

CALORIES 327; FAT 6.9g (sat 1.3g, mono 3.5g, poly 2g); PROTEIN 28.5g;
CARB 34.2g; FIBER 1.3g; CHOL 66mg; IRON 1.4mg; SODIUM 976mg; CALC 27mg

Japanese curly noodles,
made from wheat flour,
are long and wavy with
a delicate texture
and mild flavor. Their
Japanese name, *chuka
soba,* translates to "Chinese
noodle."

INGREDIENT SPOTLIGHT

Rigatoni with Spinach and Blue Cheese

1	teaspoon olive oil
3/4	cup chopped onion
4	garlic cloves, minced
6	cups fresh spinach leaves, chopped
1 1/3	cups chopped seeded tomato
1/2	cup fat-free, less-sodium chicken broth
8	cups hot cooked rigatoni (about 16 ounces uncooked tube-shaped pasta)
1/2	cup (2 ounces) crumbled blue cheese
1/4	cup pine nuts, toasted

1. Heat oil in a large nonstick skillet over medium heat. Add onion, and cook 20 minutes or until golden brown, stirring frequently. Add garlic, and sauté 1 minute. Add spinach, tomato, and broth; cook 3 minutes, stirring occasionally. Combine spinach mixture, pasta, cheese, and pine nuts in a large bowl; toss well to coat. **Yield:** 5 servings (serving size: 1 1/2 cups).

CALORIES 432; FAT 10.1g (sat 3.1g, mono 3.3g, poly 2.6g); PROTEIN 17.7g; CARB 69.8g; FIBER 7.5g; CHOL 9mg; IRON 5.9mg; SODIUM 267mg; CALC 155mg

Garlicky Spaghetti with Beans and Greens

Canned beans are a great pantry staple with lots of protein and fiber. To help reduce sodium in regular canned beans, we rinse and drain them.

8	ounces uncooked spaghetti
3/4	teaspoon kosher salt, divided
3	tablespoons extra-virgin olive oil
2	tablespoons minced fresh garlic
1/2	teaspoon crushed red pepper
2	cups grape tomatoes, halved
1	(16-ounce) can cannellini beans or other white beans, rinsed and drained
5	ounces arugula leaves
2	tablespoons fresh lemon juice
1/2	cup (2 ounces) grated Parmesan cheese

1. Cook pasta according to package directions, omitting salt and fat. Drain pasta in a colander over a bowl, reserving 1/2 cup pasta water. Place pasta in a small bowl. Add 1/4 teaspoon salt, tossing gently. Set aside, and keep warm.
2. Return pan to medium heat. Add oil, garlic, and pepper, and cook 2 minutes or until garlic is lightly browned, stirring occasionally. Stir in remaining 1/2 teaspoon salt, tomatoes, and beans; cook 2 minutes. Add pasta; cook 4 minutes, stirring frequently. Add reserved pasta water and arugula, tossing gently to combine. Remove from heat. Stir in lemon juice and cheese. Serve immediately. **Yield:** 6 servings (serving size: about 1 1/3 cups).

CALORIES 290; FAT 10.5g (sat 2.7g, mono 5.8g, poly 1.3g); PROTEIN 11.3g; CARB 38.1g; FIBER 3.7g; CHOL 8mg; IRON 2.4mg; SODIUM 469mg; CALC 173mg

Garlicky Spaghetti with Beans and Greens

20 MINUTES

Lemon-Basil Shrimp and Pasta

3	quarts water
8	ounces uncooked spaghetti
1	pound peeled and deveined large shrimp
1/4	cup chopped fresh basil
3	tablespoons drained capers
2	tablespoons extra-virgin olive oil
2	tablespoons fresh lemon juice
1/2	teaspoon salt
2	cups baby spinach

1. Bring 3 quarts water to a boil in a Dutch oven. Add pasta; cook 8 minutes. Add shrimp to pan; cook 3 minutes or until shrimp are done and pasta is al dente. Drain. Place pasta mixture in a large bowl. Stir in basil and next 4 ingredients. Place 1/2 cup spinach on each of 4 plates; top each serving with 1 1/2 cups pasta mixture. **Yield:** 4 servings.

CALORIES 397; FAT 9.6g (sat 1.5g, mono 5.3g, poly 1.8g); PROTEIN 31g; CARB 44.9g; FIBER 2.4g; CHOL 172mg; IRON 5.4mg; SODIUM 666mg; CALC 88mg

15 MINUTES

Tortellini and Broccoli Alfredo

1   (9-ounce) package refrigerated three-cheese
      tortellini
1   (12-ounce) package fresh broccoli florets
1   (1.6-ounce) envelope Alfredo sauce mix (such
      as Knorr)
1½ cups fat-free milk
2   teaspoons light butter
⅛   teaspoon ground nutmeg
¼   cup preshredded fresh Parmesan cheese
¼   teaspoon freshly ground black pepper

1. Cook tortellini according to package
directions, omitting salt and fat; add broccoli during the last 3 minutes of cooking
time. Drain well.
2. While pasta cooks, prepare sauce mix
according to package directions, using fat-
free milk, butter, and nutmeg.
3. Combine sauce and pasta and broccoli
mixture; toss well to coat. Top each serving
evenly with Parmesan cheese and pepper.
Yield: 5 servings (serving size: 1 cup).

CALORIES 268; FAT 8g (sat 3.7g, mono 1.6g, poly 2.5g); PROTEIN 15g; CARB 36.1g;
FIBER 3.3g; CHOL 27mg; IRON 1.5mg; SODIUM 785mg; CALC 253mg

20 MINUTES

Tortellini with Peas and Prosciutto

Prosciutto is cured Italian ham that's usually thinly sliced and eaten raw or lightly cooked. Look for it in the specialty section of your supermarket's deli.

1   (20-ounce) package fresh cheese or meat tortellini
1   (10-ounce) package frozen petite green peas, thawed
1   teaspoon butter
1   teaspoon bottled minced garlic
2   cups fat-free half-and-half
1.1 ounces all-purpose flour (about ¼ cup)
¼   cup plus 2 tablespoons pregrated Romano cheese
4   ounces prosciutto or lean ham, coarsely chopped
½   cup finely chopped fresh basil
¼   teaspoon salt
¼   teaspoon black pepper

1. Cook tortellini according to package directions, omitting salt and fat. Add peas during last minute of cooking. Drain pasta and peas; place in a large bowl.
2. While pasta cooks, melt butter in a medium saucepan. Add garlic; sauté 30 seconds. Combine half-and-half and flour in a small bowl, stirring with a whisk; add to pan. Bring to a simmer; cook 3 to 4 minutes or until thickened, stirring constantly with a whisk.
3. Toss half-and-half sauce, cheese, and remaining ingredients with pasta. **Yield:** 8 servings (serving size: 1 cup).

CALORIES 343; FAT 8.3g (sat 4.1g, mono 2.6g, poly 1.4g); PROTEIN 16.4g; CARB 47.3g; FIBER 3.5g; CHOL 39mg; IRON 2mg; SODIUM 707mg; CALC 212mg

15 MINUTES

Pasta with Prosciutto and Spinach

make it a meal *Add watermelon, cantaloupe, and honeydew melon wedges as a side dish to complete the menu.*

1   (9-ounce) package fresh cheese tortellini (such as DiGiorno)
1   tablespoon pine nuts
1   teaspoon olive oil
6   large garlic cloves, finely chopped
1   (6-ounce) package fresh baby spinach
¼   cup (1 ounce) preshredded Parmesan cheese
¼   teaspoon black pepper
2   ounces prosciutto, thinly sliced

1. Cook pasta according to package directions, omitting salt and fat; drain. Transfer pasta to a large bowl.
2. Heat a large nonstick skillet over medium heat. Add nuts to pan; cook 1½ minutes or until toasted, stirring occasionally. Add nuts to bowl.
3. Heat oil in pan over medium heat. Add garlic to pan; cook 2 minutes, stirring occasionally. Add spinach to pan; cook 2 minutes or until spinach wilts, stirring constantly. Add spinach mixture, cheese, and remaining ingredients to bowl; toss well. **Yield:** 4 servings (serving size: 1 cup).

CALORIES 292; FAT 9.2g (sat 3.2g, mono 2.3g, poly 1.1g); PROTEIN 14.6g; CARB 38.8g; FIBER 3.8g; CHOL 32mg; IRON 1.8mg; SODIUM 618mg; CALC 103mg

Fresh tortellini is available with a variety of fillings, including cheese, chicken, and mushroom. Look for fresh tortellini in the refrigerated section of your grocery store.

INGREDIENT SPOTLIGHT

Vermouth Scallops over Vermicelli

*If you don't have vermouth or dry white
wine, you can use ½ cup fat-free, less-
sodium chicken broth.*

4   ounces uncooked vermicelli
1   teaspoon olive oil
1   teaspoon butter
¾   pound sea scallops
2   teaspoons capers
¼   teaspoon salt
¼   teaspoon coarsely ground black pepper
½   cup dry vermouth or dry white wine

1. Cook pasta according to package directions, omitting salt and fat.
2. While pasta cooks, heat oil and butter
over medium-high heat in a large nonstick
skillet. Add scallops; cook 3 minutes on
each side until browned and cooked
through. Add capers, salt, pepper, and vermouth. Cook 30 seconds. Spoon mixture
over pasta. **Yield:** 2 servings (serving size:
1 cup scallop mixture, ¼ cup sauce, and 1
cup pasta).

CALORIES 332; FAT 5.9g (sat 1.7g, mono 2.6g, poly 1.4g); PROTEIN 31.4g;
CARB 20.4g; FIBER 1.1g; CHOL 61mg; IRON 1.4mg; SODIUM 677mg; CALC 48mg

Vermouth Scallops over
Vermicelli

Ziti with Tuscan Porcini Mushroom Sauce

*Intensely flavored dried porcini, along with
fresh button mushrooms, give this dish a
real Tuscan touch. Any dried mushroom will
work well in this recipe, but authentic
Italian porcini are worth the extra cost.*

¾   cup fat-free, less-sodium chicken broth
¼   cup chopped dried porcini mushrooms
     (about ¼ ounce)
1   tablespoon olive oil
3   cups sliced button mushrooms (8 ounces)
1   teaspoon minced fresh or ¼ teaspoon dried
     rosemary
⅛   teaspoon salt
2   garlic cloves, minced
4   quarts water
3   cups uncooked ziti (about 8 ounces short
     tube-shaped pasta) or other short pasta
¼   cup (1 ounce) grated fresh Parmesan cheese
1   tablespoon finely chopped parsley
¼   teaspoon black pepper

1. Combine broth and porcini mushrooms in
a small microwave-safe bowl. Cover with
wax paper; microwave at HIGH 2 minutes;
let stand 10 minutes.
2. Heat oil in a large nonstick skillet over
medium-high heat. Add button mush-
rooms, rosemary, salt, and garlic; sauté
3 minutes. Add broth mixture and porcini
mushrooms to pan; remove from heat.
3. Bring water to a boil in a large stockpot.
Add ziti, and return to a boil. Cook, uncovered, 10 minutes or until al dente, stirring
occasionally. Drain. Stir ziti into mushroom
mixture, and cook 3 minutes or until thoroughly heated. Stir in cheese, parsley, and
pepper. **Yield:** 4 servings (serving size:
1½ cups).

CALORIES 295; FAT 6.4g (sat 1.8g, mono 3.1g, poly 0.8g); PROTEIN 11.8g;
CARB 47.6g; FIBER 2.5g; CHOL 5mg; IRON 3.2mg; SODIUM 284mg; CALC 105mg

MEATLESS
MAIN DISHES

Chickpea and Spinach Curry

20
MINUTES

Black Bean and Corn Tostadas

To save time, buy prechopped onion and bell pepper, as well as a bag of preshredded lettuce.

5   (5½-inch) corn tortillas
Cooking spray
2   teaspoons canola oil
⅓   cup diced onion
⅓   cup diced green bell pepper
1   (15.5-ounce) can black beans, rinsed and drained
1   cup frozen whole-kernel corn, thawed
¾   cup refrigerated fresh salsa
1½   teaspoons chili powder
½   teaspoon dried oregano
½   teaspoon ground cumin
¼   teaspoon salt
⅛   teaspoon coarsely ground black pepper
1¼   cups shredded iceberg lettuce
10   tablespoons refrigerated fresh salsa
5   tablespoons fat-free sour cream
¾   cup (3 ounces) reduced-fat shredded cheddar cheese
5   teaspoons minced fresh cilantro

1. Preheat oven to 350°.
2. Coat tortillas with cooking spray; place on a baking sheet. Bake at 350° for 10 minutes or until crisp, turning after 7 minutes.
3. While tortillas bake, heat oil in a large nonstick skillet over medium-high heat. Add onion and bell pepper, and sauté 4 minutes or until onion is lightly browned. Stir in beans and next 7 ingredients. Cook 2 minutes.
4. Place tortillas on plates. Top each tortilla with about ½ cup bean mixture, ¼ cup lettuce, 2 tablespoons salsa, 1 tablespoon sour cream, about 2 tablespoons cheese, and 1 teaspoon cilantro. **Yield:** 5 servings (serving size: 1 tostada).

CALORIES 194; FAT 3.9g (sat 0.9g, mono 1.9g, poly 1g); PROTEIN 9.8g; CARB 31g; FIBER 5.3g; CHOL 6mg; IRON 1.3mg; SODIUM 535mg; CALC 140mg

MINUTES

Chickpea and Spinach Curry

1   cup coarsely chopped onion
1½   tablespoons bottled ground fresh ginger (such as Spice World)
1   teaspoon olive oil
1½   teaspoons sugar
1½   teaspoons red curry powder (such as McCormick)
1   (19-ounce) can chickpeas (garbanzo beans), rinsed and drained
1   (14.5-ounce) can diced tomatoes, undrained
4   cups fresh spinach
½   cup water
¼   teaspoon salt

1. Place onion and ginger in a food processor; pulse until minced.
2. Heat oil in a large nonstick skillet over medium-high heat. Add onion mixture, sugar, and curry to pan; sauté 3 minutes. Add chickpeas and tomatoes; simmer 2 minutes. Stir in spinach, water, and salt; cook 1 minute or until spinach wilts. **Yield:** 3 servings (serving size: 1⅓ cups chickpea mixture).

CALORIES 247; FAT 4g (sat 0.6g, mono 1.6g, poly 0.9g); PROTEIN 11.1g; CARB 45g; FIBER 8.4g; CHOL 1mg; IRON 5mg; SODIUM 857mg; CALC 194mg

COOKING CLASS: *how to cut an avocado*

Holding the knife steady, rotate the fruit so the knife moves around the pit, cutting the entire avocado. Remove the knife; then slowly and gently twist the two sides away from each other to separate. Strike the pit, and pierce it with the blade. Then twist and remove the knife; the pit will come with it. Use the knife's tip to cut the flesh in horizontal and vertical rows. Remove the flesh gently with a spoon.

 MINUTES

Double-Bean Burritos

Serve with your favorite salsa for dipping. We recommend a fresh refrigerated salsa found in the produce section of your supermarket.

1 (3½-ounce) bag boil-in-bag brown rice
1 cup chunky bottled salsa
1 (15-ounce) can black beans, rinsed and drained
6 (10-inch) flour tortillas
6 tablespoons bean dip (such as Frito Lay)
¾ cup (3 ounces) shredded Monterey Jack cheese with jalapeño peppers
1 peeled avocado, cut into 6 slices
12 fresh cilantro sprigs
6 lime wedges (optional)

1. Cook rice according to package directions, omitting salt and fat.
2. While rice cooks, combine salsa and black beans in a small saucepan; cook over medium heat 5 minutes or until thoroughly heated. Stack tortillas; wrap stack in damp paper towels. Microwave at HIGH 25 seconds or until warm.
3. Spread 1 tablespoon bean dip over each tortilla; top each tortilla with ¼ cup rice, ⅓ cup black bean mixture, 2 tablespoons cheese, 1 avocado slice, and 2 cilantro sprigs; roll up. Serve with lime wedges, if desired. **Yield:** 6 servings (serving size: 1 burrito).

CALORIES 503; FAT 16.4g (sat 4.9g, mono 7.5g, poly 2g); PROTEIN 16.1g; CARB 72.9g; FIBER 7.7g; CHOL 18mg; IRON 4.1mg; SODIUM 905mg; CALC 211mg

 MINUTES

Black Bean Tacos

Seitan has a neutral flavor and a chewy, meatlike texture. Look for it in the refrigerated sections of health food stores or Asian markets.

2 teaspoons olive oil
¾ cup chopped onion
½ teaspoon dried oregano
2 garlic cloves, minced
1 jalapeño pepper, seeded and minced
1 tablespoon dry sherry
1 tablespoon low-sodium soy sauce
1 (15-ounce) can black beans, undrained
1 (8-ounce) package seitan (wheat gluten), finely chopped
½ teaspoon black pepper
12 taco shells
2 cups shredded romaine lettuce
Avocado Salsa (recipe on page 161)

1. Heat oil in a large nonstick skillet over medium heat. Add onion, oregano, garlic, and jalapeño; cook 8 minutes, stirring frequently. Stir in sherry, soy sauce, beans, and seitan; bring to a boil. Cook 7 minutes or until liquid almost evaporates. Sprinkle with black pepper.
2. Prepare taco shells according to package directions. Spoon about ⅓ cup bean mixture into each shell; top each taco with about 2½ tablespoons lettuce and about 2½ tablespoons Avocado Salsa. **Yield:** 6 servings (serving size: 2 tacos).

CALORIES 283; FAT 9.3g (sat 1.2g, mono 5.7g, poly 1.6g); PROTEIN 20.4g; CARB 30g; FIBER 7.6g; CHOL 0mg; IRON 2.8mg; SODIUM 792mg; CALC 58mg

avocado salsa

- 1 cup finely chopped tomato
- ½ cup chopped fresh cilantro
- ½ cup chopped peeled avocado
- 2 tablespoons finely chopped red onion
- 3 tablespoons fresh lime juice
- ¼ teaspoon sea salt
- 1 garlic clove, minced
- 1 jalapeño pepper, seeded and minced

1. Combine all ingredients in a bowl; lightly mash with a fork. **Yield:** 2 cups (serving size: about ¼ cup).

CALORIES 24; FAT 1.5g (sat 0.2g, mono 0.9g, poly 0.2g); PROTEIN 0.5g; CARB 2.7g; FIBER 0.9g; CHOL 0mg; IRON 0.2mg; SODIUM 75mg; CALC 5mg

Black Bean Tacos

20 MINUTES

Poblano, Mango, and Black Bean Quesadillas

1   teaspoon olive oil
1½   cups presliced onion
½   teaspoon dried oregano
¼   teaspoon salt
⅛   teaspoon black pepper
1   poblano chile, seeded and chopped
1   (15-ounce) can black beans, rinsed and
     drained
1   cup jarred sliced peeled mango (such as
     Del Monte SunFresh)
⅓   cup cubed peeled avocado
4   (8-inch) fat-free flour tortillas
Cooking spray
½   cup (2 ounces) shredded reduced-fat sharp
     cheddar cheese

1. Preheat broiler.
2. Heat oil in a large nonstick skillet over medium-high heat. Add onion, oregano, salt, pepper, and poblano, and sauté 5 minutes or until onion is tender. Add beans; cook 1 minute or until thoroughly heated. Remove from heat, and stir in mango and avocado.
3. Place flour tortillas on a baking sheet coated with cooking spray. Arrange about ¾ cup bean mixture on half of each tortilla, leaving a ½-inch border. Sprinkle 2 tablespoons cheddar cheese over bean mixture, and fold tortilla in half. Lightly coat tortillas with cooking spray. Broil 3 minutes or until cheddar cheese melts. **Yield:** 4 servings (serving size: 1 quesadilla).

CALORIES 334; FAT 9.3g (sat 2.9g, mono 3.5g, poly 0.9g); PROTEIN 13.2g; CARB 54.5g; FIBER 7.2g; CHOL 10mg; IRON 3mg; SODIUM 753mg; CALC 253mg

make it a meal *The sweetness of the mango balances the snappiness of the chile. Top the quesadillas with fat-free sour cream and salsa, and serve with spinach and carrot salad.*

20 MINUTES

Sweet Potato, Black Bean, and Goat Cheese Quesadillas

2½ cups frozen cut sweet potatoes (such as Ore-Ida Steam n' Mash)
1 tablespoon water
1 (15-ounce) can no-salt-added black beans, rinsed and drained
⅓ cup minced fresh cilantro
¼ teaspoon freshly ground black pepper
⅛ teaspoon salt
⅓ cup bottled roasted red bell peppers
1 tablespoon chopped chipotle chile in adobo sauce
¼ cup reduced-fat sour cream
4 (10-inch) flour tortillas
¾ cup (3 ounces) crumbled goat cheese
Cooking spray

1. Combine sweet potato and 1 tablespoon water in a medium-size microwave-safe bowl; cover with wax paper. Microwave at HIGH 4 minutes or until potato is tender, stirring after 2 minutes. Stir in beans and next 3 ingredients.
2. While potatoes cook, place roasted red bell peppers, chipotle chile, and sour cream in a blender; process until smooth. Set aside.
3. Spoon ¾ cup sweet potato mixture on half of each tortilla, leaving a ¼-inch margin. Top evenly with cheese. Fold each tortilla in half.
4. Heat a large nonstick skillet over medium heat. Coat pan and both sides of each tortilla with cooking spray. Place 2 quesadillas in pan. Cook 2 to 3 minutes on each side or until lightly browned. Repeat with remaining quesadillas. Cut each quesadilla into 4 wedges, and serve immediately with red bell pepper sauce. **Yield:** 4 servings (serving size: 4 quesadilla wedges and about 2 tablespoons sauce).

CALORIES 415; FAT 7.4g (sat 4.4g, mono 2.4g, poly 0.5g); PROTEIN 16.1g; CARB 70.8g; FIBER 10.4g; CHOL 15mg; IRON 3.1mg; SODIUM 727mg; CALC 215mg

15 MINUTES

Soba with Herbed Edamame Sauce

1 cup frozen blanched shelled edamame (green soybeans)
6 tablespoons chopped dry-roasted cashews, divided
1 cup loosely packed fresh basil leaves
1 cup loosely packed fresh cilantro leaves
6 tablespoons (1½ ounces) grated fresh pecorino Romano cheese
¼ cup fresh lemon juice
¼ cup extra-virgin olive oil
1 teaspoon salt
¼ teaspoon freshly ground black pepper
3 garlic cloves, peeled
1 cup hot water
6 cups hot cooked soba (about 1 pound uncooked buckwheat noodles)
Cilantro sprigs (optional)
Lime wedges (optional)

1. Prepare edamame according to package directions, omitting salt.
2. Place edamame, ¼ cup cashews, basil, and next 7 ingredients in a food processor; process 1 minute or until finely chopped.
3. With food processor on, slowly pour hot water through food chute; process 2 minutes or until smooth. Serve over soba, and sprinkle with remaining 2 tablespoons cashews. Garnish with cilantro sprigs and lime wedges, if desired. **Yield:** 7 servings (serving size: about 1 cup noodles, about ⅓ cup sauce, and about 1 teaspoon cashews).

CALORIES 408; FAT 13.8g (sat 2.6g, mono 8.1g, poly 2.1g); PROTEIN 18g; CARB 58.6g; FIBER 4.5g; CHOL 5mg; IRON 2.5mg; SODIUM 562mg; CALC 112mg

Protein-rich soba noodles, made from a combination of buckwheat flour and wheat flour, are native to Japan. Look for them in the ethnic or pasta section of natural food and grocery stores or in specialty Asian markets.

INGREDIENT SPOTLIGHT

 MINUTES

Black-Eyed Pea Cakes with Adobo Cream

¼ cup fat-free sour cream
1 teaspoon adobo sauce
1 (15.8-ounce) can no-salt-added black-eyed peas, rinsed and drained
¼ cup dry breadcrumbs
1 tablespoon finely chopped onion
½ teaspoon bottled minced garlic
½ teaspoon ground cumin
½ teaspoon salt
¼ teaspoon black pepper
1 large egg, lightly beaten
1 large egg white, lightly beaten
1½ teaspoons olive oil
¼ cup (about 1 ounce) shredded Monterey Jack cheese

1. Combine sour cream and adobo sauce in a small bowl.
2. Place beans in a medium bowl; partially mash beans with a fork. Stir in breadcrumbs and next 7 ingredients. With floured hands, divide pea mixture into 4 equal portions, shaping each portion into a ½-inch-thick patty.
3. Heat oil in a large nonstick skillet over medium-high heat. Add patties to pan; cook 2 minutes on each side or until golden and thoroughly heated. Remove from pan; top each cake with 1 tablespoon cheese. Serve with sour cream mixture. **Yield:** 4 servings (serving size: 1 patty and about 1 tablespoon sour cream mixture).

CALORIES 173; FAT 6.3g (sat 2.1g, mono 2.4g, poly 0.9g); PROTEIN 10.2g; CARB 19.3g; FIBER 3.6g; CHOL 59mg; IRON 2mg; SODIUM 462mg; CALC 118mg

Italian-Style Eggplant

Italian-Style Eggplant

2O MINUTES

Italian-Style Eggplant

make it a meal *Serve this dish with a simple green salad for a light meal. If you want something heartier, serve it with ¾ cup hot cooked spaghetti per serving.*

1   large egg, lightly beaten
1   tablespoon water
⅔   cup Italian-seasoned breadcrumbs
¼   teaspoon freshly ground black pepper
1   large eggplant, cut crosswise into
     8 (½-inch-thick) slices
Cooking spray
½   cup pizza sauce (such as Ragu Homestyle)
1   cup (4 ounces) shredded part-skim
     mozzarella cheese

1. Preheat broiler.
2. Combine egg and water in a shallow bowl. Combine breadcrumbs and pepper in another shallow bowl. Dip eggplant slices into egg mixture, coating both sides; dredge in breadcrumbs, turning to coat both sides.
3. Line a baking sheet with foil; coat with cooking spray. Place eggplant on baking sheet; broil 5 to 7 minutes on each side or until eggplant is golden brown and tender. Spoon 1 tablespoon pizza sauce onto each eggplant slice; top with cheese. Return to broiler, and broil 1 to 2 minutes or until cheese melts. **Yield:** 4 servings (serving size: 2 eggplant slices).

CALORIES 224; FAT 8g (sat 4.3g, mono 2.6g, poly 1g); PROTEIN 13.6g; CARB 25.3g; FIBER 6.2g; CHOL 60mg; IRON 1.9mg; SODIUM 555mg; CALC 260mg

15 MINUTES

Mushroom Pasta

To make this a truly vegetarian dish, use vegetable broth instead of chicken broth.

12   ounces uncooked medium egg noodles
1   tablespoon olive oil
1½   teaspoons all-purpose flour
3   cups sliced cremini mushrooms
2   (8-ounce) packages presliced button
      mushrooms
1   cup fat-free, less-sodium chicken broth
½   cup white wine
1   tablespoon fresh lemon juice
½   teaspoon salt
2   tablespoons butter
¾   teaspoon black pepper
½   cup (2 ounces) preshredded fresh Parmesan
      cheese

1. Cook noodles according to package directions, omitting salt and fat.
2. While noodles cook, combine oil and flour in a large Dutch oven over medium-high heat; sauté 1 minute. Add mushrooms; sauté 2 minutes. Add broth, wine, juice, and salt; cook 8 minutes or until sauce is slightly thick.
3. Stir in butter and pepper. Add pasta; toss to coat. Stir in cheese. **Yield:** 5 servings (serving size: 2 cups).

CALORIES 434; FAT 13.9g (sat 6.1g, mono 5.2g, poly 1.4g); PROTEIN 19.2g; CARB 55.1g; FIBER 3.8g; CHOL 86mg; IRON 4.6mg; SODIUM 613mg; CALC 187mg

Eggplants come in an assortment of colors, shapes, and sizes, and they have virtually no fat. Look for eggplants that have smooth, shiny skin and are firm but slightly springy. Store them in a cool place, and use them within two days.

INGREDIENT SPOTLIGHT

30

Barley-Mushroom Pilaf

make it a meal *Here's a flavorful one-dish meal that can easily transition to a side dish. Substitute vegetable broth for the chicken broth, if you prefer.*

3	cups fat-free, less-sodium chicken broth
1/3	cup dried porcini mushrooms, chopped (about 1/3 ounce)
1 1/2	cups uncooked quick-cooking barley
2	tablespoons olive oil
3	cups quartered shiitake mushroom caps (about 8 ounces)
2	cups chopped onion
3/4	teaspoon salt
1/2	teaspoon dried rosemary
1	(8-ounce) package presliced mushrooms
1/4	cup dry Marsala
2	teaspoons sherry vinegar

1. Combine broth and porcini in a large saucepan. Bring to a boil; stir in barley. Cover, reduce heat, and simmer 12 minutes or until tender.
2. While barley cooks, heat oil in a Dutch oven over medium-high heat. Add shiitake, onion, salt, rosemary, and presliced mushrooms; sauté 5 minutes. Stir in Marsala; cook 1 minute. Stir in barley mixture and vinegar; cook 2 minutes or until thoroughly heated, stirring frequently. **Yield:** 4 servings (serving size: 1 1/2 cups).

CALORIES 415; FAT 8.7g (sat 1.3g, mono 5.2g, poly 1.5g); PROTEIN 15.3g; CARB 66.6g; FIBER 15g; CHOL 0mg; IRON 4.6mg; SODIUM 805mg; CALC 46mg

Stack shiitake mushroom caps before quartering or slicing them—it's much faster than cutting them one by one.

MAKE IT FASTER

20 MINUTES

Creamy Spinach-Mushroom Skillet Enchiladas

2   teaspoons olive oil
1   teaspoon bottled minced garlic
½   teaspoon chili powder
½   teaspoon ground cumin
1   (8-ounce) package presliced mushrooms
1   (6-ounce) package fresh baby spinach (about 6 cups)
¼   teaspoon salt
2   tablespoons light cream cheese with onions and chives
1   (16-ounce) bottle green salsa, divided
8   (6-inch) corn tortillas
⅓   cup (1½ ounces) shredded Monterey Jack cheese
¼   cup fat-free sour cream
Cilantro sprigs (optional)

1. Preheat broiler.
2. Heat olive oil in a large skillet over medium-high heat. Add garlic, chili powder, cumin, and mushrooms; sauté 5 minutes. Add spinach and salt; cook 1 minute or until spinach wilts, stirring frequently. Drain; return mushroom mixture to pan. Add cream cheese; cook 2 minutes or until cream cheese melts, stirring frequently. Place mushroom mixture in a bowl, and set aside.
3. Heat 1 cup salsa in a saucepan over low heat. Dredge both sides of each tortilla in warm salsa using tongs, and stack tortillas on a plate. Spoon 1 heaping tablespoon mushroom mixture into center of each tortilla; fold in half, and arrange in skillet, overlapping slightly. Top with remaining salsa, and sprinkle with cheese. Wrap handle of skillet with foil, and broil enchiladas 4 minutes or until cheese melts. Top with sour cream, and garnish with cilantro sprigs, if desired. **Yield:** 4 servings (serving size: 2 enchiladas and 1 tablespoon sour cream).

CALORIES 273; FAT 8.7g (sat 3.6g, mono 2.9g, poly 1g); PROTEIN 10.1g; CARB 39.4g; FIBER 6.7g; CHOL 15mg; IRON 2.7mg; SODIUM 806mg; CALC 330mg

Polenta Gratin with Mushrooms and Fontina

15 MINUTES

Polenta Gratin with Mushrooms and Fontina

1   (16-ounce) tube of polenta, cut into ¼-inch-thick slices
Cooking spray
1   (8-ounce) package presliced mushrooms
1   teaspoon bottled minced garlic
¼   teaspoon salt
⅓   cup sun-dried tomato Alfredo sauce (such as Classico)
¼   cup chopped fresh basil
¼   cup (1 ounce) shredded fontina cheese

1. Preheat oven to 500°.
2. Arrange polenta slices in an 11 x 7–inch baking dish coated with cooking spray, allowing slices to overlap.
3. Heat a medium nonstick skillet over medium-high heat; coat pan with cooking spray. Add mushrooms; cook 2 minutes, stirring frequently. Stir in garlic and salt. Cover, reduce heat, and cook 2 minutes. Stir in Alfredo sauce and basil.
4. Spoon mushroom mixture evenly over polenta. Top evenly with cheese. Bake at 500° for 7 minutes or until thoroughly heated. **Yield:** 3 servings.

CALORIES 221; FAT 7.4g (sat 3.9g, mono 1.7g, poly 1.2g); PROTEIN 8.3g; CARB 28.7g; FIBER 4.2g; CHOL 29mg; IRON 2.4mg; SODIUM 739mg; CALC 82mg

20 MINUTES

Polenta with Mushrooms, Zucchini, and Mozzarella

Olive oil–flavored cooking spray
1   (16-ounce) tube of polenta, cut into 8 slices
3   cups diced zucchini (about 2 medium)
1   (8-ounce) package presliced mushrooms
1   (14.5-ounce) can diced tomatoes with basil, garlic, and oregano, drained
1   cup (4 ounces) preshredded part-skim mozzarella cheese
Freshly ground black pepper (optional)

1. Heat a large nonstick skillet over medium-high heat; coat pan with cooking spray. Add polenta rounds, and cook 3 minutes on each side or until lightly browned. Remove from pan; set aside, and keep warm.
2. Add zucchini and mushrooms to pan; sauté 7 minutes or until tender. Stir in tomatoes, and cook 1 minute or until thoroughly heated.
3. Place 2 polenta rounds on each of 4 serving plates. Spoon vegetable mixture over polenta. Top with cheese. Sprinkle with pepper, if desired. **Yield:** 4 servings (serving size: 2 polenta rounds, 1 cup vegetable mixture, and $1/4$ cup cheese).

CALORIES 230; FAT 6.1g (sat 3.6g, mono 2.1g, poly 0.3g); PROTEIN 12.7g; CARB 30g; FIBER 5g; CHOL 15mg; IRON 2.2mg; SODIUM 566mg; CALC 264mg

Look for plain and flavored 16-ounce tubes of precooked polenta in the produce section of your supermarket. They work well in recipes in which polenta is cut into slices or cubes.

INGREDIENT SPOTLIGHT

20 MINUTES

Polenta with Olives, Tomatoes, and Feta

Precooked refrigerated polenta is an excellent base for this quick vegetarian meal for two. You'll find it in the produce section of the supermarket in a variety of flavors.

Cooking spray
½ (16-ounce) package prepared refrigerated basil and garlic-flavored polenta (such as Marjon), cut into 6 slices
4 teaspoons chopped fresh oregano, divided
1 (14.5-ounce) can no-salt-added diced tomatoes, undrained
6 pitted kalamata olives, quartered
⅛ teaspoon freshly ground black pepper
½ cup crumbled reduced-fat feta cheese
Oregano sprigs (optional)

1. Heat a large nonstick skillet over medium-high heat. Coat pan with cooking spray. Add polenta, and cook 4 to 5 minutes on each side or until browned. Remove from pan, and sprinkle polenta with 2 teaspoons chopped oregano; cover and keep warm.
2. Add tomatoes, kalamata olives, pepper, and remaining 2 teaspoons oregano to pan; bring to a boil. Reduce heat, and simmer 2 minutes until thoroughly heated.
3. Place 3 polenta slices in each bowl; top each serving with ¾ cup tomato mixture. Sprinkle each with ¼ cup feta cheese. Garnish with oregano sprigs, if desired. **Yield:** 2 servings.

CALORIES 235; FAT 7.6g (sat 3.4g, mono 3g, poly 1.1g); PROTEIN 10.5g; CARB 31.2g; FIBER 4.7g; CHOL 10mg; IRON 1.4mg; SODIUM 1148mg; CALC 146mg

15 MINUTES

Cannellini-Stuffed Portobello Mushrooms

make it a meal *Pasta sauce, cannellini beans, and cheese make a tasty meatless stuffing for the mushrooms. You can serve this dish with a tossed green salad.*

4 (4-inch) portobello caps
Cooking spray
½ cup part-skim ricotta cheese
¼ teaspoon salt
¼ teaspoon garlic powder
¼ teaspoon dried rosemary, crushed
¾ cup bottled pasta sauce
1 (16-ounce) can cannellini beans, rinsed and drained
½ cup (2 ounces) preshredded part-skim mozzarella cheese

1. Preheat broiler.
2. Remove gills from undersides of mushrooms using a spoon; discard gills. Place caps, smooth side up, on a baking sheet coated with cooking spray; broil 2 minutes. Turn caps over; broil 2 minutes.
3. Combine ricotta, salt, garlic powder, and rosemary, stirring well. Spread 2 tablespoons cheese mixture in each cap. Spoon 3 tablespoons pasta sauce over cheese mixture in each serving. Divide beans evenly among caps; sprinkle each serving with 2 tablespoons mozzarella. Broil 3 minutes or until cheese melts. **Yield:** 4 servings (serving size: 1 stuffed mushroom cap).

CALORIES 187; FAT 6.1g (sat 3g, mono 1.1g, poly 0.8g); PROTEIN 13g; CARB 20.5g; FIBER 4.9g; CHOL 16mg; IRON 2mg; SODIUM 654mg; CALC 240mg

COOKING CLASS: *how to remove gills*

When choosing portobellos, be sure to check under the cap to avoid selecting those with flattened gills. Use a spoon to remove the dark-colored gills; this will prevent the mushrooms from turning black.

 MINUTES

Spinach and Cheese–Stuffed Portobello Caps

4   large portobello caps
Cooking spray
¼   teaspoon salt, divided
1   cup fat-free ricotta cheese
¼   teaspoon garlic powder
¼   teaspoon ground black pepper
½   (10-ounce) package frozen chopped spinach, thawed and drained thoroughly
⅓   cup chopped bottled roasted red bell peppers
¾   cup tomato sauce
½   cup (2 ounces) shredded part-skim mozzarella
½   teaspoon dried oregano

1. Preheat oven to 400°.
2. Remove brown gills from undersides of mushrooms using a spoon; discard gills. Place mushrooms, stem sides up, on a baking sheet coated with cooking spray. Sprinkle with ⅛ teaspoon salt. Bake at 400° for 5 minutes.
3. While mushrooms bake, combine ricotta, garlic powder, black pepper, and remaining ⅛ teaspoon salt in a medium bowl, stirring well. Gently stir in spinach and bell pepper. Divide mixture evenly among mushroom caps. Top evenly with tomato sauce and cheese. Sprinkle evenly with oregano. Bake at 400° for 8 minutes. Increase oven temperature to broil. Broil 1½ minutes or until cheese is melted. **Yield:** 2 servings (serving size: 2 mushroom caps).

CALORIES 305; FAT 6.9g (sat 4.1g, mono 0g, poly 0.1g); PROTEIN 22.9g; CARB 31.6g; FIBER 6.2g; CHOL 42mg; IRON 2.8mg; SODIUM 949mg; CALC 466mg

 MINUTES

Grilled Portobello–Goat Cheese Pitas

make it a meal *If the tomatoes are ripe, skip grilling them. Serve with a tropical fruit salad of mangoes, cantaloupe, and pineapple sprinkled with toasted coconut.*

1½   teaspoons bottled minced garlic
1   teaspoon olive oil
4   (6-inch) pita rounds
½   teaspoon salt, divided
¼   teaspoon black pepper, divided
1   (6-ounce) package portobello mushrooms
2   medium tomatoes, cut into ¼-inch-thick slices
⅓   cup (3 ounces) goat cheese
½   cup chopped fresh basil

1. Preheat a grill pan over medium heat.
2. Combine garlic and oil; brush evenly over pitas. Sprinkle ¼ teaspoon salt and ⅛ teaspoon pepper evenly over pitas. Place pitas in pan, and cook 2 minutes on each side or until toasted.
3. Sprinkle ¼ teaspoon salt and ⅛ teaspoon pepper evenly over mushrooms and tomatoes. Place mushrooms in pan; cook 6 minutes or until tender, turning once. Remove mushrooms from pan. Add tomatoes to pan; cook 1 minute.
4. Spread goat cheese evenly over pitas. Arrange mushrooms and tomatoes evenly over pitas. Sprinkle with basil. **Yield:** 4 servings (serving size: 1 topped pita).

CALORIES 283; FAT 8.5g (sat 4.7g, mono 2.4g, poly 0.7g); PROTEIN 11.9g; CARB 39.8g; FIBER 2.9g; CHOL 17mg; IRON 2.7mg; SODIUM 731mg; CALC 133mg

 15 MINUTES

Stuffed Portobello Mushrooms

While panko (Japanese breadcrumbs) works best in this dish, you can substitute freshly made coarse breadcrumbs, if necessary.

4   (6-inch) portobello mushrooms, stems
      removed
Cooking spray
1   cup chopped red tomato
1   cup chopped yellow tomato
1   cup panko (Japanese breadcrumbs)
1   cup (4 ounces) preshredded part-skim
      mozzarella cheese
¼   cup chopped fresh chives
¼   teaspoon salt
¼   teaspoon black pepper

1. Preheat broiler.
2. Remove brown gills from undersides of mushrooms using a spoon; discard gills. Place mushrooms, smooth sides up, on a foil-lined baking sheet coated with cooking spray. Broil mushrooms 5 minutes.
3. While mushrooms broil, combine tomatoes, panko, cheese, and chives.
4. Turn mushrooms over; sprinkle evenly with salt and pepper. Divide tomato mixture evenly among mushrooms. Broil 5 minutes or until cheese melts. **Yield:** 4 servings (serving size: 1 stuffed mushroom).

CALORIES184; FAT 5.3g (sat 2.9g, mono 1.3g, poly 0.2g); PROTEIN 12.6g;
CARB 21.6g; FIBER 3.5g; CHOL 16mg; IRON 1.3mg; SODIUM 325mg; CALC 209mg

15 MINUTES

Brown Butter Gnocchi with Spinach and Pine Nuts

If you haven't tried gnocchi before now, don't wait any longer. This recipe will become your brand-new go-to weeknight dish.

1   (16-ounce) package vacuum-packed gnocchi (such as Vigo)
2   tablespoons butter
2   tablespoons pine nuts
2   garlic cloves, minced
1   (10-ounce) package fresh spinach, torn
¼   teaspoon salt
¼   teaspoon freshly ground black pepper
¼   cup (1 ounce) finely shredded Parmesan cheese

1. Cook gnocchi according to package directions, omitting salt and fat; drain.
2. Heat butter in a large nonstick skillet over medium heat. Add pine nuts to pan; cook 3 minutes or until butter and nuts are lightly browned, stirring constantly. Add garlic to pan; cook 1 minute. Add gnocchi and spinach to pan; cook 1 minute or until spinach wilts, stirring constantly. Stir in salt and pepper. Sprinkle with Parmesan cheese. **Yield:** 4 servings (serving size: 1 cup gnocchi mixture and 1 tablespoon cheese).

CALORIES 289; FAT 10.8g (sat 5.1g, mono 2.9g, poly 1.8g); PROTEIN 9.5g; CARB 40.3g; FIBER 1.8g; CHOL 20mg; IRON 2.2mg; SODIUM 877mg; CALC 164mg

20 MINUTES

Fold-Over Quesadillas

make it a meal *Fresh salsa and cilantro brighten up these simple quesadillas. Serve with a tossed green salad and a side of black beans to round out the meal.*

1   (4.5-ounce) can chopped green chiles
4   (8-inch) flour tortillas
1½ cups (6 ounces) shredded part-skim
      mozzarella cheese
⅓   cup finely chopped red onion
½   teaspoon ground cumin
Cooking spray
½   cup fat-free sour cream
¼   cup refrigerated fresh salsa
¼   cup chopped fresh cilantro

1. Spoon 2 tablespoons chiles over half of each tortilla, spreading evenly. Sprinkle cheese, onion, and cumin over chiles. Fold tortillas in half.
2. Heat a large nonstick skillet over medium heat. Coat pan with cooking spray. Add 2 quesadillas; cook 2 minutes. Turn and cook 2 minutes or until cheese melts. Remove from pan; keep warm. Repeat with remaining quesadillas. Cut each quesadilla into 3 wedges. Serve with sour cream, salsa, and cilantro. **Yield:** 4 servings (serving size: 3 wedges, 2 tablespoons sour cream, 1 tablespoon salsa, and 1 tablespoon cilantro).

CALORIES 314; FAT 10.1g (sat 5.4g, mono 2.8g, poly 1.8g); PROTEIN 18.2g; CARB 37.3g; FIBER 4.3g; CHOL 30mg; IRON 2.4mg; SODIUM 647mg; CALC 476mg

Use refrigerated fresh salsa found in the produce section of your supermarket. It's faster than making your own and has far less sodium than the bottled stuff.

INGREDIENT SPOTLIGHT

20 MINUTES

Zucchini, Olive, and Cheese Quesadillas

Surprise and delight your family tonight with a new spin on an old Mexican classic. These Mediterranean flavor-inspired quesadillas are a nice change of pace from the usual bean, cheese, and salsa recipe.

1   teaspoon olive oil
Cooking spray
⅓   cup finely chopped onion
½   teaspoon bottled minced garlic
1¼ cups shredded zucchini
¼   teaspoon dried oregano
⅛   teaspoon salt
⅛   teaspoon black pepper
4   (8-inch) fat-free flour tortillas
½   cup (2 ounces) preshredded part-skim
      mozzarella cheese, divided
½   cup diced tomato, divided
¼   cup chopped pitted kalamata olives, divided
¼   cup (1 ounce) crumbled feta cheese, divided

1. Heat olive oil in a large nonstick skillet coated with cooking spray over medium-high heat. Add onion and garlic; sauté 1 minute. Add zucchini; sauté 2 minutes or until lightly browned. Remove from heat; stir in oregano, salt, and pepper. Remove from pan.
2. Wipe pan clean with paper towels, and coat with cooking spray. Heat pan over medium heat. Add 1 tortilla to pan, and sprinkle with ¼ cup mozzarella. Top with half of zucchini mixture, ¼ cup tomato, 2 tablespoons olives, 2 tablespoons feta, and 1 tortilla. Cook 3 minutes or until lightly browned on bottom. Carefully turn quesadilla, and cook 2 minutes or until lightly browned. Place quesadilla on a cutting board; cut in half using a serrated knife. Repeat procedure with remaining tortillas, mozzarella, zucchini mixture, tomato, olives, and feta. Serve warm. **Yield:** 4 servings.

CALORIES 235; FAT 7.9g (sat 3.6g, mono 3.1g, poly 0.5g); PROTEIN 8.7g; CARB 23.7g; FIBER 3.8g; CHOL 14mg; IRON 0.7mg; SODIUM 632mg; CALC 160mg

15 MINUTES

Curried Couscous with Broccoli and Feta

Although filling and delicious enough as a meatless main dish, you can always add meat, such as chopped chicken or thin strips of flank steak, for the family carnivores.

1³⁄₄ cups water
1   cup uncooked couscous
1¹⁄₂ cups small broccoli florets
¹⁄₂ cup finely chopped red onion
¹⁄₃ cup shredded carrot
¹⁄₄ cup raisins
¹⁄₄ cup dry-roasted cashews, chopped
2   tablespoons white wine vinegar
1¹⁄₂ tablespoons olive oil
1   tablespoon sugar
1¹⁄₂ teaspoons curry powder
1   teaspoon bottled minced fresh ginger
³⁄₄ teaspoon salt
1   (15-ounce) can chickpeas (garbanzo beans), rinsed and drained
³⁄₄ cup (3 ounces) crumbled feta cheese

1. Bring 1³⁄₄ cups water to a boil in a medium saucepan; gradually stir in couscous. Remove from heat; cover and let stand 5 minutes. Fluff with a fork.
2. While couscous stands, steam broccoli florets, covered, 3 minutes or until tender.
3. Combine couscous, broccoli, onion, and next 10 ingredients, tossing gently. Sprinkle with cheese. **Yield:** 5 servings (serving size: about 1¹⁄₄ cups).

CALORIES 402; FAT 12.2g (sat 3.8g, mono 5.8g, poly 1.6g); PROTEIN 13.4g; CARB 61.4g; FIBER 7.4g; CHOL 15mg; IRON 2.7mg; SODIUM 827mg; CALC 145mg

Using bagged broccoli florets and preshredded carrots all but eliminates the prep with this vegetarian entrée.

MAKE IT FASTER

30 MINUTES

Huevos Rancheros with Zucchini and Green Pepper

make it a meal *Entertain at brunch with this casual main dish. Serve a pineapple and melon compote on the side tossed with fresh mint sprigs.*

1   teaspoon olive oil
Cooking spray
1¹⁄₂ cups diced zucchini
¹⁄₂ cup diced green bell pepper
¹⁄₄ cup water
¹⁄₄ teaspoon salt
¹⁄₄ teaspoon ground cumin
¹⁄₈ teaspoon freshly ground black pepper
1   (10-ounce) can diced tomatoes with green chiles, undrained
4   (6-inch) corn tortillas
4   large eggs
¹⁄₃ cup (1¹⁄₄ ounces) preshredded reduced-fat cheddar cheese
2   teaspoons chopped fresh cilantro

1. Heat oil in a large nonstick skillet coated with cooking spray over medium-high heat. Add zucchini and bell pepper; sauté 6 minutes or until lightly browned. Add water and next 4 ingredients. Stir to combine. Cover and simmer 3 minutes.
2. Warm tortillas according to package directions.
3. Break 1 egg into a small custard cup. Slip egg onto tomato mixture; repeat procedure with remaining eggs. Cover and simmer 3 minutes or until eggs are done. Sprinkle with cheese. Cover and cook 30 seconds or until cheese melts.
4. Place 1 tortilla on each of 4 plates. Spoon 1 egg and ³⁄₄ cup tomato mixture onto each tortilla. Sprinkle with ¹⁄₂ teaspoon cilantro. **Yield:** 4 servings.

CALORIES 248; FAT 8.5g (sat 2.1g, mono 2.9g, poly 0.9g); PROTEIN 13.2g; CARB 31.5g; FIBER 4.1g; CHOL 214mg; IRON 2.6mg; SODIUM 679mg; CALC 155mg

Quick Vegetarian Paella

2	tablespoons extra-virgin olive oil
2	cups chopped onion
2	cups (1-inch) chopped green bell pepper
1	cup sliced cremini mushrooms
2	garlic cloves, minced
3	cups uncooked quick-cooking brown rice
2	cups fat-free, less-sodium vegetable broth (such as Swanson Certified Organic)
1	cup water
1	teaspoon saffron threads, crushed, or ground turmeric
½	teaspoon dried thyme
2	cups chopped tomato
1	cup frozen green peas
½	cup pimiento-stuffed olives, chopped
2	tablespoons chopped fresh flat-leaf parsley
¼	teaspoon freshly ground black pepper
1	(14-ounce) can artichoke hearts, drained and coarsely chopped

Chopped fresh flat-leaf parsley (optional)

1. Heat olive oil in a stockpot over medium-high heat. Add onion, bell pepper, mushrooms, and garlic; sauté 5 minutes. Stir in rice and next 4 ingredients; bring to a boil. Cover, reduce heat, and simmer 10 minutes. **2**. Stir in tomato, green peas, olives, 2 tablespoons parsley, black pepper, and artichoke hearts. Cook 3 minutes or until rice is tender and mixture is thoroughly heated. Garnish with additional chopped fresh parsley, if desired. **Yield:** 5 servings (serving size: about 2 cups).

CALORIES 350; FAT 8.9g (sat 1g, mono 5.1g, poly 0.9g); PROTEIN 10.8g; CARB 62g; FIBER 7.2g; CHOL 0mg; IRON 3.4mg; SODIUM 686mg; CALC 78mg

make it a meal. *Complete the menu with steamed green beans and packaged mixed baby greens tossed with bottled orange sections and toasted almond slices.*

Italian Eggs over
Spinach and Polenta

Italian Eggs over Spinach and Polenta

This breakfast is good any time of day.

1   (16-ounce) tube of polenta, cut into 12 slices
Cooking spray
2   cups fat-free tomato-basil pasta sauce
1   (6-ounce) package fresh baby spinach
4   large eggs
1/2 cup (2 ounces) shredded Asiago cheese

1. Preheat broiler.
2. Arrange polenta slices on a baking sheet coated with cooking spray. Coat tops of polenta with cooking spray. Broil 3 minutes or until thoroughly heated.
3. While polenta heats, bring sauce to a simmer in a large nonstick skillet over medium-high heat. Stir in spinach; cover and cook 1 minute or until spinach wilts. Stir to combine. Make 4 indentations in top of spinach mixture using back of a wooden spoon. Break 1 egg into each indentation. Cover, reduce heat, and simmer 5 minutes or until eggs are desired degree of doneness. Sprinkle with cheese. Place 3 polenta slices on each of 4 plates; top each serving with one-fourth of spinach mixture and 1 egg. **Yield:** 4 servings.

CALORIES 264; FAT 8.8g (sat 4g, mono 2.9g, poly 0.9g); PROTEIN 15.4g; CARB 29.4g; FIBER 2.9g; CHOL 224mg; IRON 3.2mg; SODIUM 780mg; CALC 238mg

Asparagus and Basil Omelet

Cooking spray
12 asparagus spears, diagonally cut into 1-inch pieces (about 1 cup)
2   large eggs
1/2 cup egg substitute
1/4 cup water
1/4 teaspoon salt
1/4 teaspoon coarsely ground black pepper
2   tablespoons chopped fresh basil
1/2 cup (2 ounces) reduced-fat shredded Swiss cheese

1. Heat an 8-inch nonstick skillet over medium-high heat; coat pan with cooking spray. Add asparagus, and sauté 3 minutes; set aside.
2. Combine eggs and next 4 ingredients in a medium bowl; stirring with a whisk until blended.
3. Wipe pan with paper towels. Heat pan over medium heat; recoat pan with cooking spray. Add egg mixture, and cook 3 minutes or until set (do not stir). Sprinkle with asparagus, basil, and cheese. Loosen omelet with a spatula; fold in half. Cook 1 to 2 minutes or until cheese melts. Slide omelet onto a plate. Cut in half. **Yield:** 2 servings (serving size: 1/2 omelet).

CALORIES 203; FAT 7.7g (sat 2.6g, mono 3.2g, poly 1.9g); PROTEIN 24.1g; CARB 6.7g; FIBER 2.1g; CHOL 191mg; IRON 4.5mg; SODIUM 548mg; CALC 360mg

Asparagus and
Basil Omelet

When slicing onions, start at the end opposite the root. Slice the top off the onion, leaving the root intact. Remove the papery skin, and slice the onion vertically. Continue cutting the onion vertically into thin slices.

Onion and Fresh Herb Omelet with Mixed Greens

make it a meal *Add whole fresh strawberries and whole wheat toast for an easy weekend brunch or light supper during the week.*

Omelet:
½ cup egg substitute
¼ cup fat-free milk
1½ teaspoons minced fresh parsley
½ teaspoon minced fresh thyme
¼ teaspoon salt
⅛ teaspoon freshly ground black pepper
1 large egg
1.1 ounces all-purpose flour (about ¼ cup)
Cooking spray
2 cups vertically sliced onion
1 garlic clove, crushed

Salad:
3 cups loosely packed gourmet salad greens
1½ teaspoons red wine vinegar
1 teaspoon extra-virgin olive oil
2 tablespoons crumbled goat cheese
1½ teaspoons sliced almonds, toasted

1. To prepare omelet, combine first 7 ingredients in a small bowl, stirring with a whisk. Lightly spoon flour into a dry measuring cup; level with a knife. Add flour to egg mixture; stir well.
2. Heat a large nonstick skillet over medium-high heat. Coat pan with cooking spray. Add onion to pan; sauté 7 minutes or until browned. Add garlic; sauté 1 minute. Pour egg mixture over onion mixture in pan. Reduce heat, and cook 3 minutes or until set. Loosen omelet with a spatula, and fold in half; cook 1 minute. Cut omelet in half; place one half on each of 2 plates.
3. To prepare salad, combine salad greens, vinegar, and oil; toss well. Arrange 1½ cups greens on top of each serving; top each serving with 1 tablespoon cheese and ¾ teaspoon almonds. **Yield:** 2 servings.

CALORIES 291; FAT 9.8g (sat 2.7g, mono 4.3g, poly 2g); PROTEIN 18g; CARB 33.8g; FIBER 4.7g; CHOL 110mg; IRON 4.2mg; SODIUM 507mg; CALC 189mg

Omelet with Summer Vegetables

make it a meal *This satisfying entrée for one is good for any meal, from breakfast to dinner. Serve with fruit salad.*

Cooking spray
²/₃ cup frozen whole-kernel corn, thawed
½ cup chopped zucchini
3 tablespoons chopped green onions
¼ teaspoon salt, divided
2 tablespoons water
¼ teaspoon black pepper
3 large egg whites
1 large egg
2 tablespoons shredded smoked Gouda cheese

1. Heat a small saucepan over medium-high heat. Coat pan with cooking spray. Add corn, zucchini, onions, and ⅛ teaspoon salt to pan; sauté 4 minutes or until vegetables are crisp-tender. Remove from heat.
2. Heat a 10-inch nonstick skillet over medium-high heat. Combine ⅛ teaspoon salt, water, pepper, egg whites, and egg, stirring well with a whisk. Coat pan with cooking spray. Pour egg mixture into pan; cook until edges begin to set (about 2 minutes). Gently lift edges of omelet with a spatula, tilting pan to allow uncooked egg mixture to come in contact with pan. Spoon corn mixture onto half of omelet; sprinkle corn mixture with cheese. Loosen omelet with a spatula, and fold in half over corn mixture. Cook 2 minutes or until cheese melts. Carefully slide omelet onto a plate.
Yield: 1 serving (serving size: 1 omelet).

CALORIES 281; FAT 10.3g (sat 4.3g, mono 3.4g, poly 1.4g); PROTEIN 24.8g; CARB 25.3g; FIBER 4.2g; CHOL 229mg; IRON 2.1mg; SODIUM 947mg; CALC 162mg

15 MINUTES

Sun-Dried Tomato Omelet

Choose ready-to-use sun-dried tomatoes from the produce section of your grocery store. They are more pliable than the dry kind that require rehydration.

8   large egg whites
2   large eggs
Butter-flavored cooking spray
1/3 cup sun-dried tomatoes, packed without oil,
     chopped
3   tablespoons chopped fresh basil
1/2 cup (2 ounces) shredded part-skim
     mozzarella cheese

1. Heat a medium nonstick skillet over medium heat. Combine egg whites and eggs, stirring with a whisk until foamy.
2. Coat pan with cooking spray; pour egg mixture into pan. Cook 2 minutes or until edges begin to set. Slide front edge of a spatula between edge of omelet and pan. Gently lift edge of omelet, tilting pan to allow some uncooked egg mixture to come in contact with pan. Repeat procedure on opposite edge of omelet. Cook 3 minutes or until center is almost set.
3. Sprinkle tomatoes, basil, and cheese over omelet. Loosen omelet with a spatula; fold in half. Reduce heat to low; cover and cook 1 minute. Carefully turn omelet over; cook 1 minute or until cheese melts. Gently slide omelet onto a serving platter. Cut omelet in half, and serve immediately. **Yield:** 2 servings (serving size: 1/2 omelet).

CALORIES 288; FAT 13.9g (sat 5.5g, mono 6.2g, poly 2.1g); PROTEIN 29.4g;
CARB 9.6g; FIBER 1.6g; CHOL 195mg; IRON 2mg; SODIUM 510mg; CALC 259mg

30 MINUTES

Frittata with Mushrooms, Linguine, and Basil

Cooking spray
3   cups sliced cremini mushrooms
1 1/4 cups thinly sliced leek (about 2 large)
1/2 cup 1% low-fat milk
2   teaspoons butter, melted
3/4 teaspoon salt
1/8 teaspoon freshly ground black pepper
4   large egg whites
3   large eggs
2   cups hot cooked linguine (about 4 ounces
     uncooked pasta)
1/3 cup chopped fresh basil
1/2 cup (2 ounces) shredded part-skim
     mozzarella cheese

1. Preheat oven to 450°.
2. Heat a large nonstick skillet over medium heat. Coat pan with cooking spray. Add mushrooms and leek; cook 6 minutes or until leek is tender, stirring frequently.
3. Combine milk and next 5 ingredients in a large bowl, stirring with a whisk. Add leek mixture, pasta, and basil; toss gently to combine.
4. Heat pan over medium-low heat. Coat pan with cooking spray. Add egg mixture; cook until edges begin to set (about 4 minutes). Gently lift edge of egg mixture, tilting pan to allow some uncooked egg mixture to come in contact with pan. Cook 5 minutes or until almost set. Sprinkle evenly with cheese; wrap handle of pan with foil. Bake at 450° for 7 minutes or until golden brown. Cut into 8 wedges. **Yield:** 4 servings (serving size: 2 wedges).

CALORIES 269; FAT 8.8g (sat 4.1g, mono 2.8g, poly 0.9g); PROTEIN 18.4g;
CARB 28g; FIBER 2.8g; CHOL 174mg; IRON 2.6mg; SODIUM 661mg; CALC 177mg

15 MINUTES

Roasted Red Bell Pepper and Goat Cheese Frittata

2   large eggs
4   large egg whites
2   tablespoons chopped fresh chives
½   teaspoon salt, divided
½   teaspoon freshly ground black pepper, divided
4   teaspoons olive oil
1   cup chopped bottled roasted red bell peppers
4   green onions, chopped
1   teaspoon bottled minced garlic or 2 garlic cloves, minced
½   cup (2 ounces) crumbled goat cheese

1. Preheat broiler.
2. Combine eggs, egg whites, chives, ¼ teaspoon salt, and ¼ teaspoon black pepper in a bowl, stirring with a whisk.
3. Heat oil in an ovenproof skillet over medium heat. Add red bell peppers, onions, garlic, ¼ teaspoon salt, and ¼ teaspoon black pepper; sauté 2 minutes. Pour egg mixture over vegetables. As mixture starts to cook, gently lift edges of frittata with a spatula, and tilt pan so uncooked portion flows underneath. Cook 2 minutes; remove from heat.
4. Sprinkle cheese over frittata. Broil 2 minutes or until frittata is set and lightly browned. Cut into 4 wedges. **Yield:** 4 servings (serving size: 1 wedge).

CALORIES 146; FAT 9.6g (sat 3.3g, mono 5.2g, poly 1g); PROTEIN 9.9g; CARB 4.1g; FIBER 0.5g; CHOL 97mg; IRON 1mg; SODIUM 541mg; CALC 51mg

MAKE IT FASTER

Instead of taking the time to mince 2 garlic cloves, substitute bottled minced garlic. One teaspoon bottled minced garlic is the equivalent of 2 minced cloves.

30 MINUTES

Shiitake and Butternut Squash Frittata

Sweet butternut squash and savory Gruyère cheese provide a satisfying balance to this easy and light main course. Look for prechopped squash in your grocer's produce section.

1¼   cups prechopped peeled butternut squash, cut into ½-inch pieces
Cooking spray
2   cups sliced shiitake mushrooms caps (about 7 ounces)
4   large egg whites
4   large eggs
¼   teaspoon salt
¼   teaspoon freshly ground black pepper
½   cup (2 ounces) shredded Gruyère cheese

1. Place squash in a medium saucepan; cover with hot water. Bring to a boil; cover and cook 4 minutes or until tender. Drain well and set aside.
2. While squash cooks, heat a medium ovenproof skillet over medium-high heat. Coat pan with cooking spray. Add mushrooms; sauté 4 minutes or until lightly browned.
3. Preheat broiler. Combine egg whites and next 3 ingredients; stir with a whisk. Stir in cheese.
4. Add egg mixture and butternut squash to mushrooms in skillet. Cover and cook 5 minutes or until almost set. Broil frittata 5 minutes or until set and browned. Cut into wedges. **Yield:** 3 servings (serving size: 2 wedges).

CALORIES 271; FAT 11.6g (sat 5.2g, mono 4.9g, poly 1.4g); PROTEIN 21.2g; CARB 17.7g; FIBER 2.8g; CHOL 261mg; IRON 3.1mg; SODIUM 443mg; CALC 278mg

20 MINUTES

Vegetable and Cheddar Frittata

Similar to a French omelet, a frittata is the Italian version that resembles a crustless quiche. However, a frittata differs from an omelet in that it's finished under a broiler, cut into wedges, and left unfolded during the cooking process.

2 tablespoons chopped fresh cilantro or parsley
½ teaspoon salt, divided
¼ teaspoon pepper
4 large egg whites
3 large eggs
Cooking spray
1 cup frozen whole-kernel corn, thawed
½ cup thinly sliced green onions
16 grape or cherry tomatoes, halved
½ cup (2 ounces) shredded reduced-fat sharp cheddar cheese, divided
Chopped fresh cilantro (optional)

1. Preheat broiler.

2. Combine cilantro, ¼ teaspoon salt, and next 3 ingredients in a bowl; stir well with a whisk.

3. Heat a medium nonstick skillet over medium heat. Coat pan with cooking spray. Add corn; sauté 1 minute. Add green onions and tomato halves; sauté 1 minute. Sprinkle with remaining ¼ teaspoon salt and 6 tablespoons cheese. Pour egg mixture over tomato mixture; cook 3 minutes or until egg mixture is almost set. Tilt skillet and carefully loosen edges of frittata with a spatula; allow uncooked portion to flow underneath cooked portion. Wrap handle of skillet with foil; broil 2 minutes or until egg mixture is set. Sprinkle with remaining 2 tablespoons cheese. Cut into 4 wedges. Garnish with cilantro, if desired. **Yield:** 4 servings (serving size: 1 wedge).

CALORIES 173; FAT 6.9g (sat 3.1g, mono 2.7g, poly 0.9g); PROTEIN 14.3g; CARB 15.1g; FIBER 2.3g; CHOL 146mg; IRON 1.5mg; SODIUM 409mg; CALC 145mg

30 MINUTES

Tempeh Coconut Curry

This is a traditional southeast Asian preparation for tempeh—highly flavored with warm and hot spices, and seasoned with tangy tamarind. Begin cooking the rice before you start the curry so you can be finished in 30 minutes. Otherwise, it might take a little longer.

Curry:

1	tablespoon canola oil
2	cups finely chopped onion
1	teaspoon salt, divided
2	teaspoons tamarind pulp
1	tablespoon finely chopped peeled fresh ginger
1	tablespoon finely chopped fresh garlic
1½	teaspoons ground coriander
½	teaspoon ground turmeric
½	teaspoon crushed red pepper
1	(3-inch) cinnamon stick
3	cups chopped peeled sweet potato (about 1 pound)
1	cup water
1	(13.5-ounce) can light coconut milk
8	ounces organic tempeh, cut into ¾-inch cubes
1	tablespoon fresh lime juice
2	teaspoons low-sodium soy sauce

Rice:

1½	cups uncooked basmati rice
⅓	cup chopped fresh cilantro
¼	teaspoon salt

1. To prepare curry, heat oil in a large non-stick skillet over medium-high heat. Add onion and ½ teaspoon salt. Cook 2 minutes or until onion is tender, stirring occasionally. Stir in tamarind; cook 2 minutes, stirring to break up tamarind. Add ginger and next 5 ingredients; cook 2 minutes, stirring frequently. Add remaining ½ teaspoon salt, potato, water, milk, and tempeh; bring to a boil. Cover, reduce heat, and simmer 15 minutes or until potatoes are tender. Uncover; stir in juice and soy sauce. Simmer 3 minutes or until slightly thickened. Discard cinnamon stick.

2. To prepare rice, cook rice according to package instructions, omitting salt and fat. Stir in cilantro and ¼ teaspoon salt. Serve with curry. **Yield:** 4 servings (serving size: 1 cup curry and about 1 cup rice).

CALORIES 381; FAT 11.5g (sat 5.5g, mono 3.2g, poly 2.2g); PROTEIN 16.9g; CARB 53.7g; FIBER 6.3g; CHOL 0mg; IRON 2.9mg; SODIUM 870mg; CALC 112mg

INGREDIENT SPOTLIGHT

Tempeh is made from partly cooked soybeans inoculated with spores of a friendly mold. Good grilled, sautéed, pan-crisped, or braised, tempeh is sold in Asian markets, natural-foods stores, and in some large supermarkets.

20 MINUTES

Vegetarian Enchiladas

make it a meal *You'll love the extra kick the spicy refried beans give to the enchiladas. Serve with a side salad and a light Mexican beer.*

¾   cup fat-free spicy refried beans
4   (8-inch) flour tortillas
1   cup frozen meatless burger crumbles (such as Morningstar Farms)
¾   cup enchilada sauce
½   cup (2 ounces) reduced-fat shredded sharp cheddar cheese
Chopped green onions (optional)

1. Preheat oven to 400°.
2. Spread 3 tablespoons beans over each tortilla, leaving a ¾-inch border around edges. Sprinkle ¼ cup burger crumbles down center of each tortilla; roll up tortillas. Arrange tortillas, seam sides down, in an 8-inch square baking dish. Pour enchilada sauce over tortillas; sprinkle with cheese.
3. Bake at 400° for 15 minutes or until bubbly and cheese is melted. Top with onions, if desired. **Yield:** 4 servings (serving size: 1 enchilada).

CALORIES 258; FAT 5.2g (sat 2.2g, mono 1.1g, poly 1.8g); PROTEIN 17g; CARB 39.7g; FIBER 7.3g; CHOL 8mg; IRON 3.6mg; SODIUM 849mg; CALC 260mg

Vegetarian Enchiladas

20 MINUTES

Vegetarian Chipotle Nachos

The spicy bean mixture also makes a good filling for tacos and burritos. Look for meatless crumbles near the tofu and other soy products in the produce section.

Cooking spray
1   cup chopped green bell pepper (about 1 medium)
1   cup chopped onion (about 1 medium)
1   (12-ounce) package meatless fat-free crumbles (such as Lightlife Smart Ground)
1   (7-ounce) can chipotle chiles in adobo sauce
1   (15-ounce) can pinto beans, rinsed and drained
1   (14.5-ounce) can diced tomatoes with basil, garlic, and oregano, undrained
¼   cup chopped fresh cilantro
8   cups baked corn tortilla chips (6 ounces)
2   cups shredded romaine lettuce
1   cup diced peeled avocado (about 1 medium)
¾   cup vertically sliced red onion
¾   cup (3 ounces) shredded sharp cheddar cheese
6   tablespoons fat-free sour cream

1. Heat a large nonstick skillet over medium heat. Coat pan with cooking spray. Add bell pepper, chopped onion, and crumbles; cook 5 minutes, stirring occasionally.
2. Remove 1 chile and 1 tablespoon sauce from can; reserve remaining chiles and sauce for another use. Chop chile; add chile, sauce, beans, and tomatoes to pan. Cover, reduce heat, and simmer 5 minutes. Remove from heat; stir in cilantro.
3. Arrange 1⅓ cups chips on each of 6 plates. Top each serving with 1 cup bean mixture, ⅓ cup lettuce, about 2½ tablespoons avocado, 2 tablespoons onion, 2 tablespoons cheese, and 1 tablespoon sour cream. **Yield:** 6 servings.

CALORIES 408; FAT 11.8g (sat 4g, mono 4.2g, poly 2.5g); PROTEIN 23.8g; CARB 53.7g; FIBER 11g; CHOL 16mg; IRON 3.6mg; SODIUM 906mg; CALC 316mg

Seared Tofu with Gingered Vegetables

Seared Tofu with Gingered Vegetables

1   pound reduced-fat extra-firm tofu
1   (3½-ounce) bag boil-in-bag long-grain rice
¾   teaspoon salt, divided
1   tablespoon dark sesame oil, divided
1   tablespoon bottled minced garlic
1   tablespoon bottled ground fresh ginger
     (such as Spice World)
1   large red bell pepper, thinly sliced
1   cup sliced green onions, divided
2   tablespoons rice vinegar
1   tablespoon low-sodium soy sauce
Cooking spray
¼   teaspoon freshly ground black pepper
1   tablespoon sesame seeds, toasted
1   cup radish sprouts

1. Place tofu on several layers of paper towels; let stand 10 minutes. Cut tofu into 1-inch cubes.
2. Prepare rice according to package directions, omitting salt and fat. Add ¼ teaspoon salt to rice; fluff with a fork.
3. Heat 2 teaspoons oil in a large nonstick skillet over medium-high heat. Add garlic, ginger, and bell pepper to pan; sauté 3 minutes. Stir in ¾ cup onions, vinegar, and soy sauce; cook 30 seconds. Remove from pan. Wipe skillet with paper towels; coat pan with cooking spray.
4. Place pan over medium-high heat. Sprinkle tofu with remaining ½ teaspoon salt and black pepper. Add tofu to pan; cook 8 minutes or until golden, turning to brown on all sides. Return bell pepper mixture to pan, and cook 1 minute or until thoroughly heated. Drizzle tofu mixture with remaining 1 teaspoon oil; top with sesame seeds. Serve tofu mixture with rice; top with sprouts and remaining ¼ cup onions. **Yield:** 4 servings (serving size: about ¼ cup rice, 1 cup tofu mixture, ¼ cup sprouts, and 1 tablespoon onions).

CALORIES 325; FAT 10.2g (sat 2.6g, mono 2.7g, poly 4.6g); PROTEIN 28.2g; CARB 41.6g; FIBER 6.2g; CHOL 0mg; IRON 7.6mg; SODIUM 603mg; CALC 96mg

Vegetarian Soft Tacos

Our vegetarian recipe gets its "meatiness" from soy-based burger crumbles and its fresh, spicy flavor from refrigerated salsa.

2   cups frozen meatless burger crumbles (such as Morningstar Farms)
1   cup refrigerated fresh chunky salsa
8   (6-inch) flour tortillas
½   cup (2 ounces) reduced-fat shredded sharp cheddar cheese
1   (14.5-ounce) can diced tomatoes, drained
1½   cups shredded iceberg lettuce

1. Combine meatless burger crumbles and salsa in a nonstick skillet, and cook over medium heat 4 minutes or until thoroughly heated, stirring occasionally.
2. Spoon 2 tablespoons burger crumble mixture onto each tortilla; top each with 1 tablespoon cheese, about 2 tablespoons tomato, and 3 tablespoons lettuce. **Yield:** 8 servings (serving size: 1 taco).

CALORIES 156; FAT 4.1g (sat 1.5g, mono 1.7g, poly 0.7g); PROTEIN 11g; CARB 21.5g; FIBER 3g; CHOL 4mg; IRON 1.3mg; SODIUM 560mg; CALC 119mg

MINUTES

Stir-Fried Moo Shu Vegetable Wraps

1   tablespoon low-sodium soy sauce
8   ounces reduced-fat firm tofu, drained and cut into ³/₄-inch cubes
2   cups sliced shiitake mushroom caps (about 8 ounces mushrooms)
2   cups packaged broccoli coleslaw (such as River Ranch)
1   cup red bell pepper, cut into ¹/₄-inch strips
¹/₂   cup (¹/₂-inch) diagonally cut green onions
1   tablespoon bottled minced garlic
1   teaspoon bottled ground fresh ginger (such as Spice World)
2   teaspoons dark sesame oil
2   tablespoons hoisin sauce
¹/₄   teaspoon crushed red pepper
8   (7-inch) flour tortillas
¹/₄   cup plum sauce

1. Combine soy sauce and tofu in a small bowl. Combine mushrooms and next 5 ingredients in a medium bowl.
2. Heat oil in a large nonstick skillet over medium-high heat. Add vegetables; stir-fry 3 minutes. Add tofu; stir-fry 1 minute. Stir in hoisin sauce and crushed red pepper; stir-fry 1 minute or until vegetables are crisp-tender.
3. Stack tortillas; wrap in damp paper towels, and microwave at HIGH 25 seconds. Spread 1¹/₂ teaspoons plum sauce over each tortilla. Top each tortilla with about ¹/₃ cup tofu mixture; roll up. **Yield:** 4 servings (serving size: 2 tortillas).

CALORIES 455; FAT 10.4g (sat 2.2g, mono 4.8g, poly 2.6g); PROTEIN 16g; CARB 73.7g; FIBER 7.1g; CHOL 0mg; IRON 5.6mg; SODIUM 877mg; CALC 97mg

15 MINUTES

Sweet Hot Tofu

Replace the chicken broth with vegetable broth, if you desire. However, we prefer the flavor offered by the chicken broth.

1	(3½-ounce) bag boil-in-bag long-grain rice
2	teaspoons canola oil
1	(14-ounce) package firm reduced-fat tofu, cut into (1-inch) cubes
⅔	cup fat-free, less-sodium chicken broth
¼	cup hoisin sauce
1	tablespoon sherry
1	teaspoon cornstarch
2	teaspoons low-sodium soy sauce
1	teaspoon honey
½	teaspoon dark sesame oil
Dash of crushed red pepper	
2	teaspoons bottled minced fresh ginger
2	teaspoons bottled minced garlic
⅓	cup thinly sliced green onions

1. Prepare rice according to package directions, omitting salt and fat.

2. Heat canola oil in a large nonstick skillet over medium-high heat. Add tofu, and sauté 5 minutes or until lightly browned. Remove from skillet.

3. Combine broth and next 7 ingredients, stirring well with a whisk.

4. Add ginger, garlic, and onions to pan; sauté 30 seconds. Stir in broth mixture; cook 1 minute or until thickened, stirring constantly. Add tofu to pan; cook 30 seconds, stirring gently to coat. Place rice on each of 4 plates; top each serving with tofu mixture. **Yield:** 4 servings (serving size: about ½ cup rice and about ½ cup tofu mixture).

CALORIES 275; FAT 7.9g (sat 1g, mono 2.8g, poly 3.9g); PROTEIN 14.1g; CARB 36.1g; FIBER 3.2g; CHOL 0.5mg; IRON 2.6mg; SODIUM 425mg; CALC 55mg

MINUTES

Tofu Fried Rice

Using frozen peas and carrots plus bottled minced garlic and ginger speeds up preparation of this simple Chinese standby. Keep any leftover sake tightly capped in the refrigerator for up to three weeks, or you can substitute a tablespoon of rice wine vinegar for the sake.

2 cups uncooked instant rice
2 tablespoons vegetable oil, divided
1 (14-ounce) package reduced-fat firm tofu, drained and cut into (½-inch) cubes
2 large eggs, lightly beaten
1 cup (½-inch-thick) slices green onions
1 cup frozen peas and carrots, thawed
2 teaspoons bottled minced garlic
1 teaspoon bottled minced fresh ginger
2 tablespoons sake (rice wine)
3 tablespoons low-sodium soy sauce
1 tablespoon hoisin sauce
½ teaspoon dark sesame oil
Thinly sliced green onions (optional)

1. Cook rice according to package directions, omitting salt and fat.
2. While rice cooks, heat 1 tablespoon vegetable oil in a large nonstick skillet over medium-high heat. Add tofu; cook 4 minutes or until lightly browned, stirring occasionally. Remove from pan. Add eggs to pan; cook 1 minute or until done, breaking egg into small pieces. Remove from pan. Add 1 tablespoon vegetable oil to pan. Add 1 cup onions, peas and carrots, garlic, and ginger; sauté 2 minutes.
3. While vegetable mixture cooks, combine sake, soy sauce, hoisin sauce, and sesame oil. Add cooked rice to pan; cook 2 minutes, stirring constantly. Add tofu, egg, and soy sauce mixture; cook 30 seconds, stirring constantly. Garnish with sliced green onions, if desired. **Yield:** 4 servings (serving size: 1½ cups).

CALORIES 376; FAT 11g (sat 2g, mono 3g, poly 5.1g); PROTEIN 15.8g; CARB 50.6g; FIBER 3.2g; CHOL 106mg; IRON 3.8mg; SODIUM 629mg; CALC 79mg

MINUTES

Curried Tofu

make it a meal *If you prefer more spice ramp up the curry powder and crushed red pepper. Serve this colorful dish with white rice or rice noodles and fresh orange slices.*

2 teaspoons vegetable oil
1 (15-ounce) package reduced-fat firm tofu, drained and cut into ½-inch cubes
½ teaspoon salt
½ cup light coconut milk
1 teaspoon curry powder
1 cup precut matchstick-cut carrots
¼ teaspoon crushed red pepper
1 (15¼-ounce) can pineapple chunks in juice, drained
1 medium red bell pepper, thinly sliced
½ cup chopped fresh basil

1. Heat oil in a large nonstick skillet over medium-high heat. Add tofu, and sprinkle with salt. Cook 8 minutes or until golden brown, stirring frequently. Remove from pan; keep warm.
2. Add coconut milk and curry powder to pan, and cook 1 minute, stirring constantly. Add carrots, crushed red pepper, pineapple, and bell pepper; cook 5 minutes, stirring occasionally. Stir in tofu. Sprinkle with basil. **Yield:** 3 servings (serving size: about 1⅓ cups).

CALORIES 171; FAT 6.4g (sat 2g, mono 0.9g, poly 2.4g); PROTEIN 8.9g; CARB 21.7g; FIBER 3.6g; CHOL 0mg; IRON 2.7mg; SODIUM 508mg; CALC 99mg

Tofu comes in five varieties—silken, soft, medium, firm, and extra-firm—and most tofu is packaged in water to keep it fresh. It's best to remove some of that water from the medium to extra-firm varieties before sautéing or stir-frying.

INGREDIENT SPOTLIGHT

Cover and cook 4 minutes or until crisp-tender, stirring occasionally. Uncover; add soy sauce mixture and tofu, stirring gently to coat. Cook 2 minutes or until sauce thickens, stirring occasionally. Serve broccoli mixture over rice. **Yield:** 4 servings (serving size: 1 cup stir-fry and ¹/₂ cup rice).

CALORIES 451; FAT 8.3g (sat 1.4g, mono 2.6g, poly 3.8g); PROTEIN 16.2g; CARB 78g; FIBER 4.4g; CHOL 0mg; IRON 2.8mg; SODIUM 581mg; CALC 87mg

MINUTES

Soba Noodle Salad with Vegetables and Tofu

If you're short on time, substitute bagged sliced cabbage or coleslaw mix for the napa cabbage.

Dressing:

¹/₂	cup low-sodium soy sauce
¹/₄	cup packed brown sugar
1	tablespoon sesame seeds, toasted
2	tablespoons orange juice
1	tablespoon bottled minced or minced peeled fresh ginger
1	tablespoon rice vinegar
2	teaspoons dark sesame oil
1	teaspoon bottled minced garlic
1	teaspoon chile paste with garlic

Salad:

4	cups hot cooked soba (about 8 ounces uncooked buckwheat noodles) or whole wheat spaghetti
3	cups very thinly sliced napa (Chinese) cabbage
2	cups fresh bean sprouts
1	cup shredded carrot
¹/₂	cup chopped fresh cilantro
1	(12.3-ounce) package firm tofu, drained and cut into 1-inch cubes

1. To prepare dressing, combine first 9 ingredients in a small bowl; stir with a whisk.
2. To prepare salad, combine noodles and remaining ingredients in a large bowl. Drizzle with dressing, tossing well to coat. **Yield:** 5 servings (serving size: 2 cups).

CALORIES 336; FAT 7g (sat 1g, mono 1.8g, poly 3g); PROTEIN 15.1g; CARB 53.8g; FIBER 2.8g; CHOL 0mg; IRON 6.6mg; SODIUM 850mg; CALC 169mg

MINUTES

Broccoli-Tofu Stir-Fry

This simple meatless stir-fry has a subtle yet addictive sauce. To cut preparation time, use precut broccoli florets. They're near the salad greens in supermarkets.

1	(3¹/₂-ounce) bag boil-in-bag brown rice
2	tablespoons low-sodium soy sauce
2	tablespoons oyster sauce
2¹/₂	teaspoons cornstarch
2	teaspoons rice vinegar
2	teaspoons dark sesame oil
2	teaspoons vegetable oil
1	pound firm tofu, drained and cut into ¹/₂-inch cubes
¹/₄	teaspoon salt
2	cups broccoli florets
³/₄	cup water
1¹/₂	tablespoons bottled minced garlic

1. Cook rice according to package directions.
2. While rice cooks, combine soy sauce and next 4 ingredients in a small bowl, stirring with a whisk; set aside.
3. Heat vegetable oil in a large nonstick skillet over medium-high heat. Add tofu, and sprinkle with salt. Cook 8 minutes or until golden brown, tossing frequently. Remove tofu from pan, and keep warm. Add broccoli, water, and garlic to pan.

Rice Noodles with Tofu and Bok Choy

1   (6-ounce) package rice noodles
¼   cup low-sodium soy sauce
2   tablespoons rice vinegar
1   teaspoon sugar
1   teaspoon dark sesame oil
½   teaspoon crushed red pepper
Cooking spray
2   cups (¼-inch) red bell pepper strips
5   cups sliced bok choy
½   pound firm water-packed tofu, drained and
      cut into ½-inch cubes
3   garlic cloves, minced
½   cup thinly sliced green onions
3   tablespoons chopped fresh cilantro

1. Cook noodles in boiling water 6 minutes; drain. Combine soy sauce, vinegar, sugar, oil, and crushed red pepper, stirring well with a whisk.

2. Heat a large nonstick skillet over medium-high heat; coat pan with cooking spray. Add bell pepper strips; sauté 2 minutes. Add bok choy; sauté 1 minute. Add tofu and garlic; sauté 2 minutes. Add noodles and soy sauce mixture, and cook 2 minutes or until thoroughly heated, tossing well to coat. Sprinkle with green onions and cilantro. **Yield:** 4 servings (serving size: 2 cups).

CALORIES 281; FAT 5.2g (sat 0.8g, mono 0.9g, poly 2.3g); PROTEIN 12.9g;
CARB 46.7g; FIBER 4.2g; CHOL 0mg; IRON 3.8mg; SODIUM 575mg; CALC 190mg

Bok choy is a member of the cabbage family. It has thick white stalks with rounded dark leaves. Small heads, known as baby bok choy, are more tender than the large ones.

INGREDIENT SPOTLIGHT

MINUTES

Pad Thai with Tofu

This amazing pad thai dish rivals any Thai restaurant's menu offering. Even non-vegetarians will find it supremely flavorful and satisfying.

Sauce:

¼ cup low-sodium soy sauce
2 tablespoons rice vinegar
1 to 2 tablespoons hot sauce
1 tablespoon mirin (sweet rice wine)
1 tablespoon maple syrup

Noodles:

1 teaspoon vegetable oil
2 cups thinly sliced shiitake mushroom caps (about 5 ounces)
1 cup grated carrot
1 garlic clove, minced
8 ounces extra-firm tofu, drained and cut into ½-inch cubes
1 cup light coconut milk
2 cups shredded romaine lettuce
1 cup fresh bean sprouts
1 cup (1-inch) sliced green onion tops
1 cup chopped fresh cilantro
⅓ cup dry-roasted peanuts
8 ounces uncooked wide rice stick noodles (Banh Pho), cooked and drained
5 lime wedges

1. To prepare sauce, combine first 5 ingredients, stirring with a whisk.

2. To prepare noodles, heat oil in a large nonstick skillet over medium-high heat. Add mushrooms, carrot, and garlic; sauté 2 minutes. Add sauce and tofu; cook 1 minute. Stir in coconut milk; cook 2 minutes. Stir in lettuce and next 5 ingredients; cook 1 minute. Serve with lime wedges. **Yield:** 5 servings (serving size: 2 cups).

CALORIES 385; FAT 12.5g (sat 3g, mono 4g, poly 4.2g); PROTEIN 13.5g; CARB 55.8g; FIBER 4.6g; CHOL 0mg; IRON 7.1mg; SODIUM 868mg; CALC 365mg

MINUTES

Soy-Glazed Tofu

Added sodium and sugar tame seasoned rice vinegar's tartness, making a nice counterpoint to sesame oil, sweet orange juice, and aromatic orange rind. Drizzle the tofu with the flavorful pan sauce to serve; the sauce bolsters plain rice noodles tossed with snow peas, carrots, and bell pepper for a smart entrée.

1 (12-ounce) package firm tofu, drained and cut crosswise into 6 slices
3 tablespoons seasoned rice vinegar
2 tablespoons fresh orange juice
2 tablespoons low-sodium soy sauce
1 tablespoon brown sugar
¼ teaspoon grated orange rind
1 teaspoon dark sesame oil
2 tablespoons thinly diagonally sliced green onions
½ teaspoon sesame seeds, toasted

1. Cut each slice of tofu in half diagonally. Place tofu slices on several layers of paper towels, and cover tofu with additional paper towels; let stand 15 minutes, pressing down occasionally.

2. Combine vinegar and next 4 ingredients in a small saucepan; bring to a boil. Reduce heat and simmer, uncovered, 6 minutes or until thick and syrupy. Heat oil in a large nonstick skillet over medium-high heat. Arrange tofu slices in pan in a single layer; sauté 5 minutes on each side or until golden brown. Remove from heat; pour vinegar mixture over tofu to coat. Sprinkle with green onions and sesame seeds. Serve immediately. **Yield:** 4 servings (serving size: 3 triangles).

CALORIES 132; FAT 6.5g (sat 1.2g, mono 1.5g, poly 3.6g); PROTEIN 8.9g; CARB 9.2g; FIBER 0.1g; CHOL 0mg; IRON 1.8mg; SODIUM 419mg; CALC 68mg

MEATS

Shepherd's Pie

Superfast Kofte

Kofte, Turkish meatballs often grilled on a stick, can be made from ground lamb, beef, or a combination of both.

1/2 cup prechopped white onion
1/3 cup dry breadcrumbs
1/4 cup chopped fresh mint
2 tablespoons tomato paste
1 teaspoon bottled minced garlic
1/2 teaspoon salt
1/2 teaspoon ground cumin
1/4 teaspoon ground cinnamon
1/4 teaspoon ground red pepper
1/8 teaspoon ground allspice
1 pound lean ground round
1 large egg white, lightly beaten
Cooking spray
8 (1/4-inch-thick) slices plum tomato (about 2 tomatoes)
4 (6-inch) pitas, split
1/4 cup plain yogurt

1. Preheat broiler.
2. Combine first 12 ingredients in a large bowl; stir until just combined. Divide mixture into 8 equal portions; shape each portion into a (2-inch) patty. Place patties on a jelly-roll pan coated with cooking spray. Broil 4 minutes on each side or until desired degree of doneness. Place 1 tomato slice and 1 patty in each pita half; top each half with 1 1/2 teaspoons yogurt. **Yield:** 4 servings (serving size: 2 filled pita halves).

CALORIES 423; FAT 11.4g (sat 4.3g, mono 4.3g, poly 0.9g); PROTEIN 31.6g;
CARB 46.7g; FIBER 3.2g; CHOL 75mg; IRON 4.3mg; SODIUM 766mg; CALC 114mg

Shepherd's Pie

2 cups prepared mashed potatoes (such as Simply Potatoes)
3/4 pound ground sirloin
3/4 cup picante sauce
1/3 cup water
1 tablespoon ground cumin
2 teaspoons sugar
1/8 teaspoon salt
1 (15-ounce) can kidney beans, rinsed and drained
1/2 cup (2 ounces) preshredded reduced-fat extrasharp cheddar cheese
Freshly ground black pepper (optional)

1. Prepare mashed potatoes according to package directions; keep warm.
2. Cook beef in a large nonstick skillet over medium-high heat until browned, stirring to crumble. Stir in picante sauce, water, cumin, sugar, salt, and beans; bring to a boil. Reduce heat; simmer until mixture thickens (about 5 minutes).
3. Remove from heat. Spoon potatoes over meat mixture; sprinkle with cheese. Cover; let stand 2 minutes or until cheese melts. Sprinkle with pepper, if desired. **Yield:** 4 servings (serving size: 1 cup).

CALORIES 279; FAT 6g (sat 2.2g, mono 2.2g, poly 0.5g); PROTEIN 25.7g;
CARB 30.5g; FIBER 8g; CHOL 48mg; IRON 2.2mg; SODIUM 699mg; CALC 88mg

Asian Beef and Noodle-Filled Lettuce Cups

See the shortcut spotlight on the opposite page to learn how kitchen shears can keep you from getting bogged down when preparing these noodle-filled cups.

3	ounces uncooked rice vermicelli
12	ounces ground sirloin
2	teaspoons bottled minced garlic
½	cup matchstick-cut carrots
½	cup chopped cucumber
⅓	cup chopped red bell pepper
⅓	cup prechopped onion
3	tablespoons chopped fresh mint
¼	cup fresh lime juice
2	teaspoons sugar
2	teaspoons low-sodium soy sauce
4	Boston lettuce leaves
¼	cup chopped dry-roasted peanuts

1. Cook pasta according to package directions, omitting salt and fat. Drain and rinse under cold water; drain.

2. Heat a large nonstick skillet over medium-high heat. Add beef to pan, and cook 3 minutes, stirring to crumble. Stir in garlic, and cook 2 minutes or until browned. Stir in noodles, carrots, and next 4 ingredients. Combine juice, sugar, and soy sauce in a small bowl, stirring until sugar dissolves. Add juice mixture to beef mixture; tossing gently to coat. Arrange 1 lettuce leaf on each of 4 plates; spoon 1¼ cups beef mixture into each leaf. Top each serving with 1 tablespoon peanuts. **Yield:** 4 servings (serving size: 1 stuffed lettuce leaf).

CALORIES 270; FAT 8.6g (sat 2.2g, mono 3.7g, poly 1.9g); PROTEIN 21.2g; CARB 27.8g; FIBER 2.6g; CHOL 45mg; IRON 2.8mg; SODIUM 234mg; CALC 37mg

20 MINUTES

Quick Barbecue Flank Steak

make it a meal *Make this dish a meal with coleslaw and Texas toast. For the toast, combine 1 tablespoon softened butter and 1 minced garlic clove and spread it on 4 (1½-ounce) slices toasted sourdough bread.*

1 cup barbecue sauce
¼ cup fresh lemon juice
1 tablespoon prepared mustard
1½ teaspoons celery seeds
¼ teaspoon hot sauce
2 garlic cloves, minced
1 (1-pound) flank steak, trimmed
Cooking spray

1. Preheat broiler.
2. Combine first 6 ingredients in a large bowl; add steak, turning to coat. Remove steak from sauce, reserving sauce mixture. Place steak on a broiler pan coated with cooking spray; broil 6 minutes on each side or until desired degree of doneness. Let stand 5 minutes. Cut steak diagonally across grain into thin slices.
3. While steak stands, bring sauce mixture to a boil in a saucepan over high heat. Reduce heat, and cook 5 minutes. Serve with steak. **Yield:** 4 servings (serving size: 3 ounces steak and ¼ cup sauce).

CALORIES 234; FAT 10.1g (sat 3.9g, mono 4.1g, poly 0.8g); PROTEIN 24.6g; CARB 10.4g; FIBER 1.1g; CHOL 57mg; IRON 3.2mg; SODIUM 625mg; CALC 38mg

20 MINUTES

Broiled Flank Steak with Warm Tomato Topping

make it a meal *Let the steak stand while you heat the topping. Fill out the meal with orzo, and garnish with fresh cilantro sprigs, if desired.*

1¼ teaspoons ground cumin, divided
¾ teaspoon salt, divided
⅛ teaspoon ground red pepper
1 (1-pound) flank steak, trimmed
Cooking spray
1 teaspoon olive oil
1 teaspoon bottled minced garlic
1 jalapeño pepper, seeded and minced (about 1 tablespoon)
2 cups grape or cherry tomatoes, halved
¼ cup chopped fresh cilantro

1. Preheat broiler.
2. Combine 1 teaspoon cumin, ½ teaspoon salt, and red pepper; sprinkle evenly over steak. Place steak on a broiler pan coated with cooking spray; broil 10 minutes or until desired degree of doneness, turning once. Cut steak diagonally across grain into thin slices.
3. Heat oil in a large nonstick skillet over medium heat. Add garlic and jalapeño to pan; cook 1 minute. Add remaining ¼ teaspoon cumin, remaining ¼ teaspoon salt, and tomatoes to pan; cook 3 minutes or until tomatoes begin to soften. Remove from heat; stir in cilantro. Serve tomato topping with steak. **Yield:** 4 servings (serving size: 3 ounces steak and about ⅓ cup topping).

CALORIES 194; FAT 7.9g (sat 2.5g, mono 3.1g, poly 0.5g); PROTEIN 25.3g; CARB 4.3g; FIBER 1.2g; CHOL 37mg; IRON 2.4mg; SODIUM 514mg; CALC 38mg

SHORTCUT SPOTLIGHT

Rice vermicelli is similar to angel hair and sometimes sticks together after it is cooked. Use a pair of kitchen shears to snip through the noodles a few times to make them easier to toss with the remaining ingredients.

20 MINUTES

Flank Steak with Cucumber-Pepperoncini Relish

make it a meal *Pepperoncini peppers are yellow, wrinkled, and slightly spicy; we use both the chopped pickled pepper and pickling liquid to flavor the crunchy relish. Serve with soft pita wedges and a simple dill-garlic yogurt dip.*

1   (1-pound) flank steak, trimmed
1   tablespoon bottled minced garlic
½   teaspoon salt
¼   teaspoon black pepper
Cooking spray
1   tablespoon pickled pepperoncini pepper pickling liquid
1   tablespoon extra-virgin olive oil
½   teaspoon Dijon mustard
1   pickled pepperoncini pepper, chopped
2   tablespoons chopped fresh flat-leaf parsley
2   tablespoons crumbled feta cheese
½   English cucumber, quartered lengthwise and sliced (about 1 cup)

1. Preheat broiler.
2. Sprinkle both sides of flank steak evenly with garlic, salt, and ¼ teaspoon black pepper. Place steak on a broiler pan coated with cooking spray; broil steak 5 minutes on each side or until desired degree of doneness. Place steak on a cutting board; cover and let stand 5 minutes. Uncover; cut steak diagonally across grain into thin slices.
3. Combine pepperoncini pickling liquid, olive oil, and mustard in a medium bowl, stirring well with a whisk. Add chopped pepperoncini pepper, parsley, cheese, and cucumber to oil mixture in bowl; toss well to combine. Serve steak with relish. **Yield:** 4 servings (serving size: 3 ounces steak and ¼ cup relish).

CALORIES 219; FAT 11.1g (sat 3.8g, mono 5.2g, poly 0.6g); PROTEIN 24.9g; CARB 2.4g; FIBER 0.6g; CHOL 46mg; IRON 1.7mg; SODIUM 459mg; CALC 43mg

Flank Steak with Cucumber-Pepperoncini Relish

30 MINUTES

Ponzu-Glazed Flank Steak

2   tablespoons fresh lemon juice
2   tablespoons fresh lime juice
2   tablespoons low-sodium soy sauce
1   tablespoon honey
2   teaspoons bottled ground fresh ginger (such as Spice World)
1   (1-pound) flank steak, trimmed

1. Preheat broiler.
2. Combine first 5 ingredients in a small saucepan over medium-high heat, and bring to a boil. Cook 3 minutes, and remove from heat.
3. Place steak on a foil-lined broiler pan. Brush half of soy mixture over steak; broil 5 minutes or until browned. Turn steak over, and brush with remaining soy mixture. Broil 5 minutes or until browned. Remove from oven; wrap foil around steak. Let stand 5 minutes before slicing. Serve steak with pan juices. **Yield:** 4 servings (serving size: 3 ounces steak and 1 tablespoon pan juices).

CALORIES 188; FAT 6.2g (sat 2.3g, mono 2.2g, poly 0.2g); PROTEIN 25.1g; CARB 7.1g; FIBER 0.3g; CHOL 37mg; IRON 2.1mg; SODIUM 330mg; CALC 31mg

COOKING CLASS: *how to cut flank steak*

Flank steak has a distinct, visible grain and should be cut across this grain into ¼-inch-thick slices for maximum tenderness. Tilting your knife diagonally and slicing away from you ensures the largest surface area possible for each piece.

30
MINUTES

Beef Saté with Peanut Dipping Sauce

Flank steak cooks quickly when thinly sliced. The dipping sauce is inspired by traditional Indonesian condiments that often accompany this dish.

1   (3½-ounce) bag boil-in-bag long-grain rice
1   (1-pound) flank steak, trimmed
2   tablespoons hoisin sauce
¼   teaspoon salt
Cooking spray
2   tablespoons chopped fresh cilantro
2   tablespoons light coconut milk
1   tablespoon low-sodium soy sauce
1½   tablespoons creamy peanut butter
1   teaspoon sugar
1   teaspoon fresh lime juice
½   teaspoon red curry paste

1. Preheat broiler.
2. Cook rice according to package directions, omitting salt and fat. Drain; cover and keep warm.
3. Cut steak diagonally across grain into ¼-inch-thick slices. Combine steak and hoisin in a bowl; toss to coat. Thread steak onto each of 8 (8-inch) skewers; sprinkle evenly with salt. Place skewers on a broiler pan coated with cooking spray; broil 3 minutes on each side or until desired degree of doneness. Sprinkle skewers with cilantro.
4. Combine coconut milk and remaining ingredients in a bowl, stirring until smooth. Serve with skewers and rice. **Yield:** 4 servings (serving size: 2 skewers, ½ cup rice, and about 1 tablespoon peanut sauce).

CALORIES 306; FAT 9.4g (sat 3.4g, mono 3.8g, poly 1.2g); PROTEIN 27.6g;
CARB 26.4g; FIBER 1g; CHOL 37mg; IRON 2.8mg; SODIUM 503mg; CALC 30mg

Beef Lettuce Wraps

30 MINUTES

Beef Lettuce Wraps

make it a meal *Fill crisp lettuce leaves with sliced flank steak topped with a zesty sauce made from lime juice, brown sugar, and minced pepper. A soba noodle salad complements the meaty wraps and brings another texture to the plate.*

Cooking spray
1 (1-pound) flank steak, trimmed
¼ teaspoon kosher salt
¼ teaspoon freshly ground black pepper
3 tablespoons fresh lime juice
2 tablespoons fish sauce
4 teaspoons dark brown sugar
1 jalapeño pepper, seeded and minced
8 Bibb lettuce leaves
1 cup thinly sliced red onion
1 cup torn fresh mint
½ cup matchstick-cut English cucumber
½ cup torn fresh cilantro
2 tablespoons chopped unsalted, dry-roasted peanuts

1. Heat a grill pan over medium-high heat. Coat pan with cooking spray. Sprinkle steak with salt and pepper. Place steak in pan; cook 5 minutes on each side or until desired degree of doneness. Remove from pan; let stand 10 minutes. Cut steak diagonally across grain into thin slices.
2. Combine juice, fish sauce, sugar, and jalapeño in a medium bowl, stirring with a whisk. Reserve 4 teaspoons juice mixture in a small serving bowl. Pour remaining juice mixture in a large bowl; add steak, tossing to coat. Place 1½ ounces beef in center of each lettuce leaf; top each with 2 tablespoons onion, 2 tablespoons mint, 1 tablespoon cucumber, and 1 tablespoon cilantro. Sprinkle evenly with peanuts; roll up. Serve with reserved juice mixture. **Yield:** 4 servings (serving size: 2 wraps and 1 teaspoon sauce).

CALORIES 224; FAT 8.1g (sat 2.7g, mono 3.4g, poly 1g); PROTEIN 27g; CARB 11.2g; FIBER 2g; CHOL 39mg; IRON 2.6mg; SODIUM 755mg; CALC 61mg

20 MINUTES

Asian Beef

make it a meal *Serve atop soba noodles or vermicelli to round out your meal.*

⅓ cup chopped green onions
2 tablespoons brown sugar
3 tablespoons low-sodium soy sauce
2 tablespoons rice wine vinegar
1 teaspoon toasted sesame oil
1 teaspoon bottled minced garlic
1 teaspoon bottled minced ginger (such as Spice World)
1 pound flank steak, trimmed
Cooking spray

1. Preheat broiler.
2. Combine first 7 ingredients in a small bowl, stirring with a whisk. Place steak on a broiler rack coated with cooking spray. Pour soy mixture over steak.
3. Broil steak 3 inches from heat 5 minutes on each side or until desired degree of doneness. Let stand 5 minutes; thinly slice across grain. **Yield:** 4 servings (serving size: 3 ounces beef).

CALORIES 190; FAT 7g (sat 2.4g, mono 2.5g, poly 0.5g); PROTEIN 24.8g; CARB 5.3g; FIBER 0.2g; CHOL 37mg; IRON 2mg; SODIUM 300mg; CALC 31mg

 MINUTES

Beef and Sugar Snap Stir-Fry

3	tablespoons rice vinegar, divided
2	tablespoons low-sodium soy sauce, divided
1	(1-pound) flank steak, trimmed and thinly sliced across grain
2	teaspoons sugar
2	teaspoons hoisin sauce
¼	teaspoon salt
¼	teaspoon crushed red pepper
2	teaspoons toasted sesame oil, divided
1	cup chopped onion
1	teaspoon bottled minced ginger
½	teaspoon minced garlic
1	cup chopped red bell pepper
½	cup matchstick-cut carrots
1	(8-ounce) package fresh sugar snap peas
⅓	cup chopped green onions

1. Combine 1 tablespoon vinegar, 1 tablespoon soy sauce, and beef in a large bowl. Combine remaining 2 tablespoons vinegar, remaining 1 tablespoon soy sauce, sugar, hoisin, salt, and crushed red pepper in a small bowl; stir with a whisk.

2. Heat a large nonstick skillet over medium-high heat. Add 1 teaspoon oil to pan; swirl to coat. Add beef mixture to pan; stir-fry 2 minutes or until done. Place beef mixture in a bowl. Heat remaining 1 teaspoon oil in pan over medium-high heat. Add onion to pan; sauté 1 minute. Add ginger and garlic; sauté 15 seconds. Stir in bell pepper, carrot, and peas; sauté 3 minutes. Add vinegar mixture and beef mixture to pan; cook 2 minutes or until thoroughly heated. Remove from heat; stir in green onions. **Yield:** 4 servings (serving size: 1½ cups).

CALORIES 254; FAT 8.2g (sat 2.7g, mono 2.2g, poly 0.4g); PROTEIN 26.6g; CARB 16.7g; FIBER 3.4g; CHOL 37mg; IRON 2.7mg; SODIUM 526mg; CALC 63mg

Hoisin Flank Steak with
Asian Cucumber Salad

20 MINUTES

Hoisin Flank Steak with Asian Cucumber Salad

3 tablespoons hoisin sauce
1 teaspoon bottled ground fresh ginger
½ teaspoon grated orange rind
1 (1-pound) flank steak, trimmed
Cooking spray
2 cups thinly sliced seeded peeled cucumber
¼ cup thinly vertically sliced red onion
¼ cup matchstick-cut carrots
1 tablespoon sugar
1 tablespoon chopped fresh cilantro
2 tablespoons fresh lime juice
2 teaspoons fish sauce
⅛ teaspoon salt

1. Preheat broiler.
2. Combine first 3 ingredients in a small bowl. Brush steak with half of hoisin mixture. Place steak on a broiler pan coated with cooking spray. Broil 6 minutes. Turn steak over; brush with remaining hoisin mixture. Broil 6 minutes or until desired degree of doneness. Place steak on a cutting board; let stand 5 minutes.
3. Combine cucumber and remaining ingredients in a bowl; toss to combine. Cut steak diagonally across grain into thin slices. Serve with cucumber salad. **Yield:** 4 servings (serving size: 3 ounces steak and ½ cup salad).

CALORIES 213; FAT 7.7g (sat 2.9g, mono 2.8g, poly 0.3g); PROTEIN 24.6g; CARB 11.5g; FIBER 0.7g; CHOL 38mg; IRON 1.7mg; SODIUM 501mg; CALC 30mg

Mongolian Beef

15 MINUTES

Mongolian Beef

Make this traditional Chinese dish in less time than it takes to order the take-out version.

1 tablespoon dark sesame oil
2 teaspoons minced garlic
4 green onions, cut into 1-inch pieces
1 (1-pound) flank steak, trimmed and cut crosswise into thin strips
¼ cup water
2 tablespoons low-sodium soy sauce
4 teaspoons cornstarch
2 teaspoons crushed red pepper flakes
2 teaspoons brown sugar
Toasted sesame seeds (optional)

1. Heat oil in a large nonstick skillet over medium-high heat; add garlic and green onions, and cook, stirring frequently, 1 minute. Add beef, and cook 5 minutes or until beef is browned, stirring frequently.
2. While beef cooks, combine water and next 4 ingredients in a small bowl. Pour mixture over beef; cook 1 to 2 minutes or until sauce is thickened and beef is cooked through. Garnish with sesame seeds, if desired. **Yield:** 4 servings (serving size: 1 cup).

CALORIES 229; FAT 10.2g (sat 2.9g, mono 4.9g, poly 2.3g); PROTEIN 25.4g; CARB 7.6g; FIBER 0.7g; CHOL 37mg; IRON 2.3mg; SODIUM 366mg; CALC 47mg

Hoisin sauce is made with soybeans, sugar, vinegar, and spices. Sweet and fairly thick, it's often used in marinades for barbecuing and roasting and also in dipping sauces.

INGREDIENT SPOTLIGHT

Flank Steak and Edamame
with Wasabi Dressing

20

Flank Steak and Edamame with Wasabi Dressing

Wasabi paste is an intensely hot, green paste that is used anywhere horseradish would be used.

1   (1-pound) flank steak, trimmed
2   tablespoons plus 2 teaspoons low-sodium
     soy sauce, divided
½   teaspoon salt
½   teaspoon black pepper
Cooking spray
2   teaspoons dark sesame oil
1   tablespoon bottled ground fresh ginger (such
     as Spice World)
2   teaspoons bottled minced garlic
1   (10-ounce) package frozen shelled edamame
     (green soybeans), thawed
¼   cup rice vinegar
2   teaspoons wasabi paste

1. Heat a grill pan over medium-high heat. Rub steak with 2 teaspoons soy sauce; sprinkle with salt and pepper. Coat pan with cooking spray. Add steak to pan. Cook 5 minutes on each side or until desired degree of doneness. Remove from pan; let stand 10 minutes. Cut steak diagonally across grain into ½-inch-thick slices.
2. Heat oil in a large nonstick skillet over medium heat. Add ginger and garlic; sauté

1 minute, stirring occasionally. Add remaining 2 tablespoons soy sauce and edamame to pan; cook 2 minutes.
3. Combine vinegar and wasabi paste in a bowl, stirring until smooth. Place ½ cup edamame mixture on each of 4 plates. Top each serving with 3 ounces steak; drizzle each with 1 tablespoon vinegar mixture. **Yield:** 4 servings.

CALORIES 253; FAT 11.9g (sat 3g, mono 3.7g, poly 3.9g); PROTEIN 27.7g; CARB 5.9g; FIBER 0.1g; CHOL 28mg; IRON 2.8mg; SODIUM 653mg; CALC 64mg

20

Ancho-Rubbed Flank Steak

make it a meal *Roasted, simply seasoned potato wedges and a tartly dressed salad topped with smoky bacon complement this satisfying main dish.*

½   teaspoon kosher salt
½   teaspoon brown sugar
½   teaspoon ground ancho chile powder
¼   teaspoon ground cumin
Dash of freshly ground black pepper
1   (1-pound) flank steak, trimmed
2   teaspoons olive oil

1. Combine first 5 ingredients in a small bowl; rub evenly over both sides of steak.
2. Heat oil in a large skillet over medium-high heat. Add steak; cook 3 minutes on each side or until desired degree of doneness. Let stand 5 minutes; cut steak diagonally across grain into thin slices. **Yield:** 4 servings (serving size: 3 ounces).

CALORIES 175; FAT 7.8g (sat 2.6g, mono 3.8g, poly 0.5g); PROTEIN 23.8g; CARB 0.8g; FIBER 0.1g; CHOL 37mg; IRON 1.5mg; SODIUM 286mg; CALC 19mg

Fresh lime juice adds flavor you can't get with bottled juice. A juicer makes getting juice super quick. For small jobs, we recommend a handheld juicer.

SHORTCUT SPOTLIGHT

2O

Thai Basil Beef with Rice Noodles

8	cups water
1	(1-pound) flank steak, trimmed
¼	teaspoon salt
1½	cups (1½-inch-long) slices fresh asparagus (about 1 pound)
4	ounces uncooked wide rice sticks (rice-flour noodles)
1	tablespoon sugar
3	tablespoons fresh lime juice
1	tablespoon fish sauce
½	teaspoon Thai red curry paste
1	cup cherry tomatoes, halved
½	cup thinly sliced fresh basil

1. Heat a large grill pan over medium-high heat.
2. While pan heats, bring water to a boil in a large saucepan.
3. Add steak to grill pan; grill 5 minutes on each side or until desired degree of doneness. Sprinkle steak with salt. Cut steak across grain into thin slices.
4. While steak cooks, add asparagus to boiling water; cook 2 minutes. Remove asparagus with a slotted spoon. Add noodles to boiling water; cook 3 minutes or until done. Drain; rinse well. Cut noodles into smaller pieces; place in a medium bowl.
5. While noodles cook, combine sugar, lime juice, fish sauce, and curry paste in a large bowl. Add one-half of lime mixture to medium bowl with noodles; toss to coat. Add steak, asparagus, tomatoes, and basil to remaining lime mixture in large bowl; toss to combine. Serve steak mixture over noodles. **Yield:** 4 servings (serving size: ¹/₂ cup noodles and 1 cup steak mixture).

CALORIES 328; FAT 8.6g (sat 3.6g, mono 3.4g, poly 0.4g); PROTEIN 26.1g; CARB 34.9g; FIBER 3.6g; CHOL 54mg; IRON 3.2mg; SODIUM 615mg; CALC 50mg

Cumin-Pepper Flank Steak with
Horseradish Chimichurri

20 MINUTES

Cumin-Pepper Flank Steak with Horseradish Chimichurri

make it a meal *Chimichurri is a thick herb sauce for meat that is popular in Argentina. Serve with whole wheat flour tortillas and sautéed sliced carrots.*

Chimichurri:
- ²/₃ cup fresh flat-leaf parsley leaves
- 2 tablespoons chopped green onions
- 2 tablespoons water
- 1 tablespoon prepared horseradish
- 1 tablespoon red wine vinegar
- 1 teaspoon olive oil
- ¹/₈ teaspoon salt
- 1 garlic clove, peeled

Steak:
- 1 (1-pound) flank steak, trimmed
- 1 teaspoon ground cumin
- ¹/₂ teaspoon salt
- ¹/₄ teaspoon black pepper
- 1 teaspoon olive oil

1. To prepare chimichurri, place first 8 ingredients in a food processor; process until smooth.

2. To prepare steak, rub steak with cumin, ¹/₂ teaspoon salt, and pepper. Heat 1 teaspoon oil in a large nonstick skillet over medium-high heat. Add steak to pan; cook 3 minutes on each side or until desired degree of doneness. Remove from pan; let stand 5 minutes. Cut steak diagonally across grain into thin slices. Serve with chimichurri. **Yield:** 4 servings (serving size: 3 ounces steak and 1¹/₂ tablespoons chimichurri).

CALORIES 201; FAT 10.4g (sat 3.6g, mono 4.9g, poly 0.6g); PROTEIN 23.8g; CARB 1.8g; FIBER 0.8g; CHOL 43mg; IRON 2.4mg; SODIUM 433mg; CALC 40mg

20 MINUTES

Broiled Flank Steak with Salsa Verde

make it a meal *This piquant green sauce makes a great accompaniment to broiled or grilled pork, or steamed white fish. A little goes a long way, so use it sparingly. Serve this dish with roasted potato wedges.*

Salsa:
- 1 cup fresh cilantro leaves
- 1 cup fresh flat-leaf parsley leaves
- 3 tablespoons water
- 2 tablespoons extra-virgin olive oil
- 1 tablespoon fresh lime juice
- 2 teaspoons capers, rinsed and drained
- 1 teaspoon Dijon mustard
- 3 cornichons
- 1 garlic clove, peeled

Steak:
- 1 (1¹/₂-pound) flank steak, trimmed
- ¹/₂ teaspoon salt
- ¹/₂ teaspoon freshly ground black pepper
- Cooking spray

1. Preheat broiler.

2. To prepare salsa, place cilantro and next 8 ingredients in a food processor; process until smooth, scraping sides of bowl occasionally. Place sauce in a bowl; cover and set aside.

3. To prepare steak, sprinkle each side of steak evenly with salt and pepper. Place on a broiler pan coated with cooking spray; broil 6 minutes on each side or until desired degree of doneness. Cut steak diagonally across grain into thin slices; serve with salsa. **Yield:** 6 servings (serving size: 3 ounces steak and about 1 tablespoon salsa).

CALORIES 279; FAT 14.3g (sat 4.6g, mono 7.4g, poly 0.8g); PROTEIN 32g; CARB 3.9g; FIBER 0.3g; CHOL 62mg; IRON 2.9mg; SODIUM 364mg; CALC 37mg

Beef and Vegetable Kebabs

20 MINUTES

Beef and Vegetable Kebabs

make it a meal *Using the broiler lets you enjoy the taste of kebabs year-round; they are also great cooked on the grill. Serve the kebabs over rice.*

1   pound boneless sirloin steak, trimmed and cut into 1-inch cubes
8   (1-inch) pieces yellow bell pepper (about 1 pepper)
8   small mushrooms (about 4 ounces)
8   (1-inch) pieces green onions (about 2)
8   cherry tomatoes
1   teaspoon kosher salt
½   teaspoon dried thyme
¼   teaspoon freshly ground black pepper
Cooking spray
2   teaspoons canola oil

1. Preheat broiler.
2. Divide first 5 ingredients evenly among 4 (12-inch) skewers, and sprinkle with salt, thyme, and black pepper. Place on a broiler pan coated with cooking spray; drizzle kebabs with oil.
3. Broil 10 minutes or until desired degree of doneness, turning once. **Yield:** 4 servings (serving size: 1 kebab).

CALORIES 218; FAT 10g (sat 3.2g, mono 4.1g, poly 1.4g); PROTEIN 26.5g; CARB 4.7g; FIBER 0.7g; CHOL 56mg; IRON 2mg; SODIUM 529mg; CALC 33mg

15 MINUTES

Grilled Flank Steak with Chimichurri

The chimichurri can be made ahead or while the steak grills to keep the time under 15 minutes. Slice the grilled steak across the grain into thin strips to get the most tender bites.

1   (1-pound) flank steak, trimmed
⅛   teaspoon salt
¼   teaspoon freshly ground black pepper
Cooking spray
½   cup chopped fresh parsley
2   tablespoons chopped fresh mint
2   tablespoons finely chopped shallots
1   tablespoon capers
1   tablespoon fresh lemon juice
2   teaspoons olive oil
1   garlic clove, minced

1. Prepare grill.
2. Sprinkle beef evenly with salt and pepper. Place beef on grill rack coated with cooking spray; grill 3 to 4 minutes on each side or until desired degree of doneness. Let stand 5 minutes; cut beef diagonally across grain into thin slices.
3. While beef stands, combine parsley, mint, and remaining ingredients in a small bowl. Serve over beef. **Yield:** 4 servings (serving size: 3 ounces steak and about 2 tablespoons chimichurri).

CALORIES 199; FAT 9.5g (sat 3.3g, mono 5.5g, poly 0.6g); PROTEIN 25.1g; CARB 2.2g; FIBER 0.5g; CHOL 47mg; IRON 2.7mg; SODIUM 206mg; CALC 49mg

A broiler pan is a great kitchen tool that can help get you in and out of the kitchen quickly. Cooking under a broiler is similar to grilling, except the heat comes from above instead of below.

SHORTCUT SPOTLIGHT

Country-Fried Steak with Mushroom Gravy

We call for cubed steak, but you can buy regular sirloin steak and pound it with a rolling pin. For the mashed potatoes, you can't beat the frozen variety for speed.

3 tablespoons fat-free milk
2 large egg whites
1.5 ounces all-purpose flour (about ⅓ cup)
½ teaspoon onion powder
½ teaspoon salt
¼ teaspoon garlic powder
¼ teaspoon black pepper
4 (4-ounce) sirloin cubed steaks
2 teaspoons vegetable oil
2⅔ cups frozen mashed potatoes (such as Ore-Ida)
1⅓ cups fat-free milk
2 cups mushrooms, quartered
2½ tablespoons all-purpose flour
¼ teaspoon salt
1 (14-ounce) can fat-free, less-sodium beef broth

1. Combine 3 tablespoons milk and egg whites in a shallow dish, stirring with a whisk. Combine ⅓ cup flour and next 4 ingredients in a shallow dish. Working with 1 steak at a time, dip in egg mixture; dredge in flour mixture. Repeat procedure with remaining steaks, egg mixture, and flour mixture.
2. Heat oil in a large nonstick skillet over medium-high heat. Add steaks; cook 3 minutes on each side or until browned. Remove steaks from pan; keep warm.
3. While steaks cook, prepare mashed potatoes according to package directions, using 1⅓ cups milk. Keep warm.
4. Add mushrooms to pan; sauté 3 minutes. Combine 2½ tablespoons flour, ¼ teaspoon salt, and broth, stirring with a whisk. Add broth mixture to pan. Bring to a boil; cook 1 minute, stirring constantly. Spoon over steaks. Serve with mashed potatoes.
Yield: 4 servings (serving size: 1 steak, about ⅓ cup gravy, and about 1 cup mashed potatoes).

CALORIES 436; FAT 14.7g (sat 5.1g, mono 4.8g, poly 2.2g); PROTEIN 38.2g; CARB 34.7g; FIBER 1.9g; CHOL 189mg; IRON 4.6mg; SODIUM 759mg; CALC 147mg

Spicy Orange Beef

make it a meal *Orange juice, crushed red pepper, and sesame oil add allure to this saucy Chinese entrée. A side of sliced cucumbers dressed with rice vinegar and a pinch of sugar would offer a good balance for this spicy meal.*

1	(3 ½-ounce) bag boil-in-bag brown rice
½	teaspoon salt
1	teaspoon bottled minced garlic
½	teaspoon crushed red pepper
1	pound boneless sirloin steak, cut into ¼-inch strips
½	teaspoon grated orange rind
¼	cup fresh orange juice
1	tablespoon cornstarch
2	tablespoons low-sodium soy sauce
1	teaspoon dark sesame oil
¾	cup (1-inch) slices green onions

1. Cook rice according to package directions, omitting salt and fat. Combine rice and salt, tossing well.

2. Combine garlic, pepper, and beef, tossing well.

3. Combine rind, juice, cornstarch, and soy sauce, stirring with a whisk.

4. Heat oil in a large nonstick skillet over medium-high heat. Add beef mixture and onions; sauté 2 minutes. Add juice mixture; cook 2 minutes or until sauce thickens, stirring frequently. Serve beef mixture over rice. **Yield:** 4 servings (serving size: ½ cup beef mixture and about ⅓ cup rice).

CALORIES 274; FAT 6.8g (sat 1.9g, mono 2.4g, poly 0.7g); PROTEIN 26.5g; CARB 24.9g; FIBER 2.1g; CHOL 69mg; IRON 3.7mg; SODIUM 627mg; CALC 25mg

COOKING CLASS: *how to test the grill*

The best way to measure the temperature of an open fire is the time-honored hand test. Simply hold your hand about 3 inches above the grate, and then time how long you can keep your hand there. Three seconds indicates medium-high heat.

Grilled Steak with Caper-Herb Sauce

make it a meal *Serve with grilled garlic bread to soak up every last drop of the flavorful caper-herb sauce.*

1   (1-pound) boneless sirloin steak
¼   teaspoon salt
¼   teaspoon freshly ground black pepper
Cooking spray
1   cup fresh flat-leaf parsley leaves
1   cup fresh basil leaves
2   tablespoons thinly sliced green onions
2   tablespoons extra-virgin olive oil
2   tablespoons fat-free, less-sodium chicken broth
1   tablespoon capers
1   tablespoon fresh lemon juice
1   garlic clove, chopped
1   canned anchovy fillet, chopped

1. Prepare grill to medium-high heat.
2. Sprinkle steak with salt and pepper. Place steak on grill rack coated with cooking spray; grill 6 minutes on each side. Let stand 10 minutes.
3. Place parsley and remaining ingredients in a food processor; process until blended. Cut steak diagonally across grain into thin slices. Serve with sauce. **Yield:** 4 servings (serving size: 3 ounces steak and about 1 tablespoon sauce).

CALORIES 194; FAT 13g (sat 3.2g, mono 7.3g, poly 1.2g); PROTEIN 16.3g; CARB 2.4g; FIBER 1.1g; CHOL 42mg; IRON 3.5mg; SODIUM 295mg; CALC 45mg

Balsamic-Glazed Filet Mignon

make it a meal *Pair this steak with classic sides like mashed potatoes and steamed green beans. The menu comes together easily enough for a weeknight meal, but it's sophisticated enough to share with guests.*

4   (4-ounce) beef tenderloin steaks
¼   teaspoon salt
¼   teaspoon freshly ground black pepper
Cooking spray
2   teaspoons bottled minced garlic
⅛   teaspoon crushed red pepper
3   tablespoons dry sherry
2   tablespoons low-sodium soy sauce
1   tablespoon balsamic vinegar
2   teaspoons honey

1. Sprinkle both sides of steaks evenly with salt and black pepper. Heat a large nonstick skillet over medium-high heat. Coat pan with cooking spray. Add steaks to pan; cook 3 minutes on each side or until desired degree of doneness. Remove steaks from pan; keep warm.
2. Add garlic and red pepper to pan; sauté 30 seconds. Add sherry to pan; bring to a boil. Cook 30 seconds. Add soy sauce and remaining ingredients; bring to a boil, stirring occasionally. Reduce heat, and cook 1 minute. Serve with steaks. **Yield:** 4 servings (serving size: 1 steak and about 1 tablespoon sauce).

CALORIES 215; FAT 9.2g (sat 3.4g, mono 3.5g, poly 0.7g); PROTEIN 24g; CARB 4.7g; FIBER 0.1g; CHOL 70mg; IRON 3.3mg; SODIUM 406mg; CALC 9.7mg

Balsamic and Black Pepper
Filet Mignon

3. Broil 6 minutes; turn steaks over. Broil an additional 5 minutes or until desired degree of doneness. Serve immediately. **Yield:** 4 servings (serving size: 1 steak).

CALORIES 215; FAT 8.9g (sat 3g, mono 3.5g, poly 0.7g); PROTEIN 24.7g; CARB 8.3g; FIBER 0.1g; CHOL 72mg; IRON 2.3mg; SODIUM 491mg; CALC 37mg

20 MINUTES

Sirloin Steaks with Mushroom Sauce and Chive-Garlic Potatoes

4   (4-ounce) boneless sirloin steaks, trimmed (about 1 inch thick)
3/8 teaspoon black pepper, divided
1/4 teaspoon salt, divided
1   tablespoon olive oil
1   (8-ounce) package sliced cremini mushrooms
1/2 cup dry red wine
1/2 cup water
2   teaspoons all-purpose flour
1   (24-ounce) package refrigerated mashed potatoes
1/3 cup chopped fresh chives
1/2 teaspoon garlic powder

1. Sprinkle steaks evenly with 1/4 teaspoon pepper and 1/8 teaspoon salt. Heat oil in a large nonstick skillet over medium-high heat. Reduce heat to medium. Add steaks to pan; cook 2 minutes on each side or until desired degree of doneness. Remove from pan; keep warm.
2. Add mushrooms to pan; cook 5 minutes or until tender and beginning to brown, stirring frequently. Combine wine, 1/2 cup water, flour, remaining 1/8 teaspoon pepper, and remaining 1/8 teaspoon salt; stir well with a whisk. Add wine mixture to pan; bring to a boil. Cook 2 minutes or until thick; stir constantly. Remove from heat.
3. Prepare potatoes according to package directions. Stir in chives and garlic powder. Place 3/4 cup potatoes on each of 4 plates. Top each with 1 steak and about 1/4 cup mushroom sauce. **Yield:** 4 servings.

CALORIES 326; FAT 10.4g (sat 3.4g, mono 4.9g, poly 0.7g); PROTEIN 28.4g; CARB 29.8g; FIBER 3.6g; CHOL 69mg; IRON 4.1mg; SODIUM 682mg; CALC 46mg

15 MINUTES

Balsamic and Black Pepper Filet Mignon

make it a meal *Serve the steak with fast-cooking long-grain and wild rice pilaf tossed with dried fruit.*

2   tablespoons molasses
2   teaspoons balsamic vinegar
4   (4-ounce) beef tenderloin steaks, trimmed (1 inch thick)
Cooking spray
3/4 teaspoon salt
3/4 teaspoon black pepper

1. Preheat broiler.
2. Combine molasses and vinegar in a medium bowl, stirring with a whisk. Add steaks, turning to coat. Place steaks on a baking sheet coated with cooking spray. Sprinkle steaks with salt and pepper.

The leanest, most tender, and most expensive cuts of beef come from the loin: beef tenderloin, Porterhouse, T-bone, filet mignon, and New York strip steaks.

INGREDIENT SPOTLIGHT

Sirloin Steaks with Mushroom
Sauce and Chive-Garlic Potatoes

COOKING CLASS: *how to peel a shallot*

When peeling a shallot, remove a couple of the outer layers along with the peel. You might need an extra shallot to make up for the discarded layers, but this method is a lot faster than removing only the thin peel.

....

15
MINUTES

Brandy and Mustard–Glazed Tenderloin Steaks

make it a meal *Serve this dish with mashed potatoes drizzled with olive oil. Place fresh broccoli florets in a bowl with a small amount of water. Microwave three minutes or until crisp-tender; garnish with grated lemon rind, if desired.*

4   (4-ounce) beef tenderloin steaks
¼   teaspoon salt
⅛   teaspoon black pepper
2   teaspoons butter
¼   cup minced shallots
½   cup fat-free, less-sodium beef broth
1   tablespoon Dijon mustard
2   tablespoons brandy

1. Heat a large nonstick skillet over medium heat. Sprinkle both sides of steaks evenly with salt and pepper. Add steaks to pan; cook 3 minutes on each side or until browned. Remove steaks from pan, and keep warm.
2. Melt butter in pan. Add shallots to pan; cook 2 minutes, stirring occasionally. Add broth and mustard to pan; cook 1 minute or until sauce thickens, stirring occasionally. Stir in brandy. Return steaks to pan, and cook 1 minute on each side or until desired degree of doneness. Serve sauce with steaks. **Yield:** 4 servings (serving size: 1 steak and 4 teaspoons sauce).

CALORIES 218; FAT 9.3g (sat 3.9g, mono 3.5g, poly 0.4g); PROTEIN 25.7g; CARB 2.7g; FIBER 0.2g; CHOL 81mg; IRON 2.1mg; SODIUM 371mg; CALC 34mg

20
MINUTES

Beef Tenderloin Steaks with Port Reduction and Blue Cheese

make it a meal *Add Brussels sprouts and wild rice to this entertaining-worthy dish. Use a large skillet to accommodate cooking the four steaks at once. If they're crowded in a small pan, the steaks will "steam," affecting the meat's texture.*

4   (4-ounce) beef tenderloin steaks, trimmed
¼   teaspoon salt
¼   teaspoon black pepper
Cooking spray
¾   cup port or other sweet red wine
2   tablespoons jellied cranberry sauce
2   tablespoons fat-free, less-sodium beef broth
⅛   teaspoon salt
⅛   teaspoon black pepper
1   garlic clove, minced
2   tablespoons crumbled blue cheese

1. Heat a large cast-iron skillet over medium-high heat. Sprinkle steaks with ¼ teaspoon salt and ¼ teaspoon pepper; coat steaks with cooking spray. Add steaks to pan; cook 4 minutes on each side or until desired degree of doneness. Remove steaks from pan; keep warm.
2. Add port, cranberry sauce, broth, ⅛ teaspoon salt, ⅛ teaspoon pepper, and garlic to pan, scraping pan to loosen browned bits. Reduce heat, and cook until liquid is reduced to ¼ cup (about 4 minutes). Serve steaks with sauce; top with cheese. **Yield:** 4 servings (serving size: 1 steak, 1 tablespoon sauce, and 1½ teaspoons cheese).

CALORIES 282; FAT 10.2g (sat 4.1g, mono 3.8g, poly 0.4g); PROTEIN 24.7g; CARB 9.8g; FIBER 0.2g; CHOL 73mg; IRON 3.3mg; SODIUM 361mg; CALC 35mg

20 MINUTES

Filet Mignon with Arugula Salad

make it a meal *Arugula, a peppery salad green, makes a tasty bed for pan-seared steak. Asiago garlic bread is a fitting accompaniment.*

Cooking spray
4 (4-ounce) beef tenderloin steaks, trimmed
½ teaspoon salt, divided
¼ teaspoon black pepper, divided
2 teaspoons butter
½ cup prechopped red onion
1 (8-ounce) package presliced cremini mushrooms
2 tablespoons fresh lemon juice
1 (5-ounce) bag baby arugula

1. Heat a large nonstick skillet over medium-high heat. Coat pan with cooking spray. Sprinkle beef with ¼ teaspoon salt and ⅛ teaspoon pepper. Add beef to pan; cook 4 minutes on each side or until desired degree of doneness. Remove beef from pan; keep warm.

2. Melt butter in pan; coat pan with cooking spray. Add remaining ¼ teaspoon salt, remaining ⅛ teaspoon pepper, red onion, and mushrooms to pan; sauté 4 minutes or until mushrooms release their liquid. Combine juice and arugula in a large bowl. Add mushroom mixture to arugula mixture; toss gently to combine. Arrange 1½ cups salad mixture on each of 4 plates; top each serving with 1 steak. **Yield:** 4 servings.

CALORIES 191; FAT 8.9g (sat 3.8g, mono 3.1g, poly 0.5g); PROTEIN 20.5g; CARB 7g; FIBER 1.8g; CHOL 59mg; IRON 3.3mg; SODIUM 349mg; CALC 72mg

Filet Mignon with Sherry-Mushroom Sauce

make it a meal *Jazz up frozen mashed potatoes by drizzling them with a bit of truffle oil for a quick but impressive side to accompany this easy dish. Place fresh green beans in a bowl with a little water. Microwave 3 minutes or until the beans are done.*

4	(4-ounce) beef tenderloin steaks, trimmed (1 inch thick)
½	teaspoon salt
¼	teaspoon black pepper
2	teaspoons butter, divided
1½	cups presliced mushrooms
2	tablespoons chopped shallots
1	teaspoon bottled minced garlic
½	cup fat-free, less-sodium beef broth
¼	cup dry sherry
2	teaspoons cornstarch
2	teaspoons water

1. Sprinkle beef with salt and pepper. Melt 1 teaspoon butter in a large nonstick skillet over medium-high heat. Add beef to pan; cook 3 ½ minutes on each side or until desired degree of doneness. Remove beef from pan; keep warm.

2. Melt remaining 1 teaspoon butter in pan. Add mushrooms, shallots, and garlic to pan; sauté 3 minutes. Stir in broth and sherry. Combine cornstarch and 2 teaspoons water in a bowl, stirring until smooth. Add cornstarch mixture to pan; bring to a boil. Cook 1 minute, stirring constantly. **Yield:** 4 servings (serving size: 1 steak and about ¼ cup sauce).

CALORIES 219; FAT 10.5g (sat 4.4g, mono 3.8g, poly 0.4g); PROTEIN 25.3g; CARB 3.3g; FIBER 0.4g; CHOL 76mg; IRON 3.3mg; SODIUM 420mg; CALC 12mg

Filet Mignon with Port and Mustard Sauce

15 MINUTES

Filet Mignon with Port and Mustard Sauce

make it a meal *Port, a fortified dessert wine, has a distinctively smooth sweetness. If you don't have port, substitute red wine. Serve with sour cream and chive mashed potatoes and fresh green beans.*

Cooking spray
4   (4-ounce) beef tenderloin steaks, trimmed
¼   teaspoon salt
¼   teaspoon black pepper
½   cup port or other sweet red wine
3   tablespoons chopped shallots
½   cup fat-free, less-sodium beef broth
1   tablespoon Dijon mustard

1. Heat a large nonstick skillet over medium-high heat. Coat pan with cooking spray. Sprinkle both sides of steaks with salt and pepper. Add steaks to pan; cook 3 ½ minutes on each side or until desired degree of doneness. Remove steaks from pan; cover and keep warm.
2. Add port and shallots to pan. Cook 1 minute or until liquid almost evaporates, scraping pan to loosen browned bits. Stir in broth; cook until reduced to ⅓ cup (about 1 minute). Remove from heat ; stir in mustard. Serve steaks with sauce. **Yield:** 4 servings (serving size: 1 steak and about 1½ tablespoons sauce).

CALORIES 217; FAT 9.3g (sat 3.4g, mono 3.6g, poly 0.5g); PROTEIN 24.3g; CARB 3.8g; FIBER 0.1g; CHOL 70mg; IRON 3.4mg; SODIUM 361mg; CALC 17mg

MAKE IT FASTER

Purchasing presliced mushrooms saves you time in the kitchen. Just be sure to give them a quick wash before using them. The time saved from slicing them is well worth it.

15 MINUTES

Filet Mignon with Fresh Herb and Garlic Rub

make it a meal *The filet mignon comes from the small end of the tenderloin. Serve it with roasted red potato wedges and steamed broccoli florets. Place florets in a microwave-safe bowl with a little water. Cover with wax paper and microwave at HIGH 3 minutes or until crisp tender.*

2   teaspoons bottled minced garlic
1½   teaspoons minced fresh basil
1½   teaspoons minced fresh thyme
1½   teaspoons minced fresh rosemary
½   teaspoon salt
¼   teaspoon black pepper
4   (4-ounce) beef tenderloin steaks, trimmed (1 inch thick)
Cooking spray

1. Combine first 6 ingredients in a small bowl; rub evenly over steaks.
2. Heat a large nonstick skillet over medium-high heat. Coat pan with cooking spray. Add steaks to the pan, and cook 4 minutes on each side or until desired degree of doneness. **Yield:** 4 servings (serving size: 1 steak).

CALORIES 189; FAT 8.8g (sat 3.2g, mono 3.2g, poly 0.3g); PROTEIN 24.1g; CARB 0.8g; FIBER 0.2g; CHOL 71mg; IRON 3.1mg; SODIUM 349mg; CALC 9mg

Filet Mignon with Sweet Bourbon-Coffee Sauce

make it a meal *The bourbon and sugar round out the sharp coffee flavor to make a rich sauce for the beef. Roast refrigerated potato wedges for a quick side.*

½   cup water
3   tablespoons bourbon
1½   teaspoons sugar
½   teaspoon beef-flavored bouillon granules
½   teaspoon instant coffee granules
½   teaspoon black pepper
¼   teaspoon salt
4   (4-ounce) beef tenderloin steaks, trimmed (about 1 inch thick)
Cooking spray
2   tablespoons chopped fresh parsley

1. Combine first 5 ingredients in a small bowl; set aside.
2. Sprinkle pepper and salt over both sides of steaks. Heat a medium nonstick skillet over medium-high heat. Coat pan with cooking spray. Add steaks; cook 2 minutes on each side. Reduce heat to medium; cook steaks 2 minutes or until desired degree of doneness. Transfer steaks to a platter; cover and keep warm.
3. Add bourbon mixture to pan; cook over medium-high heat until mixture has reduced to ¼ cup (about 3 minutes). Serve sauce over beef; sprinkle with parsley. **Yield:** 4 servings (serving size: 1 steak, 1 tablespoon sauce, and 1½ teaspoons parsley).

CALORIES 178; FAT 5.3g (sat 2g, mono 2.1g, poly 0.2g); PROTEIN 22.4g; CARB 2.1g; FIBER 0.1g; CHOL 52mg; IRON 1.5mg; SODIUM 371mg; CALC 21mg

Pepper and Garlic–Crusted Tenderloin Steaks with Port Sauce

make it a meal *Serve with long-grain and wild rice pilaf and steamed green beans.*

2   teaspoons black peppercorns
½   teaspoon salt
3   garlic cloves, minced
4   (4-ounce) beef tenderloin steaks, trimmed (1 inch thick)
Cooking spray
¼   cup port wine
¼   cup canned beef broth
1   tablespoon chopped fresh thyme

1. Place peppercorns in a small zip-top plastic bag; seal. Crush peppercorns using a meat mallet or small heavy skillet. Combine peppercorns, salt, and garlic in a bowl; rub evenly over steaks.
2. Heat a large nonstick skillet over medium-high heat. Coat pan with cooking spray. Add steaks to pan. Reduce heat; cook 4 minutes on each side or until desired degree of doneness. Remove steaks from pan. Cover and keep warm.
3. Add port and broth to pan, stirring to loosen browned bits. Cook until reduced to ¼ cup (about 3 minutes). Place 1 steak on each of 4 plates; drizzle each serving with 1 tablespoon sauce. Sprinkle each serving with ¾ teaspoon thyme. **Yield:** 4 servings.

CALORIES 205; FAT 7.4g (sat 2.7g, mono 3g, poly 0.3g); PROTEIN 25.5g; CARB 6g; FIBER 0.4g; CHOL 76mg; IRON 2.1mg; SODIUM 389mg; CALC 36mg

Black peppercorns are the strongest spice in flavor and bite, and are the world's most popular spice. They're picked when slightly underripe and then air-dried, which results in their dark color.

INGREDIENT SPOTLIGHT

Spicy Filet Mignon with Grilled Sweet Onion

make it a meal *If you can't find sweet onions such as Vidalia, white or yellow onions will work fine, too. Serve with a tossed green salad.*

Cooking spray
2   cups vertically sliced Vidalia or other sweet onion
⅛   teaspoon salt
⅛   teaspoon black pepper
1   teaspoon garlic powder
½   teaspoon ground cumin
½   teaspoon dried oregano
¼   teaspoon salt
¼   teaspoon ground red pepper
¼   teaspoon black pepper
4   (4-ounce) filet mignons

1. Heat a grill pan over medium-high heat. Coat pan with cooking spray. Add onion; sprinkle with ⅛ teaspoon salt and ⅛ teaspoon black pepper. Cook 8 minutes or until browned, stirring occasionally. Remove from pan; keep warm.

2. Combine garlic powder and next 5 ingredients in a small bowl. Sprinkle garlic mixture over both sides of beef. Add beef to pan. Grill 5 minutes on each side or until desired degree of doneness. Serve with onion mixture. **Yield:** 4 servings (serving size: 1 filet and ¼ cup onion mixture).

CALORIES 313; FAT 22g (sat 8.7g, mono 9.2g, poly 0.9g); PROTEIN 21g; CARB 6.7g; FIBER 1.1g; CHOL 74mg; IRON 3mg; SODIUM 269mg; CALC 27mg

Steaks with Tuscan-Style Cannellini Salad

Cannellini, large white kidney beans, are common in Tuscan dishes. If you don't have cannellini, you can use any white bean, such as Great Northern or navy beans.

2   cups chopped plum tomato (about ½ pound)
1   tablespoon chopped fresh rosemary
1   tablespoon chopped fresh parsley
2   tablespoons balsamic vinegar
2   teaspoons bottled minced garlic
1   teaspoon extra-virgin olive oil
1   (16-ounce) can cannellini beans, rinsed and drained
¾   teaspoon salt, divided
¾   teaspoon cracked black pepper, divided
4   (4-ounce) beef tenderloin steaks, trimmed (1 inch thick)
Cooking spray

1. Combine tomato, rosemary, parsley, vinegar, garlic, oil, and beans in a large bowl, stirring well. Sprinkle ¼ teaspoon salt and ¼ teaspoon pepper over bean mixture; stir to combine.

2. Heat a grill pan over medium-high heat. Sprinkle steaks evenly with remaining ½ teaspoon salt and remaining ½ teaspoon pepper. Coat pan with cooking spray. Add steaks to pan; cook 3 minutes on each side or until desired degree of doneness. Serve with bean mixture. **Yield:** 4 servings (serving size: 1 steak and ½ cup bean mixture).

CALORIES 291; FAT 11.2g (sat 3.9g, mono 4.8g, poly 0.9g); PROTEIN 27.7g; CARB 18.2g; FIBER 4.6g; CHOL 71mg; IRON 3.4mg; SODIUM 700mg; CALC 59mg

Steak au Poivre

2O

Tenderloin Steaks with Red Onion Marmalade

make it a meal *Serve this company-worthy entrée with garlic mashed potatoes and sautéed green beans, and pour a bottle of cabernet sauvignon.*

Cooking spray
1   large red onion, sliced and separated into rings (about 2 cups)
2   tablespoons red wine vinegar
2   tablespoons honey
1/2   teaspoon salt, divided
1   teaspoon dried thyme
1/4   teaspoon freshly ground black pepper
4   (4-ounce) beef tenderloin steaks, trimmed (1 inch thick)

1. Preheat broiler.
2. Heat a large nonstick skillet over medium-high heat. Coat pan with cooking spray. Add onion to pan. Cover and cook 3 minutes. Add vinegar, honey, and 1/4 teaspoon salt to pan. Reduce heat, and simmer, uncovered, 8 minutes or until slightly thick, stirring occasionally.
3. Sprinkle remaining 1/4 teaspoon salt, thyme, and pepper evenly over beef. Place beef on a broiler pan coated with cooking spray; broil 4 minutes on each side or until desired degree of doneness. Serve with onion mixture. **Yield:** 4 servings (serving size: 1 steak and 1/3 cup marmalade).

CALORIES 289; FAT 11.4g (sat 4.3g, mono 4.3g, poly 0.4g); PROTEIN 32.5g; CARB 12.6g; FIBER 0.8g; CHOL 95mg; IRON 4.7mg; SODIUM 369mg; CALC 25mg

Steak au Poivre

15

Steak au Poivre

You can substitute 1/4 cup additional beef broth for the brandy, if you prefer.

1 1/2 teaspoons coarsely ground black pepper
2   (4-ounce) beef tenderloin steaks, trimmed (1 inch thick)
Cooking spray
1/4   cup brandy
1/2   cup fat-free, less-sodium beef broth
1/4   teaspoon salt
3   tablespoons reduced-fat sour cream

1. Press coarsely ground black pepper onto both sides of steaks.
2. Coat steaks with cooking spray. Heat a nonstick skillet over medium-high heat. Cook steaks 4 minutes on each side or until desired degree of doneness. Transfer to warm serving plates; set aside. Keep warm.
3. Add brandy to pan; let simmer 30 seconds or until liquid is reduced to a glaze. Add beef broth and salt. Simmer, uncovered, 3 minutes or until liquid is reduced by half.
4. Remove pan from heat; stir in sour cream. Serve sauce with steak. **Yield:** 2 servings (serving size: 1 steak and about 2 tablespoons sauce).

CALORIES 251; FAT 9g (sat 3.9g, mono 4.5g, poly 0.5g); PROTEIN 19.4g; CARB 4g; FIBER 0.4g; CHOL 61mg; IRON 2.5mg; SODIUM 463mg; CALC 11mg

INGREDIENT SPOTLIGHT

Plum tomatoes, also called Roma or Italian, are an egg-shaped variety that can be either yellow or red. They're not as sweet as beefsteak or globe varieties, but they have a lower water content and fewer seeds.

COOKING CLASS: *how to dredge veal cutlets*

To dredge veal scaloppini—a super-thin veal cutlet—place flour in a shallow baking dish or pie plate. Drag the meat through the flour, making sure the cutlets have an even dusting of flour on both sides. Gently shake the cutlets to remove excess flour.

Veal Marsala

2. Melt butter in a large nonstick skillet over medium-high heat. Add veal, and cook 1½ minutes. Turn veal over; cook 1 minute. Remove veal from pan.

3. Add wine to pan, scraping pan to loosen browned bits. Add consommé mixture, mushrooms, and salt; bring to a boil. Reduce heat; simmer 3 minutes or until thick. Return veal to pan; sprinkle with parsley. **Yield:** 4 servings (serving size: 3 ounces veal and about 2 tablespoons sauce).

CALORIES 193; FAT 6.1g (sat 3g, mono 1.1g, poly 0.4g); PROTEIN 26g; CARB 7.5g; FIBER 0.4g; CHOL 102mg; IRON 1.9mg; SODIUM 481mg; CALC 24mg

15 MINUTES

Thyme-Scented Tenderloin

2	teaspoons dried thyme
½	teaspoon salt
¼	teaspoon freshly ground black pepper
4	garlic cloves, minced
4	(4-ounce) beef tenderloin steaks (½ inch thick), trimmed

Cooking spray

1. Combine first 4 ingredients in a small bowl, and rub on both sides of steaks.
2. Heat a 10-inch cast-iron skillet over medium heat. Coat pan with cooking spray. Add steaks; cook 4 minutes on each side or to desired degree of doneness. **Yield:** 4 servings (serving size: 1 steak).

CALORIES 157; FAT 7.6g (sat 3g, mono 3.9g, poly 0.6g); PROTEIN 18.3g; CARB 2.6g; FIBER 0.9g; CHOL 53mg; IRON 2.4mg; SODIUM 334mg; CALC 39mg

15 MINUTES

Veal Marsala

make it a meal *Serve the veal over vermicelli, linguine, or egg noodles.*

1	pound veal scaloppine
1.1	ounces all-purpose flour (about ¼ cup), divided
⅔	cup beef consommé
1	tablespoon butter
½	cup dry Marsala wine
1	cup presliced mushrooms
¼	teaspoon salt
1	tablespoon chopped fresh parsley

1. Dredge veal in 3 tablespoons flour. Combine 1 tablespoon flour and consommé, stirring with a whisk; set aside.

 MINUTES

Rosemary-Grilled Veal Chops

make it a meal *Serve this dish with steamed green beans and grilled slices of refrigerated polenta.*

4   (6-ounce) lean veal loin chops (½ inch thick), trimmed
Olive oil–flavored cooking spray
1½   teaspoons dried rosemary, crushed
³/₄   teaspoon lemon pepper
Lemon wedges (optional)

1. Prepare grill.
2. Spray both sides of veal with cooking spray. Combine rosemary and lemon pepper; rub over veal chops.
3. Place veal on grill rack coated with cooking spray; grill 6 minutes on each side or until done. Serve with lemon wedges, if desired. **Yield:** 4 servings (serving size: 1 chop).

CALORIES 200; FAT 5.9g (sat 1.8g, mono 2.8g, poly 1.2g); PROTEIN 34.3g;
CARB 0.3g; FIBER 0.2g; CHOL 136mg; IRON 1.4mg; SODIUM 177mg; CALC 34mg

15 MINUTES

Veal Piccata

make it a meal *Enjoy this lemony Italian favorite with simple steamed green beans and mashed sweet potatoes. You can also use this recipe with pounded chicken breasts instead of veal.*

2   tablespoons all-purpose flour
Dash of salt
¼   teaspoon black pepper
1   tablespoon water
1   large egg white
⅓   cup Italian-seasoned breadcrumbs
4   (2-ounce) veal cutlets
2   teaspoons olive oil
1   cup fat-free, less-sodium chicken broth
1   teaspoon grated lemon rind
2   to 3 tablespoons fresh lemon juice
1   tablespoon capers, drained and rinsed
Lemon wedges (optional)
Flat-leaf parsley sprigs (optional)

1. Combine flour, salt, and pepper in a shallow dish. Combine water and egg white in another shallow dish, stirring with a whisk. Place breadcrumbs in a third shallow dish. Working with 1 cutlet at a time, dredge in flour mixture. Dip floured cutlet in egg white mixture; dredge in breadcrumbs.
2. Heat oil in a large nonstick skillet over medium-high heat. Add cutlets to pan; cook 2 minutes on each side or until lightly browned. Remove from pan; keep warm.
3. Add broth, rind, juice, and capers to pan; simmer 2 minutes, stirring constantly. Pour over cutlets; serve immediately. Garnish with lemon wedges and parsley sprigs, if desired. **Yield:** 2 servings (serving size: 2 cutlets and 3 tablespoons sauce).

CALORIES 281; FAT 7.6g (sat 1.2g, mono 4g, poly 0.6g); PROTEIN 30.4g;
CARB 21.2g; FIBER 1.3g; CHOL 89mg; IRON 2.2mg; SODIUM 964mg; CALC 89mg

MAKE IT FASTER

Although making your own breadcrumbs is extremely easy and economical, consider purchasing breadcrumbs from the grocery store to save even more time. If you do choose to make your own, simply place the bread in a food processor and pulse until the crumbs reach the desired consistency.

20 MINUTES

Herbed Lamb Chops with Pomegranate Reduction

make it a meal *These delicious lamb chops topped with sweet pomegranate sauce offer great flavor with minimal effort. Serve with a side of couscous.*

Cooking spray
8   (3-ounce) lamb rib chops, trimmed
½   teaspoon black pepper
¼   teaspoon salt
¼   teaspoon chopped fresh thyme
¾   cup pomegranate juice
1   teaspoon Dijon mustard
½   teaspoon honey
2   tablespoons minced shallots
1   teaspoon bottled minced garlic
1   teaspoon cornstarch
1   teaspoon water
1   tablespoon chopped fresh chives
⅛   teaspoon salt
⅛   teaspoon black pepper

1. Preheat broiler.
2. Coat a foil-lined baking sheet with cooking spray. Place lamb on prepared pan. Sprinkle lamb evenly with ½ teaspoon pepper, ¼ teaspoon salt, and thyme. Broil 5 minutes on each side.
3. Combine juice, mustard, and honey in a small bowl. Heat a small saucepan over medium-high heat. Coat pan with cooking spray. Add shallots and garlic to pan; sauté 1 minute. Stir in juice mixture; bring to a boil. Reduce heat and cook until reduced to ½ cup (about 5 minutes). Combine cornstarch and water in a small bowl; stir until smooth. Add cornstarch mixture to pan; bring to a boil. Cook 1 minute, stirring constantly. Remove from heat; stir in chives, ⅛ teaspoon salt, and ⅛ teaspoon pepper. Serve with lamb. **Yield:** 4 servings (serving size: 2 lamb chops and 2 tablespoons sauce).

CALORIES 264; FAT 16.6g (sat 8g, mono 6.5g, poly 0.6g); PROTEIN 18.6g; CARB 9.2g; FIBER 0.2g; CHOL 65mg; IRON 1.6mg; SODIUM 307mg; CALC 27mg

20 MINUTES

Lamb Rib Chops with Raisin-Almond Couscous

Lamb chops cook quickly and taste delicious spiced with coriander and cumin.

1½   cups water
⅓   cup golden raisins
1   teaspoon kosher salt, divided
¾   cup couscous
¼   teaspoon ground cumin
¼   teaspoon ground coriander
¼   teaspoon black pepper
8   (3-ounce) lamb rib chops, trimmed
¼   cup sliced almonds
¼   cup chopped fresh flat-leaf parsley

1. Preheat broiler.
2. Combine 1½ cups water, raisins, and ½ teaspoon salt in a medium saucepan; bring to a boil. Add couscous to pan. Remove from heat; cover and let stand 5 minutes. Fluff with a fork.
3. Combine remaining ½ teaspoon salt, cumin, coriander, and pepper. Rub spice mixture evenly over lamb. Place lamb on a jelly-roll pan lined with aluminum foil. Broil lamb 10 minutes or until desired degree of doneness, turning once.
4. Heat a small skillet over medium heat. Add almonds to pan; cook 3 minutes or until lightly toasted, stirring constantly. Add almonds and parsley to couscous mixture; stir to combine. Serve with lamb. **Yield:** 4 servings (serving size: 2 lamb chops and ¾ cup couscous).

CALORIES 328; FAT 10.9g (sat 3g, mono 5.2g, poly 1.3g); PROTEIN 20.8g; CARB 36.3g; FIBER 3g; CHOL 50mg; IRON 1.9mg; SODIUM 523mg; CALC 50mg

Broiled Lamb with Cilantro-Papaya Salsa

Broiled Lamb with Cilantro-Papaya Salsa

make it a meal *Plain couscous pairs well with these succulent Indian-spiced lamb chops.*

2   teaspoons garam masala
½   teaspoon salt, divided
¼   teaspoon black pepper
12 (3-ounce) lamb loin chops, trimmed
1   cup diced peeled papaya (about 1 medium)
½   cup prechopped red onion
¼   cup chopped fresh cilantro
1   tablespoon fresh lemon juice
1   teaspoon chopped jalapeño pepper

1. Preheat broiler.
2. Combine garam masala, ¼ teaspoon salt, and black pepper. Rub both sides of lamb chops with garam masala mixture. Arrange lamb in a single layer on a broiler pan; broil 4 minutes on each side or until desired degree of doneness. Remove from heat; sprinkle with remaining ¼ teaspoon salt.
3. While lamb cooks, combine papaya and remaining ingredients; stir well. Serve with lamb. **Yield:** 6 servings (serving size: 2 lamb chops and ¼ cup salsa).

CALORIES 160; FAT 5.6g (sat 2g, mono 2.2g, poly 0.5g); PROTEIN 19.7g; CARB 7.2g; FIBER 1.5g; CHOL 61mg; IRON 1.9mg; SODIUM 261mg; CALC 34mg

Cherry-Glazed Pan-Seared Lamb Chops

Cooking spray
2   teaspoons dried rosemary
½   teaspoon salt
½   teaspoon black pepper, divided
8   (4-ounce) lamb loin chops, trimmed
2   teaspoons bottled minced garlic
½   cup fat-free, less-sodium beef broth
½   cup cherry preserves
¼   cup balsamic vinegar
Parsley sprigs (optional)

1. Heat a large nonstick skillet over medium-high heat. Coat pan with cooking spray. Combine rosemary, salt, and ¼ teaspoon pepper in a small bowl, stirring well. Rub spice mixture evenly over both sides of lamb. Add lamb to pan; cook 5 minutes on each side. Remove lamb from pan. Wipe pan clean with paper towels.
2. Return pan to medium heat; recoat with cooking spray. Add garlic to pan; cook 30 seconds. Add remaining ¼ teaspoon pepper and broth; cook 1 minute, scraping pan to loosen browned bits. Stir in preserves and vinegar; cook 3 minutes or until slightly thick. Return lamb to pan; turn to coat. Cook 1 minute or until desired degree of doneness. Garnish with parsley sprigs, if desired. **Yield:** 4 servings (serving size: 2 lamb chops and 3 tablespoons glaze).

CALORIES 370; FAT 17.6g (sat 7.4g, mono 7.4g, poly 1.3g); PROTEIN 22.6g; CARB 29.2g; FIBER 0.4g; CHOL 84mg; IRON 1.8mg; SODIUM 422mg; CALC 29mg

Lamb is a lean meat so it's very important that you watch the cooking time and temperature carefully to make sure the meat doesn't overcook and become tough.

INGREDIENT SPOTLIGHT

Broiled Cumin Lamb Chops with Curried Couscous

Lamb:

2   teaspoons ground cumin
1   teaspoon ground coriander
½   teaspoon salt
1   tablespoon honey
8   (4-ounce) lamb loin chops, trimmed
Cooking spray

Couscous:

1   cup chopped onion
½   cup dried cranberries
¾   cup water
½   cup orange juice
1   teaspoon curry powder
¼   teaspoon salt
1   cup uncooked couscous
2   tablespoons chopped fresh cilantro

1. Preheat broiler.

2. To prepare lamb, combine first 3 ingredients in a bowl. Brush honey evenly over both sides of lamb; sprinkle evenly with spice mixture. Arrange lamb in a single layer on a broiler pan coated with cooking spray; broil 4 minutes on each side or until desired degree of doneness.

3. To prepare couscous, heat a nonstick saucepan over medium-high heat. Coat pan with cooking spray. Add onion to pan; sauté 2 minutes. Stir in cranberries and next 4 ingredients; bring to a boil. Remove from heat; stir in couscous. Cover and let stand 5 minutes. Add cilantro; fluff with a fork. **Yield:** 4 servings (serving size: 2 lamb chops and about 1 cup couscous mixture).

CALORIES 510; FAT 18.7g (sat 9g, mono 7g, poly 1g); PROTEIN 26.9g; CARB 56.8g; FIBER 4.1g; CHOL 95mg; IRON 3mg; SODIUM 493mg; CALC 54mg

Five-Spice Lamb Chops with Citrus-Raisin Couscous

make it a meal *Just the right amount of hot and sweet—five-spice studded lamb chops are delicious. Add a side of steamed green beans.*

¾ cup orange juice
½ cup fat-free, less-sodium chicken broth
⅓ cup golden raisins
1 cup uncooked couscous
¼ cup hoisin sauce
2 tablespoons honey
1 tablespoon seasoned rice vinegar
1 teaspoon chili garlic sauce (such as Lee Kum Kee)
¼ teaspoon five-spice powder
Cooking spray
¼ teaspoon black pepper
⅛ teaspoon salt
8 (4-ounce) lamb loin chops, trimmed

1. Combine first 3 ingredients in a medium saucepan; bring to a boil. Add couscous to pan. Remove from heat; cover and let stand 5 minutes. Fluff with a fork.
2. Combine hoisin and next 4 ingredients in a small bowl. Heat a large nonstick skillet over medium-high heat. Coat pan with cooking spray. Sprinkle pepper and salt over lamb. Add lamb to pan; cook 5 minutes on each side or until desired degree of doneness. Add hoisin mixture to pan; cook 1 minute or until thoroughly heated, turning to coat lamb. Spoon sauce over lamb; serve with couscous. **Yield:** 4 servings (serving size: 2 chops, ¾ cup couscous, and about 1½ tablespoons sauce).

CALORIES 428; FAT 6.5g (sat 2.1g, mono 2.4g, poly 0.9g); PROTEIN 26.2g; CARB 66.1g; FIBER 3.3g; CHOL 61mg; IRON 2.9mg; SODIUM 549mg; CALC 41mg

15 MINUTES

Lamb Chops in Fennel-Tomato-Caper Sauce

8   (4-ounce) lamb loin chops, trimmed
¼   teaspoon salt, divided
¼   teaspoon black pepper, divided
Cooking spray
½   cup prechopped onion
1   teaspoon bottled minced garlic
½   teaspoon fennel seeds
1   tablespoon capers
1   (14.5-ounce) can diced tomatoes, undrained

1. Heat a large nonstick skillet over medium-high heat. Sprinkle lamb chops with ⅛ teaspoon salt and ⅛ teaspoon black pepper. Coat pan with cooking spray. Add lamb to pan; cook 2 minutes on each side or until lightly browned. Remove lamb from pan. Add remaining ⅛ teaspoon salt, remaining ⅛ teaspoon black pepper, onion, and garlic to pan; sauté 2 minutes.
2. Place fennel seeds in a heavy-duty zip-top plastic bag; seal. Crush seeds with a rolling pin. Add seeds, capers, and tomatoes to pan; bring to a boil. Return lamb to pan. Cover, reduce heat, and cook 6 minutes or until desired degree of doneness. **Yield:** 4 servings (serving size: 2 lamb chops and ¹/₂ cup sauce).

CALORIES 228; FAT 7.8g (sat 2.8g, mono 3.1g, poly 0.7g); PROTEIN 28.3g; CARB 9.6g; FIBER 1.1g; CHOL 86mg; IRON 3.3mg; SODIUM 551mg; CALC 75mg

Chinese five-spice powder is a fragrant blend of cinnamon, cloves, fennel seed, star anise, and Szechuan peppercorns. The licorice-like anise and fennel melded with the sweet pungent cloves and cinnamon contrast the woodsy flavor of peppercorn.

INGREDIENT SPOTLIGHT

20 MINUTES

Herbes de Provence Lamb Chops with Orzo

make it a meal *Garnish each plate with a lemon wedge and thyme sprig, and pair with a glass of fruity red wine to create a Provençal menu.*

1   cup uncooked orzo
²/₃   cup torn spinach
½   cup chopped red bell pepper
⅓   cup sliced green onions
2   teaspoons grated lemon rind
2   teaspoons chopped fresh parsley
2   teaspoons olive oil
½   teaspoon salt, divided
1   tablespoon dried herbes de Provence
1   tablespoon Dijon mustard
¼   teaspoon freshly ground black pepper
8   (3-ounce) lamb loin chops
Cooking spray

1. Preheat broiler.
2. Prepare pasta according to package directions, omitting salt and fat. Drain. Combine pasta, spinach, and next 5 ingredients in a medium bowl. Stir in ¹/₄ teaspoon salt.
3. Combine remaining ¹/₄ teaspoon salt, herbes de Provence, mustard, and pepper in a small bowl. Rub lamb evenly with herb mixture. Place on a broiler pan coated with cooking spray; broil 6 minutes, turning once halfway through cooking, or until desired degree of doneness. Serve with pasta mixture. **Yield:** 4 servings (serving size: 2 lamb chops and ¹/₂ cup pasta mixture).

CALORIES 471; FAT 15.6g (sat 4.8g, mono 7.1g, poly 1.1g); PROTEIN 44.1g; CARB 35.3g; FIBER 2.9g; CHOL 121mg; IRON 4.4mg; SODIUM 499mg; CALC 48mg

Peach Spiced Lamb Chops

Mint-Grilled Lamb Chops

In a heart-healthy diet, no more than 30 percent of your calories should come from fat. But not every food you eat has to fall under the 30 percent limit. For instance, when you serve lamb chops (which are naturally higher in fat), be sure to serve a low-fat side dish such as pasta or rice to keep your total fat percentage down at a healthy level.

⅓ cup fresh mint leaves, chopped
2 tablespoons plain low-fat yogurt
2 garlic cloves, crushed
4 (4-ounce) lean lamb loin chops (about 1 inch thick)
1 small lemon, cut in half
Cooking spray
Mint sprigs (optional)

1. Combine first 3 ingredients in a small bowl.
2. Prepare grill.
3. Trim fat from lamb chops. Rub lemon halves on both sides of lamb. Place lamb on grill rack coated with cooking spray; cover and grill 4 minutes. Turn lamb; spread mint mixture evenly over lamb. Cook 3 additional minutes or to desired degree of doneness. Garnish with mint sprigs, if desired. **Yield:** 2 servings (serving size: 2 chops and 1 tablespoon mint mixture).

CALORIES 158; FAT 5.7g (sat 2.3g, mono 2.7g, poly 0.7g); PROTEIN 23.7g; CARB 1.4g; FIBER 0.2g; CHOL 73mg; IRON 2.4mg; SODIUM 77mg; CALC 31mg

MINUTES

Peach Spiced Lamb Chops

make it a meal *Use the same spicy-sweet glaze for pork chops. Accompany with sautéed Broccolini and couscous.*

1 tablespoon brown sugar
1 teaspoon salt
1 teaspoon onion powder
1 teaspoon chili powder
1 teaspoon paprika
½ teaspoon dried oregano
¼ teaspoon ground ginger
¼ teaspoon ground allspice
¼ teaspoon black pepper
8 (4-ounce) bone-in lamb loin chops, trimmed
Cooking spray
⅓ cup peach preserves

1. Combine first 9 ingredients in a small bowl; rub spice mixture evenly over both sides of lamb chops.
2. Heat a grill pan over medium-high heat. Coat pan with cooking spray. Add lamb chops to pan, and cook 3 ½ minutes on each side. Brush each chop with about 1 teaspoon preserves. Turn chops over, and cook 1 minute. Brush chops with remaining preserves. Remove from heat. **Yield:** 4 servings (serving size: 2 chops).

CALORIES 361; FAT 15.5g (sat 7g, mono 6.2g, poly 0.7g); PROTEIN 32.3g; CARB 21.8g; FIBER 0.4g; CHOL 103mg; IRON 3mg; SODIUM 690mg; CALC 37mg

Mint is a versatile herb that is used in both sweet and savory dishes. It comes in many varieties, but spearmint is the preferred choice for cooking.

INGREDIENT SPOTLIGHT

Lamb Chops with Herb Vinaigrette

make it a meal *Add garlic mashed potatoes and steamed broccoli florets. If you have bottled roasted red bell peppers in your refrigerator, you can substitute them for the pimiento.*

½   teaspoon salt, divided
½   teaspoon black pepper
8   (4-ounce) lamb loin chops
2   tablespoons finely chopped shallots
1½ tablespoons water
1   tablespoon red wine vinegar
1½ teaspoons lemon juice
1½ teaspoons extra-virgin olive oil
1   teaspoon Dijon mustard
1½ tablespoons finely chopped fresh flat-leaf parsley
1½ tablespoons finely chopped fresh tarragon
1   tablespoon finely chopped fresh mint
1   tablespoon finely chopped pimiento

1. Preheat broiler.
2. Sprinkle ¼ teaspoon salt and pepper over lamb. Place lamb on the rack of a broiler pan or roasting pan; place rack in pan. Broil 5 minutes on each side or until desired degree of doneness.
3. Combine shallots, 1½ tablespoons water, and vinegar in a small microwave-safe bowl; microwave at HIGH 30 seconds. Stir in remaining ¼ teaspoon salt, juice, oil, and mustard, stirring with a whisk. Add parsley and remaining ingredients, stirring well. Serve vinaigrette over lamb. **Yield:** 4 servings (serving size: 2 chops and 1 tablespoon vinaigrette).

CALORIES 349; FAT 15.2g (sat 5.1g, mono 6.7g, poly 1.4g); PROTEIN 47.7g; CARB 1.9g; FIBER 0.2g; CHOL 150mg; IRON 4.6mg; SODIUM 482mg; CALC 37mg

COOKING CLASS: *how to deglaze a pan*

Adding broth to a pan after you've cooked meat and then scraping the bottom to loosen the browned bits adds flavor. In the recipe on the opposite page, it begins the process of making a scrumptious raspberry glaze.

Pan-Seared Pork Chops with Dried Fruit

 MINUTES

Pan-Seared Pork Chops with Dried Fruit

make it a meal Serve this saucy dish with plain couscous or quick-cooking brown rice. Add a savory green salad or steamed vegetables to balance the sweetness of the pork chops.

Cooking spray
4   (6-ounce) bone-in center-cut pork chops (about ¹/₂ inch thick)
¹/₄   teaspoon salt
¹/₄   teaspoon freshly ground black pepper
¹/₃   cup sliced shallots
1   cup fat-free, less-sodium chicken broth
1   (7-ounce) package dried mixed fruit bits (such as SunMaid)

1. Heat a large nonstick skillet over medium-high heat. Coat pan with cooking spray. Sprinkle both sides of pork with salt and pepper. Add pork to pan; cook 3 minutes on each side or until lightly browned. Remove from pan, and set aside.
2. Add shallots to pan; cook 1 minute, stirring constantly. Add broth and fruit; cover and simmer 1 minute. Return pork to pan, and cook 1 minute or until thoroughly heated. **Yield:** 4 servings (serving size: 1 pork chop and ¹/₃ cup sauce).

CALORIES 380; FAT 12.6g (sat 4.5g, mono 5.5g, poly 0.9g); PROTEIN 28.5g; CARB 38.7g; FIBER 4.7g; CHOL 76mg; IRON 1.8mg; SODIUM 299mg; CALC 56mg

 MINUTES

Rosemary-Grilled Lamb Chops

¹/₄   cup balsamic vinegar
1   tablespoon lemon juice
1   tablespoon dried rosemary, crushed
¹/₄   teaspoon garlic powder
¹/₄   teaspoon freshly ground black pepper
4   (4-ounce) lean lamb loin chops (1 inch thick)
Cooking spray

1. Prepare grill.
2. Combine first 5 ingredients in a small bowl.
3. Trim fat from lamb. Place lamb on grill rack coated with cooking spray; cover and grill 4 to 5 minutes on each side or until desired degree of doneness, basting occasionally with vinegar mixture. **Yield:** 2 servings (serving size: 2 chops).

CALORIES 341; FAT 11.8g (sat 4.6g, mono 6.2g, poly 0.9g); PROTEIN 46.7g; CARB 7.7g; FIBER 0.9g; CHOL 145mg; IRON 5.2mg; SODIUM 153mg; CALC 48mg

ES

Pork Chops with Ancho Chile Rub and Raspberry Glaze

make it a meal *Ancho chile powder, made from dried poblano peppers, adds a mild heat, which is mellowed by the sweetness of the preserves in the glaze. Serve this dish with smashed red potatoes.*

2 teaspoons ancho chile powder
½ teaspoon salt
¼ teaspoon dried thyme
4 (6-ounce) bone-in center-cut pork chops (about ½ inch thick)
Cooking spray
¼ cup fat-free, less-sodium beef broth
2 tablespoons seedless raspberry preserves

1. Combine first 3 ingredients in a small bowl, stirring well. Rub spice mixture evenly over pork. Heat a large nonstick skillet over medium heat. Coat pan with cooking spray. Add pork to pan, and cook 3 minutes on each side or until desired degree of doneness. Remove from pan, and keep warm.
2. Add broth to pan, and cook 30 seconds, scraping pan to loosen browned bits. Increase heat to medium-high. Add preserves to pan; cook 1 minute or until slightly thick, stirring constantly with a whisk. Brush pork with glaze. **Yield:** 4 servings (serving size: 1 pork chop and 1½ tablespoons glaze).

CALORIES 187; FAT 6g (sat 2g, mono 2.9g, poly 1.1g); PROTEIN 25.2g; CARB 6.8g; FIBER 0.2g; CHOL 70mg; IRON 0.1mg; SODIUM 398mg; CALC 1.3mg

15 MINUTES

Cinnamon-Spiced Pork and Plums

½   teaspoon ground cinnamon
¼   teaspoon salt
¼   teaspoon ground cloves
¼   teaspoon coarsely ground black pepper
4   (4-ounce) boneless center-cut loin pork chops (about ½ inch thick)
1   teaspoon olive oil
¼   cup finely chopped shallots
1   teaspoon butter
1   cup pitted dried plums, halved (about 4 ounces)
⅓   cup dry white wine
⅓   cup fat-free, less-sodium chicken broth
2   tablespoons chopped fresh parsley

1. Combine first 4 ingredients in a small bowl; sprinkle evenly over pork. Heat 1 teaspoon olive oil in a large nonstick skillet over medium-high heat. Add pork, and cook 2 minutes on each side or until browned. Add shallots and butter; cook 30 seconds or until butter melts, stirring frequently. Add plums, wine, and broth, turning pork to coat. Cover, reduce heat to medium-low, and cook 2 minutes or until pork is done. Sprinkle with parsley. **Yield:** 4 servings (serving size: 1 pork chop, ¼ cup sauce, and 1½ teaspoons parsley).

CALORIES 334; FAT 12.3g (sat 4.3g, mono 5.7g, poly 1g); PROTEIN 32g; CARB 20.6g; FIBER 2.7g; CHOL 94mg; IRON 2.1mg; SODIUM 252mg; CALC 43mg

Apricot Pork Chops

Apricot Pork Chops

30 MINUTES

Apricot Pork Chops

make it a meal *Peach preserves or orange marmalade can be used instead of apricot preserves. Serve these tangy chops with a dressed baked potato and sugar snap peas.*

Cooking spray
4   (4-ounce) boneless loin pork chops
¼   cup prechopped onion
¼   cup apricot preserves
1   tablespoon low-sodium soy sauce
2   teaspoons bottled minced garlic
¼   teaspoon salt
¼   cup sliced green onions

1. Heat a large nonstick skillet over medium-high heat. Coat pan with cooking spray. Add pork to pan; cook 6 minutes on each side or until done. Remove from pan; keep warm.
2. Add prechopped onion to pan; sauté 4 minutes or until lightly browned. Stir in preserves, soy sauce, garlic, and salt; cook 3 minutes or until thickened. Add pork to pan, turning to coat. Sprinkle with green onions. **Yield:** 4 servings (serving size: 1 pork chop and 1 tablespoon sauce).

CALORIES 231; FAT 8.3g (sat 2.5g, mono 3.6g, poly 1.2g); PROTEIN 23.9g; CARB 15.2g; FIBER 0.5g; CHOL 73mg; IRON 1.2mg; SODIUM 345mg; CALC 24mg

15 MINUTES

Balsamic-Plum Glazed Pork Chops

make it a meal *Port wine, plum preserves, and balsamic vinegar combine for the sweet and savory glaze. Couscous and green beans complete the meal.*

1   teaspoon butter
4   (4-ounce) boneless center-cut loin pork chops (about ½ inch thick)
¾   teaspoon salt, divided
¼   teaspoon freshly ground black pepper
Cooking spray
2   tablespoons chopped shallots
1   teaspoon bottled minced garlic
¼   cup port wine
2   tablespoons balsamic vinegar
⅓   cup plum preserves
Chopped fresh parsley (optional)

1. Melt butter in a large nonstick skillet over medium-high heat. Sprinkle pork evenly with ½ teaspoon salt and pepper. Add pork to pan; cook 3½ minutes on each side. Remove from pan.
2. Coat pan with cooking spray. Add shallots and garlic to pan; sauté 30 seconds. Add port and vinegar to pan; cook 30 seconds, stirring occasionally. Stir in remaining ¼ teaspoon salt and plum preserves; cook 30 seconds or until smooth, stirring constantly. Return pork to pan; cook 30 seconds or until desired degree of doneness, turning to coat. Sprinkle with parsley, if desired. **Yield:** 4 servings (serving size: 1 pork chop and about 1 tablespoon glaze).

CALORIES 281; FAT 9.5g (sat 3.6g, mono 4.2g, poly 0.6g); PROTEIN 25.3g; CARB 20.5g; FIBER 0.1g; CHOL 71mg; IRON 0.8mg; SODIUM 508mg; CALC 31mg

Using prechopped onion—found in the produce section of your supermarket—is one way to get dinner on the table even faster.

MAKE IT FASTER

Pork Chops Marsala

3. Return pork to pan; cook 2 minutes or until desired degree of doneness, turning to coat. Sprinkle with salt and pepper. **Yield:** 4 servings (serving size: 1 pork chop and ¹/₂ cup sauce).

CALORIES 242; FAT 6.8g (sat 2.5g, mono 2.9g, poly 0.6g); PROTEIN 27g; CARB 15.4g; FIBER 1.1g; CHOL 67mg; IRON 2.1mg; SODIUM 299mg; CALC 44mg

15
MINUTES

Curried Pork Chops with Mango Sauce

¹/₂	cup diced peeled mango
¹/₃	cup fat-free, less-sodium chicken broth
2	tablespoons fresh lime juice
2	teaspoons olive oil
1	teaspoon honey
1	teaspoon curry powder, divided
¹/₈	teaspoon salt
4	(4-ounce) boneless loin pork chops, trimmed (about 1 inch thick)
¹/₂	teaspoon salt

Cooking spray

1. Place first 5 ingredients in a food processor; process until smooth. Stir in ¹/₂ teaspoon curry powder and ¹/₈ teaspoon salt; set aside.
2. Sprinkle chops with remaining ¹/₂ teaspoon curry powder and ¹/₂ teaspoon salt. Coat chops with cooking spray. Heat a large nonstick skillet over medium-high heat; add chops. Cook 4 or 5 minutes on each side or until done. Serve chops with mango sauce. **Yield:** 4 servings (serving size: 1 chop and about 3 tablespoons mango sauce).

CALORIES 202; FAT 8.9g (sat 2.7g, mono 5.2g, poly 0.9g); PROTEIN 23.7g; CARB 6g; FIBER 0.5g; CHOL 67mg; IRON 1.1mg; SODIUM 458mg; CALC 22mg

20
MINUTES

Pork Chops Marsala

6	tablespoons all-purpose flour, divided
4	(4-ounce) boneless center-cut loin pork chops (about ¹/₂ inch thick)

Cooking spray
¹/₃	cup minced shallots (about 2)
2	teaspoons bottled minced garlic
1	(8-ounce) package presliced mushrooms
2	teaspoons chopped fresh thyme
1	cup fat-free, less-sodium chicken broth
¹/₄	cup Marsala wine or dry sherry
¹/₄	teaspoon salt
¹/₄	teaspoon black pepper

1. Heat a large nonstick skillet over medium-high heat. Place ¹/₄ cup flour in a shallow dish. Dredge pork in flour. Coat pan with cooking spray. Add pork to pan; cook 4 minutes on each side or until browned. Remove pork from pan.
2. Add shallots, garlic, and mushrooms to pan; sauté 3 minutes or until moisture evaporates. Add remaining 2 tablespoons flour and thyme, and cook 1 minute, stirring well. Combine broth and Marsala, stirring until smooth. Gradually add broth mixture to pan, stirring constantly with a whisk; bring to a boil. Reduce heat and simmer 2 minutes or until sauce thickens.

Dicing and peeling mango can be time consuming. Use peeled mango slices from a jar to minimize your prep time.

MAKE IT FASTER

 MINUTES

Peppered Pork and Pears

If you don't have pear brandy, substitute regular brandy or additional chicken broth. Serve with egg noodles.

1 teaspoon olive oil
4 (4-ounce) boneless center-cut loin pork chops (about ½ inch thick)
2 teaspoons coarsely ground mixed peppercorns or black pepper
½ teaspoon salt, divided
1 teaspoon butter
1 cup thinly sliced leek (about 1 large)
2 firm Bartlett pears, cored and cut lengthwise into ½-inch-thick slices
⅓ cup fat-free, less-sodium chicken broth
¼ cup white wine
2 tablespoons pear brandy
1 tablespoon chopped fresh sage
Sage leaves (optional)

1. Heat oil in a large nonstick skillet over medium-high heat. Sprinkle pork with pepper and ¼ teaspoon salt. Add pork to pan; cook 4 minutes on each side or until browned. Remove pork from pan; cover and keep warm.
2. Add butter and leek to pan; sauté 2 minutes or until leek is tender. Add pears. Reduce heat to medium; cook about 2 minutes, stirring gently. Add broth, wine, brandy, chopped sage, and remaining ¼ teaspoon salt; bring to a boil. Cook until sauce is slightly thickened (about 2 minutes). Spoon sauce over pork. Garnish with sage leaves, if desired. **Yield:** 4 servings (serving size: 1 pork chop and 1 cup pear mixture).

CALORIES 259; FAT 7.5g (sat 2.4g, mono 3.5g, poly 0.6g); PROTEIN 24.8g; CARB 16.8g; FIBER 3.3g; CHOL 73mg; IRON 1.7mg; SODIUM 384mg; CALC 43mg

20 MINUTES

Pork Chops with Ginger-Cherry Sauce

1	teaspoon dark sesame oil
4	(4-ounce) center-cut boneless pork chops, trimmed
½	teaspoon salt
¼	teaspoon freshly ground black pepper
½	cup cherry preserves
2	teaspoons low-sodium soy sauce
1	teaspoon bottled ground fresh ginger (such as Spice World)
1	teaspoon seasoned rice vinegar

1. Heat oil in a nonstick skillet over medium-high heat. Sprinkle pork with salt and pepper; add to pan. Cook 4 minutes on each side; remove pork from pan.

2. Combine preserves and remaining ingredients in a small bowl. Add preserves mixture to pan; reduce heat, and cook 2 minutes or until slightly thickened, stirring constantly. Return pork to pan; cook 2 minutes or until thoroughly heated. **Yield:** 4 servings (serving size: 1 pork chop and 2 tablespoons sauce).

CALORIES 275; FAT 7.8g (sat 2.6g, mono 3.4g, poly 1g); PROTEIN 23.5g; CARB 26.8g; FIBER 0.1g; CHOL 67mg; IRON 1mg; SODIUM 453mg; CALC 19mg

15 MINUTES

Pork Chops with Bourbon-Peach Sauce

4	(4-ounce) boneless center-cut loin pork chops (about ¼ inch thick)
¾	teaspoon salt
¼	teaspoon black pepper
¼	teaspoon ground red pepper
	Cooking spray
1	tablespoon minced shallots
1	teaspoon minced bottled garlic
1½	cups frozen sliced peaches
½	cup fat-free, less-sodium chicken broth
2	teaspoons brown sugar
2	fresh thyme sprigs
2	tablespoons bourbon
2	teaspoons butter

1. Sprinkle pork with salt and peppers. Heat a large skillet over medium-high heat. Coat pan with cooking spray. Add pork to pan; cook 2 ½ minutes on each side or until browned. Remove pork from pan, and keep warm.
2. Add shallots and garlic to pan; sauté 30 seconds. Add peaches and broth to pan; sauté 2 minutes. Add sugar and thyme to pan; cook 1 minute. Add bourbon and butter to pan; cook 4 ½ minutes or until butter melts and sauce is slightly thickened. Discard thyme sprigs. Serve with pork. **Yield:** 4 servings (serving size: 1 chop and ¼ cup sauce).

CALORIES 233; FAT 8.4g (sat 3.6g, mono 3.4g, poly 0.5g); PROTEIN 24.7g; CARB 8.6g; FIBER 0.9g; CHOL 70mg; IRON 0.8mg; SODIUM 560mg; CALC 30mg

20 MINUTES

Pork Strips with Peanut Sauce and Rice Noodles

Rice noodles soak up liquid quickly, so if you're not serving immediately, reserve about ¼ cup cooked sauce, and add to remaining pork mixture just before serving.

½	cup boiling water
¼	cup reduced-fat peanut butter
2	tablespoons rice vinegar
2	tablespoons low-sodium soy sauce
1	teaspoon bottled minced garlic
1	teaspoon bottled ground fresh ginger (such as Spice World)
2	teaspoons fresh lime juice
1	teaspoon sesame oil
1	teaspoon chile paste with garlic (such as Sambal oelek)
1	teaspoon honey
½	teaspoon cornstarch
	Cooking spray
4	(4-ounce) boneless loin pork chops, trimmed and cut into ½-inch strips
1	red bell pepper, seeded and thinly sliced (about 2 cups)
1	(6-ounce) package rice noodles
½	cup thinly sliced green onions
	Lime wedges (optional)

1. Combine first 11 ingredients in a bowl, stirring with a whisk; set aside.
2. Heat a large nonstick skillet over medium-high heat. Coat pan with cooking spray. Add pork and pepper; cook 6 minutes or until pork is done. Add peanut butter mixture to pan, stirring well to coat pork; bring to a boil. Reduce heat, and simmer 1 minute.
3. Cook rice noodles according to package directions, omitting salt and fat; drain. Add noodles to pork mixture, tossing gently. Sprinkle with sliced green onions. Serve with lime wedges, if desired. **Yield:** 4 servings (serving size: 2 cups pork mixture and 2 tablespoons green onions).

CALORIES 461; FAT 15.8g (sat 4g, mono 4.1g, poly 1.7g); PROTEIN 29.6g; CARB 49.9g; FIBER 2.3g; CHOL 73mg; IRON 2mg; SODIUM 563mg; CALC 28mg

Peanut butter creates the base for the flavorful sauce in the recipe for Pork Strips with Peanut Sauce and Rice Noodles. When used sparingly, peanut butter can be part of a healthy diet.

INGREDIENT SPOTLIGHT

COOKING CLASS: *how to chop an apple*

Pierce the center of the apple with an apple corer, and rotate it to remove the core. Use a paring knife to slice the apple in half vertically. Place the apple halves, cut side down, on a cutting board. Cut through the skin to create wedges or thinner slices. Chop the wedges into bite-sized pieces with the paring knife.

 20 MINUTES

Pork with Lemon-Caper Sauce

1.5 ounces all-purpose flour (about ⅓ cup)
⅛ teaspoon salt
3 tablespoons Italian-seasoned breadcrumbs
3 tablespoons preshredded fresh Parmesan cheese
¼ teaspoon black pepper
1 large egg white, lightly beaten
4 (4-ounce) boneless center-cut pork chops (about ½ inch thick)
Cooking spray
2 teaspoons olive oil
½ cup fat-free, less-sodium chicken broth
1 tablespoon dry white wine
¼ teaspoon grated lemon rind
1 tablespoon fresh lemon juice
2 teaspoons capers, rinsed and drained

1. Combine flour and salt in a shallow dish. Place breadcrumbs, cheese, and pepper in a shallow dish; place egg white in another shallow dish. Dredge pork in flour mixture, dip in egg white, and dredge in breadcrumb mixture. Coat pork with cooking spray.
2. Heat oil in a large nonstick skillet over medium-high heat. Add pork to pan; cook 4 minutes on each side or until done. Remove from pan; keep warm. Add broth and remaining ingredients to pan, scraping pan to loosen browned bits. Cook 2 minutes or until reduced to ¼ cup (about 2 minutes). Serve with pork. **Yield:** 4 servings (serving size: 1 chop and 1 tablespoon sauce).

CALORIES 256; FAT 10.1g (sat 3.3g, mono 4.9g, poly 0.8g); PROTEIN 28.2g; CARB 11.5g; FIBER 0.7g; CHOL 68mg; IRON 1.5mg; SODIUM 419mg; CALC 82mg

 20 MINUTES

Quick Choucroute

2 teaspoons canola oil
1 pound boneless center-cut loin pork chops, cut into ½-inch slices
⅛ teaspoon kosher salt
¼ teaspoon freshly ground black pepper
1 cup chopped Golden Delicious apple (about 1)
¾ cup thinly sliced onion (about 1 medium)
1 bay leaf
1 (12-ounce) bottle light beer
2 cups sauerkraut, rinsed and drained
½ pound low-fat smoked sausage, cut diagonally into ½-inch slices
⅓ cup chopped fresh parsley
2 tablespoons prepared horseradish
1 tablespoon whole-grain mustard

1. Heat oil in a large nonstick skillet over medium-high heat. Sprinkle pork with salt and pepper. Add pork to pan; sauté 2 minutes. Remove pork from pan; keep warm.
2. Add apple, onion, and bay leaf to pan; cook 2 minutes or until onion is lightly browned. Add beer, scraping pan to loosen browned bits. Add sauerkraut and sausage; bring to a simmer, and cook 5 minutes. Return pork to pan; cover and cook 2 minutes or until pork is thoroughly heated. Discard bay leaf, and stir in parsley. Serve with horseradish and mustard. **Yield:** 4 servings (serving size: 2 cups pork mixture, 1½ teaspoons horseradish, and ¾ teaspoon mustard).

CALORIES 307; FAT 11g (sat 3.3g, mono 5.1g, poly 1.5g); PROTEIN 31g; CARB 19.9g; FIBER 3.3g; CHOL 84mg; IRON 3.2mg; SODIUM 837mg; CALC 53mg

Skillet Pork and Warm Pineapple Salsa

make it a meal *Either fresh or canned pineapple chunks work well in this recipe. If you like a spicier kick, remember that smaller jalapeño peppers are typically hotter than the larger ones. Serve with rice and steamed snow peas.*

2   teaspoons olive oil, divided
4   (4-ounce) boneless loin pork chops
1   teaspoon salt-free Jamaican jerk seasoning (such as Spice Islands)
½   teaspoon salt
⅛   teaspoon ground red pepper
1⅓ cups pineapple chunks
½   cup coarsely chopped onion
1   tablespoon fresh lime juice
1   small jalapeño pepper, seeded and chopped

1. Heat 1 teaspoon oil in a large nonstick skillet over medium-high heat. Sprinkle both sides of pork with jerk seasoning, salt, and red pepper. Add pork to pan; cook 4 minutes on each side or until done. Remove pork from pan; cover and keep warm.
2. Add remaining 1 teaspoon oil to skillet. Add pineapple, reserving 2 tablespoons juice. Add onion, and cook 2 minutes or until lightly browned, stirring frequently. Stir in lime juice, jalapeño, and reserved pineapple juice. Serve warm salsa over pork.
Yield: 4 servings (serving size: 1 chop and ½ cup salsa).

CALORIES 235; FAT 7.5g (sat 2g, mono 3.9g, poly 0.7g); PROTEIN 24.5g; CARB 17.2g; FIBER 1g; CHOL 70mg; IRON 1.3mg; SODIUM 490mg; CALC 32mg

Smoked Paprika Pork Chops with Bell Pepper and Corn Relish

15 MINUTES

Smoked Paprika Pork Chops with Bell Pepper and Corn Relish

make it a meal *Accompany the pork chops with refrigerated potato wedges tossed with garlic powder, ground red pepper, and salt, and roasted until crisp. They're the perfect accompaniment to the spicy chops and are so much faster than cutting and peeling your own potatoes.*

1	tablespoon olive oil
½	cup prechopped red onion
2	teaspoons bottled minced fresh ginger
⅓	cup chopped red bell pepper
1	teaspoon ground coriander
¼	teaspoon dried thyme
1	(15.5-ounce) can no salt-added whole kernel corn, drained
1	teaspoon cider vinegar
¾	teaspoon salt, divided
¼	teaspoon black pepper, divided
1½	teaspoons smoked sweet paprika
4	(4-ounce) center-cut boneless pork loin chops, trimmed
	Cooking spray

1. Heat olive oil in a large nonstick skillet over medium-high heat. Add red onion and ginger; sauté 2 minutes or until tender. Add chopped red bell pepper, ground coriander, dried thyme, and corn; cook 3 minutes or until bell pepper is tender, stirring occasionally. Stir in cider vinegar, ¼ teaspoon salt, and ⅛ teaspoon black pepper; cook 1 minute, stirring constantly. Spoon relish into a bowl.

2. Combine remaining ½ teaspoon salt, ⅛ teaspoon black pepper, and paprika; sprinkle evenly over pork. Coat pan with cooking spray. Add pork to pan; cook 4 minutes on each side or until done. Serve with relish. **Yield:** 4 servings (serving size: 1 pork chop and about ⅓ cup relish).

CALORIES 263; FAT 8.9g (sat 2.5g, mono 4.5g, poly 1.2g); PROTEIN 27.2g; CARB 19.8g; FIBER 1.4g; CHOL 62mg; IRON 1.6mg; SODIUM 508mg; CALC 39mg

15 MINUTES

Southwestern Pork Chops

4	(4-ounce) boneless loin pork chops, trimmed
½	teaspoon garlic salt
½	teaspoon freshly ground black pepper
½	cup bottled chunky salsa
2	tablespoons fresh lime juice
	Cooking spray
	Chopped fresh cilantro or parsley (optional)

1. Sprinkle pork chops with garlic salt and pepper. Combine salsa and juice; set aside.
2. Heat a large nonstick skillet over medium-high heat. Coat chops with cooking spray; add to pan. Cook 4 minutes on each side or until done. Add salsa mixture to pan; cook over medium heat 1 minute or until thoroughly heated. Serve immediately. Sprinkle with cilantro or parsley, if desired. **Yield:** 4 servings (serving size: 1 pork chop and about 2 tablespoons sauce).

CALORIES 171; FAT 6.5g (sat 2.4g, mono 3.4g, poly 0.7g); PROTEIN 23.4g; CARB 2.8g; FIBER 0.9g; CHOL 67mg; IRON 0.9mg; SODIUM 360mg; CALC 20mg

MINUTES

Spiced Pork Chops with Apple Chutney

Chutney:

1 tablespoon butter
5 cups (¼-inch) cubed peeled apple (about 3 apples)
¼ cup dried cranberries
3 tablespoons brown sugar
3 tablespoons cider vinegar
2 teaspoons minced peeled fresh ginger
¼ teaspoon salt
¼ teaspoon dry mustard
⅛ teaspoon ground allspice

Pork:

¾ teaspoon ground chipotle chile pepper
½ teaspoon salt
½ teaspoon garlic powder
½ teaspoon ground coriander
¼ teaspoon black pepper
4 (4-ounce) boneless center-cut pork loin chops, trimmed
Cooking spray

1. To prepare chutney, melt butter in a non-stick skillet over medium-high heat. Add apple; sauté 4 minutes or until lightly browned. Add cranberries and next 6 ingredients; bring to a boil. Reduce heat, and simmer 8 minutes or until apples are tender; stir occasionally.

2. To prepare pork, while chutney simmers, heat a grill pan over medium-high heat. Combine chipotle and next 4 ingredients; sprinkle over pork. Coat grill pan with cooking spray. Add pork to pan; cook 4 minutes on each side or until done. Serve with chutney. **Yield:** 4 servings (serving size: 1 chop and about ⅓ cup chutney).

CALORIES 321; FAT 9.6g (sat 4.2g, mono 3.6g, poly 0.7g); PROTEIN 24.4g; CARB 34.6g; FIBER 2.4g; CHOL 72mg; IRON 1.1mg; SODIUM 520mg; CALC 45mg

make it a meal *Indulge in a heart-warming, family-friendly dinner of spicy chops and a fragrant chutney topping. Slender haricots verts make a pretty and quick-cooking complement to the meal.*

MINUTES

Wasabi and Panko-Crusted Pork with Gingered Soy Sauce

²/₃ cup panko (Japanese breadcrumbs)
1   large egg white, lightly beaten
4   (4-ounce) boneless center-cut loin pork chops (about ½ inch thick)
1   teaspoon peanut oil
Cooking spray
⅛   teaspoon salt
1   tablespoon bottled ground fresh ginger (such as Spice World)
⅓   cup fat-free, less-sodium chicken broth
2   tablespoons sake or dry sherry
2   tablespoons low-sodium soy sauce
2   teaspoons sugar
1   teaspoon wasabi paste
⅓   cup thinly sliced green onions

1. Place panko in a shallow dish. Place egg white in another shallow dish. Dip pork in egg white; dredge in panko.
2. Heat peanut oil in a large nonstick skillet coated with cooking spray over medium-high heat; add pork. Cook 4 minutes on each side or until done. Remove pork from pan; sprinkle with salt.
3. Reduce heat to medium. Add ginger to pan; cook 30 seconds, stirring constantly. Combine broth and next 4 ingredients in a small bowl, stirring well with a whisk. Add broth mixture to pan, scraping pan to loosen browned bits. Stir in green onions. Spoon sauce over pork. **Yield:** 4 servings (serving size: 1 pork chop and about 1 tablespoon sauce).

CALORIES 215; FAT 6.8g (sat 2.1g, mono 2.9g, poly 0.8g); PROTEIN 24.5g; CARB 10.8g; FIBER 0.9g; CHOL 65mg; IRON 1.1mg; SODIUM 454mg; CALC 15mg

Coconut Curried Pork, Snow Pea, and Mango Stir-Fry

15 MINUTES

Coconut Curried Pork, Snow Pea, and Mango Stir-Fry

2   (3½-ounce) bags boil-in-bag long-grain rice
1   (1-pound) pork tenderloin, trimmed
1   tablespoon canola oil
1   teaspoon red curry powder
1   cup snow peas
⅓   cup light coconut milk
1   tablespoon fish sauce
1   teaspoon red curry paste (such as Thai Kitchen)
1   cup bottled mango, cut into ½-inch pieces
½   cup sliced green onions, divided
2   tablespoons shredded coconut
4   lime wedges (optional)

1. Prepare rice according to package directions, omitting salt and fat; drain. Cut pork into 1-inch cubes. Heat oil in a large nonstick skillet over medium-high heat. Sprinkle pork evenly with curry powder. Add pork and snow peas to pan; stir-fry 3 minutes.
2. Combine coconut milk, fish sauce, and curry paste, stirring well. Add milk mixture to pan; bring to a simmer. Stir in mango and ¼ cup onions; cook 1 minute or until thoroughly heated. Remove from heat. Place 1 cup rice on each of 4 plates; top each serving with 1¼ cups pork mixture. Sprinkle each serving with 1 tablespoon of remaining ¼ cup onions and 1½ teaspoons shredded coconut. Serve with lime wedges, if desired. **Yield:** 4 servings.

CALORIES 429; FAT 9.7g (sat 3.5g, mono 3.9g, poly 1.6g); PROTEIN 29.7g; CARB 54.8g; FIBER 2.3g; CHOL 74mg; IRON 4mg; SODIUM 454mg; CALC 38mg

20 MINUTES

Hoisin Pork and Snow Pea Stir-Fry

4   ounces uncooked rice noodles or rice
2   tablespoons low-sodium soy sauce, divided
1   (1-pound) pork tenderloin, trimmed and thinly sliced
¾   cup fat-free, less-sodium chicken broth
¼   cup hoisin sauce
1   tablespoon cornstarch
1   tablespoon honey
4   teaspoons dark sesame oil, divided
3   cups snow peas, trimmed (about ½ pound)
½   cup sliced red bell pepper
1   tablespoon bottled ground fresh ginger
1   teaspoon bottled minced garlic
½   cup chopped green onions

1. Prepare rice noodles according to package directions, omitting salt and fat. Drain and keep warm.
2. Combine 1 tablespoon soy sauce and pork, tossing to coat. Set aside.
3. Combine remaining 1 tablespoon soy sauce, broth, hoisin, cornstarch, and honey in a medium bowl, stirring with a whisk until smooth.
4. Heat 1 tablespoon sesame oil in a large nonstick skillet over medium-high heat. Add pork mixture to pan; sauté 3 minutes or until browned. Remove pork from pan. Add remaining 1 teaspoon sesame oil to pan. Stir in peas, bell pepper, ginger, and garlic; sauté 30 seconds. Return pork mixture to pan; stir in broth mixture. Simmer 2 minutes or until thick, stirring occasionally. Remove from heat, and stir in green onions. Serve pork mixture over noodles. **Yield:** 4 servings (serving size: ¾ cup noodles and about 1 cup pork mixture).

CALORIES 395; FAT 9.6g (sat 2.1g, mono 3.7g, poly 2.5g); PROTEIN 28.1g; CARB 43.7g; FIBER 2.4g; CHOL 74mg; IRON 2.5mg; SODIUM 690mg; CALC 53mg

Orange Pork with Scallions

spray. Add pork to pan; sauté 3 minutes or until desired degree of doneness; stir frequently. Remove pork from pan.

3. Heat oil in pan. Add carrots, $1/4$ cup water, ginger, and garlic to pan; cook $1^{1}/_{2}$ minutes, scraping pan to loosen browned bits. Return pork to pan. Stir in broth mixture; bring to a boil. Cook 30 seconds. Stir in $1/3$ cup onions. Serve immediately. Garnish with sliced onions, if desired. **Yield:** 4 servings (serving size: about 1 cup pork mixture).

CALORIES 214; FAT 6.9g (sat 1.9g, mono 3.1g, poly 1g); PROTEIN 24.1g; CARB 12.7g; FIBER 2.2g; CHOL 65mg; IRON 1.7mg; SODIUM 586mg; CALC 37mg

Orange Pork with Scallions

make it a meal *An easy, basic stir-fry comes to life when served over rice noodles or rice. For an extra punch of flavor and crunch consider adding cashews.*

1	(1-pound) pork tenderloin
2	tablespoons cornstarch, divided
$1/3$	cup fat-free, less-sodium chicken broth
$1/4$	cup orange juice
2	tablespoons low-sodium soy sauce
1	teaspoon chili garlic sauce
$1/4$	teaspoon salt

Cooking spray

$1^{1}/_{2}$	teaspoons canola oil
2	cups matchstick-cut carrots
$1/4$	cup water
2	teaspoons bottled ground fresh ginger (such as Spice World)
2	teaspoons bottled minced garlic
$1/3$	cup diagonally cut green onions

Sliced green onions (optional)

1. Cut pork into 2 x $1/4$-inch-wide strips. Combine pork and 1 tablespoon cornstarch in a bowl; toss well. Combine remaining 1 tablespoon cornstarch, broth, and next 4 ingredients.

2. Heat a large nonstick skillet over medium-high heat. Coat pan with cooking

Pork Tenderloin with Ginger-Soy Sauce

1	teaspoon canola oil
1	(1-pound) pork tenderloin, trimmed and cut crosswise into 8 pieces
$1/4$	teaspoon salt
$1/4$	teaspoon black pepper
$1/4$	cup water
1	tablespoon bottled minced fresh ginger
2	tablespoons rice vinegar
1	tablespoon water
1	tablespoon low-sodium soy sauce
1	teaspoon sugar
$1/2$	teaspoon dark sesame oil
$1/4$	cup chopped green onions

1. Heat canola oil in a large nonstick skillet over medium-high heat.

2. Flatten each piece of pork to 1-inch thickness with fingertips; sprinkle with salt and pepper. Add pork to pan; cook 5 minutes on each side or until desired degree of doneness. Remove pork from pan; keep warm.

3. Add $1/4$ cup water to pan, scraping to loosen browned bits. Add ginger and next 5 ingredients to pan; cook over medium-low heat 2 minutes. Stir in onions; serve sauce over pork. **Yield:** 4 servings (serving size: about 3 ounces pork and about 1 tablespoon sauce).

CALORIES 165; FAT 5.6g (sat 1.6g, mono 2.2g, poly 1.3g); PROTEIN 24.1g; CARB 3.1g; FIBER 0.4g; CHOL 74mg; IRON 1.6mg; SODIUM 338mg; CALC 8mg

COOKING CLASS: *how to prepare pork tenderloin*

When preparing pork tenderloin, remove the silver skin, which is the thin, shiny membrane that runs along the surface of the meat. Leaving it on can cause the tenderloin to toughen and lose shape during cooking.

15 MINUTES

Pork and Stir-Fried Vegetables with Spicy Asian Sauce

make it a meal *Use your favorite sliced vegetables in place of the zucchini and bell pepper; mushrooms and water chestnuts would also be good. To round out the meal, serve with quick-cooking rice stick noodles.*

1   teaspoon canola oil
¼   cup hoisin sauce
¼   cup ketchup
1   teaspoon low-sodium soy sauce
½   teaspoon bottled minced garlic
⅛   to ¼ teaspoon ground red pepper
1   (1-pound) pork tenderloin, trimmed and cut into ½-inch pieces
1   teaspoon black pepper
¼   teaspoon salt
2   teaspoons dark sesame oil
1   cup presliced zucchini
1   cup presliced red bell pepper
1   teaspoon bottled ground fresh ginger (such as Spice World)
½   cup chopped green onions
1   teaspoon toasted sesame seeds

1. Heat canola oil in a large nonstick skillet over medium-high heat. Combine hoisin sauce and next 4 ingredients, stirring until blended; set side. Add pork to pan; sprinkle with black pepper and salt. Cook 3 minutes on each side or until done. Remove from pan. Add sesame oil to pan. Add zucchini, bell pepper, and ginger; stir-fry 4 minutes or until bell pepper is tender. Stir in onions and pork. Add hoisin mixture to pan; toss to coat. Sprinkle with sesame seeds. **Yield:** 4 servings (serving size: about 1 cup).

CALORIES 244; FAT 8.5g (sat 1.9g, mono 3.6g, poly 2.3g); PROTEIN 25.6g; CARB 15.6g; FIBER 1.7g; CHOL 74mg; IRON 2mg; SODIUM 678mg; CALC 24mg

 MINUTES

Szechuan Pork

6	ounces soba (buckwheat) noodles, uncooked
2	teaspoons dark sesame oil
1	(1-pound) pork tenderloin, trimmed and cut into 2-inch strips
1	tablespoon chili garlic sauce (such as Lee Kum Kee)
1	teaspoon bottled ground fresh ginger (such as Spice World)
³/₄	cup red bell pepper strips (about 1 small pepper)
¹/₄	cup fat-free, less-sodium chicken broth
1¹/₂	tablespoons low-sodium soy sauce
1	tablespoon peanut butter
³/₄	cup (2-inch) diagonally cut green onions (about 4 green onions)

1. Cook noodles according to package directions. Drain and rinse with cold water; drain.

2. Heat oil in a large nonstick skillet over medium-high heat. Add pork, chili garlic sauce, and ginger to pan; stir-fry 2 minutes. Add bell pepper to pan; stir-fry 2 minutes. Add broth, soy sauce, and peanut butter to pan. Reduce heat to low; cook 1 minute or until sauce is slightly thick. Stir in onions. Serve over noodles. **Yield:** 4 servings (serving size: 1 cup pork mixture and ¹/₂ cup noodles).

CALORIES 338; FAT 8.6g (sat 2.2g, mono 3.5g, poly 1.9g); PROTEIN 30.4g; CARB 36.8g; FIBER 1.7g; CHOL 63mg; IRON 2.9mg; SODIUM 693mg; CALC 40mg

make it a meal *Fresh sliced pineapple makes a nice companion for this one-dish meal.*

Pork Vindaloo

2   (3½-ounce) bags boil-in-bag brown rice
2   teaspoons canola oil
1   (8-ounce) container prechopped onion
1   (1-pound) pork tenderloin, trimmed and cut
    into 1-inch pieces
1¼ teaspoons garam masala
1   teaspoon garlic powder
1   teaspoon mustard seeds
2   teaspoons bottled ground fresh ginger (such
    as Spice World)
¼   to ½ teaspoon ground red pepper
¼   cup fat-free, less-sodium chicken broth
1   (14.5-ounce) can petite diced tomatoes,
    undrained
1   (8-ounce) can tomato sauce
2   tablespoons chopped fresh cilantro
1   tablespoon red wine vinegar

1. Prepare rice according to package directions, omitting salt and fat; set aside.
2. Heat oil in a large nonstick skillet over
medium-high heat. Add onion to pan; sauté
2 minutes. Combine pork and next 5 ingredients; toss well. Add pork mixture to pan;
sauté 5 minutes or until lightly browned.
3. Add broth to pan, scraping bottom of pan
to loosen browned bits. Add tomatoes and
tomato sauce; cook 3 minutes, stirring occasionally. Remove from heat; stir in cilantro
and vinegar. Serve over rice. **Yield:** 4 servings (serving size: 1 cup pork mixture and
about ³/4 cup rice).

CALORIES 392; FAT 7.8g (sat 1.6g, mono 3.3g, poly 1.2g); PROTEIN 31.2g;
CARB 51.8g; FIBER 4.4g; CHOL 74mg; IRON 3.1mg; SODIUM 678mg; CALC 107mg

Garam masala is an
Indian spice blend
that typically
includes black
pepper, cardamom,
cinnamon, cloves,
and cumin.

INGREDIENT SPOTLIGHT

Pork Tenderloin with Exotic Mushrooms

make it a meal *Enjoy this pork version
of creamy Stroganoff; it has a short prep
time. Serve with steamed broccoli.*

8   ounces uncooked wide egg noodles
1   (1-pound) pork tenderloin, trimmed
Cooking spray
1   teaspoon olive oil
1   teaspoon salt
½   teaspoon dried thyme
½   teaspoon freshly ground black pepper
1   (8-ounce) package presliced exotic
    mushroom blend (such as shiitake, cremini,
    and oyster)
½   cup water
1   tablespoon all-purpose flour
2   tablespoons Worcestershire sauce
1   (8-ounce) carton reduced-fat sour cream
2   tablespoons chopped fresh parsley

1. Cook pasta according to package directions, omitting salt and fat. Drain; keep
warm. Cut pork crosswise into 4 pieces; cut
each piece in half lengthwise. Slice each half
into thin strips.
2. Heat a large nonstick skillet over
medium-high heat. Coat pan with cooking
spray. Add olive oil. Add pork, salt, thyme,
pepper, and mushrooms to pan; sauté
4 minutes or until pork is desired degree
of doneness and mushrooms are tender.
Remove from heat.
3. Combine water, flour, and Worcestershire
sauce in a medium bowl, stirring with a
whisk until smooth. Stir in sour cream. Add
sour cream mixture to pan, stirring to combine. Return pan to medium-high heat.
Bring to a boil; cook 1 minute or until sauce
thickens, stirring constantly. Serve the
pork mixture over noodles; sprinkle with
parsley. Serve immediately. **Yield:** 4 servings (serving size: 1 cup pork mixture, 1¼
cups noodles, and 1½ teaspoons parsley).

CALORIES 479; FAT 15.5g (sat 7g, mono 5.7g, poly 1.1g); PROTEIN 34.8g;
CARB 50.2g; FIBER 2.7g; CHOL 98mg; IRON 4.4mg; SODIUM 760mg; CALC 97mg

Pork Medallions with
Apricot-Orange
Sauce

MINUTES

Pork Medallions with Apricot-Orange Sauce

1 tablespoon olive oil, divided
1 (1-pound) pork tenderloin, cut into 8 (1-inch-thick) slices
1/2 teaspoon salt
1/4 teaspoon black pepper
1 cup thinly sliced onion
1/2 cup dried apricots, sliced
1/2 cup fat-free, less-sodium chicken broth
2 tablespoons fresh orange juice
2 teaspoons bottled minced garlic
1/8 teaspoon black pepper
1 tablespoon chopped fresh flat-leaf parsley

1. Heat 2 teaspoons oil in a large nonstick skillet over medium-high heat. Sprinkle pork evenly with salt and 1/4 teaspoon pepper. Add pork to pan; cook 3 minutes on each side or until browned. Remove from pan; keep warm.
2. Heat remaining 1 teaspoon oil in pan. Add onion to pan; sauté 3 minutes or until tender. Stir in apricots, broth, juice, garlic, and 1/8 teaspoon pepper; bring to a boil. Cook 2 minutes or until slightly thickened. Remove from heat; stir in parsley. Serve sauce with pork. **Yield:** 4 servings (serving size: 2 pork slices and 1/4 cup sauce).

CALORIES 236; FAT 7.6g (sat 1.8g, mono 4g, poly 0.7g); PROTEIN 23.8g; CARB 15.8g; FIBER 1.6g; CHOL 63mg; IRON 2.2mg; SODIUM 390mg; CALC 23mg

15
MINUTES

Maple-Balsamic-Glazed Pork Medallions

make it a meal *Serve with whipped sweet potatoes and sautéed broccoli rabe.*

1/4 cup maple syrup
3 tablespoons balsamic vinegar
2 teaspoons Dijon mustard
1 (1-pound) pork tenderloin, trimmed
2 teaspoons olive oil
1/2 teaspoon salt
1/4 teaspoon freshly ground black pepper

1. Combine syrup and vinegar in a small saucepan; bring to a boil. Cook until reduced to 1/3 cup (about 3 minutes), stirring occasionally. Remove from heat; stir in mustard.
2. Cut pork crosswise into 8 pieces. Place each pork piece between 2 sheets of heavy-duty plastic wrap; pound to 1/4-inch thickness using a meat mallet or small heavy skillet. Heat oil in a large nonstick skillet over medium-high heat. Sprinkle pork evenly with salt and pepper. Add pork to pan; cook 3 minutes on each side. Add vinegar mixture; cook 1 minute or until desired degree of doneness, turning pork to coat. Place 2 pork medallions on each of 4 plates; drizzle about 1 tablespoon syrup mixture over each serving. **Yield:** 4 servings.

CALORIES 214; FAT 6.4g (sat 1.7g, mono 3.3g, poly 0.7g); PROTEIN 22.7g; CARB 15.3g; FIBER 0.1g; CHOL 63mg; IRON 1.5mg; SODIUM 409mg; CALC 22mg

Maple syrup isn't just for pancakes. It also adds dimension to savory dishes with its clean, unique flavor. Whatever maple syrup you use, make sure the label says "pure maple syrup." You'll know you're getting the best.

INGREDIENT SPOTLIGHT

15 MINUTES

Pork Medallions with Red Currant Sauce

make it a meal *Red currant jelly renders the sauce a vibrant crimson, though you can use any variety of fruit jelly. Add quick-cooking grits and a Caesar salad on the side.*

$\frac{1}{2}$ teaspoon dried thyme
$\frac{1}{2}$ teaspoon salt
$\frac{1}{4}$ teaspoon smoked paprika
$\frac{1}{4}$ teaspoon dried rubbed sage
$\frac{1}{8}$ teaspoon black pepper
1 (1-pound) pork tenderloin, trimmed
Cooking spray
$\frac{1}{3}$ cup red currant jelly
3 tablespoons cider vinegar
2 tablespoons chopped fresh chives

1. Combine first 5 ingredients in a small bowl. Cut pork crosswise into 8 (1-inch-thick) pieces. Place each piece between 2 pieces of heavy-duty plastic wrap, and pound to $\frac{1}{2}$-inch thickness using a meat mallet or small heavy skillet. Rub pork with spice mixture.
2. Heat a large nonstick skillet over medium-high heat. Coat pan with cooking spray. Add pork to pan, and cook 3 minutes on each side. Remove pork from pan, and keep warm.
3. Add jelly to pan; cook 30 seconds, scraping pan to loosen browned bits. Remove from heat; stir in vinegar. Serve sauce with pork; sprinkle with chives. **Yield:** 4 servings (serving size: 2 medallions, 1 tablespoon sauce, and $1\frac{1}{2}$ teaspoons chives).

CALORIES 202; FAT 3.9g (sat 1.3g, mono 1.6g, poly 0.3g); PROTEIN 22.6g; CARB 17.8g; FIBER 0.3g; CHOL 63mg; IRON 1.4mg; SODIUM 341mg; CALC 10mg

Pork Medallions with Balsamic-Shallot Sauce

make it a meal *Complement this entrée with Parmesan cheese stirred into quick-cooking polenta and an iceberg wedge drizzled with buttermilk dressing.*

1   (1-pound) pork tenderloin, trimmed
½   teaspoon salt
½   teaspoon dried thyme
⅛   teaspoon black pepper
⅛   teaspoon ground allspice
Cooking spray
¼   cup finely chopped shallots
1   teaspoon butter
1   tablespoon brown sugar
3   tablespoons balsamic vinegar

1. Cut tenderloin crosswise into 8 pieces. Place each piece between 2 sheets of heavy-duty plastic wrap; pound each piece to ¹/₂-inch thickness using a meat mallet or small, heavy skillet. Combine salt, thyme, pepper, and allspice, and rub over both sides of pork.
2. Heat a large nonstick skillet over medium-high heat. Coat pan with cooking spray. Add pork to pan, and cook 2 minutes on each side or until done. Remove pork from pan; keep warm.
3. Reduce heat to medium. Add shallots and butter to pan; cook 2 minutes, stirring occasionally. Add brown sugar and vinegar to pan; cook 30 seconds or until sugar melts, stirring constantly. Spoon sauce over pork.
Yield: 4 servings (serving size: 2 medallions and about 1 tablespoon sauce).

CALORIES 226; FAT 6.4g (sat 2.5g, mono 2.4g, poly 0.5g); PROTEIN 32.3g; CARB 7.3g; FIBER 0.2g; CHOL 92mg; IRON 2mg; SODIUM 371mg; CALC 19mg

Pork Medallions with Nectarine-Cranberry Chutney

make it a meal *Sweet-tart cranberries and fresh summer nectarines go well with lean pork. Serve with pistachio-studded rice.*

Chutney:
1   tablespoon butter, divided
⅓   cup finely chopped onion
2   cups chopped nectarine (about 3 nectarines)
⅓   cup sweetened dried cranberries
1   tablespoon balsamic vinegar
¼   teaspoon salt
¼   teaspoon ground cinnamon
⅛   teaspoon ground cloves
Pork:
1   (1-pound) pork tenderloin, trimmed
½   teaspoon salt
¼   teaspoon freshly ground black pepper
Cooking spray

1. To prepare chutney, melt 1 teaspoon butter in a medium saucepan over medium heat. Add onion; cook 4 minutes or until tender. Add nectarine, cranberries, and vinegar; cook 3 minutes or until nectarine is tender. Remove from heat; stir in ¹/₄ teaspoon salt, cinnamon, cloves, and remaining 2 teaspoons butter.
2. To prepare pork, cut pork crosswise into 8 (1-inch-thick) slices. Place each slice between 2 sheets of heavy-duty plastic wrap; pound to ¹/₂-inch thickness using a meat mallet or small heavy skillet. Sprinkle pork evenly with ¹/₂ teaspoon salt and pepper. Heat a large nonstick skillet over medium-high heat. Coat pan with cooking spray. Add pork; cook 3 minutes on each side or until desired degree of doneness. Serve pork with chutney. **Yield:** 4 servings (serving size: 2 medallions and about ¹/₃ cup chutney).

CALORIES 233; FAT 7.6g (sat 3.4g, mono 2.8g, poly 0.7g); PROTEIN 18.4g; CARB 23.1g; FIBER 1.6g; CHOL 64mg; IRON 1.4mg; SODIUM 507mg; CALC 12mg

POULTRY

15
MINUTES

Chicken-Chile Tostadas

If you can't find ground chicken, grind your own by putting raw skinless, boneless chicken in a food processor. Pulse with the chopping blade until roughly chopped for the best texture. Tortillas are usually fried for tostadas, but here the tortillas are baked for a crunchy texture.

1	tablespoon olive oil
1	cup prechopped onion
1	teaspoon bottled minced garlic
1/2	teaspoon ground cumin
1/2	teaspoon ground chipotle chile pepper
1/4	teaspoon ground cinnamon
1	pound ground chicken breast
1/2	cup bottled fat-free salsa
1/4	cup water
1/2	teaspoon salt
2	tablespoons chopped fresh cilantro
1	teaspoon lime juice
4	(6-inch) corn tortillas
1	cup shredded iceberg lettuce
1	cup (4 ounces) preshredded reduced-fat Mexican cheese blend or cheddar cheese
1/4	cup reduced-fat sour cream

1. Preheat oven to 400°.
2. Heat oil in a large nonstick skillet over medium-high heat. Add onion and garlic; sauté 2 minutes or until onion begins to soften. Add cumin, chipotle, and cinnamon; cook 30 seconds, stirring constantly. Add chicken; cook 4 minutes or until chicken is done, stirring to crumble. Add salsa, water, and salt; cook 3 minutes or until slightly thickened. Stir in cilantro and lime juice; remove from heat.
3. While chicken cooks, place tortillas directly on oven rack; bake at 400° for 5 minutes or until slightly crisp. Place 1 tortilla on each of 4 plates; top each tortilla with 1/4 cup lettuce, 3/4 cup chicken mixture, 1/4 cup cheese, and 1 tablespoon sour cream.
Yield: 4 servings.

CALORIES 341; FAT 11.6g (sat 5.2g, mono 3g, poly 0.9g); PROTEIN 35.9g;
CARB 21.7g; FIBER 2.6g; CHOL 86mg; IRON 1.6mg; SODIUM 751mg; CALC 296mg

Thai Chicken in Cabbage Leaves

15
MINUTES

Thai Chicken in Cabbage Leaves

make it a meal *The ground chicken filling has seasonings similar to those in* larb, *a popular Thai appetizer. Add sticky rice and sautéed fresh snow peas with chopped red bell pepper to complete the meal. Squeeze a lime wedge over the chicken for extra zip.*

1	cup water
3/4	cup vertically sliced red onion
1	pound ground chicken breast
3	tablespoons finely chopped fresh mint
2	tablespoons finely chopped fresh cilantro
3	tablespoons fresh lime juice
4	teaspoons Thai fish sauce
1/4	to 1/2 teaspoon crushed red pepper
16	napa (Chinese) cabbage leaves (about 1 head)

Lime wedges (optional)

1. Heat a nonstick skillet over medium-high heat. Add first 3 ingredients to pan. Cook 5 minutes or until chicken is done, stirring to crumble. Drain. Return chicken mixture to pan; stir in mint, cilantro, juice, fish sauce, and pepper.
2. Spoon about 3 tablespoons chicken mixture onto each cabbage leaf. Serve with lime wedges, if desired. **Yield:** 4 servings (serving size: 4 stuffed leaves).

CALORIES 147; FAT 0.6g (sat 0.2g, mono 0.1g, poly 0.1g); PROTEIN 26.7g;
CARB 8.5g; FIBER 2.4g; CHOL 66mg; IRON 0.2mg; SODIUM 557mg; CALC 77mg

Black-Eyed Peas and Rice
with Andouille Sausage

20 MINUTES

Black-Eyed Peas and Rice with Andouille Sausage

make it a meal *Corn bread makes a nice accompaniment to round out this one-dish meal. Andouille sausage is a bit spicy. If you prefer a milder flavor, substitute regular chicken, turkey, or pork sausage.*

1   (3 1/2-ounce) bag boil-in-bag long-grain rice
1   teaspoon olive oil
1/2   cup prechopped onion
1   teaspoon bottled minced garlic
1/2   teaspoon Cajun seasoning
6   ounces chicken andouille sausage, sliced (such as Amy's)
1   cup fat-free, less-sodium chicken broth
1   (15-ounce) can black-eyed peas, rinsed and drained
1   (14.5-ounce) can no-salt-added diced tomatoes, undrained
1   teaspoon hot pepper sauce (such as Tabasco)
1/2   cup thinly sliced green onions

1. Place rice in an 8-inch square baking dish; cover with water. Microwave at HIGH 6 minutes; drain.
2. Heat 1 teaspoon olive oil in a large saucepan over medium heat. Add 1/2 cup chopped onion, 1 teaspoon minced garlic, and Cajun seasoning to pan, and cook 2 minutes, stirring frequently. Stir in sausage, and cook 1 minute. Add rice, chicken broth, black-eyed peas, and tomatoes to pan; bring to a boil. Reduce heat, and simmer 4 minutes or until rice is tender. Stir in hot pepper sauce. Ladle about 1 1/4 cups mixture into each of 4 bowls, and sprinkle each serving with 2 tablespoons green onions. **Yield:** 4 servings.

CALORIES 251; FAT 4.9g (sat 1.5g, mono 1.7g, poly 0.8g); PROTEIN 13.4g; CARB 37.7g; FIBER 5g; CHOL 46mg; IRON 3.3mg; SODIUM 714mg; CALC 102mg

20 MINUTES

Quick Chicken and Dumplings

In this recipe, flour tortillas stand in for the traditional biscuit dough.

1   tablespoon butter
1/2   cup prechopped onion
2   cups chopped roasted skinless, boneless chicken breasts
1   (10-ounce) box frozen mixed vegetables, thawed
1 1/2   cups water
1   tablespoon all-purpose flour
1   (14-ounce) can fat-free, less-sodium chicken broth
1/4   teaspoon salt
1/4   teaspoon black pepper
1   bay leaf
8   (6-inch) flour tortillas, cut into 1/2-inch strips
1   tablespoon chopped fresh parsley

1. Melt butter in a large saucepan over medium-high heat. Add onion; sauté 5 minutes or until tender. Stir in chicken and vegetables; cook 3 minutes or until thoroughly heated, stirring constantly.
2. While chicken mixture cooks, combine water, flour, and broth. Gradually stir broth mixture into chicken mixture. Stir in salt, pepper, and bay leaf; bring to a boil. Reduce heat, and simmer 3 minutes. Stir in tortilla strips, and cook 2 minutes or until tortilla strips soften. Remove from heat; stir in parsley. Discard bay leaf. Serve immediately. **Yield:** 4 servings (serving size: about 1 1/2 cups).

CALORIES 366; FAT 9.3g (sat 3.1g, mono 3.9g, poly 1.4g); PROTEIN 29.8g; CARB 40.3g; FIBER 5.3g; CHOL 67mg; IRON 3.4mg; SODIUM 652mg; CALC 104mg

Mango, Chicken, and Chorizo Quesadillas

Chorizo, smoked pork sausage spiced with cumin and garlic, is often used in Spanish cooking.

1   link Spanish chorizo sausage (about
     3 1/4 ounces), diced
1 1/4 cups shredded roasted skinless, boneless
     chicken breast
4   (8-inch) fat-free flour tortillas
3/4   cup (3 ounces) shredded reduced-fat
     Mexican cheese blend
1/2   cup chopped peeled mango
4   teaspoons chopped fresh cilantro
Cooking spray
1/2   cup fat-free roasted corn salsa
1/4   cup fat-free sour cream
Cilantro sprigs (optional)

1. Heat a large nonstick skillet over medium-high heat. Add sausage to pan; sauté 1 minute. Stir in chicken; sauté 2 minutes or until thoroughly heated. Remove sausage mixture from pan; set aside. Wipe pan with a paper towel.
2. Sprinkle half of each tortilla with 3 tablespoons cheese; top with 1/4 cup sausage mixture, 2 tablespoons mango, and 1 teaspoon cilantro. Carefully fold tortillas in half, pressing gently to seal.
3. Return pan to medium heat. Coat pan with cooking spray. Add 2 filled tortillas to pan; cook 2 minutes on each side or until lightly browned. Repeat with cooking spray and remaining filled tortillas. Top each serving with 2 tablespoons salsa and 1 tablespoon sour cream. Garnish with cilantro sprigs, if desired. **Yield:** 4 servings (serving size: 1 quesadilla).

CALORIES 362; FAT 12.3g (sat 4.9g, mono 3.3g, poly 0.9g); PROTEIN 27.9g; CARB 34.1g; FIBER 2.4g; CHOL 67mg; IRON 1.1mg; SODIUM 910mg; CALC 247mg

Chicken, Mushroom, and Gruyère Quesadillas

1   teaspoon olive oil
1   cup presliced mushrooms
1/2   cup thinly sliced onion
1/8   teaspoon salt
1/8   teaspoon freshly ground black pepper
1   teaspoon bottled minced garlic
1   tablespoon sherry or red wine vinegar
2   (10-inch) fat-free flour tortillas
1   cup shredded cooked chicken breast (about
     8 ounces)
1   cup arugula
1/2   cup (2 ounces) shredded Gruyère cheese
Cooking spray

1. Heat a large nonstick skillet over medium-high heat. Add olive oil to pan; swirl to coat. Add mushrooms, sliced onion, salt, and pepper to pan; sauté 5 minutes. Stir in garlic, and sauté 30 seconds. Add sherry; cook 30 seconds or until liquid almost evaporates.
2. Arrange half of mushroom mixture over half of each tortilla. Top each tortilla with 1/2 cup chicken, 1/2 cup arugula, and 1/4 cup cheese; fold tortillas in half.
3. Wipe pan clean with a paper towel. Heat pan over medium heat. Coat pan with cooking spray. Add tortillas to pan. Place a heavy skillet on top of tortillas; cook 2 minutes on each side or until crisp. **Yield:** 4 servings (serving size: 1/2 quesadilla).

CALORIES 270; FAT 8.9g (sat 3.7g, mono 3g, poly 0.8g); PROTEIN 25.2g; CARB 20.3g; FIBER 3g; CHOL 64mg; IRON 1.7mg; SODIUM 391mg; CALC 242mg

Gruyère has a smooth yet pliable texture with a mild nutty or toasty flavor. This semifirm cheese also has fruity or sweet hints and a pale yellow interior.

INGREDIENT SPOTLIGHT

Chicken, Mushroom, and Gruyère Quesadillas

15MINUTES

Mexican Chicken Baked Potato

Dive into this healthy loaded baked potato for a filling one-dish meal.

1   (8-ounce) baking potato
½   cup shredded roasted chicken breast
¾   cup refrigerated fresh salsa
2   tablespoons preshredded, reduced-fat Mexican blend cheese
1   tablespoon reduced-fat sour cream
1   tablespoon chopped green onions

1. Pierce potato with a fork; place on a paper towel in microwave oven. Microwave at HIGH 6 to 7 minutes or until done.
2. Combine chicken and salsa in a small microwave-safe bowl. Microwave at HIGH 1 minute or until chicken is thoroughly heated.
3. Cut potato in half lengthwise; spoon chicken over potato. Top with cheese, sour cream, and green onions. **Yield:** 1 serving.

CALORIES 403; FAT 5.9g (sat 3g, mono 2g, poly 0.8g); PROTEIN 29.8g;
CARB 48.8g; FIBER 3g; CHOL 77mg; IRON 1.5mg; SODIUM 631mg; CALC 124mg

Go ahead and eat the skin—potatoes are a great source of fiber, as well as vitamin B$_6$, potassium, and iron.

INGREDIENT SPOTLIGHT

15MINUTES

Soft Black Bean Tostadas

Salsa:
½   cup chopped peeled avocado
½   cup chopped seeded tomato
¼   cup thinly sliced green onions
2   teaspoons fresh lime juice
¼   teaspoon salt

Remaining Ingredients:
2   tablespoons water
2   tablespoons fresh lime juice
½   teaspoon ground cumin
⅛   teaspoon salt
⅛   teaspoon ground red pepper
1   (15-ounce) can black beans, rinsed and drained
4   (8-inch) flour tortillas
1   cup shredded roasted skinless, boneless chicken breast
¾   cup (3 ounces) preshredded Monterey Jack cheese
1   cup shredded iceberg lettuce
½   cup fat-free sour cream

1. Preheat broiler.
2. To prepare salsa, combine first 5 ingredients in a small bowl. Toss gently, and set aside.
3. Place 2 tablespoons water, lime juice, cumin, salt, ground red pepper, and black beans in a blender; process until smooth.
4. Place tortillas on a baking sheet, and spread about ¼ cup black bean mixture evenly over each tortilla. Top each evenly with ¼ cup chicken and 3 tablespoons cheese. Broil 2 minutes or until cheese melts and tortilla edges are just beginning to brown.
5. Top each tortilla with ¼ cup lettuce, ¼ cup salsa, and 2 tablespoons sour cream. Cut each tortilla into 4 wedges. **Yield:** 4 servings (serving size: 1 tostada).

CALORIES 410; FAT 14.4g (sat 5.9g, mono 5.9g, poly 1.4g); PROTEIN 25.3g;
CARB 47.7g; FIBER 7.2g; CHOL 49mg; IRON 3.7mg; SODIUM 858mg;
CALC 264mg

Speedy Chicken and Cheese Enchiladas

sauce; bring to a boil. Cover, reduce heat, and simmer 5 minutes.
3. Combine chicken, ³⁄₄ cup cheese, and cumin, tossing well.
4. Wrap tortillas in paper towels; microwave at HIGH 30 seconds or until warm. Spoon ¼ cup chicken mixture in center of each tortilla; roll up. Place tortillas, seam sides down, in an 11 x 7–inch baking dish coated with cooking spray. Pour sauce mixture over enchiladas; broil 3 minutes or until thoroughly heated. Sprinkle remaining ¼ cup cheese evenly over enchiladas, and broil 1 minute or until cheese melts. Serve with sour cream and cilantro. **Yield:** 4 servings (serving size: 2 enchiladas, 1 tablespoon sour cream, and 1 tablespoon cilantro).

CALORIES 364; FAT 10.9g (sat 4.9g, mono 2.9g, poly 1.4g); PROTEIN 29.7g; CARB 37.2g; FIBER 4.1g; CHOL 70mg; IRON 1.7mg; SODIUM 701mg; CALC 339mg

Speedy Chicken and Cheese Enchiladas

Rotisserie chicken and prechopped vegetables make this a quick casserole.

Cooking spray
1   cup prechopped white onion
1   cup prechopped bell pepper
1   (10-ounce) can enchilada sauce (such as Old El Paso)
2   cups chopped skinless, boneless rotisserie chicken breast (about 8 ounces)
1   cup (4 ounces) preshredded, reduced-fat Mexican blend cheese, divided
½   teaspoon ground cumin
8   (6-inch) corn tortillas
¼   cup fat-free sour cream
¼   cup chopped fresh cilantro

1. Preheat broiler.
2. Heat a large nonstick skillet over medium-high heat. Coat pan with cooking spray. Add onion and pepper; sauté 2 minutes or until crisp-tender. Add enchilada

Chicken Burritos

Traditional chicken burritos get a healthy face-lift from whole wheat tortillas and a boost of flavor from jalapeño-infused cheddar and fresh lime juice.

2   cups shredded cooked chicken breast
1   cup (4 ounces) 50% reduced-fat shredded cheddar cheese with jalapeño pepper
2   tablespoons chopped fresh cilantro
2   tablespoons fresh lime juice
4   (8-inch) 98% fat-free whole wheat tortillas
Salsa (optional)

1. Toss together first 4 ingredients in a bowl. Spoon chicken mixture evenly down center of each tortilla. Fold in ends, and roll up tortilla. Tightly wrap each burrito in wax paper; arrange in a circle along edge of microwave turntable. Microwave at HIGH 1½ minutes or until hot. Serve immediately with salsa, if desired. **Yield:** 4 servings (serving size: 1 burrito).

CALORIES 308; FAT 7.6g (sat 3.8g, mono 2.5g, poly 1.2g); PROTEIN 33.9g; CARB 24.7g; FIBER 2g; CHOL 75mg; IRON 0.7mg; SODIUM 564mg; CALC 255mg

Spicy Asian Lettuce Wraps

2½ ounces bean threads (cellophane noodles)
¼ cup minced fresh cilantro
¼ cup low-sodium soy sauce
1 tablespoon chile paste with garlic
2 teaspoons dark sesame oil
2 cups chopped roasted skinless, boneless chicken
12 large Boston or Romaine lettuce leaves

1. Cover bean threads with boiling water. Let stand 5 minutes or until softened. Drain; rinse under cool water. Chop noodles.

2. While bean threads soak, combine cilantro, soy sauce, chile paste, and oil in a large bowl, stirring with a whisk. Add noodles and chicken to soy sauce mixture; toss well to coat. Spoon about ⅓ cup chicken mixture down center of each lettuce leaf; roll up. **Yield:** 4 servings (serving size: 3 lettuce wraps).

CALORIES 213; FAT 4.9g (sat 1g, mono 1.8g, poly 1.5g); PROTEIN 23.2g; CARB 18.3g; FIBER 0.7g; CHOL 60mg; IRON 1.7mg; SODIUM 641mg; CALC 31mg

make it a meal *Use roasted chicken and rice noodles to fill these creative lettuce wraps for a no-cook weeknight meal. Serve with orange slices for a bright, refreshing dessert.*

2O

Chicken, Cashew, and Red Pepper Stir-Fry

make it a meal *This dish balances salty, sweet, tangy, and spicy ingredients. Spoon it alongside a quick rice pilaf.*

3 3/4 teaspoons cornstarch, divided
2   tablespoons low-sodium soy sauce, divided
2   teaspoons dry sherry
1   teaspoon rice wine vinegar
3/4   teaspoon sugar
1/2   teaspoon hot pepper sauce (such as Tabasco)
1   pound chicken breast tenders, cut lengthwise into thin strips
1/2   cup coarsely chopped unsalted cashews
2   tablespoons canola oil
2   cups julienne-cut red bell pepper (about 1 large)
1   teaspoon minced garlic
1/2   teaspoon minced peeled fresh ginger
3   tablespoons thinly sliced green onions

1. Combine 1 teaspoon cornstarch, 1 tablespoon soy sauce, and next 4 ingredients in a small bowl; stir with a whisk.
2. Combine remaining 2 3/4 teaspoons cornstarch, remaining 1 tablespoon soy sauce, and chicken in a medium bowl; toss well to coat.
3. Heat a large nonstick skillet over medium-high heat. Add cashews to pan; cook 3 minutes or until lightly toasted, stirring frequently. Remove from pan.
4. Add oil to pan, swirling to coat. Add chicken mixture to pan; sauté 2 minutes or until lightly browned. Remove chicken from pan; place in a bowl. Add bell pepper to pan; sauté 2 minutes, stirring occasionally. Add garlic and ginger, and cook 30 seconds. Add chicken and cornstarch mixture to pan; cook 1 minute or until sauce is slightly thick. Sprinkle with cashews and green onions. **Yield:** 4 servings (serving size: 1 cup).

CALORIES 324; FAT 16.6g (sat 2.5g, mono 9.2g, poly 3.8g); PROTEIN 30g; CARB 13.5g; FIBER 2g; CHOL 66mg; IRON 2.4mg; SODIUM 350mg; CALC 33mg

15

Chicken Lettuce Wraps with Sweet and Spicy Sauce

You can serve these casual wraps already assembled at the table or buffet style.

3   tablespoons unsalted, dry-roasted peanuts
3   tablespoons hoisin sauce
2   tablespoons cider vinegar
2   teaspoons low-sodium soy sauce
1   teaspoon bottled ground fresh ginger (such as Spice World)
1   teaspoon dark sesame oil
1/2   teaspoon crushed red pepper
1/2   teaspoon bottled minced garlic
2   cups packaged cabbage-and-carrot coleslaw
1   cup canned sliced water chestnuts, drained
8   ounces grilled chicken breast strips (such as Louis Rich)
12   Bibb lettuce leaves

1. Place peanuts in a small nonstick skillet over medium-high heat; cook 3 minutes or until lightly browned, shaking pan frequently. Remove pan from heat; set aside.
2. Combine hoisin, vinegar, soy sauce, ginger, oil, pepper, and garlic in a small bowl, stirring well with a whisk.
3. Combine peanuts, coleslaw, water chestnuts, and chicken in a medium bowl, and toss well.
4. Spoon about 1/3 cup chicken mixture in the center of each lettuce leaf; top each with 2 teaspoons sauce. Roll up; secure with a wooden pick. **Yield:** 4 servings (serving size: 3 wraps).

CALORIES 197; FAT 7.4g (sat 1.4g, mono 2.9g, poly 2.1g); PROTEIN 16.5g; CARB 18.2g; FIBER 3.4g; CHOL 37mg; IRON 1.9mg; SODIUM 825mg; CALC 40mg

COOKING CLASS: *how to de-kernel corn*

To de-kernel corn, cut about ½ inch from the tip of an ear to create a flat base on which to stand the cob while removing the kernels. Stand the cob upright in a pie plate or bowl to catch the kernels, and use a sharp knife to slice away the kernels in a slow, sawing motion.

30 MINUTES

Chicken and Summer Vegetable Tostadas

make it a meal *The tostadas can easily become soft tacos if you skip broiling the tortillas. Serve with black beans.*

1	teaspoon ground cumin
¼	teaspoon salt
¼	teaspoon black pepper
2	teaspoons canola oil
12	ounces chicken breast tenders
1	cup chopped red onion (about 1)
1	cup fresh corn kernels (about 2 ears)
1	cup chopped zucchini (about 4 ounces)
½	cup green salsa
3	tablespoons chopped fresh cilantro, divided
4	(8-inch) fat-free flour tortillas
	Cooking spray
1	cup (4 ounces) shredded Monterey Jack cheese

1. Preheat broiler.
2. Combine first 3 ingredients, stirring well. Heat oil in a large nonstick skillet over medium-high heat. Sprinkle spice mixture evenly over chicken. Add chicken to pan; sauté 3 minutes. Add onion, corn, and zucchini to pan; sauté 2 minutes or until chicken is done. Stir in salsa and 2 tablespoons cilantro. Cook 2 minutes or until liquid almost evaporates, stirring frequently.
3. Working with 2 tortillas at a time, arrange tortillas in a single layer on a baking sheet; lightly coat tortillas with cooking spray. Broil 3 minutes or until lightly browned. Spoon about ¾ cup chicken mixture in the center of each tortilla; sprinkle each serving with ¼ cup cheese. Broil an additional 2 minutes or until cheese melts. Repeat procedure with remaining tortillas, chicken mixture, and cheese. Sprinkle each serving with about ¾ teaspoon of remaining cilantro. Serve immediately. **Yield:** 4 servings.

CALORIES 398; FAT 13.1g (sat 5.9g, mono 4.1g, poly 1.2g); PROTEIN 32.5g; CARB 36.7g; FIBER 3.1g; CHOL 75mg; IRON 1.4mg; SODIUM 799mg; CALC 236mg

Last-Minute
Chicken Fajitas

20
MINUTES

Chicken Paprikash

make it a meal *Serve this saucy dish with egg noodles tossed with a bit of butter, caraway seeds, salt, and pepper.*

1	tablespoon canola oil
1	pound chicken breast tenders, cut into 1-inch strips
1	cup prechopped onion
1	cup thinly sliced red bell pepper (about 1 medium)
1½	teaspoons bottled minced garlic
¼	cup whipping cream
1	tablespoon paprika
1	tablespoon tomato paste
1	teaspoon caraway seeds
½	teaspoon salt
¼	teaspoon black pepper
1	(14.5-ounce) can diced tomatoes, undrained

1. Heat canola oil in a large nonstick skillet over medium heat. Add chicken; cook 5 minutes or until browned, stirring occasionally. Remove from pan, and keep warm. **2.** Add onion, bell pepper, and garlic to pan; sauté 4 minutes or until tender. Return chicken to pan. Stir in cream and remaining ingredients; cover and simmer 5 minutes or until chicken is done and sauce is slightly thick. **Yield:** 4 servings (serving size: 1 cup).

CALORIES 241; FAT 8.2g (sat 2.4g, mono 3.3g, poly 1.7g); PROTEIN 28.4g; CARB 12.9g; FIBER 3.1g; CHOL 76mg; IRON 1.8mg; SODIUM 507mg; CALC 51mg

15
MINUTES

Last-Minute Chicken Fajitas

With only five simple ingredients on-hand you can have steaming fajitas on your table in less than 15 minutes.

	Cooking spray
1	pound chicken breast tenders, cut into strips
2	tablespoons salt-free fajita seasoning
1	(16-ounce) package frozen bell pepper stir-fry
8	(6-inch) flour tortillas, warmed
½	cup (2 ounces) reduced-fat shredded cheddar cheese
	Salsa (optional)

1. Heat a large nonstick skillet over medium-high heat; coat pan with cooking spray. Add chicken and seasoning; sauté 2 minutes. Add bell pepper stir-fry, and sauté 2 minutes or until chicken is done. **2.** Spoon ½ cup chicken mixture down center of each tortilla; sprinkle each with 1 tablespoon cheese. Roll up. Top with salsa, if desired. **Yield:** 4 servings (serving size: 2 fajitas).

CALORIES 356; FAT 7.8g (sat 2.2g, mono 3.4g, poly 2.1g); PROTEIN 31.7g; CARB 37.4g; FIBER 3.2g; CHOL 65mg; IRON 1.5mg; SODIUM 573mg; CALC 108mg

Chicken Paprikash

15 MINUTES

Creole Chicken and Vegetables

make it a meal *Enjoy the flavor of summer anytime by using frozen bell peppers and frozen okra in this speedy Creole dish. For a filling meal, serve it over rice.*

Cooking spray
1   pound chicken breast tenders
2   cups frozen pepper stir-fry (such as Bird's Eye), thawed
1   cup frozen cut okra, thawed
³/₄   cup thinly sliced celery
³/₄   teaspoon sugar
¹/₂   teaspoon salt
¹/₂   teaspoon dried thyme
¹/₄   teaspoon ground red pepper
1   (14.5-ounce) can diced tomatoes, undrained
¹/₄   cup chopped fresh parsley
1   tablespoon butter

1. Heat a large nonstick skillet over medium-high heat. Coat pan with cooking spray. Add chicken; cook 3 minutes on each side or until browned. Add pepper stir-fry and next 6 ingredients, stirring to combine. Pour tomatoes over chicken mixture; bring to a boil. Cover, reduce heat, and simmer 5 minutes. Uncover; cook 3 minutes. Add parsley and butter, stirring until butter melts. **Yield:** 4 servings (serving size: 1 cup).

CALORIES 199; FAT 4.4g (sat 1.8g, mono 1.5g, poly 0.5g); PROTEIN 28.3g; CARB 11g; FIBER 3.2g; CHOL 73mg; IRON 1.9mg; SODIUM 550mg; CALC 71mg

Frozen okra makes a great stand-in for fresh. Not only is it just as healthy, frozen okra saves you time from having to cut up the fresh produce. And frozen okra is available year-round.

INGREDIENT SPOTLIGHT

15 MINUTES

Chicken Strips with Blue Cheese Dressing

make it a meal *Pair this fiery entrée with cool, crunchy carrot and celery sticks.*

Chicken:
¹/₂   cup low-fat buttermilk
¹/₂   teaspoon hot sauce
2.25 ounces all-purpose flour (about ¹/₂ cup)
¹/₂   teaspoon paprika
¹/₂   teaspoon ground red pepper
¹/₂   teaspoon freshly ground black pepper
¹/₄   teaspoon salt
1   pound chicken breast tenders
1   tablespoon canola oil

Dressing:
¹/₂   cup fat-free mayonnaise
¹/₄   cup (1 ounce) crumbled blue cheese
1   tablespoon red wine vinegar
1   teaspoon bottled minced garlic
¹/₄   teaspoon salt
¹/₄   teaspoon freshly ground black pepper

1. To prepare chicken, combine buttermilk and hot sauce in a shallow dish. Lightly spoon flour into a dry measuring cup; level with a knife. Combine flour and next 4 ingredients in a shallow dish. Dip chicken in buttermilk mixture, and dredge chicken in flour mixture.
2. Heat oil in a large nonstick skillet over medium-high heat. Add chicken; cook 4 minutes on each side or until done. Remove from pan. Set aside, and keep warm.
3. While chicken cooks, prepare dressing. Combine fat-free mayonnaise and next 5 ingredients in a small bowl. Serve with chicken strips. **Yield:** 4 servings (serving size: about 3 chicken tenders and 2 tablespoons dressing).

CALORIES 281; FAT 8.7g (sat 2.6g, mono 3.2g, poly 1.5g); PROTEIN 30.8g; CARB 18.4g; FIBER 1.3g; CHOL 77mg; IRON 1.9mg; SODIUM 771mg; CALC 101mg

Chicken Strips with Blue Cheese Dressing

 MINUTES

Thai Chicken Sauté

1	(3½-ounce) bag boil-in-bag rice
1½	pounds chicken breast tenders
1	tablespoon cornstarch
1	tablespoon fish sauce
4	teaspoons canola oil, divided
1	cup sliced onion
2	teaspoons bottled minced garlic
1	teaspoon bottled ground fresh ginger (such as Spice World)
½	cup light coconut milk
2	tablespoons Sriracha (hot chile sauce, such as Huy Fong)
1	tablespoon sugar
1	tablespoon fresh lime juice
2	tablespoons chopped fresh cilantro
4	lime wedges

1. Cook rice according to package directions, omitting salt and fat. Keep warm.

2. Toss chicken with cornstarch and fish sauce. Heat 1 tablespoon oil in a large non-stick skillet over medium-high heat. Add chicken to pan; sauté 5 minutes. Remove chicken from pan. Heat remaining 1 teaspoon oil in pan. Add onion, garlic, and ginger to pan; sauté 1 minute. Return chicken to pan; cook 1 minute or until done. Stir in coconut milk, Sriracha, sugar, and juice; cook 45 seconds or until thoroughly heated. Sprinkle each serving with 1½ teaspoons cilantro. Serve chicken mixture over rice with lime wedges. **Yield:** 4 servings (serving size: 1½ cups chicken mixture, ½ cup rice, and 1 lime wedge).

CALORIES 403; FAT 10.8g (sat 3.1g, mono 4.3g, poly 2.4g); PROTEIN 42.6g; CARB 31.4g; FIBER 0.5g; CHOL 108mg; IRON 2.4mg; SODIUM 650mg; CALC 32mg

Spicy Basque-Style Chicken

Chicken Yakitori on Watercress

make it a meal Yakitori, *which means "grilled fowl" in Japanese, is traditionally served on skewers, but this skillet version is just as tasty and even easier. The sweet-salty chicken and sauce make a lovely main-dish salad when served on watercress with a side of sticky rice.*

2	tablespoons low-sodium soy sauce
2	tablespoons rice wine vinegar
2	tablespoons mirin
1½	tablespoons dark sesame oil
2	teaspoons sugar
¼	teaspoon crushed red pepper
1	pound chicken breast tenders
Cooking spray	
½	cup sliced green onions
4	cups trimmed watercress (about 1 bunch)
¼	cup sliced radishes

1. Combine first 6 ingredients in a large bowl. Reserve half of marinade.
2. Add chicken to marinade in bowl, turning to coat. Let stand 5 minutes.
3. While chicken marinates, heat a large nonstick skillet over medium-high heat. Coat pan with cooking spray. Drain chicken; discard marinade. Add chicken to pan, and cook 4 minutes on each side or until done.
4. Remove pan from heat; add reserved marinade and onions. Toss to coat.
5. Divide watercress evenly among 4 plates. Divide chicken mixture evenly among servings; top evenly with radishes and sauce.
Yield: 4 servings (serving size: 4 ounces chicken, 1 cup watercress, about 2 tablespoons sauce, and 1 tablespoon radishes).

CALORIES 174; FAT 4g (sat 0.8g, mono 1.4g, poly 1.4g); PROTEIN 27.2g; CARB 4.7g; FIBER 0.8g; CHOL 66mg; IRON 1mg; SODIUM 225mg; CALC 56mg

Spicy Basque-Style Chicken

make it a meal *Serve this dish with saffron rice to soak up the tasty sauce.*

1	teaspoon smoked paprika
¼	teaspoon black pepper
1	pound chicken breast tenders
2	teaspoons olive oil
2	teaspoons bottled minced garlic
¼	cup sliced green olives
2	(10-ounce) cans diced tomatoes and green chiles, undrained
¼	cup finely chopped prosciutto
2	tablespoons chopped fresh parsley

1. Combine paprika and pepper; sprinkle evenly over chicken. Heat oil in a large non-stick skillet over medium-high heat. Add chicken to pan; cook 4 minutes. Add garlic to pan; cook 30 seconds. Turn chicken over. Add olives and tomatoes to pan; bring to a boil. Reduce heat, and simmer 6 minutes.
2. Remove chicken from pan. Increase heat to medium-high, and cook 2 minutes, stirring occasionally. Sprinkle with prosciutto and parsley. **Yield:** 4 servings (serving size: 3 ounces chicken, about ½ cup sauce, 1 tablespoon prosciutto, and 1½ teaspoons parsley).

CALORIES 264; FAT 9g (sat 1.6g, mono 4g, poly 2.2g); PROTEIN 36.2g; CARB 8g; FIBER 0.3g; CHOL 94mg; IRON 1.4mg; SODIUM 876mg; CALC 92mg

Chicken and Mushroom Tacos

20 MINUTES

Greek Chicken with Capers and Orzo

Orzo is a rice-shaped pasta common in Mediterranean cooking. You can also substitute couscous or tiny star pasta.

1 cup uncooked orzo (rice-shaped pasta)
Cooking spray
12 ounces chicken breast tenders
1 tablespoon salt-free dried Greek seasoning blend
2 tablespoons capers
2 tablespoons fresh lemon juice
2 tablespoons extra-virgin olive oil
1 teaspoon bottled minced garlic
½ teaspoon salt
1 large red bell pepper, cut into thin strips
½ cup finely chopped green onions

1. Cook orzo according to package directions, omitting salt and fat. Drain.
2. While orzo cooks, heat a 12-inch nonstick skillet over medium-high heat. Coat pan with cooking spray. Add chicken; cook 3 minutes on each side or until done. Remove chicken from pan; cover and keep warm.
3. Combine Greek seasoning and next 5 ingredients; set aside.
4. Recoat pan with cooking spray. Add bell pepper, and sauté 2 minutes. Add onions; sauté 1 minute or until peppers begin to brown. Return chicken to pan. Stir in caper mixture, tossing gently to coat chicken. Spoon chicken mixture over orzo. Serve immediately. **Yield:** 4 servings (serving size: ³/₄ cup chicken mixture and about ¹/₂ cup orzo).

CALORIES 337; FAT 9g (sat 1.5g, mono 5.7g, poly 1g); PROTEIN 26.3g; CARB 37.2g; FIBER 2.4g; CHOL 49mg; IRON 2.7mg; SODIUM 514mg; CALC 41mg

15 MINUTES

Chicken and Mushroom Tacos

make it a meal *Add a side of fat-free refried beans topped with your favorite salsa.*

Cooking spray
1¾ cups thinly vertically sliced onion
1 jalapeño pepper, seeded and minced
¼ teaspoon sugar
2 cups presliced mushrooms
1 tablespoon bottled minced garlic
¼ cup Madeira wine or dry sherry
2 cups chopped cooked chicken breast (about 8 ounces)
8 (6-inch) corn tortillas
1 cup (4 ounces) shredded reduced-fat sharp cheddar cheese
¼ cup light sour cream

1. Heat a large nonstick skillet over medium-high heat. Coat pan with cooking spray. Add onion; sauté 2 minutes. Add jalapeño; sauté 2 minutes. Sprinkle sugar over onion mixture; sauté 1 minute. Remove onion mixture from pan.
2. Return pan to heat; recoat with cooking spray. Add mushrooms and garlic to pan; sauté 1 minute. Add Madeira to pan; cover, reduce heat, and simmer 2 minutes.

Uncover; cook 2 minutes or until liquid evaporates, stirring frequently. Stir in onion mixture and chicken; cook 3 minutes or until thoroughly heated.

3. Warm tortillas according to package directions. Spoon about ⅓ cup chicken mixture onto each tortilla. Top each tortilla with 2 tablespoons cheese; fold in half. Serve with sour cream. **Yield:** 4 servings (serving size: 2 tacos and 1 tablespoon sour cream).

CALORIES 383; FAT 11g (sat 5.6g, mono 2.8g, poly 1.3g); PROTEIN 29.9g; CARB 36.3g; FIBER 4g; CHOL 73mg; IRON 1.7mg; SODIUM 389mg; CALC 316mg

Spicy Chicken and Snow Peas

20

Spicy Chicken and Snow Peas

A mixture of snow peas, carrots, and red bell peppers coupled with crunchy peanuts and spicy chile paste creates an amazingly tasty, quick, and easy weeknight dish.

1 (3½-ounce) bag boil-in-bag long-grain rice
2 tablespoons sugar
3 tablespoons low-sodium soy sauce
2 tablespoons rice vinegar
2 teaspoons chile paste with garlic (such as sambal oelek)
1 teaspoon bottled ground fresh ginger (such as Spice World)
Cooking spray
1 teaspoon dark sesame oil
1½ cups matchstick-cut carrots
1 cup thinly sliced red bell pepper
2 cups chopped cooked chicken breast
2 cups snow peas, trimmed
¼ teaspoon salt
⅓ cup unsalted, dry-roasted peanuts

1. Cook rice according to package directions, omitting salt and fat. Keep warm.
2. Combine sugar and next 4 ingredients in a small bowl. Heat a large nonstick skillet over medium-high heat. Coat pan with cooking spray. Add oil to pan. Add carrots and pepper to pan; sauté 2 minutes. Add chicken and peas to pan; sauté 1 minute. Transfer chicken mixture to a large bowl; stir in salt.

3. Return pan to heat. Add soy sauce mixture to pan; bring to a boil. Cook until reduced to ¼ cup (about 1½ minutes), stirring constantly. Arrange about ½ cup rice in each of 4 bowls; top each serving with about 1¼ cups chicken mixture. Drizzle 1 tablespoon sauce over each serving; sprinkle each serving with about 4 teaspoons peanuts. **Yield:** 4 servings.

CALORIES 293; FAT 9.9g (sat 1.8g, mono 4.3g, poly 3g); PROTEIN 27.3g; CARB 24.7g; FIBER 3.8g; CHOL 60mg; IRON 2.4mg; SODIUM 667mg; CALC 48mg

INGREDIENT SPOTLIGHT

Sambal oelek (chile paste with garlic) is a Chinese condiment that is often added to stews as a flavoring. It's essentially pureed fresh chiles, but some varieties have bean paste or garlic added. We prefer the basic variety. This somewhat thin sauce has intense heat. Stir it into sauces and marinades.

20 MINUTES

Chicken and Cashews

make it a meal *Top tender chicken with an inspired Asian sauce loaded with cashews, ginger, honey, and sesame oil. Pair this entrée with a simple rice pilaf.*

3	tablespoons low-sodium soy sauce, divided
2	tablespoons dry sherry
4	teaspoons cornstarch, divided
1	pound skinless, boneless chicken breast, cut into bite-sized pieces
½	cup fat-free, less-sodium chicken broth
2	tablespoons oyster sauce
1	tablespoon honey
2	teaspoons sesame oil, divided
¾	cup chopped onion
½	cup chopped celery
½	cup chopped red bell pepper
1	tablespoon grated peeled fresh ginger
2	garlic cloves, minced
½	cup chopped green onions (about 3 green onions)
¼	cup chopped unsalted dry-roasted cashews

1. Combine 1 tablespoon soy sauce, sherry, 2 teaspoons cornstarch, and chicken in a large bowl; toss well to coat. Combine remaining 2 tablespoons soy sauce, remaining 2 teaspoons cornstarch, broth, oyster sauce, and honey in a small bowl.
2. Heat 1 teaspoon oil in a large nonstick skillet over medium-high heat. Add chicken mixture to pan; sauté 3 minutes. Remove from pan. Heat remaining 1 teaspoon oil in pan. Add onion, celery, and bell pepper to pan; sauté 2 minutes. Add ginger and garlic; sauté 1 minute. Return chicken mixture to pan; sauté 1 minute. Stir in broth mixture. Bring to a boil; cook 1 minute, stirring constantly. Remove from heat. Sprinkle with green onions and cashews. **Yield:** 4 servings (serving size: about ¾ cup).

CALORIES 257; FAT 9g (sat 1.9g, mono 4.2g, poly 2.3g); PROTEIN 26g; CARB 17g; FIBER 1.9g; CHOL 63mg; IRON 2mg; SODIUM 584mg; CALC 45mg

15 MINUTES

Spicy Chicken Quesadillas

make it a meal *Fresh herbs and pickled jalapeños brighten up these simple quesadillas. Serve them with a tossed green salad and a side of black beans to round out the meal.*

¼	cup thinly sliced green onions (about 2)
2	tablespoons chopped cilantro
1	tablespoon chopped pickled jalapeño peppers
1	cup chopped cooked chicken (about 8 ounces), divided
4	(8-inch) flour tortillas
¾	cup (3 ounces) reduced-fat shredded cheddar cheese, divided

Cooking spray
¾ cup salsa

1. Combine first 3 ingredients in a small bowl; stir until blended.
2. Place ¼ cup chopped chicken over half of 1 tortilla. Sprinkle with 3 tablespoons cheese and 1 tablespoon onion mixture; fold in half. Repeat procedure with remaining tortillas, chicken, cheese, and onion mixture.
3. Heat a large nonstick skillet over medium-high heat. Coat pan with cooking spray. Place 2 quesadillas in pan. Cook 2 minutes on each side or until lightly browned. Repeat procedure with remaining quesadillas. Cut each quesadilla in half. Serve with salsa. **Yield:** 4 servings (serving size: 1 quesadilla and 3 tablespoons salsa).

CALORIES 328; FAT 10.9g (sat 4.8g, mono 4.1g, poly 1.5g); PROTEIN 27.9g; CARB 29.4g; FIBER 2.1g; CHOL 65mg; IRON 2.5mg; SODIUM 786mg; CALC 248mg

Using precut vegetables such as celery, onion, and bell pepper will shave even more time off the Chicken and Cashews dish.

MAKE IT FASTER

Sweet and Sour Chicken

1	tablespoon olive oil
1	tablespoon bottled minced garlic
1	teaspoon bottled ground fresh ginger (such as Spice World)
¼	teaspoon crushed red pepper
1½	pounds skinless, boneless chicken breast, cut into ½-inch pieces
¾	cup chopped onion
½	cup chopped celery
½	cup chopped red bell pepper
1	(15¼-ounce) can pineapple chunks in juice, undrained
⅓	cup reduced-sodium soy sauce
2	tablespoons dry sherry
1½	tablespoons cornstarch
2	teaspoons brown sugar
¼	cup dry-roasted chopped cashews

1. Heat oil in a large nonstick skillet over medium-high heat. Add garlic, ginger, red pepper, and chicken to pan; sauté 5 minutes or until chicken is done. Remove chicken mixture from pan; set aside.
2. Add onion, celery, and bell pepper to pan, and sauté 4 minutes or until crisp-tender. Drain pineapple, reserving ½ cup juice. Add 1 cup pineapple chunks to pan; cook 30 seconds. Reserve remaining pineapple for another use. Combine reserved ½ cup juice, soy sauce, sherry, cornstarch, and sugar in a bowl, stirring with a whisk until smooth.
3. Return chicken mixture to pan. Stir in juice mixture; bring to boil. Cook 1 minute. Sprinkle with cashews. **Yield:** 4 servings (serving size: about 1 cup).

CALORIES 388; FAT 11.6g (sat 2.4g, mono 6.2g, poly 2g); PROTEIN 41.5g;
CARB 28.9g; FIBER 2.1g; CHOL 101mg; IRON 2.7mg; SODIUM 858mg; CALC 58mg

Braised Chicken with
Red Potatoes and
Tarragon Broth

Chicken Biryani

make it a meal *Serve with a salad of
thinly sliced cucumber and plum tomato
wedges topped with a yogurt dressing.
Combine ⅓ cup plain low-fat yogurt,
1 tablespoon chopped green onions,
1 teaspoon fresh lemon juice, ¼ teaspoon
ground cumin, ⅛ teaspoon salt, and a dash
of ground red pepper.*

2	teaspoons canola oil
1	pound skinless, boneless chicken breast, cut into 1-inch pieces
1	cup chopped onion (about 1 medium onion)
1	jalapeño pepper, seeded and minced
1	teaspoon minced fresh ginger
1½	teaspoons garam masala
¾	teaspoon ground cumin
½	teaspoon salt
2	garlic cloves, minced
2	cups chopped plum tomato (about 2 tomatoes)
1	cup uncooked basmati rice
⅓	cup golden raisins
1	(14-ounce) can fat-free, less-sodium chicken broth
¼	cup chopped fresh cilantro
¼	cup sliced almonds
4	lime wedges

1. Heat oil in a large nonstick skillet over
medium-high heat. Add chicken to pan;
sauté 3 minutes. Add onion and jalapeño;
sauté 3 minutes. Add ginger, garam masala,
cumin, salt, and garlic; sauté 30 seconds.
Add tomato, rice, raisins, and broth; bring
to a boil. Cover, reduce heat, and simmer
15 minutes or until rice is tender. Stir in
cilantro. Sprinkle with almonds; serve with
lime wedges. **Yield:** 4 servings (serving size:
1½ cups rice mixture, 1 tablespoon
almonds, and 1 lime wedge).

CALORIES 437; FAT 9.1g (sat 1.4g, mono 4.6g, poly 2.3g); PROTEIN 29.8g;
CARB 63.2g; FIBER 4.5g; CHOL 66mg; IRON 3.4mg; SODIUM 555mg;
CALC 58mg

Braised Chicken with Red Potatoes and Tarragon Broth

make it a meal *Serve this one-dish meal
with a green salad and crusty bread.*

2	teaspoons olive oil
⅓	cup finely chopped shallots (about 2 small)
1	pound skinless, boneless chicken breast halves, cut into bite-sized pieces
2½	cups fat-free, less-sodium chicken broth
½	cup dry white wine
1	teaspoon chopped fresh tarragon
½	teaspoon salt
¼	teaspoon freshly ground black pepper
1	(12-ounce) package red potato wedges (such as Simply Potatoes), cut into ½-inch pieces
2	tablespoons chopped fresh flat-leaf parsley

1. Heat oil in a large saucepan over medium-
high heat. Add shallots to pan; sauté 1 minute. Add chicken to pan; sauté 2 minutes or
until browned. Add broth, wine, tarragon,
salt, and pepper; bring to a boil. Simmer 5
minutes, stirring occasionally. Add potatoes; simmer 5 minutes or until potatoes
are tender. Remove from heat; stir in parsley. **Yield:** 4 servings (serving size: 1¼
cups).

CALORIES 227; FAT 3.9g (sat 0.7g, mono 2.1g, poly 0.6g); PROTEIN 29.2g;
CARB 16.2g; FIBER 1.8g; CHOL 66mg; IRON 1.6mg; SODIUM 831mg; CALC 33mg

20 MINUTES

Country Captain Chicken

1   tablespoon curry powder
¼   teaspoon salt
¼   teaspoon black pepper
1   pound skinless, boneless chicken breast, cut
     into ¾-inch pieces
1½   tablespoons olive oil
2½   cups vertically sliced onion (about 2 medium)
¾   cup thinly sliced green bell pepper (about
     1 medium)
2   garlic cloves, minced
⅔   cup fat-free, less-sodium chicken broth
¼   cup dried currants
2   tablespoons chopped fresh thyme, divided
1   (14.5-ounce) can diced tomatoes with
     jalapeño, undrained
½   cup sliced almonds, toasted

1. Combine curry powder, salt, and black pepper. Sprinkle chicken with curry mixture.

2. Heat oil in a large nonstick skillet over medium-high heat. Add chicken mixture to pan; sauté 5 minutes. Add onion, bell pepper, and garlic; sauté 3 minutes. Add broth, currants, 1 tablespoon thyme, and tomatoes; bring to a boil. Reduce heat, and simmer 5 minutes. Stir in remaining 1 tablespoon thyme; cook 1 minute. Sprinkle with almonds. **Yield:** 4 servings (serving size: 1½ cups chicken mixture and 1 tablespoon almonds).

CALORIES 314; FAT 11.2g (sat 1.4g, mono 7g, poly 1.9g); PROTEIN 30.5g; CARB 23.2g; FIBER 4.6g; CHOL 66mg; IRON 2.6mg; SODIUM 683mg; CALC 86mg

Sriracha-Glazed Chicken and Onions over Rice

1 (3½-ounce) bag boil-in-bag long-grain rice
3 tablespoons hoisin sauce
1 tablespoon ketchup
1¼ teaspoons Sriracha (hot chile sauce, such as Huy Fong)
1½ tablespoons canola oil
1½ cups presliced onion
1 tablespoon bottled minced fresh ginger
1 tablespoon bottled minced garlic
¾ teaspoon curry powder
1 pound skinless, boneless chicken breast, cut into 1-inch-thick slices

1. Prepare rice according to package directions, omitting salt and fat.
2. While rice cooks, combine hoisin, ketchup, and Sriracha in a small bowl.
3. Heat oil in a large nonstick skillet over medium-high heat. Add onion; sauté 3 minutes or until tender. Add ginger and remaining ingredients; sauté 6 minutes or until chicken is done. Stir in hoisin mixture; cook 1 minute, tossing to coat. Serve over rice.
Yield: 4 servings (serving size: ¾ cup chicken mixture and about ½ cup rice).

CALORIES 326; FAT 7.3g (sat 0.9g, mono 3.6g, poly 2.1g); PROTEIN 29.5g; CARB 34g; FIBER 2.2g; CHOL 66mg; IRON 2mg; SODIUM 338mg; CALC 35mg

Fiesta Chicken Tacos with Mango and Jicama Salad

make it a meal *Try this with a side of chipotle refritos. Combine 1 tablespoon fresh lime juice, 1 teaspoon minced canned chipotle chile in adobo sauce, 1 (16-ounce) can refried beans, and 1 minced garlic clove in a saucepan. Cook over medium heat 5 minutes or until thoroughly heated. Sprinkle with 2 teaspoons chopped fresh cilantro.*

Salad:

³/₄ cup (3-inch) julienne-cut peeled jicama
½ cup sliced peeled ripe mango
¼ cup presliced red onion
1 tablespoon fresh lime juice
½ teaspoon sugar
1½ teaspoons chopped fresh cilantro
¼ teaspoon salt
Dash of black pepper

Tacos:

1 tablespoon olive oil, divided
1 pound skinless, boneless chicken breast, cut into thin strips
½ teaspoon chili powder
½ teaspoon ground cumin
⅛ teaspoon ground chipotle chile pepper
1 cup presliced red bell pepper
1 cup presliced red onion
¼ teaspoon salt
8 (6-inch) corn tortillas
1 cup mixed salad greens

1. To prepare salad, combine first 8 ingredients.
2. To prepare tacos, heat 2 teaspoons oil in a large nonstick skillet over medium-high heat. Sprinkle chicken evenly with chili powder, cumin, and chipotle pepper. Add chicken mixture to pan; sauté 3 minutes. Remove from pan.
3. Heat remaining 1 teaspoon oil in pan. Add bell pepper and 1 cup onion; cook 3 minutes or until crisp-tender. Return chicken mixture to pan; cook 2 minutes or until chicken is done. Sprinkle with ¼ teaspoon salt.

4. Heat tortillas according to package directions. Arrange 2 tablespoons mixed greens, about ¹/₃ cup chicken mixture, and about 2 tablespoons salad in each tortilla; fold over. **Yield:** 4 servings (serving size: 2 tacos).

CALORIES 320; FAT 6.4g (sat 1.1g, mono 3.2g, poly 1.3g); PROTEIN 30.4g; CARB 36.1g; FIBER 5.8g; CHOL 66mg; IRON 2.2mg; SODIUM 471mg; CALC 129mg

Chicken Cacciatore

1 (3½-ounce) bag boil-in-bag brown rice
1 teaspoon olive oil
1 pound skinless, boneless chicken breast, cut into 1-inch pieces
Cooking spray
1 cup frozen chopped green bell pepper
1¾ cups tomato-basil pasta sauce (such as Classico)
¼ cup water

1. Cook rice according to package directions, omitting salt and fat. Drain rice, and remove from bag.
2. While rice cooks, heat oil in a large non-stick skillet over medium-high heat. Coat chicken with cooking spray; add chicken and bell pepper to pan. Cook, stirring frequently, 5 minutes or until chicken is lightly browned.
3. Add pasta sauce and water to pan; bring to a boil. Reduce heat, and simmer, uncovered, 5 minutes. Serve over rice. **Yield:** 3 servings (serving size: 1 cup chicken mixture and ²/₃ cup rice).

CALORIES 278; FAT 6.5g (sat 1.3g, mono 3.1g, poly 1.9g); PROTEIN 34.2g; CARB 19.8g; FIBER 3.2g; CHOL 88mg; IRON 2.1mg; SODIUM 531mg; CALC 116mg

In this quick and easy version of chicken cacciatore, we've relied on the flavors in a commercial pasta sauce and served the chicken mixture over brown rice.

MAKE IT FASTER

COOKING CLASS: *how to grill fruit*

When grilled, fruit becomes even more succulent and juicy. Firm fruits hold up best on the grill, while softer fruits, such as peaches and plums, require a little more attention and shouldn't be too ripe. If overcooked, soft fruits can become mushy.

 20 MINUTES

Barbecue Chicken with Grilled Peaches

Place the peaches on the grill after turning the chicken so they'll both be ready at the same time.

4	(6-ounce) skinless, boneless chicken breast halves
2	teaspoons salt-free barbecue seasoning (such as Mrs. Dash Chicken Grilling Blend)
¼	teaspoon salt, divided
½	cup low-sugar apricot spread (such as Smucker's)
2	tablespoons white wine vinegar
1	tablespoon grated peeled fresh ginger
Cooking spray	
4	large ripe peaches, halved and pitted

1. Prepare grill.
2. Sprinkle chicken with barbecue seasoning and ⅛ teaspoon salt.
3. Combine apricot spread, vinegar, ginger, and remaining ⅛ teaspoon salt in a small bowl.
4. Place chicken on grill rack coated with cooking spray; grill 7 minutes on each side or until done, basting occasionally with glaze. Place peach halves on grill rack, cut sides down. Grill 3 minutes on each side or until peaches are soft, basting occasionally with glaze. **Yield:** 4 servings (serving size: 1 chicken breast half and 2 peach halves).

CALORIES 295; FAT 4.4g (sat 1.2g, mono 2g, poly 1.1g); PROTEIN 35.8g; CARB 27.2g; FIBER 2.4g; CHOL 99mg; IRON 1.6mg; SODIUM 687mg; CALC 28mg

15 MINUTES

Black Pepper Citrus Chicken

Be sure to use fresh, coarsely ground black pepper in this dish; finely ground pepper will overpower the chicken.

1	tablespoon canola oil, divided
1¼	teaspoons freshly ground black pepper, divided
¼	teaspoon salt
4	(6-ounce) skinless, boneless chicken breast halves
1	cup vertically sliced onion
2	teaspoons bottled minced garlic
¼	cup white wine
2	tablespoons fresh orange juice
1	tablespoon fresh lemon juice
2	tablespoons chopped fresh parsley

1. Heat 1 teaspoon oil in a large nonstick skillet over medium-high heat. Sprinkle ½ teaspoon pepper and salt over chicken. Add chicken to pan; cook 2 minutes on each side or until browned. Remove chicken from pan; keep warm. Add remaining 2 teaspoons oil to pan. Add onion and garlic to pan; sauté 2 minutes. Add wine; cook 1 minute. Return chicken to pan. Add remaining ¾ teaspoon pepper and juices. Cover, reduce heat, and simmer 4 minutes or until chicken is done. Sprinkle with parsley. **Yield:** 4 servings (serving size: 1 chicken breast half and 2 tablespoons onion mixture).

CALORIES 240; FAT 5.9g (sat 0.8g, mono 2.6g, poly 1.5g); PROTEIN 39.6g; CARB 3.8g; FIBER 0.5g; CHOL 99mg; IRON 1.5mg; SODIUM 259mg; CALC 29mg

20 MINUTES

Chicken-Peanut Chow Mein

1   cup precut matchstick-cut carrots
1   cup snow peas, trimmed
2   (6-ounce) packages chow mein noodles
1   tablespoon dark sesame oil, divided
½   pound skinless, boneless chicken breast
3   tablespoons low-sodium soy sauce, divided
¾   cup fat-free, less-sodium chicken broth
2   tablespoons oyster sauce
1   teaspoon sugar
¼   teaspoon crushed red pepper
1   cup presliced mushrooms
2   teaspoons bottled fresh ground ginger (such as Spice World)
1   cup (1-inch) sliced green onions
2   tablespoons dry-roasted peanuts, coarsely chopped

1. Cook carrots, snow peas, and noodles in boiling water 3 minutes; drain.

2. Heat 2 teaspoons oil in a large nonstick skillet over medium-high heat. Cut chicken crosswise into thin strips. Add chicken and 1 tablespoon soy sauce to pan, and stir-fry 3 minutes. Remove chicken from pan, and keep warm.

3. Combine remaining 2 tablespoons soy sauce, broth, oyster sauce, sugar, and pepper, stirring well. Heat remaining 1 teaspoon oil over medium-high heat. Add mushrooms and ginger to pan; stir-fry 3 minutes. Add broth mixture, and cook 1 minute. Add noodle mixture and chicken to pan; cook 1 minute, tossing to combine. Sprinkle with onions and peanuts. **Yield:** 4 servings (serving size: 1½ cups noodle mixture, ¼ cup onions, and 1½ teaspoons peanuts).

CALORIES 471; FAT 8.7g (sat 1.4g, mono 3g, poly 2.6g); PROTEIN 27.8g;
CARB 72.6g; FIBER 2.7g; CHOL 33mg; IRON 2.2mg; SODIUM 807mg; CALC 43mg

20 MINUTES

Chicken and Mushrooms in Garlic White Wine Sauce

4	ounces uncooked medium egg noodles
1	pound skinless, boneless chicken breast halves
2	tablespoons all-purpose flour, divided
1/2	teaspoon salt, divided
1/4	teaspoon black pepper, divided
2	tablespoons olive oil, divided
1	tablespoon bottled minced garlic
1/2	teaspoon dried tarragon
1	(8-ounce) package presliced mushrooms
1/2	cup dry white wine
1/2	cup fat-free, less-sodium chicken broth
1/4	cup grated Parmesan cheese

1. Cook noodles according to package directions, omitting salt and fat. Drain, and keep warm.

2. Cut chicken into 1-inch pieces; place in a shallow dish. Combine 1 tablespoon flour, 1/4 teaspoon salt, and 1/8 teaspoon pepper, stirring well with a whisk. Sprinkle flour mixture over chicken; toss to coat.

3. Heat 1 tablespoon oil in a large nonstick skillet over medium-high heat. Add chicken to pan; sauté 4 minutes or until browned. Remove chicken from pan. Add remaining 1 tablespoon oil to pan. Add garlic, tarragon, and mushrooms to pan; sauté 3 minutes or until liquid evaporates and mushrooms darken. Add wine to pan; cook 1 minute. Stir in remaining 1 tablespoon flour; cook 1 minute, stirring constantly. Stir in broth, remaining 1/4 teaspoon salt, and remaining 1/8 teaspoon pepper; cook 1 minute or until slightly thick, stirring frequently.

4. Return chicken to the pan. Cover and simmer 2 minutes. Uncover; cook 1 minute or until chicken is done. Stir in noodles; cook 1 minute or until thoroughly heated. Place about 1 1/2 cups chicken mixture on each of 4 plates; top each serving with 1 tablespoon cheese. **Yield:** 4 servings.

CALORIES 350; FAT 11.1g (sat 2.6g, mono 6.2g, poly 1.4g); PROTEIN 34.3g; CARB 26.5g; FIBER 1.2g; CHOL 99mg; IRON 2.5mg; SODIUM 502mg; CALC 91mg

Chicken Parmesan with Red Wine Sauce

This is the perfect last-minute dish to prepare when friends drop by for a casual supper.

½ cup Italian-seasoned breadcrumbs
½ teaspoon dried Italian seasoning
4 (6-ounce) skinless, boneless chicken breast halves
1 large egg white, lightly beaten
½ teaspoon black pepper, divided
⅛ teaspoon salt
1 tablespoon olive oil
Dash of ground red pepper
½ cup dry red wine
2 cups low-sodium tomato-basil pasta sauce (such as Amy's)
4 teaspoons grated Parmesan cheese
½ cup (2 ounces) shredded part-skim mozzarella cheese

1. Combine breadcrumbs and Italian seasoning in a shallow dish. Dip chicken in egg white; sprinkle with ¼ teaspoon black pepper and salt, and dredge in breadcrumbs.
2. Heat oil in a large nonstick skillet over medium-high heat. Add chicken; cook 3 minutes on each side. Remove chicken from pan; keep warm. Add remaining ¼ teaspoon black pepper, red pepper, and wine to pan, scraping pan to loosen browned bits. Cook 1 minute. Add pasta sauce; cook 1 minute or until bubbly.
3. Arrange chicken over sauce; top each breast half with a spoonful of sauce, and sprinkle evenly with cheeses. Cover, reduce heat, and simmer 5 minutes or until chicken is done and cheeses melt. **Yield:** 4 servings (serving size: 1 chicken breast half, about ⅓ cup sauce, 1 teaspoon Parmesan cheese, and 2 tablespoons mozzarella cheese).

CALORIES 387; FAT 11.7g (sat 3.9g, mono 5.6g, poly 2g); PROTEIN 43.9g; CARB 23.2g; FIBER 1.6g; CHOL 109mg; IRON 3.5mg; SODIUM 698mg; CALC 194mg

Cheesy Chile Chicken

4 (6-ounce) skinless, boneless chicken breast halves
¼ teaspoon salt
1 teaspoon ground black pepper
¼ teaspoon ground red pepper
½ teaspoon paprika
½ teaspoon garlic powder
2 teaspoons olive oil
1 (4.5-ounce) can diced green chiles
½ cup (2 ounces) shredded reduced-fat Monterey Jack cheese

1. Place each chicken breast half between 2 sheets of heavy-duty plastic wrap; pound to ½-inch thickness, using a meat mallet or rolling pin. Combine salt and next 4 ingredients; sprinkle over chicken.
2. Heat oil in a large skillet over medium-high heat. Add chicken, and cook 3 minutes on each side or until golden brown. Remove pan from heat; top chicken with chiles and cheese. Cover and let stand 2 minutes or until cheese melts. **Yield:** 4 servings (serving size: 1 chicken breast half).

CALORIES 261; FAT 8.8g (sat 3g, mono 4.3g, poly 1.4g); PROTEIN 39.5g; CARB 3.6g; FIBER 1.2g; CHOL 109mg; IRON 1.4mg; SODIUM 344mg; CALC 159mg

20 MINUTES

Chicken Breasts with Avocado, Tomato, and Cucumber Salsa

make it a meal *Baked tortilla chips make a crunchy companion for this simple summer supper. Try the salsa another night on grilled fish or shrimp.*

Cooking spray
- ¾ teaspoon salt, divided
- ¼ teaspoon chipotle chile powder
- 4 (6-ounce) skinless, boneless chicken breast halves
- 1¼ cups coarsely chopped seeded peeled cucumber (about 1 large)
- 1 cup grape tomatoes, halved
- ½ cup prechopped red onion
- ½ cup chopped peeled avocado
- 2 tablespoons chopped fresh cilantro
- 2 tablespoons fresh lime juice
- 1 jalapeño pepper, seeded and finely chopped

1. Heat a grill pan over medium-high heat. Coat pan with cooking spray. Sprinkle ½ teaspoon salt and ¼ teaspoon chipotle chile powder evenly over chicken; add chicken to pan. Cook 6 minutes on each side or until done, and remove from heat.

2. Combine remaining ¼ teaspoon salt, cucumber, tomatoes, onion, and remaining ingredients in a medium bowl, tossing well. Serve with chicken. **Yield:** 4 servings (serving size: 1 chicken breast half and ¾ cup salsa).

CALORIES 243; FAT 7.6g (sat 1.6g, mono 3.5g, poly 1.3g); PROTEIN 35.6g; CARB 7.3g; FIBER 2.7g; CHOL 94mg; IRON 1.7mg; SODIUM 533mg; CALC 34mg

20 MINUTES

Chicken Puttanesca with Angel Hair Pasta

8   ounces uncooked angel hair pasta
2   teaspoons olive oil
4   (6-ounce) skinless, boneless chicken breast
     halves
½   teaspoon salt
2   cups tomato-basil pasta sauce (such as
     Muir Glen Organic)
¼   cup pitted and coarsely chopped kalamata
     olives
1   tablespoon capers
¼   teaspoon crushed red pepper
¼   cup (1 ounce) preshredded Parmesan cheese
Chopped fresh basil or basil sprigs (optional)

1. Cook pasta according to package directions, omitting salt and fat. Drain and keep warm.
2. Heat oil in a large nonstick skillet over medium-high heat. Cut chicken into 1-inch pieces. Add chicken to pan; sprinkle evenly with salt. Cook chicken 5 minutes or until lightly browned, stirring occasionally. Stir in pasta sauce, olives, capers, and pepper; bring to a simmer. Cook 5 minutes or until chicken is done, stirring frequently. Arrange 1 cup pasta on each of 4 plates; top with 1½ cups chicken mixture. Sprinkle each serving with 1 tablespoon cheese. Garnish with chopped basil or basil sprigs, if desired. **Yield:** 4 servings.

CALORIES 530; FAT 12.4g (sat 2.8g, mono 6.6g, poly 2g); PROTEIN 51.8g;
CARB 55g; FIBER 2.1g; CHOL 104mg; IRON 4.2mg; SODIUM 971mg; CALC 165mg

15 MINUTES

Chicken Breasts with Tomatoes and Olives

(pictured on cover)

make it a meal *Kalamata and picholine olives add salty savor. Serve over couscous with dressed greens for an easy supper.*

4   (6-ounce) skinless, boneless chicken breast
     halves
¼   teaspoon salt
¼   teaspoon freshly ground black pepper
Cooking spray
1   cup multicolored cherry or grape tomatoes,
     halved
3   tablespoons oil and vinegar dressing, divided
20   olives, halved
½   cup (2 ounces) crumbled feta cheese
Torn basil leaves (optional)

1. Prepare grill to medium-high heat. Sprinkle chicken evenly with salt and pepper. Place on grill rack coated with cooking spray; grill 6 minutes on each side or until chicken is done. Keep warm.
2. While chicken grills, combine tomatoes, 1½ tablespoons dressing, and olives in a skillet over medium heat; cook 2 minutes or until tomatoes soften slightly and mixture is thoroughly heated, stirring occasionally.
3. Brush chicken with remaining dressing. Cut each chicken breast half into ¾-inch slices. Top each serving with ¼ cup tomato mixture; sprinkle with 2 tablespoons cheese and basil, if desired. **Yield:** 4 servings.

CALORIES 348; FAT 17.3g (sat 4.4g, mono 5g, poly 1.2g); PROTEIN 41.9g;
CARB 3.9g; FIBER 0.6g; CHOL 111mg; IRON 1.6mg; SODIUM 810mg; CALC 100mg

Instead of shredding your own, buy preshredded Parmesan from the deli section of your local supermarket. It's a little way to save time on meal preparation.

MAKE IT FASTER

20 MINUTES

Chicken with Dried Plums and Sage

make it a meal *Add quick-cooking whole wheat couscous and steamed green beans.*

4	(6-ounce) skinless, boneless chicken breast halves
2	tablespoons chopped fresh sage, divided
½	teaspoon salt
¼	teaspoon black pepper, divided
4	teaspoons olive oil, divided
2	cups thinly sliced onion (about 1 large)
½	cup dry white wine
½	cup fat-free, less-sodium chicken broth
12	pitted dried plums, halved
1½	teaspoons balsamic vinegar

1. Place each chicken breast half between 2 sheets of heavy-duty plastic wrap; pound to ¹/₂-inch thickness using a meat mallet or small heavy skillet. Sprinkle chicken with 1 tablespoon sage, salt, and ¹/₈ teaspoon pepper.
2. Heat 2 teaspoons oil in a large nonstick skillet over medium heat. Add chicken to pan; cook 3 minutes on each side or until done. Remove chicken from pan; keep warm. Heat remaining 2 teaspoons oil in pan. Add onion to pan; cook 3 minutes or until tender. Stir in wine and broth; bring to a boil. Add remaining 1 tablespoon sage and dried plums to pan; cook 4 minutes or until mixture thickens. Stir in remaining ¹/₈ teaspoon pepper and vinegar. **Yield:** 4 servings (serving size: 1 chicken breast half and about ¹/₂ cup sauce).

CALORIES 301; FAT 8.7g (sat 1.8g, mono 4.7g, poly 1.4g); PROTEIN 35.4g; CARB 19.8g; FIBER 2.3g; CHOL 94mg; IRON 1.6mg; SODIUM 438mg; CALC 49mg

20 MINUTES

Chicken with Caper-Tomato Salsa

Fresh salsa plus a few garden vegetables creates a winning topping for juicy chicken breasts. Serve with ½ cup orzo.

4	(6-ounce) skinless, boneless chicken breast halves
2	tablespoons Italian-seasoned breadcrumbs
2	teaspoons olive oil
2	tablespoons water
³/₄	cup refrigerated fresh salsa
¹/₃	cup diced plum tomato
¹/₃	cup diced zucchini
2	tablespoons chopped ripe olives
2	teaspoons capers

1. Place chicken breast halves between 2 sheets of heavy-duty plastic wrap; pound to ¹/₂-inch thickness using a meat mallet or small heavy skillet. Sprinkle chicken with breadcrumbs.
2. Heat oil in a large nonstick skillet over medium-high heat. Add chicken; cook 2 minutes on each side or until browned. Reduce heat to low; add 2 tablespoons water. Cover; cook 8 minutes or until done.
3. While chicken cooks, combine salsa and next 4 ingredients in a bowl; stir well. Serve salsa mixture over chicken. **Yield:** 4 servings (serving size: 1 chicken breast half and about ¹/₃ cup salsa).

CALORIES 241; FAT 7g (sat 1.6g, mono 4g, poly 1.3g); PROTEIN 35.1g; CARB 5.3g; FIBER 0.6g; CHOL 99mg; IRON 1.6mg; SODIUM 331mg; CALC 31mg

Chopping fresh olives can be time consuming. To make this recipe even faster, consider purchasing canned chopped olives, instead.

MAKE IT FASTER

Chicken with Sherry-Soy Reduction Sauce

make it a meal *Serve with bagged salad greens and quick-cooking rice noodles.*

Cooking spray
4   (6-ounce) skinless, boneless chicken breast halves
¼   teaspoon salt
¼   teaspoon freshly ground black pepper
⅓   cup dry sherry
1   tablespoon sugar
2   tablespoons low-sodium soy sauce
2   tablespoons red wine vinegar
⅛   teaspoon crushed red pepper
1   teaspoon sesame oil
¼   cup thinly sliced green onions

1. Heat a large nonstick skillet over medium-high heat. Coat pan with cooking spray. Sprinkle chicken with salt and black pepper. Add chicken to pan; cook 4 minutes on each side or until lightly browned. Remove from pan; keep warm.
2. Add sherry, sugar, soy sauce, vinegar, and red pepper to pan; scrape pan to loosen browned bits. Bring to a boil; cook 1 minute. Stir in oil. Serve sauce over chicken, and sprinkle with onions. **Yield:** 4 servings (serving size: 1 chicken breast half, 1 tablespoon sauce, and 1 tablespoon onions).

CALORIES 230; FAT 3.3g (sat 0.7g, mono 1g, poly 1g); PROTEIN 39.9g; CARB 4.7g; FIBER 0.3g; CHOL 99mg; IRON 1.6mg; SODIUM 528mg; CALC 27mg

20 MINUTES
Chicken with Southwestern Salsa

1	tablespoon canola oil, divided
1	teaspoon ground cumin, divided
³/₄	teaspoon ground coriander, divided
¹/₂	teaspoon salt
¹/₄	teaspoon black pepper
¹/₈	teaspoon ground red pepper
4	(6-ounce) skinless, boneless chicken breast halves
¹/₂	cup prechopped onion
1	teaspoon bottled minced garlic
¹/₃	cup chopped plum tomato
¹/₄	cup chopped fresh cilantro
2	tablespoons fresh lime juice
1	(15¹/₂-ounce) can black beans, rinsed and drained
1	(8³/₄-ounce) can no-salt-added whole kernel corn, drained

1. Heat 2 teaspoons oil in a large nonstick skillet over medium-high heat. Combine ¹/₂ teaspoon cumin, ¹/₂ teaspoon coriander, salt, black pepper, and red pepper; sprinkle mixture evenly over chicken. Add chicken to pan; cook 7 minutes on each side or until done.

2. While chicken cooks, heat the remaining 1 teaspoon oil in a small skillet over medium-high heat. Add onion to pan; sauté 1 minute. Add garlic to pan; sauté 30 seconds. Transfer onion mixture to a large bowl; add remaining ¹/₂ teaspoon cumin, remaining ¹/₄ teaspoon coriander, tomato, and remaining ingredients to onion mixture, tossing well. Serve with chicken.

Yield: 4 servings (serving size: 1 chicken breast half and ³/₄ cup salsa).

CALORIES 317; FAT 8.7g (sat 1.4g, mono 3.5g, poly 1.9g); PROTEIN 39g; CARB 24.4g; FIBER 5.2g; CHOL 94mg; IRON 2.2mg; SODIUM 705mg; CALC 50mg

2O MINUTES

Greek Chicken

make it a meal *Bottled minced garlic is a real time-saver—especially with a recipe that calls for a whole tablespoon. Once you open the bottle, be sure to store it in the refrigerator and check the "use by" date before adding it to a dish. Serve this garlic-infused chicken over ½-cup servings of cooked rice garnished with chopped fresh parsley.*

4 (6-ounce) skinless, boneless chicken breast halves
Cooking spray
1 (14.5-ounce) can diced tomatoes with basil, garlic, and oregano, undrained
¼ cup pitted kalamata olives, sliced
1 tablespoon bottled minced garlic
¼ teaspoon black pepper
¼ cup (1 ounce) crumbled feta cheese

1. Place a large nonstick skillet over medium-high heat. Coat pan and chicken with cooking spray; place chicken in pan. Cook 3 minutes on each side or until chicken is browned.
2. Reduce heat to medium; add tomatoes, olives, garlic, and pepper. Cover and cook 11 minutes or until chicken is done. Remove from heat, and sprinkle with feta cheese. **Yield:** 4 servings (serving size: 1 chicken breast and about ½ cup sauce).

CALORIES 279; FAT 8.2g (sat 2.5g, mono 4.3g, poly 1.3g); PROTEIN 37.1g; CARB 10.9g; FIBER 1.2g; CHOL 102mg; IRON 2.8mg; SODIUM 835mg; CALC 113mg

Feta is a fresh Greek cheese that is tangy and salty as a result of the brine in which it's cured. A choice addition to salads, feta is also good for fillings, sauces, and pasta dishes.

INGREDIENT SPOTLIGHT

2O MINUTES

Cuban-Style Chicken

make it a meal *Toss a green salad while the chicken cooks, then serve it with rice for a complete meal. To save time, use drained canned pineapple tidbits in place of fresh fruit.*

½ cup diced fresh pineapple
2 tablespoons rice vinegar
1 tablespoon orange marmalade
1 (15-ounce) can black beans, rinsed and drained
¼ teaspoon ground red pepper, divided
½ teaspoon salt
½ teaspoon paprika
4 (6-ounce) skinless, boneless chicken breast halves
Cooking spray
¼ cup chopped fresh cilantro

1. Combine first 4 ingredients in a medium saucepan; add ⅛ teaspoon pepper. Bring to a simmer over medium heat; cook 1 minute or until thoroughly heated. Keep warm.
2. Heat a large nonstick skillet over medium heat. Combine the remaining ⅛ teaspoon pepper, salt, and paprika, and sprinkle evenly over chicken. Coat chicken with cooking spray. Add chicken to pan; cook 5 minutes on each side or until done. Serve with bean mixture; sprinkle with cilantro. **Yield:** 4 servings (serving size: 1 chicken breast half, ½ cup bean mixture, and 1 tablespoon cilantro).

CALORIES 293; FAT 2.7g (sat 0.6g, mono 0.5g, poly 0.5g); PROTEIN 45.2g; CARB 22.4g; FIBER 6.2g; CHOL 99mg; IRON 2.9mg; SODIUM 632mg; CALC 57mg

Grilled Sesame-Ginger Chicken

15 MINUTES

Hoisin-Glazed Chicken Breasts

Adding the remaining glaze on the chicken after broiling intensifies the flavor. Be sure to use a clean spoon or brush when adding the final amount of hoisin mixture—you don't want it to come in contact with any utensils that touched raw chicken.

¼ cup hoisin sauce
1 tablespoon fresh lime juice
1 tablespoon low-sodium soy sauce
2 teaspoons bottled minced garlic
2 teaspoons dark sesame oil
¾ teaspoon bottled minced fresh ginger
Cooking spray
4 (6-ounce) skinless, boneless chicken breast halves
4 lime wedges

1. Preheat broiler.
2. Combine first 6 ingredients. Remove 2 tablespoons of hoisin mixture, and reserve to brush on cooked chicken. Line a shallow roasting pan with foil; coat foil with cooking spray. Place chicken on prepared pan. Brush 2 tablespoons of hoisin mixture evenly over chicken; broil 5 minutes. Turn chicken over; brush with 2 tablespoons of hoisin mixture. Broil 5 minutes or until chicken is done. Spoon reserved 2 tablespoons of hoisin mixture over cooked chicken. Serve with lime wedges. **Yield:** 4 servings (serving size: 1 chicken breast half and 1 lime wedge).

CALORIES 249; FAT 4.9g (sat 1g, mono 1.6g, poly 1.7g); PROTEIN 40.2g; CARB 8.4g; FIBER 0.5g; CHOL 99mg; IRON 1.4mg; SODIUM 520mg; CALC 26mg

15 MINUTES

Grilled Sesame-Ginger Chicken

 Stir 1 tablespoon sliced green onions and 1 teaspoon toasted sesame seeds into each ½ cup serving of cooked white rice to make your meal complete.

2 tablespoons low-sodium soy sauce
2 tablespoons honey
1 tablespoon toasted sesame seeds
2 teaspoons minced peeled fresh ginger
4 (6-ounce) skinless, boneless chicken breast halves
Cooking spray
Sliced green onions (optional)

1. Prepare grill.
2. Combine first 4 ingredients in a small bowl, stirring with a whisk.
3. Place each chicken breast half between 2 sheets of heavy-duty plastic wrap; pound to ½-inch thickness using a meat mallet or small heavy skillet.
4. Place chicken on grill rack coated with cooking spray; grill 5 to 6 minutes on each side or until chicken is done, basting occasionally with sesame seed mixture. Place on a serving platter; garnish with green onions, if desired. Serve immediately. **Yield:** 4 servings (serving size: 1 chicken breast half).

CALORIES 232; FAT 4.9g (sat 1.3g, mono 2.1g, poly 1.4g); PROTEIN 35.2g; CARB 10.2g; FIBER 0.4g; CHOL 99mg; IRON 1.5mg; SODIUM 383mg; CALC 23mg

15 MINUTES

Grilled Chicken with Roasted Red Pepper Sauce

make it a meal *Pair this delicious grilled favorite with a simple green salad.*

1   (7-ounce) bottle roasted red bell peppers, drained
2   teaspoons olive oil
1   tablespoon chopped fresh cilantro
1   teaspoon fresh lime juice
½   teaspoon salt, divided
4   (6-ounce) skinless, boneless chicken breast halves
¼   teaspoon freshly ground black pepper
Cooking spray

1. Prepare grill.
2. Place roasted red bell peppers and next 3 ingredients in a blender or food processor; process until smooth. Stir in ¼ teaspoon salt, and set aside.
3. Sprinkle chicken evenly with remaining ¼ teaspoon salt and black pepper. Place chicken on grill rack coated with cooking spray over medium-high heat. Grill, covered, 5 to 6 minutes on each side or until done.
4. While chicken grills, place bell pepper sauce in a small saucepan; cook over medium heat until warm. Serve with chicken. **Yield:** 4 servings (serving size: 1 chicken breast half and 3 tablespoons sauce).

CALORIES 211; FAT 6.2g (sat 1.4g, mono 3.5g, poly 1.2g); PROTEIN 34.3g; CARB 1.7g; FIBER 0.1g; CHOL 99mg; IRON 1.3mg; SODIUM 503mg; CALC 20mg

Jamaican Chicken with Mango Salsa

Readers raved about the sweet 'n' spicy salsa that tops Jamaican jerk chicken. Make the salsa up to two days ahead to save time in the kitchen the day you make this dish.

½ teaspoon Jamaican jerk seasoning (such as Spice Islands)
½ teaspoon salt, divided
4 (6-ounce) skinless, boneless chicken breast halves
Cooking spray
¼ cup minced fresh cilantro
¼ cup finely chopped red onion
1 tablespoon chopped fresh mint
1 teaspoon brown sugar
2 teaspoons fresh lime juice
¼ teaspoon black pepper
¼ teaspoon crushed red pepper
1 (16-ounce) jar sliced peeled mango, drained and chopped (such as Del Monte SunFresh)

1. Heat a large nonstick skillet over medium-high heat. Sprinkle seasoning and ¼ teaspoon of salt evenly over chicken. Coat chicken with cooking spray. Add chicken to pan; cook 4 minutes on each side or until done.

2. While chicken cooks, combine ¼ teaspoon salt, cilantro, and remaining ingredients. Serve salsa with chicken. **Yield:** 4 servings (serving size: 1 chicken breast half and about ½ cup salsa).

CALORIES 244; FAT 2.4g (sat 0.6g, mono 0.6g, poly 0.5g); PROTEIN 39.8g; CARB 14.7g; FIBER 1.6g; CHOL 99mg; IRON 1.5mg; SODIUM 445mg; CALC 33mg

MINUTES

Lemon-Basil Chicken with Basil Aioli

Chicken:
½ cup chopped fresh basil
⅓ cup chopped green onions
2 tablespoons fresh lemon juice
2 tablespoons white wine vinegar
½ teaspoon lemon pepper
¼ teaspoon freshly ground black pepper
4 (6-ounce) skinless, boneless chicken breast halves
Cooking spray

Basil Aioli:
¼ cup finely chopped fresh basil
2 tablespoons low-fat mayonnaise
1 tablespoon fresh lemon juice
1½ teaspoons Dijon mustard
¾ teaspoon bottled minced garlic
½ teaspoon olive oil

1. To prepare chicken, combine first 6 ingredients in a large bowl. Add chicken to basil mixture, turning to coat.
2. Heat a large nonstick skillet over medium-high heat. Coat pan with cooking spray. Add chicken to pan; cook 8 minutes on each side or until done.
3. While chicken cooks, prepare aioli. Combine ¼ cup basil and remaining ingredients in a small bowl, stirring with a whisk. Serve with chicken. **Yield:** 4 servings (serving size: 1 chicken breast half and 1 tablespoon aioli).

CALORIES 284; FAT 10.3g (sat 1.7g, mono 1.4g, poly 0.6g); PROTEIN 40.1g; CARB 6.1g; FIBER 1g; CHOL 106mg; IRON 1.9mg; SODIUM 410mg; CALC 51mg

MINUTES

Moroccan Chicken with Fruit and Olive Topping

make it a meal *The pairing of dried fruit and olives is also characteristic of other North African cuisines, such as Tunisian and Algerian. Serve over Israeli couscous, a pearl-like pasta; sprinkle with chopped green onions.*

1 tablespoon olive oil, divided
½ teaspoon salt
¼ teaspoon black pepper
¼ teaspoon dried thyme
4 (6-ounce) skinless, boneless chicken breast halves
½ cup prechopped onion
2 teaspoons bottled minced garlic
¾ cup dried mixed fruit
½ cup dry white wine
½ cup fat-free, less-sodium chicken broth
¼ cup chopped pitted green olives
⅛ teaspoon salt
⅛ teaspoon black pepper

1. Heat 2 teaspoons oil in a large nonstick skillet over medium-high heat. Sprinkle ½ teaspoon salt, ¼ teaspoon pepper, and thyme evenly over chicken. Add chicken to pan, and cook 4 minutes on each side or until done. Remove from pan; cover and keep warm.
2. Heat remaining 1 teaspoon oil in pan. Add onion to pan; sauté 2 minutes until tender. Add garlic to pan; sauté 30 seconds. Add fruit and remaining ingredients to pan; cook 5 minutes or until liquid almost evaporates. **Yield:** 4 servings (serving size: 1 chicken breast half and about ⅓ cup fruit mixture).

CALORIES 346; FAT 7.5g (sat 1g, mono 4.3g, poly 1.3g); PROTEIN 40.6g; CARB 26g; FIBER 2.1g; CHOL 99mg; IRON 2.4mg; SODIUM 591mg; CALC 45mg

Basil is one of the most important culinary herbs. Sweet basil, the most common type, tastes like a cross between licorice and cloves.

INGREDIENT SPOTLIGHT

COOKING CLASS: *how to pan-sear chicken*

To pan-sear chicken make sure the skillet is hot. The key is to seal in the juices by forming an outer crust, and the best way to do this is to minimize turning the chicken in the pan.

Pan-Seared Chicken with Italian Salsa Verde

The fresh flavors of parsley and mint carry the piquant capers, garlic, and vinegar in this simple chicken recipe. It's especially good atop fettuccine.

1	tablespoon all-purpose flour
¼	teaspoon salt
¼	teaspoon freshly ground black pepper
4	(6-ounce) skinless, boneless chicken breast halves
5	teaspoons olive oil, divided
¾	cup fresh flat-leaf parsley leaves
2	tablespoons water
2	tablespoons red wine vinegar
1	teaspoon bottled minced garlic
1	teaspoon capers, rinsed and drained
4	(2-inch) fresh mint sprigs
1	(2-ounce) slice peasant bread, crust removed

1. Combine first 4 ingredients in a large zip-top plastic bag; seal and shake well to coat. Heat 1 tablespoon oil in a large nonstick skillet over medium-high heat. Add chicken to pan, and cook 6 minutes on each side or until done.

2. Place remaining 2 teaspoons oil, parsley, and remaining ingredients except bread in a food processor; process 10 seconds or until finely chopped. Tear peasant bread into pieces; add to the processor, and process 4 seconds or until well blended. Thinly slice each chicken breast half, and serve topped with salsa verde. **Yield:** 4 servings (serving size: 1 chicken breast half and 2 tablespoons salsa verde).

CALORIES 280; FAT 8.3g (sat 1.5g, mono 4.7g, poly 1.3g); PROTEIN 40.9g; CARB 8.1g; FIBER 1g; CHOL 99mg; IRON 2.7mg; SODIUM 345mg; CALC 51mg

Seared Chicken with Tomatillo-Avocado Salsa

20 MINUTES

Seared Chicken Breast with Pan Gravy

make it a meal *This is a lightened version of a classic family-friendly recipe. Rather than deep-fat frying the chicken, we lightly floured and then browned it in a minimal amount of olive oil to seal in the natural juices. Serve with mashed potatoes and steamed carrots.*

4   (6-ounce) skinless, boneless chicken breast
    halves
1   tablespoon chopped fresh thyme
½   teaspoon salt
½   teaspoon coarsely ground black pepper
1.1 ounces (about ¼ cup) plus 1 tablespoon
    all-purpose flour, divided
1   tablespoon olive oil
¼   cup minced shallots (1 medium)
1   cup fat-free, less-sodium chicken broth
1   tablespoon fresh lemon juice
¼   teaspoon coarsely ground black pepper

1. Place each chicken breast half between 2 sheets of heavy-duty plastic wrap; pound to ¼-inch thickness using a meat mallet or small heavy skillet.
2. Sprinkle chicken with thyme, salt, and pepper. Place ¼ cup flour in a shallow dish. Dredge chicken in flour.
3. Heat oil in a large skillet over medium-high heat. Add chicken; cook 2 to 3 minutes on each side or until done. Remove chicken from skillet; keep warm. Add shallots; cook 1 minute.
4. Stir in chicken broth and remaining 1 tablespoon flour, scraping pan to loosen browned bits. Simmer 3 to 4 minutes or until gravy is reduced and slightly thickened. Add lemon juice and ¼ teaspoon pepper. Spoon gravy over chicken. **Yield:** 4 servings (serving size: 1 chicken breast half and 3 tablespoons gravy).

CALORIES 262; FAT 7.6g (sat 1.6g, mono 4.4g, poly 1.5g); PROTEIN 35.9g; CARB 10.1g; FIBER 0.5g; CHOL 99mg; IRON 1.9mg; SODIUM 512mg; CALC 28mg

20 MINUTES

Seared Chicken with Tomatillo-Avocado Salsa

make it a meal *Serve with baked tortilla chips, reduced-fat sour cream, and frozen margaritas for a quick, festive dinner.*

4   ounces tomatillos (3 tomatillos)
¾   cup peeled chopped avocado
⅓   cup sliced radish
¼   cup chopped fresh cilantro
2   tablespoons fresh lime juice
½   teaspoon salt
¼   teaspoon crushed red pepper
Cooking spray
4   (6-ounce) skinless, boneless chicken breast
    halves
1½ teaspoons poultry seasoning

1. Discard husks and stems from the tomatillos, and finely chop. Combine tomatillos and next 6 ingredients in a medium bowl.
2. Heat a large nonstick skillet over medium-high heat. Coat pan with cooking spray. Sprinkle chicken evenly with seasoning. Add chicken to pan; cook 3 minutes. Turn chicken over. Reduce heat, and cook 5 minutes or until done. Serve chicken with tomatillo mixture. **Yield:** 4 servings (serving size: 1 chicken breast half and ½ cup tomatillo mixture).

CALORIES 199; FAT 6.2g (sat 1.2g, mono 3.1g, poly 1g); PROTEIN 30.5g; CARB 4.9g; FIBER 2.2g; CHOL 74mg; IRON 1.5mg; SODIUM 529mg; CALC 25mg

30 MINUTES

Sicilian Chicken

make it a meal *Sicilian olives are large green olives marinated in herbs; you can substitute Spanish manzanilla olives. Accompany with orzo pasta and Chianti, if you're pouring wine.*

4	(6-ounce) skinless, boneless chicken breast halves
$1/2$	teaspoon salt
$1/2$	teaspoon black pepper
1	tablespoon olive oil
3	tablespoons all-purpose flour
$1/2$	cup dry white wine
$1/2$	cup sliced Sicilian olives
$1/4$	cup golden raisins
1	tablespoon balsamic vinegar
1	teaspoon dried oregano
1	(14.5-ounce) can diced no-salt-added tomatoes, undrained
$1/4$	cup chopped fresh basil

1. Place each chicken breast half between 2 sheets of heavy-duty plastic wrap; pound each breast half to $1/2$-inch thickness using a meat mallet or heavy skillet. Sprinkle both sides of chicken with salt and pepper.
2. Heat oil in a large nonstick skillet over medium-high heat. Place flour in a shallow dish; dredge chicken in flour. Add chicken to pan; cook 3 minutes on each side or until lightly browned. Add wine; cook 1 minute. Add olives and next 4 ingredients; bring to a boil. Reduce heat, and simmer 8 minutes or until chicken is done. Sprinkle with basil.
Yield: 4 servings (serving size: 1 chicken breast half and about 6 tablespoons sauce).

CALORIES 304; FAT 6.8g (sat 1.2g, mono 3.9g, poly 1g); PROTEIN 41.3g; CARB 18.2g; FIBER 2.6g; CHOL 99mg; IRON 2.5mg; SODIUM 671mg; CALC 59mg

30 MINUTES

Sesame-Orange Chicken

make it a meal *Ground sesame seeds thicken the sauce as it cooks. Serve with a salad and bread.*

2	tablespoons sesame seeds, toasted
1	tablespoon grated orange rind
$1/4$	teaspoon salt, divided

Dash of ground red pepper

4	(6-ounce) skinless, boneless chicken breast halves
2	teaspoons canola oil
1	teaspoon butter
1	cup fat-free, less-sodium chicken broth
$1/3$	cup orange juice
1	tablespoon whipping cream

1. Place sesame seeds, rind, $1/8$ teaspoon salt, and pepper in a food processor; process until mixture resembles coarse meal.
2. Place each chicken breast half between 2 sheets of heavy-duty plastic wrap; pound to $1/4$-inch thickness using a meat mallet or rolling pin. Sprinkle chicken evenly with $1/8$ teaspoon salt.
3. Heat oil and butter in a large nonstick skillet over medium heat until butter melts. Add chicken; cook 6 minutes on each side or until done. Remove chicken from pan, and keep warm.
4. Add ground sesame mixture to pan, stirring with a whisk. Add broth, and bring to a boil, scraping pan to loosen browned bits. Cook broth mixture until reduced to $2/3$ cup (about 3 minutes). Add orange juice and cream; cook 30 seconds, stirring constantly. Serve sauce over chicken. **Yield:** 4 servings (serving size: 1 chicken breast half and 3 tablespoons sauce).

CALORIES 271; FAT 9.1g (sat 2.5g, mono 3.4g, poly 2.2g); PROTEIN 41.1g; CARB 4g; FIBER 0.7g; CHOL 106mg; IRON 1.9mg; SODIUM 377mg; CALC 70mg

Skillet Barbecued Chicken

make it a meal *You'll love this skillet chicken slathered with spicy barbecue sauce, melted cheese, and smoky bacon. Serve with refrigerated mashed potatoes to keep the prep time short.*

4   (6-ounce) skinless, boneless chicken breast
    halves
2   teaspoons olive oil
Cooking spray
¼   teaspoon black pepper
¼   cup bottled smoky barbecue sauce (such as
    KC Masterpiece)
½   cup (2 ounces) 50% reduced-fat shredded
    cheddar cheese with jalapeño pepper (such
    as Cabot)
2   tablespoons real bacon pieces (such as
    Hormel)
3   tablespoons chopped green onions

1. Place each chicken breast half between 2 sheets of heavy-duty plastic wrap; pound to ½-inch thickness using a meat mallet or small heavy skillet.

2. Heat oil in a large nonstick skillet coated with cooking spray over medium-high heat. Sprinkle chicken evenly with pepper. Add chicken to pan, and cook 4 to 5 minutes on each side or until chicken is lightly browned and done.

3. Brush 1 tablespoon barbecue sauce over each chicken breast half; top each with 2 tablespoons cheese and 1½ teaspoons bacon pieces. Cover, reduce heat to medium-low, and cook 2 minutes or until cheese melts. Sprinkle each with about 2 teaspoons green onions. **Yield:** 4 servings (serving size: 1 breast half).

CALORIES 286; FAT 9.7g (sat 4.2g, mono 4.1g, poly 1.2g); PROTEIN 39.7g;
CARB 8.4g; FIBER 0.2g; CHOL 109mg; IRON 1.4mg; SODIUM 371mg; CALC 142mg

2O
MINUTES

Sweet Chicken and Green Peppers

make it a meal *While the chicken cooks prepare a bag of boil-in-bag rice. Toss the rice with chopped green onions before serving.*

³/₄ cup water
3 tablespoons ketchup
1 teaspoon Worcestershire sauce
½ teaspoon dried oregano
½ teaspoon freshly ground black pepper
Cooking spray
4 (6-ounce) skinless, boneless chicken breast
   halves
1 green bell pepper, cut into thin strips

1. Combine first 5 ingredients; stir well.
2. Heat a large nonstick skillet over medium-high heat; coat pan with cooking spray. Add chicken; cook 5 minutes on each side or until done. Place chicken on a serving platter, and keep warm.
3. Add bell pepper to pan; add ketchup mixture. Cook 5 minutes or until bell pepper is tender and sauce is slightly thick. Spoon sauce over chicken. **Yield:** 4 servings (serving size: 1 chicken breast half and ¼ cup sauce).

CALORIES 203; FAT 4.1g (sat 1.1g, mono 1.8g, poly 1.1g); PROTEIN 34.9g; CARB 5.1g; FIBER 0.6g; CHOL 99mg; IRON 1.6mg; SODIUM 222mg; CALC 28mg

Citrus Chicken

Spiced Grilled Chicken Breasts with Corn-Pepper Relish

Substitute an equal amount of chopped fresh cilantro for the minced parsley in the relish, if desired.

1   teaspoon chili powder
$^1/_2$ teaspoon salt
$^1/_2$ teaspoon ground cumin
$^1/_4$ teaspoon paprika
$^1/_8$ teaspoon ground red pepper
$^1/_8$ teaspoon black pepper
4   (6-ounce) skinless, boneless chicken breast halves
1   tablespoon canola oil
2   cups frozen whole-kernel corn, thawed
1   cup diced red bell pepper
3   tablespoons prechopped onion
2   tablespoons minced fresh parsley
2   tablespoons fresh lime juice
Dash of black pepper

1. Combine first 6 ingredients in a small bowl. Rub spice mixture over both sides of chicken breasts.
2. Heat oil in a grill pan over medium-high heat. Add chicken; cook 5 minutes on each side or until done.
3. While chicken cooks, combine corn and remaining ingredients in a bowl. Serve with chicken. **Yield:** 4 servings (serving size: 1 chicken breast and $^1/_2$ cup of relish).

CALORIES 333; FAT 9g (sat 1.7g, mono 3.9g, poly 2.5g); PROTEIN 42.7g; CARB 21.5g; FIBER 3.3g; CHOL 108mg; IRON 2.2mg; SODIUM 397mg; CALC 35mg

Citrus Chicken

$^1/_4$ cup orange juice
$^1/_2$ teaspoon grated lime rind
2   tablespoons fresh lime juice
2   tablespoons chopped fresh thyme
2   teaspoons bottled minced garlic
1   teaspoon grated orange rind
$^1/_4$ teaspoon salt
$^1/_8$ teaspoon ground red pepper
1   pound skinless, boneless chicken cutlets
1   tablespoon olive oil
Cooking spray
6   cups bagged prewashed baby spinach

1. Combine first 8 ingredients in a small bowl, stirring well with a whisk. Pour $^1/_4$ cup juice mixture into a large zip-top plastic bag. Add chicken to bag. Seal; let stand 5 minutes. Add oil to remaining juice mixture; stir well with a whisk.
2. Heat a large nonstick skillet over medium-high heat. Coat pan with cooking spray. Remove chicken from bag; discard marinade. Add chicken to pan; cook 4 minutes on each side or until done. Place $1^1/_2$ cups spinach on each of 4 plates. Divide chicken evenly among servings; top each serving with 1 tablespoon juice mixture. **Yield:** 4 servings.

CALORIES 183; FAT 4.9g (sat 0.9g, mono 2.8g, poly 0.7g); PROTEIN 27.4g; CARB 7.1g; FIBER 2.1g; CHOL 66mg; IRON 2.3mg; SODIUM 278mg; CALC 50mg

Bagged prewashed baby spinach helps make this recipe faster. The stems are tender and do not need to be removed.

MAKE IT FASTER

COOKING CLASS: *how to pound chicken*

Pounding chicken breast halves ensures they'll cook quickly and evenly. Place the breasts between plastic wrap. Pound to ¼-inch thickness using a meat mallet or small heavy skillet.

15 MINUTES

Peanutty Baked Chicken Cutlets

make it a meal *A quick spritz of cooking spray on the cutlets before they hit the hot oven enhances the crispness and color of the crust. Serve with baked sweet potatoes and broccoli spears.*

2   tablespoons honey
2   tablespoons Dijon mustard
⅓   cup peanuts
1   cup panko (Japanese breadcrumbs)
4   (½-inch-thick) chicken breast cutlets (about 1 pound)
Cooking spray
¼   cup peach chutney

1. Preheat oven to 500°.
2. Combine honey and mustard in a small bowl; stir well. Place peanuts in a food processor; pulse until finely chopped. Combine peanuts and panko in a shallow bowl.
3. Brush each cutlet with honey mixture; dredge cutlets in panko mixture. Place cutlets on a baking sheet coated with cooking spray; lightly coat cutlets with cooking spray. Bake at 500° for 8 minutes or until done. Serve with chutney. **Yield:** 4 servings (serving size: 1 cutlet and 1 tablespoon chutney).

CALORIES 282; FAT 7.8g (sat 1.5g, mono 3.3g, poly 2g); PROTEIN 27.2g;
CARB 25.6g; FIBER 1.6g; CHOL 63mg; IRON 1.1mg; SODIUM 299mg; CALC 22mg

20 MINUTES

Pan-Roasted Chicken Cutlets with Maple-Mustard Dill Sauce

make it a meal *Serve with a side of orange-scented couscous to bring out the orange flavors in the sauce.*

4   (6-ounce) skinless, boneless chicken breast halves
¼   teaspoon salt
¼   teaspoon black pepper
Cooking spray
2   tablespoons chopped red onion
6   tablespoons maple syrup
¼   cup Dijon mustard
1   tablespoon water
1   teaspoon chopped fresh dill
1   teaspoon grated orange rind

1. Place each chicken breast half between 2 sheets of heavy-duty plastic wrap; pound each to ¼-inch thickness using a meat mallet or small heavy skillet. Sprinkle chicken evenly with salt and pepper. Heat a large nonstick skillet over medium-high heat. Coat pan with cooking spray. Add chicken to pan; cook 4 minutes on each side or until done. Remove chicken from pan.
2. Reduce heat to medium. Add onion to pan; cook 1 minute. Add syrup and remaining ingredients; cook 1 minute or until thoroughly heated, stirring frequently. Serve sauce with chicken. **Yield:** 4 servings (serving size: 1 chicken breast half and about 2 tablespoons sauce).

CALORIES 287; FAT 3.5g (sat 0.6g, mono 1g, poly 0.9g); PROTEIN 40.3g;
CARB 22.5g; FIBER 0.3g; CHOL 99mg; IRON 2mg; SODIUM 640mg; CALC 63mg

 MINUTES

Peanut-Crusted Chicken with Pineapple Salsa

1 cup chopped fresh pineapple
2 tablespoons chopped fresh cilantro
1 tablespoon finely chopped red onion
1/3 cup unsalted, dry-roasted peanuts
1 (1-ounce) slice white bread
1/2 teaspoon salt
1/8 teaspoon black pepper
4 (4-ounce) chicken cutlets
1 1/2 teaspoons canola oil
Cooking spray
Cilantro sprigs (optional)

1. Combine first 3 ingredients in a small bowl, tossing well.
2. Place peanuts and bread slice in a food processor; process until finely chopped. Sprinkle salt and pepper evenly over chicken. Dredge chicken in breadcrumb mixture.
3. Heat oil in a large nonstick skillet over medium-high heat. Coat pan with cooking spray. Add chicken to pan; cook 2 minutes on each side or until done. Serve chicken with pineapple mixture. Garnish with cilantro sprigs, if desired. **Yield:** 4 servings (serving size: 1 cutlet and 1/4 cup salsa).

CALORIES 219; FAT 7.4g (sat 1.1g, mono 3.4g, poly 2.1g); PROTEIN 28.9g; CARB 9.1g; FIBER 1.3g; CHOL 66mg; IRON 1.2mg; SODIUM 398mg; CALC 27mg

make it a meal *Pick up a container of fresh pineapple chunks in the produce section of the supermarket; chop into half-inch pieces for the salsa. Serve with steamed broccoli and warm rolls to complete the dinner.*

30
MINUTES

Chicken Drumsticks with Apricot Glaze

Speed preparation by reducing the glaze while the chicken broils.

8   (4-ounce) chicken drumsticks, skinned
¼   teaspoon salt
⅛   teaspoon black pepper
Cooking spray
½   cup apricot spread (such as Polaner All Fruit)
1   tablespoon dark brown sugar
2   tablespoons cider vinegar
1   tablespoon low-sodium soy sauce
1   teaspoon bottled ground fresh ginger (such as Spice World)
¼   teaspoon crushed red pepper

1. Preheat broiler.
2. Line bottom of a broiler pan with foil. Sprinkle chicken with salt and black pepper. Place chicken on the rack of a broiler pan coated with cooking spray; place rack in pan. Broil chicken 12 minutes, turning once.
3. While chicken cooks, combine apricot spread and remaining ingredients in a small saucepan; bring to a boil over medium heat. Cook 5 minutes or until reduced to ½ cup, stirring frequently. Brush ¼ cup apricot mixture evenly over chicken; broil 2 minutes. Brush remaining apricot mixture over chicken; broil 2 minutes or until done.
Yield: 4 servings (serving size: 2 drumsticks).

CALORIES 232; FAT 3.9g (sat 1g, mono 1.2g, poly 0.9g); PROTEIN 23.6g; CARB 24.3g; FIBER 0.1g; CHOL 87mg; IRON 1.4mg; SODIUM 382mg; CALC 17mg

Jamaican Chicken Thighs

15
MINUTES

Jamaican Chicken Thighs

make it a meal *Reasonably priced chicken thighs make a Caribbean-accented meal when seasoned with classic island spices and sautéed. Serve alongside peaches tossed with lime juice and cilantro or fresh pineapple with cilantro.*

2   teaspoons garlic powder
1   teaspoon onion powder
½   teaspoon ground ginger
½   teaspoon dried thyme
½   teaspoon ground allspice
¼   teaspoon salt
¼   teaspoon ground nutmeg
¼   teaspoon ground red pepper
⅛   teaspoon freshly ground black pepper
8   skinless, boneless chicken thighs
Cooking spray

1. Combine first 9 ingredients in a small bowl. Rub spice mixture evenly over chicken. Heat a large nonstick skillet over medium-high heat. Coat pan with cooking spray. Add chicken, and cook 5 minutes on each side or until done. **Yield:** 4 servings (serving size: 2 thighs).

CALORIES 175; FAT 5.5g (sat 1.4g, mono 1.7g, poly 1.4g); PROTEIN 27.5g; CARB 2.2g; FIBER 0.6g; CHOL 115mg; IRON 1.7mg; SODIUM 265mg; CALC 22mg

Grilled Thai-Spiced Chicken

make it a meal *Enjoy a two-thigh serving with grilled red bell peppers and cooked white rice.*

8   (3-ounce) skinless, boneless chicken thighs
½   teaspoon salt
¼   teaspoon black pepper
4   teaspoons red curry paste
Cooking spray
1   tablespoon chopped fresh cilantro

1. Prepare grill.
2. Sprinkle chicken with salt and pepper; spread curry paste evenly over chicken.
3. Place chicken on grill rack coated with cooking spray; cover and grill 5 minutes on each side or until chicken is done. Sprinkle with cilantro. **Yield:** 4 servings (serving size: 2 thighs).

CALORIES 186; FAT 4g (sat 1.1g, mono 1.9g, poly 0.9g); PROTEIN 34.3g; CARB 0.8g; FIBER 0g; CHOL 94mg; IRON 1.1mg; SODIUM 463mg; CALC 18mg

Chicken thighs have a slightly higher fat content than the very lean chicken breast. After you remove the skin, chicken thighs have less total fat than the same amount of beef sirloin or tenderloin, a pork chop, or a portion of salmon.

INGREDIENT SPOTLIGHT

Jamaican-Spiced Chicken Thighs

make it a meal *Complete the menu with mashed sweet potatoes and a mixed green salad. For more heat, leave the seeds in the jalapeño.*

¼   cup minced red onion
1   tablespoon sugar
1   tablespoon finely chopped seeded jalapeño pepper
2   teaspoons cider vinegar
2   teaspoons low-sodium soy sauce
½   teaspoon salt
½   teaspoon ground allspice
½   teaspoon dried thyme
½   teaspoon black pepper
¼   teaspoon ground red pepper
8   skinless, boneless chicken thighs (about 1½ pounds)
Cooking spray

1. Combine first 10 ingredients in a large bowl; add chicken, tossing to coat. Heat a grill pan over medium-high heat. Coat pan with cooking spray. Add chicken to pan; cook 4 minutes. Turn chicken over; cook 6 minutes or until done. **Yield:** 4 servings (serving size: 2 chicken thighs).

CALORIES 187; FAT 5.7g (sat 1.4g, mono 1.7g, poly 1.4g); PROTEIN 27.5g; CARB 5g; FIBER 0.5g; CHOL 115mg; IRON 1.6mg; SODIUM 503mg; CALC 21mg

Orange Sweet-and-Sour Chicken Thighs with Bell Peppers

1   (3½-ounce) bag boil-in-bag long-grain rice
1½   tablespoons canola oil, divided
1   pound skinless, boneless chicken thighs
¼   teaspoon salt
1   cup orange juice
1   tablespoon cornstarch
2   tablespoons rice vinegar
3   tablespoons low-sodium soy sauce
2   tablespoons honey
1   cup prechopped onion
1   teaspoon bottled minced garlic
1   teaspoon bottled minced fresh ginger
1   green bell pepper, cut into ¼-inch strips
1   red bell pepper, cut into ¼-inch strips

1. Cook rice according to package directions, omitting salt and fat.
2. While rice cooks, heat 1 tablespoon canola oil in a large nonstick skillet over medium-high heat. Sprinkle chicken with salt. Add chicken to pan, and cook 3 minutes on each side or until done. Remove chicken from pan, and cut into thin strips.
3. While chicken cooks, combine orange juice, cornstarch, vinegar, soy sauce, and honey, stirring with a whisk.
4. Add remaining 1½ teaspoons oil to pan. Add onion, garlic, and ginger; sauté 1 minute. Add green bell pepper and red bell pepper strips, and sauté 2 minutes. Add orange juice mixture, and bring to a boil.

Reduce heat, and simmer 1 minute. Add chicken to pan, and cook 1 minute or until thoroughly heated. Serve over rice. **Yield:** 4 servings (serving size: ¾ cup rice and 1¼ cups chicken mixture).

CALORIES 382; FAT 9.9g (sat 1.5g, mono 4.5g, poly 2.7g); PROTEIN 26.5g; CARB 45.9g; FIBER 1.9g; CHOL 94mg; IRON 2.4mg; SODIUM 705mg; CALC 38mg

Spiced Chicken Thighs with Yogurt Sauce

The yogurt sauce's cooling effect balances the heat of the chicken.

1   cup uncooked couscous
1   teaspoon ground cumin
1   teaspoon ground coriander
1   teaspoon ground turmeric
¼   teaspoon ground ginger
¼   teaspoon ground red pepper
½   teaspoon salt, divided
8   skinless, boneless chicken thighs (about 1½ pounds)
Cooking spray
¼   cup chopped fresh cilantro
1   teaspoon bottled minced garlic
1   (6-ounce) carton plain fat-free yogurt
Cilantro sprigs (optional)

1. Cook couscous according to package directions, omitting salt and fat.
2. Combine cumin and next 4 ingredients in a bowl; stir in ¼ teaspoon salt. Sprinkle spice mixture over chicken. Heat a large nonstick skillet over medium heat. Coat pan with cooking spray. Add chicken to pan, and cook 6 minutes on each side or until done.
3. Combine remaining ¼ teaspoon salt, chopped cilantro, garlic, and yogurt in a bowl, stirring well. Serve with chicken and couscous. Garnish with cilantro sprigs, if desired. **Yield:** 4 servings (serving size: 2 chicken thighs, about ¼ cup yogurt mixture, and ½ cup couscous).

CALORIES 335; FAT 11.7g (sat 3.3g, mono 4.4g, poly 2.7g); PROTEIN 32.6g; CARB 22.5g; FIBER 1.5g; CHOL 100mg; IRON 2.2mg; SODIUM 425mg; CALC 111mg

Choose bell peppers with brightly colored, glossy skins. They should be free of soft spots and wrinkles, which are signs of aging, and their stems should be firm and green.

INGREDIENT SPOTLIGHT

15MINUTES

Spicy Honey-Brushed Chicken Thighs

make it a meal *Skinless, boneless thighs cook quickly and are more flavorful than white meat, so they need fewer ingredients. Serve with garlic-roasted potato wedges and a salad or broccolini.*

2 teaspoons garlic powder
2 teaspoons chili powder
1 teaspoon salt
1 teaspoon ground cumin
1 teaspoon paprika
$^1/_2$ teaspoon ground red pepper
8 skinless, boneless chicken thighs
Cooking spray
6 tablespoons honey
2 teaspoons cider vinegar

1. Preheat broiler.
2. Combine first 6 ingredients in a large bowl. Add chicken to bowl; toss to coat. Place chicken on a broiler pan coated with cooking spray. Broil chicken 5 minutes on each side.
3. Combine honey and vinegar in a small bowl, stirring well. Remove chicken from oven; brush $^1/_4$ cup honey mixture on chicken. Broil 1 minute. Remove chicken from oven, and turn over. Brush chicken with remaining honey mixture. Broil 1 additional minute or until chicken is done. **Yield:** 4 servings (serving size: 2 chicken thighs).

CALORIES 321; FAT 11g (sat 3g, mono 4.1g, poly 2.5g); PROTEIN 28g; CARB 27.9g; FIBER 0.6g; CHOL 99mg; IRON 2.1mg; SODIUM 676mg; CALC 21mg

20MINUTES

Duck with Olives and Couscous

1 cup water
$^3/_4$ cup couscous
$^1/_4$ teaspoon salt
1 tablespoon olive oil
4 (6-ounce) boneless duck breast halves, skinned
1$^1/_4$ cups fat-free, less-sodium chicken broth
$^1/_2$ cup dry white wine
$^1/_4$ cup minced shallots
1 teaspoon dried herbes de Provence
1$^1/_2$ teaspoons tomato paste
1 (3-inch) cinnamon stick
$^1/_4$ cup chopped pitted green olives

1. Bring water to a boil in a medium saucepan; gradually stir in couscous and salt. Remove from heat; cover and let stand 5 minutes. Fluff with a fork.
2. While couscous stands, heat oil in a large nonstick skillet over medium-high heat. Add duck; cook 3 minutes on each side or until browned. Combine broth and next 5 ingredients in a bowl, stirring with a whisk. Add broth mixture to pan. Cover, reduce heat, and simmer 3 minutes. Remove duck from pan; keep warm. Bring broth mixture to a boil; cook, uncovered, 2 minutes. Stir in olives; cook 1 minute. Discard cinnamon stick. Spoon about $^1/_2$ cup couscous onto each of 4 plates. Top each serving with 1 duck breast half, sliced, and about $^1/_4$ cup sauce. **Yield:** 4 servings.

CALORIES 376; FAT 11.7g (sat 2.9g, mono 5.2g, poly 1.4g); PROTEIN 38.3g; CARB 22.3g; FIBER 2g; CHOL 131mg; IRON 9mg; SODIUM 480mg; CALC 45mg

COOKING CLASS: *how to measure honey*

When measuring honey, lightly coat your measuring cup or spoon with cooking spray first, and all of the honey will slide out easily.

15 MINUTES

Duck with Port and Cranberry-Cherry Sauce

This rich sauce pairs well with duck breast, chicken, or pork.

1½ tablespoons butter, divided
3 tablespoons chopped shallots
½ cup port
¼ cup red currant jelly
1 tablespoon red wine vinegar
1 teaspoon sugar
¼ cup sweetened dried cranberries
3 tablespoons dried tart cherries
¾ teaspoon salt, divided
¼ teaspoon black pepper, divided
2 teaspoons olive oil
4 (6-ounce) boneless duck breast halves, skinned

1. Melt 1½ teaspoons butter over medium-high heat in a medium saucepan. Add shallots; sauté 1 minute. Add port, jelly, vinegar, and sugar; cook 2 minutes or until sugar dissolves. Stir in cranberries and cherries; cook 2 minutes or until slightly thick. Remove from heat. Stir in remaining 1 tablespoon butter, ¼ teaspoon salt, and ⅛ teaspoon pepper.

2. While sauce cooks, heat oil in a medium nonstick skillet over medium-high heat. Sprinkle duck with remaining ½ teaspoon salt and remaining ⅛ teaspoon pepper. Add duck to pan; cook 4 minutes on each side or until desired degree of doneness. Serve with sauce. **Yield:** 4 servings (serving size: 1 duck breast half and about 3 tablespoons sauce).

CALORIES 371; FAT 9.8g (sat 3.8g, mono 3.9g, poly 0.9g); PROTEIN 35.7g; CARB 30.1g; FIBER 1.5g; CHOL 194mg; IRON 6.2mg; SODIUM 610mg; CALC 27mg

Gnocchi with Turkey Ragù

make it a meal *Gnocchi are Italian potato-based dumplings. They float to the top of the water when they're done. Serve them with breadsticks.*

1	(16-ounce) package gnocchi
	Cooking spray
8	ounces ground turkey breast
1	cup chopped onion
¾	cup chopped red bell pepper
1	tablespoon bottled minced garlic
1	teaspoon dried basil
¼	teaspoon fennel seeds
½	cup dry white wine
3	tablespoons tomato paste
1	(14.5-ounce) can diced tomatoes with basil, garlic, and oregano
1	tablespoon finely grated fresh Romano cheese
½	teaspoon black pepper
	Basil sprigs (optional)

1. Cook gnocchi according to package directions, omitting salt and fat. Drain.

2. Heat a large nonstick skillet over medium-high heat. Coat pan with cooking spray. Add turkey to pan; cook 3 minutes or until browned, stirring to crumble. Drain. Add onion and next 4 ingredients; sauté 2 minutes. Return turkey to pan. Stir in wine; cook 2 minutes. Stir in tomato paste and tomatoes; cook 4 minutes, stirring occasionally. Remove from heat; stir in cheese and black pepper. Place about 1 cup gnocchi in each of 4 shallow bowls; top each serving with about ½ cup sauce. Garnish with basil, if desired. **Yield:** 4 servings.

CALORIES 317; FAT 9.7g (sat 5.5g, mono 2.3g, poly 0.5g); PROTEIN 18.7g; CARB 38g; FIBER 3.7g; CHOL 45mg; IRON 2.8mg; SODIUM 651mg; CALC 131mg

15 MINUTES

Turkey Picadillo

make it a meal *To serve, wrap the picadillo in a warm flour tortilla or spoon it over brown rice.*

1¼	pounds ground turkey breast
2	teaspoons ground cumin
1	(15-ounce) can seasoned diced tomato sauce or chili (such as Hunt's)
¼	cup water
½	cup raisins
1	tablespoon cider vinegar
¼	teaspoon black pepper
¼	cup presliced green onions

1. Heat a large nonstick skillet over medium-high heat; add turkey and cumin. Cook 7 minutes or until turkey is browned, stirring to crumble. Stir in tomato sauce and next 4 ingredients; bring to a boil. Cover, reduce heat, and simmer 5 minutes. Sprinkle with green onions before serving. **Yield:** 4 servings (serving size: about 1 cup).

CALORIES 315; FAT 10.5g (sat 3.2g, mono 4.8g, poly 2.3g); PROTEIN 31.7g; CARB 25.9g; FIBER 3.1g; CHOL 89mg; IRON 2.7mg; SODIUM 897mg; CALC 75mg

Ground turkey can be a lean substitute for ground beef, but be sure to read the labels carefully at the store because the fat content varies. "Ground turkey breast" is the leanest at about 3% fat; it contains white meat only and no skin. Regular ground turkey contains white and dark meat and some skin; it is about 10% fat. Frozen ground turkey is usually all dark meat and skin; it is 15% fat.

INGREDIENT SPOTLIGHT

---

20 MINUTES

Barley Sausage Skillet

make it a meal *Madeira is a slightly sweet Portuguese fortified wine. Substitute sherry or a fruity white wine, if necessary. Serve with broccoli sautéed with garlic and lemon, and corn bread.*

1	(14-ounce) can fat-free, less-sodium chicken broth
1	cup quick-cooking barley
	Cooking spray
8	ounces hot turkey Italian sausage
1	teaspoon olive oil
1	cup chopped onion
½	cup chopped red bell pepper
1	(8-ounce) package presliced mushrooms
2	teaspoons bottled minced garlic
2	tablespoons Madeira wine
¼	cup thinly sliced fresh basil
⅛	teaspoon black pepper

1. Place broth in a small saucepan; bring to a boil. Add barley to pan. Cover, reduce heat, and simmer 10 minutes or until liquid is absorbed.
2. Heat a large nonstick skillet over medium-high heat. Coat pan with cooking spray. Remove casings from sausage. Add sausage to pan; cook 3 minutes, stirring to crumble. Transfer to a bowl. Heat oil in pan over medium-high heat. Add onion, bell pepper, and mushrooms; sauté 4 minutes or until liquid evaporates. Add garlic; sauté 1 minute. Return sausage to pan. Stir in Madeira; sauté 2 minutes. Add barley; cook 1 minute or until thoroughly heated. Remove from heat; stir in basil and black pepper. **Yield:** 4 servings (serving size: 1¼ cups).

CALORIES 337; FAT 8.1g (sat 3.7g, mono 2.6g, poly 1.6g); PROTEIN 17.6g; CARB 49.1g; FIBER 9.6g; CHOL 34mg; IRON 3mg; SODIUM 537mg; CALC 49mg

MINUTES

20

One-Dish Chicken and Kielbasa Rice

The turmeric, chicken broth, and sausage add layers of flavor to the rice. If you want to splurge, you can substitute a few crushed saffron threads for the turmeric.

2   cups fat-free, less-sodium chicken broth
1/8 teaspoon ground turmeric
8   ounces turkey kielbasa, cut into 1/2-inch pieces
2   cups long-grain parboiled rice (such as Uncle Ben's)
2   teaspoons olive oil
8   ounces skinless, boneless chicken thighs, cut into bite-sized pieces
1   cup prechopped onion
1   cup prechopped green bell pepper
1/2 cup frozen green peas
1/4 cup sliced pitted stuffed manzanilla (or green) olives
1   tablespoon bottled minced garlic

1. Combine first 3 ingredients in a medium saucepan; bring to a boil. Stir in rice. Cover, reduce heat, and simmer 5 minutes. Remove from heat; let stand 5 minutes.
2. Heat olive oil in a large skillet over high heat. Add chicken pieces; cook 2 minutes or until browned, stirring occasionally. Add onion and bell pepper; sauté 4 minutes or until tender. Stir in peas, sliced olives, and garlic; sauté 1 minute. Add rice mixture; cook 1 minute or until thoroughly heated, stirring constantly. **Yield:** 4 servings (serving size: 1 1/2 cups).

CALORIES 428; FAT 11.5g (sat 2.6g, mono 5.4g, poly 2.4g); PROTEIN 26.7g; CARB 53.1g; FIBER 4g; CHOL 84mg; IRON 5.2mg; SODIUM 891mg; CALC 60mg

15 MINUTES

Balsamic Turkey with Sweet Red Bell Peppers

When slicing the red bell pepper into rings, be sure to remove the white pithy part of the pepper—it can lend a bitter taste to the dish.

6   (2-ounce) turkey breast cutlets (about 3/4 pound)
1/4 teaspoon salt
1/4 teaspoon garlic powder
1/4 teaspoon black pepper
2   teaspoons olive oil
Cooking spray
1   large red bell pepper, cut into rings
1/4 cup balsamic vinegar

1. Rub turkey with salt, garlic powder, and black pepper. Heat oil in a large nonstick skillet coated with cooking spray over medium-high heat. Add turkey, and cook 2 minutes on each side or until lightly browned. Transfer cutlets to a serving platter, and keep warm.
2. Add red bell pepper to pan, and cook 3 minutes or until crisp-tender, stirring constantly. Transfer to serving platter with turkey.
3. Add vinegar to pan, and cook 1 minute or until reduced by half. Spoon over turkey. **Yield:** 2 servings (serving size: 3 cutlets, 1/2 of bell pepper mixture, and 1 tablespoon vinegar).

CALORIES 265; FAT 5.4g (sat 0.8g, mono 3.8g, poly 0.7g); PROTEIN 42.8g; CARB 9.5g; FIBER 1.3g; CHOL 68mg; IRON 2.9mg; SODIUM 456mg; CALC 16mg

When our recipes call for chicken broth, we use fat-free, less sodium chicken broth. Swanson Natural Goodness is the brand we prefer.

INGREDIENT SPOTLIGHT

15 MINUTES

Orange-Glazed Turkey with Cranberry Rice

make it a meal *Combine hot cooked rice with dried cranberries for a supereasy and festive side dish to accompany the turkey.*

1   (8.8-ounce) pouch microwaveable cooked brown rice (such as Uncle Ben's Ready Rice)
1/2 cup orange-flavored sweetened dried cranberries (such as Craisins)
2   tablespoons chopped pecans, toasted
1/8 teaspoon salt
1 1/2 pounds turkey cutlets (about 12 cutlets)
1/4 teaspoon salt, divided
Butter-flavored cooking spray
1/3 cup low-sugar orange marmalade

1. Prepare rice in microwave according to package directions. Place cranberries in a medium bowl. Pour hot rice over cranberries; let stand 1 minute. Stir pecans and 1/8 teaspoon salt into rice mixture; cover and keep warm.

2. Sprinkle turkey cutlets evenly with 1/8 teaspoon salt. Heat a large nonstick skillet over medium-high heat. Coat pan with cooking spray.

3. Add cutlets to pan, salted side down. Cook 1 minute; coat cutlets with cooking spray, and sprinkle with remaining 1/8 teaspoon salt. Turn cutlets; cook 1 minute. Transfer turkey to a platter. Turn off heat; add marmalade to hot skillet, and stir 30 seconds. Return turkey and accumulated juices to skillet, turning to coat cutlets.

4. Place turkey cutlets on serving plates; spoon sauce over cutlets. Serve with rice mixture. **Yield:** 4 servings (serving size: about 3 cutlets, about 1/2 cup rice, and 1/2 tablespoon sauce).

CALORIES 359; FAT 4.1g (sat 0.4g, mono 2.3g, poly 1.3g); PROTEIN 44.2g; CARB 35.2g; FIBER 2.1g; CHOL 68mg; IRON 2.3mg; SODIUM 378mg; CALC 12mg

20 MINUTES

Turkey and Cranberry Port Wine Sauce

Use cranberry sauce left over from your holiday meal to make this easy supper. The recipe calls for shallots, which have a milder, sweeter flavor than onions. A sweet onion will work, as well.

1 tablespoon canola oil
4 (4-ounce) turkey breast cutlets
½ teaspoon salt, divided
½ teaspoon black pepper, divided
1 tablespoon butter
¼ cup chopped shallots
⅔ cup whole-berry cranberry sauce
¼ cup port wine
1 tablespoon chopped fresh sage
1 tablespoon red wine vinegar
Whole sage leaves (optional)

1. Heat oil in a large nonstick skillet over medium-high heat. Sprinkle turkey with ¼ teaspoon salt and ¼ teaspoon pepper. Add turkey to pan, and cook 5 minutes on each side or until done. Transfer turkey to a plate.
2. Melt butter in pan. Add shallots; sauté 30 seconds. Reduce heat to medium; stir in cranberry sauce, wine, chopped sage, vinegar, remaining ¼ teaspoon salt, and remaining ¼ teaspoon pepper. Cook 2 minutes or until slightly thickened, stirring occasionally.
3. Return turkey to pan. Cook 1 minute or until thoroughly heated. Serve with sauce. Garnish with sage leaves, if desired. **Yield:** 4 servings (serving size: 1 cutlet and ¼ cup sauce).

CALORIES 276; FAT 6.9g (sat 1.7g, mono 3.2g, poly 1.1g); PROTEIN 28.4g;
CARB 21.5g; FIBER 0.8g; CHOL 53mg; IRON 1.7mg; SODIUM 428mg; CALC 16mg

Port is a sweet fortified wine that is most often served after a meal, but it can also add a rich sweetness to foods when it's used in cooking. Once you open a bottle, you can use it for several months. Most ports do not need to be chilled.

INGREDIENT SPOTLIGHT

20 MINUTES

Turkey Cutlets with Prosciutto

4 (4-ounce) turkey breast cutlets
⅛ teaspoon salt
⅛ teaspoon black pepper
1½ ounces prosciutto, julienned
2 teaspoons finely chopped fresh sage
1 tablespoon olive oil
3 tablespoons finely chopped shallots
⅓ cup dry white wine

1. Place each cutlet between 2 sheets of heavy-duty plastic wrap; pound to ¼-inch thickness using a meat mallet or small heavy skillet. Sprinkle both sides of each cutlet with salt and pepper. Divide prosciutto into 4 equal portions; place 1 portion in the center of each cutlet. Sprinkle each portion with ½ teaspoon sage. Roll up cutlets, jelly-roll fashion, starting with narrow end.
2. Heat oil in a large nonstick skillet over medium-high heat. Add cutlets to pan; cook 6 minutes or until thoroughly cooked, turning to brown on all sides. Remove cutlets from pan; cover and keep warm. Reduce heat to medium-low. Add shallots to pan; cook 2 minutes, stirring occasionally. Add wine; bring to a simmer. Cook 30 seconds. Serve with cutlets. **Yield:** 4 servings (serving size: 1 cutlet and 1 tablespoon sauce).

CALORIES 180; FAT 5.2g (sat 1.1g, mono 2.5g, poly 0.5g); PROTEIN 31.1g; CARB 1.6g;
FIBER 0.1g; CHOL 54mg; IRON 1.8mg; SODIUM 380mg; CALC 7mg

SOUPS, SALADS &
SANDWICHES

Chilled Orange-Peach Soup

If you don't have time to peel and slice raw fruit, reach for frozen. You'll save time and also be able to enjoy fresh-tasting fruit soups year-round. You can partially thaw frozen fruit in the microwave by placing it in a microwave-safe dish and heating at MEDIUM-LOW for about 6 minutes, stirring once.

MAKE IT FASTER

15 MINUTES

Chilled Orange-Peach Soup

For added creaminess and visual appeal, swirl yogurt into the colorful soup.

1   (16-ounce) package frozen sliced peaches, partially thawed
¼   cup water
1½ cups orange juice
½   cup peach nectar
½   cup vanilla fat-free yogurt
2   tablespoons honey
Additional vanilla fat-free yogurt (optional)

1. Place peaches and water in a food processor; process until smooth. Add orange juice, nectar, and yogurt; process until well blended. With processor on, slowly add honey through food chute; process until well blended. Serve immediately, or cover and chill.
2. To serve, ladle soup into individual bowls. If desired, top each with a dollop of additional yogurt; swirl yogurt using tip of a knife. **Yield:** 6 servings (serving size: about 1 cup).

CALORIES 106; FAT 0.1g (sat 0.1g, mono 0g, poly 0g); PROTEIN 2.1g; CARB 25.5g; FIBER 1.4g; CHOL 0mg; IRON 0.4mg; SODIUM 16mg; CALC 49mg

15 MINUTES

Chilled Strawberry-Ginger Soup

This sweet, aromatic soup is ideal for a refreshing summer lunch. Make sure to add the honey while the blender is on so that it doesn't get too cold and clump at the bottom of the blender.

1   (16-ounce) package frozen unsweetened strawberries, partially thawed
1   (15-ounce) can pear halves in juice, undrained
½   cup frozen orange juice concentrate, thawed
1   tablespoon grated fresh ginger
¼   cup honey

1. Place first 4 ingredients in a blender. With blender on, slowly add honey. Process 3 minutes or until smooth, stopping once to scrape down sides. Serve immediately, or cover and chill up to 1 hour. **Yield:** 5 servings (serving size: about 1 cup).

CALORIES 212; FAT 0.3g (sat 0g, mono 0.1g, poly 0.1g); PROTEIN 1.3g; CARB 54.8g; FIBER 3.6g; CHOL 0mg; IRON 1.2mg; SODIUM 8mg; CALC 33mg

Cool and Creamy Tropical Fruit Soup

This beautifully colored soup is full of fresh taste. It makes a great snack or a refreshing summer dessert.

2	cups hulled fresh strawberries
12	ounces unsweetened pineapple juice
1	ripe mango, peeled and seeded
½	cup fat-free half-and-half
2	tablespoons sugar
1	teaspoon grated peeled fresh ginger
⅛	teaspoon crushed red pepper

Fresh strawberries (optional)

1. Place first 7 ingredients in a blender; process until smooth. Serve immediately, or cover and chill until ready to serve. Garnish with additional strawberries, if desired. **Yield:** 4 servings (serving size: about 1 cup).

CALORIES 154; FAT 0.3g (sat 0.1g, mono 0.1g, poly 0.1g); PROTEIN 1.1g; CARB 36g; FIBER 2.3g; CHOL 0mg; IRON 0.6mg; SODIUM 34mg; CALC 48mg

Cool and Creamy
Tropical Fruit Soup

Corn and Potato Chowder

make it a meal *Ideal for a weeknight supper, this vegetarian-friendly corn-studded soup can be made ahead and reheated just before serving. Ladle a bowl alongside a green salad and slice of hearty bread.*

Cooking spray

1½	cups prechopped green bell pepper
1	cup chopped green onions, divided (about 1 bunch)
2	cups frozen corn kernels
1¼	cups water
1	teaspoon seafood seasoning (such as Old Bay)
¾	teaspoon dried thyme leaves
⅛	teaspoon ground red pepper
1	pound baking potatoes, cut into ½-inch pieces
1	cup half-and-half
¼	cup chopped parsley
¾	teaspoon salt
½	cup (2 ounces) shredded reduced-fat sharp cheddar cheese

1. Heat a Dutch oven over medium-high heat. Coat pan with cooking spray. Add bell pepper and ¾ cup green onions, and sauté 4 minutes or until lightly browned.
2. Increase heat to high; add corn and next 5 ingredients; bring to a boil. Cover, reduce heat, and simmer 10 minutes or until potatoes are tender. Remove from heat, and stir in half-and-half, chopped parsley, and salt. Ladle about 1½ cups soup in each of 4 bowls; sprinkle each with 2 tablespoons cheese and 1 tablespoon of remaining green onions. **Yield:** 4 servings.

CALORIES 343; FAT 10.2g (sat 6.4g, mono 3.1g, poly 0.5g); PROTEIN 11.5g; CARB 53.3g; FIBER 7g; CHOL 41mg; IRON 2.5mg; SODIUM 654mg; CALC 219mg

30 MINUTES

Herbed Fish and Red Potato Chowder

2   bacon slices
3   cups diced red potato (about 1 pound)
1   cup chopped onion
3   tablespoons all-purpose flour
2   (8-ounce) bottles clam juice
2   cups 2% reduced-fat milk
1   tablespoon chopped fresh thyme
¼   teaspoon salt
¼   teaspoon black pepper
12   ounces skinless halibut fillets, cut into 1-inch pieces
2   tablespoons chopped fresh flat-leaf parsley

1. Cook bacon in a Dutch oven over medium-high heat until crisp. Remove bacon from pan. Reserve 1 tablespoon drippings in pan; discard remaining drippings. Cool bacon, and crumble. Set bacon aside. Add potato and onion to drippings in pan; sauté 3 minutes or until onion is tender. Add flour to pan; cook 1 minute, stirring constantly. Stir in clam juice; bring to a boil. Cover, reduce heat, and simmer 6 minutes or until potatoes are tender. Stir in milk; bring to a simmer over medium-high heat, stirring constantly (do not boil). Stir in thyme, salt, pepper, and fish; cook 3 minutes or until fish flakes easily when tested with a fork or until desired degree of doneness. Stir in parsley. Sprinkle with bacon. **Yield:** 4 servings (serving size: 2 cups).

CALORIES 307; FAT 8.1g (sat 3.5g, mono 3g, poly 0.9g); PROTEIN 24.4g; CARB 33.9g; FIBER 2.5g; CHOL 57mg; IRON 2.2mg; SODIUM 611mg; CALC 198mg

The small, pointed serrano chile is about 1½ inches long. It may be smaller than the similar jalapeño, but it's about twice as fierce. As it matures, it turns from bright green to scarlet red and then yellow.

INGREDIENT SPOTLIGHT

Southwest Shrimp and Corn Chowder

30 MINUTES

Southwest Shrimp and Corn Chowder

make it a meal *Quesadillas and a side of salsa are quick and easy accompaniments for rounding out your meal.*

2   tablespoons butter
1   cup chopped green onions
½   cup chopped red bell pepper
2   tablespoons finely chopped serrano chile (about 1 small)
1   (4.5-ounce) can chopped green chiles, undrained
3   tablespoons all-purpose flour
1½   cups 2% reduced-fat milk
1½   cups fat-free, less-sodium chicken broth
1½   cups frozen Southern-style hash brown potatoes, diced, thawed
½   teaspoon salt
½   teaspoon ground cumin
1   (15.25-ounce) can whole-kernel corn with red and green peppers, drained
1   pound peeled and deveined small shrimp
2   tablespoons chopped fresh cilantro

1. Melt butter in a large Dutch oven over medium-high heat. Add onions, bell pepper, and serrano chile to pan; sauté 2 minutes or until tender, stirring frequently. Add canned chiles to pan; cook 1 minute. Add flour to pan; cook 1 minute, stirring constantly. Stir in milk and next 5 ingredients; bring to a boil. Cook 5 minutes or until slightly thick. Stir in shrimp; cook 1 minute or until shrimp are done. Remove from heat; stir in cilantro. **Yield:** 6 servings (serving size: about 1 cup).

CALORIES 212; FAT 6.7g (sat 3.4g, mono 1.5g, poly 0.7g); PROTEIN 19.3g; CARB 18.3g; FIBER 2.2g; CHOL 130mg; IRON 2.5mg; SODIUM 702mg; CALC 131mg;

20 MINUTES

Chicken Corn Chowder

make it a meal *Corn kernels pureed with milk create the rich, smooth texture of classic chowder. A tossed salad offers complementary textures and flavors.*

1   tablespoon butter
6   green onions
2   tablespoons all-purpose flour
2   cups chopped cooked chicken breast
¼   teaspoon salt
¼   teaspoon freshly ground black pepper
2   (10-ounce) packages frozen corn kernels, thawed and divided
1   (14-ounce) can fat-free, less-sodium chicken broth
2   cups fat-free milk
½   cup (2 ounces) preshredded cheddar cheese

1. Melt butter in a Dutch oven over medium-high heat. Remove green tops from green onions. Chop green onion tops, and set aside. Thinly slice white portion of each onion. Add sliced onions to pan; sauté 2 minutes. Add flour; cook 1 minute, stirring constantly with a whisk. Stir in chicken, salt, pepper, 1 package of corn, and broth; bring to a boil. Reduce heat, and simmer 5 minutes.
2. While mixture simmers, place remaining corn and milk in a blender; process until smooth. Add milk mixture to pan; simmer 2 minutes or until thoroughly heated. Ladle 2 cups chowder into each of 4 soup bowls; sprinkle evenly with green onion tops. Top each serving with 2 tablespoons cheese. **Yield:** 4 servings.

CALORIES 394; FAT 11.5g (sat 5.8g, mono 3.4g, poly 1.4g); PROTEIN 35.5g; CARB 40.7g; FIBER 4.5g; CHOL 84mg; IRON 2.2mg; SODIUM 534mg; CALC 293mg

15 MINUTES

Avocado Soup with Citrus-Shrimp Relish

make it a meal *This lovely no-cook soup makes a refreshing entrée with a green salad.*

Relish:
2	tablespoons chopped fresh cilantro
1	teaspoon grated lemon rind
1	teaspoon finely chopped red onion
1	teaspoon extra-virgin olive oil
8	ounces peeled and deveined medium shrimp, steamed and coarsely chopped

Soup:
2	cups fat-free, less-sodium chicken broth
1¾	cups chopped avocado (about 2)
1	cup water
1	cup rinsed and drained canned navy beans
½	cup fat-free plain yogurt
1½	tablespoons fresh lemon juice
¼	teaspoon salt
¼	teaspoon black pepper
¼	teaspoon hot pepper sauce (such as Tabasco)
1	small jalapeño pepper, seeded and chopped
¼	cup (1 ounce) crumbled queso fresco cheese

1. To prepare relish, combine first 5 ingredients in a small bowl, tossing gently.
2. To prepare soup, place broth and next 9 ingredients in a blender, and puree until smooth, scraping sides. Ladle 1¼ cups avocado mixture into each of 4 bowls; top each serving with ¼ cup shrimp mixture and 1 tablespoon cheese. **Yield:** 4 servings.

CALORIES 292; FAT 13.2g (sat 2.2g, mono 7.8g, poly 2.6g); PROTEIN 23.9g; CARB 22.5g; FIBER 7.3g; CHOL 118mg; IRON 3.4mg; SODIUM 832mg; CALC 146mg

Avocado Soup with
Citrus-Shrimp Relish

15 MINUTES

Creamy Cucumber Gazpacho

Here's a twist on the classic using cool, refreshing cucumber instead.

2	English cucumbers (about 1¾ pounds), peeled and coarsely chopped
2	cups fat-free, less-sodium chicken broth
3	tablespoons white wine vinegar
1	garlic clove, minced
¼	teaspoon salt
¼	teaspoon freshly ground black pepper
3	cups fat-free sour cream
	Finely chopped English cucumber (optional)

1. Place first 6 ingredients in a blender; process until smooth. Pour cucumber mixture into a large bowl; add sour cream, stirring with a whisk until smooth.
2. Cover and chill at least 2 hours. Ladle soup into bowls; top with finely chopped cucumber, if desired. **Yield:** 8 servings (serving size: 1 cup).

CALORIES 104; FAT 0.2g (sat 0g, mono 0.1g, poly 0.1g); PROTEIN 6.9g; CARB 17.3g; FIBER 0.9g; CHOL 15mg; IRON 0.2mg; SODIUM 262mg; CALC 195mg

20
MINUTES

Tortellini-Basil Soup

If you chop the tomato and basil while the pasta cooks, your total time to prepare the recipe will be 14 minutes.

1   (32-ounce) container fat-free, less-sodium chicken broth
1   (9-ounce) package fresh cheese tortellini
1   (15.5-ounce) can cannellini beans, rinsed and drained
1   cup chopped tomato
½   cup thinly sliced fresh basil
2   tablespoons balsamic vinegar
¼   teaspoon salt
1   teaspoon freshly ground black pepper

1. Bring broth to a boil in a Dutch oven. Add tortellini; cook 6 minutes or until tender.

Stir in beans and tomato. Reduce heat; simmer 3 to 4 minutes or until thoroughly heated.
2. Remove from heat; stir in basil, vinegar, and salt. Ladle soup into individual bowls; sprinkle evenly with pepper. **Yield:** 6 servings (serving size: 1 cup).

CALORIES 234; FAT 2.1g (sat 0.8g, mono 1.1g, poly 0.1g); PROTEIN 14.9g; CARB 39.3g; FIBER 8.2g; CHOL 7mg; IRON 4.9mg; SODIUM 541mg; CALC 140mg

Fresh tortellini is available with a variety of fillings, including cheese. Look for fresh tortellini in the refrigerated section of your grocery store.

INGREDIENT SPOTLIGHT

15 MINUTES

Spicy Vegetarian Black Bean Soup

2 (15-ounce) cans black beans, rinsed and drained
1 (16-ounce) package frozen pepper stir-fry, slightly thawed
1 (12-ounce) package frozen meatless burger crumbles (such as Morningstar Farms or Boca)
1 (16-ounce) bottle chunky salsa
1 (14-ounce) can organic vegetable broth (such as Swanson Certified Organic)
2 teaspoons salt-free Mexican seasoning
½ cup (2 ounces) shredded 50% reduced-fat Monterey Jack cheese with jalapeño peppers (such as Cabot)

1. Mash half of beans with the back of a fork or a potato masher. Combine mashed beans and remaining beans in a large Dutch oven. Add pepper stir-fry and next 4 ingredients; bring to a boil. Reduce heat, and simmer, uncovered, 8 minutes. Ladle soup into bowls; top with shredded cheese. **Yield:** 8 servings (serving size: 1 cup soup and 1 tablespoon cheese).

CALORIES 151; FAT 3.2g (sat 0.8g, mono 0.5g, poly 1.7g); PROTEIN 14.1g; CARB 19.9g; FIBER 5.5g; CHOL 5mg; IRON 2.4mg; SODIUM 941mg; CALC 88mg

15
MINUTES

Southwestern Two-Bean Soup

Cheese is an optional topping that makes this soup even heartier, but you can always top it with fat-free sour cream instead.

Olive oil–flavored cooking spray
1   cup frozen chopped onion
¹/₂ teaspoon garlic powder
1   (19-ounce) can cannellini beans, rinsed and drained
1   (16-ounce) can kidney beans, rinsed and drained
1   (14-ounce) can fat-free, less-sodium chicken broth
2   (4¹/₂-ounce) cans chopped green chiles
1   tablespoon ground cumin
¹/₄ teaspoon salt
1   tablespoon fresh lime juice
Shredded Monterey Jack cheese (optional)
Chopped fresh cilantro (optional)

1. Heat a large saucepan over medium-high heat; coat pan with cooking spray. Add onion and garlic powder; sauté 3 minutes or until tender.
2. Mash half of cannellini beans, and add to onion mixture. Add remaining cannellini beans and kidney beans. Stir in broth and next 3 ingredients. Bring to a boil; cover, reduce heat, and simmer 5 minutes. Remove from heat; add lime juice. Ladle soup into bowls. Top with cheese and cilantro, if desired. **Yield:** 4 servings (serving size: 1¹/₄ cups).

CALORIES 181; FAT 1.8g (sat 0g, mono 0.8g, poly 1g); PROTEIN 9.8g; CARB 32.2g; FIBER 10.6g; CHOL 0mg; IRON 2.6mg; SODIUM 543mg; CALC 90mg

MINUTES

Spicy Tomato and White Bean Soup

make it a meal *Pair this soup with a simple grilled cheese sandwich for a quick and satisfying meal.*

1   (14-ounce) can fat-free, less-sodium chicken broth, divided
2   teaspoons chili powder
1   teaspoon ground cumin
1   (16-ounce) can navy beans, rinsed and drained
1   medium poblano chile, halved and seeded
¹/₂ onion, cut into ¹/₂-inch-thick wedges
1   pint grape tomatoes
¹/₄ cup chopped fresh cilantro
2   tablespoons fresh lime juice
1   tablespoon extra-virgin olive oil
¹/₂ teaspoon salt
Cilantro sprigs (optional)

1. Combine 1 cup broth, chili powder, cumin, and beans in a Dutch oven over medium-high heat. Place remaining broth, poblano, and onion in a food processor; pulse until vegetables are chopped. Add onion mixture to pan.
2. Add tomatoes and cilantro to food processor, and process until coarsely chopped. Add tomato mixture to pan; bring to a boil. Cover, reduce heat, and simmer 5 minutes or until vegetables are tender. Remove from heat; stir in juice, olive oil, and salt. Garnish with cilantro sprigs, if desired. **Yield:** 4 servings (serving size: 1 cup).

CALORIES 157; FAT 4.3g (sat 0.6g, mono 2.6g, poly 0.6g); PROTEIN 8.1g; CARB 23.1g; FIBER 6g; CHOL 0mg; IRON 2.4mg; SODIUM 828mg; CALC 65mg

Olive oil–flavored cooking spray is used in place of regular cooking spray in this dish. Made with extra-virgin olive oil, this spray is more healthful and gives an olive-oil flavor.

INGREDIENT SPOTLIGHT

COOKING CLASS: *how to purchase beef*

To make sure you're buying lean ground beef, read the label to determine the percentage of fat rather than relying on the name of the specific cut. The percentage of lean to fat is usually listed on the label near the name of the cut. Ground beef with 10% fat or less is sometimes labeled "ground sirloin" or "extra-lean."

20 MINUTES

Three-Bean Chili

2   teaspoons olive oil
1   cup prechopped onion
½   cup prechopped green bell pepper
2   teaspoons bottled minced garlic
¾   cup water
2   tablespoons tomato paste
2   teaspoons chili powder
2   teaspoons ground cumin
¼   teaspoon black pepper
1   (15½-ounce) can garbanzo beans, rinsed and drained
1   (15½-ounce) can red kidney beans, rinsed and drained
1   (15½-ounce) can black beans, rinsed and drained
1   (14½-ounce) can organic vegetable broth (such as Swanson Certified Organic)
1   (14½-ounce) can no-salt-added diced tomatoes, undrained
1   tablespoon yellow cornmeal
¼   cup chopped fresh cilantro
6   tablespoons reduced-fat sour cream

1. Heat olive oil in a large saucepan over medium-high heat. Add onion, bell pepper, and garlic to pan; sauté 3 minutes. Stir in ¾ cup water and next 9 ingredients; bring to a boil. Reduce heat, and simmer 8 minutes. Stir in cornmeal; cook 2 minutes. Remove from heat; stir in cilantro. Serve with sour cream. **Yield:** 6 servings (serving size: 1¹⁄₃ cups chili and 1 tablespoon sour cream).

CALORIES 180; FAT 4.9g (sat 1.5g, mono 1.7g, poly 0.3g); PROTEIN 8.4g; CARB 29.5g; FIBER 8.6g; CHOL 5mg; IRON 2.3mg; SODIUM 714mg; CALC 86mg

15 MINUTES

Spicy Beef and Black Bean Chili

There's no need for this beef and black bean chili to simmer a long time. It's full of flavor after 7 minutes. Top it with a dollop of sour cream, and garnish it with green onions or fresh cilantro sprigs, if desired.

1   pound ground sirloin
1   tablespoon 40%-less-sodium taco seasoning
1   (15-ounce) can whole-kernel corn, drained
1   (15-ounce) can black beans, undrained
1   (10-ounce) can diced tomatoes and green chiles, drained
1   (10-ounce) can diced tomatoes and green chiles, undrained
1   cup water
½   teaspoon black pepper
6   tablespoons reduced-fat sour cream
Chopped green onions or cilantro sprigs (optional)

1. Cook beef in a medium Dutch oven over medium-high heat until browned, stirring to crumble. Drain, if necessary; return beef to pan. Stir in taco seasoning and next 6 ingredients; cover and bring to a boil. Reduce heat, and simmer 7 minutes or until thoroughly heated. Ladle chili into bowls; top each with 1 tablespoon sour cream. Garnish with green onions or cilantro sprigs, if desired. **Yield:** 6 servings (serving size: 1 cup).

CALORIES 207; FAT 5.6g (sat 2.5g, mono 1.2g, poly 0.5g); PROTEIN 19.2g; CARB 20.4g; FIBER 5g; CHOL 46mg; IRON 1.8mg; SODIUM 722mg; CALC 167mg

20

Quick Bean Soup

2   teaspoons canola oil
2   cups prechopped onion
³/₄   cup prechopped green bell pepper
1   cup refrigerated fresh salsa
1   teaspoon ground cumin
1   (16-ounce) can kidney beans, rinsed and
     drained
1   (16-ounce) can pinto beans, rinsed and
     drained
1   (15-ounce) can black beans, rinsed and
     drained
2   (14.5-ounce) cans stewed tomatoes,
     undrained and chopped
1   (14-ounce) can fat-free, less-sodium chicken
     broth
Fresh flat-leaf parsley leaves (optional)

1. Heat oil in a Dutch oven over medium-high heat. Add onion and bell pepper; sauté 4 minutes or until tender. Add salsa and next 6 ingredients; bring to a boil, stirring occasionally. Cover, reduce heat, and simmer 7 minutes. Garnish with parsley, if desired. **Yield:** 10 servings (serving size: 1 cup).

CALORIES 128; FAT 1.5g (sat 0.2g, mono 0.7g, poly 0.4g); PROTEIN 6.1g; CARB 21.9g; FIBER 6.2g; CHOL 0mg; IRON 2.3mg; SODIUM 516mg; CALC 67mg

Easy Texas Chili

COOKING CLASS: *how to prepare lemongrass*

To use lemongrass, discard the tough outer leaves and about 2 to 3 inches of the thick root end. This will leave the tender stalk, which can be sliced or chopped, or in the case of Thai Hot and Sour Soup with Shrimp (at right), halved and crushed.

15 MINUTES

Spicy Shrimp and Rice Soup

make it a meal *Serve this soup with spiced baked wontons on the side.*

4	cups fat-free, less-sodium chicken broth
2	cups water
1	cup instant long-grain rice (such as Minute brand)
1	tablespoon canola oil
1	teaspoon bottled minced garlic
½	teaspoon crushed red pepper
1½	pounds large shrimp, peeled and deveined
4	lime wedges

Bean sprouts (optional)
Sliced green onions (optional)
Chopped fresh cilantro (optional)
Sliced jalapeño pepper (optional)

1. Combine chicken broth and water in a large saucepan, and bring to a boil. Stir in instant long-grain rice, and bring to a boil. Remove from heat, and let stand 5 minutes. **2.** Heat canola oil in a large nonstick skillet over medium-high heat. Add garlic, red pepper, and shrimp; sauté 3 minutes or until shrimp are done. Stir shrimp mixture into broth mixture. Divide soup evenly among 4 bowls, and serve with lime wedges. Top each serving with sprouts, onions, cilantro, and jalapeño, if desired. **Yield:** 4 servings (serving size: about 1½ cups soup and 1 lime wedge).

CALORIES 315; FAT 6.9g (sat 1.1g, mono 3.1g, poly 1.6g); PROTEIN 38.8g; CARB 21.1g; FIBER 1.6g; CHOL 259mg; IRON 5.2mg; SODIUM 644mg; CALC 113mg

20 MINUTES

Easy Texas Chili

1	pound ground round
⅔	cup prechopped onion
1	teaspoon bottled minced garlic
1½	cups hot water
1	tablespoon chili powder
1	teaspoon salt
1	(16-ounce) can chili beans, undrained
1	(6-ounce) can tomato paste

1. Cook meat, onion, and garlic in a Dutch oven over medium-high heat until meat is browned, stirring to crumble. Drain in a colander; return to pan. **2.** Stir in water and remaining ingredients. Cover, reduce heat, and simmer 13 minutes, stirring occasionally. **Yield:** 6 servings (serving size: 1 cup).

CALORIES 226; FAT 10.5g (sat 4.5g, mono 4.8g, poly 0.7g); PROTEIN 19.9g; CARB 16.2g; FIBER 4.9g; CHOL 46mg; IRON 5.1mg; SODIUM 1,094mg; CALC 50mg

Thai Hot and Sour Soup with Shrimp

6   cups fat-free, less-sodium chicken broth
4   kaffir lime leaves
1   (4-inch) lemongrass stalk, halved and crushed
½   habanero chile pepper, minced
1   cup thinly sliced shiitake mushrooms (about 2 ounces)
½   pound large shrimp, peeled and deveined
¼   cup fresh lime juice
2   teaspoons fish sauce
1   medium tomato, cut into wedges
2   green onions, thinly sliced (about ½ cup)
1   cup light coconut milk
2   tablespoons chopped fresh cilantro

1. Combine chicken broth, kaffir lime leaves, lemongrass, and habanero in a large saucepan; bring to a boil. Cook 5 minutes. Add mushrooms and shrimp to pan; cook 3 minutes or until shrimp are done. Add juice, fish sauce, tomato, and onions to pan; cook 2 minutes. Remove from heat; stir in coconut milk and cilantro. Discard lemongrass stalk and lime leaves. **Yield:** 4 servings (serving size: 2 cups).

CALORIES 135; FAT 4.4g (sat 3.1g, mono 0.3g, poly 0.5g); PROTEIN 16.6g; CARB 8.4g; FIBER 2.2g; CHOL 86mg; IRON 2.7mg; SODIUM 838mg; CALC 63mg

Sausage and Chicken Gumbo

Frozen vegetables and boil-in-bag rice help get dinner on the table in a flash. For a spicier bowl, bump up the amount of ground red pepper or consider adding hot sauce at the table.

1   (3½-ounce) bag boil-in-bag rice
2   tablespoons all-purpose flour
1   tablespoon vegetable oil
1   cup frozen chopped onion
1   cup frozen chopped green bell pepper
1   cup frozen cut okra
1   cup chopped celery
1   teaspoon bottled minced garlic
½   teaspoon dried thyme
¼   teaspoon ground red pepper
2   cups chopped roasted skinless, boneless chicken breast (about 2 breasts)
8   ounces turkey kielbasa, cut into 1-inch pieces
1   (14½-ounce) can diced tomatoes with peppers and onion
1   (14½-ounce) can fat-free, less-sodium chicken broth

1. Cook rice according to package directions, omitting salt and fat.

2. While rice cooks, combine flour and oil in a Dutch oven; saute over medium-high heat 3 minutes. Add onion and next 6 ingredients; cook 3 minutes or until tender, stirring frequently.

3. Stir in chicken, kielbasa, tomatoes, and broth, and cook 6 minutes or until thoroughly heated. Serve over rice. **Yield:** 4 servings (serving size: 1½ cups gumbo and ½ cup rice).

CALORIES 369; FAT 11.3g (sat 2.7g, mono 4.8g, poly 3g); PROTEIN 29.4g; CARB 37g; FIBER 3g; CHOL 77mg; IRON 2.2mg; SODIUM 949mg; CALC 92mg

Chipotle Chicken Tortilla Soup

15
MINUTES

Chipotle Chicken Tortilla Soup

make it a meal *If you like spicy food, you'll love this. Purchase corn muffins from your supermarket bakery to round out the meal.*

1 tablespoon canola oil
1½ teaspoons bottled minced garlic
¾ pound chicken breast tenders, cut into bite-sized pieces
1 teaspoon chipotle chile powder
1 teaspoon ground cumin
1 cup water
¼ teaspoon salt
1 (14-ounce) can fat-free, less-sodium chicken broth
1 (14.5-ounce) can stewed tomatoes, undrained
1 cup crushed baked tortilla chips
¼ cup chopped fresh cilantro
1 lime, cut into 4 wedges

1. Heat oil in a large saucepan over medium-high heat. Add minced garlic and chicken; sauté 2 minutes. Add chile powder and cumin; stir well. Add water, salt, broth, and tomatoes; bring to a boil. Cover, reduce heat, and simmer 5 minutes. Top each serving with tortilla chips and cilantro, and serve with lime wedges. **Yield:** 4 servings (serving size: 1¼ cups soup, ¼ cup chips, 1 tablespoon cilantro, and 1 lime wedge).

CALORIES 228; FAT 5.4g (sat 0.6g, mono 2.5g, poly 1.7g); PROTEIN 22.9g; CARB 21.8g; FIBER 3.5g; CHOL 49mg; IRON 1.7mg; SODIUM 873mg; CALC 62mg

15
MINUTES

Nana's Chicken Pastina Soup

You can substitute orzo or alphabets for pastina in this Sicilian-style chicken soup.

½ cup water
2 (14-ounce) cans fat-free, less-sodium chicken broth
2¼ cups prechopped celery, onion, and carrot mix
½ teaspoon black pepper
⅛ teaspoon salt
1 pound chicken breast tenders (cut into 1-inch cubes)
¼ cup (1½ ounces) uncooked pastina (tiny star-shaped pasta)
3 tablespoons commercial pesto
2 tablespoons fresh lemon juice
¼ cup (1 ounce) preshredded fresh Parmesan cheese

1. Bring water and broth to a boil in a large saucepan. Stir in celery mix, pepper, salt, and chicken; bring to a boil. Add pasta; cook 4 minutes. Stir in pesto and juice, and simmer 1 minute. Sprinkle with cheese. **Yield:** 4 servings (serving size: 1½ cups soup and about 2 teaspoons cheese).

CALORIES 288; FAT 9.1g (sat 2.5g, mono 5.2g, poly 1g); PROTEIN 33.7g; CARB 16.3g; FIBER 2.7g; CHOL 73mg; IRON 699mg; SODIUM 2mg; CALC 156mg

Instead of making pesto, we used commercial pesto to speed up preparation time. As an added convenience, commercial pesto is available year-round at your local supermarket.

MAKE IT FASTER

Wild Rice and
Mushroom Soup
with Chicken

Wild Rice and Mushroom Soup with Chicken

make it a meal *Add sliced whole wheat French bread and mixed salad greens to complete the menu.*

4   cups fat-free, less-sodium chicken broth, divided
1   (2.75-ounce) package quick-cooking wild rice (such as Gourmet House)
1   tablespoon olive oil
½   cup prechopped onion
½   cup chopped red bell pepper
⅓   cup matchstick-cut carrots
1   teaspoon bottled minced garlic
½   teaspoon dried thyme
1   teaspoon butter
2   (4-ounce) packages presliced exotic mushroom blend (such as shiitake, cremini, and oyster)
2   cups shredded cooked chicken breast
⅛   teaspoon salt
⅛   teaspoon black pepper

1. Bring 1⅓ cups broth to a boil in a medium saucepan; add rice to pan. Cover, reduce heat, and simmer 5 minutes or until liquid is absorbed. Set aside.
2. Heat oil in a Dutch oven over medium-high heat. Add onion and next 4 ingredients to pan; sauté 3 minutes, stirring occasionally. Stir in butter and mushrooms; sauté 3 minutes or until lightly browned. Add remaining 2⅔ cups broth, rice, chicken, salt, and pepper to pan; cook 3 minutes or until thoroughly heated, stirring occasionally. **Yield:** 4 servings (serving size: 1½ cups).

CALORIES 281; FAT 7.5g (sat 1.9g, mono 3.8g, poly 1.3g); PROTEIN 28.9g; CARB 23g; FIBER 4g; CHOL 62mg; IRON 2.8mg; SODIUM 541mg; CALC 42mg

Sante Fe Ravioletti Soup

Ravioletti is smaller than ravioli, so the tiny pillows fit perfectly in your spoon.

2   (14-ounce) cans fat-free, less-sodium chicken broth
1   (7-ounce) package three-cheese ravioletti (such as Buitoni)
1   (16-ounce) container refrigerated fresh salsa
1   (15-ounce) can no-salt-added black beans, rinsed and drained
1   (10-ounce) package diced cooked chicken (such as Tyson)
1   teaspoon bottled minced garlic
¼   cup chopped fresh cilantro
Reduced-fat sour cream (optional)

1. Bring broth to a boil in a large saucepan over high heat. Add ravioletti, and cook 3 minutes. Stir in salsa and next 3 ingredients. Cook 5 minutes or until thoroughly heated, stirring occasionally; stir in cilantro.
2. Ladle soup into bowls; top with sour cream, if desired. **Yield:** 6 servings (serving size: about 1¼ cups soup).

CALORIES 204; FAT 3.4g (sat 1.5g, mono 1.3g, poly 0.6g); PROTEIN 18g; CARB 20.7g; FIBER 2.6g; CHOL 30mg; IRON 1.1mg; SODIUM 766mg; CALC 59mg

30 MINUTES

Asian Chicken, Edamame, and Noodle Soup

Look for refrigerated cooked, shelled edamame in the produce section of your supermarket. Substitute the frozen uncooked variety for the refrigerated version, if desired.

2   cups chopped roasted chicken breast
1   (10-ounce) package refrigerated cooked, shelled edamame
1   (32-ounce) carton fat-free, less-sodium chicken broth
1   (3-ounce) package Oriental or teriyaki chicken–flavored ramen noodles
1   cup thinly sliced green onions (about 6 onions)

1. Combine first 3 ingredients in a Dutch oven; bring to a boil. Cover, reduce heat to low, and simmer 12 minutes. Break noodles into 1-inch pieces. Add noodles, contents of flavoring packet, and green onions to pan; cook 3 minutes. Serve immediately. **Yield:** 6 servings (serving size: about 1 cup).

CALORIES 219; FAT 5.9g (sat 1.6g, mono 1.7g, poly 2.4g); PROTEIN 23.8g; CARB 16.2g; FIBER 3.3g; CHOL 40mg; IRON 2.2mg; SODIUM 749mg; CALC 51mg

INGREDIENT SPOTLIGHT

Japanese curly noodles, made from wheat flour, are long and wavy with a delicate texture and mild flavor. They are commonly referred to as ramen noodles or chucka soba. These noodles are a staple in quick-and-easy cuisine. Look for them in the Asian section of your supermarket.

20 MINUTES

Chipotle Turkey and Corn Soup

Stacking the turkey cutlets and then thinly slicing them will save you some time during preparation. You can freeze leftover chipotle chiles in the adobo sauce (package the chiles individually with a little sauce in small plastic freezer bags) and use them in salsas, with pork, or for Mexican-inspired scrambled eggs.

1   tablespoon canola oil
1   pound turkey cutlets, cut into thin strips
2   teaspoons adobo sauce
1   to 2 teaspoons chopped canned chipotle chiles in adobo sauce
2   (14-ounce) cans fat-free, less-sodium chicken broth
1   (14 3/4-ounce) can cream-style corn
1/4   cup chopped fresh cilantro, divided
1/4   teaspoon salt
1/2   cup crushed lime-flavored tortilla chips (about 1 1/2 ounces)
4   lime wedges

1. Heat canola oil in a large saucepan over medium-high heat. Add turkey; cook 3 minutes or until browned, stirring occasionally. Stir in adobo sauce, chiles, chicken broth, and corn; bring to a boil. Reduce heat to medium-low; simmer 5 minutes. Stir in 3 tablespoons cilantro and salt. Divide soup evenly among 4 bowls; sprinkle evenly with remaining cilantro and crushed chips. Serve with lime wedges. **Yield:** 4 servings (serving size: 1 1/2 cups soup, 3/4 teaspoon cilantro, 2 tablespoons chips, and 1 lime wedge).

CALORIES 263; FAT 5.5g (sat 0.7g, mono 2.8g, poly 1.6g); PROTEIN 32g; CARB 22.1g; FIBER 2.8g; CHOL 45mg; IRON 2.3mg; SODIUM 943mg; CALC 25mg

20 MINUTES

Pasta Fagioli Soup

make it a meal *This Italian soup derives its name—fagioli—and its high fiber content from kidney beans. Serve it with crusty Italian bread and a Caesar salad for a quick weeknight supper.*

12   ounces Santa Fe chicken sausage, halved
        lengthwise and sliced (such as Amy's)
3   cups fat-free, less-sodium chicken broth
½   cup uncooked small seashell pasta
2   cups coarsely chopped zucchini (about
        2 small zucchini)
1   (14.5-ounce) can stewed tomatoes,
        undrained
1   teaspoon dried basil
1   teaspoon dried oregano
1   (15-ounce) can kidney beans, rinsed and
        drained
⅓   cup (about 1½ ounces) shredded Asiago
        cheese

1. Heat a large saucepan over high heat. Add sausage; cook 2 minutes, stirring constantly. Add broth and pasta; bring to a boil. Cover, reduce heat, and simmer 4 minutes. Add zucchini and tomatoes; bring to a boil. Cover, reduce heat, and simmer 2 minutes. Stir in basil, oregano, and beans; cover and simmer 3 minutes or until pasta and zucchini are tender. Sprinkle with cheese.
Yield: 5 servings (serving size: about 1⅓ cups soup and about 1 tablespoon Asiago cheese).

CALORIES 319; FAT 9.2g (sat 3.3g, mono 3.8g, poly 0.8g); PROTEIN 21.9g;
CARB 39.7g; FIBER 9.6g; CHOL 56mg; IRON 4.4mg; SODIUM 858mg; CALC 56mg

20 MINUTES

Sausage, Escarole, and White Bean Ragout

make it a meal *The flavorful sausage and bold escarole are filling additions to this French-accented stew. Substitute mustard greens to mimic the bitter flavor of escarole, or use spinach for milder flavor. Serve with a crusty baguette or rolls.*

12   ounces sweet turkey Italian sausage
Cooking spray
1   cup prechopped onion
1   cup cubed peeled red potatoes (about
        6 ounces)
⅓   cup chardonnay or other dry white wine
1   tablespoon bottled minced garlic
1   (16-ounce) can cannellini beans or other
        white beans, rinsed and drained
1   (14-ounce) can fat-free, less-sodium chicken
        broth
4   cups sliced escarole (about 4 ounces)
1   teaspoon chopped fresh rosemary
2   tablespoons grated fresh Parmesan cheese

1. Remove casings from sausage.
2. Heat a large nonstick skillet over medium-high heat. Coat pan with cooking spray. Add Italian sausage and onion to pan, and cook 4 minutes or until sausage browns, stirring to crumble. Drain sausage mixture well; return to pan. Stir in potatoes, wine, garlic, beans, and chicken broth; bring to a simmer. Cover and cook 7 minutes. Stir in escarole and rosemary, and cook 4 minutes or until escarole wilts, stirring occasionally. Ladle 1¼ cups soup into each of 4 shallow bowls, and sprinkle each serving evenly with 1½ teaspoons cheese.
Yield: 4 servings (serving size: 1¼ cups soup and 1½ teaspoons cheese).

CALORIES 254; FAT 9.2g (sat 2.9g, mono 3.2g, poly 2.7g); PROTEIN 21g; CARB 21.2g;
FIBER 4.9g; CHOL 74mg; IRON 2.6mg; SODIUM 929mg; CALC 86mg

Escarole is the mildest of the endive varieties. It has broad bright green leaves that curl slightly. Escarole has only a hint of the characteristic bitterness of Belgian and curly endives.

INGREDIENT SPOTLIGHT

Sausage and Spinach Soup

Fresh herbs are added after the soup cooks so they'll retain their bright color and flavor.
You can substitute 1 teaspoon of dried herbs for each tablespoon of fresh, but add them
with the tomatoes. Serve this soup with a toasted baguette.

10	ounces sweet turkey Italian sausage
	Cooking spray
1	cup prechopped onion
2	teaspoons bottled minced garlic
½	cup water
1	(15-ounce) can cannellini beans, rinsed and drained
1	(14.5-ounce) can organic stewed tomatoes, undrained (such as Muir Glen)
1	(14-ounce) can fat-free, less-sodium chicken broth
2	cups baby spinach
1	tablespoon chopped fresh basil
2	teaspoons chopped fresh oregano
2	tablespoons grated fresh Romano cheese

1. Remove casings from sausage. Cook sausage in a large saucepan coated with cooking spray over high heat until browned, stirring to crumble. Add onion and 2 teaspoons garlic to pan; cook 2 minutes. Stir in ½ cup water, beans, tomatoes, and broth. Cover and bring to a boil. Uncover and cook 3 minutes or until slightly thick. Remove from heat, and stir in spinach, basil, and oregano. Ladle 1½ cups soup into each of 4 bowls, and sprinkle each serving with 1½ teaspoons cheese. **Yield:** 4 servings.

CALORIES 261; FAT 8.6g (sat 2.8g, mono 2.7g, poly 2.5g); PROTEIN 20.9g; CARB 23.1g; FIBER 5.4g; CHOL 62mg; IRON 3.4mg; SODIUM 842mg; CALC 105mg

20 MINUTES

Spicy Andouille Posole

Andouille sausage contributes its spicy, smoky essence to this hominy-based Mexican stew.

- 1 teaspoon olive oil
- 2 links (6.5 ounces) andouille sausage, thinly sliced
- 1 red bell pepper, cut into 1-inch pieces
- 1 large zucchini, diced (about 8 ounces)
- 2½ cups fat-free, less-sodium chicken broth
- 1 (15.5-ounce) can white hominy, rinsed and drained
- 2 teaspoons pureed chipotle chiles in adobo sauce (about 1 chile)
- ¼ cup chopped fresh cilantro

1. Heat oil in a large saucepan over medium-high heat; add andouille, and cook 1 minute. Add bell pepper and zucchini; cook, stirring occasionally, 1 minute.
2. Add broth, hominy, and chile. Bring to a boil; reduce heat, and simmer, uncovered, 8 minutes or until vegetables are tender. Sprinkle with cilantro before serving. **Yield:** 4 servings (serving size: about 1⅓ cups).

CALORIES 196; FAT 10.5g (sat 3.6g, mono 5.2g, poly 1.6g); PROTEIN 10.1g; CARB 15.6g; FIBER 3.3g; CHOL 33mg; IRON 1.8mg; SODIUM 897mg; CALC 26mg

Hominy is made of dried corn kernels from which the hull and germ have been removed. Hominy is sold canned, ready to eat, or dried. Look for canned hominy alongside the corn in the canned vegetable section of your supermarket.

INGREDIENT SPOTLIGHT

30 MINUTES

Southwestern Pork Soup

make it a meal *Substitute chicken for pork in this dish, if you prefer. Pink beans are similar to pinto beans, but smaller; if you can't find pink beans, substitute pintos. Add cheddar corn bread and orange slices to round out the meal.*

Cooking spray
- 1 cup prechopped onion
- ⅔ cup prechopped green bell pepper
- 1 tablespoon bottled minced garlic
- 1 jalapeño pepper, seeded and minced
- 1 pound pork tenderloin, trimmed and cut into bite-sized pieces
- 2 cups fat-free, less-sodium chicken broth
- 2 teaspoons chili powder
- 1 teaspoon ground cumin
- ½ teaspoon salt
- ¼ teaspoon black pepper
- 1 (15-ounce) can pink beans, rinsed and drained
- 1 (14-ounce) can diced tomatoes, undrained
- 2 tablespoons chopped fresh cilantro
- 1 cup diced avocado

1. Heat a small nonstick Dutch oven over medium-heat. Coat pan with cooking spray. Add onion, bell pepper, garlic, and jalapeño to pan; sauté 2 minutes. Add pork; cook 3 minutes. Add broth and next 6 ingredients; bring to a boil. Partially cover, reduce heat, and simmer 6 minutes or until pork is done, stirring occasionally. Remove from heat, and stir in cilantro. Serve with avocado. **Yield:** 4 servings (serving size: about 1¾ cups soup and ¼ cup avocado).

CALORIES 310; FAT 10.5g (sat 2.4g, mono 5.5g, poly 1.4g); PROTEIN 30.6g; CARB 24.5g; FIBER 8.3g; CHOL 74mg; IRON 3.7mg; SODIUM 911mg; CALC 82mg

2O
MINUTES

Red Bean Stew with Pasta

1	tablespoon olive oil
1½	cups presliced mushrooms
1	cup diced carrot
1½	cups water
¼	teaspoon black pepper
1	(15-ounce) can kidney beans, rinsed and drained
1	(14.5-ounce) can diced tomatoes, undrained
1	(14-ounce) can less-sodium beef broth
1	cup uncooked ditalini (about 4 ounces short tube-shaped pasta)
2	tablespoons commercial pesto
¼	cup (1 ounce) grated fresh Parmesan cheese

1. Heat olive oil in a Dutch oven over medium-high heat. Add mushrooms and carrot; sauté 4 minutes. Stir in water and next 4 ingredients. Cover; bring to a boil. Stir in pasta; cook, uncovered, 11 minutes or until pasta is done. Stir in pesto; sprinkle each serving with cheese. **Yield:** 4 servings (serving size: 1½ cups stew and 1 tablespoon cheese).

CALORIES 324; FAT 10.2g (sat 2.3g, mono 4.7g, poly 1.7g); PROTEIN 15.2g; CARB 43.7g; FIBER 10.4g; CHOL 6mg; IRON 3.1mg; SODIUM 560mg; CALC 150mg

Graters, whether handheld or box, are a handy kitchen tool that speeds up preparation time. Use the smaller holes for grating hard cheese or chocolate. For ingredients like cheddar cheese or carrots, the largest holes work best.

SHORTCUT SPOTLIGHT

Cioppino-Style Seafood Stew

1½   tablespoons olive oil
½   cup prechopped onion
1½   teaspoons bottled minced garlic
¼   teaspoon crushed red pepper
1   pound mussels, scrubbed and debearded
8   ounces sea scallops
8   ounces peeled and deveined medium shrimp
½   cup clam juice
¼   cup chopped fresh flat-leaf parsley
1   (14.5-ounce) can diced tomatoes, undrained

1. Heat olive oil in a Dutch oven over medium-high heat. Add onion, garlic, and red pepper to pan; sauté 2 minutes. Add mussels, scallops, and shrimp to pan; sauté 1 minute. Stir in ½ cup clam juice, parsley, and diced tomatoes; bring to a boil. Cover, reduce heat, and simmer 10 minutes or until mussels open, and discard any unopened shells. **Yield:** 4 servings (serving size: 2 cups).

CALORIES 289; FAT 9.3g (sat 1.5g, mono 4.8g, poly 1.7g); PROTEIN 36.2g; CARB 13.8g; FIBER 1.5g; CHOL 138mg; IRON 6.4mg; SODIUM 726mg; CALC 88mg

Ginger-Apple Salad

Waldorf Salad

1   (8-ounce) can pineapple tidbits in juice, undrained
2   cups chopped Granny Smith apple
1   tablespoon lemon juice
1   cup chopped celery
¼   cup light mayonnaise
3   tablespoons raisins
Lettuce leaves (optional)

1. Drain pineapple tidbits, reserving 1 tablespoon pineapple juice.
2. Combine apple, reserved 1 tablespoon pineapple juice, and lemon juice in a medium bowl, tossing to coat apples. Stir in pineapple, celery, mayonnaise, and raisins. Serve immediately, or cover and chill. Serve on lettuce leaves, if desired. **Yield:** 6 servings (serving size: ²/₃ cup).

CALORIES 95; FAT 3.4g (sat 0.5g, mono 0.8g, poly 2g); PROTEIN 0.7g; CARB 17.2g; FIBER 1.3g; CHOL 3mg; IRON 0.3mg; SODIUM 98mg; CALC 16mg

Ginger-Apple Salad

Crystallized ginger adds a peppery note to this crisp apple salad, which garnered rave reviews in our Test Kitchens.

2½ cups chopped Granny Smith apple (1 large)
2   cups chopped Gala apple (1 large)
½   cup chopped pecans, toasted
¼   cup dried sweet cherries
3   tablespoons chopped crystallized ginger
2   tablespoons thawed orange juice concentrate
1   tablespoon lemon juice
1   tablespoon honey

1. Combine all ingredients in a large bowl; toss well. Let stand 8 to 10 minutes before serving. **Yield:** 10 servings (serving size: ¹/₂ cup).

CALORIES 93; FAT 4.3g (sat 0.4g, mono 2.6g, poly 1.3g); PROTEIN 1g; CARB 13.9g; FIBER 1.7g; CHOL 0mg; IRON 0.4mg; SODIUM 2mg; CALC 13mg

Grapefruit and Fennel Salad

The fresh fennel in this unique salad has a subtle licorice flavor, which complements grilled chicken, fish, or pork.

2   tablespoons extra-virgin olive oil
½   teaspoon salt
¼   teaspoon freshly ground black pepper
1   fennel bulb, halved and thinly sliced
1   cup drained refrigerated red grapefruit sections
¼   cup coarsely chopped pimiento-stuffed olives

1. Combine oil, salt, and pepper in a large bowl; stir with a whisk. Add fennel, grapefruit sections, and olives; toss gently to combine. **Yield:** 7 servings (serving size: ¹/₂ cup).

CALORIES 70; FAT 5.3g (sat 0.6g, mono 3.4g, poly 1.2g); PROTEIN 0.6g; CARB 5.7g; FIBER 1.5g; CHOL 0mg; IRON 0.3mg; SODIUM 322mg; CALC 21mg

 15 MINUTES

Melon Salad

Watermelon and cantaloupe are two luscious summer fruits that are packed with an abundance of vitamins and nutrients.

4   cups cubed seeded watermelon
1½   cups cubed peeled honeydew melon
1½   cups cubed peeled cantaloupe
¼   cup fresh lime juice (about 2 limes)
2   tablespoons chopped fresh mint
2   tablespoons honey
1   teaspoon canola oil

1. Combine first 3 ingredients in a large bowl.

2. Combine lime juice and remaining 3 ingredients in a small bowl, stirring with a whisk. Drizzle over fruit; toss gently to coat. Cover and chill until ready to serve. **Yield:** 7 servings (serving size: 1 cup).

CALORIES 77; FAT 0.9g (sat 0.1g, mono 0.4g, poly 0.3g); PROTEIN 1.1g; CARB 18.4g; FIBER 1g; CHOL 0mg; IRON 0.4mg; SODIUM 13mg; CALC 14mg

Take advantage of your grocery store's cubed fresh fruit from the produce section to speed things along.

MAKE IT FASTER

Cucumber and
Honeydew Salad

COOKING CLASS: *how to peel an orange*

To quickly peel an orange, cut the top and bottom portions from the fruit to create a stable cutting surface. Next, stand the fruit upright, then use a paring knife to slice downward in a long, slow curve to remove the rind and the white pith.

 MINUTES

Cucumber and Honeydew Salad

Fresh mint, lime juice, and sweet honeydew are a refreshing combination in this side.

2   cups cubed honeydew melon
2   cups chopped English cucumber
2   tablespoons chopped fresh mint
2   tablespoons fresh lime juice
2   tablespoons finely chopped red onion
⅛   teaspoon salt
Mint sprigs (optional)

1. Combine first 6 ingredients in a large bowl; toss gently to coat.
2. Cover and chill until ready to serve. Garnish with mint sprigs, if desired. **Yield:** 4 servings (serving size: 1 cup).

CALORIES 42; FAT 0.2g (sat 0.1g, mono 0g, poly 0.1g); PROTEIN 0.9g; CARB 10.6g; FIBER 1.1g; CHOL 0mg; IRON 0.4mg; SODIUM 89mg; CALC 18mg

 MINUTES

Sicilian Orange Salad

make it a meal *This winter salad is usually prepared with blood oranges. But in this version, we tested with more readily available navel oranges, and the salad was terrific. Serve with your favorite grilled fish.*

4   small navel oranges (about 2 ¼ pounds)
½   small red onion, cut in half lengthwise and thinly sliced (about ½ cup)
½   cup coarsely chopped pitted Sicilian green olives
1   tablespoon chopped fresh flat-leaf parsley
1   teaspoon olive oil
¼   teaspoon freshly ground black pepper
⅛   teaspoon salt

1. Peel and section oranges over a bowl; squeeze membranes to extract juice. Set sections aside, reserving ½ cup juice. Discard membranes.
2. Combine orange sections, onion, olives, and parsley in a medium bowl. Combine reserved ½ cup juice, oil, pepper, and salt; stir well with a whisk. Pour over salad; toss gently. Serve immediately, or cover and chill until ready to serve. **Yield:** 4 servings (serving size: ¾ cup).

CALORIES 122; FAT 5.3g (sat 0.5g, mono 3.9g, poly 0.8g); PROTEIN 1.8g; CARB 20g; FIBER 3.8g; CHOL 0mg; IRON 0.7mg; SODIUM 305mg; CALC 90mg

15 MINUTES

Cranberry Salad

Keep in mind that this recipe needs time to chill, so be sure to make it at least four hours before you're ready to serve it. It's ideal for the holidays when paired with turkey or pork.

2   (0.3-ounce) packages sugar-free black cherry–flavored gelatin
1   cup boiling water
1   cup canned whole-berry cranberry sauce
1   cup ice water
1   (20-ounce) can crushed pineapple in juice, drained
½   cup chopped pecans

1. Combine gelatin and boiling water in an 11 x 7–inch baking dish; stir until gelatin is dissolved. Add cranberry sauce and ice water, stirring well. Add pineapple and pecans; stir. Cover and chill 4 hours or until set. **Yield:** 8 servings (serving size: ³/₄ cup).

CALORIES 129; FAT 5.4g (sat 0.5g, mono 3.2g, poly 1.6g); PROTEIN 1.4g; CARB 21.1g; FIBER 2g; CHOL 0mg; IRON 0.5mg; SODIUM 9mg; CALC 13mg

15 MINUTES

Garden Salad

Keep this salad easy by using prepackaged salad greens; feel free to substitute other varieties, if desired.

3   cups sweet baby greens (such as Fresh Express)
½   small red bell pepper, cut into thin strips
2   green onions, thinly sliced
3   tablespoons light honey Dijon dressing (such as Good Seasons)
Freshly ground black pepper

1. Combine first 3 ingredients in a medium bowl; drizzle with dressing. Toss well, and sprinkle with pepper. **Yield:** 2 servings (serving size: 1³/₄ cups).

CALORIES 49; FAT 1.7g (sat 0.8g, mono 0.8g, poly 0.1g); PROTEIN 1.6g; CARB 7.6g; FIBER 1.9g; CHOL 0mg; IRON 1.3mg; SODIUM 167mg; CALC 52mg

15 MINUTES

Mixed Greens with Goat Cheese Croutons

make it a meal *Toasted baguette slices topped with velvety goat cheese make the crouton the star of this simple side salad. Serve with roasted chicken or pork.*

4   cups mixed baby salad greens
2   small tomatoes, cut into wedges
¼   cup light cranberry-walnut vinaigrette (such as Newman's Own)
3   tablespoons goat cheese
4   (¼-inch-thick) slices diagonally cut whole wheat baguette, toasted

1. Combine first 3 ingredients in a medium bowl; toss gently to coat.
2. Spread goat cheese evenly on croutons. Divide salad among plates, and top with croutons. **Yield:** 4 servings (serving size: 1 cup salad and 1 crouton).

CALORIES 104; FAT 4.7g (sat 1.8g, mono 1.4g, poly 1.4g); PROTEIN 4.5g; CARB 12.1g; FIBER 2.1g; CHOL 8mg; IRON 1.3mg; SODIUM 212mg; CALC 307mg

15 MINUTES

Baby Arugula, Pear, and Gorgonzola Salad

Arugula is a peppery salad green that adds bite to this salad. You can substitute baby spinach leaves for the arugula if you want a milder flavor.

2   Bartlett pears, cored and sliced
1   (5-ounce) package baby arugula
½   cup refrigerated fat-free raspberry vinaigrette (such as Naturally Fresh)
¼   cup (1 ounce) crumbled Gorgonzola cheese
2   tablespoons chopped walnuts, toasted
½   teaspoon freshly ground black pepper

1. Combine all ingredients in a large bowl; toss gently to coat. Serve immediately. **Yield:** 6 servings (serving size: 2 cups).

CALORIES 82; FAT 3.1g (sat 1.2g, mono 0.5g, poly 1.3g); PROTEIN 2.3g; CARB 11.7g; FIBER 1g; CHOL 4mg; IRON 0.5mg; SODIUM 267mg; CALC 71mg

Baby Arugula, Pear, and
Gorgonzola Salad

COOKING CLASS: *how to toast walnuts*

To toast walnuts, cook them in a dry skillet over medium heat for
1 to 2 minutes, stirring constantly. Remove them from the heat as
soon as you begin to smell that wonderful nutty aroma.

Raspberry-Greens Salad

This recipe calls for the drier, crumbled form of goat cheese so that it can be sprinkled over the salad.

⅓ cup fat-free raspberry vinaigrette
1 (5-ounce) package mixed baby salad greens
2 cups raspberries
¼ cup (1 ounce) crumbled goat cheese
¼ cup pecan pieces, toasted

1. Pour vinaigrette over salad greens; toss gently to coat. Place about 1 cup lettuce mixture on each of 6 plates. Top each serving with ⅓ cup raspberries, 2 teaspoons goat cheese, and 2 teaspoons pecans. **Yield:** 6 servings.

CALORIES 86; FAT 4.9g (sat 1g, mono 2.5g, poly 1.3g); PROTEIN 2.2g; CARB 9.4g; FIBER 3.7g; CHOL 4mg; IRON 0.7mg; SODIUM 153mg; CALC 40mg

Wedge Salad

It's not just restaurant fare anymore. The wedge-style salad is a fun, easy, and different way to serve iceberg to your family.

3 precooked bacon slices
1 head iceberg lettuce, cut into 6 wedges
1 large tomato, diced (about 1¾ cups)
⅓ cup light blue cheese dressing (such as Marie's)
¼ cup sliced green onions

1. Heat bacon according to package directions; crumble and set aside.
2. Place 1 lettuce wedge on each of 6 plates.
3. Top wedges with diced tomato and bacon. Drizzle dressing over top, and sprinkle evenly with sliced green onions. **Yield:** 6 servings (serving size: 1 lettuce wedge, about ¼ cup tomato, 1½ teaspoons crumbled bacon, about 2½ teaspoons dressing, and 2 teaspoons green onions).

CALORIES 66; FAT 3.7g (sat 1g, mono 0.4g, poly 2.2g); PROTEIN 2.3g; CARB 7.1g; FIBER 3.1g; CHOL 6mg; IRON 0.7mg; SODIUM 170mg; CALC 18mg

Bistro Dinner Salad

This is a perfect light and quick yet refined meal. The mustard tarragon vinaigrette complements the slightly bitter salad greens, while the pear adds a hint of sweetness.

3 tablespoons finely chopped walnuts
4 large eggs
Cooking spray
2 bacon slices (uncooked)
8 cups gourmet salad greens
¼ cup (1 ounce) crumbled blue cheese
1 Bartlett pear, cored and thinly sliced
1 tablespoon white wine vinegar
1 tablespoon extra-virgin olive oil
½ teaspoon dried tarragon
½ teaspoon Dijon mustard
4 (1-inch-thick) slices French bread baguette, toasted

1. Place nuts in a small skillet; cook over medium-high heat 3 minutes or until lightly browned, shaking pan frequently. Remove from heat; set aside.
2. Break 1 egg into each of 4 (6-ounce) custard cups coated with cooking spray. Cover with plastic wrap, and microwave at HIGH 40 seconds or until set; let stand 1 minute. Remove eggs from cups; drain on paper towels.
3. Cook bacon in a skillet over medium-high heat until crisp; cool slightly. Remove bacon from pan, reserving 1 teaspoon drippings. Crumble bacon. Combine walnuts, bacon, greens, blue cheese, and pear in a large bowl.
4. Combine 1 teaspoon reserved drippings, vinegar, oil, tarragon, and mustard in a small bowl; stir with a whisk. Drizzle over greens mixture; toss gently. Arrange 2 cups salad mixture on each of 4 serving plates; top each serving with 1 egg and 1 toast slice. **Yield:** 4 servings.

CALORIES 393; FAT 17g (sat 4.7g, mono 6.9g, poly 3.2g); PROTEIN 16.9g; CARB 44.7g; FIBER 8.8g; CHOL 222mg; IRON 3.1mg; SODIUM 605mg; CALC 150mg

 MINUTES

Red Grapefruit and Feta Salad

Toss the dressing and salad right before serving so that the tender gourmet greens will stay crisp and not wilt.

6	cups gourmet salad greens
1	cup red grapefruit sections (about 2 large)
3	tablespoons fresh red grapefruit juice
2	teaspoons extra-virgin olive oil
1	teaspoon honey
1/4	teaspoon salt
1/8	teaspoon coarsely ground black pepper
1/4	cup (1 ounce) crumbled feta cheese

1. Combine gourmet salad greens and grapefruit sections in a large bowl.
2. Combine grapefruit juice and next 4 ingredients in a small bowl, stirring with a whisk. Pour over salad mixture; toss gently to coat. Divide evenly among plates. Sprinkle each serving with cheese. **Yield:** 4 servings (serving size: about 1^1/$_2$ cups salad and 1 tablespoon cheese).

CALORIES 88; FAT 4.1g (sat 1.4g, mono 2g, poly 0.5g); PROTEIN 2.8g; CARB 11.9g; FIBER 2.5g; CHOL 6mg; IRON 1.2mg; SODIUM 246mg; CALC 89mg

Zucchini, Parmesan, and Mâche Salad

This recipe proves that minimalism in the kitchen pays off. Lemon and salty Parmesan cheese perfectly complement the raw zucchini. If mâche is unavailable, substitute baby spinach or arugula.

1	small lemon
2	medium zucchini, thinly sliced
¼	cup (about 1 ounce) shaved Parmigiano-Reggiano cheese
2	tablespoons olive oil
½	teaspoon kosher salt
¼	teaspoon freshly ground black pepper
1	(3½-ounce) container mâche

1. Grate ½ teaspoon lemon rind; squeeze lemon to yield 1 tablespoon juice. Combine lemon rind, juice, zucchini, and next 4 ingredients in a large bowl, and toss. Let stand at room temperature 15 minutes.
2. Add mâche, and toss well to coat. Serve immediately. **Yield:** 4 servings (serving size: 1⅓ cups).

CALORIES 110; FAT 9.1g (sat 2.4g, mono 5.7g, poly 0.9g); PROTEIN 4.4g; CARB 4.9g; FIBER 1.7g; CHOL 5mg; IRON 0.6mg; SODIUM 374mg; CALC 101mg

Mandarin Orange Salad

Honey-roasted almonds add a sweet crunch to this fruited spinach salad. Look for a package of the almonds in the produce section of your grocery store.

1   (6-ounce) package fresh baby spinach
½   cup diced red onion
1   (15-ounce) can mandarin oranges in light syrup, drained
¼   cup orange juice
1   teaspoon sugar
1   teaspoon grated peeled fresh ginger
1   teaspoon low-sodium soy sauce
1   teaspoon dark sesame oil
¼   cup honey-roasted sliced almonds (such as Sunkist Almond Accents)

1. Combine first 3 ingredients; toss.
2. Combine orange juice and next 4 ingredients. Pour juice mixture over spinach mixture, and toss gently. Sprinkle with almonds. **Yield:** 6 servings (serving size: 1¹/₃ cups).

CALORIES 83; FAT 3.2g (sat 0.1g, mono 1.9g, poly 1.2g); PROTEIN 1.9g; CARB 12.7g; FIBER 1.3g; CHOL 0mg; IRON 1.3mg; SODIUM 112mg; CALC 43mg

If you are unfamiliar with fresh ginger, you might be puzzled about how to deal with the papery brown skin and gnarled root. Simply use a vegetable peeler to remove the tough skin and reveal the flesh. It's quick and easy.

SHORTCUT SPOTLIGHT

Caesar Salad

Creamy dressing, crunchy croutons, and a characteristic Mediterranean bite make Caesar salad hard to turn down.

2   romaine hearts, halved lengthwise
4   tablespoons light Caesar dressing
4   tablespoons grated fresh Parmesan cheese
4   large-cut Caesar-flavored croutons, halved

1. Top each romaine half with 1 tablespoon dressing, 1 tablespoon cheese, and 2 crouton halves. **Yield:** 4 servings (serving size: 1 romaine half).

CALORIES 95; FAT 5.8g (sat 1.5g, mono 1.4g, poly 2.8g); PROTEIN 4.9g; CARB 7g; FIBER 1.2g; CHOL 10mg; IRON 1.3mg; SODIUM 329mg; CALC 149mg

Romaine and Apple Salad

Romaine lettuce leaves grow in heads and range in color from dark green outer leaves to a yellowish-green heart in the center. It adds crisp texture to the salad along with the Fuji apple.

4   cups torn romaine lettuce
6   tablespoons pecan pieces, toasted
1   Fuji apple, thinly sliced
¼   cup fat-free balsamic vinaigrette
1   ounce shaved fresh Parmesan cheese

1. Combine first 3 ingredients in a large bowl. Add vinaigrette; toss to coat. Place 1¹/₂ cups salad on each of 4 plates; top evenly with Parmesan. Serve immediately. **Yield:** 4 servings.

CALORIES 147; FAT 10.3g (sat 1.7g, mono 5.8g, poly 2.7g); PROTEIN 4.8g; CARB 11.2g; FIBER 3.1g; CHOL 6mg; IRON 1.1mg; SODIUM 331mg; CALC 130mg

15 MINUTES

Sautéed Escarole, Corn, and White Bean Salad

Escarole's bitter flavor mellows when cooked. Combine it with fresh corn and white beans for a refreshing dish.

2   heads escarole, quartered lengthwise and rinsed
Cooking spray
2   ounces pancetta, chopped
1   medium zucchini, quartered and cut into julienne strips
1   garlic clove, minced
1   cup fresh corn kernels
½   cup chopped fresh flat-leaf parsley
1   (15-ounce) can navy beans, rinsed and drained
2   tablespoons red wine vinegar
1   teaspoon extra-virgin olive oil
½   teaspoon black pepper

1. Heat a large nonstick skillet over medium-high heat. Add escarole to pan; cook 3 minutes or until wilted, turning frequently. Trim white stem ends from each escarole quarter; roughly chop.
2. Wipe pan with a paper towel. Return pan to medium-high heat. Coat pan with cooking spray. Add pancetta, zucchini, and garlic to pan; cook 2 minutes or until zucchini is tender. Add corn; cook 1 minute. Combine escarole, corn mixture, parsley, and beans in a large bowl. Add vinegar and remaining ingredients; toss well to coat. Serve immediately. **Yield:** 4 servings (serving size: about 1¾ cups).

CALORIES 210; FAT 7.2g (sat 2.4g, mono 3.1g, poly 1g); PROTEIN 12.6g; CARB 32.7g; FIBER 14.4g; CHOL 10mg; IRON 4.1mg; SODIUM 634mg; CALC 199mg

Sautéed Escarole, Corn, and White Bean Salad

15 MINUTES

Fresh Greek Salad

Using a variety of fresh vegetables enhances both the taste and appearance of a salad. During the summer months, the vegetables in this salad are at their peak and are readily available at any grocery store.

4   cups torn romaine lettuce
2   cups halved grape tomatoes
1   cup sliced cucumber
½   cup chopped red onion
¼   cup crumbled feta cheese
¼   cup fat-free red wine vinaigrette
8   pitted kalamata olives

1. Combine all ingredients in a large bowl; toss well to coat. Serve immediately. **Yield:** 5 servings (serving size: 1 cup).

CALORIES 71; FAT 3.5g (sat 1.4g, mono 1.6g, poly 0.3g); PROTEIN 2.5g; CARB 8.5g; FIBER 2g; CHOL 7mg; IRON 0.7mg; SODIUM 349mg; CALC 64mg

Fresh Greek
Salad

Crunchy Coleslaw with
Green Peas

COOKING CLASS: *how to cut an onion*

When an onion is cut, it releases gases that can mix with the moisture in your eyes to form a mild sulfuric acid that causes tears. To avoid weeping while chopping an onion, peel and chill the onion in the refrigerator before slicing.

 MINUTES

Crunchy Coleslaw with Green Peas

Using frozen peas saves time and lets you prepare this recipe year-round. Opt for blanched early spring peas when they're available.

4   cups shredded coleslaw mix
½   cup frozen green peas, thawed
½   cup chopped yellow bell pepper
½   cup matchstick-cut carrots
¼   cup finely chopped onion
3   tablespoons cider vinegar
2   tablespoons sugar
1½   teaspoons canola oil
¼   teaspoon salt

1. Combine all ingredients in a large bowl; toss gently to coat. Serve immediately. **Yield:** 8 servings (serving size: about ²/₃ cup).

CALORIES 43; FAT 0.9g (sat 0.1g, mono 0.5g, poly 0.3g); PROTEIN 1g; CARB 7.8g; FIBER 1.5g; CHOL 0mg; IRON 0.2mg; SODIUM 91mg; CALC 7mg

 MINUTES

Tangy Slaw

Prepare and refrigerate this salad several hours before serving, if you like. For more color in the dish, toss in red bell pepper strips.

¼   cup creamy mustard blend (such as Dijonnaise)
3   tablespoons sugar
2   tablespoons cider vinegar
1   tablespoon apple cider
2   tablespoons sweet pickle relish
1   (7-ounce) package shredded cabbage

1. Combine first 4 ingredients; stir well with a whisk. Combine pickle relish and cabbage in a bowl; pour dressing over slaw, and toss gently. Cover and chill. **Yield:** 4 servings (serving size: ¹/₂ cup).

CALORIES 77; FAT 0.1g (sat 0g, mono 0g, poly 0g); PROTEIN 0.7g; CARB 18.5g; FIBER 1.3g; CHOL 0mg; IRON 0.3mg; SODIUM 282mg; CALC 21mg

COOKING CLASS: *how to prepare jicama*

To prepare jicama, remove the skin with a sharp vegetable peeler, and then cut the white flesh into strips according to the recipe. Because jicama doesn't brown or become soggy after it is cut, it makes a nice addition to crudité platters and salads.

 MINUTES

Sweet Lemon-Jicama Slaw

This crunchy, refreshing, citrusy slaw features jicama, a Mexican root vegetable with a texture similar to a water chestnut.

2   cups matchstick-cut peeled jicama
¼   cup thinly sliced red onion
2   jalapeño peppers, seeded and finely chopped
1   teaspoon grated fresh lemon rind
3   tablespoons fresh lemon juice
2   tablespoons sugar
2   tablespoons chopped fresh cilantro
1   teaspoon canola oil

1. Combine all ingredients in a medium bowl; toss well. **Yield:** 5 servings (serving size: about ¹/₂ cup).

CALORIES 52; FAT 1g (sat 0.1g, mono 0.6g, poly 0.3g); PROTEIN 0.5g; CARB 11g; FIBER 2.7g; CHOL 0mg; IRON 0.4mg; SODIUM 3mg; CALC 9mg

 MINUTES

Broccoli Salad

We used light mayonnaise and fat-free yogurt to lower the fat and calories in this classic salad. Reduced amounts of real bacon and regular cheese provide maximum flavor. If you prefer a bit of sweetness, mix in ¼ cup golden raisins.

⅓   cup light mayonnaise
¼   cup plain fat-free yogurt
3   tablespoons sugar
1   tablespoon white vinegar
⅓   cup chopped red onion
⅓   cup (1.3 ounces) shredded mild cheddar cheese
1   (12-ounce) package broccoli florets, cut into bite-sized pieces
3   precooked bacon slices, crumbled
¼   teaspoon freshly ground black pepper

1. Combine first 4 ingredients in a medium bowl. Add onion and remaining ingredients; toss gently to coat. **Yield:** 8 servings (serving size: ³/₄ cup).

CALORIES 98; FAT 5.8g (sat 1.7g, mono 1.8g, poly 2.2g); PROTEIN 3.6g; CARB 9.2g; FIBER 1.3g; CHOL 10mg; IRON 0.4mg; SODIUM 174mg; CALC 65mg

20
MINUTES

Asparagus–Goat Cheese Salad

We use a bottled balsamic vinaigrette, but you can always make a homemade version if you have more time to spare.

1   pound asparagus spears, trimmed
¼   cup plus 1 tablespoon balsamic vinaigrette, divided
6   cups torn butter lettuce
½   cup (2 ounces) crumbled goat cheese
Freshly ground black pepper (optional)

1. Cook asparagus in boiling water 5 minutes; drain and plunge into ice water. Let stand 4 minutes or until cold. Drain and toss with 1 tablespoon vinaigrette.
2. Divide lettuce evenly among salad plates. Divide asparagus among salads; drizzle remaining ¼ cup vinaigrette over lettuce and asparagus. Sprinkle with cheese and, if desired, pepper. **Yield:** 4 servings (serving size: 1½ cups lettuce, about 5 asparagus spears, 1 tablespoon dressing, and 2 tablespoons cheese).

CALORIES 128; FAT 9g (sat 2.8g, mono 3.4g, poly 2.7g); PROTEIN 6.3g; CARB 8.2g;
FIBER 3g; CHOL 7mg; IRON 2.6mg; SODIUM 290mg; CALC 73mg

Edamame Salad

1	(10-ounce) package fully cooked refrigerated shelled edamame (green soybeans)
1	large navel orange, peeled and sectioned
¼	cup minced red onion
1	tablespoon chopped fresh mint
1	teaspoon sugar
2	teaspoons fresh orange juice
1	teaspoon seasoned rice vinegar
1	teaspoon extra-virgin olive oil
½	teaspoon salt
¼	teaspoon black pepper

1. Combine first 4 ingredients in a large bowl.

2. Combine sugar and next 5 ingredients. Pour over edamame mixture; toss gently to coat. **Yield:** 4 servings (serving size: about ¹/₂ cup).

CALORIES 133; FAT 4.1g (sat 0.2g, mono 1.9g, poly 1.8g); PROTEIN 8g; CARB 15.6g; FIBER 4.8g; CHOL 0mg; IRON 1.7mg; SODIUM 349mg; CALC 66mg

Carrot Salad with Grapes

Grapes add a twist to a traditional carrot salad that's usually filled with the smaller, dried variety—raisins.

¼ cup light mayonnaise
2 tablespoons orange juice
1 teaspoon sugar
6 medium carrots, shredded
⅔ cup seedless red grape halves

1. Combine first 3 ingredients in a large bowl, stirring with a whisk until blended. Add carrots and grapes, tossing well to coat. Let stand 5 minutes. **Yield:** 4 servings (serving size: ¾ cup).

CALORIES 101; FAT 5.1g (sat 0.8g, mono 1.3g, poly 2.9g); PROTEIN 0.9g; CARB 13.9g; FIBER 2g; CHOL 5mg; IRON 0.4mg; SODIUM 163mg; CALC 34mg

Black-Eyed Pea Salad

Grapes contain resveratrol, which helps protect them from fungus. Resveratrol has anti-inflammatory properties and may help prevent heart disease and several kinds of cancer. Additionally, grapes provide potassium and are packed with flavonoids that also may help prevent cancer and heart disease.

INGREDIENT SPOTLIGHT

Black-Eyed Pea Salad

make it a meal *Prepare this salad an hour or so before you plan to serve, and then chill. The zesty flavors of the Italian dressing, tomatoes and green chiles, and fresh cilantro will mingle with the peas and other vegetables. This salad serves double duty as a fresh side for grilled chicken or pork tenderloin and as a salsa-like appetizer when paired with tortilla chips.*

1 (15.8-ounce) can black-eyed peas, rinsed and drained
1 (11-ounce) can shoepeg white corn, drained
1 cup chopped seeded cucumber (1 small)
1 cup finely chopped celery (3 stalks)
½ cup finely chopped red onion (½ medium)
½ cup finely chopped fresh cilantro
1 (10-ounce) can diced tomatoes and green chiles (such as Rotel), drained
¾ cup roasted red pepper Italian dressing with Parmesan (such as Kraft)
½ teaspoon black pepper

1. Combine all ingredients in a large bowl; cover and chill. Serve with a slotted spoon. **Yield:** 7 servings (serving size: ¾ cup).

CALORIES 111; FAT 2.3g (sat 0.1g, mono 0.6g, poly 1.4g); PROTEIN 3.3g; CARB 19.1g; FIBER 2.6g; CHOL 0mg; IRON 0.7mg; SODIUM 487mg; CALC 23mg

Gazpacho Salad

Classic Caprese

At first glance, you might think that the vinegar has been accidentally omitted; however, this salad traditionally has no vinegar at all.

2 medium tomatoes, each cut into 6 slices
8 ounces fresh mozzarella cheese, cut into 12 slices
20 fresh basil leaves
4 teaspoons extra-virgin olive oil
½ teaspoon salt
½ teaspoon freshly ground black pepper

1. Arrange 3 tomato slices, 3 cheese slices, and 5 basil leaves on each of 4 salad plates; drizzle each with 1 teaspoon oil, and sprinkle each with ¹/₈ teaspoon salt and ¹/₈ teaspoon pepper. Serve immediately. **Yield:** 4 servings.

CALORIES 207; FAT 16.8g (sat 8.8g, mono 6.9g, poly 1g); PROTEIN 10.2g; CARB 2.2g; FIBER 0.2g; CHOL 45mg; IRON 0.9mg; SODIUM 379mg; CALC 337mg

MINUTES

Gazpacho Salad

Gazpacho Salad allows you to enjoy the refreshing flavors of the classic chilled soup in a salad form. For a more colorful presentation, slice off alternating strips of the peel before chopping the cucumber.

1 pint grape tomatoes, halved
1 cup coarsely chopped cucumber
³/₄ cup coarsely chopped yellow bell pepper
½ cup coarsely chopped red onion
2 garlic cloves, crushed
¼ cup fat-free zesty Italian dressing
¼ teaspoon salt
¼ teaspoon freshly ground black pepper

1. Combine all ingredients in a medium bowl, stirring well. Serve immediately, or cover and chill. **Yield:** 4 servings (serving size: 1 cup).

CALORIES 49; FAT 1.1g (sat 0.1g, mono 0.4g, poly 0.6g); PROTEIN 1.3g; CARB 8g; FIBER 2.1g; CHOL 0mg; IRON 0.5mg; SODIUM 261mg; CALC 27mg

INGREDIENT SPOTLIGHT

Fresh mozzarella marries smooth, creamy texture with milky, mild flavor. Although traditionally made from buffalo's milk, most fresh mozzarella is made with cow's milk. It's stored in a brine, which helps keep it moist.

Minted Vegetable Salad

4 cups chopped seeded tomato
1½ cups chopped cucumber
1 cup chopped red bell or yellow pepper
1 cup sliced green onions
1 cup chopped fresh parsley
½ cup chopped radishes
⅓ cup chopped fresh mint
⅓ cup chopped pitted kalamata olives
¼ cup fresh lemon juice
2 tablespoons olive oil
1 garlic clove, minced
½ teaspoon black pepper
¼ teaspoon salt

1. Place first 8 ingredients in a large bowl.
2. Combine lemon juice and next 4 ingredients in a small bowl, stirring with a whisk. Pour dressing over salad; toss well. Serve immediately, or cover and chill until ready to serve. **Yield:** 7 servings (serving size: 1 cup).

CALORIES 92; FAT 6.1g (sat 0.8g, mono 4.2g, poly 0.9g); PROTEIN 2.1g; CARB 9.5g; FIBER 2.7g; CHOL 0mg; IRON 1.3mg; SODIUM 202mg; CALC 46mg

20 MINUTES

Feta and Pepperoncini Barley Salad

make it a meal *Serve cantaloupe wedges and warm pita bread to complete the menu. Barley and navy beans are excellent sources of dietary fiber in this salad.*

1½ cups water
⅔ cup uncooked quick-cooking barley
1 cup (4 ounces) crumbled feta cheese with basil and sun-dried tomatoes
1 cup halved grape or cherry tomatoes
½ cup finely chopped pepperoncini peppers
½ cup chopped bottled roasted red bell pepper
2 tablespoons chopped fresh basil
1 tablespoon capers, drained
1 tablespoon cider vinegar
1 tablespoon extra-virgin olive oil
½ teaspoon bottled minced garlic
1 (16-ounce) can navy beans, rinsed and drained

1. Bring 1½ cups water to a boil in a medium saucepan; add barley. Cover, reduce heat, and simmer 18 minutes or until liquid is absorbed and barley is tender. Drain and rinse under cold water, and drain well.

2. While barley cooks, combine feta cheese, tomatoes, peppers, basil, capers, vinegar, olive oil, garlic, and navy beans in a large bowl; toss well. Add cooked barley; toss gently until combined. Serve immediately.
Yield: 4 servings (serving size: 1¼ cups).

CALORIES 317; FAT 10.8g (sat 5g, mono 4g, poly 1.1g); PROTEIN 14.3g; CARB 42.6g; FIBER 10.5g; CHOL 25mg; IRON 4.2mg; SODIUM 973mg; CALC 250mg

15 MINUTES

Quinoa Salad with Toasted Pistachios and Dried Pineapple

Fluffy quinoa offers a crunchy texture to this filling salad. Toast the quinoa before cooking if you prefer a nuttier flavor.

1½ cups water
¾ cup uncooked quinoa
¼ cup shelled, chopped pistachios (about 1 ounce)
2 cups rotisserie chicken breast, chopped
⅓ cup chopped green onions
⅓ cup chopped dried pineapple
1 tablespoon toasted sesame oil
1½ teaspoons bottled ground fresh ginger (such as Spice World)
½ teaspoon ground cumin
½ teaspoon salt
¼ teaspoon crushed red pepper

1. Boil water in a small saucepan. Add quinoa. Cover, reduce heat, and simmer 12 minutes.
2. Heat a small skillet over medium-high heat. Add chopped pistachios, and cook 2 minutes or until lightly toasted, stirring frequently. Transfer pistachios to a large bowl; add cooked quinoa and remaining ingredients to bowl. Toss gently to coat.
Yield: 4 cups (serving size: 1 cup).

CALORIES 344; FAT 10.7g (sat 1.6g, mono 4.7g, poly 3.7g); PROTEIN 27g; CARB 32.5g; FIBER 3.7g; CHOL 60mg; IRON 3.2mg; SODIUM 362mg; CALC 42mg

INGREDIENT SPOTLIGHT

Pita is a round yeast flatbread that's traditional in many Middle Eastern and Mediterranean cuisines. It is used to scoop up sauces and dips, and it can be opened into a pocket for sandwich fillings. Because pita bread tends to dry out quickly, store it in a tightly sealed plastic bag.

Fattoush

Fattoush (fah-TOOSH) is the Middle Eastern version of bread salad, made with torn bits of pita and lots of late-summer vegetables. This version is a main dish, thanks to the addition of chicken and kidney beans.

¼   cup fresh lemon juice
2   tablespoons extra-virgin olive oil
1   teaspoon Dijon mustard
¼   teaspoon salt
¼   teaspoon black pepper
8   cups chopped romaine lettuce
2   cups shredded cooked chicken breast
1½   cups chopped peeled cucumber
1   cup thinly sliced fennel bulb
⅓   cup thinly sliced green onions
¼   cup chopped fresh mint
¼   cup chopped fresh flat-leaf parsley
2   (6-inch) pitas, torn into bite-sized pieces
1   (15-ounce) can kidney beans, rinsed and
     drained
1   pint cherry tomatoes, halved

1. Combine first 5 ingredients in a bowl, stirring with a whisk.
2. Combine lettuce and remaining ingredients in a large bowl; toss gently. Drizzle juice mixture over chicken mixture; toss to coat. Serve immediately. **Yield:** 4 servings (serving size: 2 cups).

CALORIES 400; FAT 13.4g (sat 2.6g, mono 7.1g, poly 2.2g); PROTEIN 30.3g; CARB 40.9g; FIBER 9.4g; CHOL 59mg; IRON 4.1mg; SODIUM 566mg; CALC 163mg

15 MINUTES

Panzanella

Traditionally, panzanella, a bread and vegetable salad, was a perfect way for Italians to use stale bread. Here, we used toasted bread slices, but a leftover baguette would work great, too.

1	cup coarsely chopped plum tomato
1	cup coarsely chopped English cucumber
1/3	cup thinly sliced red onion
1/4	cup diced fresh mozzarella cheese
2	(1.5-ounce) slices multigrain bread, toasted and cubed
1/4	cup light Italian vinaigrette with basil and Romano cheese (such as Ken's Steak House)

1. Combine first 5 ingredients in a large bowl. Add vinaigrette; toss to combine. Serve immediately. **Yield:** 6 servings (serving size: 1 cup).

CALORIES 84; FAT 2.9g (sat 0.7g, mono 0.9g, poly 1.3g); PROTEIN 3.7g; CARB 10.6g; FIBER 2.3g; CHOL 5mg; IRON 0.5mg; SODIUM 228mg; CALC 114mg

English cucumbers naturally have fewer seeds and are larger than regular cucumbers. Because there's no need to seed them, they can be prepared faster. Find them in most major grocery stores individually wrapped in plastic.

INGREDIENT SPOTLIGHT

Orange-Scented Couscous Salad with Almonds, Cilantro, and Cucumber

Orange-Scented Couscous Salad with Almonds, Cilantro, and Cucumber

make it a meal *Cut wonton wrappers into wedges, coat with cooking spray, and sprinkle with sesame seeds. Bake them until they are crisp, and serve with the salad.*

1   cup orange juice, divided
1/2   cup water
1   teaspoon salt, divided
1   teaspoon ground coriander
1/4   teaspoon ground cinnamon
1/4   teaspoon black pepper, divided
1   cup uncooked couscous
1/4   cup sweetened dried cranberries
1/4   cup sliced almonds
1 1/2   cups chopped, cooked chicken breast
1   cup chopped cucumber
1/3   cup prechopped red onion
3   tablespoons chopped fresh cilantro
1   tablespoon fresh lime juice
2   teaspoons Dijon mustard
1 1/2   tablespoons extra-virgin olive oil

1. Combine 3/4 cup orange juice, water, 1/2 teaspoon salt, coriander, cinnamon, and 1/8 teaspoon pepper in a saucepan; bring to a boil. Remove from heat; add couscous and cranberries. Cover and let stand 5 minutes; fluff with a fork. Transfer couscous mixture to a large bowl.
2. Heat a small skillet over medium heat. Add nuts to pan; cook 3 minutes or until toasted, stirring frequently. Add nuts, chicken, and next 3 ingredients to couscous; toss.
3. Combine remaining 1/4 cup orange juice, 1/2 teaspoon salt, 1/8 teaspoon pepper, lime juice, and mustard, stirring with a whisk. Gradually add oil to juice mixture, stirring constantly with a whisk. Drizzle juice mixture over couscous mixture, tossing to coat. **Yield:** 4 servings (serving size: 1 1/2 cups).

CALORIES 396; FAT 10.7g (sat 1.5g, mono 6.4g, poly 1.8g); PROTEIN 24.1g; CARB 49.7g; FIBER 4.1g; CHOL 45mg; IRON 1.4mg; SODIUM 690mg; CALC 58mg

Chicken-Couscous Bibb Salad

Rinsing the couscous with cold water cools it quickly. Drain it well before mixing it with the chicken. Bring this salad to the table with whole wheat pitas and hummus.

1/2   cup water
1/3   cup uncooked couscous
2   cups chopped cooked chicken breast
1   cup chopped cucumber
1/2   cup finely chopped red onion
1/2   cup chopped fresh mint
1/4   cup chopped fresh parsley
2   tablespoons fresh lemon juice
2   teaspoons chopped fresh oregano
1   tablespoon extra-virgin olive oil
1/2   teaspoon salt
12   Bibb lettuce leaves

1. Bring 1/2 cup water to a boil in a small saucepan; stir in couscous. Remove from heat, cover, and let stand 5 minutes. Fluff with a fork. Place couscous in a fine-mesh strainer; rinse with cold water. Drain.
2. Combine couscous, chicken, and next 6 ingredients in a medium bowl. Stir in oil and salt. Place 3 lettuce leaves on each of 4 plates; spoon about 1/4 cup chicken mixture in center of each leaf. **Yield:** 4 servings (serving size: 3 lettuce cups).

CALORIES 225; FAT 6.3g (sat 1.2g, mono 3.4g, poly 1g); PROTEIN 24.9g; CARB 16.6g; FIBER 2.4g; CHOL 60mg; IRON 2.3mg; SODIUM 355mg; CALC 64mg

Summer Black Bean and Pasta Salad

Drain the pasta, and rinse it immediately with cold water to cool it quickly. If you can't find ditalini pasta, substitute tubetti or small elbow macaroni.

¾ cup uncooked ditalini (very short tube-shaped macaroni, 3 ounces)
1½ cups halved grape tomatoes
¾ cup diced peeled avocado
½ cup chopped seeded poblano chile (about 1)
½ cup chopped cucumber
⅓ cup chopped red onion
2 tablespoons chopped fresh cilantro
1 (15-ounce) can black beans, rinsed and drained
2 teaspoons grated lime rind
2 tablespoons fresh lime juice
1 tablespoon cider vinegar
2 teaspoons extra-virgin olive oil
¾ teaspoon bottled minced garlic
¾ teaspoon salt
⅛ teaspoon ground red pepper
1 medium lime, cut in 4 wedges

1. Cook pasta according to package directions, omitting salt and fat. Drain and cool completely.
2. Combine tomatoes, avocado, poblano, cucumber, onion, cilantro, and beans in a medium bowl, stirring well. Combine rind, juice, vinegar, oil, garlic, salt, and pepper in a small bowl, stirring well with a whisk. Add

pasta and lime mixture to bean mixture; toss to combine. Serve with lime wedges. **Yield:** 4 servings (serving size: 1½ cups pasta and 1 lime wedge).

CALORIES 214; FAT 7.1g (sat 1.1g, mono 4.4g, poly 0.9g); PROTEIN 7.3g; CARB 35.5g; FIBER 7.2g; CHOL 0mg; IRON 2.4mg; SODIUM 656mg; CALC 47mg

Southwestern Couscous Salad

You can use boneless, skinless chicken breast halves instead of turkey.

Cooking spray
1 (1-pound) turkey tenderloin, cut into 1-inch pieces
½ teaspoon salt, divided
¼ teaspoon black pepper, divided
2 cups fat-free, less-sodium chicken broth
2 cups frozen corn kernels
1½ cups uncooked couscous
1 cup diced plum tomato (about 2 medium)
½ cup prechopped green bell pepper
¼ cup chopped fresh cilantro
¼ cup fresh lime juice
2 tablespoons canola oil
1 teaspoon ground cumin
1 teaspoon hot pepper sauce (such as Tabasco)

1. Heat a large nonstick skillet over medium-high heat. Coat pan with cooking spray. Sprinkle turkey with ¼ teaspoon salt and ⅛ teaspoon pepper. Add turkey to pan; sauté 6 minutes.
2. Place broth in a medium saucepan; bring to a boil. Add corn to pan; cook 3 minutes. Add couscous to pan. Remove from heat; cover and let stand 5 minutes. Fluff with a fork.
3. Combine remaining ¼ teaspoon salt, remaining ⅛ teaspoon pepper, tomato, and remaining ingredients in a large bowl. Add turkey and couscous mixture to bowl, and toss well. **Yield:** 6 servings (serving size: 1⅔ cups).

CALORIES 353; FAT 6.1g (sat 0.7g, mono 3.1g, poly 1.9g); PROTEIN 27g; CARB 47.7g; FIBER 4.5g; CHOL 47mg; IRON 2mg; SODIUM 377mg; CALC 34mg

SHORTCUT SPOTLIGHT

For the best flavor, fresh lime juice can't be beat. A citrus press is a quick and easy way to get a lot of juice from your lime. To get the most juice, bring your lime to room temperature before pressing it.

15 MINUTES

Antipasto Salad

1   (9-ounce) package fresh light four-cheese ravioli
1   (14-ounce) can quartered artichoke hearts, drained and roughly chopped
2   tablespoons chopped drained oil-packed sun-dried tomato halves
¼   cup sliced ripe olives
¼   cup torn fresh basil leaves
½   cup fat-free balsamic vinaigrette

1. Cook pasta according to package directions, omitting salt; drain.
2. Combine cooked pasta, artichokes, and remaining ingredients in a large bowl. Serve immediately. **Yield:** 4 servings (serving size: 1¼ cups).

CALORIES 231; FAT 4.3g (sat 1.6g, mono 1.4g, poly 1.2g); PROTEIN 10.5g; CARB 38.8g; FIBER 2.8g; CHOL 25mg; IRON 2.3mg; SODIUM 941mg; CALC 86mg

Soba Noodle Salad with Citrus Vinaigrette

Look for soba noodles, often labeled buckwheat noodles, in the Asian section of your supermarket.

1	(8-ounce) package soba noodles
1¼	cups frozen shelled edamame (green soybeans)
¾	cup matchstick-cut carrots
⅓	cup sliced green onions
2	tablespoons chopped fresh cilantro
1½	teaspoons chopped serrano chile
1	pound peeled and deveined medium shrimp
¼	teaspoon salt
¼	teaspoon black pepper
	Cooking spray
2	tablespoons fresh orange juice
2	tablespoons fresh lime juice
1	tablespoon low-sodium soy sauce
1	tablespoon dark sesame oil
1	tablespoon olive oil

1. Cook noodles in boiling water 7 minutes or until almost al dente. Add edamame to pan; cook 1 minute or until thoroughly heated. Drain. Place noodle mixture in a large bowl. Add carrots, onions, cilantro, and chile; toss.

2. Heat a large skillet over medium-high heat. Sprinkle shrimp with salt and pepper. Coat pan with cooking spray. Add shrimp; cook 1½ minutes on each side. Add shrimp to noodle mixture.

3. Combine orange juice and remaining ingredients in a bowl, stirring well with a whisk. Drizzle juice mixture over noodle mixture; toss well. **Yield:** 4 servings (serving size: about 2 cups).

CALORIES 418; FAT 10.2g (sat 1.3g, mono 4.3g, poly 2.4g); PROTEIN 31.9g; CARB 52.4g; FIBER 3.4g; CHOL 168mg; IRON 5.5mg; SODIUM 922mg; CALC 101mg

15 MINUTES

Pesto Tortellini and Zucchini Salad

make it a meal *Serve this fragrant, colorful salad with warm whole wheat rolls and precut fresh cantaloupe or honeydew melon. Look for fresh tortellini in the refrigerated section of your supermarket. You can substitute yellow squash for zucchini.*

2   (9-ounce) packages fresh three-cheese tortellini
Cooking spray
2   teaspoons bottled minced garlic
4   cups zucchini, halved and thinly sliced (about 2 zucchini)
2   cups chopped plum tomato (about 4 tomatoes)
3   tablespoons commercial pesto
½   teaspoon salt
¼   teaspoon freshly ground black pepper
2   tablespoons shredded Parmesan cheese

1. Cook pasta according to package directions, omitting salt and fat; drain. Reserve ¼ cup cooking liquid.
2. While pasta cooks, heat a large nonstick skillet over medium-high heat. Coat pan with cooking spray. Add garlic and zucchini, and sauté 5 minutes or until zucchini is tender. Combine pasta mixture, zucchini mixture, and tomato in a large bowl, tossing gently to coat.
3. Combine reserved ¼ cup cooking liquid, pesto, salt, and pepper in a small bowl. Drizzle over pasta, tossing gently to coat. Sprinkle with cheese. **Yield:** 6 servings (serving size: about 2 cups pasta mixture and 1 teaspoon cheese).

CALORIES 336; FAT 11.2g (sat 4.4g, mono 4.4g, poly 1g); PROTEIN 14.9g; CARB 45.9g; FIBER 3.3g; CHOL 39mg; IRON 2.1mg; SODIUM 586mg; CALC 220mg

15 MINUTES

Warm Tortellini and Cherry Tomato Salad

Extra-virgin olive oil and two kinds of vinegar make an easy, classic dressing for this pasta-and-vegetable salad. You can also try this with chicken or mushroom tortellini or cheese ravioli.

2   (9-ounce) packages fresh cheese tortellini
1½ cups (1½-inch-long) slices fresh asparagus (about 1 pound)
3   tablespoons red wine vinegar
1   tablespoon balsamic vinegar
1   tablespoon extra-virgin olive oil
¼   teaspoon black pepper
4   cups trimmed arugula
1½ cups halved cherry tomatoes
¾   cup (3 ounces) pregrated fresh Parmesan cheese
½   cup thinly sliced red onion
⅓   cup thinly sliced fresh basil
1   (14-ounce) can artichoke hearts, drained and quartered

1. Cook pasta according to package directions, omitting salt and fat. Add asparagus to pasta during last 2 minutes of cook time. Drain.
2. While pasta cooks, combine vinegars, oil, and pepper in a large bowl, stirring with a whisk. Add pasta mixture, arugula, and remaining ingredients; toss to coat. **Yield:** 6 servings (serving size: 1½ cups).

CALORIES 403; FAT 11.6g (sat 5.7g, mono 4.4g, poly 0.6g); PROTEIN 21.7g; CARB 52.4g; FIBER 7.9g; CHOL 50mg; IRON 1.9mg; SODIUM 725mg; CALC 415mg

To speed up the process, we used a can of artichoke hearts instead of cutting up an artichoke.

MAKE IT FASTER

MINUTES

Mediterranean Salmon Salad

Shorter pastas like orzo generally cook faster than the longer varieties, and it's what's used in this recipe.

½   cup uncooked orzo
2   (6-ounce) salmon fillets (about 1 inch thick)
¼   teaspoon salt
¼   teaspoon dried oregano
⅛   teaspoon black pepper
Cooking spray
2   cups torn spinach
½   cup chopped red bell pepper
¼   cup chopped green onions
4   kalamata olives, pitted and chopped
3   tablespoons fresh lemon juice
2   tablespoons crumbled feta cheese

1. Preheat broiler.
2. Cook pasta according to package directions, omitting salt and fat.
3. Sprinkle salmon evenly with salt, oregano, and black pepper. Place on a broiler pan coated with cooking spray. Broil 10 minutes or until fish flakes easily when tested with a fork or until desired degree of doneness. Let stand 5 minutes; break into bite-sized pieces with 2 forks.
4. Combine pasta, salmon, spinach, and remaining ingredients in a medium bowl; toss well. **Yield:** 4 servings (serving size: 1 cup).

CALORIES 231; FAT 7.7g (sat 1.6g, mono 2.7g, poly 2.3g); PROTEIN 20.3g; CARB 19.3g; FIBER 1.8g; CHOL 49mg; IRON 1.3mg; SODIUM 310mg; CALC 56mg

In a pinch, use canned drained salmon—and flake it with two forks—in place of the broiled fillets.

MAKE IT FASTER

Pan-Grilled Thai Tuna Salad

make it a meal *Precut matchstick carrots and bottled fresh orange sections are time-savers. Pair with a side of crunchy rice crackers and prepare a refreshing dessert to follow the spicy salad.*

Cooking spray
2   (6-ounce) Yellowfin tuna steaks (about 1 inch thick)
¼   teaspoon salt
⅛   teaspoon black pepper
4   cups thinly sliced napa (Chinese) cabbage
1   cup thinly sliced cucumber
½   cup matchstick-cut carrots
⅓   cup presliced red onion
1   navel orange, sectioned and chopped
1   tablespoon sugar
2   tablespoons chopped fresh cilantro
2   tablespoons fresh lime juice
2   tablespoons rice vinegar
½   teaspoon dark sesame oil
¼   teaspoon sambal oelek (ground fresh chile paste) or Sriracha (hot chile sauce, such as Huy Fong)

1. Heat a grill pan over medium-high heat. Coat pan with cooking spray. Sprinkle fish evenly with salt and pepper. Add fish to pan; cook 2 minutes on each side or until desired degree of doneness. Transfer to a cutting board.
2. Combine cabbage and next 4 ingredients in a large bowl. Combine sugar and remaining ingredients in a small bowl, stirring well with a whisk. Reserve 1 tablespoon dressing. Drizzle remaining dressing over salad; toss gently to coat. Divide salad mixture evenly between 2 plates. Cut each tuna steak across the grain into ¼-inch slices; arrange over salad mixture. Drizzle 1½ teaspoons reserved dressing over each serving. **Yield:** 2 servings.

CALORIES 307; FAT 3g (sat 0.6g, mono 0.8g, poly 1g); PROTEIN 41.8g; CARB 28.4g; FIBER 5.2g; CHOL 74mg; IRON 1.6mg; SODIUM 398mg; CALC 201mg

15 MINUTES

Mixed Greens Salad with Smoked Trout, Pistachios, and Cranberries

2   tablespoons raspberry vinegar
2   tablespoons fat-free, less-sodium chicken
     broth
1   tablespoon honey
1   teaspoon extra-virgin olive oil
¼   teaspoon freshly ground black pepper
¼   cup dried cranberries
⅓   cup (1½ ounces) goat cheese
8   (½-ounce) slices French bread
6   cups gourmet salad greens
1   (7-ounce) smoked rainbow trout
2   tablespoons dry-roasted pistachios

1. Preheat broiler.
2. Combine first 5 ingredients in a small bowl, stirring with a whisk. Add cranberries; let stand 5 minutes.
3. Spread about 1 teaspoon goat cheese on each bread slice. Arrange bread slices in a single layer on a baking sheet. Broil bread slices 1 minute.
4. Place 1½ cups salad greens on each of 4 plates. Top each serving with 1¾ ounces trout and 1½ teaspoons pistachios. Drizzle about 4 teaspoons dressing over each serving. Place 2 cheese toasts on each plate.
Yield: 4 servings.

CALORIES 226; FAT 9.9g (sat 3g, mono 3.7g, poly 2.2g); PROTEIN 17.4g; CARB 29.2g;
FIBER 3.6g; CHOL 44mg; IRON 2.6mg; SODIUM 875mg; CALC 88mg

COOKING CLASS: *how to sear scallops*

For the best sear on scallops, pat them dry with paper towels before seasoning and cooking them. Add the scallops, a few at a time, and wait for them to sizzle before adding more. If you add too many at once, the pan will lose heat, the scallops will take longer to brown, and they may overcook, resulting in tough, dry scallops.

 MINUTES

Seared Scallop Salad

Seared Scallop Salad

2	teaspoons bottled ground fresh ginger (such as Spice World)
1	teaspoon bottled minced garlic
2	teaspoons olive oil
¼	teaspoon salt
¼	teaspoon black pepper
1½	pounds large sea scallops
	Cooking spray
4	cups packaged gourmet salad greens
2	cups halved cherry tomatoes (about 1 pound)
1	cup preshredded carrot
1	cup sliced cucumber
¼	cup prechopped red onion
¼	cup light red wine vinaigrette

1. Combine first 6 ingredients in a large bowl; toss gently to coat. Heat a large non-stick skillet over medium-high heat. Coat pan with cooking spray. Add scallop mixture to pan; cook 3 minutes on each side or until done. Combine greens and remaining ingredients in a large bowl, and toss well. Divide salad evenly among 4 plates; top evenly with scallops. **Yield:** 4 servings (serving size: 1¾ cups salad and about 3 scallops).

CALORIES 235; FAT 4.1g (sat 0.5g, mono 1.8g, poly 0.9g); PROTEIN 30.7g; CARB 18g; FIBER 3.3g; CHOL 56mg; IRON 1.8mg; SODIUM 680mg; CALC 92mg

 MINUTES

Shrimp and Avocado Salad with Creole Sauce

½	cup low-fat mayonnaise
¼	cup sliced red onion
1	tablespoon chopped fresh flat-leaf parsley
2	tablespoons fresh lemon juice
2	tablespoons Creole mustard
1	teaspoon bottled minced garlic
¼	teaspoon ground red pepper
⅛	teaspoon paprika
8	cups torn Boston lettuce (about 4 small heads)
1½	pounds cooked peeled and deveined large shrimp
½	peeled avocado, thinly sliced

1. Combine first 8 ingredients in a large bowl. Add lettuce and shrimp to bowl; toss well to coat. Place about 2 cups salad on each of 4 plates; arrange one-fourth of avocado slices around each serving. **Yield:** 4 servings.

CALORIES 280; FAT 8g (sat 1.2g, mono 3.3g, poly 2.4g); PROTEIN 37.7g; CARB 14.1g; FIBER 2.6g; CHOL 332mg; IRON 6mg; SODIUM 753mg; CALC 109mg

Lemon-Splashed Shrimp Salad

Purchase peeled and deveined shrimp to save prep time. Chop, measure, and prepare the remaining ingredients while the pasta water comes to a boil. Chock-full of colorful ingredients, this makes a summery one-dish meal.

8   cups water
2/3   cup uncooked rotini (corkscrew pasta)
1½   pounds large shrimp, peeled and deveined
1   cup halved cherry tomatoes
3/4   cup sliced celery
½   cup chopped avocado
½   cup chopped seeded poblano pepper
2   tablespoons chopped fresh cilantro
2   teaspoons grated lemon rind
3   tablespoons fresh lemon juice
2   teaspoons extra-virgin olive oil
3/4   teaspoon kosher salt

1. Bring 8 cups water to a boil in a large saucepan. Add pasta to pan; cook 5 minutes or until almost tender. Add shrimp to pan; cook 3 minutes or until done. Drain. Rinse with cold water; drain well. Combine pasta mixture, tomatoes, celery, avocado, poblano, cilantro, rind, juice, olive oil, and salt in a bowl; toss well. **Yield:** 4 servings (serving size: about 1³/₄ cups).

CALORIES 250; FAT 6.9g (sat 1.2g, mono 3.8g, poly 1.2g); PROTEIN 30.3g; CARB 17g; FIBER 2.6g; CHOL 252mg; IRON 5.1mg; SODIUM 667mg; CALC 74mg

Mango and Shrimp Salad

Shrimp and Calamari Salad

Here's a quick and easy recipe that's ideal for a summer supper. Precut matchstick carrots and prechopped red onion help speed preparation.

6   cups water
³/₄   pound large shrimp, peeled and deveined
³/₄   pound cleaned, skinless squid
1¹/₂ cups thinly sliced fennel (about ¹/₂ bulb)
1   cup thinly sliced celery
¹/₂   cup precut matchstick-cut carrots
¹/₄   cup prechopped red onion
3   tablespoons chopped fresh parsley
3   tablespoons fresh lemon juice
1   tablespoon extra-virgin olive oil
³/₄   teaspoon salt
¹/₄   teaspoon freshly ground black pepper
4   cups mixed salad greens

1. Bring water to a boil in a large saucepan. Add shrimp to pan, and cook 3 minutes. Add squid to pan; cook 1 minute or until done. Drain and rinse with cold water; drain and cool.
2. Combine fennel and next 8 ingredients in a large bowl. Add shrimp mixture to bowl; toss well. Arrange 1 cup greens on each of 4 plates; top each serving with about 1¹/₂ cups shrimp mixture. **Yield:** 4 servings.

CALORIES 238; FAT 6.5g (sat 1.1g, mono 3g, poly 1.4g); PROTEIN 32.4g; CARB 12g; FIBER 3g; CHOL 327mg; IRON 3.9mg; SODIUM 667mg; CALC 142mg

Mango and Shrimp Salad

Look for bottled mango in the refrigerated food section of the produce department.

2   cups water
5   tablespoons lemon juice, divided
¹/₄   teaspoon salt
¹/₄   teaspoon crushed red pepper flakes
1   bay leaf
1   pound peeled and deveined shrimp
1   to 2 tablespoons chili sauce
1   tablespoon sesame oil
1   cup halved grape tomatoes
1   cup bottled chopped mango
¹/₂   cup sliced bottled red bell pepper
8   Bibb lettuce leaves

1. Combine water, 1 tablespoon juice, salt, red pepper flakes, and bay leaf in a large saucepan; bring to a boil. Add shrimp. Cover, reduce heat, and simmer 3 minutes or until shrimp are done. Drain shrimp, and discard bay leaf. Set shrimp aside.
2. Combine remaining ¹/₄ cup juice, chili sauce, and oil in a large bowl; stir with a whisk. Gently stir in shrimp, tomatoes, mango, and bell pepper. Line 4 plates evenly with lettuce leaves. Divide salad among plates. **Yield:** 4 servings (serving size: 1 cup of salad and 2 lettuce leaves).

CALORIES 168; FAT 4.6g (sat 0.8g, mono 1.6g, poly 1.9g); PROTEIN 18.7g; CARB 13.6g; FIBER 1.6g; CHOL 166mg; IRON 3.1mg; SODIUM 472mg; CALC 46mg

It can often be difficult to find squid at your local supermarket. If you can't find it, simply double the shrimp. Either shrimp or squid is perfect with this salad.

INGREDIENT SPOTLIGHT

 MINUTES

Thai Shrimp Salad with Spicy-Sour Dressing

4	ounces uncooked linguine
12	ounces peeled and deveined medium shrimp
½	cup fresh lime juice
1	tablespoon sugar
1	tablespoon Sriracha (hot chile sauce, such as Huy Fong)
1	teaspoon fish sauce
4	cups torn romaine lettuce
1¼	cups vertically sliced red onion
¼	cup matchstick-cut carrots
½	cup chopped fresh mint leaves
¼	cup chopped fresh cilantro
⅓	cup chopped dry-roasted cashews, unsalted

1. Cook pasta according to package directions, omitting salt and fat. Add shrimp to pan during last 3 minutes of cook time. Drain and rinse with cold water. Drain.
2. Combine juice, sugar, Sriracha, and fish sauce in a large bowl, stirring until sugar dissolves. Add pasta mixture, lettuce, and next 4 ingredients to juice mixture; toss to coat. Place about 2 cups pasta mixture on each of 4 plates. Sprinkle each serving with 4 teaspoons cashews. **Yield:** 4 servings.

CALORIES 305; FAT 6.5g (sat 1.3g, mono 3.3g, poly 1.4g); PROTEIN 23g; CARB 37.6g; FIBER 2.9g; CHOL 166mg; IRON 5.8mg; SODIUM 414mg; CALC 88mg

20
MINUTES

Thai Beef Salad

1	cup loosely packed fresh cilantro leaves
¼	cup fresh lime juice (about 3 limes)
2	tablespoons low-sodium soy sauce
1½	tablespoons Thai fish sauce
1	tablespoon honey
2	teaspoons grated orange rind
2	garlic cloves, peeled
½	small serrano chile
2	teaspoons olive oil
4	(4-ounce) beef tenderloin steaks, trimmed
¼	teaspoon black pepper
⅛	teaspoon salt
2	cups shredded Napa cabbage
1	cup grated, seeded, peeled cucumber
⅓	cup thinly sliced green onions
3	tablespoons chopped fresh basil
1	(12-ounce) package broccoli coleslaw
1	(11-ounce) can mandarin oranges in light syrup, drained

1. Place first 8 ingredients in a food processor; process until smooth.

2. Heat oil in a large nonstick skillet over medium-high heat. Sprinkle steak evenly on both sides with pepper and salt. Add steak to pan; cook 4 minutes on each side or until desired degree of doneness. Remove steak from pan, and let stand 5 minutes. Thinly slice steak.

3. Combine cabbage and remaining ingredients in a large bowl. Drizzle slaw mixture with cilantro mixture; toss. Arrange 2 cups slaw mixture on each of 4 plates, and top each serving with 3 ounces beef. **Yield:** 4 servings.

CALORIES 313; FAT 11.8g (sat 4g, mono 5.5g, poly 0.6g); PROTEIN 28.2g; CARB 22.6g; FIBER 5g; CHOL 71mg; IRON 2.8mg; SODIUM 883mg; CALC 105mg

You'll find napa cabbage in various shapes, from round to more elongated. Similar in appearance to romaine lettuce, it is thin and delicate with a mild flavor.

INGREDIENT SPOTLIGHT

Steak Salad with Creamy Ranch Dressing

Steak:
- ½ teaspoon garlic powder
- ½ teaspoon brown sugar
- ½ teaspoon ground red pepper
- ¼ teaspoon salt
- ¼ teaspoon black pepper
- 1 (1-pound) boneless sirloin steak, trimmed (about ½ inch thick)
- Cooking spray

Salad:
- 4 (1-ounce) slices sourdough bread
- 1 garlic clove, halved
- 2 cups grape tomatoes
- 1 cup halved and sliced cucumber
- 1 cup sliced red onion
- 1 (16-ounce) bag classic iceberg salad mix (such as Dole's)
- ½ cup fat-free ranch dressing

1. Heat a nonstick grill pan over medium-high heat.
2. Preheat broiler.
3. To prepare steak, combine first 5 ingredients; rub evenly over both sides of steak. Coat grill pan with cooking spray. Cook steak 4 minutes on each side or until desired degree of doneness. Remove from pan; let stand 5 minutes. Cut steak diagonally across grain into thin slices.
4. While steak stands, prepare salad. Place bread slices on a baking sheet. Broil 2 minutes on each side or until lightly browned. Rub cut sides of garlic halves over bread slices. Cut bread into (¾-inch) cubes. Combine bread cubes, tomatoes, cucumber, onion, and lettuce in a large bowl. Add dressing, tossing gently to coat. Divide salad evenly among 4 plates; top with steak. **Yield:** 4 servings (serving size: 3 cups salad and about 3 ounces meat).

CALORIES 334; FAT 7.5g (sat 2.6g, mono 3.1g, poly 0.6g); PROTEIN 29.2g; CARB 37g; FIBER 4.8g; CHOL 67mg; IRON 3.6mg; SODIUM 733mg; CALC 73mg

Steak Salad with Creamy Ranch Dressing

Roast Beef with Fruit and Mixed Greens

When you stop at your grocer's deli, ask for one thick slice of roast beef that weighs ¾ pound instead of the usual thin slices; then cube the meat when you get home. Or you can substitute leftover lean pork loin, ham, or chicken.

- 1 (10-ounce) bag mixed salad greens
- 1 cup blueberries
- 1 cup seedless red grapes, halved
- 2 medium peaches, halved, pitted, and thinly sliced
- ¾ pound low-sodium deli roast beef (such as Boar's Head), cubed
- ½ cup fat-free balsamic vinaigrette

1. Combine first 5 ingredients in a large bowl. Drizzle with vinaigrette; toss gently to coat. Serve immediately. **Yield:** 4 servings (serving size: 3 cups).

CALORIES 226; FAT 4.4g (sat 1.6g, mono 1.7g, poly 1g); PROTEIN 24.9g; CARB 25.4g; FIBER 3.6g; CHOL 46mg; IRON 3.5mg; SODIUM 541mg; CALC 45mg

 MINUTES

Spinach Salad with Spiced Pork and Ginger Dressing

make it a meal *Crisp flatbread can round out this satisfying salad supper.*

1   (1-pound) pork tenderloin, trimmed
1   tablespoon Sriracha (hot chile sauce, such as Huy Fong)
2   tablespoons brown sugar
1/2 teaspoon garlic powder
1/4 teaspoon salt
Cooking spray
3   cups baby spinach leaves
2   cups thinly sliced Napa cabbage
1   cup red bell pepper strips
1/4 cup low-fat sesame ginger dressing (such as Newman's Own)

1. Cut pork crosswise into $^1/_2$-inch slices; flatten each slice slightly with hand. Combine pork and Sriracha in a bowl, tossing to coat. Add sugar, garlic powder, and salt; toss well.
2. Heat a large nonstick skillet over medium-high heat. Coat pan with cooking spray. Add pork mixture to pan, and cook 3 minutes on each side or until done. Remove from heat; keep warm.
3. Combine spinach, cabbage, and bell pepper in a large bowl. Add sesame ginger dressing; toss well. Arrange $1^1/_2$ cups spinach mixture in each of 4 shallow bowls; top each serving with 3 ounces pork. **Yield:** 4 servings.

CALORIES 202; FAT 4.7g (sat 1.4g, mono 1.8g, poly 0.5g); PROTEIN 25g; CARB 14.7g; FIBER 1.9g; CHOL 74mg; IRON 2.2mg; SODIUM 490mg; CALC 56mg

MINUTES

Warm Spinach Salad with Pork and Pears

make it a meal *A loaf of whole-grain or sesame seed bread completes the dinner. Blue cheese balances the sweetness of the pears and raisins; choose a premium variety such as Maytag for more intensity.*

Cooking spray
1   (1-pound) pork tenderloin, trimmed and cut crosswise into 12 slices
½   teaspoon salt, divided
¼   teaspoon black pepper, divided
3   tablespoons water
3   tablespoons sherry vinegar or red wine vinegar
1   tablespoon extra-virgin olive oil
2   cups thinly sliced Anjou or Bartlett pear (about 2)
¼   cup golden raisins
1   (5-ounce) package baby spinach
2   tablespoons crumbled blue cheese

1. Heat a large nonstick skillet over medium-high heat. Coat pan with cooking spray. Sprinkle pork evenly with ¼ teaspoon salt and ⅛ teaspoon pepper. Add pork to pan; cook 4 minutes on each side or until browned.
2. Combine remaining ¼ teaspoon salt, remaining ⅛ teaspoon pepper, 3 tablespoons water, vinegar, and oil in a small bowl, stirring with a whisk.
3. Combine pear, raisins, and spinach in a large bowl; toss well. Arrange 2 cups spinach mixture on each of 4 plates, and drizzle evenly with vinegar mixture. Top each serving with 3 pork slices and 1½ teaspoons cheese. **Yield:** 4 servings.

CALORIES 296; FAT 10.1g (sat 3g, mono 4.8g, poly 0.8g); PROTEIN 25.5g; CARB 27.4g; FIBER 4.5g; CHOL 68mg; IRON 2.8mg; SODIUM 471mg; CALC 117mg

MINUTES

Asian Chicken Salad

make it a meal *Put this on the table with soft breadsticks and a dessert of vanilla yogurt topped with fresh berries. If you want wine, try chilled sake.*

2   tablespoons seasoned rice vinegar
1   tablespoon low-sodium soy sauce
1   tablespoon dark sesame oil
1   teaspoon bottled ground fresh ginger (such as Spice World)
1   teaspoon honey
6   cups gourmet salad greens
2   cups chopped cooked chicken
1   cup matchstick-cut carrots
1   cup snow peas, trimmed and cut lengthwise into thin strips
2   tablespoons sliced almonds, toasted

1. Combine vinegar, soy sauce, sesame oil, ginger, and honey in a large bowl, stirring well with a whisk. Add salad greens, chicken, carrots, and snow peas; toss gently to coat. Sprinkle with almonds. **Yield:** 4 servings (serving size: 1 ¾ cups).

CALORIES 172; FAT 6g (sat 0.9g, mono 2.7g, poly 2g); PROTEIN 19.6g; CARB 10.9g; FIBER 3.5g; CHOL 38mg; IRON 1.6mg; SODIUM 538mg; CALC 73mg

The distinctively robust and sharp flavor of blue cheese drives people to love it or hate it. Its most distinguishable feature is its white interior, which is streaked with bluish veins. The texture can vary from crumbly to creamy. Blue cheese pairs well with fruits, such as apples, pears, and strawberries, which balance and accentuate its flavor.

INGREDIENT SPOTLIGHT

15 MINUTES

Chicken, Carrot, and Cucumber Salad

make it a meal *Serve this chunky salad with pita wedges or pita chips. Purchase pita chips or make your own by spraying pita wedges with cooking spray, sprinkling them with a little shredded Parmesan cheese, and baking them at 400° for about 10 minutes.*

2	cups chopped cooked chicken breast (about 1 pound)
1¼	cups chopped seeded cucumber
½	cup matchstick-cut carrots
½	cup sliced radishes
⅓	cup chopped green onions
¼	cup light mayonnaise
2	tablespoons chopped fresh cilantro
1	teaspoon bottled minced garlic
¼	teaspoon salt
¼	teaspoon ground cumin
⅛	teaspoon black pepper
4	green leaf lettuce leaves
4	(6-inch) whole wheat pitas, each cut into 8 wedges

1. Combine first 5 ingredients in a large bowl. Combine mayonnaise and next 5 ingredients in a small bowl, stirring with a whisk. Add mayonnaise mixture to chicken mixture; stir until combined.
2. Place 1 lettuce leaf on each of 4 plates; top each leaf with about 1 cup chicken mixture. Place 8 pita wedges on each serving. **Yield:** 4 servings.

CALORIES 382; FAT 10.4g (sat 2.1g, mono 2.7g, poly 4.3g); PROTEIN 40.7g; CARB 31.4g; FIBER 5.1g; CHOL 102mg; IRON 3mg; SODIUM 621mg; CALC 56mg

Basil Chicken Salad

15 MINUTES

Basil Chicken Salad

make it a meal *Spoon the chicken salad onto a bed of fresh spinach, adding two or three slices of fresh tomato on the side.*

3	cups chopped rotisserie chicken breast
½	cup light mayonnaise
¼	cup chopped fresh basil
¼	cup finely chopped pecans
¼	cup shredded fresh Parmesan cheese
1	tablespoon Dijon mustard
¼	teaspoon freshly ground black pepper

1. Combine all ingredients in a large bowl, stirring well to coat. Cover and chill. **Yield:** 6 servings (serving size: ¹/₂ cup).

CALORIES 238; FAT 14g (sat 2.8g, mono 5g, poly 6g); PROTEIN 23.7g; CARB 3.2g; FIBER 0.6g; CHOL 70mg; IRON 1mg; SODIUM 338mg; CALC 67mg

A freshly prepared or prepackaged rotisserie chicken from the grocery is a time-saving ingredient for quick and easy main-dish salads. A 2-pound rotisserie chicken yields about 3 cups of chopped chicken.

MAKE IT FASTER

Chicken and Strawberry Salad

make it a meal *Pair this simple, no-cook meal with toasted buttery baguette slices.*

Dressing:

1	tablespoon sugar
2	tablespoons red wine vinegar
1	tablespoon water
$\frac{1}{8}$	teaspoon salt
$\frac{1}{8}$	teaspoon freshly ground black pepper
2	tablespoons extra-virgin olive oil

Salad:

4	cups torn romaine lettuce
4	cups arugula
2	cups quartered strawberries
$\frac{1}{3}$	cup vertically sliced red onion
12	ounces skinless, boneless rotisserie chicken breast, sliced
2	tablespoons unsalted cashews, halved
$\frac{1}{2}$	cup (2 ounces) crumbled blue cheese

1. To prepare dressing, combine first 5 ingredients in a small bowl. Gradually drizzle in oil, stirring constantly with a whisk.

2. To prepare salad, combine romaine and next 4 ingredients in a bowl; toss gently. Place about 2 cups chicken mixture on each of 4 plates. Top each serving with $1\frac{1}{2}$ teaspoons cashews and 2 tablespoons cheese. Drizzle about 4 teaspoons dressing over each serving. **Yield:** 4 servings.

CALORIES 333; FAT 16.4g (sat 4.9g, mono 8.3g, poly 2.1g); PROTEIN 32g; CARB 14.8g; FIBER 3.5g; CHOL 83mg; IRON 2.5mg; SODIUM 347mg; CALC 156mg

Herbed Greek Chicken Salad

make it a meal *Serve with toasted pita wedges to round out your meal.*

1	teaspoon dried oregano
½	teaspoon garlic powder
¾	teaspoon black pepper, divided
½	teaspoon salt, divided
	Cooking spray
1	pound skinless, boneless chicken breast, cut into 1-inch cubes
5	teaspoons fresh lemon juice, divided
1	cup plain fat-free yogurt
2	teaspoons tahini (sesame-seed paste)
1	teaspoon bottled minced garlic
8	cups chopped romaine lettuce
1	cup peeled chopped English cucumber
1	cup grape tomatoes, halved
6	pitted kalamata olives, halved
¼	cup (1 ounce) crumbled feta cheese

1. Combine oregano, garlic powder, ½ teaspoon pepper, and ¼ teaspoon salt in a bowl. Heat a nonstick skillet over medium-high heat. Coat pan with cooking spray. Add chicken and spice mixture; sauté until chicken is done. Drizzle with 1 tablespoon juice; stir. Remove from pan.

2. Combine remaining 2 teaspoons juice, remaining ¼ teaspoon salt, remaining ¼ teaspoon pepper, yogurt, tahini, and garlic in a small bowl; stir well. Combine lettuce, cucumber, tomatoes, and olives. Place 2 ½ cups lettuce mixture on each of 4 plates. Top each serving with ½ cup chicken mixture and 1 tablespoon cheese. Drizzle each serving with 3 tablespoons yogurt mixture. **Yield:** 4 servings.

CALORIES 243; FAT 7.7g (sat 2.3g, mono 2.9g, poly 1.6g); PROTEIN 29.7g; CARB 13.4g; FIBER 3.5g; CHOL 70mg; IRON 2.5mg; SODIUM 578mg; CALC 216mg

COOKING CLASS: *how to cook orzo*

Orzo, which means "barley" in Italian, is a common addition to sides, soups, and salads. The rice-shaped pasta is available in short plump grains and long thin grains. Eight ounces (or 1¼ cups) of dry orzo yields 2½ cups of cooked orzo in about 6 minutes.

15
MINUTES

Chicken-Orzo Salad with Goat Cheese

make it a meal *Leftover salad is also good the next day for lunch; stir in a handful of arugula to add a fresh touch, if you have extra on hand. Serve with pita wedges.*

1¼	cups uncooked orzo (rice-shaped pasta)
3	cups chopped grilled chicken breast strips (such as Tyson)
1½	cups trimmed arugula
1	cup grape tomatoes, halved
½	cup chopped red bell pepper
¼	cup prechopped red onion
2	tablespoons chopped fresh basil
1	teaspoon chopped fresh oregano
2	tablespoons red wine vinegar
1	tablespoon extra-virgin olive oil
⅛	teaspoon salt
⅛	teaspoon black pepper
6	tablespoons (1½ ounces) crumbled goat cheese

1. Cook pasta according to package directions, omitting salt and fat; drain well.
2. Combine pasta, chicken, and next 6 ingredients in a large bowl; toss well.
3. Combine vinegar, oil, salt, and black pepper in a small bowl, stirring with a whisk. Drizzle vinegar mixture over pasta mixture; toss well to coat. Sprinkle with cheese. **Yield:** 6 servings (serving size: 1⅓ cups salad and 1 tablespoon cheese).

CALORIES 295; FAT 7.7g (sat 2.9g, mono 2.8g, poly 1.1g); PROTEIN 24.4g; CARB 32.1g; FIBER 2g; CHOL 55mg; IRON 2.4mg; SODIUM 788mg; CALC 40mg

15
MINUTES

Chicken Cobb Salad

make it a meal *Bacon, blue cheese, avocado, and chicken are all ingredients in the classic Cobb salad. Serve with a chilled summer soup or sandwich for a light and refreshing meal.*

	Cooking spray
1½	pounds skinless, boneless chicken breast cutlets
¼	teaspoon salt
¼	teaspoon black pepper
8	cups mixed greens
1	cup cherry tomatoes, halved
⅓	cup diced peeled avocado
2	tablespoons sliced green onions
⅓	cup fat-free Italian dressing
2	tablespoons crumbled blue cheese
1	bacon slice, cooked and crumbled

1. Heat a large nonstick skillet over medium-high heat. Coat pan with cooking spray. Sprinkle chicken with salt and pepper. Add chicken to pan; cook 5 minutes on each side or until done. Cut into ½-inch slices.
2. Combine greens, tomatoes, avocado, and onions in a large bowl. Drizzle greens mixture with dressing; toss gently to coat. Arrange about 2 cups greens mixture on each of 4 salad plates. Top each serving with 4 ounces chicken, 1½ teaspoons cheese, and about ½ teaspoon bacon. **Yield:** 4 servings.

CALORIES 263; FAT 8g (sat 2.4g, mono 3.2g, poly 1.4g); PROTEIN 37.9g; CARB 8.9g; FIBER 3.7g; CHOL 99mg; IRON 2.6mg; SODIUM 606mg; CALC 89mg

15 MINUTES

Italian Chicken Salad

Leftover or rotisserie chicken from the deli speeds this fresh dish to the table.

Dressing:
1	tablespoon olive oil
1	tablespoon fresh lemon juice
1	tablespoon red wine vinegar
½	teaspoon bottled minced garlic
½	teaspoon sugar
¼	teaspoon freshly ground black pepper
⅛	teaspoon salt

Salad:
3	cups cubed cooked chicken breast
1	cup finely chopped red bell pepper
2	tablespoons finely chopped fresh parsley
1	teaspoon dried oregano
½	teaspoon dried basil
10	pitted ripe olives, halved
1	(14-ounce) can quartered artichoke hearts, drained

1. To prepare dressing, combine first 7 ingredients in a medium bowl, stirring with a whisk.

2. To prepare salad, combine chicken and remaining ingredients in a large bowl. Pour dressing over salad, and toss gently to combine. **Yield:** 4 servings (serving size: 1¼ cups).

CALORIES 262; FAT 9.4g (sat 1.5g, mono 3.8g, poly 1.2g); PROTEIN 34.6g; CARB 8.3g; FIBER 1.1g; CHOL 89mg; IRON 2.5mg; SODIUM 395mg; CALC 31mg

---

Red and white wine vinegars are two versatile vinegars that work well in just about any dish. Wine vinegars, like wine itself, vary in flavor according to the type of grape from which they're made, where the grapes are grown, and how the vinegar is stored and aged.

INGREDIENT SPOTLIGHT

---

20 MINUTES

Spiced Chicken and Greens with Pomegranate Dressing

Chicken:
	Cooking spray
1	teaspoon chili powder
¼	teaspoon salt
4	(6-ounce) skinless, boneless chicken breast halves

Dressing:
⅓	cup pomegranate juice
3	tablespoons red wine vinegar
2	teaspoons sugar
2	teaspoons canola oil
¼	teaspoon salt
¼	teaspoon crushed red pepper

Salad:
1	(5-ounce) package gourmet salad greens
½	cup thinly sliced red onion
¾	cup orange sections (about 2 medium oranges)
⅓	cup dried cranberries
¼	cup (1 ounce) crumbled Gorgonzola cheese

1. To prepare chicken, heat a large nonstick skillet over medium heat. Coat pan with cooking spray. Sprinkle chili powder and salt over chicken. Add chicken to pan; cook 5 minutes on each side or until done. Remove chicken from pan; let stand 3 minutes. Cut chicken across grain into thin slices; set aside.

2. To prepare dressing, combine juice and next 5 ingredients in a small bowl; stir well with whisk.

3. To prepare salad, place greens on a serving platter; top with onion, orange, cranberries, and chicken slices. Sprinkle evenly with cheese; pour dressing over salad. **Yield:** 4 servings (serving size: 2 cups salad, about 4½ ounces chicken, and 2 tablespoons dressing).

CALORIES 333; FAT 6.7g (sat 2.3g, mono 2.4g, poly 1.2g); PROTEIN 42.2g; CARB 27.1g; FIBER 5.4g; CHOL 105mg; IRON 2mg; SODIUM 527mg; CALC 115mg

Roast Chicken Salad with Peaches, Goat Cheese, and Pecans

The 8-ingredient vinaigrette, made with pantry staples, takes just minutes to make. Use a store-bought rotisserie chicken to save time in the kitchen. Serve with herbed bread.

2½ tablespoons balsamic vinegar
1½ tablespoons extra-virgin olive oil
1½ tablespoons minced shallots
2½ teaspoons fresh lemon juice
2½ teaspoons maple syrup
¾ teaspoon Dijon mustard
¼ teaspoon kosher salt
¼ teaspoon freshly ground black pepper
2 cups shredded skinless, boneless rotisserie chicken breast
2 cups sliced peeled peaches
½ cup vertically sliced red onion
¼ cup chopped pecans, toasted
1 (5-ounce) package gourmet salad greens
2 tablespoons crumbled goat cheese

1. Combine first 8 ingredients, and stir with a whisk.
2. Combine chicken and remaining ingredients except cheese in a large bowl. Add vinegar mixture; toss gently. Sprinkle with cheese. **Yield:** 4 servings (serving size: about 1¾ cups salad and 1½ teaspoons cheese).

CALORIES 285; FAT 14g (sat 2.4g, mono 7.8g, poly 2.8g); PROTEIN 24.6g; CARB 16g; FIBER 2.9g; CHOL 61mg; IRON 1.9mg; SODIUM 203mg; CALC 54mg

Stir-Fried Chicken Salad

¼ cup fat-free, less-sodium chicken broth
2 tablespoons rice wine vinegar
1 tablespoon Thai fish sauce
1 tablespoon low-sodium soy sauce
1 tablespoon bottled chopped garlic
2 teaspoons sugar
1 pound skinless, boneless chicken breast tenders
1 tablespoon peanut oil
4 cups mixed salad greens
¼ cup chopped fresh basil
½ cup thinly sliced red onion
2 tablespoons finely chopped unsalted, dry-roasted peanuts
Lime wedges (optional)

1. Combine first 6 ingredients in a medium bowl. Add chicken to broth mixture, stirring to coat. Let stand 3 minutes.

2. Heat oil in a large nonstick skillet over medium-high heat. Drain chicken, reserving marinade. Add chicken to pan; cook 4 minutes or until done, stirring frequently. Stir in reserved marinade. Reduce heat; cook 1 minute or until slightly thickened. Remove pan from heat.

3. Combine greens and basil in a large bowl. Add chicken mixture, tossing to coat. Place 1¼ cups salad mixture on each of 4 plates. Top each serving with 2 tablespoons onion and 1½ teaspoons peanuts. Serve immediately. Serve with lime wedges, if desired. **Yield:** 4 servings.

CALORIES 214; FAT 7.2g (sat 1.3g, mono 3g, poly 2.2g); PROTEIN 29.1g; CARB 8g; FIBER 2g; CHOL 66mg; IRON 2mg; SODIUM 594mg; CALC 60mg

15 MINUTES

Quick Romaine Salad with Pan-Grilled Chicken

1   pound chicken breast tenders
½   teaspoon kosher salt
¼   teaspoon black pepper, divided
Cooking spray
3   tablespoons reduced-fat mayonnaise
2   tablespoons fresh lemon juice
1   tablespoon water
2   teaspoons extra-virgin olive oil
1   teaspoon capers
1   teaspoon bottled minced garlic
1   teaspoon anchovy paste
1   teaspoon Dijon mustard
2   (10-ounce) packages chopped romaine lettuce

1. Heat a grill pan over medium-high heat. Sprinkle chicken with salt and ⅛ teaspoon pepper. Coat pan with cooking spray. Add chicken to pan; cook 3 minutes on each side or until done. Remove chicken from pan.
2. While chicken cooks, place remaining ⅛ teaspoon black pepper, mayonnaise, and next 7 ingredients in a blender; process until smooth.
3. Cut chicken into ½-inch pieces. Combine chicken and lettuce in a large bowl; drizzle with mayonnaise mixture. Toss to coat. Serve immediately. **Yield:** 4 servings (serving size: about 2½ cups salad and 3 ounces chicken).

CALORIES 203; FAT 6.4g (sat 1.1g, mono 3g, poly 1.6g); PROTEIN 28.2g; CARB 7.8g; FIBER 1.8g; CHOL 67mg; IRON 2.8mg; SODIUM 650mg; CALC 90mg

20 MINUTES

Turkey Taco Salad

1   pound ground turkey breast
2   tablespoons 40%-less-sodium taco seasoning
2   tablespoons water
1   tomato, chopped
1   (15-ounce) can kidney beans, rinsed and drained
1   (15-ounce) can chickpeas (garbanzo beans), rinsed and drained
1   (2¼-ounce) can sliced ripe olives, drained
1   small avocado, peeled and diced
1   cup refrigerated fresh salsa
½   cup reduced-fat sour cream
8   ounces light tortilla chips
1   (10-ounce) package torn romaine lettuce (about 8 cups)
½   cup (2 ounces) preshredded reduced-fat 4-cheese Mexican blend cheese

1. Heat a large nonstick skillet over medium-high heat until hot. Add turkey; cook 7 minutes or until browned, stirring to crumble. Drain, if necessary, and return turkey to pan. Stir in taco seasoning and 2 tablespoons water; cook 1 minute.
2. Combine turkey mixture, tomato, and next 4 ingredients in a large bowl.
3. Combine salsa and sour cream in a small bowl.
4. To serve, place 6 chips on each of 8 plates; top chips evenly with lettuce, turkey mixture, and cheese. Serve with sour cream mixture. **Yield:** 8 servings (serving size: 6 chips, about 1 cup lettuce, ¾ cup turkey mixture, 1 tablespoon cheese, and 3 tablespoons sour cream mixture).

CALORIES 342; FAT 12.2g (sat 3.5g, mono 6g, poly 2.6g); PROTEIN 19.7g; CARB 39.7g; FIBER 6.4g; CHOL 56mg; IRON 2.7mg; SODIUM 612mg; CALC 137mg

INGREDIENT SPOTLIGHT

One anchovy fillet is equivalent to ½ teaspoon anchovy paste. The paste is formed by mixing pounded anchovies with vinegar and spices. Anchovy paste is normally sold in a tube and can be found in your local supermarket. Leftover anchovy paste can be refrigerated for up to one month.

Turkey and Blue Cheese Salad

⅓ cup light ranch dressing
1 tablespoon 1% low-fat milk
1 teaspoon bottled minced garlic
½ teaspoon dried dill
¼ teaspoon salt
1 cup chopped plum tomato
½ cup chopped celery
½ cup chopped green onions
4 ounces roasted turkey, cut into thin strips
2 ounces crumbled blue cheese

1 (8-ounce) bag preshredded lettuce
1 (15½-ounce) can chickpeas (garbanzo beans), rinsed and drained
1 Anaheim chile, sliced into thin rounds

1. Combine first 5 ingredients in a small bowl; set aside.
2. Combine tomato, celery, and remaining ingredients in a large bowl; pour dressing over salad. Toss gently to coat. **Yield:** 4 servings (serving size: about 2 cups).

CALORIES 232; FAT 7.7g (sat 2.8g, mono 1.9g, poly 1.4g); PROTEIN 16.5g; CARB 24.2g; FIBER 5.5g; CHOL 34mg; IRON 2.3mg; SODIUM 774mg; CALC 136mg

Romaine and Turkey Salad with Creamy Avocado Dressing

make it a meal *Served with crisp parmesan toasts, it's a complete meal.*

¼ cup low-fat buttermilk
1 tablespoon light mayonnaise
1 tablespoon fresh lime juice
½ teaspoon salt
⅛ teaspoon ground red pepper
1 garlic clove, peeled
½ ripe peeled avocado, seeded and coarsely mashed
8 (½-ounce) slices diagonally cut French bread (about ½ inch thick)
¼ cup (1 ounce) preshredded Parmesan cheese
4 cups bagged chopped romaine lettuce
2 cups diced roasted turkey breast (about 8 ounces)
½ cup thinly sliced green onions
2 tablespoons chopped fresh cilantro

1. Place first 7 ingredients in a blender; process until smooth, scraping sides. Set aside.
2. Preheat broiler.
3. Arrange bread slices in a single layer on a baking sheet. Sprinkle 1½ teaspoons cheese on each bread slice. Broil bread slices 2 minutes or until lightly browned.
4. Combine lettuce and remaining ingredients in a large bowl. Drizzle buttermilk mixture over lettuce mixture; toss gently to coat. Serve with cheese toasts. **Yield:** 4 servings (serving size: about 1½ cups salad and 2 cheese toasts).

CALORIES 260; FAT 8g (sat 2.4g, mono 3.5g, poly 1g); PROTEIN 24.2g; CARB 22.8g; FIBER 4g; CHOL 53mg; IRON 2.6mg; SODIUM 694mg; CALC 171mg

Romaine and Turkey Salad with Creamy Avocado Dressing

California Crab Wraps

Choosing canned lump crabmeat instead of refrigerated crabmeat from the seafood department is a budget-friendly way to enjoy this meal any night of the week.

1½ cups diced plum tomato (about 3 tomatoes)
½ cup prechopped red onion
½ cup diced avocado (about ½ avocado)
1 tablespoon fresh lime juice
½ teaspoon ground cumin
¼ teaspoon salt
⅛ teaspoon ground black pepper
1¼ cups canned lump crabmeat (such as Chicken of the Sea)
½ cup (4 ounces) ⅓-less-fat cream cheese
¼ cup chopped fresh cilantro
4 (10-inch) whole wheat flour tortillas
4 romaine lettuce leaves, trimmed

1. Combine first 7 ingredients in a small bowl; set aside.
2. Combine crabmeat, cream cheese, and cilantro in a small bowl; spread evenly down center of each tortilla. Place 1 lettuce leaf over crabmeat mixture. Spoon tomato mixture evenly over lettuce, and roll up. **Yield:** 4 servings (serving size: 1 wrap).

CALORIES 312; FAT 11.7g (sat 0.9g, mono 2.7g, poly 1.1g); PROTEIN 18.5g; CARB 44.8g; FIBER 6g; CHOL 58mg; IRON 2.5mg; SODIUM 602mg; CALC 100mg

Mediterranean
Tuna Salad Pitas

Tuscan Tuna Sandwiches

make it a meal *You can serve the sandwiches with baked potato chips.*

¼	cup finely chopped fennel bulb
¼	cup prechopped red onion
¼	cup chopped fresh basil
2	tablespoons drained capers
2	tablespoons fresh lemon juice
2	tablespoons extra-virgin olive oil
¼	teaspoon black pepper
2	(6-ounce) cans solid white tuna in water, drained
1	(4-ounce) jar chopped roasted red bell peppers, drained
8	(1-ounce) slices sourdough bread, toasted

1. Combine chopped fennel, red onion, ¼ cup basil, capers, lemon juice, olive oil, ¼ teaspoon black pepper, tuna, and bell peppers in a bowl, stirring well. Spoon ½ cup tuna mixture on each of 4 bread slices. Top each serving with 1 bread slice. Cut each sandwich in half diagonally. **Yield:** 4 servings (serving size: 1 sandwich).

CALORIES 292; FAT 10g (sat 1.6g, mono 5.6g, poly 1.7g); PROTEIN 25.2g; CARB 24.3g; FIBER 3.3g; CHOL 36mg; IRON 2.4mg; SODIUM 878mg; CALC 85mg

Mediterranean Tuna Salad Pitas

make it a meal *Slice some fresh orange wedges to serve alongside the pitas.*

2	(6-ounce) cans albacore tuna in water, drained and flaked
½	cup bottled roasted red bell peppers, finely chopped
½	(14-ounce) can quartered artichoke hearts, rinsed, drained, and finely chopped
¼	cup finely chopped flat-leaf parsley
¼	cup chopped pitted kalamata olives
2	tablespoons capers
1	tablespoon extra-virgin olive oil
1	tablespoon fresh lemon juice
½	teaspoon freshly ground black pepper
¼	teaspoon salt
4	(6-inch) pitas, cut in half
4	curly leaf lettuce leaves, torn in half

1. Combine first 10 ingredients in a medium bowl, stirring well. Line each pita half with a lettuce leaf. Fill each with about ½ cup tuna salad. **Yield:** 4 servings (serving size: 2 pita halves).

CALORIES 311; FAT 6.7g (sat 0.8g, mono 4.3g, poly 1.5g); PROTEIN 24.1g; CARB 39.2g; FIBER 2.6g; CHOL 27mg; IRON 3.5mg; SODIUM 935mg; CALC 63mg

INGREDIENT SPOTLIGHT

When buying canned tuna, follow these recommendations: A healthy diet includes up to 12 ounces (or approximately two meals) of low-mercury fish per week. Canned light tuna is low in mercury. Canned albacore (or white) tuna contains more mercury than canned light. Consume no more than 6 ounces of canned albacore tuna per week.

Pineapple Chicken Salad Pitas

2 ½ cups chopped cooked chicken breast
(about 1 pound)
½ cup matchstick-cut carrots
⅓ cup sliced almonds, toasted
⅓ cup light mayonnaise
¼ cup finely chopped green onions
¼ cup plain fat-free yogurt
1 tablespoon Worcestershire sauce
½ teaspoon garlic powder
¼ teaspoon salt
¼ teaspoon black pepper
1 (8-ounce) can crushed pineapple in juice,
drained
4 (6-inch) whole wheat pitas, each cut in half
8 romaine lettuce leaves

1. Combine first 11 ingredients in a large
bowl, stirring well. Line each pita half with
1 lettuce leaf; fill each half with ⅓ cup
chicken mixture. **Yield:** 4 servings (serving
size: 2 stuffed pita halves).

CALORIES 471; FAT 15.5g (sat 2.5g, mono 5.4g, poly 6.2g); PROTEIN 36.8g;
CARB 48.8g; FIBER 7.2g; CHOL 82mg; IRON 3.9mg; SODIUM 776mg; CALC 98mg

Southwestern Chicken Wraps

15 MINUTES

Mediterranean Chicken Salad Pitas

make it a meal *Greek yogurt has a thick, rich consistency similar to sour cream. Add honeydew melon and cantaloupe slices on the side.*

1   cup plain whole-milk Greek yogurt (such as Fage Total Classic)
2   tablespoons lemon juice
½   teaspoon ground cumin
¼   teaspoon crushed red pepper
3   cups chopped cooked chicken
1   cup chopped red bell pepper (about 1 large)
½   cup chopped pitted green olives (about 20 small)
½   cup diced red onion
¼   cup chopped fresh cilantro
1   (15-ounce) can no-salt-added chickpeas (garbanzo beans), rinsed and drained
6   (6-inch) whole wheat pitas, cut in half
12 Bibb lettuce leaves
6   (⅛-inch-thick) slices tomato, cut in half

1. Combine first 4 ingredients in a small bowl; set aside. Combine chicken and next 5 ingredients in a large bowl. Add yogurt mixture to chicken mixture; toss gently to coat. Line each pita half with 1 lettuce leaf and 1 tomato piece; add ½ cup chicken mixture to each pita half. **Yield:** 6 servings (serving size: 2 stuffed pita halves).

CALORIES 404; FAT 10.2g (sat 3.8g, mono 4g, poly 1.5g); PROTEIN 33.6g; CARB 46.4g; FIBER 6g; CHOL 66mg; IRON 3.4mg; SODIUM 575mg; CALC 110mg

15 MINUTES

Southwestern Chicken Wraps

You can serve these wraps immediately, or wrap them in parchment paper or plastic wrap and chill them up to 8 hours for a quick and hearty lunch.

2   (6-ounce) packages grilled chicken strips
½   cup refrigerated fresh salsa
2½   cups mixed salad greens
½   cup canned pinto beans, rinsed and drained
½   ripe avocado, diced
5   (8-inch) flour tortillas

1. Combine chicken and salsa; stir. Add greens, beans, and avocado; toss.
2. Spoon 1 cup mixture down center of each tortilla; roll up tortillas. Wrap each tightly in parchment paper. **Yield:** 5 servings (serving size: 1 wrap).

CALORIES 277; FAT 6.5g (sat 1.1g, mono 3.6g, poly 1.7g); PROTEIN 21.9g; CARB 34.4g; FIBER 5.6g; CHOL 44mg; IRON 3.4mg; SODIUM 1,156mg; CALC 132mg

Fresh salsa is a quick and healthy alternative to the bottled salsas that are loaded with sodium. Plus nothing tastes better than fresh. Look for fresh salsa in the produce section of your supermarket.

INGREDIENT SPOTLIGHT

Curried Chicken Salad Sandwiches

BST Sandwiches

make it a meal *We replaced the traditional BLT's lettuce with baby spinach for an updated twist and added nutrients. Serve with baked potato chips.*

- 8 center-cut bacon slices
- 1/3 cup light mayonnaise, divided
- 8 (0.8-ounce) slices light wheat bread, toasted
- 1 cup fresh baby spinach
- 8 (1/4-inch-thick) slices tomato
- 1/8 teaspoon salt
- 1/8 teaspoon black pepper

1. Cook bacon in a large skillet over medium heat until crisp. Drain on paper towels.
2. Spread 2 teaspoons mayonnaise on each bread slice. Divide spinach evenly among 4 bread slices; top with 2 tomato slices and 2 bacon slices. Sprinkle sandwiches evenly with salt and pepper. Top with remaining bread slices, mayonnaise sides down. Cut sandwiches diagonally into halves, if desired. **Yield:** 4 servings (serving size: 1 sandwich).

CALORIES 237; FAT 11.6g (sat 3g, mono 3.7g, poly 4.8g); PROTEIN 10.1g; CARB 25.3g; FIBER 3.2g; CHOL 19mg; IRON 1.9mg; SODIUM 706mg; CALC 42mg

Curried Chicken Salad Sandwiches

If you don't want to make all eight sandwiches at once, simply keep the chicken salad in the refrigerator and assemble the sandwiches as desired.

- 1/2 cup light mayonnaise
- 1/4 cup plain low-fat yogurt
- 1 teaspoon curry powder
- 1 teaspoon lemon juice
- 1/2 teaspoon salt
- 4 cups shredded cooked chicken breast
- 1/2 cup seedless red grapes, halved
- 1/2 cup chopped walnuts, toasted
- 1 (8-ounce) can pineapple tidbits in juice, drained
- 1/3 cup diced red onion
- 16 slices whole wheat double-fiber bread (such as Nature's Own)
- 8 lettuce leaves

1. Combine first 5 ingredients in a large bowl. Add chicken and next 4 ingredients; stir well to combine.
2. Top each of 8 bread slices with 1/2 cup chicken salad. Top each with a lettuce leaf and a bread slice. **Yield:** 8 servings (serving size: 1 sandwich).

CALORIES 342; FAT 13.4g (sat 2.1g, mono 3.1g, poly 8.1g); PROTEIN 29.8g; CARB 34.7g; FIBER 11.1g; CHOL 65mg; IRON 3.5mg; SODIUM 593mg; CALC 43mg

BST Sandwiches

Middle Eastern
Chicken Salad
Wraps

MINUTES

Middle Eastern Chicken Salad Wraps

Salad dressing and roasted garlic hummus combine with lettuce and chicken breast for a no-cook sandwich.

6   cups chopped romaine lettuce
1½   cups chopped cooked chicken breast
½   cup chopped bottled roasted red bell peppers
¼   cup light Caesar dressing (such as Ken's)
½   cup hummus with roasted garlic
4   (10-inch) whole wheat flatbread wraps (such as Toufayan)

1. Combine first 4 ingredients. Spread 2 tablespoons hummus over each wrap; top each wrap with about 2 cups lettuce mixture; roll up. Cut each wrap in half crosswise. **Yield:** 4 servings (serving size: 2 halves).

CALORIES 336; FAT 8.1g (sat 1.1g, mono 2.6g, poly 3.4g); PROTEIN 25.8g; CARB 41.2g; FIBER 10.8g; CHOL 50mg; IRON 3.2mg; SODIUM 591mg; CALC 76mg

Bottled salad dressings are quick convenience products that help speed up your meal preparation. They are speedier than homemade versions.

MAKE IT FASTER

MINUTES

Smoked Turkey Wraps

If you're tired of turkey and mayo on whole wheat, try a turkey wrap. It gets a boost of flavor from mango chutney and cream cheese.

½   cup tub-style fat-free cream cheese, softened
⅓   cup mango chutney
4   (10-inch) flour tortillas
1⅓   cups thinly sliced romaine lettuce
½   pound thinly sliced deli smoked turkey
12   (⅛-inch-thick) slices cucumber
8   (¼-inch-thick) slices tomato, halved
⅓   cup slivered red onion

1. Spread 2 tablespoons cream cheese and about 4 teaspoons chutney over each tortilla, leaving a 1-inch border around edge. Divide lettuce, turkey, cucumber, tomato, and onion evenly among tortillas; roll up. **Yield:** 4 servings (serving size: 1 wrap).

CALORIES 332; FAT 2.5g (sat 0.8g, mono 1.2g, poly 0.5g); PROTEIN 23.8g; CARB 50g; FIBER 5.8g; CHOL 30mg; IRON 1.8mg; SODIUM 1,131mg; CALC 168mg

Smoked Turkey Wrap

Dried Cherry–Toasted Almond Turkey Salad Sandwiches

Dried Cherry–Toasted Almond Turkey Salad Sandwiches

Dried Cherry–Toasted Almond Turkey Salad Sandwiches

make it a meal If you don't have leftover turkey, go to the deli section of your local grocery store and ask for a thick, eight-ounce cut of roasted turkey breast meat. For a quick meal, serve with baked chips.

- ¼ cup slivered almonds (about 1 ounce)
- ¼ cup plain fat-free yogurt
- 3 tablespoons low-fat mayonnaise
- 1 teaspoon bottled ground fresh ginger (such as Spice World)
- ⅛ teaspoon crushed red pepper
- ¾ cup thinly sliced celery
- ¼ cup chopped red onion
- ¼ cup dried cherries
- ¼ cup golden raisins
- 8 ounces roasted turkey breast, chopped
- 4 (6-inch) whole wheat pitas, cut in half

1. Heat a small nonstick skillet over medium-high heat. Add almonds; cook 2 minutes or until toasted, stirring constantly. Remove from heat; set aside.
2. Combine yogurt, mayonnaise, ginger, and pepper in a medium bowl. Add almonds, celery, and next 4 ingredients, stirring well to combine. Spoon ⅓ cup turkey mixture into each pita half. **Yield:** 4 servings (serving size: 2 stuffed pita halves).

CALORIES 398; FAT 8.7g (sat 1.4g, mono 4.1g, poly 2.4g); PROTEIN 25.9g; CARB 56.1g; FIBER 6.9g; CHOL 51mg; IRON 3.5mg; SODIUM 501mg; CALC 93mg

Balsamic Turkey–Goat Cheese Sandwiches

These sandwiches are a great way to use leftover turkey, but rotisserie chicken would make a fine substitute. You can also substitute tub-style light cream cheese for the goat cheese, too.

- ½ (4-ounce) package semisoft goat cheese
- 8 (1.5-ounce) slices sourdough French bread, lightly toasted
- 2½ cups shredded cooked turkey
- 3 tablespoons balsamic vinegar
- 12 large fresh basil leaves
- ⅓ cup sliced English cucumber (about 12 slices)

1. Spread goat cheese evenly over bread slices. Layer turkey evenly over goat cheese on 4 bread slices; drizzle turkey with balsamic vinegar. Top with basil, cucumber, and remaining bread slices, cheese sides down. **Yield:** 4 servings (serving size: 1 sandwich).

CALORIES 400; FAT 6.3g (sat 3.5g, mono 1.6g, poly 1.2g); PROTEIN 33.5g; CARB 50.7g; FIBER 2.2g; CHOL 67mg; IRON 4.5mg; SODIUM 664mg; CALC 92mg

Golden raisins come from the same grape as dark raisins—the Thompson seedless grape—but they're sprayed with sulphur dioxide to prevent darkening and are not dried as long. Raisins add a burst of sweetness to these turkey salad sandwiches.

INGREDIENT SPOTLIGHT

Ham and Turkey Rollups

Thai Beef Rolls

Thai Beef Rolls

make it a meal *These wrap sandwiches take just a few minutes to assemble and make a quick lunch or supper. Serve with rice crackers and sautéed zucchini.*

1½	tablespoons fresh lime juice
1	tablespoon dark sesame oil
1	tablespoon bottled ground fresh ginger (such as Spice World)
1	tablespoon bottled minced garlic
2	teaspoons fish sauce
¾	teaspoon sugar
4	(8-inch) flour tortillas
2	cups torn Boston lettuce
12	ounces thinly sliced deli roast beef
½	cup matchstick-cut carrots
¼	cup chopped fresh mint

1. Combine first 6 ingredients in a small bowl, stirring well with a whisk. Place tortillas on a work surface; brush lightly with 2 teaspoons juice mixture. Arrange ½ cup lettuce on each tortilla; top each with 3 ounces beef. Combine carrots and mint; arrange about 3 tablespoons carrot mixture over each serving. Drizzle each serving with about 1 tablespoon remaining juice mixture; roll up. **Yield:** 4 wraps (serving size: 1 wrap).

CALORIES 294; FAT 9.5g (sat 1.8g, mono 2.8g, poly 2g); PROTEIN 22.5g; CARB 30.3g; FIBER 1.1g; CHOL 47mg; IRON 3.8mg; SODIUM 967mg; CALC 127mg

Ham and Turkey Rollups

Jazz up your sack lunch with this quick and easy rollup. Wrap each rollup tightly in parchment paper to keep it from falling apart. Most deli meats are quite high in sodium, so be sure to use reduced-sodium ham and turkey.

½	cup chopped bottled roasted red bell peppers
1	(4-ounce) tub light garlic-and-herbs spreadable cheese (such as Alouette light)
6	(8-inch) flour tortillas (such as Mission)
3	cups firmly packed fresh baby spinach leaves
6	ounces thinly sliced reduced-sodium ham (such as Boar's Head)
6	ounces thinly sliced reduced-sodium turkey breast (such as Boar's Head)

1. Pat peppers dry with paper towels.
2. Combine peppers and cheese in a small bowl, stirring until blended.
3. Spread cheese mixture evenly over 6 tortillas. Arrange ½ cup spinach on each tortilla. Top each with ham and turkey. Roll up wraps; cut in half. **Yield:** 6 servings (serving size: 2 halves).

CALORIES 193; FAT 5.9g (sat 3.2g, mono 1.3g, poly 1.4g); PROTEIN 17g; CARB 27.1g; FIBER 2.6g; CHOL 54mg; IRON 2.5mg; SODIUM 1,059mg; CALC 53mg

15 MINUTES

Grilled Mozzarella Sandwiches with Spinach and Pesto

make it a meal *We've refined the flavors of the traditional grilled cheese sandwich by using creamy mozzarella, fresh spinach, and a hint of pesto. Pair it with a bowl of ready-made tomato-basil soup.*

2   tablespoons light mayonnaise
2   teaspoons pesto
4   (²/₃-ounce) slices light whole wheat bread
4   (²/₃-ounce) slices part-skim mozzarella cheese
12   baby spinach leaves (about ¼ cup)
Butter-flavored cooking spray

1. Combine mayonnaise and pesto in a small bowl. Spread pesto mixture evenly on 1 side of each bread slice. Top each of 2 bread slices with 1 cheese slice, 6 spinach leaves, 1 cheese slice, and 1 bread slice. Coat both sides of sandwiches with cooking spray.
2. Heat a large nonstick skillet over medium heat; coat pan with cooking spray. Place sandwiches, coated sides down, in pan; cook 3 minutes on each side or until lightly browned and cheese melts. **Yield:** 2 servings (serving size: 1 sandwich).

CALORIES 264; FAT 16.5g (sat 6.3g, mono 6.1g, poly 4.1g); PROTEIN 14.7g; CARB 19g; FIBER 4.4g; CHOL 27mg; IRON 2.5mg; SODIUM 533mg; CALC 367mg

COOKING CLASS: *how to press panini*

Panini are pressed Italian-style sandwiches. If you don't have a panini press simply place a heavy skillet on the sandwiches as they cook. You can even weigh down a lighter skillet with a sack of flour or canned goods.

MINUTES

Panini Margherita

16 (⅛-inch-thick) slices plum tomato (2 large tomatoes)
8   (1-ounce) slices rustic French bread loaf
¼   teaspoon salt
¼   teaspoon freshly ground black pepper
1   cup (4 ounces) shredded part-skim mozzarella cheese
12 fresh basil leaves
8   teaspoons extra-virgin olive oil, divided
Cooking spray

1. Divide tomato slices evenly among 4 bread slices, and sprinkle evenly with salt and pepper. Sprinkle cheese evenly over tomatoes. Arrange basil leaves evenly over cheese; cover with remaining bread slices. Drizzle 1 teaspoon olive oil over top of each sandwich; coat with cooking spray.
2. Place a grill pan or large nonstick skillet over medium-high heat until hot. Place sandwiches, oil sides down, in pan. Drizzle 1 teaspoon oil over top of each sandwich, and coat with cooking spray. Place a piece of foil over sandwiches in pan; place a heavy skillet on top of foil to press sandwiches. Cook 2 minutes or until bottom bread slices are golden brown. Turn sandwiches over; replace foil and heavy skillet. Cook 2 minutes or until bottom bread slices are golden brown. Serve immediately. **Yield:** 4 servings (serving size: 1 sandwich).

CALORIES 325; FAT 16.6g (sat 4.9g, mono 8.6g, poly 3.1g); PROTEIN 12.7g; CARB 32g; FIBER 1.4g; CHOL 15mg; IRON 2.1mg; SODIUM 561mg; CALC 243mg

MINUTES

Portobello Cheeseburgers

Portobello mushrooms are well paired with pungent Gorgonzola cheese. Use crumbled blue cheese to save even more time.

2   teaspoons olive oil
4   (4-inch) portobello mushroom caps
¼   teaspoon salt
¼   teaspoon black pepper
1   tablespoon bottled minced garlic
¼   cup (1 ounce) crumbled Gorgonzola cheese
3   tablespoons reduced-fat mayonnaise
4   (2-ounce) sandwich rolls
2   cups trimmed arugula
½   cup sliced bottled roasted red bell peppers

1. Heat oil in a large nonstick skillet over medium-high heat. Sprinkle mushrooms with salt and pepper. Add mushrooms to pan; sauté 4 minutes or until tender, turning once. Add garlic to pan; sauté 30 seconds. Remove from heat.
2. Combine cheese and mayonnaise, stirring well. Spread about 2 tablespoons mayonnaise mixture over bottom half of each roll; top each serving with ½ cup arugula and 2 tablespoons peppers. Place 1 mushroom on each serving, and top with top halves of rolls. **Yield:** 4 servings (serving size: 1 burger).

CALORIES 278; FAT 9.9g (sat 3g, mono 1.7g, poly 0.4g); PROTEIN 9.3g; CARB 33.7g; FIBER 2.4g; CHOL 6mg; IRON 1.7mg; SODIUM 726mg; CALC 129mg

Succotash Burritos

down center of each tortilla. Top evenly with 1 tablespoon salsa and 1 tablespoon cheese. Fold top and bottom of each tortilla toward center; roll up burrito-style. Garnish with cilantro sprigs, if desired. **Yield:** 5 servings (serving size: 1 burrito).

CALORIES 291; FAT 8g (sat 1.7g, mono 4.7g, poly 1.5g); PROTEIN 13.9g; CARB 43.5g; FIBER 6g; CHOL 0mg; IRON 4.4mg; SODIUM 347mg; CALC 205mg

20 MINUTES

Falafel Pitas

¼ cup plain dry breadcrumbs
¼ cup fresh flat-leaf parsley leaves
2 tablespoons chopped green onions
1 teaspoon ground cumin
½ teaspoon ground coriander
¼ teaspoon salt
1 (15-ounce) can chickpeas, rinsed and drained
1 large egg
1 garlic clove, chopped
Dash of ground red pepper
Cooking spray
¼ cup shredded seeded peeled cucumber
¼ cup plain 2% low-fat Greek yogurt
1 teaspoon fresh lemon juice
⅛ teaspoon salt
2 (6-inch) whole wheat pitas, halved
4 Bibb lettuce leaves
8 (¼-inch-thick) slices tomato

1. Place first 10 ingredients in a food processor. Process until finely chopped. Divide mixture into 4 equal portions; shape each portion into a ½-inch-thick patty. Heat a large nonstick skillet over medium-high heat. Coat pan with cooking spray. Add patties to pan; cook 3 minutes on each side or until lightly browned.
2. Combine cucumber, yogurt, juice, and ⅛ teaspoon salt in a small bowl. Line each pita half with 1 lettuce leaf and 2 tomato slices. Place 1 patty in each pita half. Top each patty with about 1 tablespoon cucumber mixture. **Yield:** 4 servings (serving size: 1 stuffed pita half).

CALORIES 220; FAT 4.4g (sat 0.8g, mono 1.2g, poly 1.5g); PROTEIN 10.4g; CARB 37.2g; FIBER 6.7g; CHOL 54mg; IRON 3.2mg; SODIUM 617mg; CALC 83mg

20 MINUTES

Succotash Burritos

Fresh soybeans (edamame) are high in protein and fiber. They take the place of lima beans in this updated succotash recipe. Look for ready-to-eat, fully cooked edamame in the produce section of your supermarket.

2 teaspoons olive oil
1 (10-ounce) package (about 1¾ cups) refrigerated fully cooked shelled edamame (such as Melissa's)
1½ cups frozen corn, thawed
½ cup chopped red bell pepper
¼ cup chopped red onion
1 garlic clove, minced
½ teaspoon ground cumin
¼ teaspoon salt
¼ teaspoon black pepper
5 (10-inch) spinach- or sun-dried tomato-flavored tortillas, warmed
5 tablespoons salsa
5 tablespoons shredded reduced-fat Monterey Jack cheese
Cilantro sprigs (optional)

1. Heat oil in a large nonstick skillet over medium-high heat. Add edamame and next 4 ingredients. Sauté 5 minutes or until bell pepper and onion are tender. Add cumin, salt, and black pepper.
2. Spoon about ⅔ cup vegetable mixture

Falafel Pitas

 MINUTES

Pan-Seared Shrimp Po' Boys

⅓   cup reduced-fat mayonnaise
2   tablespoons sweet pickle relish
1   tablespoon chopped shallots
1   teaspoon capers, chopped
¼   teaspoon hot pepper sauce (such as Tabasco)
1   pound peeled and deveined large shrimp
1½   teaspoons salt-free Cajun seasoning
2   teaspoons olive oil
4   (2½-ounce) hoagie rolls
½   cup shredded romaine lettuce
8   thin tomato slices
4   thin red onion slices

1. Combine first 5 ingredients in a small bowl. Heat a large nonstick skillet over medium-high heat. Combine shrimp and Cajun seasoning in a bowl; toss well. Add olive oil to pan, and swirl to coat. Add shrimp to pan; cook 2 minutes on each side or until done.

2. Cut each roll in half horizontally. Top bottom half of each roll with 2 tablespoons lettuce, 2 tomato slices, 1 onion slice, and one quarter of shrimp. Spread top half of each roll with about 2 tablespoons mayonnaise mixture; place on top of sandwich. **Yield:** 4 servings (serving size: 1 sandwich).

CALORIES 401; FAT 12.1g (sat 2.8g, mono 4.6g, poly 3.2g); PROTEIN 30.7g; CARB 44.2g; FIBER 2.7g; CHOL 172mg; IRON 4.4mg; SODIUM 944mg; CALC 152mg

make it a meal *Serve a New Orleans classic featuring a homemade five-ingredient tartar sauce made with pantry staples. Carrot and cabbage slaw makes for a crunchy side dish.*

30 MINUTES

Fresh Salmon-Cilantro Burgers

make it a meal *Skip the beef, and serve a Mexican-inspired salmon burger topped with a fresh lime-cilantro mayonnaise sauce. A spinach salad with a sweet, slightly spicy Asian-influenced dressing makes a tasty accompaniment.*

¼ cup reduced-fat mayonnaise
1 tablespoon chopped fresh cilantro
1 tablespoon fresh lime juice
⅛ teaspoon salt
⅛ teaspoon freshly ground black pepper
1 (1-pound) salmon fillet, skinned and cut into 1-inch pieces
¼ cup dry breadcrumbs
2 tablespoons fresh cilantro leaves
2 tablespoons chopped green onions
1 tablespoon chopped seeded jalapeño pepper
2 tablespoons fresh lime juice
½ teaspoon salt
¼ teaspoon freshly ground black pepper
Cooking spray
4 (1½-ounce) hamburger buns with sesame seeds, toasted
12 (¼-inch-thick) slices English cucumber
4 leaf lettuce leaves

1. Combine first 5 ingredients in a small bowl; cover and chill.
2. Place salmon in a food processor; pulse until coarsely chopped. Add breadcrumbs and next 6 ingredients; pulse 4 times or until well blended. Divide salmon mixture into 4 equal portions, shaping each into a ¾-inch-thick patty.
3. Heat a grill pan over medium-high heat. Coat pan with cooking spray. Add patties to pan; cook 2 minutes. Carefully turn patties over; cook 2 minutes or until done.
4. Spread about 1 tablespoon mayonnaise mixture over bottom half of each hamburger bun. Top each serving with 1 salmon patty, 3 cucumber slices, 1 lettuce leaf, and top half of bun. **Yield:** 4 servings (serving size: 1 burger).

CALORIES 341; FAT 11.5g (sat 2g, mono 2.9g, poly 4.9g); PROTEIN 31.6g; CARB 30.9g; FIBER 1.8g; CHOL 66mg; IRON 2.2mg; SODIUM 816mg; CALC 67mg

20 MINUTES

Catfish Sandwiches with Creole Mayonnaise

make it a meal *Fillets work well in these sandwiches. You can substitute tilapia or basa for catfish. Serve with coleslaw and vegetable chips.*

Cooking spray
4 (6-ounce) catfish fillets
1½ teaspoons Cajun seasoning
4 (1½-ounce) hamburger buns
3 tablespoons fat-free mayonnaise
1½ teaspoons minced shallots
1¼ teaspoons whole-grain Dijon mustard
½ teaspoon fresh lemon juice
4 curly leaf lettuce leaves
4 (¼-inch-thick) slices tomato
8 teaspoons sweet pickle relish

1. Heat a grill pan over medium-high heat. Coat pan with cooking spray. Sprinkle fillets evenly with seasoning. Add fillets to pan; cook 4 minutes. Turn over; cook 3 minutes or until fish flakes easily when tested with a fork or until desired degree of doneness.
2. Place buns, cut sides down, in pan; cook 1 minute or until toasted. Remove from pan.
3. Combine mayonnaise, shallots, mustard, and juice, stirring well. Line bottom half of each bun with 1 lettuce leaf; top each serving with 1 fillet and 1 tomato slice. Spoon 2 teaspoons relish on top of each tomato. Spread 1 tablespoon mayonnaise mixture over cut side of each top half of buns; place on top of each sandwich. **Yield:** 4 servings (serving size: 1 sandwich).

CALORIES 319; FAT 11.6g (sat 2.7g, mono 5.1g, poly 2.9g); PROTEIN 24.5g; CARB 28.4g; FIBER 1.3g; CHOL 60mg; IRON 2.3mg; SODIUM 674mg; CALC 76mg

Cornmeal Crusted Tilapia
Sandwiches with Lime Butter

20 MINUTES

Cornmeal Crusted Tilapia Sandwiches with Lime Butter

make it a meal *Plate with grapes and coleslaw for a weeknight supper.*

3   tablespoons yellow cornmeal
1   tablespoon chili powder
1   teaspoon ground cumin
½   teaspoon salt
½   teaspoon ground coriander
⅛   teaspoon ground red pepper
4   (6-ounce) tilapia fillets
Cooking spray
2   tablespoons butter, softened
1   teaspoon grated lime rind
½   teaspoon fresh lime juice
4   (1½-ounce) French bread rolls, toasted
4   (¼-inch-thick) slices tomato
1   cup shredded red leaf lettuce

1. Preheat broiler.
2. Combine first 6 ingredients in a shallow dish. Coat both sides of fish with cooking spray. Dredge fish in cornmeal mixture.
3. Place fish on a broiler pan coated with cooking spray. Broil 10 minutes or until fish flakes easily with a fork or until desired degree of doneness.
4. Combine butter, rind, and juice in a small bowl; stir well.
5. Spread 1½ teaspoons butter mixture over cut side of each of 4 roll tops. Place

1 fillet, 1 tomato slice, and ¼ cup lettuce on each of 4 roll bottoms. Place top halves of rolls on sandwiches. **Yield:** 4 servings (serving size: 1 sandwich).

CALORIES 345; FAT 9.9g (sat 4.6g, mono 2.3g, poly 1g); PROTEIN 39.2g; CARB 26.3g; FIBER 2g; CHOL 100mg; IRON 2.6mg; SODIUM 708mg; CALC 68mg

20 MINUTES

Indian-Spiced Chicken Burgers

make it a meal *Serve these burgers with cucumber spears.*

Patties:
¼   cup presliced green onions
1   tablespoon lemon juice
2   teaspoons garam masala
1   teaspoon bottled ground fresh ginger (such as Spice World)
¼   teaspoon salt
¼   teaspoon ground red pepper
1   pound ground chicken
Cooking spray
Remaining Ingredients:
¼   cup 2% low-fat Greek yogurt
1½   teaspoons chopped fresh mint
⅛   teaspoon salt
¼   cup hot mango chutney
4   (1½-ounce) hamburger buns
1   cup fresh spinach leaves

1. To prepare patties, combine first 7 ingredients in a large bowl. Divide mixture into 4 equal portions, shaping each into a ½-inch-thick patty. Heat a large nonstick skillet over medium-high heat. Coat pan with cooking spray. Add patties to pan; cook 7 minutes on each side or until done.
2. Combine yogurt, mint, and ⅛ teaspoon salt. Spread 1 tablespoon chutney on bottom halves of 4 buns; top each with 1 patty, 1 tablespoon yogurt mixture, ¼ cup spinach, and a bun top. **Yield:** 4 servings (serving size: 1 burger).

CALORIES 364; FAT 14.5g (sat 4.8g, mono 4g, poly 3.8g); PROTEIN 25g; CARB 34.4g; FIBER 1.6g; CHOL 137mg; IRON 3.3mg; SODIUM 766mg; CALC 130mg

Honey Barbecue Chicken Sandwiches

A Southern specialty, this sandwich is often made with chicken or pork that has been cooked slowly over low heat. To deliver a juicy barbecue sandwich with a similar flavor but a faster prep time, we used store-bought rotisserie chicken.

1	(10-ounce) package angel hair coleslaw
1/3	cup light coleslaw dressing
3	cups shredded roasted chicken
6	tablespoons honey barbecue sauce
6	(1.6-ounce) light wheat hamburger buns, toasted

1. Combine coleslaw and dressing in a bowl; toss well. Let stand 10 minutes.

2. Place ¹/₂ cup chicken, ¹/₂ cup coleslaw mixture, and 1 tablespoon barbecue sauce on bottom half of each bun. Top with remaining halves of buns. Serve immediately. **Yield: 6 servings (serving size: 1 sandwich).**

CALORIES 280; FAT 6.8g (sat 1.2g, mono 2.7g, poly 2.8g); PROTEIN 26.9g; CARB 37g; FIBER 5.8g; CHOL 72mg; IRON 2.4mg; SODIUM 610mg; CALC 59mg

Chicken Souvlaki

½   cup (2 ounces) crumbled feta cheese
½   cup plain Greek yogurt
1   tablespoon chopped fresh dill
1   tablespoon extra-virgin olive oil, divided
1¼ teaspoons bottled minced garlic, divided
½   teaspoon dried oregano
2   cups sliced roasted skinless, boneless chicken
    breast
4   (6-inch) pitas, cut in half
1   cup shredded iceberg lettuce
½   cup chopped peeled cucumber
½   cup chopped plum tomato
¼   cup thinly sliced red onion

1. Combine feta cheese, yogurt, dill, 1 teaspoon oil, and ¼ teaspoon garlic in a small bowl, stirring well.
2. Heat remaining 2 teaspoons olive oil in a large skillet over medium-high heat. Add remaining 1 teaspoon garlic and oregano to pan, and sauté 20 seconds. Add chicken, and cook 2 minutes or until thoroughly heated. Place ¼ cup chicken mixture in each pita half, and top with 2 tablespoons yogurt mixture, 2 tablespoons shredded lettuce, 1 tablespoon cucumber, and 1 tablespoon tomato. Divide onion evenly among pitas.
Yield: 4 servings (serving size: 2 stuffed pita halves).

CALORIES 414; FAT 13.7g (sat 6.4g, mono 4.7g, poly 1.4g); PROTEIN 32.3g; CARB 38g; FIBER 2g; CHOL 81mg; IRON 2.8mg; SODIUM 595mg; CALC 187mg

Open-Faced Chicken and Muenster Sandwiches with Apricot-Dijon Spread

4   teaspoons apricot preserves
4   teaspoons Dijon mustard
4   (2-ounce) slices country bread
Cooking spray
1   cup thinly sliced Ambrosia or Fuji apple
     (about ⅓ pound)
¼   cup presliced onion
2½ cups bagged prewashed spinach
2   cups shredded skinless, boneless rotisserie
     chicken breast (about 12 ounces)
4   (1-ounce) slices Muenster cheese

1. Preheat broiler.
2. Combine preserves and mustard in a small bowl; stir with a whisk. Spread 1 side of each bread slice with 2 teaspoons mustard mixture. Place bread slices, mustard mixture side up, on a baking sheet coated with cooking spray.
3. Heat a large skillet over medium-high heat. Coat pan with cooking spray. Add apple and onion to pan; cook 3 minutes or until tender, stirring occasionally. Add spinach; cook 1 minute or until spinach begins to wilt. Layer each of 4 bread slices with ¼ cup spinach mixture, ½ cup chicken, and 1 cheese slice. Place sandwiches on a baking sheet coated with cooking spray; broil 1½ minutes or until cheese is bubbly. Remove from heat, and serve immediately. **Yield:** 4 servings (serving size: 1 sandwich).

CALORIES 440; FAT 13.2g (sat 6.3g, mono 3.8g, poly 1.4g); PROTEIN 38.7g; CARB 40g; FIBER 2.4g; CHOL 100mg; IRON 3.6mg; SODIUM 750mg; CALC 286mg

A panini press is great for making sandwiches quickly. You can find one at most kitchen stores.

SHORTCUT SPOTLIGHT

Grilled Chicken Caesar Panini

Grilled Chicken Caesar Panini

If you don't have a panini press, place these sandwiches in a large nonstick skillet over medium heat. Place a piece of foil over the sandwiches; top with a heavy skillet. Cook 2 to 3 minutes on each side or until the sandwiches are golden and cheese melts.

¼   cup light Caesar dressing
8   (0.5-ounce) slices Italian bread
4   (0.8-ounce) slices reduced-fat provolone
     cheese (such as Alpine Lace)
2   cups shredded cooked chicken breast
1   cup baby arugula or baby spinach
Olive oil–flavored cooking spray

1. Preheat panini press.
2. Spread ½ tablespoon dressing on each bread slice. Top each of 4 bread slices with 1 slice cheese, ½ cup chicken, ¼ cup arugula, and a remaining bread slice. Coat sandwiches with cooking spray; place on panini press, and cook 4 to 5 minutes or until golden brown. **Yield:** 4 servings (serving size: 1 sandwich).

CALORIES 300; FAT 11.2g (sat 3.9g, mono 4g, poly 3.3g); PROTEIN 30.5g; CARB 17.7g; FIBER 0.9g; CHOL 75mg; IRON 1.7mg; SODIUM 546mg; CALC 73mg

COOKING CLASS: *how to freeze pesto*

Thanks to olive oil, pesto retains its bright color when frozen. Just drop a tablespoon of pesto into each section of an ice cube tray, and freeze. Remove the cubes, and transfer them to a heavy-duty zip-top plastic bag. Or skip the ice tray, and spoon the pesto directly into a plastic bag or container to freeze. Let the pesto thaw for a few hours before you use it.

15 MINUTES

Grilled Chicken and Tomato Pesto Baguettes

Work quickly when assembling this sandwich so that the grilled chicken and bell pepper retain enough heat to melt the cheese.

1   (8.5-ounce) thin whole wheat baguette
2   (8-ounce) skinless, boneless chicken breast halves
¼   teaspoon salt
⅛   teaspoon black pepper
1   red bell pepper, seeded and quartered
Cooking spray
¼   cup sun-dried tomato pesto (such as Classico)
4   curly leaf lettuce leaves
4   (0.7-ounce) slices low-fat Swiss cheese, cut in half lengthwise

1. Prepare grill.
2. Cut baguette in half lengthwise. Hollow out top half of baguette, leaving a ¹/₂-inch border; reserve torn bread for another use. Set aside.
3. Place chicken breast halves between 2 large sheets of heavy-duty plastic wrap; pound to ¹/₂-inch thickness using a meat mallet or small heavy skillet. Sprinkle chicken with salt and pepper.
4. Flatten bell pepper quarters with hands. Coat chicken breasts and bell pepper quarters with cooking spray; place on grill rack. Cover and grill 8 minutes or until chicken is done and bell peppers are tender, turning once. Place cut sides of baguette halves on grill during last 2 minutes of grilling to lightly toast. Cut each chicken breast in half crosswise.
5. Spread both cut halves of baguette with pesto. Top bottom half with lettuce leaves, chicken breast halves, bell pepper quarters, and cheese slices. Place top half of baguette on top of cheese. Cut crosswise into 4 equal portions. **Yield:** 4 servings (serving size: ¹/₄ of baguette).

CALORIES 335; FAT 4.2g (sat 1.1g, mono 1.7g, poly 1.3g); PROTEIN 37.1g; CARB 33.1g; FIBER 2g; CHOL 71mg; IRON 2.8mg; SODIUM 880mg; CALC 160mg

Mediterranean Turkey Burgers

5 minutes or until both sides are browned, turning once.

3. Place arugula in a bowl. Drizzle juice over arugula; toss gently. Remove top bread half from sandwich. Arrange arugula mixture over chicken. Replace top bread half. Cut sandwich into 4 equal portions. **Yield:** 4 servings (serving size: $^1/_4$ sandwich).

CALORIES 381; FAT 12.7g (sat 6.1g, mono 4.7g, poly 1g); PROTEIN 24.7g; CARB 42.6g; FIBER 1.2g; CHOL 70mg; IRON 2.6mg; SODIUM 591mg; CALC 71mg

20
MINUTES

Mediterranean Turkey Burgers

make it a meal *Serve a light-and-fresh turkey burger flavored with pesto and feta cheese. Prepare a spicy and creamy tzatziki sauce to spread on the burgers or to serve on the side for dipping.*

$^1/_2$ cup panko (Japanese breadcrumbs)
$^1/_4$ cup (1 ounce) crumbled feta cheese
1 tablespoon minced red onion
2 tablespoons commercial pesto
$^1/_4$ teaspoon salt
$^1/_4$ teaspoon freshly ground black pepper
1 pound ground turkey breast
1 garlic clove, minced
Cooking spray
2 cups arugula
2 (6-inch) whole wheat pitas, toasted and halved

1. Combine first 8 ingredients in a bowl; mix until combined. Divide panko mixture into 4 portions, shaping each into a $^1/_2$-inch-thick oval patty.
2. Heat a nonstick grill pan over medium-high heat. Coat pan with cooking spray. Add patties to pan; cook 6 minutes on each side or until done. Place 1 patty and $^1/_2$ cup arugula in each pita half. **Yield:** 4 servings (serving size: 1 stuffed pita half).

CALORIES 303; FAT 8.8g (sat 2.9g, mono 4.1g, poly 0.8g); PROTEIN 33g; CARB 24.3g; FIBER 3g; CHOL 56mg; IRON 1.9mg; SODIUM 595mg; CALC 101mg

15
MINUTES

Chicken Panini with Fig Jam

Ciabatta is a long, flat Italian bread loaf. Serve with pickle spears.

$^1/_4$ cup fig jam
1 (8-ounce) ciabatta, cut lengthwise
$^1/_4$ cup crumbled blue cheese
2 tablespoons butter, softened
8 ounces sliced cooked chicken breast
$^1/_8$ teaspoon freshly ground black pepper
2 cups arugula leaves
1 teaspoon fresh lemon juice

1. Spread jam over cut side of top half of bread. Combine cheese and butter in a bowl, stirring until smooth. Spread cheese mixture over cut side of bottom half of bread. Arrange chicken evenly over cheese mixture; sprinkle with pepper. Place top half of bread, jam side down, over chicken.
2. Heat a large nonstick skillet over medium heat, and add sandwich to pan. Place a heavy cast-iron skillet on sandwich; cook

30 MINUTES

Open-Faced Turkey Patty Melt

make it a meal *The traditional patty melt gets a makeover with ground turkey, but substitute ground chicken or ground sirloin, if you prefer. Pair sandwiches with vegetable chips.*

1	teaspoon olive oil
1	cup vertically sliced Vidalia or other sweet onion
¼	cup part-skim ricotta cheese
1½	teaspoons Worcestershire sauce
½	teaspoon black pepper
1	pound ground turkey breast
1	large egg white

Cooking spray

4	(1-ounce) slices reduced-fat Swiss cheese
4	slices light rye bread
¼	cup country-style Dijon mustard

1. Heat oil in a large nonstick skillet over medium heat. Add onion to pan. Cook 5 minutes or until lightly browned; stir occasionally. Transfer onion to a bowl.
2. Preheat broiler.
3. Combine cheese and next 4 ingredients. Divide turkey mixture into 4 equal portions, shaping each into a ¹/₂-inch-thick patty. Return pan to medium heat. Coat pan with cooking spray. Add patties to pan; cook 4 minutes or until brown. Turn patties over; cook 1 minute. Top each patty with 1 cheese slice; cook 3 minutes or until cheese melts and patties are done.
4. Place bread slices in a single layer on a baking sheet; broil 2 minutes or until toasted. Spread 1 tablespoon mustard on each bread slice; top each serving with 1 patty. Divide onion mixture evenly among sandwiches. **Yield:** 4 servings (serving size: 1 sandwich).

CALORIES 348; FAT 9g (sat 4g, mono 2.2g, poly 2.6g); PROTEIN 43.4g; CARB 22.4g; FIBER 1.5g; CHOL 50mg; IRON 2.1mg; SODIUM 848mg; CALC 325mg

20 MINUTES

Feta-Stuffed Turkey Burgers

¼	cup finely chopped red onion
1	teaspoon dried oregano
1	teaspoon grated lemon rind
½	teaspoon salt
¼	teaspoon freshly ground black pepper
1	pound ground turkey
6	tablespoons (1½ ounces) crumbled feta cheese

Cooking spray

¼	cup grated English cucumber
¼	cup plain fat-free yogurt
1	tablespoon chopped fresh mint
4	(¼-inch-thick) slices tomato
4	green leaf lettuce leaves
4	(2-ounce) Kaiser rolls or hamburger buns

1. Combine first 6 ingredients. Divide mixture into 4 portions. Indent center of each portion; place 1¹/₂ tablespoons feta into each. Fold turkey mixture around cheese; shape each portion into a ¹/₂-inch-thick patty.
2. Heat grill pan over medium-high heat. Coat pan with cooking spray. Add patties; cook 5 minutes on each side.
3. Combine cucumber, yogurt, and mint in a small bowl. Arrange 1 turkey patty, 1 tomato slice, 1 lettuce leaf, and 2 tablespoons yogurt mixture on bottom half of each roll. Top with top halves of rolls. **Yield:** 4 servings.

CALORIES 386; FAT 13.7g (sat 4.5g, mono 4.3g, poly 3g); PROTEIN 30.2g; CARB 34g; FIBER 2.3g; CHOL 109mg; IRON 3.9mg; SODIUM 897mg; CALC 198mg;

INGREDIENT SPOTLIGHT

Oregano has an aromatic, warm flavor. It's commonly used in Greek and Italian cooking. Although fresh is best, dried oregano is handy, especially when it comes to convenience and last-minute meal preparation.

Feta-Stuffed
Turkey Burgers

20 MINUTES

Tex-Mex Chipotle Sloppy Joes

make it a meal *Make a quick black bean and corn salad to serve with these sandwiches. The turkey can also be served over rice or as a taco or enchilada filling.*

1	teaspoon olive oil
½	cup prechopped onion
1	tablespoon bottled minced garlic
2	teaspoons minced seeded jalapeño pepper
1	teaspoon sugar
1	teaspoon ground cumin
1	teaspoon chili powder
½	teaspoon ground coriander
¼	teaspoon ground chipotle chile powder
1	pound ground turkey breast
1½	cups bottled mild salsa
1	tablespoon chopped fresh cilantro
4	(2½-ounce) Kaiser rolls, cut in half horizontally

1. Heat oil in a large nonstick skillet over medium-high heat. Add onion, garlic, and jalapeño; sauté 2 minutes or until soft. Add sugar and next 5 ingredients; cook 5 minutes or until turkey is browned, stirring to crumble. Stir in salsa; cook 4 minutes or until slightly thick. Stir in cilantro. Spread about ¾ cup turkey mixture on bottom half of each roll, and cover with top half of each roll. **Yield:** 4 servings (serving size: 1 sandwich).

CALORIES 397; FAT 5.4g (sat 0.9g, mono 1.9g, poly 1.6g); PROTEIN 35.4g; CARB 44.8g; FIBER 2.5g; CHOL 70mg; IRON 4.1mg; SODIUM 870mg; CALC 92mg

15 MINUTES

Turkey Reuben Sandwiches

make it a meal *Smoked turkey stands in for corned beef in this lightened variation of a deli favorite. Serve with a pickle wedge and chips.*

2	tablespoons Dijon mustard
8	slices rye bread
4	(1-ounce) slices reduced-fat, reduced-sodium Swiss cheese (such as Alpine Lace)
8	ounces smoked turkey, thinly sliced
⅔	cup sauerkraut, drained and rinsed
¼	cup fat-free Thousand Island dressing
1	tablespoon canola oil, divided

1. Spread about ¾ teaspoon mustard over each bread slice. Place 1 cheese slice on each of 4 bread slices. Divide turkey evenly over cheese. Top each serving with 2½ tablespoons sauerkraut and 1 tablespoon dressing. Top each serving with 1 bread slice, mustard sides down.
2. Heat 1½ teaspoons canola oil in a large nonstick skillet over medium-high heat. Add 2 sandwiches to pan; top with another heavy skillet. Cook 3 minutes on each side or until golden; remove sandwiches from pan, and keep warm. Repeat procedure with remaining oil and sandwiches. **Yield:** 4 servings (serving size: 1 sandwich).

CALORIES 255; FAT 10.7g (sat 4.8g, mono 3.9g, poly 1.5g); PROTEIN 19.6g; CARB 18.9g; FIBER 3.4g; CHOL 44mg; IRON 0.7mg; SODIUM 865mg; CALC 311mg

Mustards are an excellent low-calorie, low-saturated fat option for adding tons of flavor to sandwiches. Dijon is a great choice because it has only has 15 calories per tablespoon, no fat, and about 360 milligrams of sodium.

INGREDIENT SPOTLIGHT

20 MINUTES

Grilled Sausage, Onion, and Pepper Sandwiches

The balsamic vinegar adds a sweetness that pairs nicely with Italian spices in the sausage. This recipe calls for a lot of onions; be sure to stir them frequently in the pan so they cook evenly. The filling for the sandwich is also good over egg noodles.

Cooking spray
4   cups thinly sliced Oso Sweet or other sweet onion
4   (4-ounce) turkey Italian sausage links, halved lengthwise
3   tablespoons balsamic vinegar
1   (7-ounce) bottle roasted red bell peppers, drained and thinly sliced
¼   teaspoon black pepper
1   (8-ounce) French bread baguette, halved lengthwise

1. Heat a large grill pan over medium-high heat. Coat pan with cooking spray. Add onion and sausage; cook 1 minute. Sprinkle with vinegar; cook 14 minutes or until sausage is done, turning occasionally. Add bell peppers; cook 1 minute. Sprinkle with black pepper. Arrange sausage mixture evenly over bottom half of bread; top with top half. Cut into 5 sandwiches. **Yield:** 5 servings (serving size: 1 sandwich).

CALORIES 388; FAT 11.4g (sat 3.2g, mono 4.5g, poly 3.3g); PROTEIN 23.4g; CARB 48.2g; FIBER 6.1g; CHOL 76mg; IRON 3.3mg; SODIUM 900mg; CALC 121mg

Grilled Turkey and Ham Sandwiches

15 MINUTES

Grilled Turkey and Ham Sandwiches

make it a meal *Enjoy a grilled sandwich with carrot sticks and tomato soup.*

1   tablespoon light mayonnaise
1   teaspoon Dijon mustard
8   (1-ounce) slices country white bread
4   (1-ounce) slices deli, lower-salt turkey breast
4   (½-ounce) slices deli, lower-salt ham
4   (½-ounce) slices reduced-fat cheddar cheese
8   (¼-inch-thick) slices tomato
Cooking spray

1. Combine mayonnaise and mustard in a small bowl. Spread about 1 teaspoon mayonnaise mixture over 1 side of each of 4 bread slices. Top each slice with 1 turkey slice, 1 ham slice, 1 cheese slice, and 2 tomato slices. Top with remaining bread slices.
2. Heat a large nonstick skillet over medium heat. Coat pan with cooking spray. Add sandwiches to pan; cook 4 minutes or until lightly browned. Turn sandwiches over; cook 2 minutes or until cheese melts. **Yield:** 4 sandwiches (serving size: 1 sandwich).

CALORIES 237; FAT 5.8g (sat 1.8g, mono 0.9g, poly 0.9g); PROTEIN 18.4g; CARB 29.1g; FIBER 0.4g; CHOL 28mg; IRON 1.1mg; SODIUM 781mg; CALC 166mg

15 MINUTES

Quick Pork Picadillo Sandwiches

make it a meal *Round out the meal with a side of sweet potato chips, or eat it with rice and beans like they do in Cuba.*

1½	cups chopped onion (about 1 medium)
1	teaspoon bottled minced garlic
1	pound lean ground pork
½	cup golden raisins
1	tablespoon chili powder
2	tablespoons red wine vinegar
1	teaspoon pumpkin pie spice
½	teaspoon salt
1	(28-ounce) can diced tomatoes, drained
¼	cup sliced pimiento-stuffed green olives
8	(1½-ounce) whole wheat hamburger buns

1. Cook onion, garlic, and pork in a large nonstick skillet over medium-high heat 5 minutes or until browned, stirring to crumble. Drain and return mixture to pan. Stir in raisins and next 5 ingredients. Reduce heat, and cook 5 minutes, stirring occasionally. Stir in olives. Spread about ²/₃ cup picadillo mixture on bottom half of each bun; cover with top half of bun. **Yield:** 8 servings (serving size: 1 sandwich).

CALORIES 289; FAT 9.2g (sat 2.5g, mono 4.2g, poly 1.9g); PROTEIN 15.8g; CARB 37.7g; FIBER 3.3g; CHOL 43mg; IRON 1.6mg; SODIUM 754mg; CALC 64mg

Picadillo, a Cuban favorite, includes many spices that give it its authentic flavor. Here, we've used a combination of pumpkin pie spice and chili powder to make short work of the usual long list of spices that go into traditional picadillo.

MAKE IT FASTER

Mozzarella, Ham, and Basil Panini

15 MINUTES

Pulled-Pork Sandwiches

These sandwiches are quick enough for lunch, but filling enough for dinner. With the help of a store-bought pork au jus, these fuss-free sandwiches can be ready in less than 15 minutes.

1   (17-ounce) package precooked pork roast au jus
2½ cups preshredded cabbage
½   cup light sweet Vidalia onion dressing (such as Ken's Steak House)
¾   teaspoon ground cumin
6   (1.6-ounce) whole wheat hamburger buns
Dill pickle slices (optional)

1. Heat pork according to package directions.
2. Combine cabbage and dressing; set aside.
3. Transfer pork to a medium bowl, reserving ¼ cup juices. Remove and discard any fat from pork. Shred pork with 2 forks. Stir in reserved juices and cumin. Spoon ⅓ cup pork onto bottom half of each bun; spoon ¼ cup slaw mixture over pork. Top with pickle slices, if desired. Cover with top halves of buns. **Yield:** 6 servings (serving size: 1 sandwich).

CALORIES 284; FAT 9.4g (sat 2.3g, mono 4.3g, poly 2.6g); PROTEIN 20.8g; CARB 31.8g; FIBER 4g; CHOL 49mg; IRON 1.4mg; SODIUM 650mg; CALC 75mg

Pulled-Pork Sandwiches

15 MINUTES

Mozzarella, Ham, and Basil Panini

make it a meal *Serve these simple pressed sandwiches with a pickle and some vegetable chips.*

1   (16-ounce) loaf ciabatta, cut in half horizontally
4   teaspoons Dijon mustard
4   teaspoons balsamic vinegar
1⅓ cups (8 ounces) thinly sliced fresh mozzarella cheese
12 fresh basil leaves
8   ounces sliced 33%-less-sodium cooked deli ham (such as Healthy Choice)
2   sweetened hot cherry peppers, sliced
1   large plum tomato, thinly sliced
Cooking spray

1. Brush cut side of the bottom bread half with mustard; brush cut side of top half with vinegar. Top bottom half with mozzarella, basil, ham, peppers, and tomato. Top with remaining bread half.
2. Heat a large nonstick skillet over medium heat. Coat pan with cooking spray. Add sandwich to pan; top with another heavy skillet. Cook 3 minutes on each side or until golden. Cut sandwich into 6 wedges. **Yield:** 6 servings (serving size: 1 wedge).

CALORIES 371; FAT 12.5g (sat 6.1g, mono 5g, poly 0.6g); PROTEIN 20.2g; CARB 44.9g; FIBER 1.8g; CHOL 46mg; IRON 3mg; SODIUM 976mg; CALC 220mg

Prosciutto, Mozzarella, and Arugula Panini

4	teaspoons balsamic vinegar
2	teaspoons extra-virgin olive oil
1/4	teaspoon black pepper
1	garlic clove, minced
1	(7-ounce) loaf ciabatta, cut in half horizontally
16	very thin slices prosciutto (about 4 ounces)
4	(3/4-ounce) slices part-skim mozzarella cheese
8	(1/4-inch-thick) slices tomato (2 medium tomatoes)
2	cups lightly packed trimmed arugula or spinach
	Olive oil–flavored cooking spray

1. Combine first 4 ingredients in a small bowl; stir well with a whisk.
2. Brush cut sides of bread with vinaigrette. Arrange prosciutto and next 3 ingredients over bottom half of bread; replace top half of bread. Cut loaf in half crosswise, and coat with cooking spray.
3. Heat a large grill pan or nonstick skillet over medium heat. Add sandwich halves to pan. Place a heavy skillet on top of sandwiches to weigh them down. Cook 3 minutes on each side or until bread is toasted and cheese melts. Cut each sandwich half in half again to form 4 equal portions. Serve immediately. **Yield:** 4 servings (serving size: 1/4 of loaf).

CALORIES 289; FAT 11.5g (sat 4.2g, mono 6.2g, poly 1g); PROTEIN 16.6g; CARB 30.2g; FIBER 1.1g; CHOL 28mg; IRON 2.2mg; SODIUM 883mg; CALC 177mg

Domestic prosciutto is fine for flavoring sauces, soups, and stews, but when you're really spotlighting the ham, go for prosciutto di Parma. In Italy, it's considered the ultimate indulgence.

INGREDIENT SPOTLIGHT

Cheddar Burgers with
Red Onion Jam

20

Asian Beef Lettuce Wraps

1	pound 93% lean ground beef
¼	cup matchstick-cut carrots
2	tablespoons minced peeled fresh ginger
¼	cup low-sodium soy sauce
1	tablespoon rice vinegar
¼	teaspoon dark sesame oil
⅛	teaspoon crushed red pepper
½	cup thinly sliced green onions
¼	cup chopped fresh cilantro
2	tablespoons chopped fresh mint
8	iceberg lettuce leaves
1	cup thinly sliced cucumber

Lime wedges

1. Heat a large nonstick skillet over medium-high heat until hot. Add beef, carrots, and ginger; sauté 6 minutes or until beef is browned, stirring to crumble beef. Drain, if necessary, and return beef mixture to pan. Stir in soy sauce and next 3 ingredients; cook 1 minute.
2. Remove beef mixture from heat; stir in green onions, cilantro, and mint. Spoon beef filling evenly into center of each lettuce leaf; top evenly with sliced cucumber. Serve with lime wedges. **Yield:** 4 servings (serving size: 2 wraps).

CALORIES 158; FAT 5.5g (sat 2.1g, mono 2.4g, poly 0.8g); PROTEIN 23.7g; CARB 5g; FIBER 1.3g; CHOL 60mg; IRON 2.6mg; SODIUM 606mg; CALC 25mg

30

Cheddar Burgers with Red Onion Jam

make it a meal *A quick five-ingredient sauce tops cheesy homemade burgers to make an easy, delicious dinner in no time. Serve with baked chips and blue cheese dip. For heightened flavor, add ¼ teaspoon black pepper to the beef.*

Jam:

1	teaspoon olive oil
4	cups vertically sliced red onion
4	teaspoons sugar
4	teaspoons red wine vinegar
¾	teaspoon chopped fresh thyme

Burgers:

¾	teaspoon chopped fresh oregano
½	teaspoon salt
¼	teaspoon garlic powder
1	pound extra-lean ground round

Cooking spray

4	(½-ounce) slices white cheddar cheese
4	(1½-ounce) hamburger buns, toasted
4	teaspoons canola mayonnaise

1. Prepare grill to medium-high heat.
2. To prepare jam, heat a large nonstick skillet over medium-high heat. Add oil to pan; swirl to coat. Add onion; sauté 5 minutes. Reduce heat to medium-low; stir in sugar, vinegar, and thyme. Cover and cook 10 minutes or until onion is very tender. Remove from heat.
3. To prepare burgers, combine oregano, salt, garlic powder, and beef. Divide mixture into 4 equal portions, shaping each into a ½-inch-thick patty. Place on grill rack coated with cooking spray; cook 2 minutes. Turn patties over. Place 1 cheese slice on each patty; cook 2 minutes or until done.
4. Spread cut sides of each bun with ½ teaspoon mayonnaise. Place 1 patty on bottom half of each bun; top each with ¼ cup onion jam and bun top. **Yield:** 4 servings (serving size: 1 burger).

CALORIES 395; FAT 13.9g (sat 5.7g, mono 5.2g, poly 1.6g); PROTEIN 33.8g; CARB 36.1g; FIBER 3g; CHOL 75mg; IRON 3.3mg; SODIUM 696mg; CALC 190mg

20 MINUTES

Smoky Chili Joes

Cooking spray
½ pound extra-lean ground beef
½ cup prechopped onion
1 teaspoon bottled minced garlic
1 teaspoon ground cumin
½ teaspoon chili powder
⅛ teaspoon chipotle chile powder
¼ cup ketchup
1 (15-ounce) can red kidney beans, rinsed and drained
1 (14.5-ounce) can diced tomatoes with green pepper and onions, undrained
6 (1½-ounce) hamburger buns
6 tablespoons shredded sharp cheddar cheese
12 sandwich-cut bread-and-butter pickles

1. Heat a large nonstick skillet over medium-high heat. Coat pan with cooking spray. Add beef to pan; cook 4 minutes or until browned, stirring to crumble. Add onion and garlic to pan; cook 2 minutes, stirring frequently. Add cumin, chili powder, and chipotle chile powder, and cook 30 seconds. Stir in ketchup, beans, and tomatoes; cook 6 minutes or until slightly thickened. Spoon about ⅔ cup beef mixture over 6 bottom bun halves, and top each with 1 tablespoon cheese and 2 pickles. Top with remaining bun halves. **Yield:** 6 servings (serving size: 1 sandwich).

CALORIES 334; FAT 8.1g (sat 3.1g, mono 2g, poly 1g); PROTEIN 22.2g; CARB 49.6g; FIBER 8.1g; CHOL 21mg; IRON 2.7mg; SODIUM 866mg; CALC 132mg

Chipotle chile peppers in adobo sauce are smoked jalapeños canned in a sauce of tomatoes, onions, garlic, spices, and vinegar. Taking a cue from Mexican cooks, we often reach for these to add complex, smoky flavor to a dish.

INGREDIENT SPOTLIGHT

20 MINUTES

Chipotle Barbecue Burgers with Slaw

make it a meal *The cool sour cream dressing in the slaw balances the spiciness of chiles in the burger. Toast the buns while the patties cook. Serve with baked sweet potato chips.*

½ cup dry breadcrumbs
2 tablespoons barbecue sauce
1 tablespoon chopped chipotle chiles, canned in adobo sauce
1 teaspoon bottled minced garlic
1 pound lean ground beef
1 large egg
Cooking spray
2 cups cabbage-and-carrot coleslaw
1 tablespoon reduced-fat mayonnaise
1 tablespoon reduced-fat sour cream
1 teaspoon sugar
1 teaspoon cider vinegar
⅛ teaspoon salt
⅛ teaspoon black pepper
4 (1½-ounce) hamburger buns

1. Combine first 6 ingredients. Divide mixture into 4 equal portions, shaping each into a ½-inch-thick patty.
2. Heat a large nonstick skillet over medium-high heat. Coat pan with cooking spray. Add patties to pan; cook 4 minutes on each side or until a meat thermometer registers 160°.
3. Combine coleslaw and next 6 ingredients in a large bowl; toss well. Place 1 patty on bottom half of each bun; top each serving with ½ cup coleslaw mixture and top half of bun. **Yield:** 4 servings (serving size: 1 burger).

CALORIES 358; FAT 9.1g (sat 3g, mono 2.7g, poly 1.9g); PROTEIN 32.1g; CARB 36.3g; FIBER 2.6g; CHOL 115mg; IRON 4.3mg; SODIUM 609mg; CALC 112mg

20 MINUTES

Onion-Smothered Italian Burgers

1   teaspoon olive oil
2   cups thinly sliced Vidalia or other
    sweet onion
2   teaspoons sugar
¼   teaspoon salt
⅛   teaspoon black pepper
1   tablespoon balsamic vinegar
3   tablespoons preshredded fresh Parmesan
    cheese
2   tablespoons tomato paste
1   teaspoon dried oregano
½   teaspoon garlic powder
¼   teaspoon dried basil
1   pound ground beef, extra lean
Cooking spray
4   (1½-ounce) hamburger buns

1. Heat oil in a large nonstick skillet over medium-high heat. Add onion, sugar, salt, and pepper to pan. Cook 6 minutes or until lightly browned, stirring occasionally. Add vinegar to pan; cook 30 seconds, stirring constantly.

2. Combine cheese and next 5 ingredients in a medium bowl; shape meat mixture into 4 (3-inch) patties. Heat a grill pan over medium-high heat. Coat pan with cooking spray. Add patties to pan. Cook 5 minutes on each side or until desired degree of doneness. Place 1 patty on bottom half of each bun; top each patty with ¼ cup onion mixture and top half of each bun. **Yield:** 4 servings (serving size: 1 burger).

CALORIES 330; FAT 8.9g (sat 3g, mono 3.7g, poly 1.5g); PROTEIN 28.9g; CARB 33.7g; FIBER 2.9g; CHOL 65mg; IRON 4mg; SODIUM 541mg; CALC 142mg

make it a meal *Serve corn on the cob as a quick and easy side dish and low-fat strawberry ice cream for dessert.*

30 MINUTES

Chipotle Sloppy Joes

make it a meal *Add Mexican-inspired spice to this traditional family favorite. Plate with pickle chips and a simple slaw.*

Cooking spray
2½ cups presliced Vidalia or other sweet onion
1 (7-ounce) can chipotle chiles in adobo sauce
1 pound ground sirloin
½ cup prechopped green bell pepper
2 tablespoons tomato paste
1 teaspoon kosher salt
½ teaspoon ground cumin
1 (8-ounce) can no-salt-added tomato sauce
5 (1½-ounce) hamburger buns, toasted

1. Heat a small nonstick skillet over medium-high heat. Coat pan with cooking spray. Add onion to pan; cover and cook 8 minutes or until golden brown, stirring frequently. Remove from heat; set aside.
2. Remove 1 teaspoon adobo sauce from can; set aside. Remove 1 chipotle chile from can; chop and set aside. Reserve remaining chiles and adobo sauce for another use.

Tomato paste is a richly flavored tomato concentrate made from ripened tomatoes that have been cooked for several hours, strained, and reduced. The result is a thick red paste that's perfect for adding hearty flavor to sauces. Spoon tablespoonfuls of leftover paste onto a baking sheet, and freeze. Store the frozen paste in a heavy-duty plastic freezer bag. It'll be measured and ready for your next recipe.

INGREDIENT SPOTLIGHT

3. Heat a large nonstick skillet over medium-high heat. Coat pan with cooking spray. Add beef to pan; cook 4 minutes or until browned, stirring to crumble. Add bell pepper to pan; sauté 2 minutes. Stir in chopped chipotle chile, adobo sauce, tomato paste, and next 3 ingredients; cook 3 minutes, stirring occasionally. Spoon ½ cup beef mixture over bottom half of each bun, and top evenly with onions and top half of bun. **Yield:** 5 servings (serving size: 1 sandwich).

CALORIES 273; FAT 6.1g (sat 2.1g, mono 2.1g, poly 1.3g); PROTEIN 23.3g; CARB 32.1g; FIBER 3.4g; CHOL 48mg; IRON 3.7mg; SODIUM 724mg; CALC 84mg

15 MINUTES

Steak and Cheese Sandwiches with Mushrooms

1 teaspoon olive oil
2 cups presliced onion
2 cups green bell pepper strips
2 teaspoons bottled minced garlic
1 cup presliced mushrooms
¾ pound top round steak, trimmed and cut into thin strips
¼ teaspoon salt
⅛ teaspoon black pepper
2 teaspoons Worcestershire sauce
4 (0.6-ounce) slices reduced-fat provolone cheese, cut in half
4 (2½-ounce) hoagie rolls with sesame seeds

1. Heat oil in a large nonstick skillet over medium-high heat. Add onion, bell pepper, and garlic to pan; sauté 3 minutes. Add mushrooms to pan; sauté 4 minutes. Sprinkle beef with salt and black pepper. Add beef to pan; sauté 3 minutes or until browned, stirring occasionally. Stir in Worcestershire sauce; cook 1 minute.
2. Place 1 cheese slice half on bottom half of each roll, and top each serving with one-fourth of beef mixture. Top with remaining cheese slice halves and tops of rolls. **Yield:** 4 servings (serving size: 1 sandwich).

CALORIES 384; FAT 9.8g (sat 4.1g, mono 2.9g, poly 0.4g); PROTEIN 32.9g; CARB 44.9g; FIBER 4.1g; CHOL 43mg; IRON 4.7mg; SODIUM 580mg; CALC 231mg

Beefy Jicama Wraps

make it a meal *Serve this plentiful sandwich with a cup of fresh grapes for an easy, fun, family-friendly supper.*

½ pound lean boneless sirloin steak
½ teaspoon canola oil
⅛ teaspoon salt
¼ teaspoon black pepper
1 cup (¼-inch) julienne-cut peeled jicama (about ½ small jicama)
½ cup sliced red onion
1 tablespoon fresh lime juice
½ teaspoon chili powder
2 (8-inch) 96% fat-free flour tortillas
¼ cup refrigerated fresh salsa

1. Cut steak across grain into very thin strips. Heat oil in a large nonstick skillet over medium-high heat. Add meat; sprinkle with salt and pepper. Cook 4 minutes or until meat is browned, turning occasionally. **2.** Stir in jicama and next 3 ingredients; cook 2 minutes, stirring frequently. **3.** Cover tortillas with wax paper or damp paper towels. Microwave at HIGH 20 seconds or until warm. Spoon filling evenly down center of each tortilla. Roll up; serve immediately with salsa. **Yield:** 2 servings (serving size: 1 wrap and 2 tablespoons salsa).

CALORIES 343; FAT 8g (sat 2.5g, mono 4.5g, poly 0.9g); PROTEIN 29.4g; CARB 34.9g; FIBER 5.7g; CHOL 67mg; IRON 2.5mg; SODIUM 651mg; CALC 24mg

Open-Faced Steak, Pear, and Gorgonzola Sandwiches

Cooking spray
1   pound flank steak, trimmed
½   teaspoon salt
½   teaspoon freshly ground black pepper
1   cup thinly sliced red onion, separated into rings (about ½ onion)
2   small Bartlett pears
3   tablespoons bottled lemon juice, divided
2   tablespoons white wine vinegar
1   tablespoon water
1   teaspoon olive oil
1   teaspoon bottled minced garlic
6   cups prewashed gourmet salad greens
¼   cup (1 ounce) crumbled Gorgonzola cheese
6   (2.8-ounce) Mediterranean-style white flatbread (such as Toufayan)

1. Heat a large cast-iron skillet over medium-high heat. Coat pan with cooking spray. Sprinkle both sides of steak with salt and pepper. Add steak to pan; cook 6 minutes. Turn steak; add onion to pan. Lightly coat onion with cooking spray. Cook steak an additional 6 minutes or until desired degree of doneness, stirring onion frequently. Transfer steak to a cutting board. Cook onion an additional 2 minutes or until tender and lightly browned. Remove pan from heat.
2. Core pears; cut into thin slices. Place pears in a large bowl. Drizzle pears with 2 tablespoons lemon juice; toss well to coat. Combine remaining 1 tablespoon lemon juice, vinegar, water, olive oil, and garlic in a small bowl; stir well with a whisk. Add salad greens and cheese to pear mixture. Drizzle with oil mixture; toss to coat.
3. Cut steak diagonally into thin slices. Top each flatbread with about 7 slices (about 2 ounces) steak and about 1⅓ cups salad mixture. **Yield:** 6 servings (serving size: 1 sandwich).

CALORIES 397; FAT 9.4g (sat 3.3g, mono 3.7g, poly 1g); PROTEIN 26.7g; CARB 54.2g; FIBER 11.4g; CHOL 31mg; IRON 4.6mg; SODIUM 435mg; CALC 145mg

Greek Steak Pitas

make it a meal *Serve a Mediterranean-inspired meal in minutes. These stackers are stuffed with bright flavors including Greek seasoning, lemon juice, red onion, and feta cheese. Creamy hummus rounds out this meal.*

½   cup red wine vinegar
1   teaspoon Greek seasoning (such as McCormick)
⅛   teaspoon black pepper
1   (1-pound) flank steak, trimmed
½   teaspoon kosher salt, divided
1   teaspoon butter
1   teaspoon olive oil
2   tablespoons lemon juice
1   teaspoon minced garlic
1   (6-ounce) package fresh baby spinach
4   (6-inch) pitas, cut in half
½   cup thinly sliced red onion
24   slices English cucumber
½   cup (2 ounces) crumbled feta cheese

1. Combine first 3 ingredients in a large zip-top plastic bag; add steak to bag. Marinate 3 minutes, turning once. Remove steak from bag; discard marinade. Sprinkle steak with ¼ teaspoon salt. Heat a large skillet over medium-high heat. Add butter and oil. Add steak; cook 5 minutes on each side or until desired doneness. Let stand 2 minutes. Cut steak across grain into thin slices.
2. Return pan to heat. Add juice, garlic, and spinach; sauté 1 minute. Remove from heat; add remaining salt.
3. Spoon 2 tablespoons spinach mixture into each pita half. Place 1 tablespoon onion, 3 cucumber slices, and 1½ ounces steak in each pita half; sprinkle 1 tablespoon cheese in each pita half. **Yield:** 4 servings (serving size: 2 filled pita halves).

CALORIES 427; FAT 13.3g (sat 6.5g, mono 4.7g, poly 0.6g); PROTEIN 35.5g; CARB 39.1g; FIBER 2.6g; CHOL 53mg; IRON 6mg; SODIUM 730mg; CALC 215mg

SIDE DISHES

20 MINUTES

Sautéed Apples and Fennel

We recommend using Braeburn apples because they hold up well when sautéed.

2 teaspoons olive oil
½ cup thinly sliced fennel bulb
½ cup thinly sliced sweet onion
2 Braeburn apples, halved, cored, and thinly sliced
1 teaspoon minced fresh rosemary
¼ teaspoon salt
¼ teaspoon freshly ground black pepper

1. Heat oil in a large nonstick skillet over medium heat until hot. Add fennel and onion. Sauté 5 minutes. Add apple; cook, stirring frequently, 8 minutes or until tender and golden. Stir in rosemary, salt, and pepper; cook, stirring constantly, 1 minute. **Yield:** 4 servings (serving size: about ½ cup).

CALORIES 67; FAT 2.5g (sat 0.4g, mono 1.7g, poly 0.4g); PROTEIN 0.5g; CARB 11.8g; FIBER 2.3g; CHOL 0mg; IRON 0.3mg; SODIUM 152mg; CALC 11mg

With its short stems, feathery green leaves, and rounded white bulb, fennel is easily mistaken for a bunch of plump celery. But its mild, sweet flavor, which is similar to licorice or anise, sets it apart. Look for small, heavy, white fennel bulbs that are firm and free of cracks, browning, or moist areas. The stalks should be crisp, with feathery, bright green fronds. Trim the stalks about an inch above the bulb. Keep the root end intact so the bulb will hold together as it's sliced.

30 MINUTES

Chunky Cranberry Applesauce

5 Gala apples, peeled and thinly sliced
1 cup fresh or frozen cranberries
½ cup water
¼ cup sugar
1 teaspoon grated fresh orange rind

1. Combine first 3 ingredients in a Dutch oven. Bring to a boil; cover, reduce heat, and simmer 15 minutes or until apple slices are tender, stirring occasionally.
2. Stir in sugar and orange rind; remove from heat. Mash with a potato masher until chunky. **Yield:** 7 servings (serving size: ½ cup).

CALORIES 80; FAT 0.1g (sat 0g, mono 0g, poly 0.1g); PROTEIN 0.3g; CARB 20.9g; FIBER 1.8g; CHOL 0mg; IRON 0.1mg; SODIUM 0mg; CALC 9mg

15 MINUTES

Warm Pear Applesauce

When you see how quick, easy, and delicious homemade applesauce can be, you'll never go back to the store-bought kind.

2½ cups chopped peeled Granny Smith apple (2 medium)
2 cups chopped peeled Bosc pear (2 large)
½ teaspoon ground cinnamon
1 tablespoon fresh lemon juice
1 tablespoon sugar
1⁄16 teaspoon salt

1. Combine apple and pear in a medium microwave-safe bowl. Microwave at HIGH 10 minutes or until tender. Mash fruit with the back of a wooden spoon.
2. Stir in cinnamon and remaining ingredients. **Yield:** 4 servings (serving size: about ½ cup).

CALORIES 92; FAT 0.2g (sat 0g, mono 0g, poly 0.1g); PROTEIN 0.5g; CARB 24.6g; FIBER 3.6g; CHOL 0mg; IRON 0.3mg; SODIUM 38mg; CALC 18mg

MINUTES

Berry Slaw

The longer this slaw chills, the juicier and more condensed it becomes. If you serve it immediately, you will actually get double the amount (8 cups).

6   cups thinly sliced green cabbage
1½ cups sliced strawberries
½   cup dried cranberries
¼   cup raspberry-flavored vinegar
¼   cup cranberry juice cocktail
½   teaspoon salt
½   teaspoon white pepper

1. Combine all ingredients in a medium bowl; stir well. Cover and chill 8 hours, stirring occasionally. **Yield:** 4 servings (serving size: 1 cup).

CALORIES 109; FAT 0.5g (sat 0.1g, mono 0.1g, poly 0.2g); PROTEIN 2.2g; CARB 26.5g; FIBER 4.9g; CHOL 0mg; IRON 1.2mg; SODIUM 317mg; CALC 68mg

Grilled Nectarines with
Blue Cheese

4. Place nectarines on a serving platter. Spoon about 1 teaspoon cranberries and 1 teaspoon vinaigrette mixture into center of each half. Sprinkle cheese evenly over nectarines. Serve warm. **Yield:** 8 servings (serving size: 1 stuffed nectarine half).

CALORIES 115; FAT 4.2g (sat 1.1g, mono 0.9g, poly 2.2g); PROTEIN 1.5g; CARB 20g; FIBER 1.4g; CHOL 2mg; IRON 0.2mg; SODIUM 107mg; CALC 22mg

MINUTES

Grilled Nectarines with Blue Cheese

make it a meal *Grill the nectarines alongside chicken breasts or pork tenderloin as a simple side dish that gets high marks for flavor and appearance.*

½   cup light raspberry-walnut vinaigrette (such as Ken's)
3   tablespoons honey
4   ripe nectarines, halved and pitted
3   tablespoons sweetened dried cranberries
Cooking spray
3   tablespoons crumbled blue cheese

1. Prepare grill.
2. Combine vinaigrette and honey in a small microwave-safe bowl. Brush vinaigrette mixture over nectarine halves until both sides are evenly coated. Add dried cranberries to remaining vinaigrette mixture in bowl. Cover cranberry mixture with plastic wrap, and vent; microwave at HIGH 1 minute or until mixture begins to boil. Set aside.
3. Place nectarines, cut sides down, on grill rack coated with cooking spray. Grill 4 to 6 minutes on each side or until nectarines are tender.

15 MINUTES

Fresh Pears with Ginger

make it a meal *Serve these simple, sweet pears with roasted pork, chicken, or turkey.*

2   tablespoons honey
2   tablespoons lemon juice
2   tablespoons minced crystallized ginger
3   ripe pears, sliced

1. Combine first 3 ingredients in a medium bowl. Add pear slices, and toss well. **Yield:** 4 servings (serving size: 1 cup).

CALORIES 90; FAT 0.1g (sat 0g, mono 0g, poly 0g); PROTEIN 0.3g; CARB 24.2g; FIBER 2g; CHOL 0mg; IRON 0.4mg; SODIUM 3mg; CALC 16mg

Pears are as versatile as apples, especially during their peak season. Test for ripeness by applying light thumb pressure near the stem— if the pear is ripe, there will be a slight give. If the pears aren't ripe, place them on a kitchen counter in a brown paper bag, and check them daily. It may take three to five days for them to fully ripen.

INGREDIENT SPOTLIGHT

Spiced Winter Fruit

Spiced Winter Fruit

Topped with low-fat vanilla ice cream, this also makes a simple elegant holiday dessert. This dish will hold up for up to three days if it's refrigerated in an airtight container. To serve, reheat it over low heat.

1 cup packed light brown sugar
1 teaspoon ground ginger
1 teaspoon ground cinnamon
¹⁄₂ teaspoon ground nutmeg
2 tablespoons butter or stick margarine
2 quinces, each cut into 8 wedges (about ³⁄₄ pound)
3 cups sliced peeled Bartlett or Anjou pear (about 1¹⁄₂ pounds)
2¹⁄₂ cups sliced peeled Granny Smith apple (about 1¹⁄₂ pounds)
¹⁄₄ teaspoon freshly ground black pepper
Cinnamon sticks (optional)

1. Combine first 4 ingredients in a small bowl; set aside.
2. Melt butter in a large nonstick skillet over medium heat. Add quinces; cover and cook 6 minutes, stirring occasionally. Add sugar mixture, pear, and apple; cover and cook 12 minutes, stirring occasionally. Stir in pepper; garnish with cinnamon sticks, if desired. **Yield:** 8 servings (serving size: ³⁄₄ cup).

CALORIES 219; FAT 3.6g (sat 1.9g, mono 0.9g, poly 0.3g); PROTEIN 0.7g; CARB 50.1g; FIBER 4.5g; CHOL 8mg; IRON 1.1mg; SODIUM 38mg; CALC 38mg

Balsamic-Glazed Oranges

make it a meal *These orange slices, drenched with a richly flavored syrup, are the perfect partner for dark-meat poultry such as duck breast or chicken thighs or drumsticks.*

2 tablespoons packed brown sugar
2 tablespoons balsamic vinegar
2 oranges, peeled and cut into ¹⁄₄-inch-thick slices
¹⁄₂ teaspoon chopped fresh mint (optional)

1. Combine sugar and vinegar in a small saucepan. Bring to a boil. Cook mixture until reduced to 2 tablespoons (about 1 minute), stirring constantly; remove the mixture from heat. Divide orange slices evenly between 2 salad plates. Drizzle each serving with 1 tablespoon vinegar glaze. Garnish with chopped mint, if desired. **Yield:** 2 servings.

CALORIES 96; FAT 0.2g (sat 0g, mono 0g, poly 0g); PROTEIN 1.2g; CARB 24.4g; FIBER 5.8g; CHOL 0mg; IRON 0.4mg; SODIUM 4mg; CALC 60mg

INGREDIENT SPOTLIGHT

Quince is a yellow-skinned fruit that looks and tastes like a cross between an apple and a pear, but it turns pink when it's cooked. Cooking also mellows the tartness. (If you can't find quince, just use two additional apples or pears cut into wedges.)

MINUTES

Plantain Chips

Use plantains that are moderately ripe (mottled-looking) for this recipe.

1   tablespoon olive oil
2   medium plantains, peeled and cut into
     ¼-inch diagonal slices (about 2 cups)
¼   teaspoon salt
⅛   teaspoon ground red pepper

1. Heat oil in a large nonstick skillet over medium heat. Add the plantain slices; cook 3 minutes on each side or until browned. Sprinkle salt and pepper over chips. **Yield:** 4 servings (serving size: ½ cup).

CALORIES 190; FAT 3.9g (sat 0.5g, mono 2.5g, poly 0.3g); PROTEIN 1.7g; CARB 42g; FIBER 0.7g; CHOL 0mg; IRON 0.8mg; SODIUM 152mg; CALC 4mg

Plantain Chips

MINUTES

Asian Caramelized Pineapple

make it a meal *Served warm or at room temperature, this interesting side pairs nicely with pork chops.*

1½   teaspoons canola oil
1½   tablespoons minced red onion
1   large garlic clove, minced
2   cups diced fresh pineapple
1   tablespoon low-sodium soy sauce
1½   teaspoons chopped seeded red jalapeño
     pepper
1½   teaspoons fresh lime juice
1   teaspoon chopped peeled fresh ginger
1½   teaspoons chopped fresh cilantro

1. Heat oil in a large nonstick skillet over medium heat. Add onion and garlic to pan; cook 2 minutes. Add pineapple; cook 5 minutes or until lightly browned. Add soy sauce, pepper, juice, and ginger; cook 2 minutes. Remove from heat; stir in cilantro. **Yield:** 4 servings (serving size: about ½ cup).

CALORIES 61; FAT 1.9g (sat 0.1g, mono 1.1g, poly 0.6g); PROTEIN 0.9g; CARB 11.6g; FIBER 1.3g; CHOL 0mg; IRON 0.4mg; SODIUM 135mg; CALC 15mg

MINUTES

Asparagus with Balsamic Butter

make it a meal *The combination of fresh asparagus tossed with sweet balsamic vinegar, sautéed shallots, and butter makes a perfect side dish to serve with beef, pork, or fish.*

1¼   pounds asparagus spears
Cooking spray
2   tablespoons finely chopped shallots
1   tablespoon light stick butter
1   teaspoon balsamic vinegar
¼   teaspoon salt
¼   teaspoon freshly ground black pepper

1. Snap off tough ends of asparagus. Bring 1 inch of water to a boil in a large skillet; add asparagus. Cook 4 to 5 minutes or until crisp-tender. Drain and place on a serving platter.
2. While asparagus cooks, heat a large nonstick skillet over medium heat. Coat pan with cooking spray. Add shallots; sauté 1 to 2 minutes or until soft. Remove from heat; stir in butter and balsamic vinegar. Pour balsamic butter over asparagus, and sprinkle with salt and pepper. Toss well. **Yield:** 4 servings (serving size: ¼ of asparagus).

CALORIES 57; FAT 2g (sat 1.2g, mono 0.5g, poly 0.2g); PROTEIN 3.4g; CARB 6.7g; FIBER 3g; CHOL 4mg; IRON 3.2mg; SODIUM 164mg; CALC 38mg

COOKING CLASS: *how to prepare asparagus*

Be sure to snap or cut off the tough ends of the asparagus spears before cooking them. To maintain freshness, wrap a moist paper towel around the stem ends, or stand the spears upright in about 2 inches of cold water.

 MINUTES

Lemon-Sesame Asparagus

2   teaspoons low-sodium soy sauce
1   teaspoon dark sesame oil
¼   teaspoon grated fresh lemon rind
1   teaspoon fresh lemon juice
1   pound asparagus spears
Cooking spray
⅛   teaspoon salt
⅛   teaspoon freshly ground black pepper
1   teaspoon sesame seeds, toasted

1. Preheat oven to 450°.
2. Combine first 4 ingredients in a small bowl; set aside.
3. Snap off tough ends of asparagus. Place spears on a baking sheet; coat with cooking spray, and sprinkle with salt and pepper. Bake at 450° for 7 to 9 minutes or until asparagus is tender and lightly browned. Transfer asparagus to a serving dish; drizzle with soy sauce mixture. Sprinkle with toasted sesame seeds. **Yield:** 4 servings (serving size: ¼ of asparagus).

CALORIES 44; FAT 1.6g (sat 0.3g, mono 0.6g, poly 0.7g); PROTEIN 2.8g; CARB 5g; FIBER 2.5g; CHOL 0mg; IRON 2.6mg; SODIUM 179mg; CALC 23mg

MINUTES

Asparagus with Blue Cheese Vinaigrette

Asparagus has a mild flavor and a delicate texture, although it becomes tougher as it ages. During its peak season (February through June), pencil-thin spears are plentiful.

1   pound asparagus spears
1   tablespoon olive oil
2   teaspoons red wine vinegar
2   tablespoons crumbled blue cheese
2   tablespoons minced fresh chives
⅛   teaspoon freshly ground black pepper

1. Snap off tough ends of asparagus. Add water to a medium skillet to a depth of 1 inch, and bring to a boil. Add asparagus in a single layer; cook 3 minutes or until crisp-tender. Drain asparagus; arrange on a serving platter.
2. Combine oil and vinegar in a small bowl, stirring with a whisk. Add cheese and chives, stirring until well blended. Pour vinegar mixture over asparagus. Sprinkle with pepper. **Yield:** 4 servings (serving size: ¼ of asparagus).

CALORIES 74; FAT 4.7g (sat 1.3g, mono 2.8g, poly 0.5g); PROTEIN 3.5g; CARB 4.6g; FIBER 2.4g; CHOL 3mg; IRON 2.5mg; SODIUM 60mg; CALC 51mg

Zesty White Beans
and Tomatoes

Smoky Baked Beans with Peaches

Canned peaches add sweetness, while the smokiness comes from a commercial barbecue sauce. Rinsing the canned beans reduces sodium and improves their overall appearance.

Cooking spray
- ³/₄ cup finely chopped onion
- 1 (16-ounce) can pinto beans, rinsed and drained
- 1 (15.8-ounce) can Great Northern beans, rinsed and drained
- ¹/₂ cup barbecue sauce (such as KC Masterpiece Original)
- 1 (4-ounce) cup diced peaches in light syrup (such as Del Monte), undrained

1. Heat a medium saucepan over medium heat. Coat pan with cooking spray. Add onion; sauté 3 minutes or until tender. Stir in remaining ingredients. Cover and simmer 10 minutes. **Yield:** 6 servings (serving size: about ¹/₂ cup).

CALORIES 149; FAT 0.6g (sat 0.1g, mono 0.1g, poly 0.2g); PROTEIN 5.9g; CARB 31.1g; FIBER 4.9g; CHOL 0mg; IRON 1.5mg; SODIUM 250mg; CALC 49mg

 MINUTES

Zesty White Beans and Tomatoes

make it a meal *With its refreshing blend of lemon juice, fresh parsley and basil, and cherry tomatoes, here's a colorful complement to grilled beef, pork, or chicken. This is an ideal make-ahead side for a summer cookout.*

- 1 (16-ounce) can navy beans, rinsed and drained
- ¹/₂ cup quartered cherry tomatoes
- 2 tablespoons chopped fresh parsley
- 1 tablespoon chopped fresh basil
- 1 tablespoon lemon juice
- 1 tablespoon extra-virgin olive oil
- ¹/₄ teaspoon salt
- 1 garlic clove, minced

1. Combine all ingredients in a bowl. Serve at room temperature or chilled. **Yield:** 4 servings (serving size: ¹/₂ cup).

CALORIES 112; FAT 3.9g (sat 0.6g, mono 2.5g, poly 0.7g); PROTEIN 5.4g; CARB 15.2g; FIBER 3.8g; CHOL 0mg; IRON 1.5mg; SODIUM 331mg; CALC 39mg

Smoky Baked
Beans with
Peaches

20 MINUTES

Chipotle-Bacon Baked Beans

1 (28-ounce) can barbecue baked beans
3 slices precooked bacon, coarsely chopped
1 tablespoon brown sugar
1 chipotle chile, canned in adobo sauce, seeded and chopped
1 tablespoon canned adobo sauce

1. Preheat oven to 425°.
2. Combine all ingredients in an 11 x 7–inch baking dish. Bake, uncovered, at 425° for 15 minutes or until thoroughly heated. **Yield:** 6 servings (serving size: ¹/₂ cup).

CALORIES 192; FAT 2.6g (sat 0.4g, mono 1.2g, poly 0.8g); PROTEIN 7g; CARB 35.6g; FIBER 6.3g; CHOL 3mg; IRON 2.2mg; SODIUM 1,089mg; CALC 64mg

15 MINUTES

Garlic Green Beans

Use pretrimmed green beans to save time in this healthy and versatile dish that you can serve alongside almost any entrée.

1 (12-ounce) bag pretrimmed fresh green beans
1 tablespoon light stick butter
Cooking spray
1 cup grape tomatoes
2 garlic cloves, crushed
¼ teaspoon salt
¼ teaspoon freshly ground black pepper

1. Pierce green bean bag with a fork; microwave at HIGH 4 to 5 minutes or until tender. Let stand 1 minute.
2. While green beans cook, melt butter in a large nonstick skillet coated with cooking spray over medium heat. Add tomatoes and garlic; cook 1 minute, stirring constantly. Add green beans, salt, and pepper; cook 2 minutes or until thoroughly heated. **Yield:** 4 servings (serving size: ¹/₄ of green beans).

CALORIES 48; FAT 1.6g (sat 0.9g, mono 0.2g, poly 0.4g); PROTEIN 1.9g; CARB 8.4g; FIBER 3.4g; CHOL 4mg; IRON 1mg; SODIUM 178mg; CALC 38mg

15 MINUTES

Lemon-Tarragon Beans

The flavor of fresh tarragon, like other herbs, is generally much better than that of dried—but you can substitute dried, using the general rule that one part dried herbs equals three parts fresh.

1 (16-ounce) bag pretrimmed fresh green beans
¼ cup water
2 teaspoons fresh lemon juice
1 teaspoon chopped fresh tarragon
¼ teaspoon salt

1. Combine beans and water in a microwave-safe dish. Cover and microwave at HIGH 6 minutes or until tender. Drain. Toss with lemon juice, tarragon, and salt. **Yield:** 4 servings (serving size: 1 cup).

CALORIES 28; FAT 0g; PROTEIN 1.4g; CARB 7.1g; FIBER 4.1g; CHOL 0mg; IRON 0.5mg; SODIUM 145mg; CALC 56mg

15 MINUTES

Blue Cheese Green Beans

To get a robust punch with just a little cheese, use a premium blue cheese.

1 (12-ounce) bag pretrimmed fresh green beans
2 tablespoons water
1 tablespoon balsamic vinegar
2 teaspoons olive oil
2 tablespoons crumbled blue cheese

1. Place green beans and water in an 11 x 7–inch microwave-safe dish. Cover and microwave at HIGH 8 minutes or until tender; drain. Transfer beans to a serving dish; drizzle with vinegar and oil. Sprinkle with blue cheese. **Yield:** 3 servings (serving size: about 1 cup).

CALORIES 78; FAT 4.6g (sat 1.5g, mono 2.6g, poly 0.6g); PROTEIN 2.6g; CARB 7.9g; FIBER 4.1g; CHOL 4mg; IRON 0.6mg; SODIUM 87mg; CALC 86mg

Rely on bags of pretrimmed green beans, available in your supermarket's produce section, to create fresh side dishes with minimal prep work. We've used them here to make this recipe even faster.

MAKE IT FASTER

Blue Cheese Green Beans

Thyme-Scented Green Beans with Almonds

Green Beans with Cilantro

make it a meal *Give green beans a zip by adding hot pepper and fresh cilantro. Serve with grilled fish.*

1½ teaspoons olive oil
Cooking spray
1 (12-ounce) bag pretrimmed fresh green beans, diagonally cut (about 3 cups)
1 tablespoon minced fresh cilantro
1 small jalapeño pepper, seeded and minced
¼ teaspoon salt

1. Heat oil in a large nonstick skillet coated with cooking spray over medium-high heat. Add green beans; sauté 10 minutes or until tender and lightly browned.
2. Stir in minced cilantro, minced pepper, and salt. **Yield:** 4 servings (serving size: ½ cup).

CALORIES 37; FAT 1.7g (sat 0.3g, mono 1.2g, poly 0.2g); PROTEIN 1.1g; CARB 5.3g; FIBER 3.2g; CHOL 0mg; IRON 0.4mg; SODIUM 153mg; CALC 42mg

Simple Garlicky Lima Beans

This is a delicious, basic way to cook any kind of fresh shell bean or pea.

4 cups fresh lima beans
2½ cups water
1 tablespoon olive oil
2 garlic cloves, crushed
3 thyme sprigs
1 bay leaf
½ teaspoon sea salt
¼ teaspoon freshly ground black pepper

1. Sort and wash beans; drain. Combine beans and next 5 ingredients in a medium saucepan. Bring to a boil. Cover, reduce heat, and simmer 20 minutes or until tender. Discard thyme sprigs and bay leaf. Stir in salt and pepper. **Yield:** 8 servings (serving size: ½ cup).

CALORIES 105; FAT 2.4g (sat 0.4g, mono 1.3g, poly 0.5g); PROTEIN 5.4g; CARB 16.2g; FIBER 3.9g; CHOL 0mg; IRON 2.5mg; SODIUM 152mg; CALC 30mg

Thyme-Scented Green Beans with Almonds

Smoked almonds and fresh thyme update this traditional combination of flavors.

1 (12-ounce) bag pretrimmed fresh green beans
2 teaspoons butter
1 tablespoon chopped fresh thyme
¼ teaspoon salt
¼ teaspoon black pepper
1 tablespoon chopped smoked almonds

1. Pierce green bean bag with a fork; microwave at HIGH 4 to 5 minutes or until tender. Let stand 1 minute.
2. While green beans cook, melt butter in a large nonstick skillet over medium heat. Add green beans, thyme, salt, and pepper; toss gently to coat. Cook 2 minutes or until thoroughly heated. Sprinkle beans with almonds. **Yield:** 4 servings (serving size: ¼ of green beans).

CALORIES 53; FAT 3.2g (sat 1.3g, mono 1.3g, poly 0.5g); PROTEIN 1.6g; CARB 5.7g; FIBER 3.3g; CHOL 5mg; IRON 0.5mg; SODIUM 178mg; CALC 41mg

2O

Beets with Orange and Herb Vinaigrette

When selecting fresh beets, buy small to medium globes with the stems and leaves attached. They should have firm, smooth skins and no soft spots. To store them, trim the stems to about 1 inch, and keep the beets in plastic bags in the refrigerator for up to 2 weeks.

1½ pounds assorted-color beets (about
    6 medium)
2 tablespoons balsamic vinegar
2 tablespoons extra-virgin olive oil
2 tablespoons minced fresh chives
1 tablespoon minced fresh tarragon
1 teaspoon grated orange rind
¼ teaspoon salt
¼ teaspoon freshly ground black pepper

1. Remove and discard beet greens. Leave root and 1-inch stem on beets; scrub with a brush. Place beets in a microwave-safe 2-quart glass baking dish; cover with 3 layers of damp paper towels. Microwave at HIGH 10 to 12 minutes or until tender. Remove from microwave; place in ice water. Let stand 5 minutes. Drain beets. Remove root; peel and cut into thin wedges.
2. Combine beet wedges and remaining ingredients in a large bowl. **Yield:** 4 servings (serving size: ³/₄ cup).

CALORIES 144; FAT 7.3g (sat 1g, mono 5.1g, poly 1.1g); PROTEIN 2.7g; CARB 18.7g; FIBER 4.9g; CHOL 0mg; IRON 1.6mg; SODIUM 270mg; CALC 35mg

Shave minutes off the cook time for this sweet and savory side by microwaving the beets. Traditional cooking methods—baking, boiling, steaming, and roasting—can require 45 minutes or longer.

MAKE IT FASTER

Bok Choy with Ginger
and Water Chestnuts

Bok Choy with Ginger and Water Chestnuts

make it a meal *Consider serving this flavorful side with pork medallions.*

1   teaspoon dark sesame oil
1   pound bok choy, trimmed and thinly sliced (about 6 cups)
½   cup thinly sliced green onions
1   teaspoon grated peeled fresh ginger
2   garlic cloves, minced
1   (8-ounce) can diced water chestnuts, drained
3   tablespoons low-sodium soy sauce

1. Heat sesame oil in a large nonstick skillet over medium-high heat. Add bok choy and next 3 ingredients; cover and cook 5 minutes, stirring once.
2. Add water chestnuts and soy sauce to pan, and cook 1 minute. **Yield:** 4 servings (serving size: 1 cup).

CALORIES 54; FAT 1.5g (sat 0.2g, mono 0.5g, poly 0.7g); PROTEIN 2.6g; CARB 8.8g; FIBER 3.3g; CHOL 0mg; IRON 1.5mg; SODIUM 527mg; CALC 134mg

Panko-Topped Broccoli

1   (12-ounce) package fresh broccoli florets (about 5 cups)
1   tablespoon olive oil
4   garlic cloves, minced
¾   cup panko (Japanese breadcrumbs)
1   tablespoon chopped fresh flat-leaf parsley
¼   teaspoon salt
1½ teaspoons freshly ground black pepper

1. Cut large florets in half. Arrange broccoli in a vegetable steamer in a Dutch oven. Steam broccoli, covered, 6 minutes or until crisp-tender. Remove steamer from pan; pour water from pan. Return pan briefly to heat to evaporate residual water.
2. When water has evaporated, add oil to pan. Add garlic; sauté 30 seconds or until golden. Stir in breadcrumbs; remove from heat. Stir in parsley, salt, and pepper. Return broccoli to pan, and toss gently with crumb mixture. Serve immediately. **Yield:** 5 servings (serving size: 1 cup).

CALORIES 82; FAT 3.2g (sat 0.4g, mono 2.1g, poly 0.6g); PROTEIN 3.5g; CARB 10.8g; FIBER 2.4g; CHOL 0mg; IRON 0.8mg; SODIUM 162mg; CALC 40mg

Sesame Broccoli Stir-Fry

make it a meal *Pair this tangy stir-fry with grilled chicken for a low-fat weeknight meal.*

Cooking spray
1   (12-ounce) package broccoli coleslaw
1   teaspoon dark sesame oil
1   teaspoon toasted sesame seeds (such as McCormick)
4   teaspoons low-fat sesame-ginger dressing (such as Newman's Own)

1. Heat a large nonstick skillet over medium-high heat; coat pan with cooking spray. Add broccoli coleslaw; cook 7 minutes or until crisp-tender, stirring occasionally. Add oil, and cook 1 minute. Remove from heat; stir in sesame seeds and dressing. **Yield:** 4 servings (serving size: about ½ cup).

CALORIES 53; FAT 1.7g (sat 0.2g, mono 0.7g, poly 0.7g); PROTEIN 2.5g; CARB 5.8g; FIBER 2.5g; CHOL 0mg; IRON 1.8mg; SODIUM 90mg; CALC 20mg

Steamed Broccoli with Lemon and Marjoram

Fresh lemon juice adds zing to this simple steamed broccoli.

4   cups broccoli florets
½   teaspoon dried marjoram
½   tablespoon fresh lemon juice
⅛   teaspoon salt

1. Arrange broccoli in a vegetable steamer; sprinkle with marjoram. Steam, covered, 5 minutes or until crisp-tender.
2. Place broccoli in a serving bowl; toss with lemon juice and salt. Serve immediately. **Yield:** 3 servings (serving size: about 1 cup).

CALORIES 27; FAT 0.3g (sat 0.1g, mono 0g, poly 0.2g); PROTEIN 2.8g; CARB 5.2g; FIBER 2.8g; CHOL 0mg; IRON 0.9mg; SODIUM 124mg; CALC 48mg

Broccoli with Red Pepper Flakes and Toasted Garlic

The bold, straightforward flavors of garlic and crushed red pepper make this classic Mediterranean broccoli dish appealing.

2   teaspoons olive oil
6   cups broccoli florets (about 1 head)
¼   teaspoon kosher salt
¼   teaspoon crushed red pepper
3   garlic cloves, thinly sliced
¼   cup water

1. Heat olive oil in a large nonstick skillet over medium-high heat. Add broccoli, kosher salt, crushed red pepper, and sliced garlic. Sauté 2 minutes. Add ¼ cup water. Cover, reduce heat to low, and cook 2 minutes or until broccoli is crisp-tender. **Yield:** 4 servings (serving size: 1 cup).

CALORIES 53; FAT 2.7g (sat 0.4g, mono 1.7g, poly 0.4g); PROTEIN 3.3g; CARB 6.4g; FIBER 3.2g; CHOL 0mg; IRON 1mg; SODIUM 147mg; CALC 55mg

Broccoli with Red Pepper Flakes and Toasted Garlic

Brussels Sprouts with
Pancetta

30 MINUTES

Brussels Sprouts with Pancetta

1   quart water
1¼ pounds Brussels sprouts, trimmed
¾   ounce thinly sliced pancetta
1   tablespoon butter
1½ tablespoons balsamic vinegar
¼   teaspoon freshly ground black pepper
2   tablespoons chopped walnuts, toasted

1. Bring 1 quart water to a boil in a large nonstick skillet. Add Brussels sprouts, and boil 5 minutes or just until tender; drain well. Place Brussels sprouts in a serving bowl, and keep warm. Wipe pan dry with paper towels.
2. Cook pancetta in pan over medium-high heat until crisp. Remove pancetta from pan; drain on paper towels.
3. Melt butter in pan over medium heat; cook 2 minutes or until lightly browned, stirring occasionally. Stir balsamic vinegar and pepper into butter; cook 1 minute or until mixture is slightly thick. Spoon butter mixture over Brussels sprouts; sprinkle with pancetta and toasted walnuts. **Yield:** 6 servings (serving size: ½ cup).

CALORIES 90; FAT 5.1g (sat 2.5g, mono 0.8g, poly 1.6g); PROTEIN 3.5g; CARB 9.8g; FIBER 2.8g; CHOL 8mg; IRON 1.3mg; SODIUM 191mg; CALC 40mg

20 MINUTES

Roasted Brussels Sprouts

Orange rind and juice give these Brussels sprouts a pleasing hint of citrus.

1   teaspoon grated orange rind
1   tablespoon fresh orange juice
2   teaspoons olive oil
1   pound Brussels sprouts, halved
Cooking spray
½   teaspoon salt
¼   teaspoon freshly ground black pepper

1. Preheat oven to 450°.
2. Combine orange rind, orange juice, and olive oil in a small bowl. Place Brussels sprouts on a jelly-roll pan coated with cooking spray; drizzle orange juice mixture over sprouts, and toss gently to coat. Sprinkle with salt and pepper.
3. Bake at 450° for 15 to 20 minutes or until edges of sprouts look lightly browned and crisp. **Yield:** 4 servings (serving size: about ¾ cup).

CALORIES 71; FAT 2.6g (sat 0.4g, mono 1.7g, poly 0.5g); PROTEIN 3.9g; CARB 10.8g; FIBER 4.4g; CHOL 0mg; IRON 1.6mg; SODIUM 323mg; CALC 49mg

20 MINUTES

Cabbage Sauté with Apples

make it a meal *This simple sauté is the perfect accompaniment to dress up your smoked turkey sausage, pork chop, or bratwurst.*

2   teaspoons butter
2   teaspoons olive oil
1¼ cups vertically sliced red onion
1   teaspoon chopped fresh thyme
2   teaspoons Dijon mustard
½   teaspoon fennel seeds
½   teaspoon salt
1   large Granny Smith apple, cored and
     chopped (1¼ cups)
1   (10-ounce) package angel hair slaw
¼   cup apple juice
3   tablespoons cider vinegar
1   teaspoon sugar
½   teaspoon ground white pepper

1. Heat butter and oil in a large nonstick skillet over medium-high heat until butter melts. Add onion and next 4 ingredients; sauté 3 minutes or until onion is tender. Add apple and slaw; sauté 2 minutes or until cabbage begins to wilt. Stir in apple juice and remaining ingredients. Bring to a boil; reduce heat to medium. Simmer 9 minutes or until liquid evaporates, stirring occasionally. **Yield:** 5 servings (serving size: ½ cup).

CALORIES 85; FAT 3.4g (sat 1.2g, mono 1.7g, poly 0.3g); PROTEIN 1.3g; CARB 12.7g; FIBER 2.4g; CHOL 4mg; IRON 0.4mg; SODIUM 298mg; CALC 16mg

Curried Cabbage

1	tablespoon vegetable oil
½	cup minced shallots
2	garlic cloves, minced
2	tablespoons whole-grain Dijon mustard
2	teaspoons curry powder
1	teaspoon ground turmeric
12	cups thinly sliced green cabbage (about 3 pounds)
¼	cup fat-free, less-sodium chicken broth
¼	cup rice vinegar
½	teaspoon salt
¼	teaspoon black pepper

1. Heat oil in a large nonstick skillet over medium-high heat. Add shallots and garlic; sauté 2 minutes. Add mustard, curry, and turmeric; cook 1 minute, stirring constantly. Stir in cabbage and remaining ingredients; cook 5 minutes or until tender, stirring frequently. **Yield:** 8 servings (serving size: ²/₃ cup).

CALORIES 58; FAT 2.3g (sat 0.4g, mono 0.7g, poly 1g); PROTEIN 1.8g; CARB 8.4g; FIBER 2.8g; CHOL 0mg; IRON 1mg; SODIUM 244mg; CALC 58mg

make it a meal *The pungent flavors of turmeric, mustard, and curry powder go well with grilled pork loin or lamb.*

Lemon-Honey Glazed Carrots

15 MINUTES

Maple-Glazed Carrots

1½ cups sliced carrots (about 4 large)
2   tablespoons reduced-calorie maple syrup
1   teaspoon butter
¼   teaspoon salt-free herb-and-spice blend

1. Place all ingredients in a small microwave-safe bowl. Cover and microwave at HIGH 6 minutes or until tender, stirring every 2 minutes. **Yield:** 2 servings (serving size: about ½ cup).

CALORIES 64; FAT 2.1g (sat 1.2g, mono 0.5g, poly 0.2g); PROTEIN 0.9g; CARB 12.2g; FIBER 2.6g; CHOL 5mg; IRON 0.3mg; SODIUM 103mg; CALC 31mg

15 MINUTES

Lemon-Honey Glazed Carrots

Sweet and tender, these carrots are a pleasing partner for just about any entrée.

1   (16-ounce) package fresh baby carrots
2   tablespoons honey
1   tablespoon light stick butter
2   teaspoons lemon juice
¼   teaspoon salt

1. Combine all ingredients in a medium microwave-safe dish. Cover and microwave at HIGH 8 to 10 minutes or until tender, stirring after 4 minutes. **Yield:** 4 servings (serving size: about ½ cup).

CALORIES 64; FAT 1.9g (sat 1.1g, mono 0.5g, poly 0.1g); PROTEIN 0.4g; CARB 12.5g; FIBER 1.3g; CHOL 5mg; IRON 0.5mg; SODIUM 194mg; CALC 16mg

15 MINUTES

Moroccan Carrots

Presliced carrots from the produce department are quickest and easiest, but carrots that you peel and slice yourself may have the freshest flavor.

4   cups diagonally cut carrot (about 1¼ pounds)
2   teaspoons olive oil
3   garlic cloves, thinly sliced
¼   teaspoon cumin seeds
1½ tablespoons chopped fresh cilantro
1   teaspoon honey
½   teaspoon salt
½   teaspoon freshly ground black pepper
¼   teaspoon ground cumin

1. Steam carrots, covered, 8 minutes or until tender. Drain.
2. While carrots steam, heat oil in a large nonstick skillet over medium heat. Add garlic and cumin seeds; sauté 1½ minutes or until lightly browned. Stir in carrots, cilantro, and remaining ingredients. **Yield:** 4 servings (serving size: about 1 cup).

CALORIES 81; FAT 2.6g (sat 0.4g, mono 1.7g, poly 0.4g); PROTEIN 1.4g; CARB 14.2g; FIBER 3.6g; CHOL 0mg; IRON 0.6mg; SODIUM 380mg; CALC 48mg

Steaming helps vegetables retain their water-soluble vitamins. It's a quick and easy process, especially when you use a collapsible metal vegetable steamer.

SHORTCUT SPOTLIGHT

Middle Eastern Roasted Cauliflower

15 MINUTES

Spicy Honey-Roasted Carrots

Top these carrots with a few fresh grinds of black pepper for an extra kick.

1   tablespoon honey
1   tablespoon orange juice
¼   teaspoon hot sauce
¼   cup raisins
1   (16-ounce) package fresh baby carrots
Olive oil–flavored cooking spray
½   teaspoon salt

1. Preheat oven to 475°.
2. Combine first 4 ingredients in a small bowl.
3. Place carrots in a single layer on a jelly-roll pan; coat carrots with cooking spray, and sprinkle with salt. Bake at 475° for 13 minutes, stirring occasionally. Add honey mixture; toss to coat. Bake an additional minute or until lightly browned and crisp-tender. **Yield:** 4 servings (serving size: about ½ cup).

CALORIES 90; FAT 0.4g (sat 0g, mono 0.2g, poly 0.1g); PROTEIN 1.1g; CARB 22g; FIBER 3.8g; CHOL 0mg; IRON 1.3mg; SODIUM 393mg; CALC 42mg

Give your food a bit of pungent flavor with a sprinkle of cracked or freshly ground pepper with the quick turn of a peppermill. It's a must-have kitchen gadget for quick cooking.

SHORTCUT SPOTLIGHT

20 MINUTES

Middle Eastern Roasted Cauliflower

Instead of cutting a head of cauliflower into florets, you can use 2 (10⅜-ounce) packages of florets.

6   cups cauliflower florets (about 1 head)
1   tablespoon olive oil
½   teaspoon salt
½   teaspoon freshly ground black pepper
½   teaspoon ground cumin
¼   teaspoon curry powder
⅛   teaspoon ground cinnamon
½   cup canned petite diced tomatoes, drained
¼   cup raisins
1   tablespoon chopped fresh parsley

1. Preheat oven to 500°.
2. Combine first 7 ingredients in a large bowl; toss well. Place cauliflower on a foil-lined jelly-roll pan. Bake at 500° for 12 minutes or until lightly browned, stirring once after 5 minutes.
3. Combine tomatoes, raisins, and parsley in a large bowl. Stir in cauliflower. Serve warm or at room temperature. **Yield:** 8 servings (serving size: ¾ cup).

CALORIES 47; FAT 2g (sat 0.3g, mono 1.3g, poly 0.3g); PROTEIN 1.4g; CARB 7.2g; FIBER 1.8g; CHOL 0mg; IRON 0.5mg; SODIUM 163mg; CALC 23mg

MINUTES

Cauliflower with Cheddar Sauce

1 small head cauliflower (about 1¼ pounds)
Cooking spray
¼ cup light mayonnaise
¼ cup (1 ounce) preshredded reduced-fat sharp cheddar cheese
2 tablespoons chopped green onions
2 teaspoons Dijon mustard
⅛ teaspoon freshly ground black pepper

1. Preheat oven to 425°.
2. Remove large outer leaves of cauliflower. Cut cauliflower into large florets. Steam, covered, 6 minutes or until crisp-tender; drain. Place florets in an 8-inch square baking dish coated with cooking spray.
3. Combine mayonnaise and next 3 ingredients in a small bowl. Spread cheese mixture evenly over florets. Bake at 425° for 4 minutes or until thoroughly heated and cheese melts. Sprinkle with pepper. **Yield:** 4 servings (serving size: ¼ of cauliflower).

CALORIES 92; FAT 6.6g (sat 1.9g, mono 1.7g, poly 2.9g); PROTEIN 3.3g; CARB 5.9g; FIBER 1.8g; CHOL 10mg; IRON 0.6mg; SODIUM 201mg; CALC 73mg

 MINUTES

Skillet Corn

1 tablespoon butter
3 cups frozen whole-kernel corn, thawed
¼ cup chopped red bell pepper
¼ teaspoon salt
⅛ teaspoon freshly ground black pepper
¼ cup chopped green onions

1. Heat butter in a cast-iron skillet over medium-high heat. Add corn, bell pepper, salt, and black pepper. Cook 4 minutes, stirring frequently. Stir in onions, and cook 5 minutes or until corn is lightly browned, stirring frequently. **Yield:** 4 servings (serving size: ½ cup).

CALORIES 151; FAT 3.8g (sat 2g, mono 1.1g, poly 0.6g); PROTEIN 4.2g; CARB 30g; FIBER 3.9g; CHOL 8mg; IRON 0.9mg; SODIUM 177mg; CALC 12mg

 MINUTES

Creamed Corn with Ham

Our version of Southern creamed corn captures the flavor of traditional recipes but saves time by using canned corn.

2 (15¼-ounce) cans whole-kernel corn, drained and divided
2 tablespoons all-purpose flour
1½ cups fat-free milk
2 teaspoons sugar
¼ teaspoon salt
2 teaspoons butter
¼ cup finely diced ham
¼ cup finely chopped onion
½ teaspoon bottled minced garlic

1. Place 1 cup corn, flour, and next 3 ingredients in a food processor; process until almost smooth.
2. Melt butter in a large nonstick skillet over medium heat. Add ham, onion, and garlic; cook 3 minutes or until lightly browned. Add puréed corn mixture and remaining corn; cook 11 minutes or until slightly thickened, stirring occasionally. **Yield:** 6 servings (serving size: ½ cup).

CALORIES 148; FAT 2.6g (sat 0.9g, mono 0.8g, poly 0.7g); PROTEIN 5.5g; CARB 25.4g; FIBER 3.2g; CHOL 10mg; IRON 0.6mg; SODIUM 408mg; CALC 65mg

Grilled Corn on the Cob
with Chive Butter

Cilantro-Lime Corn on the Cob

To save time, purchase partially shucked corn in cellophane-wrapped packages at your grocery store.

4   large ears shucked corn
3   tablespoons light stick butter, softened
1   tablespoon chopped fresh cilantro
1   tablespoon fresh lime juice
1   teaspoon paprika
¼   teaspoon salt

1. Place corn in a microwave-safe baking dish; cover dish with wax paper. Microwave at HIGH 7 minutes or until tender.
2. While corn is cooking, combine butter and remaining ingredients in a small bowl. Brush butter mixture evenly over cooked corn. **Yield:** 4 servings (serving size: 1 ear).

CALORIES 175; FAT 7.1g (sat 3.6g, mono 2.3g, poly 1.2g); PROTEIN 5g; CARB 27.8g; FIBER 4.1g; CHOL 10mg; IRON 1mg; SODIUM 214mg; CALC 9mg

MINUTES

Grilled Corn on the Cob with Chive Butter

Grilling vegetables, like corn, adds depth of flavor, sweetness, and an appealing char-grilled appearance to your plate.

8   ears shucked corn
Cooking spray
¼   cup light stick butter, softened
2   tablespoons chopped fresh chives

1. Prepare grill.
2. Coat corn with cooking spray. Place corn on grill rack; cover and grill 6 minutes on each side or until slightly charred.
3. While corn grills, combine butter and chives. Brush butter mixture over grilled corn. **Yield:** 8 servings (serving size: 1 ear of corn).

CALORIES 110; FAT 4.6g (sat 2.4g, mono 1.4g, poly 0.6g); PROTEIN 3.1g; CARB 17.2g; FIBER 2.5g; CHOL 8mg; IRON 0.5mg; SODIUM 43mg; CALC 6mg

Cilantro-Lime
Corn on the Cob

Lemon Couscous

make it a meal *You'll need a little less than half of a 10-ounce box of couscous. Serve with fish or chicken for a supereasy supper.*

¾ cup fat-free, less-sodium chicken broth
1 tablespoon lemon rind
2 tablespoons fresh lemon juice
⅔ cup uncooked couscous
3 tablespoons pine nuts, toasted
2 tablespoons chopped fresh parsley
1 (2-ounce) jar sliced pimiento, drained and chopped

1. Combine first 3 ingredients in a saucepan; bring to a boil. Gradually stir in couscous. Remove from heat; cover and let stand 5 minutes. Fluff with a fork; stir in remaining ingredients. **Yield:** 5 servings (serving size: about ½ cup).

CALORIES 128; FAT 3.7g (sat 0.3g, mono 1.2g, poly 2.2g); PROTEIN 4g; CARB 19.9g; FIBER 1.8g; CHOL 0mg; IRON 0.8mg; SODIUM 87mg; CALC 13mg

Couscous, regarded by many as a grain, is actually pasta made from semolina (coarsely ground durum wheat). In some regions, however, couscous is made from coarsely ground barley or millet. Its earthy flavor is famously friendly to seasonings. And it's versatile, working well as a side dish, entrée, or salad.

INGREDIENT SPOTLIGHT

Summer Corn and Rice with Basil

Cucumber and fresh basil add a dash of summer to this warm side salad. Enjoy it year-round by using frozen corn, but when corn is at its peak, substitute fresh kernels cut from the cob. Leave any remaining English cucumber in its original wrapper, cover the cut end with plastic wrap, and store it in the refrigerator for up to a week.

1½ cups frozen shoepeg white corn
Olive oil–flavored cooking spray
1 (8.8-ounce) pouch microwaveable cooked long-grain rice (such as Uncle Ben's Ready Rice)
1½ cups chopped English cucumber
⅓ cup reduced-fat olive oil vinaigrette (such as Ken's Lite)
1 teaspoon fresh lemon juice
½ cup thinly sliced fresh basil
⅛ teaspoon salt
¼ teaspoon freshly ground black pepper

1. Heat a large nonstick skillet over medium-high heat. Add corn; coat with cooking spray. Cook, stirring often, 4 minutes or until lightly browned.
2. While corn cooks, microwave rice according to package directions.
3. Place corn and rice in a medium bowl. Stir in cucumber and remaining ingredients. Toss gently, and serve immediately. **Yield:** 7 servings (serving size: ½ cup).

CALORIES 100; FAT 2.9g (sat 0.2g, mono 2.2g, poly 0.4g); PROTEIN 1.9g; CARB 17g; FIBER 1.4g; CHOL 0mg; IRON 0.8mg; SODIUM 153mg; CALC 15mg

Cucumber-and-Feta Couscous

make it a meal *Add cooked chicken or shrimp to this couscous for a quick one-dish meal.*

1	cup water
¾	cup uncooked couscous
½	cup diced English cucumber
½	cup diced tomato
¼	cup diced red onion
1	tablespoon olive oil
1	tablespoon fresh lemon juice
½	cup (2 ounces) crumbled feta cheese

1. Bring 1 cup water to a boil in a medium saucepan; gradually stir in couscous. Remove from heat; cover and let stand 5 minutes. Fluff with a fork.

2. While couscous stands, place cucumber and next 4 ingredients in a serving bowl. Add couscous and cheese; toss gently with a fork. **Yield:** 6 servings (serving size: ½ cup).

CALORIES 134; FAT 4.5g (sat 1.8g, mono 2.1g, poly 0.4g); PROTEIN 4.4g; CARB 18.8g; FIBER 1.5g; CHOL 11mg; IRON 0.4mg; SODIUM 109mg; CALC 57mg

MINUTES

Pine Nut and Apricot Couscous

Apricots and pine nuts contribute a delightful hint of sweetness to plain couscous.

1   cup fat-free, less-sodium chicken broth
³/₄   cup uncooked plain couscous
¹/₄   teaspoon kosher salt
¹/₄   teaspoon freshly ground pepper
2   tablespoons pine nuts, toasted
2   tablespoons dried apricots, chopped

1. Bring broth to a boil over medium-high heat in a medium saucepan; stir in couscous, salt, and pepper. Cover and remove from heat; let stand 5 minutes. Add pine nuts and apricots, and toss with a fork. **Yield:** 6 servings (serving size: about ¹/₂ cup).

CALORIES 111; FAT 2g (sat 0.4g, mono 0.6g, poly 1g); PROTEIN 3.8g; CARB 19.2g; FIBER 1.5g; CHOL 0mg; IRON 0.5mg; SODIUM 180mg; CALC 8.6mg

MINUTES

Spinach and Onion Couscous

make it a meal *This couscous can be prepared and served in the same microwave-safe bowl. Pair it with Mediterranean Cod (recipe on page 58).*

³/₄   cup water
¹/₄   cup finely chopped red onion
¹/₄   teaspoon salt
1   (6-ounce) package fresh baby spinach, coarsely chopped
¹/₂   cup uncooked couscous

1. Combine first 3 ingredients in a medium microwave-safe bowl. Cover with heavy-duty plastic wrap, and vent. Microwave at HIGH 2 minutes.
2. Add spinach and couscous to onion mixture; cover and microwave at HIGH 2 minutes. Let stand, covered, 5 minutes; fluff with a fork. Serve immediately. **Yield:** 4 servings (serving size: ³/₄ cup).

CALORIES 103; FAT 0.2g (sat 0g, mono 0.1g, poly 0.1g); PROTEIN 3.9g; CARB 22.2g; FIBER 3.3g; CHOL 0mg; IRON 1.6mg; SODIUM 215mg; CALC 38mg

MINUTES

Israeli Couscous with Almonds and Mint

Browning the couscous adds nutty flavor to this delicious pasta.

1   teaspoon extra-virgin olive oil
³/₄   cup Israeli couscous
1¹/₂ cups fat-free, less-sodium chicken broth
¹/₈   teaspoon salt
3   tablespoons slivered almonds, toasted
2   tablespoons chopped fresh mint

1. Heat oil in a medium saucepan over medium heat. Add couscous to pan; cook 3 minutes or until lightly browned, stirring frequently. Add broth and salt. Bring to a boil; cover, reduce heat, and simmer 8 minutes or until liquid is absorbed. Stir in almonds and mint. Serve immediately. **Yield:** 4 servings (serving size: about ¹/₂ cup).

CALORIES 188; FAT 4.3g (sat 0.4g, mono 2.6g, poly 1.2g); PROTEIN 6g; CARB 31.6g; FIBER 2.2g; CHOL 0mg; IRON 0.2mg; SODIUM 288mg; CALC 15mg

Pearl-like Israeli couscous, also known as maftoul, has larger-sized grains than couscous and takes on the consistency of macaroni when prepared. It cooks longer than regular couscous due to its size, but its size also allows it to absorb plenty of liquid and flavor.

INGREDIENT SPOTLIGHT

Grilled Eggplant

Creamy Cheese Grits

2½ cups fat-free, less-sodium chicken broth
1⅓ cups water
1 cup uncooked stone-ground yellow grits
1 garlic clove, pressed
⅓ cup (1.3 ounces) reduced-fat shredded sharp cheddar cheese
⅓ cup (2.6 ounces) ⅓-less-fat cream cheese

1. Combine first 4 ingredients in a 4-quart saucepan. Bring to a boil; partially cover, reduce heat, and simmer 19 minutes or until thick, stirring occasionally.
2. Add cheeses to pan, stirring until cheeses melt. **Yield:** 8 servings (serving size: ½ cup).

CALORIES 115; FAT 3.4g (sat 2.1g, mono 1.1g, poly 0.2g); PROTEIN 4.3g; CARB 16.5g; FIBER 0.5g; CHOL 10mg; IRON 0.8mg; SODIUM 213mg; CALC 41mg

---

15
MINUTES

Grilled Eggplant

Serve this quick and easy eggplant with almost any Italian entrée.

1 (1¼-pound) eggplant, cut crosswise into ½-inch-thick slices
Olive oil–flavored cooking spray
1½ teaspoons dried Italian seasoning
¼ teaspoon freshly ground black pepper
⅛ teaspoon salt

1. Prepare grill.
2. Coat eggplant slices with cooking spray. Sprinkle with Italian seasoning, pepper, and salt.
3. Place eggplant on grill rack coated with cooking spray; grill 3 to 4 minutes on each side or until tender. **Yield:** 4 servings (serving size: about 3 slices eggplant).

CALORIES 34; FAT 0.5g (sat 0.1g, mono 0.2g, poly 0.1g); PROTEIN 1.4g; CARB 7.9g; FIBER 4.8g; CHOL 0mg; IRON 0.4mg; SODIUM 77mg; CALC 13mg

---

30
MINUTES

Green Chile–Cheese Grits

Canned chopped green chiles and jalapeño-infused cheddar cheese pump up the flavor of traditional cheese grits.

2 cups fat-free milk
2 cups water
1 teaspoon bottled minced garlic
1¼ cups uncooked quick-cooking grits
2 tablespoons canned chopped green chiles, drained
¾ teaspoon salt
¾ cup (3 ounces) reduced-fat shredded jalapeño cheddar cheese (such as Cabot)

1. Combine first 3 ingredients in a medium saucepan, and bring to a boil. Reduce heat to low, and slowly add grits, stirring constantly with a whisk. Add chiles and salt. Cook 5 to 7 minutes or until thick, stirring frequently. Remove from heat, and add cheese, stirring until cheese melts. Serve immediately. **Yield:** 10 servings (serving size: ½ cup).

CALORIES 112; FAT 1.7g (sat 1g, mono 0.5g, poly 0.1g); PROTEIN 5.8g; CARB 18.2g; FIBER 0.4g; CHOL 6mg; IRON 0.8mg; SODIUM 260mg; CALC 112mg

COOKING CLASS: *how to clean kale*

To clean kale, pull apart the bunch; remove and discard any yellowed or limp leaves. Wash greens in cool water, agitating with your hands. Replace the water two or three times, until there are no traces of dirt. Pat dry with paper towels or use a salad spinner. Place on a cutting board, and cut away tough stems. To remove the hard center vein, fold the leaf in half and tear or cut away.

Kale with Lemon-Balsamic Butter

until lightly browned. Stir in raisins, juice, and vinegar; cook 30 seconds, stirring constantly with a whisk. Pour butter mixture over kale. Sprinkle with salt and pepper; toss well to coat. **Yield:** 10 servings (serving size: about 1 cup).

CALORIES 151; FAT 4.7g (sat 2.3g, mono 1.1g, poly 0.7g); PROTEIN 6.3g; CARB 25.5g; FIBER 4.9g; CHOL 9mg; IRON 3.4mg; SODIUM 289mg; CALC 252mg

30 MINUTES

Lemon-Garlic Linguine

make it a meal *Lemon juice, garlic, and extra-virgin olive oil lend a delicate fresh taste to this quick and easy pasta dish. Serve it with baked fish or chicken.*

8   ounces uncooked linguine
1   tablespoon extra-virgin olive oil, divided
3   garlic cloves, minced
1   teaspoon grated fresh lemon rind
1   tablespoon fresh lemon juice
½   teaspoon salt
¼   teaspoon freshly ground black pepper

1. Cook pasta according to package directions, omitting salt and fat; drain and place in a bowl.
2. While pasta cooks, heat a small nonstick skillet over medium heat. Add 1 teaspoon oil, garlic, and lemon rind. Cook 1 to 2 minutes, stirring constantly.
3. Add garlic mixture, remaining 2 teaspoons oil, lemon juice, salt, and pepper to pasta; toss well. Serve immediately. **Yield:** 8 servings (serving size: ½ cup).

CALORIES 121; FAT 2.2g (sat 0.4g, mono 1.5g, poly 0.3g); PROTEIN 4g; CARB 21.7g; FIBER 1g; CHOL 0mg; IRON 0.9mg; SODIUM 147mg; CALC 6mg

15 MINUTES

Kale with Lemon-Balsamic Butter

If you like spicy foods, add a dash of crushed red pepper to heat things up.

4   (1-pound) bunches kale
4   quarts water
3   tablespoons butter
½   cup raisins
3   tablespoons fresh lemon juice
3   tablespoons balsamic vinegar
¾   teaspoon fine sea salt
¼   teaspoon freshly ground black pepper

1. Bring water to a boil in an 8-quart stockpot. Remove stems and center ribs from kale. Wash and pat dry. Coarsely chop to measure 24 cups. Add kale; cover and cook 3 minutes. Drain well; place kale in a bowl.
2. Melt butter in a small skillet over medium-high heat; cook 3 minutes or

Grilled Okra

Grilling adds a whole new taste sensation to veggies. Purchase firm and brightly colored okra pods that are less than 4 inches long; they should be more tender than larger pods.

8	(12-inch) wooden skewers
1	pound small okra pods
1	tablespoon extra-virgin olive oil
1	teaspoon minced garlic
½	teaspoon salt
½	teaspoon freshly ground black pepper

1. Soak skewers in water 30 minutes.
2. Prepare grill.
3. Divide okra pods evenly among skewers (thread okra pods with 2 skewers to ease grilling). Combine olive oil and remaining ingredients; brush over okra.
4. Grill okra 4 to 6 minutes on each side or until crisp-tender. Serve immediately.
Yield: 4 servings (serving size: about 7 pods).

CALORIES 70; FAT 3.7g (sat 0.5g, mono 2.5g, poly 0.6g); PROTEIN 2.3g; CARB 8.4g; FIBER 3.7g; CHOL 0mg; IRON 0.9mg; SODIUM 300mg; CALC 94mg

Lemon-Basil Orzo with Parmesan

15 MINUTES

Okra, Corn, and Tomatoes

1	(14 1/2-ounce) can Cajun-style stewed tomatoes
2 1/2	cups frozen cut okra
1	cup frozen whole kernel corn

1. Combine tomatoes, okra, and corn in a large saucepan. Bring to a boil; cover, reduce heat to medium, and cook 10 minutes or until vegetables are tender, stirring occasionally. **Yield:** 6 servings (serving size: 1/2 cup).

CALORIES 56; FAT 0.2g (sat 0g, mono 0.1g, poly 0.1g); PROTEIN 1.9g; CARB 13.6g; FIBER 3.2g; CHOL 0mg; IRON 0.5mg; SODIUM 254mg; CALC 12mg

20 MINUTES

Orange-Basil Orzo Pilaf

1	(32-ounce) carton fat-free, less-sodium chicken broth
12	ounces uncooked orzo
1	tablespoon butter
1 1/4	cups finely diced carrot (about 2 medium)
3/4	cup finely diced onion (about 1 small)
3/4	cup finely diced celery (about 2 stalks)
1	teaspoon bottled minced garlic
1/4	cup chopped fresh basil
2	teaspoons grated fresh orange rind
2	tablespoons fresh orange juice
1/2	teaspoon salt
1/4	teaspoon freshly ground black pepper

1. Place broth in a medium saucepan; bring broth to a boil. Add orzo; reduce heat, and simmer 9 minutes or until tender. Drain.
2. While orzo cooks, melt butter in a large nonstick skillet over medium heat. Add carrot and next 3 ingredients; sauté 5 to 7 minutes or until tender. Add cooked orzo, basil, and remaining ingredients; stir well to combine. **Yield:** 10 servings (serving size: 1/2 cup).

CALORIES 146; FAT 2g (sat 0.7g, mono 0.5g, poly 0.6g); PROTEIN 4.6g; CARB 26.6g; FIBER 1.9g; CHOL 3mg; IRON 0.2mg; SODIUM 363mg; CALC 22mg

15 MINUTES

Lemon-Basil Orzo with Parmesan

To get the best cheese flavor, use fresh Parmigiano-Reggiano cheese. This premium Italian Parmesan cheese has a sharp, complex flavor that's perfect with pasta. You can wrap the cheese tightly in plastic and keep it in your refrigerator for up to six months.

3/4	cup uncooked orzo
2	teaspoons olive oil
2	teaspoons grated fresh lemon rind
2	garlic cloves, minced
1/4	cup chopped fresh basil
2	tablespoons grated fresh Parmigiano-Reggiano cheese
1/4	teaspoon salt
1/4	teaspoon black pepper
	Basil sprigs (optional)

1. Cook orzo according to package directions, omitting salt and fat. Drain.
2. While orzo cooks, heat oil in a medium nonstick skillet over medium-high heat. Add lemon rind and garlic, and sauté 1 minute. Remove from heat.
3. Add orzo, chopped basil, and next 3 ingredients to pan; toss well. Garnish with basil sprigs, if desired. Serve immediately. **Yield:** 4 servings (serving size: 1/2 cup).

CALORIES 158; FAT 4g (sat 1.1g, mono 2.2g, poly 0.7g); PROTEIN 5.7g; CARB 24.7g; FIBER 1.4g; CHOL 3mg; IRON 0.2mg; SODIUM 211mg; CALC 59mg

Minted Peas

2. Combine peas and remaining ingredients in a medium bowl; toss gently to coat. **Yield:** 4 servings (serving size: about $^1/_2$ cup).

CALORIES 64; FAT 0.8g (sat 0.3g, mono 0.3g, poly 0.1g); PROTEIN 4.5g; CARB 10.1g; FIBER 3.1g; CHOL 1mg; IRON 1.1mg; SODIUM 112mg; CALC 42mg

 MINUTES

Herbed English Peas with Mushrooms

1	teaspoon canola oil
$^1/_2$	cup thinly sliced onion
$1^1/_2$	cups presliced fresh mushrooms
$1^1/_2$	cups frozen petite green peas, thawed
2	tablespoons water
1	teaspoon dried tarragon
$^1/_4$	teaspoon salt
$^1/_8$	teaspoon black pepper

1. Heat canola oil in a large nonstick skillet over medium heat. Add onion; cook 4 minutes or until tender, stirring often. Add mushrooms; cook 4 minutes or until tender, stirring often. Stir in peas and remaining ingredients; cover and cook 4 minutes or just until peas are tender. **Yield:** 4 servings (serving size: $^1/_2$ cup).

CALORIES 70; FAT 1.3g (sat 0.1g, mono 0.7g, poly 0.4g); PROTEIN 3.1g; CARB 11.3g; FIBER 3.4g; CHOL 0mg; IRON 0.9mg; SODIUM 223mg; CALC 21mg

 MINUTES

Minted Peas

make it a meal *A sprinkle of fresh mint adds just-picked flavor to frozen green peas and makes this a fresh-tasting accompaniment for lamb chops.*

2	cups frozen petite green peas
1	tablespoon water
1	teaspoon butter
1	tablespoon chopped fresh mint
$^1/_8$	teaspoon salt

1. Place peas and water in a microwave-safe bowl. Cover and microwave at HIGH 7 minutes, stirring after 3 minutes.
2. Add butter, mint, and salt to peas; toss to coat. **Yield:** 3 servings (serving size: $^1/_2$ cup).

CALORIES 81; FAT 1.3g (sat 0.8g, mono 0.3g, poly 0.1g); PROTEIN 4g; CARB 12g; FIBER 4.1g; CHOL 3mg; IRON 1.1mg; SODIUM 305mg; CALC 2mg

 MINUTES

Parmesan Peas

2	cups frozen petite green peas
1	tablespoon grated fresh Parmesan cheese
2	teaspoons grated lemon rind
1	teaspoon fresh lemon juice

1. Place peas in a colander, and rinse under cool water until thawed; drain well.

Tarragon is native to Siberia and western Asia, though it is primarily used in France. It's often added to white wine vinegar, lending a sweet, delicate licorice-like perfume and flavor. Heat diminishes tarragon's flavor, so add tarragon toward the end of cooking, or use it as a garnish. A little goes a long way.

INGREDIENT SPOTLIGHT

Gingered Sugar Snap Peas

Gingered Sugar Snap Peas

2   teaspoons olive oil
1   pound fresh sugar snap peas, trimmed
2   teaspoons grated peeled fresh ginger
1   garlic clove, minced
1   teaspoon coarsely chopped walnuts, toasted
¼   teaspoon salt

1. Heat oil in a large nonstick skillet over medium-high heat. Add peas, and cook 5 minutes or until crisp-tender, stirring occasionally.
2. Add ginger and remaining ingredients; cook 1 minute, stirring constantly. **Yield:** 5 servings (serving size: about ³/₄ cup).

CALORIES 74; FAT 2.1g (sat 0.3g, mono 1.4g, poly 0.4g); PROTEIN 2.3g; CARB 6.8g;
FIBER 2.2g; CHOL 0mg; IRON 0.8mg; SODIUM 129mg; CALC 44mg

Zesty Sugar Snap Peas

Butter-flavored cooking spray
1   pound fresh sugar snap peas, trimmed
2   teaspoons lemon pepper seasoning

1. Heat a large nonstick skillet over medium-high heat. Coat pan with cooking spray. Add peas, and sauté 3 minutes or until crisp-tender. Coat peas lightly with additional cooking spray, and sprinkle with lemon pepper seasoning. **Yield:** 4 servings (serving size: about ³/₄ cup).

CALORIES 68; FAT 0.2g (sat 0g, mono 0.2g, poly 0g); PROTEIN 2.7g; CARB 8g;
FIBER 2.7g; CHOL 0mg; IRON 1mg; SODIUM 13mg; CALC 53mg

15 MINUTES

Orange-Sesame Snow Peas

Snow peas are best—and will keep their fresh crunch—when you cook them just enough to bring out the bright green color.

3   tablespoons thawed orange juice
    concentrate
1   tablespoon low-sodium soy sauce
1   teaspoon toasted sesame seeds
1½ teaspoons dark sesame oil
⅛   teaspoon crushed red pepper
3   cups snow peas, trimmed (about ¾ pound)

1. Combine first 5 ingredients in a small bowl.
2. Heat a large nonstick skillet over medium-high heat; add juice mixture and peas. Cook 3 minutes, stirring often. Serve immediately. **Yield:** 4 servings (serving size: ½ cup).

CALORIES 90; FAT 2.1g (sat 0.3g, mono 0.9g, poly 0.9g); PROTEIN 2.5g;
CARB 11.2g; FIBER 2.2g; CHOL 0mg; IRON 0.9mg; SODIUM 165mg; CALC 45mg

15 MINUTES

Mushroom and Pepper Skillet

Cooking spray
1½ cups red bell pepper strips (1 large)
1   (8-ounce) package presliced fresh
    mushrooms
2   tablespoons water
1   tablespoon low-sodium soy sauce
2   green onions, thinly sliced

1. Heat a large nonstick skillet over medium-high heat. Coat pan with cooking spray. Add pepper strips and next 3 ingredients. Cover and cook 4 minutes; stir well. Cover and cook 3 minutes or until crisp-tender. Remove from heat; stir in green onions. **Yield:** 4 servings (serving size: about ½ cup).

CALORIES 40; FAT 0.3g (sat 0.1g, mono 0g, poly 0.2g); PROTEIN 2g; CARB 8.2g;
FIBER 2.9g; CHOL 0mg; IRON 0.6mg; SODIUM 154mg; CALC 10mg

INGREDIENT SPOTLIGHT

Orange juice concentrate is a convenience product that's always good to have on hand. Not only is it useful for fruity beverages, but it also adds a sweet tanginess to this snow pea recipe.

Bell Pepper Sauté

Many grocery stores carry multipacks of green, red, and yellow bell peppers that are often less expensive than each pepper purchased separately.

1   tablespoon olive oil
1   large yellow bell pepper, seeded and cut
    into julienne strips
1   large green bell pepper, seeded and cut into
    julienne strips
1   large red bell pepper, seeded and cut into
    julienne strips
2   shallots, chopped
⅛   tablespoon salt
2   tablespoons chopped fresh parsley
¼   teaspoon black pepper

1. Heat oil in a large nonstick skillet over medium-high heat. Add bell peppers and shallots to pan; sprinkle vegetables with salt. Cook 5 minutes or until bell peppers are crisp-tender. Stir in chopped fresh parsley and black pepper; cook 1 minute. **Yield:** 5 servings (serving size: about 1 cup).

CALORIES 54; FAT 3g (sat 0.5g, mono 2g, poly 0.5g); PROTEIN 1.2g; CARB 7.1g;
FIBER 1.9g; CHOL 0mg; IRON 0.6mg; SODIUM 64mg; CALC 14mg

COOKING CLASS: *how to cut bell pepper*

To cut bell pepper strips, slice off the top of the pepper. Cut the pepper into quarters. Discard the stem, seeds, and white membranes. Slice each pepper quarter either crosswise or lengthwise into ¼-inch-thick strips.

Bell Pepper Sauté

30 MINUTES

Pretty Pepper Kebabs

These pepper kebabs are a colorful side dish for any grilled entrée.

2 tablespoons olive oil
2 tablespoons balsamic vinegar
1 teaspoon dried oregano
3 small bell peppers in assorted colors, seeded and cut into 1-inch pieces
1 small onion, cut into wedges
¼ teaspoon salt
¼ teaspoon black pepper
Cooking spray

1. Prepare grill.
2. Combine first 3 ingredients in a large zip-top plastic bag. Add bell peppers and onion; seal bag, and shake, tossing to coat. Remove vegetables from bag; discard marinade.
3. Alternately thread vegetables onto 4 (10-inch) metal skewers. Sprinkle each kebab evenly with salt and black pepper. Place kebabs on grill rack coated with cooking spray; cover and grill 10 minutes or until tender, turning occasionally. **Yield:** 4 servings (serving size: 1 kebab).

CALORIES 88; FAT 6.9g (sat 1g, mono 4.9g, poly 0.8g); PROTEIN 0.8g; CARB 6.2g; FIBER 1.6g; CHOL 0mg; IRON 0.5mg; SODIUM 152mg; CALC 14mg

15 MINUTES

Cheesy Polenta with Garlic and Sage

make it a meal *Polenta is a staple northern Italian side dish made with cornmeal. It has a soft texture similar to grits. This cheesy version is especially good with grilled or roasted meats.*

1 teaspoon olive oil
2 garlic cloves, minced
1 cup water
1 cup fat-free milk
½ teaspoon salt
½ cup yellow cornmeal
⅓ cup (3 ounces) ⅓-less-fat cream cheese
2 tablespoons minced fresh sage
2 tablespoons grated fresh pecorino Romano cheese
¼ teaspoon black pepper

1. Heat oil in a medium saucepan over medium heat. Add garlic; sauté 1 minute or until golden. Remove garlic from pan, and set aside.
2. Add water, milk, and salt to pan; bring to a boil. Add cornmeal, stirring with a whisk. Cook 2 minutes or until thick, stirring frequently with a whisk.
3. Remove from heat; add cream cheese, sage, Romano cheese, pepper, and reserved garlic. Stir until cheeses melt. Serve immediately. **Yield:** 5 servings (serving size: ½ cup).

CALORIES 139; FAT 5.4g (sat 3.1g, mono 1.9g, poly 0.4g); PROTEIN 5.4g; CARB 16.4g; FIBER 0.5g; CHOL 15mg; IRON 0.4mg; SODIUM 375mg; CALC 116mg

20 MINUTES

Roasted Fingerling Potatoes with Rosemary

Kosher salt's unique texture helps it adhere to food surfaces, making it ideal for enhancing simply seasoned finished dishes.

1½ pounds fingerling potatoes, sliced lengthwise
1 tablespoon olive oil
1 tablespoon chopped fresh rosemary
½ teaspoon kosher salt
½ teaspoon freshly ground black pepper

1. Preheat oven to 475°.
2. Combine potato, olive oil, and rosemary in a large bowl, tossing to coat potato. Arrange potato in a single layer on a baking sheet. Bake at 475° for 15 minutes or until potato is browned and tender. Sprinkle with salt and pepper. **Yield:** 8 servings (serving size: ¹/₂ cup).

CALORIES 86; FAT 1.7g (sat 0.2g, mono 1.2g, poly 0.2g); PROTEIN 2g; CARB 15.2g; FIBER 1.1g; CHOL 0mg; IRON 0.5mg; SODIUM 123mg; CALC 1mg

15 MINUTES

Feta Mashed Potatoes

Feta lends a distinctive flavor to packaged mashed potatoes. The result: a top-rated side dish suitable for family or guests.

1 (24-ounce) package refrigerated sour cream and chive mashed potatoes (such as Simply Potatoes)
3 tablespoons crumbled feta cheese
¼ teaspoon dried oregano
¼ teaspoon black pepper

1. Heat potatoes in microwave according to package directions. Add feta, oregano, and pepper; stir well. **Yield:** 6 servings (serving size: ¹/₂ cup).

CALORIES 117; FAT 4.2g (sat 2.7g, mono 0.9g, poly 0.5g); PROTEIN 3.6g; CARB 16.8g; FIBER 1.7g; CHOL 16mg; IRON 0.4mg; SODIUM 456mg; CALC 87mg

15 MINUTES

New Potatoes in Seasoned Butter

Just a little bit of lime juice kicks up the flavor in these potatoes.

1 pound small new potatoes, unpeeled and quartered (about 5 to 6 potatoes)
1 tablespoon butter, melted
1½ teaspoons lime juice
³/₄ teaspoon paprika
¼ teaspoon salt
3 tablespoons chopped fresh parsley

1. Steam potatoes, covered, 10 to 12 minutes or until tender. Transfer to a large serving bowl, and keep warm.
2. Combine butter and next 3 ingredients in a small bowl, stirring well. Add butter mixture to potatoes, and toss. Sprinkle with parsley, and toss gently. **Yield:** 4 servings (serving size: ²/₃ cup).

CALORIES 98; FAT 2.9g (sat 1.8g, mono 0.7g, poly 0.1g); PROTEIN 3g; CARB 14.6g; FIBER 3g; CHOL 8mg; IRON 0.7mg; SODIUM 287mg; CALC 6mg

New Potatoes in Seasoned Butter

2O
MINUTES

Creamy Herbed Mashed Potatoes

4	cups cubed peeled Yukon gold potato (about 2 pounds)
½	cup 2% reduced-fat milk
¼	cup low-fat sour cream
3	tablespoons butter
3	tablespoons chopped fresh chives
2	tablespoons chopped fresh parsley
½	teaspoon salt
¼	teaspoon freshly ground black pepper

1. Place potato in a saucepan; cover with water. Bring to a boil; cover, reduce heat, and simmer 10 minutes or until tender. Drain. Return potato to pan. Add milk and remaining ingredients; mash with a potato masher to desired consistency. **Yield:** 6 servings (serving size: ³/₄ cup).

CALORIES 215; FAT 7.1g (sat 4.5g, mono 1.8g, poly 0.3g); PROTEIN 4.5g; CARB 34.5g; FIBER 2.4g; CHOL 20mg; IRON 0.7mg; SODIUM 280mg; CALC 51mg

15 MINUTES

Grilled Sweet Potatoes

Use commercial salad dressing to quickly and easily glaze these grilled sweet potatoes.

3 small sweet potatoes, peeled
1 tablespoon light honey mustard dressing (such as Ken's)
½ tablespoon light stick butter, melted
Cooking spray

1. Prepare grill.
2. Cut each sweet potato lengthwise into 4 slices. Arrange potato slices in a single layer on a large microwave-safe dish. Microwave at HIGH 5 minutes or just until tender.
3. While potatoes cook, combine honey mustard dressing and butter in a small bowl. Brush potatoes with half of honey-mustard mixture. Place potato slices on grill rack coated with cooking spray. Grill potato slices 8 to 10 minutes, turning after 4 minutes to brush potato slices with remaining honey mustard mixture. **Yield:** 3 servings (serving size: 4 potato slices).

CALORIES 77; FAT 1.9g (sat 0.7g, mono 0.5g, poly 0.6g); PROTEIN 2.5g; CARB 14.3g; FIBER 2g; CHOL 3mg; IRON 0.4mg; SODIUM 69mg; CALC 23mg

Sweet potatoes are actually not potatoes at all—they're members of the morning glory family and are warm-weather plants. (Potatoes grow best at high altitudes and in cold climates.) Though marginally higher in calories than white potatoes, sweet potatoes are nutrient powerhouses.

INGREDIENT SPOTLIGHT

30 MINUTES

Sweet Potato Fries

2 medium sweet potatoes (about 1¼ pounds), cut lengthwise into thin strips
1 tablespoon chopped fresh rosemary
1 tablespoon olive oil
½ teaspoon freshly ground black pepper
¼ teaspoon kosher salt
¼ teaspoon garlic powder

1. Preheat oven to 475°.
2. Combine all ingredients in a bowl; toss well. Arrange potato in a single layer on a baking sheet.
3. Bake at 475° for 25 minutes or until lightly browned and tender, turning once. **Yield:** 4 servings (serving size: about ½ cup).

CALORIES 154; FAT 3.5g (sat 0.5g, mono 2.5g, poly 0.4g); PROTEIN 2.3g; CARB 28.9g; FIBER 4.4g; CHOL 0mg; IRON 0.9mg; SODIUM 196mg; CALC 45mg

30 MINUTES

Spicy Sweet Potatoes

Sweet potatoes are packed with fiber and vitamins A and C. We used a chipotle seasoning blend, but you can substitute another blend, if you prefer.

2 teaspoons salt-free southwest chipotle seasoning blend (such as Mrs. Dash)
2 teaspoons olive oil
1 teaspoon fresh lime juice
¼ teaspoon salt
2 large sweet potatoes (about 1¾ pounds), peeled and each cut into 8 wedges
Cooking spray

1. Preheat oven to 450°.
2. Combine first 4 ingredients in a bowl. Add potatoes, and toss well to coat.
3. Place potatoes on a baking sheet coated with cooking spray. Bake at 450° for 25 minutes or until tender. Serve immediately. **Yield:** 4 servings (serving size: 4 wedges).

CALORIES 160; FAT 2.5g (sat 0.4g, mono 1.6g, poly 0.5g); PROTEIN 3.1g; CARB 32.2g; FIBER 5.1g; CHOL 0mg; IRON 1.1mg; SODIUM 201mg; CALC 59mg

Sweet Potato Fries

20 MINUTES

Sweet Potatoes with Orange-Honey Butter

make it a meal *Get a healthy dose of vitamins A and C with these rich and buttery sweet potatoes. Serve them with turkey cutlets or loin pork chops.*

4	(6-ounce) sweet potatoes
2	tablespoons butter, softened
2	teaspoons honey
¼	teaspoon vanilla extract
¼	teaspoon grated orange rind

1. Microwave sweet potatoes at HIGH 8 or 9 minutes or until tender, rearranging after 5 minutes. Wrap in a towel. Let stand 5 minutes.
2. While sweet potatoes cook, combine butter and next 3 ingredients in a small bowl.
3. Cut potatoes in half within ¹/₂ inch of bottom, and push open. Fluff sweet potatoes with a fork, and top with orange-honey butter. **Yield:** 4 servings (serving size: 1 potato and 1¹/₂ teaspoons orange-honey butter).

CALORIES 193; FAT 5.7g (sat 3.6g, mono 1.5g, poly 0.2g); PROTEIN 2.7g; CARB 33.1g; FIBER 5.3g; CHOL 15mg; IRON 1mg; SODIUM 132mg; CALC 28mg

15 MINUTES

Southwestern Rice

make it a meal *Serve this superfast rice dish with chicken fajitas, enchiladas, or tacos.*

1¹/₂	cups fat-free, less-sodium chicken broth
³/₄	teaspoon fajita seasoning
1¹/₂	cups uncooked instant long-grain rice
¼	cup thinly sliced green onions

1. Bring broth and seasoning to a boil in a medium saucepan; stir in rice. Remove from heat; let stand 7 minutes or until liquid is absorbed. Stir in green onions. **Yield:** 6 servings (serving size: ¹/₂ cup).

CALORIES 102; FAT 0.4g (sat 0g, mono 0.3g, poly 0.1g); PROTEIN 2.6g; CARB 21.4g; FIBER 0.6g; CHOL 0mg; IRON 1.5mg; SODIUM 211mg; CALC 10mg

15 MINUTES

Fruited Curry Rice

Transform plain instant rice into a fruity curry rice by adding dried fruit, cilantro, and curry powder.

1	cup water
1	teaspoon butter
¹/₂	teaspoon curry powder
¼	teaspoon salt
1	cup uncooked instant long-grain rice
¹/₂	cup chopped tropical dried fruit
¼	cup chopped fresh cilantro

1. Bring water to a boil in a medium saucepan. Add butter and next 4 ingredients; stir gently. Remove from heat. Cover and let stand 5 minutes or until water is absorbed.
2. Add cilantro, and fluff with a fork. **Yield:** 4 servings (serving size: ¹/₂ cup).

CALORIES 177; FAT 1.9g (sat 1.1g, mono 0.5g, poly 0.2g); PROTEIN 1.9g; CARB 37.1g; FIBER 1.6g; CHOL 3mg; IRON 1.7mg; SODIUM 183mg; CALC 29mg

Fruited Curry Rice

2O
MINUTES

Rapid Risotto

Preparing risotto in the microwave makes a traditionally labor-intensive dish quick and virtually hands-off. The creamy texture is the same you achieve with 45 minutes of stirring on the stovetop. If you prefer to omit the wine, just add ½ cup more vegetable broth.

1¾ cups organic vegetable broth (such as Swanson Certified Organic)
1   cup uncooked Arborio rice or other short-grain rice
½   cup dry white wine
½   cup frozen chopped onion
1   tablespoon olive oil
1   cup finely chopped plum tomato
½   cup (2 ounces) preshredded fresh Parmesan cheese
½   teaspoon freshly ground black pepper
⅛   teaspoon salt
2   tablespoons chopped fresh parsley

1. Combine first 5 ingredients in a 1½-quart microwave-safe dish. Cover with plastic wrap, and vent. Microwave at HIGH 12 to 15 minutes or until liquid is almost absorbed. Remove from microwave; add tomato and next 3 ingredients, stirring well. Cover and let stand until ready to serve. Stir in parsley just before serving. **Yield:** 8 servings (serving size: ½ cup).

CALORIES 153; FAT 4.1g (sat 1.4g, mono 2.3g, poly 0.3g); PROTEIN 4.6g; CARB 22.2g; FIBER 1.5g; CHOL 6.3mg; IRON 0.2mg; SODIUM 264mg; CALC 82mg

Yellow Rice

4   cups water
½   teaspoon salt
½   teaspoon ground turmeric
1   bay leaf
1   (3½-ounce) bag boil-in-bag brown rice

1. Combine water, salt, turmeric, and bay leaf in a medium bowl. Add boil-in-bag rice, pressing down into liquid to thoroughly moisten. Microwave, uncovered, at HIGH 12 to 13 minutes or until tender; drain well, discarding liquid and bay leaf. Cut bag open, and return rice to bowl; fluff with a fork. **Yield:** 4 servings (serving size: ½ cup).

CALORIES 93; FAT 0.6g (sat 0g, mono 0.3g, poly 0.3g); PROTEIN 2.2g; CARB 19.5g; FIBER 1.1g; CHOL 0mg; IRON 0.7mg; SODIUM 301mg; CALC 5mg

Bay leaves infuse recipes with a woodsy flavor. If your grocery store doesn't carry fresh bay leaves, substitute good-quality dried bay leaves (such as Spice Island).

INGREDIENT SPOTLIGHT

Brown Rice and Onion Pilaf

1   (5.3-ounce) package boil-in-bag
    brown rice
Cooking spray
1   cup chopped Vidalia or other sweet onion
1½ cups spinach, coarsely chopped
¼   cup pine nuts, toasted
4   sun-dried tomato halves, chopped
¼   teaspoon salt
⅛   teaspoon freshly ground black pepper

1. Cook rice according to package directions,
omitting salt and fat.
2. While rice cooks, heat a medium nonstick
skillet over medium-high heat; coat pan
with cooking spray. Add onion to pan, and
cook 5 to 6 minutes or until browned, stirring frequently. Remove from heat. Stir in
cooked rice, spinach, and remaining ingredients; toss gently until spinach wilts. **Yield:**
6 servings (serving size: about ¹/₂ cup).

CALORIES 141; FAT 3.7g (sat 0.7g, mono 1.2g, poly 1.7g); PROTEIN 3.2g; CARB 23.6g;
FIBER 2.5g; CHOL 0mg; IRON 1mg; SODIUM 112mg; CALC 27mg

Nutty Brown Rice

*This hearty, whole-grain side dish is ready
in under 15 minutes thanks to boil-in-bag
brown rice.*

1   (3½-ounce) bag boil-in-bag brown rice
    (such as Success Rice)
3   cups fat-free, less-sodium chicken broth
⅛   teaspoon freshly ground black pepper
¼   cup chopped pecans, toasted
2   teaspoons light stick butter

1. Prepare rice according to package directions, omitting salt and fat and substituting 3 cups chicken broth for the water;
drain well. Stir in black pepper, toasted
pecans, and butter. Serve immediately.
Yield: 4 servings (serving size: ¹/₂ cup).

CALORIES 107; FAT 7.8g (sat 1.3g, mono 4g, poly 2.3g); PROTEIN 2.1g; CARB 7.4g;
FIBER 1.1g; CHOL 2mg; IRON 0.3mg; SODIUM 423mg; CALC 10mg

Coconut-Pineapple-Ginger Rice

make it a meal *Serve this tropical-
flavored rice with a mild white fish for a
healthy evening meal.*

1   (8-ounce) can pineapple tidbits in juice
3¾ cups water
1   (3½-ounce) package boil-in-bag jasmine
    rice
Butter-flavored cooking spray
1   tablespoon minced peeled fresh ginger
1   tablespoon chopped fresh cilantro
2   tablespoons light coconut milk
¼   teaspoon salt

1. Drain pineapple, reserving juice. Combine
pineapple juice, water, and rice in a saucepan. Bring to a boil; boil, uncovered, 8 minutes. Drain well.
2. While rice cooks, heat a large nonstick
skillet over medium-high heat. Coat pan
with cooking spray. Add ginger and drained
pineapple tidbits; sauté 4 minutes or until
caramelized. Combine ginger mixture, rice,
cilantro, coconut milk, and salt. Serve
immediately. **Yield:** 4 servings (serving
size: ¹/₂ cup).

CALORIES 122; FAT 0.4g (sat 0.4g, mono 0g, poly 0g); PROTEIN 2g; CARB 29.3g;
FIBER 0.5g; CHOL 0mg; IRON 1mg; SODIUM 148mg; CALC 8mg

30 MINUTES

Green Onion Rice

*Coconut milk adds just a touch of
sweetness to aromatic jasmine rice.*

1   cup fat-free, less-sodium chicken broth
3/4 cup light coconut milk
1/4 teaspoon salt
1   cup uncooked jasmine rice
1/3 cup thinly sliced green onions
2   tablespoons chopped fresh cilantro

1. Combine first 3 ingredients in a medium
saucepan; bring to a boil. Stir in rice. Cover,
reduce heat, and simmer 15 minutes or
until rice is tender and liquid is absorbed.
Stir in green onions and cilantro. **Yield:**
6 servings (serving size: 1/2 cup).

CALORIES 75; FAT 1.5g (sat 1.4g, mono 0.1g, poly 0g); PROTEIN 1.9g; CARB 13.8g;
FIBER 0.4g; CHOL 0mg; IRON 0.3mg; SODIUM 203mg; CALC 5mg

Green Onion Rice

20 MINUTES

Creamed Spinach

*We used light butter, light cream cheese,
and reduced-fat white cheddar cheese to
decrease fat but not taste in this comforting
side dish.*

Cooking spray
2   (12-ounce) bags fresh baby spinach
1   tablespoon light stick butter
1/3 cup finely chopped onion
2   teaspoons bottled minced garlic
1   tablespoon all-purpose flour
1/4 cup fat-free milk
1/2 cup tub-style light cream cheese, softened
1/2 cup (2 ounces) reduced-fat shredded white
     cheddar cheese (such as Kraft Cracker
     Barrel)
1/4 teaspoon freshly ground black pepper
1/4 teaspoon hot sauce

1. Heat a large Dutch oven over medium-
high heat; coat pan with cooking spray. Add
spinach; sauté 5 minutes or until spinach
wilts. Drain spinach in a colander, pressing
spinach with back of a spoon to remove as
much moisture as possible.
2. Melt butter in pan; sauté onion and garlic
over medium heat 3 minutes or until tender. Add flour, and cook, stirring constantly, 1 minute. Add milk and cheeses;
cook, stirring constantly, 2 minutes or until
cheese melts. Add spinach; cook 3 minutes
or until spinach is thoroughly heated.
Remove from heat; stir in pepper and hot
sauce. **Yield:** 4 servings (serving size: about
1/2 cup).

CALORIES 226; FAT 10.7g (sat 6.8g, mono 2.8g, poly 0.9g); PROTEIN 11.4g;
CARB 24.6g; FIBER 8.3g; CHOL 33mg; IRON 5.6mg; SODIUM 734mg;
CALC 284mg

Sautéed Lemon Spinach
and Onion

Sautéed Spinach with Raisins and Pine Nuts

4	teaspoons pine nuts
1	teaspoon olive oil
2	garlic cloves, minced
2	(6-ounce) packages fresh baby spinach
¼	teaspoon salt
¼	teaspoon freshly ground black pepper
⅛	teaspoon crushed red pepper

Dash of ground nutmeg

| ⅓ | cup golden raisins |

1. Place pine nuts in a large nonstick skillet over medium-high heat; cook 3 minutes or until lightly browned, stirring constantly. Remove from pan; set aside.

2. Heat oil in pan over medium-high heat. Add garlic; sauté 30 seconds. Add spinach; cook 4 minutes or until spinach wilts, stirring occasionally. Remove from heat; sprinkle with salt and next 3 ingredients. Add pine nuts and raisins; toss well. Serve immediately with a slotted spoon. **Yield:** 4 servings (serving size: ½ cup).

CALORIES 94; FAT 3.1g (sat 0.3g, mono 1.5g, poly 1.2g); PROTEIN 3g; CARB 14.9g; FIBER 2.7g; CHOL 0mg; IRON 3.3mg; SODIUM 212mg; CALC 91mg

Sautéed Lemon Spinach and Onion

This recipe transforms mild and tender fresh baby spinach leaves into a warm, savory side dish.

| 1 | teaspoon olive oil |

Cooking spray

½	cup chopped red onion
2	garlic cloves, minced
1	(6-ounce) package fresh baby spinach
½	teaspoon grated fresh lemon rind
2	teaspoons fresh lemon juice
¼	teaspoon salt
¼	teaspoon black pepper

1. Heat oil in a large nonstick skillet coated with cooking spray over medium heat. Add onion and garlic; sauté 3 minutes or until onion is tender.

2. Add spinach, and cook 4 minutes or just until spinach wilts. Stir in lemon rind and remaining ingredients. Serve immediately. **Yield:** 2 servings (serving size: ½ cup).

CALORIES 78; FAT 2.3g (sat 0.3g, mono 1.7g, poly 0.3g); PROTEIN 2.7g; CARB 14.4g; FIBER 4.9g; CHOL 0mg; IRON 2.9mg; SODIUM 428mg; CALC 77mg

Pine nuts are the pearly seeds from the cones of certain pine trees that are harvested throughout the Mediterranean. In American markets, most pine nuts are imported from Italy or China because domestic pine trees don't produce the same quality product. While pine nuts play an important role in Italian baking and cooking, they're also a good-for-you-snack because they're high in the "good" fats.

INGREDIENT SPOTLIGHT

15 MINUTES

Baby Spinach with Mushrooms

1	teaspoon olive oil
1	cup sliced fresh mushrooms
2	garlic cloves, minced
2	(6-ounce) packages fresh baby spinach
¼	teaspoon salt
¼	teaspoon freshly ground black pepper

1. Heat oil in a large nonstick skillet over medium-high heat. Add mushrooms; sauté 2 minutes. Add garlic; sauté 30 seconds. Add spinach in batches, and cook until spinach wilts and liquid almost evaporates, stirring frequently. Stir in salt and pepper, and serve immediately. **Yield:** 4 servings (serving size: about ½ cup).

CALORIES 38; FAT 1.2g (sat 0.2g, mono 0.8g, poly 0.2g); PROTEIN 2.9g; CARB 4.4g; FIBER 2.3g; CHOL 0mg; IRON 2.9mg; SODIUM 214mg; CALC 84mg

15 MINUTES

Swiss Chard with Garlic and Oregano

10	cups coarsely chopped Swiss chard (about 10 ounces)
1	teaspoon olive oil
1	garlic clove, minced
¼	teaspoon dried oregano
⅛	teaspoon salt
Dash of black pepper	
2	teaspoons red wine vinegar

1. Rinse Swiss chard with cold water; drain chard well.
2. Heat oil in a large nonstick skillet over medium-high heat. Add garlic, and sauté 1 minute or until slightly golden. Add chard. Cover and cook 1 minute or until chard begins to wilt. Stir in oregano, salt, and pepper. Cover and cook 5 minutes or until tender, stirring occasionally. Remove from heat; stir in vinegar. **Yield:** 2 servings (serving size: about ½ cup).

CALORIES 51; FAT 2.6g (sat 0.4g, mono 1.7g, poly 0.3g); PROTEIN 2.7g; CARB 6.1g; FIBER 2.4g; CHOL 0mg; IRON 2.8mg; SODIUM 454mg; CALC 80mg

30 MINUTES

Sunchoke Latkes

Cook the latkes soon after combining the ingredients so the mixture does not become watery; if this happens, remove the mixture from the liquid using a slotted spoon.

1½	pounds Jerusalem artichokes (sunchokes), peeled and shredded
1	pound baking potatoes, peeled and shredded
1	large carrot, peeled and shredded
1.5	ounces all-purpose flour (about ⅓ cup)
1	teaspoon salt
¼	teaspoon black pepper
1	large egg, lightly beaten
1	large egg white, lightly beaten
2½	tablespoons olive oil, divided
6	tablespoons fat-free sour cream

1. Place artichoke, potato, and carrot in a large bowl, and toss gently to combine. Lightly spoon flour into a dry measuring cup; level with a knife. Add flour, salt, and pepper to artichoke mixture; toss gently to combine. Add egg and egg white; stir just until combined.
2. Heat half of oil in a large nonstick skillet over medium-high heat. Spoon about ¼ cup artichoke mixture for each of 9 latkes into pan. Cook 3 minutes on each side or until browned. Remove from pan. Repeat with remaining oil and artichoke mixture. Serve with sour cream. **Yield:** 6 servings (serving size: 3 latkes and 1 tablespoon sour cream).

CALORIES 216; FAT 6.6g (sat 1g, mono 4.5g, poly 0.6g); PROTEIN 6.8g; CARB 32.1g; FIBER 3.1g; CHOL 38mg; IRON 3.7mg; SODIUM 445mg; CALC 54mg

SHORTCUT SPOTLIGHT

A food processor is a handy piece of equipment that can save time. Use the shredder blade to quickly shred the artichokes, potato, and carrot for this latke recipe.

Acorn Squash with
Maple Syrup

MINUTES

Acorn Squash with Maple Syrup

*Briefly microwave the whole acorn squash
to soften the shell and make it easier to cut
in half.*

1   (1-pound) acorn squash
¼   cup water
1   tablespoon light butter
1½   tablespoons maple syrup
⅛   teaspoon salt
⅛   teaspoon ground cinnamon

1. Microwave whole squash at HIGH 1 to
2 minutes. Cut squash in half lengthwise;
scoop out seeds and discard.
2. Place squash, cut-sides-down, in an
8-inch square microwave-safe baking dish;
add water to dish. Cover with plastic wrap;
pull back one corner to vent. Microwave at
HIGH 6 to 8 minutes or until tender. Transfer squash to a serving plate.
3. While squash cooks, place butter, syrup,
and salt in a small saucepan over medium
heat; bring mixture to a boil. Spoon mixture evenly over cooked squash; sprinkle
with cinnamon. **Yield:** 2 servings (serving
size: 1 squash half).

CALORIES 163; FAT 3.8g (sat 2.3g, mono 1.1g, poly 0.2g); PROTEIN 2g; CARB 33.8g;
FIBER 3.5g; CHOL 8mg; IRON 1.9mg; SODIUM 183mg; CALC 90mg

15
MINUTES

Summer Squash with Parmesan

*You can use all zucchini or all yellow squash
in this recipe, if you'd like.*

Cooking spray
1   medium zucchini, thinly sliced (about
    1½ cups)
1   medium yellow squash, thinly sliced (about
    1 cup)
1   small onion, thinly sliced (about 1 cup)
¼   teaspoon salt
¼   teaspoon freshly ground black pepper
2   teaspoons chopped fresh oregano
¼   cup (1 ounce) grated fresh Parmesan cheese

1. Heat a large nonstick skillet over
medium-high heat. Coat pan with cooking
spray. Add zucchini and next 4 ingredients;
cook 7 minutes or until vegetables are tender, stirring frequently.
2. Stir in oregano. Sprinkle cheese on top;
cook 1 minute or until cheese melts. **Yield:**
4 servings (serving size: about ½ cup).

CALORIES 59; FAT 2.2g (sat 1.1g, mono 0.9g, poly 0.2g); PROTEIN 4.5g; CARB 6.4g;
FIBER 1.5g; CHOL 5mg; IRON 0.4mg; SODIUM 275mg; CALC 119mg

Unlike winter squashes,
such as butternut or
acorn, summer squash
has edible skin and
seeds. The most
common summer
varieties are yellow squash
(also called crookneck),
pattypan squash, and zucchini.
Whether you're gathering
them from your garden or
from the supermarket bins,
choose small, firm squashes
with bright-colored,
blemish-free skins.

INGREDIENT SPOTLIGHT

Balsamic Grilled Zucchini and
Yellow Squash

15 MINUTES

Balsamic Grilled Zucchini and Yellow Squash

Summer is the peak season for squash and zucchini, and there's no better way to enjoy these vegetables than grilled to perfection.

2   large zucchini squash, halved lengthwise
2   large yellow squash, halved lengthwise
⅓   cup fat-free balsamic vinaigrette (such as Maple Grove Farms)
Cooking spray

1. Prepare grill.
2. Brush cut sides of squash with balsamic vinaigrette. Place squash on grill rack coated with cooking spray. Grill 5 minutes on each side or until squash are tender, basting with any remaining balsamic vinaigrette. Remove squash from grill, and cut into slices. **Yield:** 4 servings (serving size: about 1 cup).

CALORIES 68; FAT 0.6g (sat 0.1g, mono 0.1g, poly 0.3g); PROTEIN 3.9g; CARB 14.8g; FIBER 3.6g; CHOL 0mg; IRON 1.4mg; SODIUM 286mg; CALC 48mg

 MINUTES

Italian-Seasoned Squash Sauté

1   tablespoon olive oil
2   small zucchini squash, sliced
1   large yellow squash, halved lengthwise and sliced
1   teaspoon dried Italian seasoning
1   garlic clove, minced
2   tablespoons shredded fresh Parmesan cheese

1. Heat olive oil in a large nonstick skillet over medium-high heat. Add squash to pan, and sprinkle with Italian seasoning. Cook 4 minutes or until lightly browned, stirring occasionally. Add garlic, and sauté 1 minute. Remove from heat, and sprinkle with Parmesan cheese. **Yield:** 4 servings (serving size: about ½ cup).

CALORIES 67; FAT 4.6g (sat 1.1g, mono 2.9g, poly 0.6g); PROTEIN 2.9g; CARB 5.1g; FIBER 1.6g; CHOL 3mg; IRON 0.5mg; SODIUM 58mg; CALC 60mg

15 MINUTES

Rosemary-Asiago Zucchini

Earthy rosemary and rich, nutty Asiago cheese pair well with delicately flavored zucchini. If you can't find Asiago, fresh Parmesan works well in this recipe, too.

1   teaspoon olive oil
¾   pound zucchini, cut into ¼-inch-thick slices (about 2 medium)
1   garlic clove, minced
1   tablespoon chopped fresh rosemary
¼   teaspoon salt
⅛   teaspoon ground red pepper
2   tablespoons shredded Asiago cheese

1. Heat oil in a large nonstick skillet over medium-high heat. Add zucchini and garlic; cook 5 minutes or until lightly browned, stirring frequently. Stir in rosemary, salt, and red pepper. Sprinkle with cheese; cover and let stand 1 minute. **Yield:** 2 servings (serving size: 1 cup).

CALORIES 77; FAT 4.5g (sat 1.6g, mono 2.2g, poly 0.5g); PROTEIN 4.1g; CARB 6.7g; FIBER 2.1g; CHOL 6mg; IRON 0.7mg; SODIUM 326mg; CALC 97mg

INGREDIENT SPOTLIGHT

Fresh Asiago has a mild, nutty flavor that is similar to cheddar. Aged Asiago has a much saltier flavor and a harder, drier texture that is similar to Parmesan. Look for Asiago cheese in wheels or wedges with the other gourmet cheeses.

20 MINUTES

Oven-Fried Zucchini

3   cups (¼-inch) sliced zucchini (about 2 large)
2   tablespoons fat-free Italian dressing
¼   cup Italian-seasoned breadcrumbs
1   tablespoon grated Parmesan cheese
½   teaspoon paprika
Cooking spray

1. Preheat oven to 450°.
2. Combine zucchini and Italian dressing in a medium bowl; toss well to coat.
3. Combine breadcrumbs, cheese, and paprika in a shallow dish. Dredge zucchini in breadcrumb mixture. Place zucchini on a jelly-roll pan lined with foil and coated with cooking spray.
4. Bake at 450° for 15 minutes. **Yield:** 4 servings (serving size: about ⅔ cup).

CALORIES 54; FAT 1.1g (sat 0.4g, mono 0.3g, poly 0.4g); PROTEIN 3g; CARB 8.9g; FIBER 1.3g; CHOL 1mg; IRON 0.6mg; SODIUM 232mg; CALC 52mg

Herbed Grape Tomatoes

MINUTES

Roasted Tomatoes

2	large tomatoes, halved horizontally
1/4	teaspoon salt
1/4	teaspoon freshly ground black pepper
1/4	cup torn fresh basil
1/4	cup shredded part-skim mozzarella cheese

1. Preheat oven to 500°.
2. Place tomato halves on a broiler pan. Sprinkle cut side of tomatoes with salt and pepper; top with basil and cheese.
3. Bake tomatoes at 500° for 12 minutes or until cheese melts and is lightly browned. **Yield:** 4 servings (serving size: 1 tomato half).

CALORIES 39; FAT 1.6g (sat 0.9g, mono 0.4g, poly 0.1g); PROTEIN 2.7g; CARB 4g; FIBER 1.2g; CHOL 4mg; IRON 0.4mg; SODIUM 187mg; CALC 65mg

MINUTES

Baked Tomatoes

Use olive oil–flavored cooking spray instead of regular to get the taste of olive oil without the fat.

Olive oil–flavored cooking spray
2	large tomatoes, cut into 1/2-inch-thick slices (about 6 slices)
1/3	cup sliced green onions
3/4	teaspoon dried Italian seasoning
1/4	teaspoon salt
1/4	teaspoon freshly ground black pepper
2	garlic cloves, minced
1/4	cup (1 ounce) grated fresh Parmesan cheese

1. Preheat oven to 350°.
2. Coat a 13 x 9–inch baking dish with cooking spray. Arrange tomato slices in a single layer in dish. Sprinkle green onions and remaining ingredients over tomato slices. Bake, uncovered, at 350° for 10 minutes or until thoroughly heated and cheese melts. Serve warm. **Yield:** 6 servings (serving size: 1 slice).

CALORIES 36; FAT 1.6g (sat 0.7g, mono 0.5g, poly 0.3g); PROTEIN 2.6g; CARB 3.2g; FIBER 1.2g; CHOL 3mg; IRON 0.3mg; SODIUM 187mg; CALC 81mg

20 MINUTES

Herbed Grape Tomatoes

Roasting the grape tomatoes makes them juicy and intensifies their flavor.

2	pints grape tomatoes
1	tablespoon chopped fresh basil
1	tablespoon chopped fresh flat-leaf parsley
2	teaspoons olive oil
1/8	teaspoon salt
1/8	teaspoon freshly ground black pepper

1. Preheat oven to 425°.
2. Combine all ingredients on a large rimmed baking sheet. Toss to coat tomatoes. Bake at 425° for 13 minutes or until tomato skins pop and tomatoes begin to lose their shape, stirring after 8 minutes. **Yield:** 4 servings (serving size: 3/4 cup).

CALORIES 52; FAT 2.8g (sat 0.4g, mono 1.8g, poly 0.5g); PROTEIN 1.3g; CARB 7g; FIBER 1.7g; CHOL 0mg; IRON 0.8mg; SODIUM 87mg; CALC 10mg

##
Pesto-Vegetable Medley

30 MINUTES

Pesto-Vegetable Medley

2   pounds red potatoes, halved
1   (12-ounce) bag pretrimmed green beans
Cooking spray
1   pint grape tomatoes
5   tablespoons commercial pesto
¾   teaspoon salt
¼   teaspoon freshly ground black pepper

1. Place potatoes in a Dutch oven; cover with water. Bring to a boil; cover, reduce heat, and simmer 6 minutes. Add beans; cook 8 minutes or until potatoes are tender and beans are crisp-tender. Drain; place in a large serving bowl.
2. Wipe pan dry with a paper towel. Spray pan with cooking spray; place over medium heat. Add tomatoes; sauté 1 to 2 minutes or until slightly browned. Add to potato mixture.
3. Combine pesto, salt, and pepper. Spoon over potato mixture, and toss gently to coat. **Yield:** 12 servings (serving size: 1 cup).

CALORIES 100; FAT 3.1g (sat 0.6g, mono 1.8g, poly 0.7g); PROTEIN 2.9g; CARB 15.9g; FIBER 2.7g; CHOL 2mg; IRON 1.1mg; SODIUM 202mg; CALC 40mg

20 MINUTES

Grilled Vegetables

1   large red bell pepper, seeded and cut in half
1   tablespoon olive oil
1   large red onion, cut into ½-inch-thick slices
2   zucchini, cut diagonally into ½-inch-thick slices
2   yellow squash, cut diagonally into ½-inch-thick slices
¼   teaspoon salt
¼   teaspoon freshly ground black pepper
Cooking spray

1. Prepare grill.
2. Flatten bell pepper with palm of hand.
3. Drizzle oil evenly over bell pepper, onion, zucchini, and squash; sprinkle with salt and pepper.
4. Place onion on grill rack coated with cooking spray; grill, uncovered, 6 to 7 minutes on each side or until tender. While onion is cooking, grill bell pepper, zucchini, and squash 2 minutes on each side or until tender. Remove vegetables from grill. Cut bell pepper into ½-inch-thick slices. **Yield:** 4 servings (serving size: ¼ of vegetables).

CALORIES 87; FAT 3.8g (sat 0.6g, mono 2.5g, poly 0.6g); PROTEIN 3.2g; CARB 12.6g; FIBER 3.7g; CHOL 0mg; IRON 1mg; SODIUM 161mg; CALC 39mg

15 MINUTES

California-Style Steamed Veggies

1   (16-ounce) package frozen California-style vegetable blend
½   teaspoon grated fresh lemon rind
1   tablespoon fresh lemon juice
¼   teaspoon ground nutmeg
¼   teaspoon freshly ground black pepper
⅛   teaspoon salt

1. Place vegetable blend in a vegetable steamer over simmering water; cover and steam 8 minutes or until crisp-tender. Transfer vegetables to a bowl, and sprinkle with lemon rind, lemon juice, nutmeg, pepper, and salt; toss well. **Yield:** 4 servings (serving size: about 1 cup).

CALORIES 36; FAT 0g (sat 0g, mono 0g, poly 0g); PROTEIN 2.7g; CARB 7.2g; FIBER 2.8g; CHOL 0mg; IRON 0.5mg; SODIUM 107mg; CALC 28mg

DESSERTS

Fruit Kebabs with Lemon Dip

Toffee Dip with Apples

Many recipes call for brushing cut apples with lemon juice to prevent browning. Here, pineapple juice does the job.

- 1/2 cup (4 ounces) block-style 1/3-less-fat cream cheese, softened
- 1/3 cup packed light brown sugar
- 1/4 cup sifted powdered sugar
- 1/2 teaspoon vanilla extract
- 1/3 cup almond toffee bits (such as Hershey's Heath Bits O' Brickle)
- 1/2 cup pineapple juice
- 4 Red Delicious apples (about 2 pounds), each cored and cut into 8 wedges
- 4 Granny Smith apples (about 2 pounds), each cored and cut into 8 wedges

1. Combine first 4 ingredients in a bowl; beat with a mixer at medium speed until smooth. Stir in toffee bits.
2. Combine juice and apple wedges in a bowl; toss well. Drain apples; serve with toffee dip. **Yield:** 8 servings (serving size: 3 tablespoons dip and 8 apple wedges).

CALORIES 251; FAT 6.4g (sat 3g, mono 3.1g, poly 0.3g); PROTEIN 1.9; CARB 48.3g; FIBER 2.8g; CHOL 13mg; IRON 0.6mg; SODIUM 122mg; CALC 32mg

Fruit Kebabs with Lemon Dip

Serve skewered angel food cake and fresh fruit with a sweet lemon sauce for this light, fun dessert for two.

- 1/4 cup marshmallow creme
- 1/4 cup low-fat lemon yogurt
- 8 fresh pineapple cubes
- 1 cup (8 cubes) angel food cake
- 4 strawberries, halved
- 4 small wooden skewers

1. Combine marshmallow creme and yogurt in a small bowl, stirring well.
2. Thread pineapple cubes, cake cubes, and strawberry halves evenly onto 4 wooden skewers.
3. Serve fruit skewers with lemon dip.
Yield: 2 servings (serving size: 2 skewers and 1/4 cup dip).

CALORIES 135; FAT 0.5g (sat 0.3g, mono 0.1g, poly 0.1g); PROTEIN 2.8g; CARB 30.7g; FIBER 1.3g; CHOL 2mg; IRON 0.5mg; SODIUM 163mg; CALC 74mg

Toffee Dip with Apples

MINUTES

Bittersweet Chocolate Sauce

²/₃	cup fat-free sweetened condensed milk
½	cup Dutch process cocoa
½	cup honey
½	cup water
⅛	teaspoon salt
¼	cup butter
1	teaspoon vanilla extract

1. Combine first 5 ingredients in a small saucepan, stirring with a whisk until smooth. Bring to a boil over medium heat, stirring occasionally. Reduce heat, and simmer 1 minute. Remove from heat. Add butter and vanilla extract, stirring until butter melts. Serve warm with fresh fruit or cubed angel food cake. **Yield:** 16 servings (serving size: 2 tablespoons).

CALORIES 105; FAT 5.3g (sat 3.3g, mono 1.6g, poly 0.2g); PROTEIN 1.6g; CARB 18.3g; FIBER 0.5g; CHOL 9mg; IRON 1mg; SODIUM 52mg; CALC 35mg

Chocolate-Hazelnut Sauce

⅓ cup half-and-half
¼ cup fat-free milk
8 ounces semisweet chocolate, chopped
1¼ cups powdered sugar
¼ cup water
2 tablespoons Frangelico (hazelnut-flavored liqueur)
2 tablespoons dark corn syrup

1. Combine first 3 ingredients in a medium saucepan; cook over medium-low heat, stirring constantly, 3 minutes or until smooth. Stir in sugar and next 3 ingredients. Cook, stirring constantly, 5 minutes or until mixture is smooth. Keep warm in a fondue pot, small slow cooker, or over simmering water. **Yield:** 18 servings (serving size: 2 tablespoons fondue).

CALORIES 122; FAT 4.3g (sat 2.6g, mono 1.4g, poly 0.2g); PROTEIN 0.8g; CARB 21g; FIBER 0.7g; CHOL 1.7mg; IRON 0.4mg; SODIUM 7mg; CALC 9mg

Chocolate-Hazelnut Sauce

INGREDIENT SPOTLIGHT

Frangelico is a caramel-colored hazelnut liqueur that's produced in northern Italy. Hints of cacao, vanilla, and coffee combine with toasted hazelnuts to produce the smooth, sweet, and very pleasant liqueur that's delicious in cocktails as well as desserts. Frangelico is expensive, but it keeps indefinitely. You can purchase smaller sample bottles of liqueur. Look behind your liquor store's checkout counter for bottles that hold approximately 3 tablespoons (1.5 ounces) of liqueur.

Amaretto Strawberries over Angel Food Cake

2 cups sliced fresh strawberries
¼ cup almond-flavored liqueur (such as amaretto)
2 teaspoons sugar
8 ounces prepared angel food cake, cut into 8 (½-inch) slices
½ cup frozen fat-free whipped topping, thawed

1. Combine first 3 ingredients, and let stand 10 minutes.
2. Spoon ¼ cup strawberry mixture over each cake slice. Top each with 1 tablespoon whipped topping. **Yield:** 8 servings.

CALORIES 110; FAT 0.2g (sat 0g, mono 0g, poly 0.1g); PROTEIN 1.8g; CARB 22.8g; FIBER 1.3g; CHOL 0mg; IRON 0.3mg; SODIUM 180mg; CALC 31mg

Chocolate Cupcakes
with Vanilla Cream
Cheese Frosting

Nutritionally, egg substitute and egg whites are the same because egg substitutes are made from egg whites, corn oil, water, flavorings, and preservatives. Egg substitutes are great to use in recipes that call for just egg whites, particularly in those where the eggs aren't fully cooked because they're pasteurized.

INGREDIENT SPOTLIGHT

30 MINUTES

Chocolate Cupcakes with Vanilla Cream Cheese Frosting

Instant coffee intensifies the chocolate richness of these cupcakes. For thicker frosting, cover and chill it for 10 minutes before spreading it on the cupcakes. Refrigerate the frosted cupcakes overnight; cover them lightly with plastic wrap, or store them in an airtight container.

Cupcakes:
1   cup granulated sugar
1/2   cup egg substitute
1/4   cup canola oil
1/2   teaspoon vanilla extract
6.75 ounces all-purpose flour (about 1 1/2 cups)
1/2   cup unsweetened cocoa
1   teaspoon baking soda
1   teaspoon instant coffee granules
1/2   teaspoon baking powder
1/4   teaspoon salt
1   cup fat-free buttermilk

Frosting:
1   cup powdered sugar
1/2   teaspoon vanilla extract
Dash of salt
1   (8-ounce) block 1/3-less-fat cream cheese, softened

1. Preheat oven to 350°.
2. To prepare cupcakes, place first 4 ingredients in a large bowl; beat with a mixer at medium speed until well blended (about 2 minutes).
3. Lightly spoon flour into dry measuring cups; level with a knife. Combine flour and next 5 ingredients, stirring well with a whisk. Stir flour mixture into sugar mixture alternately with buttermilk, beginning and ending with flour mixture; mix after each addition just until blended.
4. Place 16 paper muffin cup liners in muffin cups; spoon about 2 1/2 tablespoons batter into each cup. Bake at 350° for 18 minutes or until a wooden pick inserted in center of a cupcake comes out with moist crumbs attached (do not overbake). Remove cupcakes from pans; cool on a wire rack.
5. To prepare frosting, combine powdered sugar and remaining ingredients in a medium bowl. Beat with a mixer at medium speed until combined. Increase speed to medium-high, and beat until smooth. Spread about 1 tablespoon frosting on top of each cupcake. **Yield:** 16 servings (serving size: 1 cupcake).

CALORIES 203; FAT 6.8g (sat 2.1g, mono 3g, poly 1.3g); PROTEIN 4.8g; CARB 32.4g; FIBER 1.2g; CHOL 8mg; IRON 1.3mg; SODIUM 211mg; CALC 53mg

20 MINUTES

Peach Shortcakes

Turbinado sugar, with its unique texture and amber color, adds a sweet crunch as well as an elegant appearance. Use a fork to quickly toss together the dough; over-mixing will cause the shortcakes to be tough.

1⅓ cups low-fat baking mix (such as Bisquick Heart Smart)
3 tablespoons granulated sugar, divided
⅛ teaspoon ground cinnamon
⅛ teaspoon ground nutmeg
⅓ cup 1% low-fat milk
1 tablespoon butter, melted
2 teaspoons turbinado sugar
3 cups frozen sliced peaches
½ cup frozen fat-free whipped topping, thawed

1. Preheat oven to 425°.
2. Lightly spoon baking mix into dry mea-suring cups; level with a knife. Combine baking mix, 2 tablespoons granulated sugar, cinnamon, and nutmeg; stir well. Add milk and butter, stirring just until combined.
3. Form dough into 4 (3-inch) circles on a baking sheet lined with parchment paper. Sprinkle each with ½ teaspoon turbinado sugar. Bake at 425° for 10 minutes or until lightly golden.
4. While shortcakes bake, sprinkle peaches with remaining 1 tablespoon granulated sugar, and stir well. Microwave at HIGH 3 minutes.
5. Split each shortcake in half horizontally. Top bottom halves of cakes each with ¾ cup peach mixture and 2 tablespoons whipped topping. Top with remaining cake halves. Serve warm. **Yield:** 4 servings (serving size: 1 shortcake).

CALORIES 281; FAT 5.6g (sat 2g, mono 2.6g, poly 0.7g); PROTEIN 4.7g;
CARB 55.2g; FIBER 2.6g; CHOL 9mg; IRON 1.9mg; SODIUM 467mg; CALC 177mg

30 MINUTES

Peach Turnovers

If you don't have a 6-inch round cutter, use a bowl or lid that measures 6 inches in diameter. Use the tip of a sharp knife to cut the dough.

1 (15-ounce) package refrigerated pie dough (such as Pillsbury)
2 cups chopped peeled peaches (about 4 medium)
¼ cup apricot jam, melted
1 large egg white
1 teaspoon water
2 tablespoons turbinado sugar

1. Preheat oven 450°.
2. Line 2 large baking sheets with parch-ment paper; set aside.
3. Roll each piecrust into a 14-inch circle on a lightly floured surface. Using a 6-inch round cutter, cut each crust into 4 circles. Combine peaches and jam in a medium bowl. Spread circles of dough evenly with peach mixture to within ¼ inch of edges. Fold crust over filling, pressing edges to seal.
4. Combine egg white and water with a whisk; brush turnovers with egg wash. Sprinkle turnovers with turbinado sugar; place on prepared baking sheets. Bake at 450° for 15 to 16 minutes or until crust is golden brown. **Yield:** 8 servings (serving size: 1 turnover).

CALORIES 189; FAT 7.9g (sat 2.8g, mono 4.1g, poly 0.8g); PROTEIN 1.4g; CARB 28.1g;
FIBER 0.7g; CHOL 6mg; IRON 0.2mg; SODIUM 129mg; CALC 5mg

COOKING CLASS: *how to beat eggs*

Correctly beaten egg whites are key to successful meringue cookies. Though eggs separate easier when they're cold, the egg whites beat to a greater volume when they're at room temperature. For best results, separate your eggs while they're cold. Place the egg whites in a bowl on the counter to warm while you gather the rest of the ingredients. Don't wait more than 30 minutes to beat them, though, for safety reasons.

Almond Macaroon Cookies

These cookies are similar to traditional almond macaroons, but they take much less time to prepare.

³⁄₄ cup slivered almonds
1 large egg white
Dash of salt
¹⁄₃ cup sugar
Cooking spray

1. Preheat oven to 350°.
2. Place almonds in a large nonstick skillet over medium-high heat; cook, stirring constantly, 3 minutes or until light brown and fragrant. Remove from heat, and let cool.
3. Beat egg white and salt with a mixer at high speed until foamy. Gradually add sugar, 2 tablespoons at a time, beating 6 minutes or until stiff peaks form.
4. Place almonds in a food processor; process until finely ground. Gently fold ground almonds into beaten egg whites.
5. Drop mixture by teaspoonfuls 1 inch apart onto baking sheets coated with cooking spray. Bake at 350° for 8 minutes or just until lightly browned. Let cookies cool on pans 1 minute. Remove to wire racks, and let cool completely. **Yield:** 2 dozen cookies (serving size: 2 cookies).

CALORIES 62; FAT 3.3g (sat 0.3g, mono 2.2g, poly 0.8g); PROTEIN 1.7g; CARB 7.1g; FIBER 0.8g; CHOL 0mg; IRON 0.3mg; SODIUM 17mg; CALC 18mg

Lemon-Glazed Soft-Baked Cookies

1 cup low-fat baking mix (such as reduced-fat Bisquick)
3 tablespoons granulated sugar
3 tablespoons quick-cooking oats
3 tablespoons 1% low-fat milk
2 tablespoons egg substitute
1 tablespoon butter, melted
1 teaspoon grated lemon rind
¹⁄₂ teaspoon vanilla extract
Cooking spray
6 tablespoons powdered sugar
2 teaspoons fresh lemon juice
¹⁄₄ teaspoon grated lemon rind

1. Preheat oven to 375°.
2. Lightly spoon baking mix into a dry measuring cup; level with a knife. Combine baking mix, granulated sugar, and oats in a medium bowl. Add milk and next 4 ingredients, stirring just until dry ingredients are moistened.
3. Drop by level tablespoonfuls 2 inches apart on a baking sheet coated with cooking spray. Bake at 375° for 8 minutes or until cookies are lightly browned around edges.
4. While cookies bake, combine powdered sugar, lemon juice, and lemon rind in a small bowl, stirring with a whisk. Remove cookies to a wire rack. Place wax paper under racks, and drizzle lemon glaze over warm cookies. **Yield:** 12 cookies (serving size: 1 cookie).

CALORIES 79; FAT 1.7g (sat 0.6g, mono 0.7g, poly 0.3g); PROTEIN 1.3g; CARB 14.9g; FIBER 0.3g; CHOL 3mg; IRON 0.5mg; SODIUM 123mg; CALC 45mg

Dark Chocolate
Cookies

30 MINUTES

Chewy Chocolate-Cherry Cookies

*The tartness of the cherries contrasts with
the cocoa and semisweet chocolate chips.*

4.5   ounces all-purpose flour (about 1 cup)
1/3   cup unsweetened cocoa
1/2   teaspoon baking powder
1/4   teaspoon baking soda
1/4   teaspoon salt
1   cup sugar
1/3   cup butter, softened
1   teaspoon vanilla extract
1   large egg
2/3   cup dried tart cherries
3   tablespoons semisweet chocolate chips
Cooking spray

1. Preheat oven to 350°.
2. Lightly spoon flour into a dry measuring
cup; level with a knife. Combine flour,
cocoa, baking powder, baking soda, and
salt, stirring with a whisk. Place sugar and
butter in a large bowl; beat with a mixer at
high speed until well blended. Add vanilla
and egg; beat well. With mixer on low
speed, gradually add flour mixture. Beat
just until combined. Fold in cherries and
chocolate chips.
3. Drop by tablespoonfuls 2 inches apart
onto baking sheets coated with cooking
spray. Bake at 350° for 12 minutes or just
until set. Remove from oven; cool on pans
5 minutes. Remove from pans; cool completely on wire racks. **Yield:** 30 cookies
(serving size: 1 cookie).

CALORIES 80; FAT 2.7g (sat 1.3g, mono 1.1g, poly 0.1g); PROTEIN 1.1g; CARB 13.4g;
FIBER 0.8g; CHOL 12mg; IRON 0.4mg; SODIUM 56mg; CALC 10mg

30 MINUTES

Dark Chocolate Cookies

*These irresistible cookies are slightly
crunchy on the outside and soft and chewy
on the inside.*

1   (18.25-ounce) package devil's food cake
       mix
1/4   cup strong brewed coffee (at room
       temperature)
3   tablespoons butter, melted
1   tablespoon water
1   large egg, lightly beaten
1/2   cup milk chocolate minichips
Cooking spray

1. Preheat oven to 350°.
2. Combine first 5 ingredients in a large
bowl. Beat with a mixer at medium speed
2 minutes, stopping to scrape down sides.
Stir in chocolate minichips.
3. Drop by level tablespoons 2 inches apart
on baking sheets coated with cooking spray.
Bake at 350° for 11 minutes or just until set.
Let cool on pans 2 minutes. Remove cookies
to wire racks to cool completely. **Yield:** 38
cookies (serving size: 1 cookie).

CALORIES 84; FAT 3.6g (sat 1.7g, mono 1.4g, poly 0.4g); PROTEIN 1.2g; CARB 11.8g;
FIBER 0.3g; CHOL 16mg; IRON 0.5mg; SODIUM 125mg; CALC 12mg

COOKING CLASS: *how to measure flour*

Measuring flour is the single most important factor in light baking, so we list flour amounts in our ingredient lists by weight and also give an approximate cup measure if you don't have a kitchen scale. If you're measuring using a measuring cup be sure to use dry measuring cups without spouts, stir the flour in the canister before spooning it out, and lightly spoon the flour into the measuring cup without compacting it. Finally, level off the excess flour with the flat edge of a knife.

Chocolate Chip Cookies

10.1 ounces all-purpose flour (about 2¼ cups)
1 teaspoon baking soda
¼ teaspoon salt
1 cup packed brown sugar
¾ cup granulated sugar
½ cup butter, softened
1 teaspoon vanilla extract
2 large egg whites
¾ cup semisweet chocolate chips
Cooking spray

1. Preheat oven to 350°.
2. Lightly spoon flour into dry measuring cups; level with a knife. Combine flour, baking soda, and salt, stirring with a whisk.
3. Combine sugars and butter in a large bowl; beat with a mixer at medium speed until well blended. Add vanilla and egg whites; beat 1 minute. Add flour mixture and chips; beat until blended.
4. Drop dough by level tablespoons 2 inches apart onto baking sheets coated with cooking spray. Bake at 350° for 10 minutes or until lightly browned. Cool on pans 2 minutes. Remove from pans; cool completely on wire racks. **Yield:** 4 dozen (serving size: 1 cookie).

CALORIES 88; FAT 3g (sat 1.8g, mono 0.5g, poly 0.1g); PROTEIN 1g; CARB 14.6g; FIBER 0.2g; CHOL 5mg; IRON 0.4mg; SODIUM 56mg; CALC 5mg

Double Chocolate–Oatmeal Cookies

These cookies can be stirred up, dropped on the pan, and baked to perfection in just under 20 minutes.

2 tablespoons butter, melted
½ cup sugar
¼ cup unsweetened cocoa
1 large egg
1 teaspoon vanilla extract
½ cup uncooked regular oats
2 tablespoons all-purpose flour
¼ teaspoon baking powder
Dash of salt
1 ounce white chocolate, chopped

1. Preheat oven to 350°.
2. Combine first 5 ingredients in a large bowl; beat until smooth.
3. Combine oats, flour, baking powder, and salt; add to butter mixture, stirring just until blended. Stir in chopped white chocolate. Drop by rounded tablespoonfuls 2 inches apart onto a baking sheet lined with parchment paper.
4. Bake at 350° for 9 minutes or until cookie centers are almost done. Cool 1 minute on pan. Remove from pan; cool completely on wire rack. **Yield:** about 10 servings (serving size: 1 cookie).

CALORIES 109; FAT 4.1g (sat 2.3g, mono 1.3g, poly 0.4g); PROTEIN 2.1g; CARB 17g; FIBER 1.1g; CHOL 25mg; IRON 0.7mg; SODIUM 52mg; CALC 25mg

Double Chocolate–Oatmeal Cookies

Oatmeal-Raisin Cookies

Fast, simple, and satisfying, oatmeal-raisin cookies are a sure-to-please staple in the American home. They're easy to prepare because they're made with ingredients that you probably have on hand.

½   cup granulated sugar
½   cup packed brown sugar
⅓   cup butter, softened
1   teaspoon vanilla extract
⅛   teaspoon salt
1   large egg
4.5 ounces all-purpose flour (about 1 cup)
1   cup regular oats
½   cup raisins
Cooking spray

1. Preheat oven to 350°.
2. Beat first 6 ingredients with a mixer at medium speed until light and fluffy. Lightly spoon flour into a dry measuring cup, and level with a knife. Add flour and oats to egg mixture, and beat until blended. Stir in raisins. Drop by level tablespoons 2 inches apart onto baking sheets coated with cooking spray. Bake at 350° for 15 minutes or until golden brown. Cool on pans 3 minutes. Remove cookies from pans; cool on wire racks. **Yield:** 2 dozen (serving size: 1 cookie).

CALORIES 101; FAT 3.1g (sat 1.7g, mono 0.9g, poly 0.2g); PROTEIN 1.5g; CARB 17.3g; FIBER 0.6g; CHOL 16mg; IRON 0.6mg; SODIUM 43mg; CALC 10mg

Oats contain soluble fiber, which can help lower cholesterol and reduce the risk of heart disease. They are low in fat and contain no sodium or preservatives.

INGREDIENT SPOTLIGHT

Banana-Rum-Coconut Cookies

Spicy Oatmeal Crisps

Pepper may sound like an odd ingredient for a cookie, but it complements the other spices well (although you can omit it if you prefer).

3.4 ounces all-purpose flour (about ¾ cup)
1 teaspoon ground cinnamon
½ teaspoon baking soda
½ teaspoon ground allspice
½ teaspoon grated whole nutmeg
¼ teaspoon salt
¼ teaspoon ground cloves
¼ teaspoon freshly ground black pepper
   (optional)
1 cup packed brown sugar
5 tablespoons butter or stick margarine,
   softened
1 teaspoon vanilla extract
1 large egg
½ cup regular oats
Cooking spray

1. Preheat oven to 350°.
2. Lightly spoon flour into dry measuring cups; level with a knife. Combine flour and next 6 ingredients in a medium bowl; add pepper, if desired. Beat sugar, butter, and vanilla in a large bowl with a mixer at medium speed until light and fluffy. Add egg, and beat well. Stir in flour mixture and oats.
3. Drop by level tablespoons 2 inches apart onto baking sheets coated with cooking spray. Bake at 350° for 12 minutes or until crisp. Cool on pan 2 to 3 minutes or until firm. Remove cookies from pan; cool on wire racks. **Yield:** 2 dozen (serving size: 1 cookie).

CALORIES 81; FAT 3.1g (sat 1.7g, mono 0.9g, poly 0.3g); PROTEIN 1.5g; CARB 12.2g; FIBER 0.7g; CHOL 15mg; IRON 0.6mg; SODIUM 71mg; CALC 12mg

Banana-Rum-Coconut Cookies

⅔ cup packed dark brown sugar
½ cup ripe mashed banana (about 1 medium)
½ cup reduced-fat mayonnaise
1 teaspoon rum
3.4 ounces all-purpose flour (about ¾ cup)
1 cup quick-cooking oats
½ cup flaked sweetened coconut
½ cup golden raisins
½ cup chopped walnuts
1 teaspoon baking powder
¼ teaspoon ground cinnamon
⅛ teaspoon ground nutmeg
Dash of ground ginger

1. Preheat oven to 350°.
2. Place first 4 ingredients in a large bowl; beat with a mixer at medium speed until blended. Lightly spoon flour into dry measuring cups; level with a knife. Combine flour and remaining ingredients, stirring with a whisk. Stir flour mixture into banana mixture. Drop dough by 2 tablespoonfuls onto parchment paper-lined baking sheets. Bake at 350° for 19 minutes or until lightly browned. Remove from pan; cool completely on a wire rack. **Yield:** 20 cookies (serving size: 1 cookie).

CALORIES 118; FAT 3.7g (sat 1.1g, mono 0.3g, poly 1.5g); PROTEIN 1.7g; CARB 19.9g; FIBER 1.1g; CHOL 0mg; IRON 0.6mg; SODIUM 86mg; CALC 26mg

Key Lime Coconut Snowballs

Use regular limes if the Key limes are not available. Unsweetened coconut, which is often labeled "desiccated" or "pulverized," is often sold in health-food stores. Refrigerate the balls in an airtight container for up to one day.

2/3	cup graham cracker crumbs (about 4 cookie sheets)
6	tablespoons fat-free sweetened condensed milk
1	teaspoon grated Key lime rind
1 1/2	tablespoons fresh Key lime juice
1	teaspoon vanilla extract
1	cup shredded unsweetened coconut, divided
1 1/4	cups powdered sugar

1. Combine crumbs, sweetened condensed milk, rind, juice, and vanilla in a medium bowl. Add 2/3 cup coconut, and beat with a mixer at medium speed for 1 minute or until no longer grainy. Add sugar, 1/4 cup at a time, beating until well combined. Cover and chill 20 minutes.

2. Shape crumb mixture into 24 balls, about 1 teaspoon each. Place remaining 1/3 cup coconut in a shallow bowl; roll balls in coconut. **Yield:** 12 servings (serving size: 2 balls).

CALORIES 121; FAT 2.7g (sat 2.1g, mono 0.3g, poly 0.2g); PROTEIN 1.4g; CARB 23.2g; FIBER 0.8g; CHOL 1mg; IRON 0.4mg; SODIUM 40mg; CALC 30mg

Green Pumpkinseed and Cranberry Crispy Bars

We loved this creative take on the traditional Rice Krispies bar. Green pumpkinseeds are also sometimes sold as pepitas. In humid weather, cool the bars in the refrigerator to keep them from becoming too sticky.

Cooking spray
½ cup raw green pumpkinseeds
¼ cup butter
1 (8-ounce) package miniature marshmallows (about 5 cups)
1 teaspoon vanilla extract
⅛ teaspoon salt
5 cups oven-toasted rice cereal (such as Rice Krispies)
1 cup dried cranberries

1. Heat a large nonstick skillet over medium-high heat. Coat pan with cooking spray. Add pumpkinseeds; cook 4 minutes or until seeds begin to pop and lightly brown, stirring frequently. Remove from heat; cool.
2. Lightly coat a 13 x 9–inch baking dish with cooking spray; set aside. Melt butter in a large saucepan over medium heat. Stir in marshmallows; cook 2 minutes or until smooth, stirring constantly. Remove from heat; stir in vanilla and salt. Stir in reserved seeds, cereal, and cranberries. Scrape mixture into prepared dish using a rubber spatula.
3. Lightly coat hands with cooking spray; press cereal mixture evenly into prepared dish. Cool completely. Cut into 16 bars. **Yield:** 16 servings (serving size: 1 bar).

CALORIES 152; FAT 4.9g (sat 2.2g, mono 1.4g, poly 1g); PROTEIN 1.9g; CARB 26.3g; FIBER 0.7g; CHOL 7.5mg; IRON 0.9mg; SODIUM 115mg; CALC 4.7mg

Cocoa-Cranberry Crispy Bars

When you make these crispy bars, coat the spoon with cooking spray before you stir the cereal into the marshmallow mixture.

1 (10-ounce) package large marshmallows
2 tablespoons butter
6 cups chocolate-flavored oven-toasted rice cereal (such as Cocoa Krispies)
1 cup sweetened dried cranberries or raisins
½ cup miniature semisweet chocolate chips
Cooking spray

1. Combine marshmallows and butter in a large microwave-safe bowl. Microwave at HIGH 2 minutes. Stir well; microwave 1 additional minute.
2. Combine cereal, cranberries, and chocolate chips in a large bowl. Pour marshmallow mixture over cereal mixture, stirring until combined.
3. Press cereal mixture into a 13 x 9–inch baking dish coated with cooking spray. Cool completely; cut into bars. **Yield:** 24 bars (serving size: 1 bar).

CALORIES 118; FAT 2.4g (sat 1.5g, mono 0.7g, poly 0.1g); PROTEIN 0.8g; CARB 24.7g; FIBER 0.6g; CHOL 3mg; IRON 2.5mg; SODIUM 76mg; CALC 3mg

INGREDIENT SPOTLIGHT

Pumpkinseeds, also known as pepitas, not only have a subtly sweet and nutty flavor but are also some of the most nutritious seeds you can find. In addition to providing heart-healthy fats and protein, they are a very good source of magnesium, manganese, and phosphorous. For optimal freshness, store the seeds in an airtight container in the refrigerator and use them within two months of the purchase date.

Hello Dolly Bars

These bar cookies are also known as seven-layer bars. They can create a sticky mess in the pan, so it's crucial to line it with parchment paper. Because the milk needs to seep into the graham cracker crumbs, don't pack the crumbs too tightly in the bottom of the pan.

1½   cups graham cracker crumbs (about
       9 cookie sheets)
2   tablespoons butter, melted
1   tablespoon water
⅓   cup semisweet chocolate chips
⅓   cup butterscotch morsels
⅔   cup flaked sweetened coconut
¼   cup chopped pecans, toasted
1   (15-ounce) can fat-free sweetened
       condensed milk

1. Preheat oven to 350°.
2. Line bottom and sides of a 9-inch square baking pan with parchment paper; cut off excess parchment paper around top edge of pan.
3. Place crumbs in a medium bowl. Drizzle with butter and 1 tablespoon water; toss with a fork until moist. Gently pat mixture into an even layer in prepared pan (do not press firmly). Sprinkle chips and morsels over crumb mixture. Top evenly with coconut and pecans. Drizzle milk evenly over top. Bake at 350° for 25 minutes or until lightly browned and bubbly around edges. Cool completely on a wire rack. **Yield:** 24 servings (serving size: 1 bar).

CALORIES 123; FAT 4.4g (sat 2.3g, mono 1.3g, poly 0.6g); PROTEIN 2.1g; CARB 19.1g; FIBER 0.5g; CHOL 5mg; IRON 0.3mg; SODIUM 64mg; CALC 50mg

COOKING CLASS: *how to make chocolate curls*

Chocolate curls are easy to make and are a beautiful dessert garnish for special occasions. For perfect curls, gently drag a vegetable peeler against the side of a milk chocolate candy bar. If you're making the curls ahead of time, transfer them to a container with a flat surface, such as a small baking pan; cover and store in the refrigerator until you're ready to garnish and serve the dessert.

 MINUTES

Chewy Chocolate–Peanut Butter Bars

You'll need to make these chewy peanut butter bars ahead of time since they need to chill in the refrigerator for an hour to firm up.

2/3 cup extra-chunky peanut butter
1 (14-ounce) can fat-free sweetened condensed milk, divided
1 teaspoon vanilla extract, divided
1 cup semisweet chocolate chips

1. Line an 8-inch square baking pan with foil.
2. Place peanut butter and 2/3 cup sweetened condensed milk in a medium microwave-safe bowl. Microwave at HIGH 2 1/2 minutes. Stir; microwave an additional 30 seconds. Stir in 1/2 teaspoon vanilla. Spread mixture in prepared pan, pressing into an even layer with fingers.
3. Place remaining sweetened condensed milk and chocolate chips in a medium microwave-safe bowl. Microwave at HIGH 1 1/2 minutes. Add remaining 1/2 teaspoon vanilla; stir until smooth. Pour chocolate mixture over peanut butter mixture; spread with a small spatula. Chill until firm. Cut into 20 rectangular bars. Store in an airtight container in refrigerator. **Yield:** 20 servings (serving size: 1 bar).

CALORIES 168; FAT 6.8g (sat 2.2g, mono 3g, poly 1.4g); PROTEIN 4.5g; CARB 24g; FIBER 1.2g; CHOL 3mg; IRON 0.4mg; SODIUM 63mg; CALC 77mg

 MINUTES

Frozen Peanut Butter Pie

For peanut butter purists, serve this creamy frozen pie unadorned. If you prefer a taste of chocolate with your peanut butter, try topping the pie with chocolate curls just before serving it. You'll need to make this ahead, and freeze it for eight hours before serving.

1 (8-ounce) block 1/3-less-fat cream cheese, softened
1/2 cup reduced-fat creamy peanut butter
1/2 cup packed brown sugar
1 (8-ounce) container frozen fat-free whipped topping, thawed
1 (6-ounce) reduced-fat graham cracker crust

1. Combine first 3 ingredients in a medium bowl; beat with a mixer at high speed until creamy. Fold in whipped topping. Spoon filling into crust. Cover and freeze 8 hours or overnight. **Yield:** 8 servings (serving size: 1 slice).

CALORIES 337; FAT 15.6g (sat 5.8g, mono 6.1g, poly 3.7g); PROTEIN 7.6g; CARB 41.8g; FIBER 1g; CHOL 20mg; IRON 1mg; SODIUM 313mg; CALC 32mg

20 MINUTES

Vanilla Pudding

It doesn't take much longer to make this pudding than it does to make a "cook and serve" pudding from a box—and the silky, smooth texture and authentic vanilla flavor will convince you that it's worth the effort.

¼ cup sugar
2 tablespoons cornstarch
⅛ teaspoon salt
2 cups fat-free milk
1 large egg
1 tablespoon light stick butter
1 teaspoon vanilla extract

1. Combine first 3 ingredients in a medium saucepan; gradually add milk, stirring with a whisk. Bring to a boil over medium-high heat, and cook, whisking constantly, 2 minutes or until thick. Remove from heat.
2. Beat egg with a whisk 1 minute or until frothy. Gradually whisk about one-fourth of hot milk mixture into egg; add to remaining hot milk mixture, whisking constantly. Cook over low heat, whisking constantly, 3 minutes.
3. Remove from heat; add butter and vanilla, whisking until butter melts. Spoon pudding into each of 4 bowls. Serve warm, or cover and chill, if desired. **Yield:** 4 servings (serving size: ½ cup).

CALORIES 146; FAT 3g (sat 1.5g, mono 1g, poly 0.3g); PROTEIN 6.2g; CARB 22.9g; FIBER 0g; CHOL 59mg; IRON 0.3mg; SODIUM 170mg; CALC 159mg

30 MINUTES

Jasmine Chai Rice Pudding

2 cups 1% low-fat milk, divided
1½ cups water
2 teaspoons loose chai tea (about 4 tea bags)
⅛ teaspoon salt
1 cup uncooked jasmine rice
¾ cup sweetened condensed milk
¼ cup diced dried mixed fruit
2 large egg yolks
1 tablespoon butter
6 tablespoons frozen fat-free whipped topping, thawed
2 tablespoons chopped pistachios
½ teaspoon grated orange rind

1. Combine 1 cup milk, 1½ cups water, tea, and salt in a large saucepan; bring to a boil. Remove from heat; steep 1 minute. Strain milk mixture through a fine sieve into a bowl; discard solids. Return milk mixture to pan; place pan over medium heat. Stir in rice. Cover and simmer 10 minutes. Combine remaining 1 cup milk, condensed milk, fruit, and egg yolks, stirring well with a whisk. Gradually add half of hot milk mixture to egg yolk mixture, stirring constantly with a whisk. Return milk mixture to pan; cook 10 minutes or until mixture is thick and rice is tender, stirring constantly. Remove from heat; stir in butter.
2. Place ⅔ cup rice pudding in each of 6 bowls. Top each serving with 1 tablespoon fat-free whipped topping. Combine nuts and rind, and sprinkle about 1 teaspoon nut mixture over each serving. **Yield:** 6 servings.

CALORIES 287; FAT 8.8g (sat 4.5g, mono 3g, poly 0.8g); PROTEIN 8.3g; CARB 44g; FIBER 1.1g; CHOL 90mg; IRON 0.6mg; SODIUM 169mg; CALC 223mg

Jasmine Chai Rice
Pudding

Pineapple-Strawberry
Smoothie

 15 MINUTES

Banana-Caramel Milk Shake

½ cup 1% low-fat milk
¼ cup vanilla light ice cream
2 teaspoons fat-free caramel sundae syrup
1 large banana, sliced and frozen

1. Place all ingredients in a blender; process until smooth. Serve immediately. **Yield:** 2 servings (serving size: about ¾ cup).

CALORIES 128; FAT 1.7g (sat 1g, mono 0.6g, poly 0.1g); PROTEIN 3.7g; CARB 26.5g; FIBER 1.8g; CHOL 8mg; IRON 0.2mg; SODIUM 55mg; CALC 91mg

15 MINUTES

Key Lime Floats

2 cups vanilla light ice cream (such as Edy's)
½ cup Key lime juice
1 (25-ounce) bottle lime-flavored sparkling water, chilled
Lime slices (optional)

1. Spoon ½ cup ice cream into each of 4 tall glasses. Pour 2 tablespoons Key lime juice and about ¾ cup sparkling water into each glass. Garnish with lime slices, if desired. Serve immediately with a straw. **Yield:** 4 servings (serving size: 1 float).

CALORIES 169; FAT 3.2g (sat 1.9g, mono 0.9g, poly 0.2g); PROTEIN 3.2g; CARB 32.7g; FIBER 0.2g; CHOL 18mg; IRON 0.1mg; SODIUM 56mg; CALC 108mg

 15 MINUTES

Pineapple-Strawberry Smoothie

Adding soy to your diet can lower your cholesterol and help reduce the risk of heart disease.

1 cup prechopped fresh pineapple
1 cup frozen unsweetened strawberries
1 cup vanilla light soy milk
½ cup vanilla fat-free frozen yogurt

1. Place all ingredients in a blender; process until smooth. Serve immediately. **Yield:** 2 servings (serving size: about 1⅓ cups).

CALORIES 149; FAT 1.1g (sat 0.3g, mono 0.2g, poly 0.6g); PROTEIN 4.2g; CARB 32.6g; FIBER 2.7g; CHOL 2mg; IRON 1.3mg; SODIUM 83mg; CALC 222mg

INGREDIENT SPOTLIGHT

Real Key limes are sometimes hard to find, but the bottled juice, which we use in this recipe, is available in most grocery stores. You'll find it alongside the bottled lemon juice. If you're in a pinch, you can substitute lemon juice, but it won't be as tart.

Banana-Berry Split

Satisfy your dessert craving **with** *this glorified banana split topped with colorful summer berries.*

½   cup fat-free hot fudge topping (such as Smucker's)
2   ripe bananas, quartered lengthwise
2   cups vanilla fat-free ice cream (such as Breyers)
1   cup blueberries
1   cup sliced strawberries
¼   cup unsalted, dry-roasted peanuts, chopped

1. Microwave hot fudge topping in a small microwave-safe bowl at HIGH 30 seconds or until thin and hot.

2. Place 2 banana quarters into each of 4 individual serving bowls. Top each with ½ cup ice cream, 2 tablespoons hot fudge topping, and ¼ cup each blueberries and strawberries. Sprinkle each with 1 table-spoon peanuts. **Yield:** 4 servings (serving size: 1 banana split).

CALORIES 343; FAT 4.8g (sat 0.7g, mono 2.3g, poly 1.6g); PROTEIN 7.2g;
CARB 71.5g; FIBER 4g; CHOL 0mg; IRON 0.7mg; SODIUM 186mg; CALC 94mg

Tropical-Fruit Sundaes

COOKING CLASS: *how to chop a mango*

A mango can be tricky to cut because it has a rather large seed that grows inside the fruit. To remove the flesh from a mango, begin by holding the fruit, stem end up, on a cutting board. With a sharp knife, slice the fruit lengthwise down each side of the flat pit. Holding one mango half in the palm of your hand, score the pulp in square cross-sections. Be sure that you slice to, but not through, the skin. Finally, turn the mango inside out, and cut the chunks from the skin. Chop the chunks to the desired size.

30 MINUTES

Tropical-Fruit Sundaes

Kiwi, mango, orange, lime, and pineapple flavors receive well-deserved attention in this fruit-filled sundae.

1	cup chopped kiwifruit (about 2)
1	cup chopped mango (about 1 medium)
3	tablespoons orange juice
1	tablespoon lime juice
2	cups pineapple sherbet
4	teaspoons flaked sweetened coconut, toasted

1. Combine first 4 ingredients in a small bowl; cover and chill 30 minutes. Spoon ¹/₂ cup sherbet into each of 4 dessert dishes. Top sherbet evenly with fruit mixture, and sprinkle with coconut. Serve immediately. **Yield:** 4 servings (serving size: ¹/₂ cup sherbet, ¹/₂ cup fruit, and 1 teaspoon coconut).

CALORIES 174; FAT 2.4g (sat 1.4g, mono 0.5g, poly 0.2g); PROTEIN 1.7g; CARB 38.2g; FIBER 4.6g; CHOL 0mg; IRON 0.4mg; SODIUM 37mg; CALC 61mg

 Strawberry-Mango Sorbet Sundaes

15 MINUTES

Ice Cream with Sweet-and-Sour Cherry Sauce

To enjoy this dessert all year long, use frozen cherries. If you prefer to use fresh sweet cherries during the summer months, you'll only need to cook them in the sugar mixture for two minutes.

2	tablespoons light brown sugar
1	tablespoon balsamic vinegar
2	cups frozen pitted dark sweet cherries
2	cups vanilla fat-free ice cream (such as Edy's)

1. Combine sugar and vinegar in a medium saucepan over medium heat; cook 1 minute until sugar dissolves.
2. Stir in cherries; cook 4 minutes or until thoroughly heated. Serve with ice cream. **Yield:** 4 servings (serving size: ¹/₂ cup ice cream and about ¹/₃ cup cherry sauce).

CALORIES 189; FAT 0g; PROTEIN 4g; CARB 45.7g; FIBER 0.5g; CHOL 0mg; IRON 0.3mg; SODIUM 49mg; CALC 100mg

15 MINUTES

Strawberry-Mango Sorbet Sundaes

Try experimenting with other flavored sorbets for variation. Using jarred mango instead of fresh is a big time-saver in this quick dessert.

1	(16-ounce) jar sliced peeled mango (such as Del Monte SunFresh)
1	cup diced strawberries
1	teaspoon finely chopped fresh mint
1	pint strawberry sorbet

1. Remove 1 cup mango and ¹/₃ cup juice from jar. Reserve remaining mango for another use. Dice mango; combine with reserved juice, strawberries, and mint in a medium bowl, stirring gently.
2. Place ¹/₂ cup sorbet into each of 4 stemmed glasses or bowls, and top with ¹/₂ cup fruit mixture. **Yield:** 4 servings.

CALORIES 167; FAT 0.4g (sat 0.1g, mono 0.1g, poly 0.1g); PROTEIN 0.9g; CARB 41.5g; FIBER 2.9g; CHOL 0mg; IRON 0.2mg; SODIUM 4mg; CALC 10mg

Apple-Pie Sundaes

15 MINUTES

Summer Cherries Jubilee

If you don't want to use the wine, cranberry juice produces a beautiful color and a delicious, albeit different, result.

1½	cups pitted sweet cherries
½	cup cabernet sauvignon or other dry red wine
¼	cup cherry preserves
1	tablespoon amaretto (almond-flavored liqueur)
2	teaspoons fresh lemon juice
2	cups vanilla low-fat frozen yogurt

1. Combine first 3 ingredients in a small saucepan, and bring to a boil. Reduce heat, and simmer 5 minutes, stirring frequently. Stir in liqueur and lemon juice. Serve warm over yogurt. **Yield:** 4 servings (serving size: about ⅓ cup cherry sauce and ½ cup yogurt).

CALORIES 231; FAT 1.9g (sat 1g, mono 0.5g, poly 0.2g); PROTEIN 5.2g; CARB 43.5g; FIBER 1.5g; CHOL 5mg; IRON 0.5mg; SODIUM 67mg; CALC 168mg

You need to remove the stems and pits of cherries before using them. This can be most easily and quickly done with a cherry pitter. Be aware that cherry juice can stain fabrics and countertops, so prep them near your sink. A pitter will help keep you from getting a red-stained thumb.

SHORTCUT SPOTLIGHT

15 MINUTES

Apple-Pie Sundaes

Warm, saucy spiced apples and sweet caramel topping are drizzled over fat-free vanilla ice cream and topped with crunchy granola.

1	tablespoon butter
1	medium Braeburn apple, peeled, cored, and cut into chunks (about 8.5 ounces)
¼	cup packed light brown sugar
¼	teaspoon apple-pie spice
2	cups vanilla fat-free ice cream
4	teaspoons fat-free caramel topping
¼	cup low-fat granola

1. Melt butter in a large nonstick skillet. Add apple, brown sugar, and apple-pie spice; cook 7 minutes or until apple is tender.
2. Spoon ice cream into bowls. Spoon apple mixture over ice cream; top with caramel, and sprinkle with granola. **Yield:** 4 servings (serving size: ½ cup ice cream, ¼ cup apple mixture, 1 teaspoon caramel topping, and 1 tablespoon granola).

CALORIES 251; FAT 3.3g (sat 1.9g, mono 1g, poly 0.3g); PROTEIN 3.7g; CARB 54.4g; FIBER 1.9g; CHOL 8mg; IRON 0.7mg; SODIUM 107mg; CALC 104mg

 M I N U T E S

Broiled Berries and Nectarines with Ice Cream

Blackberries and nectarines combine to form a deliciously simple dessert. Substitute freshly squeezed orange juice for the Grand Marnier, if you prefer.

4	nectarines, quartered
1	(6⅛-ounce) package blackberries (about 1¼ cups)
2	tablespoons Grand Marnier or other orange liqueur
⅓	cup packed light brown sugar
2	cups vanilla fat-free ice cream (such as Edy's)

1. Preheat broiler.

2. Arrange nectarines, cut sides up, and berries on a foil-lined jelly-roll pan; drizzle with orange liqueur, and sprinkle with brown sugar.

3. Broil 7 to 8 minutes or until nectarines are lightly browned. Serve broiled fruit over ice cream. **Yield:** 4 servings (serving size: ¹/₂ cup ice cream, 4 nectarine quarters, and about 3 tablespoons blackberries).

CALORIES 251; FAT 0.7g (sat 0g, mono 0.3g, poly 0.4g); PROTEIN 4.6g; CARB 56.5; FIBER 4.3g; CHOL 0mg; IRON 0.9mg; SODIUM 50mg; CALC 103mg

20

MINUTES

Vanilla Ice Cream with Pears and Walnuts

This deliciously simple dessert is also great made with fresh figs instead of pears.

1⅓ cups chopped pear (about 8 ounces)
Cooking spray
¼   cup honey
2   tablespoons fresh orange juice
2   cups vanilla fat-free ice cream (such as Breyers)
4   teaspoons chopped walnuts, toasted

1. Preheat oven to 400°.
2. Place pear in an 8-inch square baking dish coated with cooking spray. Combine honey and orange juice; pour over pear. Bake at 400° for 8 minutes or until pear is tender.
3. Place ½ cup ice cream in each of 4 serving bowls. Spoon pear mixture evenly over ice cream, and top with walnuts. Serve immediately. **Yield:** 4 servings (serving size: ½ cup ice cream, ¼ cup pear mixture, and 1 teaspoon walnuts).

CALORIES 216; FAT 1.7g (sat 0.2g, mono 0.2g, poly 1.2g); PROTEIN 3.7g; CARB 50.1g; FIBER 1.9g; CHOL 0mg; IRON 0.3mg; SODIUM 52mg; CALC 90mg

30 MINUTES

Chunky Plum-and-Ginger Ice Cream

Make this ice cream ahead, and you'll be ready to scoop it out for dessert any night of the week.

4 cups vanilla low-fat ice cream, softened
1 cup diced plums (about 3 plums)
1 tablespoon finely chopped crystallized ginger
6 gingersnaps

1. Combine first 3 ingredients in a freezer-safe container. Cover, and freeze until firm. Spoon ice cream into 6 small bowls, and crumble 1 gingersnap over each serving. **Yield:** 6 servings (serving size: ²/₃ cup ice cream and 1 gingersnap).

CALORIES 177; FAT 5.3g (sat 2.7g, mono 1.8g, poly 0.5g); PROTEIN 4.1g; CARB 29.8g; FIBER 0.6g; CHOL 15mg; IRON 0.7mg; SODIUM 86mg; CALC 139mg

Ripe plums yield slightly to the touch, but don't squeeze them. Let the fruit sit in your palm. It should give a little. If you buy firmer fruit, though, don't put it in the refrigerator or the kitchen window—put it in a paper bag in a dark place for a day or two. Although plums might taste sweeter, it's actually a trick on the palate. The sugar level remains the same after picking, but the acidity falls, so it only seems sweeter.

INGREDIENT SPOTLIGHT

30 MINUTES

Ice Cream Treasures

Use any combination of cereals you like. This frozen dessert would also be delicious with chocolate ice cream and chopped walnuts instead of almonds. Make it ahead, and then simply pull it out of the freezer to serve after dinner.

1½ cups (6 ounces) chocolate-covered English toffee candy bars (such as Heath), crushed
8 cups vanilla reduced-fat ice cream (such as Healthy Choice), softened
4 cups crispy rice cereal squares, crushed (such as Rice Chex)
2 cups whole-grain toasted oat cereal (such as Cheerios)
²/₃ cup packed dark brown sugar
¹/₃ cup slivered almonds, toasted
¹/₃ cup flaked sweetened coconut, toasted
2 tablespoons butter, melted

1. Stir crushed candy into ice cream. Cover and freeze until ready to use.
2. Combine cereals, brown sugar, and remaining ingredients in a large bowl, stirring until well blended. Press half of cereal mixture in bottom of a 13 x 9–inch baking pan.
3. Let ice cream stand at room temperature 20 minutes or until softened. Spread softened ice cream mixture over cereal mixture; top evenly with remaining cereal mixture. Cover and freeze 8 hours or overnight. **Yield:** 16 servings (serving size: about ³/₄ cup).

CALORIES 265; FAT 8.4g (sat 4.1g, mono 2.7g, poly 0.7g); PROTEIN 5.2g; CARB 41.7g; FIBER 1g; CHOL 25mg; IRON 3.6mg; SODIUM 194mg; CALC 156mg

Chocolate-Caramel Cheesecake Parfaits

A sweet cream cheese mixture is layered between a delectable combination of chocolate, caramel, and graham cracker crumbs. Prepare the cream cheese mixture and make the graham cracker crumbs in advance; assemble the parfaits just before serving.

¾   cup (6 ounces) block-style ⅓-less-fat cream cheese, softened
3   tablespoons light brown sugar, divided
2½ tablespoons reduced-fat sour cream
1   tablespoon fat-free milk
1   cup frozen fat-free whipped topping, thawed
½   cup graham cracker crumbs
8   teaspoons fat-free hot fudge topping
8   teaspoons fat-free caramel topping

1. Place cream cheese, 2 tablespoons brown sugar, sour cream, and milk in a medium bowl; beat with a mixer at medium speed until smooth. Gently fold in whipped topping.
2. Place remaining 1 tablespoon brown sugar and graham cracker crumbs in a small bowl; stir well. Spoon 2 heaping tablespoons cream cheese mixture into each of 4 (8-ounce) parfait glasses. Top each parfait with 1 tablespoon graham cracker crumb mixture and 1 teaspoon each fudge topping and caramel topping. Repeat layers once. **Yield:** 4 servings (serving size: 1 parfait).

CALORIES 291; FAT 11.3g (sat 6.9g, mono 3.4g, poly 0.9g); PROTEIN 6g; CARB 40.3g; FIBER 0.3g; CHOL 31mg; IRON 0.5mg; SODIUM 345mg; CALC 57mg

Black Forest Cheesecake Parfaits

In the Black Forest region of Germany, the signature dessert is layered with chocolate, cherries, and whipped cream. Here, cream cheese replaces whipped cream.

4   cups frozen unsweetened cherries
½   cup black cherry preserves
½   cup sugar
2   tablespoons fresh lemon juice
6   ounces ⅓-less-fat cream cheese
¾   cup chocolate wafer crumbs (about 15 cookies; such as Nabisco's Famous Chocolate Wafers)
Grated lemon rind (optional)

1. Combine cherries and preserves in a medium saucepan, and bring to a boil. Reduce heat to medium-low, and simmer 5 minutes. Remove from heat, and cool completely.
2. Combine sugar, juice, and cheese in a large bowl, and beat with a mixer at medium speed until smooth (about 2 minutes). Cover and chill.
3. Spoon 2 teaspoons crumbs into each of 8 (8-ounce) glasses; top each with 1½ tablespoons cream cheese mixture and 3 tablespoons cherry mixture. Repeat layers once, ending with cherry mixture. Garnish with rind, if desired. Serve immediately. **Yield:** 8 servings (serving size: 1 parfait).

CALORIES 236; FAT 6.8g (sat 3.7g, mono 2g, poly 0.7g); PROTEIN 3.5g; CARB 42.6g; FIBER 1.6g; CHOL 16mg; IRON 0.9mg; SODIUM 147mg; CALC 30mg

Grated lemon rind adds a colorful garnish to these parfaits. Get double duty from the lemon by removing the zest and then saving the remaining lemon for later. Once you remove the rind, you can refrigerate the fruit for up to a week.

INGREDIENT SPOTLIGHT

ES

Strawberry-Granola Parfaits

$1/3$ cup apricot preserves

3   cups sliced strawberries

2   cups low-fat vanilla yogurt

$1/2$ cup low-fat granola without raisins (such as Kellogg's)

2   tablespoons slivered almonds, toasted

1. Place apricot preserves in a medium microwave-safe bowl, and microwave at HIGH 10 to 15 seconds or until preserves melt. Add strawberries, and toss gently to coat.

2. Spoon $1/4$ cup yogurt into each of 4 parfait glasses; top each serving with $1/3$ cup strawberry mixture. Repeat layers with remaining yogurt and strawberry mixture. Top each serving with 2 tablespoons granola and $1^1/2$ teaspoons almonds. Serve immediately. **Yield:** 4 servings (serving size: 1 parfait).

CALORIES 279; FAT 4.2g (sat 1.4g, mono 1.4g, poly 0.6g); PROTEIN 8.7g; CARB 53.5g; FIBER 3.9g; CHOL 6mg; IRON 1mg; SODIUM 94mg; CALC 240mg

20 MINUTES

Peach and Raspberry Pavlova Parfaits

½ cup (4 ounces) ⅓-less-fat cream cheese
¼ cup sugar, divided
1 cup vanilla fat-free yogurt
2 cups sliced peeled peaches (about 6 to 7 peaches)
1 cup raspberries
1 cup vanilla meringue cookie crumbs (such as Miss Meringue Minis; about 12 mini cookies, coarsely crushed)
12 vanilla meringue mini cookies

1. Place cream cheese and 3 tablespoons sugar in a medium bowl; beat with a mixer at high speed 2 minutes or until smooth. Beat in yogurt until blended.
2. Combine 1 tablespoon sugar, peaches, and raspberries in a large bowl, tossing to coat. Let stand 5 minutes.
3. Spoon 2 tablespoons cheese mixture into each of 6 (8-ounce) glasses; top each with ¼ cup peach mixture and 2½ tablespoons cookie crumbs. Repeat layers once with remaining cheese mixture and remaining peach mixture; top each with 2 whole cookies. Cover and chill until ready to serve.
Yield: 6 servings (serving size: 1 parfait).

CALORIES 193; FAT 4.7g (sat 2.9g, mono 1.3g, poly 0.2g); PROTEIN 5.1g;
CARB 34.7g; FIBER 2.5g; CHOL 15mg; IRON 0.3mg; SODIUM 111mg; CALC 94mg

COOKING CLASS: *how to toast coconut*

Toasted coconut is a simple way to add a little sweetness and a delightful crunch to desserts, hot cereal, and other dishes. To toast a large amount of coconut to keep on hand, spread flaked sweetened coconut in a single layer on a baking sheet. Bake at 325° for 10 minutes or until the coconut is golden. Toss the coconut occasionally while baking, and keep a close eye on it to prevent overcooking. Store it in a zip-top freezer bag or an airtight container.

15 MINUTES

Winter Ambrosia

1   (15¼-ounce) can pineapple chunks in juice, drained
1   cup pink grapefruit sections
1   cup orange sections
¼   cup flaked sweetened coconut, toasted

1. Combine first 3 ingredients in a medium bowl; toss gently. Sprinkle with coconut. Cover and chill. **Yield:** 4 servings (serving size: ¾ cup).

CALORIES 102; FAT 1.5g (sat 1.2g, mono 0.1g, poly 0.1g); PROTEIN 1.2g; CARB 23g; FIBER 2.7g; CHOL 0mg; IRON 0.4mg; SODIUM 14mg; CALC 35mg

30 MINUTES

Island Ambrosia

Imagine yourself relaxing in paradise while you enjoy this easy ambrosia.

1½   cups hulled strawberries, chopped (about 12 large)
1   (8-ounce) can pineapple tidbits in juice, drained
1   large naval orange, peeled and chopped (about ¾ cup)
⅓   cup flaked sweetened coconut, toasted
1   cubed peeled kiwifruit

1. Combine all ingredients in a medium bowl; toss gently. Let stand 15 minutes before serving. **Yield:** 8 servings (serving size: ½ cup).

CALORIES 50; FAT 1.1g (sat 0.9g, mono 0.1g, poly 0.1g); PROTEIN 0.8g; CARB 10.5g; FIBER 1.8g; CHOL 0mg; IRON 0.3mg; SODIUM 10mg; CALC 23mg

Winter Ambrosia

15 MINUTES

Spirited Tropical Fruit Dessert

1	(24-ounce) jar ruby red grapefruit sections
3	tablespoons light brown sugar
3	tablespoons dark rum
2	cups fresh pineapple chunks
3	kiwifruit, peeled and cut into wedges
¼	cup flaked sweetened coconut, toasted

1. Drain grapefruit sections, reserving 2 tablespoons juice. Combine reserved juice, brown sugar, and rum in a medium bowl, stirring well. Add grapefruit sections, pine-apple, and kiwifruit. Toss gently. Serve immediately, or cover and chill. Sprinkle with toasted coconut before serving. **Yield:** 4 servings (serving size: 1 cup fruit, 1 table-spoon coconut, and 2 tablespoons juice).

CALORIES 211; FAT 1.8g (sat 1.3g, mono 0.1g, poly 0.3g); PROTEIN 2.2g; CARB 44.4g; FIBER 5.1g; CHOL 0mg; IRON 0.8mg; SODIUM 27mg; CALC 57mg

Autumn Fruit with Honey-Yogurt Sauce

Broiled Apricots with Ginger Cream

Use peaches or nectarines instead of apricots, if you wish. Peaches and nectarines are larger than apricots, so plan on one per serving.

8   small apricots, halved and pitted
3   tablespoons light brown sugar, divided
½   cup reduced-fat sour cream
1   teaspoon grated peeled fresh ginger

1. Preheat broiler.
2. Line a baking sheet with parchment paper. Place apricots, cut sides up, on pre-pared baking sheet; sprinkle with 1 table-spoon brown sugar. Broil 5 to 7 minutes or until lightly browned.
3. While apricots broil, combine remaining 2 tablespoons brown sugar, sour cream, and ginger in a small bowl. Serve apricots with sauce. **Yield:** 4 servings (serving size: 4 apricot halves and 2 tablespoons sauce).

CALORIES 117; FAT 4g (sat 2.4g, mono 1.2g, poly 0.2g); PROTEIN 2g; CARB 20.1g; FIBER 1.6g; CHOL 16mg; IRON 0.4mg; SODIUM 22mg; CALC 50mg

Autumn Fruit with Honey-Yogurt Sauce

For a superquick dessert or a satisfying snack, stir up a simple yogurt sauce to spoon over fruit.

⅔   cup vanilla low-fat yogurt
1   tablespoon honey
1   cup chopped pear
1   cup chopped red apple
1   cup seedless green grape halves
Ground nutmeg (optional)

1. Combine yogurt and honey in a small bowl; stir with a whisk.
2. Combine pear, apple, and grapes in a large bowl. Spoon ¾ cup fruit into each of 4 dessert dishes; top each with about 2 ½ tablespoons yogurt sauce. Sprinkle lightly with nutmeg, if desired. **Yield:** 4 servings.

CALORIES 108; FAT 0.5g (sat 0.3g, mono 0.1g, poly 0.1g); PROTEIN 1.9g; CARB 26.2g; FIBER 2.4g; CHOL 2mg; IRON 0.3mg; SODIUM 29mg; CALC 59mg

Look for fresh ginger in the produce section of your supermarket. Choose the freshest, youngest-looking ginger you can find. Old rhizomes are fibrous, tough, and flavorless. Store fresh ginger tightly wrapped in plastic wrap in the vegetable crisper section of your refrigerator for up to three weeks.

INGREDIENT SPOTLIGHT

COOKING CLASS: *how to flambé*

The "flambé" cooking technique is the important final step in making Bananas Foster. The alcohol is set aflame and allowed to burn off, leaving a more intense flavor. To flambé, remove the skillet from the heated cooktop, and add rum. For safety, ignite the rum using a long match. The flames will die out naturally as you stir the bananas, creating a delicious syrup that coats the fruit.

 MINUTES

Brennan's Bananas Foster

Bananas Foster is an exquisite dessert made of sliced bananas that are first sautéed in butter and sugar and then flambéed in rum and spooned over ice cream.

4 medium bananas
¼ cup butter
1 cup packed brown sugar
¼ cup crème de banane (banana liqueur)
½ teaspoon ground cinnamon
¼ cup dark rum
2 cups vanilla low-fat ice cream

1. Peel bananas; cut each banana in half lengthwise. Cut each half into 2 pieces.
2. Melt butter in a large nonstick skillet over medium heat. Stir in brown sugar, liqueur, and cinnamon. Bring to a simmer, and cook 2 minutes. Add bananas; cook 4 minutes or until tender. Remove from heat. Add rum to pan, and ignite rum with a long match. Stir bananas gently until flame dies down. Serve over ice cream.
Yield: 8 servings (serving size: ¼ cup ice cream, 2 banana pieces, and 2 tablespoons sauce).

CALORIES 290; FAT 6.9g (sat 3.4g, mono 2.4g, poly 0.3g); PROTEIN 2.2g; CARB 51.4g; FIBER 2.1g; CHOL 18mg; IRON 0.7mg; SODIUM 74mg; CALC 79mg

 MINUTES

Orange-Glazed Bananas

The subtle hint of orange adds a refreshing citrus twist to classic Bananas Foster. Prior to starting the recipe, toast the pecans in a skillet over medium heat for about one minute, stirring often.

4 firm unpeeled bananas (about 1½ pounds)
2 tablespoons light stick butter
⅓ cup packed light brown sugar
½ teaspoon grated fresh orange rind
¼ teaspoon ground cinnamon
⅓ cup fresh orange juice
1 cup vanilla light ice cream
4 teaspoons coarsely chopped pecans, toasted

1. Peel bananas; cut each banana in half crosswise, and then cut in half lengthwise. Set aside.
2. Melt butter in a large nonstick skillet over medium heat. Add sugar and next 3 ingredients; cook until mixture is syrupy and bubbly, stirring often. Add banana, and cook 3 minutes or until banana is soft, basting frequently with syrup.
3. Serve banana pieces with vanilla light ice cream, and top with toasted pecans. **Yield:** 4 servings (serving size: 4 banana pieces with syrup, ¼ cup ice cream, and 1 teaspoon pecans).

CALORIES 289; FAT 7.2g (sat 3.5g, mono 2.8g, poly 0.7g); PROTEIN 3.1g; CARB 58.1g; FIBER 3.4g; CHOL 17mg; IRON 0.9mg; SODIUM 60mg; CALC 60mg

Summer Berry Medley with Limoncello and Mint

Limoncello *(lee-mon-CHAY-low) is a lemon-flavored liqueur from Italy's Amalfi coast that is often savored after a meal. Store it in the freezer, and serve over ice. If you have trouble finding it, substitute an orange-flavored liqueur such as Grand Marnier.*

1   cup fresh raspberries
2   cups fresh blackberries
2   cups hulled fresh strawberries, quartered
2   cups fresh blueberries
¼   cup sugar
1   tablespoon grated lemon rind
2   tablespoons fresh lemon juice
2   tablespoons limoncello (lemon-flavored liqueur)
½   cup torn fresh mint leaves

1. Combine first 8 ingredients in a bowl; let stand 20 minutes. Gently stir in mint using a rubber spatula. **Yield:** 6 servings (serving size: about 1 cup).

CALORIES 136; FAT 0.8g (sat 0g, mono 0.1g, poly 0.4g); PROTEIN 1.9g; CARB 31.3g; FIBER 7.4g; CHOL 0mg; IRON 1mg; SODIUM 2mg; CALC 38mg

Zabaglione with Fresh Fruit

Zabaglione is a classic Italian dessert sauce that's usually served warm over fresh fruit or plain cake. We found that a wide metal bowl placed over a pan of simmering water produced a greater volume of sauce than a double boiler. Substitute 2 cups sliced peeled peaches or nectarines for the figs, if desired.

⅓ cup sweet Marsala wine
¼ cup sugar
4 large egg yolks
7 ripe fresh figs (about 10 ounces), quartered
2 cups mixed fresh berries (such as blueberries, raspberries, blackberries, and sliced strawberries)
1 cup fat-free canned refrigerated whipped topping (such as Reddi-wip)

1. Add water to a large saucepan to a depth of 1 inch; bring water to a simmer over high heat. Reduce heat until water is barely simmering and producing steam.
2. Combine Marsala, sugar, and egg yolks in a large metal bowl (bowl should be large enough to sit on top of saucepan but not in saucepan); beat with a mixer at medium speed until well blended. Place bowl over saucepan of simmering water; beat egg mixture 4 minutes or until thick and pale and thermometer registers 160° (mixture will hold its shape for a few moments when beaters are removed from bowl).
3. Spoon ⅔ cup zabaglione into each of 4 shallow rimmed soup bowls; top each with 7 fig quarters, ½ cup berries, and ¼ cup whipped topping. **Yield:** 4 servings.

CALORIES 229; FAT 4.9g (sat 1.6g, mono 2.1g, poly 1.1g); PROTEIN 3.9g; CARB 39.2g; FIBER 4.8g; CHOL 205mg; IRON 1.2mg; SODIUM 11mg; CALC 61mg

Orange-Mint Berries

Fresh mint and honey create a surprisingly interesting flavor when tossed with berries and orange sections.

2 large navel oranges
3 tablespoons chopped fresh mint
3 tablespoons honey
2 cups fresh strawberries, halved
1 cup fresh raspberries
1 cup fresh blueberries

1. Peel and section oranges over a medium bowl to catch juices. Coarsely chop orange sections; add to juice. Stir in mint and honey.
2. Add berries to orange mixture, and toss gently to coat. Serve immediately, or cover and chill. **Yield:** 4 servings (serving size: about 1¼ cups).

CALORIES 154; FAT 0.7g (sat 0g, mono 0.1g, poly 0.4g); PROTEIN 2.1g; CARB 39g; FIBER 6.7g; CHOL 0mg; IRON 0.9mg; SODIUM 2mg; CALC 63mg

Cantaloupe with Balsamic Berries and Cream

Here's a surprising twist on a fruit and cream sundae. Instead of using chocolate syrup we've used balsamic glaze.

12 (5-inch) slices cantaloupe
2 cups vanilla bean light ice cream (such as Edy's)
1 cup fresh raspberries
2 tablespoons balsamic glaze (such as Gia Russa)

1. Arrange 3 slices cantaloupe on each of 4 dessert plates; top each with ice cream and raspberries. Drizzle balsamic glaze over each serving. **Yield:** 4 servings (serving size: 3 slices cantaloupe, ½ cup ice cream, ¼ cup raspberries, and 1½ teaspoons balsamic glaze).

CALORIES 174; FAT 4g (sat 2.1g, mono 0g, poly 0.2g); PROTEIN 4.4g; CARB 32.6g; FIBER 2g; CHOL 20mg; IRON 0.5mg; SODIUM 71mg; CALC 79mg

Cantaloupes are the most nutritious of melons: One cup contains 74 times the vitamin A of honeydew melon, more beta carotene than a small spinach salad, almost as much vitamin C as an orange, and roughly the same amount of fiber as a slice of whole wheat bread. Skip the thumping and shaking when choosing a melon. Just look for sweet-smelling melons that have a thick netting and a golden (not green) undertone. The stem end should have a small indentation.

INGREDIENT SPOTLIGHT

Cantaloupe with Balsamic
Berries and Cream

Fresh figs are available twice a year. You'll find the first crop from June through July; the second crop begins early in September and lasts through mid-October. The figs from the first crop are larger and more flavorful than those from the second. Figs are extremely perishable, so you should either use them soon after they're purchased or store them in the refrigerator for no more than two to three days.

INGREDIENT SPOTLIGHT

15 MINUTES

Minted Fruit Compote

Serve the fruit mixture in martini glasses or stemmed dessert glasses for a quick, tasty, and elegant dessert that's a refreshing end to a summer supper.

½   cup sparkling water, chilled and divided (such as Pellegrino)
3   tablespoons honey
3   cups cubed cantaloupe
1   cup blueberries
2   tablespoons thinly sliced fresh mint

1. Combine ¼ cup sparkling water and honey in a large bowl, stirring until smooth. Add remaining ¼ cup sparkling water, cantaloupe, blueberries, and mint. **Yield:** 4 servings (serving size: 1 cup).

CALORIES 115; FAT 0.4g (sat 0.1g, mono 0g, poly 0.2g); PROTEIN 1.5g; CARB 29.4g; FIBER 1g; CHOL 0mg; IRON 0.5mg; SODIUM 24mg; CALC 22mg

30 MINUTES

Warm Figs with Honey and Gorgonzola

⅓   cup honey
2   tablespoons riesling or other slightly sweet white wine
12   ripe fresh figs (about 1 pound), halved
Cooking spray
½   cup (2 ounces) crumbled Gorgonzola cheese
1½   teaspoons ground walnuts

1. Preheat oven to 325°.
2. Combine honey and wine in a medium bowl, stirring to blend. Add figs, and toss gently to coat. Spoon figs and honey mixture into an 8-inch square baking dish coated with cooking spray. Bake at 325° for 25 minutes or until thoroughly heated.
3. Place 4 fig halves on each of 6 dessert plates, and drizzle warm honey mixture evenly over figs. Sprinkle evenly with cheese and walnuts. Serve immediately. **Yield:** 6 servings.

CALORIES 150; FAT 3.2g (sat 2.1g, mono 0.3g, poly 0.7g); PROTEIN 2.7g; CARB 30.5g; FIBER 2.6g; CHOL 8mg; IRON 0.4mg; SODIUM 130mg; CALC 79mg

Minted Fruit Compote

Brandied Mixed Fruit

MINUTES

Melon with Strawberry Sauce

Save time by purchasing watermelon cubes from the grocery store salad bar or produce section. You can substitute cantaloupe or honeydew, if it's more readily available.

1½ cups sliced strawberries
3   tablespoons orange juice
2   tablespoons sugar
4   cups cubed seedless watermelon

1. Combine strawberries, juice, and sugar in a food processor or blender; process until smooth.
2. Place 1 cup melon in each of 4 dessert dishes; top each with about ⅓ cup strawberry sauce. **Yield:** 4 servings.

CALORIES 95; FAT 0.5g (sat 0g, mono 0.1g, poly 0.2g); PROTEIN 1.4g; CARB 23.7g; FIBER 1.9g; CHOL 0mg; IRON 0.7mg; SODIUM 2mg; CALC 22mg

MINUTES

Brandied Mixed Fruit

2   cups chopped cantaloupe
1   cup chopped peeled peaches
1   cup chopped strawberries
1   cup blueberries
⅔   cup chopped peeled nectarines
1½ teaspoons grated orange rind
½   cup fresh orange juice (about 1 orange)
¼   cup sugar
2   tablespoons brandy
2   kiwifruit, peeled and coarsely chopped

1. Combine all ingredients in a large bowl; toss gently. Serve immediately, or cover and chill. **Yield:** 5 servings (serving size: about 1 cup).

CALORIES 170; FAT 0.7g (sat 0.1g, mono 0.2g, poly 0.4g); PROTEIN 2.3g; CARB 38.8g; FIBER 3.8g; CHOL 0mg; IRON 0.6mg; SODIUM 12mg; CALC 30mg

COOKING CLASS: *how to measure brown sugar*

Unlike granulated sugar, which flows freely, brown sugar isn't as refined and contains more moisture. Because it can trap air, it must be firmly packed into the measuring cup in order to get an accurate measurement. The sugar should hold the shape of the cup when it's turned out.

MINUTES

Roasted Plums with Sour Cream

4	large purple plums, cut in half and pitted
1/3	cup water
1/2	teaspoon vanilla extract
1/4	cup packed brown sugar
1/4	cup low-fat sour cream
2	tablespoons turbinado sugar

1. Preheat oven to 450°.
2. Place plums, cut sides down, in an 8-inch square baking dish. Combine water and vanilla; pour over plums. Sprinkle brown sugar over plums.
3. Bake plums at 450° for 25 to 30 minutes or until skins just start to blister.
4. Place 2 plum halves and syrup into each of 4 bowls. Top each with 1 tablespoon sour cream and 1/2 tablespoon turbinado sugar. **Yield:** 4 servings.

CALORIES 129; FAT 1g (sat 0.8g, mono 0.2g, poly 0g); PROTEIN 1g; CARB 30.9g; FIBER 1g; CHOL 5mg; IRON 0.4mg; SODIUM 15mg; CALC 17mg

MINUTES

Broiled Fruit with Sour Cream and Brown Sugar

Assemble these individual fruit desserts in ramekins before dinner, and then place them under the broiler for just two minutes to caramelize the brown sugar before serving.

6	cups cubed fresh pineapple
3	cups seedless green grapes
	Cooking spray
1	cup fresh raspberries
1	(8-ounce) carton reduced-fat sour cream
1	tablespoon orange juice
5	tablespoons packed brown sugar, divided

1. Preheat broiler.
2. Combine pineapple and grapes; toss well. Spoon pineapple mixture evenly into 9 (8- to 10-ounce) ramekins or custard cups coated with cooking spray. Sprinkle evenly with raspberries.
3. Combine sour cream, orange juice, and 2 tablespoons brown sugar, and stir well. Divide sour cream mixture evenly over fruit mixture. Sprinkle remaining 3 tablespoons brown sugar evenly over sour cream mixture.
4. Place ramekins on a baking sheet, and broil 2 minutes or until brown sugar melts and caramelizes (fruit will not be warm). Serve immediately. **Yield:** 9 servings (serving size: 1 cup).

CALORIES 156; FAT 3.3g (sat 1.9g, mono 0.9g, poly 0.2g); PROTEIN 1.9g; CARB 33.1g; FIBER 2.8g; CHOL 10mg; IRON 0.7mg; SODIUM 16mg; CALC 57mg

Moroccan-Spiced Oranges

The cinnamon-orange combination is great. You can also serve this over ice cream or frozen yogurt.

2 ½ cups orange sections, cut into ½-inch
     pieces (about 6)
¼ cup slivered almonds
2 ½ tablespoons chopped pitted dates (about 4)
1   tablespoon powdered sugar
1   tablespoon fresh lemon juice
¼ teaspoon ground cinnamon
Ground cinnamon (optional)
Grated orange rind (optional)

1. Combine first 6 ingredients in a medium bowl, tossing to combine. Cover; chill 20 minutes. Garnish with cinnamon and rind, if desired. **Yield:** 4 servings (serving size: about ½ cup).

CALORIES 167; FAT 3.6g (sat 0.3g, mono 2.2g, poly 0.9g); PROTEIN 3g; CARB 35g; FIBER 5.3g; CHOL 0mg; IRON 0.7mg; SODIUM 0mg; CALC 81mg

Lemon verbena is a lemon-scented herb that's ideal for adding a citrus burst to your recipe. Be sure to use this aromatic herb sparingly because it is potent and can easily overpower the recipe if too much is used.

INGREDIENT SPOTLIGHT

Peaches with Cava
and Lemon Verbena

MINUTES

Peaches with Cava and Lemon Verbena

10   (3-inch) lemon verbena leaves
1   (750-milliliter) bottle Cava or other
     sparkling wine
½   cup sugar
6   cups sliced peaches (about 2 pounds)
½   teaspoon minced lemon verbena leaves

1. Combine whole verbena leaves and sparkling wine in a large saucepan; bring to a boil over medium heat. Cook until reduced to 1 cup (about 15 minutes). Remove and discard whole leaves. Add sugar, stirring until dissolved. Add sliced peaches; bring to a boil. Remove from heat. Cover and chill. Stir in minced verbena leaves just before serving. **Yield:** 5 servings (serving size: 1 cup).

CALORIES 157; FAT 0.5g (sat 0g, mono 0.1g, poly 0.1g); PROTEIN 1.9g; CARB 39.5g; FIBER 2.7g; CHOL 0mg; IRON 1.1mg; SODIUM 11mg; CALC 23mg

MINUTES

Fresh Peaches with Maple-Raspberry Sauce

1   cup raspberries
¼   cup maple syrup
1½   cups vanilla light ice cream (such as Edy's)
6   small peaches (about 2 pounds), peeled and
     sliced

1. Combine raspberries and syrup in a medium bowl; gently mash raspberries with a spatula, leaving some berries whole.
2. Place ¼ cup ice cream in each of 6 stemmed glasses or bowls. Top each with peach slices and raspberry sauce. Serve immediately. **Yield:** 6 servings (serving size: ¼ cup ice cream, 1 sliced peach, and 2 tablespoons sauce).

CALORIES 159; FAT 2.1g (sat 1g, mono 0.6g, poly 0.3g); PROTEIN 3.2g; CARB 34.3g; FIBER 3.7g; CHOL 9mg; IRON 0.5mg; SODIUM 24mg; CALC 76mg

MINUTES

Fresh Peaches with Sabayon

Sabayon, which is the French version of zabaglione, is a foamy Italian custard made by whisking together egg yolks, wine, and sugar over simmering water.

¼   cup sugar
3   large egg yolks
¼   cup Marsala wine
2   tablespoons water
8   cups sliced peeled peaches (about 4 pounds)
Mint sprigs (optional)

1. Combine sugar and yolks in the top of a double boiler, beating with a mixer at medium speed until foamy. Add wine and water. Cook over simmering water until mixture reaches 160° (about 7 minutes), beating with a mixer at medium speed. Serve immediately over peaches. Garnish with fresh mint sprigs, if desired. **Yield:** 8 servings (serving size: 1 cup peaches and ½ cup sabayon).

CALORIES 125; FAT 2.1g (sat 0.6g, mono 0.8g, poly 0.3g); PROTEIN 2.2g; CARB 25.7g; FIBER 3.4g; CHOL 80mg; IRON 0.4mg; SODIUM 3mg; CALC 17mg

Egg yolks help provide the base for sabayon and zabaglione. Yolks account for one-third of an egg's weight and all of the fatty acids, such as omega-3s, about half the protein, most of the vitamins, such as A, B_{12}, E, and all of the antioxidants, such as lutein. Because it contains all the fat, and fat is higher in calories per gram than protein or carbohydrate, the yolk also has the most of the calories—76 percent.

INGREDIENT SPOTLIGHT

20
MINUTES

Grilled Peaches with Honeyed Yogurt

Make sure to clean the cooking grate thoroughly so that no residue from previously grilled foods ruins the flavor of the fruit.

½ cup plain low-fat yogurt
1 tablespoon honey
½ teaspoon vanilla extract
2 tablespoons brown sugar
1½ tablespoons butter
½ teaspoon ground cinnamon
2 large unpeeled ripe peaches, halved and pitted
¼ cup regular oats
2 tablespoons chopped walnuts, toasted

1. Combine yogurt, honey, and vanilla in a bowl; cover and chill.
2. Combine brown sugar, butter, and cinnamon in a large skillet; cook over medium heat until butter melts, stirring constantly. Remove from heat, and dip peach halves in mixture; set peach halves aside.
3. Return pan with butter mixture to heat; cook over medium-low heat 1 minute or until syrupy and bubbly, stirring often. Remove from heat; stir in oats. Spread onto parchment paper to cool.
4. While oat mixture cools, prepare grill.
5. Place peach halves on grill rack; grill, cut sides down, 2 minutes. Turn and grill 3 minutes or until tender. Place peach halves on plates; top evenly with yogurt mixture. Break cooled oat mixture into pieces; sprinkle oat mixture and walnuts over yogurt mixture. **Yield:** 4 servings (serving size: 1 stuffed peach half).

CALORIES 173; FAT 7.7g (sat 3.3g, mono 0.2g, poly 2.2g); PROTEIN 3.5g; CARB 24.6g; FIBER 2g; CHOL 13mg; IRON 1mg; SODIUM 54mg; CALC 75mg

15
MINUTES

Wine-Poached Peaches

Riesling wine is light and delicate with hints of fruitiness and spice, making it a good choice with peaches and cinnamon.

½ cup riesling or other slightly sweet white wine
¼ cup sugar
1 (3-inch) cinnamon stick, broken in half
2 (3-inch) lemon rind strips
4 medium peaches, halved and pitted (about 1 pound)

1. Combine wine and next 3 ingredients in a large skillet; bring to a boil. Add peaches, cut sides up; cover, reduce heat, and simmer 6 to 8 minutes or until tender.
2. Remove peaches from cooking liquid using a slotted spoon. Discard cinnamon sticks and lemon rind strips. Drizzle syrup from pan over peaches. **Yield:** 4 servings (serving size: 2 peach halves and 1 tablespoon syrup).

CALORIES 121; FAT 0.3g (sat 0g, mono 0.1g, poly 0.1g); PROTEIN 1.1g; CARB 25.9g; FIBER 2.7g; CHOL 0mg; IRON 3.8mg; SODIUM 0mg; CALC 7mg

15
MINUTES

Summer Fruit Salad

2 tablespoons powdered sugar
2 teaspoons fresh lemon juice
2 teaspoons Grand Marnier (orange-flavored liqueur) or orange juice
2½ cups thinly sliced peeled peaches
1 cup blueberries
1 cup raspberries

1. Combine first 3 ingredients in a large bowl, stirring with a whisk. Add peaches, blueberries, and raspberries; toss gently to coat. Serve immediately, or cover and chill until ready to serve. **Yield:** 4 servings (serving size: about 1 cup).

CALORIES 117; FAT 0.3g (sat 0g, mono 0g, poly 0.2g); PROTEIN 1.9g; CARB 27.5g; FIBER 4.3g; CHOL 0mg; IRON 0.8mg; SODIUM 13mg; CALC 10mg

KITCHEN COMPANION

Nutritional Analysis

How to Use It and Why

Glance at the end of any *Cooking Light* recipe, and you'll see how committed we are to helping you make the best of today's light cooking. With chefs, registered dietitians, home economists, and a computer system that analyzes every ingredient we use, *Cooking Light* gives you authoritative dietary detail like no other magazine. We go to such lengths so you can see how our recipes fit into your healthful eating plan. If you're trying to lose weight, the calorie and fat figures will probably help most. But if you're keeping a close eye on the sodium, cholesterol, and saturated fat in your diet, we provide those numbers, too. And because many women don't get enough iron or calcium, we can also help there, as well. Finally, there's a fiber analysis for those of us who don't get enough roughage.

Here's a helpful guide to put our nutritional analysis numbers into perspective. Remember, one size doesn't fit all, so take your lifestyle, age, and circumstances into consideration when determining your nutrition needs. For example, pregnant or breast-feeding women need more protein, calories, and calcium. And women older than 50 need 1,200mg of calcium daily, 200mg more than the amount recommended for younger women.

In Our Nutritional Analysis, We Use These Abbreviations

sat	saturated fat	**CHOL**	cholesterol
mono	monounsaturated fat	**CALC**	calcium
poly	polyunsaturated fat	**g**	gram
CARB	carbohydrates	**mg**	milligram

Daily Nutrition Guide

	Women Ages 25 to 50	Women over 50	Men over 24
Calories	2,000	2,000 or less	2,700
Protein	50g	50g	63g
Fat	65g or less	65g or less	88g or less
Saturated Fat	20g or less	20g or less	27g or less
Carbohydrates	304g	304g	410g
Fiber	25g to 35g	25g to 35g	25g to 35g
Cholesterol	300mg or less	300mg or less	300mg or less
Iron	18mg	8mg	8mg
Sodium	2,300mg or less	1,500mg or less	2,300mg or less
Calcium	1,000mg	1,200mg	1,000mg

The nutritional values used in our calculations either come from The Food Processor, Version 8.9 (ESHA Research), or are provided by food manufacturers.

Metric Equivalents

The information in the following charts is provided to help cooks outside the United States successfully use the recipes in this book. All equivalents are approximate.

Cooking/Oven Temperatures

	Fahrenheit	Celsius	Gas Mark
Freeze Water	32° F	0° C	
Room Temp.	68° F	20° C	
Boil Water	212° F	100° C	
Bake	325° F	160° C	3
	350° F	180° C	4
	375° F	190° C	5
	400° F	200° C	6
	425° F	220° C	7
	450° F	230° C	8
Broil			Grill

Liquid Ingredients by Volume

¼ tsp	=	. 1 ml				
½ tsp	=	2 ml				
1 tsp	=	5 ml				
3 tsp	=	1 tbl	=	½ fl oz	=	15 ml
2 tbls	=	⅛ cup	=	1 fl oz	=	30 ml
4 tbls	=	¼ cup	=	2 fl oz	=	60 ml
5⅓ tbls	=	⅓ cup	=	3 fl oz	=	80 ml
8 tbls	=	½ cup	=	4 fl oz	=	120 ml
10⅔ tbls	=	⅔ cup	=	5 fl oz	=	160 ml
12 tbls	=	¾ cup	=	6 fl oz	=	180 ml
16 tbls	=	1 cup	=	8 fl oz	=	240 ml
1 pt	=	2 cups	=	16 fl oz	=	480 ml
1 qt	=	4 cups	=	32 fl oz	=	960 ml
				33 fl oz	=	1000 ml = 1 l

Dry Ingredients by Weight

(To convert ounces to grams, multiply the number of ounces by 30.)

1 oz	=	1/16 lb	=	30 g
4 oz	=	¼ lb	=	120 g
8 oz	=	½ lb	=	240 g
12 oz	=	¾ lb	=	360 g
16 oz	=	1 lb	=	480 g

Length

(To convert inches to centimeters, multiply the number of inches by 2.5.)

1 in	=			2.5 cm	
6 in	=	½ ft	=	15 cm	
12 in	=	1 ft	=	30 cm	
36 in	=	3 ft =	1 yd =	90 cm	
40 in	=			100 cm	= 1 m

Equivalents for Different Types of Ingredients

Standard Cup	Fine Powder (ex. flour)	Grain (ex. rice)	Granular (ex. sugar)	Liquid Solids (ex. butter)	Liquid (ex. milk)
1	140 g	150 g	190 g	200 g	240 ml
¾	105 g	113 g	143 g	150 g	180 ml
⅔	93 g	100 g	125 g	133 g	160 ml
½	70 g	75 g	95 g	100 g	120 ml
⅓	47 g	50 g	63 g	67 g	80 ml
¼	35 g	38 g	48 g	50 g	60 ml
⅛	18 g	19 g	24 g	25 g	30 ml